THE
CHICANO
HERITAGE

This is a volume in the Arno Press collection

THE CHICANO HERITAGE

Advisory Editor
Carlos E. Cortés

Editorial Board
Rodolfo Acuña
Juan Gómez-Quiñones
George F. Rivera, Jr.

*See last pages of this volume
for a complete list of titles.*

The Spanish Archives of New Mexico

Ralph Emerson Twitchell

Volume One

ARNO PRESS
A New York Times Company
New York — 1976

Editorial Supervision: LESLIE PARR

Reprint Edition 1976 by Arno Press Inc.

Reprinted from a copy in
 The Princeton University Library

THE CHICANO HERITAGE
ISBN for complete set: 0-405-09480-9
See last pages of this volume for titles.

Manufactured in the United States of America

Library of Congress Cataloging in Publication Data

Twitchell, Ralph Emerson, 1859-1925, comp.
 The Spanish archives of New Mexico.

 (The Chicano heritage)
 Reprint of the ed. published by the Torch Press, Cedar
Rapids, Iowa.
 1. New Mexico--History--Sources. 2. New Mexico--
History--Sources--Bibliography. I. Title. II. Series.
F791.T85 1976   978.9   76-1607
ISBN 0-405-09529-5

The Spanish Archives
of New Mexico

El Palacio Reál, Santa Fe, New Mexico
Erected A. D. 1606, destroyed A. D. 1680, rebuilt A. D. 1697, restored A. D. 1911-13

The Spanish Archives of New Mexico

Compiled and chronologically arranged with historical, genealogical, geographical, and other annotations, by authority of the State of New Mexico

By
Ralph Emerson Twitchell
Of the New Mexico Bar

Volume One

THE ARTHUR H. CLARK COMPANY
GLENDALE, CALIFORNIA, U. S. A.
NINETEEN FOURTEEN

COPYRIGHT 1914 BY
RALPH EMERSON TWITCHELL

THE TORCH PRESS
CEDAR RAPIDS
IOWA

A TRIBUTE TO THE MEMORY OF
DANIEL SAWIN TWITCHELL, MY FATHER
WHOSE ANCESTOR IN AMERICA, BENJAMIN TWITCHELL, SETTLED IN DORCHESTER, MASSACHUSETTS, IN 1630, A PURITAN PIONEER, COTEMPORARY IN NEW WORLD CIVILIZATION WITH THE SPANISH CONQUISTADORES OF NEW MEXICO

PREFATORY NOTE

THE documentary period of New Mexican history begins with the *Relacion* of Alvar Nuñez Cabeza de Vaca, who, with three companions, survivors of the ill-fated expedition under Don Pamfilo Narvaez, in 1528, shipwrecked upon the coast of the Mexican Gulf, traversed the continent, finally, in 1538, meeting with other Spaniards in New Galicia near the west coast of Mexico. Thereafter came the memorable journeys of the Franciscan frayles, Juan de la Asuncion and Marcos de Niza, the negro, Estevan, who lost his life at Zuñi, the expedition under Francisco Vasquez Coronado; Friar Agustin Ruiz, with Chamuscado; Don Antonio de Espejo; Castaño de Sosa; and finally, in 1598, the first colonizer in the United States of today, Don Juan de Oñate, who located his first capital at San Gabriel, near the junction of the Rio Chama with the Rio Grande, in the county of Rio Arriba, New Mexico.

The Spanish archives of New Mexico, however, do not contain any record of the events of the explorations of the last half of the sixteenth century, nor are there any connected with the first settlement under Oñate. The earliest is one of the year 1621, a translation of which is given together with a photographic reproduction. All of the earlier archives at Santa Fe, with this exception and two others, were destroyed by the Indians in the Pueblo Rebellion of 1680. The Spaniards, in August of that year, under the governor and captain-general, Don Antonio de Otermín, were forced to evacuate the capital after a siege continuing five days, retiring to Paso del Norte, which became the seat of government and military operations of the Province until the re-conquest under General Don Diego de Vargas Zapata Lujan Ponce de Leon in 1692-94.

The Spanish archives of this State have been a subject of enduring interest ever since the occupation of New Mexico by American troops in 1846. From the time of the re-conquest until the American Occupation period the archives were well cared for by the Spanish and Mexican authorities.

The Spanish and Mexican governments were extremely zealous in the administration of the regulations governing their custody and care. At the time of the Occupation these archives were in the charge of Don Donaciano Vigil, who had been the sole custodian, during many administrations, since 1824.

On the 22d of September, 1846, Vigil was appointed secretary of New Mexico and ex-officio recorder of land titles and custodian of the archives, by General Stephen W. Kearny. In 1847, after the assassination of Governor Charles Bent, he succeeded to the civil governorship but continued as official custodian until New Mexico became a Territory of the United States in 1851.

A recital of the historical events in connection with the custody of these documents will be of interest. It is recorded that no sooner had the Americans assumed control than reports were forwarded to the authorities at Washington, declaring that the "prefect at Paso del Norte has for the last few months been very active in disposing (for his own benefit) of all lands in that vicinity that are valuable, *ante*-dating the title to such purchases." Thus early was the taint of fraud given to archives, the value of which was so little appreciated by the soldiers of the American army that during the occupation of Paso del Norte by Colonel Doniphan's troops, they, in considerable quantity, were thrown into the street to make room for office headquarters and burned.

Professor J. H. Vaughan, *A Preliminary Report on the Archives of New Mexico,* Appendix "C," *Report,* American Historical Association, 1908, p. 471, has fallen into error where he states that "The Federal authorities then in control allowed the documents to remain in the custody of the Territorial authorities, and this custody continued to be exercised without question until 1903." On the contrary, the general government, almost immediately after the Territory of New Mexico was created, took steps for their preservation. He also errs in his conclusion that "There is no question that many of the more important papers relating to, or bearing directly on, the question of land titles in the Territory were borrowed from the general stock and were not returned," for, in truth, after the segregation by Surveyor-General Pelham, the number of archives relative to land titles was materially augmented by the filing of title papers in his office by land owners.

Pursuant to the provisions of the Act of Congress of July 22, 1854 (*10 Stats.,* p. 309), under which was created the office of surveyor-general of New Mexico, the first appointee, William Pelham, was instructed, upon his arrival at Santa Fe, to make application to the governor (Merriwether) for "such of the archives as relate to grants of land by the former authorities of the country," to see that "they are kept in a place of security from fire, or other accidents, and that access is allowed only to land-owners who may find it necessary to refer to their title records," and such references "must be made under your eye or that of a sworn employe of the government."

The surveyor-general was also instructed to prepare, in duplicate, from the archives, or authoritative sources, a document exhibiting the names of all the officers of the Territory who held the power of distributing land from the earliest settlement of the Territory until the change of government, indicating the several periods of their incumbency; the nature and extent of their powers concerning lands; whether, and to what extent, and under what conditions and limitations, authority existed in the governors or political chiefs to distribute the public domain; whether, in any class of cases, they had the power to make an absolute grant; and if so, for what maximum in area; or whether subject to the affirmance of the department or supreme government; whether the Spanish surveying system was in operation, and since what period in the country, and under what organization; also, with verified copies of the original, and translations of the laws and decrees of the Mexican Republic, and regulations which may have been adopted by the general government of that republic for the disposal of the public lands in New Mexico.

Mindful of the rights of the Pueblo Indians of New Mexico, he was instructed to collect data from the records and other authentic sources relative to these Pueblos, so that Congress would understand the matter fully and be able to legislate in such a manner as would do "justice to all concerned."

In accordance with his instructions, the surveyor-general made application to Governor Merriwether for such of the archives as related to grants of land by the former authorities of the country. The governor declined to act, saying that "their selection from the large amount of papers composing the public archives of the Territory would involve an immense amount of labor and a heavy expenditure which he was not authorized to incur."

Governor Merriwether, however, graciously permitted the surveyor-general "to remove the packages containing such papers as related to the grants of land in the country from their deposit and examine them in my own office; whereupon I immediately assigned two of my clerks to separate them. On the last day of July (1855) this difficult duty was accomplished, and from one hundred and sixty-eight packages, averaging *one hundred and sixty-eight thousand papers,* of every nature and description imaginable, one thousand seven hundred and fifteen grants, conveyances of land, and other documents referring to claims to land, have been selected, and are now being arranged and classified in a systematical form in this office. It will, however, be impossible to have them properly and substantially bound, as required by your instructions, on account of the different shapes and forms in which they are to be found — some existing on large sheets of foolscap paper, while others are to be found on half-sheets, and others again, on scraps of paper which can never be bound in any convenient form."

Immediately the surveyor-general began the performance of his duties, but, as appears from the report of the commissioner of the general land office, the people of New Mexico were averse to responding to the call of the surveyor-general to produce their title papers to lands in the Territory, "some for fear of losing the evidence of their titles, inspired, it is supposed, by designing individuals."

"In many instances," says the commissioner, "the Pueblo Indians have been deterred from filing their title papers with the surveyor-general, in the apprehension they would never again get possession of them.

"Others, conscious of an indisputable possessory right of landed estates, feel perfectly secure on the subject and do not care to exhibit, much less file, their title papers, for the purpose of enabling the surveyor-general to report upon the claims to Congress for confirmation under the Act of July 22, 1854."

Pelham continued as surveyor-general until the breaking out of the Civil War, when he endeavored to make his escape from New Mexico in company with the army of Confederate invaders under the command of General H. H. Sibley, but was captured by General Canby near Alburquerque at the time of the inglorious retreat of the Texans in 1862.

Thereafter and for more than a quarter of a century the surveyor-general's office was engaged in the investigation of these private land claims, during which time, up to and including the year 1880, according to the report of the secretary of the interior, "after a lapse of nearly thirty years, more than one thousand claims have been filed with the surveyor-general, of which less than one hundred and fifty have been reported to Congress, and of the number so reported, Congress has finally acted upon seventy-one. The construction of railroads through New Mexico and Arizona, and the consequent influx of population in those Territories, render it imperatively necessary that these claims should be finally settled with the least possible delay. I have, therefore, the honor to recommend that the attention of Congress be called especially to the subject, with a view to securing action upon the claims pending before it, and upon the pending bill providing for the settlement of the remaining claims.

"On June 30, 1880, patents had been issued by the government for 4,456,158.43 acres of private land claims in New Mexico and Colorado; the largest grant for 1,714,764.94 acres, and the smallest for 1,720 acres.

"There were on the above mentioned date forty-six claims for private land grants in New Mexico and Colorado, containing an area of 4,675,173.57 acres pending in the general land office for patents, and on that date there were pending sixty private land claims in the same area for confirmation by Congress, embracing an area, so far as the same has been surveyed, of 4,294,627.475 acres.

"This condition of affairs continued until the establishment of the Court of Private Land Claims in 1891, which court began its official functions by a formal organization at Denver, Colorado, July 1, 1891, and ceased, by operation of law, June 30, 1904."

During the thirty-seven years of investigations of these private land claims by the several surveyors-general, lawyers and other interested persons became entirely familiar with the documents in the office of the surveyor-general. Much testimony was taken by that official, the major portion of which is of more than ordinary historical importance. Translations of these archives were made by a succession of official translators, notably Whiting, Miller, Ellison, Key, and Vigil, and during the existence of the court of private land claims by Flipper, Tipton, Chacón, and others, the work of all of whom has been used in this compilation. Not one of these documents has ever been mislaid or tampered with while in the custody of the representatives of the Department of the Interior.

These archives are by far the most valuable and interesting of any in the Southwest, not excepting those of California. Here we find reflected the home and business life of the early settlers. In the *expedientes, testimonios,* and other papers, numbers of which have been translated and given in full, are disclosed the pride of ancestral achievement in the conquest and pacification of the country; recitals of Indian campaigns, usages, methods of defense, the erection of forts and towers in exposed localities on the Indian frontiers; customs, civil and military; names of officers in all branches of the service; the respectful regard for the rights of the Pueblo Indians relative to their land holdings; the efforts to win over the hostile tribes and convert them to the Catholic faith; the deference for the ecclesiastics; official admonitions; wills and testaments, slaves and slavery, laws and customs, forms of official procedure, census returns; in fine, almost everything necessary for a study of the lives, manners, routine, dress, and daily occupations of the people during a period of more than two centuries. The will of General De Vargas exemplifies in many ways the picture of official life at Santa Fe; the manners of dress, the home life, the use of elaborate plate, the wearing of resplendent jewelry, the affection bestowed upon his intimates, all are found in this notable document.

Those archives which, in 1854, remained in the custody of Governor Merriwether, became a part of the official records of the executive office. On February 4, 1854, the Territorial Assembly memorialized Congress, reciting that the archives were in a ruined condition, documents of great importance being exposed and in danger of complete destruction; that the Territory was without means to care for them properly, and asking for an appropriation of fifteen thousand dollars for their care and translation into the English language. Congress did nothing. Even the Palace of the Governors was, at that time, in such poor repair, according to the governor, that it was no fit place for the sessions of the Assembly. During successive administrations recommendations were made to the Territorial legislatures for appropriations for the care of these important documents. Meanwhile many of them disappeared, and during the administration of Governor Pyle, it is said, many were carried off. In a measure this is true, but they were not destroyed, as nearly all of them found their way into private collections at Santa Fe and elsewhere.

In 1891-2, during the administration of Governor L. Bradford Prince, the Legislative Assembly authorized the expenditure of two thousand four hundred dollars for cataloguing, numbering, indexing, binding, and translating these archives, and the governor was empowered to contract with some competent person for the work, "it being understood that only such documents as contained matters of historical interest to New Mexico shall be required to be translated, and that the person with whom such contract shall be made shall also make clean copies of said documents as he may translate, with proper indexes to both Spanish and English, so as to prepare the same for publication as historical documents; such documents shall also be arranged chronologically."

Mr. Ad. F. Bandelier was employed by the governor for the purpose. All that the Territory ever received for the money paid to Mr. Bandelier was a "list" of 1074 archives, chronologically arranged, a copy of which is now in the possession of the Historical Society of New Mexico, and which has been used in this compilation. If any translations were made they were never filed with the Territorial authorities, or, if filed, have entirely disappeared. No index was ever made and no copies have ever been preserved.

Narrowly escaping destruction by fire when the first capitol was burned in 1892, the archives were placed in the custody of the secretary of the Territory. Numbers of them were used in the trial of cases before the court of private land claims.

During the last year of the administration of Governor Miguel A. Otero they were removed, by order of the general government, to Washington and placed in the Library of Congress. A full statement of how this removal was arbitrarily accomplished is contained in Professor Vaughan's monograph, where he states:

PREFATORY NOTE xvii

"After the completion of the present Territorial capitol, in 1900, and the removal of the Territorial offices from the Old Palace to the capitol building, these old documents were transferred to the office of the Territorial Secretary and stored in the vault adjoining the office. Here they were arranged, roughly, in the order of their dates, were tied in packages, and stored as carefully as was possible on the shelving in a vault available for that purpose. In 1901, however, it was clearly seen that these documents, which occupied nearly all the shelf space on one side of the vault, would have to be removed in order to make room for the current records of the office, the volume of which was constantly and rapidly increasing.

"About this time correspondence was being received from the authorities at Washington, particularly from the librarian of Congress, asking that these Spanish and Mexican archives be transferred to the Library of Congress at Washington, where they would be stored in a manner absolutely safe; also classified, indexed, and translated by persons trained in this line of work, and without expense to the Territory. Recommendations to this effect were made by the Secretary of the Territory in 1899, 1901, and 1903; and the governor, in his message to the Legislative Assembly, called the attention of that body to the circumstances on at least one occasion. No action of any kind was taken or even considered until 1903. During the winter of that year the librarian of Congress was a visitor in Santa Fe, in the month of February, and discussed the matter with the members of the Legislature and the Territorial officials. The result of this discussion was the drafting of an act which provided for the transfer of these documents to the Library of Congress, which, through the librarian, entered into certain stipulations, as to the preservation, classification, and indexing of the documents free of charge to the Territory. Through the intervention of certain persons this act was amended after its introduction so as to stipulate that all of the archives found to relate to land titles or to local and personal matter, and not of great historic importance, should be returned within one year, and that all the remainder of said archives, upon being properly analyzed and classified, should within five years of their reception at Washington be returned to New Mexico. The result was that when the act was finally passed, as amended, the authorities at Washington refused to enter into the stipulations as provided for in said act (chap. 102, *Laws of 1903*).

"The negotiations of the Library of Congress had failed to secure the records; but the incident was not closed. The authorities at Washington held that these archives were, always had been, subject to the control and supervision of the federal government. Acting on this assumption, the Secretary of the Interior, April 29, 1903, directed the governor of New Mexico to forward the archives to the Interior Department. They were accordingly expressed from Santa Fe to the department May 9, 1903. Here they were immediately turned over to the Librarian of Congress, and were held to be the property of the United States Government, the control of them in the Secretary of the Interior.

"The authority of the Secretary of the Interior to

turn these records over to the Library of Congress was alleged to be found in the following Act of Congress, approved February 25, 1903:

" 'The head of any executive department or bureau or any commission of the Government is hereby authorized, from time to time, to turn over to the Librarian of Congress, for the use of the Library of Congress, any books, maps or other material in the library of the department, bureau or commission no longer needed for its use, and in the judgment of the Librarian of Congress appropriate to the uses of the Library of Congress.' "

In this manner were these archives taken away from the custody of the Territorial officials. It seems to have required an Act of Congress to accomplish the deed. Had such a course been pursued in dealing with any other Territory, such opposition would have been raised that no Act of Congress could have been passed. No such course was pursued with California or any other Territory of the United States. Legally, the government had the right to assert its ownership and control over these documents, but morally, it was an act which is justified only by the very excellent work which has been accomplished by the Librarian of Congress since they have been in his custody.

This great collection has been stored in the Manuscripts Division of the Library of Congress. They consist, approximately, of 20,000 documents, 10,000 in manuscript containing from 1 to 200 folios, and 10,000 printed, mostly of 1 to 4 folios. Since they have been in Washington they have all been arranged chronologically; the sheets have been cleansed, pressed free of creases, and stored flat; the manuscripts are in 180 half-leather portfolios; the printed material has been, in part, repaired, mounted, and bound in half-morocco folio volumes. The unmounted portion is stored flat in manila jackets.

A calendar, in English, is being prepared, with an index. This now includes the year 1823. In this compilation this calendar has been employed, not using the numbers exactly as they have been given by the Librarian. It is stated that these archives, of enormous importance to the people of New Mexico, will eventually be restored to the State. Of course this is possible but, considering the efforts which were successfully made in securing them for the Library of Congress, such action on the part of the general government, even at the request of a sovereign State, is highly improbable. New Mexicans can congratulate themselves that the records of the court of private land claims were permitted to remain in the custody of the surveyor-general. It is of prime importance that the State have copies of all the archives at Washington; it is also essential that those in the office of the surveyor-general be handled more carefully when examined by attorneys in courts or in his office. The same sort of treatment should be accorded those as has been given the archives at Washington, and photostat copies should be made of both collections.

The *Autos* of Don Antonio de Otermín, governor and captain-general, and the *Disculpa* of Alonzo Garcia, lieutenant-general, translations of which are given, consist of the record of events transpiring at the time of the Pueblo Rebellion which have been available for this publication. There are still other *Autos* of Otermín in the archives at the City of Mexico, but the unfortunate course of events occurring in Mexico during the past few years has made it impossible to secure copies or translations. Those appearing here, so far as the writer knows, have not heretofore been published in the English language.

The statement of the private land claims investigated by the surveyor-general of New Mexico is complete, as is also that of the cases finally disposed of in the court of private land claims.

This compilation has been undertaken with the view of furnishing information promptly and accurately to those most interested — the people of New Mexico. The cost of publication has been borne in part by the State. It will be noticed that in some instances the titles are given in the Spanish language. These, however, are in the main translated and the contents of each archive, so far as is indicated by the title, are suggested to the reader. This portion of the catalogue, with some changes and other modifications, is taken from the "list" prepared by Mr. Bandelier. The method being somewhat unscientific when compared with the work performed under the direction of the librarian of Congress, which is most thorough, and the compiler lacking in that peculiar training and preparedness demanded by the rules governing this class of composition, the want of suitable intellectual equipment is apt to provoke unfavorable comment from some scholastic Pharisee.

Comment and criticism of this sort, however, coming as they usually do from persons whose range of vision is limited to the four walls of a university quadrangle, are harmless. They serve to enlarge the layman's contempt for some methods of educational training and administration.

The reading public, however, men actively engaged in the affairs of the day, have learned to expect nothing but criticism from such sources, and its value is estimated accordingly. These critics are paid for such service and, needs be, future employment must find apology. There are pleasurable exceptions, but the rule generally discloses composition from such sources so hypercritical, so self-assuring, so devoid of the ordinary elements of human interest, that it attracts hardly passing notice. The American reading public demands a popular style of treatment, combined with accuracy of statement, from whatever source obtained. The so-called scientific class, with some exceptions, usually reveals unopened leaves and a final resting place in the literary scrap-heap.

Notwithstanding the prospect of provoking such criticism, this work has been arranged with the view of demonstrating that even a catalogue may be made interesting as well as profitable reading. To be sure no "discoveries" are claimed and no missing manuscripts have been "recovered," the right of discovery having been exclusively reserved to some, who for the sake of being classified among the "Who's Who" of scholastic recognition, make occasional contributions — a term of scientific significance — to periodicals, vehicles for the publication of monographs devoted to historical research.

The thanks of the writer are tendered to the librarian of Congress for courtesies extended; to Francis C.

Wilson, Esq., of Santa Fe, New Mexico, for the use of notes relative to the land tenures of the Pueblo Indians prepared by Mr. Will M. Tipton; to Miss Florence P. Spofford, of Washington, D. C.; and to the many friends in New Mexico who have permitted the use of old documents and papers not in the archives, from which the genealogy of some of our leading New Mexican families has been established.

RALPH EMERSON TWITCHELL

Las Vegas, New Mexico
January 2, 1914

ILLUSTRATIONS

El Palacio Reál, Santa Fe, New Mexico . . *Frontispiece*	
Duke of Alburquerque	8
Oldest Archive in Office of Surveyor-General . .	16
Inscription on El Morro by General De Vargas . .	33
Inscription on El Morro by Captain Juan de Ulibarri .	49
Coat of Arms of General de Vargas	64
Facsimiles of Signatures of Governors and Captains-General	96
Don Fernando de Alencastre Norona y Silva, Duke of Linares	128
Don Baltazar de Zuniga, Marques de Valero, Duke of Arion	160
Facsimiles of Signatures of Governors of New Mexico .	192
Facsimiles of Signatues of General De Vargas and Captains	224
Don Juan de Acuña, Marqués de Casa Fuerte . .	256
Urrutia's Map of Santa Fe	289
Don Juan Antonio de Vizarron y Eguiarreta . .	320
Don Pedro de Castro Figueroa	384
Facsimiles of Distinguished New Mexicans . . .	416
Facsimiles of Signatures of Governors and Captains-General	432
Facsimiles of Signatures of Distinguished New Mexicans	448
Facsimiles of Signatures of Governors of New Mexico .	464
Facsimiles of Signatures of Governors of New Mexico	480

THE SPANISH ARCHIVES OF NEW MEXICO

IN THE OFFICE OF THE SURVEYOR-GENERAL
SANTA FE, NEW MEXICO

1 PEDRO DE ABALOS. March 26, 1685. Town of *Nuestra Señora de Guadalupe de El Paso*. Before Don Domingo Jironza Petriz de Cruzate, Governor and Captain-General.

Registration of a mine, situate forty-five leagues from the said town in the little mountain called *Fray Cristobal*. Name of mine; *Nuestra Señora del Pilar de Zaragoza*.

Pedro de Abalos was a soldier of the garrison at the El Paso presidio at the time of the registry of this mine. The property was discovered while on the campaign north with Cruzate for the recovery of the Province. He gave one-half of the mine to Alonzo Rael de Aguilar; a part to his brother, Antonio de Abalos, who was also a soldier of the garrison; also a part to Captain Juan Garcia de Noriega. Alonzo Rael de Aguilar was also a captain, married, and with his wife and children was living at Paso del Norte at the time of this registration.

On the retreat from Santa Fe, in 1680, it was at Fray Cristobal that a *junta de guerra* was begun for the consideration of the question of an immediate return to the Villa of Santa Fe, and an attempt made to drive out the victorious apostates. The safety of the women and children having been provided for, Otermín assembled the members of the *cabildo* of Santa Fe, the frayles, military officers, and prominent Spaniards who had made their escape. Fray Ayeta attended the *junta* and represented the entire body of Religious; he made offers of assistance in the way of provisions if the re-conquest was undertaken. One of the officers who addressed the *junta* was Captain Thomé Dominguez, who advised the acceptance of the offer made by the custodio, Fr. Ayeta. The strongest opponents to a return, at that time, were Francisco Gomez Robledo, Alonzo Garcia, and Pedro Duran y Chaves. The *cabildo* of Santa Fe took sides with the last named, as did also the Captains Pedro Marquez and

Sebastian de Herrera. Governor Otermín agreed with the *cabildo*, and on October 5 made announcement of his decision. The *junta* which brought about this final determination was concluded when within a few leagues of Paso del Norte.

All three of the individuals signing this archive came north with General De Vargas twelve years later.

The mine was probably situate somewhere west of the present town of Engle, Sierra county, New Mexico.

Don Domingo Jironza Petriz de Cruzate was named governor and captain-general of the province of New Mexico, referred to in all his *autos* and other official documents as *"Reino"* (kingdom), in the year 1682, succeeding Don Antonio de Otermín. Carlos II sent him as *visitador* to the Leeward Islands. He was prominent in the wars with Portugal. A copy of his commission appears later in this volume. He had been alcalde of Mestitlan when appointed governor of New Mexico. He endeavored to regain the province, but failed.

Bancroft says that he was succeeded by General Pedro Reneros de Posada. See archives in office of the surveyor-general for New Mexico, Files R. A., R. B., and R. C., from which it will be seen that as late as September 25, 1689, he was making grants of land to the pueblos of San Juan, Jemez, Pecos, and others. These archives, in my judgment, are spurious. Don Pedro Ortiz Niño Ladron de Guevarra was his secretary of government and war at the time. In 1688, Reneros de Posada was a general under Cruzate and may have been a governor and captain-general *ad interim*. He was in a campaign against the apostates as far north as the pueblo of Cia. See affidavit of Bartolomé de Ojeda, Indian of Zia, where this fact appears. Archive File R, No. A, S. G. O. Escalante says so, also. Governor Cruzate joins with Ojeda in making this affidavit, and in it the "affair" at Zia is mentioned.

Bancroft and all the rest err as to the date of the appointment of Governor Cruzate. He was appointed on or prior to the 20th day of August, 1682. See archive 1134, which I give in full as being of sufficient importance, thereby settling the conflicting statements of historical writers:

"ONE REAL. Third Seal. ONE REAL. Years one thousand six hundred and seventy-nine and eighty. (STAMP)-(STAMP).

"I, Thomas Lorenzo Manuel Manrique de la Cerda Henrique Afan de Rivera Porto Arro and Cardena, cónde de Paredes, Marqués de la Laguna, knight commander of Moraleja in the Order and Knighthood of Alcantara, at the court of His Majesty, acting viceroy and governor and captain-general of New Spain, president of the Royal Audiencia of the same, having appointed as governor and captain-general of the province of New Mexico, Captain Domingo Jironza Petriz de Cruzate and having determined in general council that it is necessary and proper in view of the authority I have conferred on the said appointee, to make distributions of land, that the governor of Viscaya be notified thereof, in order that he may confine himself to those which pertain alone to his jurisdiction, and to the end that the one and the other may reciprocally enjoy a good understanding, each confining himself within the limits of his own jurisdiction, having to do only with the demarcations of their governments, it being understood that the territory of Vizcaya extends up to the river of *Nombre de Dios,* otherwise called *Sacramento,* and that thence the territory of the government of New Mexico begins, with which declaration all controversy will cease.

"I, therefore, command the said Captain Domingo Jironza Petriz de Cruzate to notify and make known this decision to Bartolomé de Estrada of the Order of Santiago and governor and captain-general of the Royal Province of Nueva Vizcaya, so that, should he have any representation to make he may report to this government, confining himself to the Interior; and I direct said appointee that he urge and compel all Spaniards who may have fled from El Paso and other jurisdictions of the Province of New Mexico and who may now be within the territory of his jurisdiction, to return to that place, he reporting to me fully of the execution of this mandate and of whatever he may deem proper.

"MEXICO, August 20, 1682.

    "THE CONDE DE PAREDES MARQUES DE LA LAGUNA
       [rubric]

"By Command of His Excellency:
  "PEDRO VELASQUEZ DE LA CADENA."

Attached to this archive are a number of "protests," notably one from the officials of the City of Parral, in which is found a great deal of information of great value dealing with mining and agricultural matters in that country and protesting against being made a part of New Mexico.

The Sacramento river is about twenty miles north of Chihuahua. It was near this river that General Alexander W. Doniphan fought his battle with the Mexicans in 1847.

Bancroft says that Ojeda's affidavit "mystifies" him. They (the grants) have mystified others and for just what purpose they were made — *at that time* — does not clearly appear. However, these are the basic titles to the lands of the several pueblos mentioned, and upon them the government of the United States acted when the grants were confirmed to the pueblos. There is at least one prime authority, Will M. Tipton, who believes that all of these pueblo grant papers are forgeries.

After the appointment of Don Diego de Vargas Zapata Lujan Ponce de Leon as governor and captain-general of New Mexico, Cruzate was named governor of Sonora.

The Indian, Bartolomé Ojeda, subsequently fought un der De Vargas and is referred to by the latter as *"Mi Compadre!"* He fought at the battle of *Potrero Viejo*.

2 ANA DE ARCHULETA. February 1, 1696. City of *Santa Fe*. Before Diego de Vargas Zapata Lujan Ponce de Leon, Marqués de la Nava Brazinas.

Grant of a small piece of land in the City of Santa Fe. Captain Juan Garcia de la Riva; Luis Duran; Francisco de la Mora; Gregorio de Archuleta; Lorenzo Madrid; Domingo de la Barreda; Captain Bartolomé Garduño; Juan Antonio Barrios; Antonio Alvarez Castillon; Francisco Joseph Casados; Joseph Manuel Giltomey; Pedro de Roxas.

General De Vargas began making grants and allotments of land which had belonged to the Spaniards who left with Governor Otermín, before he commenced his second *entrada*. He made some shortly after his first *entrada*. This archive has a fine signature of De Vargas and those signing with him. Lorenzo Madrid was a brother of Roque Madrid, who was sergeant-major under Cruzate; Roque Madrid was one of the soldiers who escaped from the *Villa* with Otermín; he had a ranch south of the City of Santa Fe. Captain Juan Garcia de la Riva was afterward alcalde of Santa Cruz, named by De Vargas upon the re-settlement of the *Villa Nueva de Santa Cruz de la Cañada*. He was also the grantee to a piece of land south of Santa Fe in the vicinity of the old pueblo of *La Cienega*.

Of those whose names appear on this archive, in the year 1696, the date when this grant to Ana de Archuleta was made, Lorenzo Madrid (in those days the Spaniards had not eliminated the "de" from their names) was an *alcalde* at Santa Fe and a member of the *cabildo*. This body at that time and during the last year of the term of office of General De Vargas was composed of Francisco Romero de Pedraza, Lazaro de Misquia, Diego Montoya, José Garcia Jurado. Captain Lucero de Godoy was secretary of the *cabildo*.

Domingo de Barreda was secretary of government and of war.

Roque Madrid had been promoted by De Vargas from *sargento* to *teniente-general* of cavalry, and he was also *alcalde* of Santa Cruz.

3 CAPTAIN FRANCISCO MATTHEO LUZERO DE GODOY and Ana Maria, wife of Juan de Alderete, Maria Madalena and Francisca, his daughters, to Major Francisco de Anaya Almazan. April 16, 1697. City of *Santa Fe*. Before Captain Diego Arias de Quiros, Alcalde.

Conveyance of a house and land in the City of *Santa Fe*. This is an uncertified copy of the original deed.

Diego Arias de Quiros was a captain; everyone of the *alcaldes* under De Vargas and named by him was an officer in his army.

Note the date of this instrument. Bancroft says that the grantee, Francisco Anaya Almazan, was drowned in the Rio del Norte over a year before the date of this deed. He errs, because the certificate shows that the grantee "appeared." Francisco Joseph Casados was an *alcalde* of Santa Fe in 1716. Archive 10, *q. v.*

4 ANTONIO GUTIERREZ DE FIGUEROA to Antonio de Aguilera. September 18, 1698. City of *Santa Fe*. Before Diego Arias de Quiros, Alcalde.

Conveyance of land in the City of Santa Fe. Certified copy by the Alcalde.

5 OLAYA DE OTON to Inez de Aspitia. September 15, 1700. City of *Santa Fe*. Before Antonio de Aguilera, Alcalde.

Conveyance of house and land in the city of Santa Fe.

6   AGUSTIN SAES and ANTONIA MARQUEZ to Juan de Archibec. November 7, 1701. City of *Santa Fe*. Before Joseph Rodriguez, Alcalde.

House and land in the city of Santa Fe.

Juan de Archibec was "Jean L'Archiveque." His widow married Don Bernardino de Sena, to whom was granted the pueblo of *Cuyamungue* in 1731. This pueblo was in existence as late as 1696, when it was finally abandoned, and three years later it was given to the Captain Alonzo Rael de Aguilar.

7   JUAN DE ATIENZA, Protector of the Christian Indians of New Mexico. Before Don Juan Ignacio Flores Mogollon, Governor and Captain-General.

Question as to land alleged to have been granted to Joseph Quiros and Antonio Duran de Armijo by Don Pedro Rodriguez Cubero, governor and captain-general. Armijo sold his part to the Indians of Pojoaque, and Quiros sold his part to Miguel Tenorio de Alva, who also sold to the same Indians. Baltazar Trujillo claimed to have bought part of the land claimed by the Indians. This action was begun in 1715 and decided the following year. There are seventeen leaves in this archive.

Controversy relative to certain lands alleged to have been sold to the Indians of Pojoaque by some Spaniards.

The "Protector" was a sort of "Indian Agent," named by the government. His chief duty was to defend legally the rights of the Indians. These *protectores* were established at an early day. At first the prelates of the Indies, bishops and archbishops, were the protectors. Philip II established special official protectors. See *Real Cédula* of January 10, 1589. Their duties were well defined. They had no jurisdiction over the Indian and no right to meddle in his affairs. Each Indian of New Spain had to pay half a real toward defraying expenses incident to any defense that became necessary in their behalf. See *Real Cédula* of June 13, 1623. Philip IV.

This petition by Juan de Atienza, attorney for the Indians of New Mexico, relates to lands claimed by the Indians of Pojoaque. He alleges that the Indians formerly held certain lands which Governor Pedro Rodriguez Cubero saw fit to grant to Joseph de Quiros and Antonio Duran de Armijo; that the latter sold his part to the Indians, transferring to them the grant made by Governor

Rodriguez; that Quiros sold his part of the land to Miguel Tenorio de Alva, who sold it to the Indians. The petitioner further relates that almost half of the land bought of Tenorio by the Indians is claimed by Baltazar Trujillo, who states that he bought it of Tenorio, and who exhibits a certified copy of a deed to the latter from Quiros. The petitioner asks that such steps be taken as will enable him to appear before the governor of the kingdom in such manner as to secure a decision favorable to the Indians.

This petition bears no date, but was presented to Joseph Trujillo, chief alcalde and war-captain of the Villa Nueva de Santa Cruz, on May 16, 1715.

That officer then took the testimony of the following persons: Captain Miguel Tenorio de Alva, Captain Baltazar Trujillo, an Indian named Juanillo, another named Lucas de Abenbua, another named Francisco Canjuebe, alias Bollo, and three others, named respectively Miguel, Tomas, and Pablo.

This testimony seems to indicate that probably Tenorio had sold a part of the land to the Indians and another part to Trujillo, and that some of the Indians had not paid their portion of the purchase price. Tenorio appears to have considered the sale as one made to Indians individually, and not to the pueblo of Pojoaque.

After the testimony was taken on the 17th and 24th days of May, 1715, it was delivered to the Indians' attorney, Juan de Atienza, in order that he might make such use of it as he deemed proper in the interest of the Indians.

On June 12, 1715, Atienza presented to Governor Juan Ygnacio Flores Mogollon a petition setting forth the steps he had taken in the matter and asking that the governor do justice to the Indians.

The governor at once appointed Alonzo (or Alfonso) Rael de Aguilar to investigate the matter, and report to him.

This officer, on June 14, 1715, issued an order for Captain Miguel Tenorio de Alba to present to him the titles and papers upon which he based his right to sell the land in question; and on the same date he made an entry to the effect that he had personally notified Tenorio and that the latter had stated that he would obey the order.

On June 19, 1715, Tenorio made a written statement, which he presented to Rael de Aguilar, in which he calls attention to a certified copy of a deed which he presents for inspection, stating that the original thereof is in the government archives. He also refers to the grant under which Joseph de Quiros had held the lands in question, which grant he states was made to Quiros and his son-in-law, Antonio Duran de Armijo. He refers also to a memorial which he presented to the Marquis of Penuela (a former governor of New Mexico) in regard to the Indians being obliged to pay him what they still owed on the land.

The three documents referred to by Tenorio are parts of this archive. The first begins on page 1 of leaf 16. It is a copy of a deed, dated December 16, 1703, by Joseph de Quiros to Miguel Tenorio de Alba, and the correctness of the copy is certified to by Cristobal de Gongora, secretary of the town council of Santa Fe. This deed is for a portion of the land claimed by Quiros under the grant made by Governor Rodriguez. The land sold is described as consisting of three *fanegas* of corn-planting land, which, according to calculations based on data found in *"Ordenanzas de Tierras y Aguas,"* by Mariano Galvan, Paris, 1868, p. 164 (see also Hall's *Mexican Law*, p. 82), would amount to about 26.45 acres. The boundaries are described as follows: "On one side, which is that of the north, by some hills, on the south by the river; on the east by San Juan bluff; and on the west by lands of Juan Trujillo." The consideration was 130 *pesos*.

The second document cited by Tenorio begins on page 1 of leaf 14, of this archive. It consists of a petition by Antonio Duran de Armijo and Joseph de Quiros, directed to the governor and captain-general of New Mexico, asking for a grant of a piece of cultivable land located between the San Juan road and the Jacona bluffs. The boundaries were: "On the north side, the hill as we go to the new town (Santa Cruz de la Cañada); and on the south side the river which comes from Pojoaque; and on the east side the San Juan road; and on the west side the rocky bluffs (*peñascos*) which look toward Jacona." This petition was presented to Governor Pedro Rodriguez Cubero on September 10, 1701, and on that date he made the grant and ordered the chief alcalde of Santa Cruz, or his deputy, to place the grantees in possession of the land. On September 12, 1701, the chief alcalde, Roque Madrid, gave the possession with the following boundaries: "On the east side by a main road which goes to San Juan; on the west side by a precipitously crested red hill (*un*

DUKE OF ALBURQUERQUE
Viceroy of Mexico

creston colorado); on the north side by the hills; and on the south side by the river which comes down from the *pueblo of Nambé*.

Immediately after this act of possession, in a different handwriting from any in the muniments, is the following: "I transfer this grant to Francisco Canjuebe (Francisco Joseph Casados being witness) and he agrees to pay me at harvest time." There is no signature.

The *third* document referred to by Tenorio is leaf 13 of this archive. It is what he terms a memorial. In it he sets forth that he had sold to the Indians of Pojoaque about three fanegas of corn planting land, for the same price for which he had bought it — 130 *pesos*, and that after the lapse of two years they were still in arrears on the payment. He asks that they be compelled to pay him what they owed him. In a marginal note dated April 10, 1712, the Marquis of Peñuela, then governor of New Mexico, to whom the memorial was directed, told Tenorio to apply to the chief alcalde of Santa Cruz, or his deputy, and ordered the latter to compel the Indians to pay the debt or to cease using the land, which upon the re-payment to the Indians of what they had advanced on it might be sold by its owner to whomsoever he saw fit.

Tenorio's statement of June 19, 1715, when presented to Rael de Aguilar, was accompanied by the titles to the land and other documentary evidence, as is shown by a marginal note on the first page of leaf 9.

After Tenorio's statement the next document, in chronological order, is a petition by Juan de Atienza, attorney for the Indians, calling attention to the proceedings had in the time of Governor Juan Ignacio Flores Mogollon, and asks that they be examined, and that justice be done to the Indians.

This petition was presented to Felix Martinez, governor of New Mexico, and on April 30, 1716, he issued an order in which he states that as Alonso [Alfonso] Rael de Aguilar had acted in connection with such proceedings he was directed to present them to the governor for the latter's examination and decision.

Near the bottom of the second page of leaf 16, following the certified copy of the deed from Joseph de Quiros to Miguel Tenorio de Alba, is Rael de Aguilar's statement that the proceedings had not been concluded on account of the absence from Santa Fe of Juan de Atienza, and because Rael de Aguilar's commission had expired when Governor Martinez succeeded Governor Flores. But he transmits the proceedings uncompleted to the governor to be deposited in the archives.

8 DIEGO ARIAS DE QUIROS, July 24, 1715. City of Santa Fe.

Relative to the opening of a spring in the *Cienega*. The court house and a number of private residences now occupy this tract, which was granted to the *cabildo* of Santa Fe, August 20, 1715, as appears by the following, on file in the office of the surveyor-general. File 4.

Copy of documents of 1715 referring to the *cienega*, to the streets of Santa Fe, and their being obstructed by buildings; mention is made of the *"Calle Real de San Francisco"* and of the old church of the same name *on the plaza*. There is also a grant to the Captain Diego Arias de Quiros of a spring and reservoir which he had constructed in the *cienega*.

"I, Don Juan Ygnacio Flores Mogollon, governor and captain-general of this kingdom and provinces of New Mexico, and commander of its forces and garrisons for his majesty, &c. WHEREAS, on the 24th day of the month of July past, the illustrious *cabildo* of this town made a presentation to me with regard to various matters, and one of them was that, whereas the swamp (*cienega*) that lies to one side of this castle, looking to the east, is royal domain, that it should be adjudicated as municipal land (*propios*) of the town, in the name of his majesty, so that the inhabitants may enjoy the benefit and use of cutting hay for their animals as they have done heretofore and are doing until now, and because in an order I issued at the foot of said presentation on the 27th day of the said month of July, making provisions with regard to the other points stated to me in said representation, I say that because this petition is so justified, and because the said swamp (*cienega*) is royal domain, I make it the grant in the name of his majesty (whom may God preserve), and I order that a portion of it should be executed by virtue of the faculty conferred on me on account of my office, I grant to the said illustrious *cabildo* the said swamp (*cienega*) in the condition in which it is at present, for the reason that a piece thereof has been adjudicated to Captain Diego Arias de Quiros, on which he has introduced himself for many days by farming on it; likewise did I grant him a small spring of [torn] that he had taken out making a tank in order to be able to irrigate [torn]. As all appears from the proceedings that [torn] spring or tank were formed [torn], *cabildo*, and that he may become acquainted with all the points of his representation, and the condition with which I have made the said grant for the said tank and piece of swamp (*cienega*), farmed by the said Captain Diego Arias, in order that said illustrious *cabildo* may ask whenever he fails in any of the circumstances with which I made him the grant; and likewise shall it be able to ask as against other persons that having obstructed the inlets and outlets, and ancient streets of this town, I order that *testimonio* of said proceedings shall be given to it literally, said proceedings being now in the office of the secretary of this government, in order that said illustrious *cabildo* may keep it in its archive, and that it may there always appear; and of this grant, with regard that the swamp (*cienega*) has been adjudicated to it record shall be made (*se tomare razon*) in the book of grants and entries of this government. It is done at this town of Santa Fe, of New Mexico, on the 20th day of August, 1715, and I signed it with my secretary of government and war.

"DON JUAN YGNACIO FLORES MOGOLLON

"By command of his excellency the governor and captain-general: ROQUE DE PINTTO [rubric]

"Secretary of Government and War.

"I made the record on said day (*toma la razon*)."

The question of title to lands in the "*cienega*" was not finally settled until the Congress of the United States empowered the City of Santa Fe to make quit-claim to lands held within the areas prescribed by the act. The title was in question shortly before the American Occupation, during the administration of Governor Mariano Martinez.

9 JUAN ALONZO DE MONDRAGON and SEBASTIANA TRUXILLO to Francisca Antonio De Eguijosa. *Villa Nueva de Santa Cruz*, May 19, 1716. Before Juan Garcia de las Rivas, Alcalde.

Conveyance of lands. This property is located in the present county of *Rio Arriba*, New Mexico.

10 CRISTOBAL MARTIN and ANTONIO DE MORAGA to Captain Diego Arias de Quiros. 1716. City of *Santa Fe*. Before Francisco Joseph Cassados, Alcalde.

12   THE SPANISH ARCHIVES OF NEW MEXICO

      Conveyance of lands in the city of *Santa Fe*. This item is in a very badly damaged condition.

11   BERNARDO CASILLAS to Juan Estevan de Apodaca. City of *Santa Fe*. December 29, 1716.

      Conveyance of house and lands. County of *Santa Fe*. Before Juan Garcia de las Rivas, Alcalde.

12   DIEGO ARIAS DE QUIROS. March 23, 1717. City of *Santa Fe*. Before Juan Paez Hurtado, Governor and Captain-General.

      Grant of a lead mine, situate five leagues from *Santa Fe*, between *La Cienega* and *La Cieneguilla*. This is in the southern part of the county of Santa Fe, near the mining district at one time called the Bonanza; about nine miles from Los Cerrillos, on the line of the Atchison, Topeka and Santa Fe Railway. In this locality afterwards were found and located many prospects, and mines bearing silver, lead, and zinc. The famous turquoise mines are close by.

      De Vargas re-assumed the office of governor and captain-general on November 10, 1703. In the spring of the year following he inaugurated and led a campaign against the Faraon Apaches, in the Sandia mountains; he was taken ill while upon this campaign and died suddenly at Bernalillo, April 8, 1704. His remains were taken to Santa Fe and were buried in the church. See archive 1027; his will.

      Bancroft says that Don Francisco Cuervo y Valdez assumed the office of governor *ad interim* on March 10, 1705. This is a mistake. Six months before this date, August 4, 1704, he was already in office, as a suit at law involving the title to lands was tried before him. See archive 295, *Antonio Bas Gonzales vs. Diego Arias de Quiros*. Don Juan Paez Hurtado, the friend of De Vargas, did not serve, as Bancroft says, until March 10, 1705, for the reason that on August 4, 1704, he was present at this trial and signed the proceedings.

13   JUAN DE ARCHIVEQUE. 1721.

      Inventory and partition of his estate; made by the Captain Bueno de Bohorquez y Corcuera. In the City of *Santa Fe*. The item contains ninety-eight pages.

      With it is a document of four pages, being a certified copy of an order of the viceroy of New Spain defining the boundary line between *Nueva Vizcaya* and *Nuevo Mexico*. The original order was dated at the City of Mexico, August 2, 1682. See note to archive 6, *ante.*

Ad. F. Bandelier was the first writer in English to identify this man as the Jean L'Archeveque of the ill-fated La Salle expedition. An account of his purchase from the Texas Indians by Governor Alonzo Leon is given by Palacio Rivas in his *A Través de Los Siglos,* published several years prior to Mr. Bandelier's article appearing in the *Nation,* August 30, 1888, as follows:

"Two months ago, while searching the archives of the Pueblo of *Ka-Po* or Santa Clara (New Mexico) for documents of historical import, in behalf of the Hemenway Southwestern Archaeological Expedition, my attention was drawn, among others, to the great number of manuscripts called in Spanish *Diligencias matrimoniales.* They are investigations made on the petition of parties applying for license to marry, and consist in the main of the application of him or her, and of the examination of witnesses in regard to the standing of the applicants, their relations towards each other, etc. Among these I found one at Santa Clara headed: 'Ynformacion de Pedro Meusnier, frances.— 1699.' The fact that Frenchmen should be found in New Mexico at such an early date, and in face of the stringent laws of Spain against the admittance of foreigners into the colonies, appeared interesting. My interest soon increased upon discovering that Meusnier had come over to America in the fleet commanded by 'Monsieur de La Sala' in 1684. This is testified to by two witnesses, one of whom signs himself Juan de Archeveque, while the other, rather illiterate, has not signed, but states in his deposition that he is a native of La Rochelle, and his name is given as 'Santiago Groslee.' Both these witnesses claim to have come over with Meusnier in the same fleet, and in the year 1684 also. Both Meusnier and Archeveque were in 1699 soldiers of the garrison of Santa Fe; Groslee was a resident of that town.

"There was only one L'Archeveque in La Salle's ill-fated expedition, and the evidence seemed quite conclusive that this was the one whose signature I had before me at Santa Clara. Mr. Parkman, to whom I communicated the fact, also inclined to the belief that he was the fellow who enticed La Salle into the fatal snare, while Groslee seemed to be Grollet, the sailor. I have since found the latter as Grolle and Groli in two official documents now in my possession. As late as 1705 he was a resident of the little town of Bernalillo, on the Rio Grande. Of Meusnier I have not been able to find any further trace as yet.

"But the chief interest to me rested in the person of L'Archeveque, the more so since there is to-day in New Mexico a family calling themselves Archibeque, and of whom it is surmised, at least, that they are of French descent. Furthermore, I had met, in documents antedating 1720, the name and declarations of a Captain Juan de Archeveque. It was but natural to suspect that the Captain of the War Councils of 1715 and of 1720 was the same man as the private soldier of 1699; the more so since at the latter council, where the project of the ill-fated reconnoissance to the Arkansas river was discussed, the said Capt. Archibeque strongly recommended it, alleging in its favor, along other reasons, that it would procure definite information in regard to 'his countrymen the French.'

"Researches at the archives of the U. S. Surveyor-General's office at Santa Fe brought to light documents which impart valuable information. There is in the first place a transfer to Juan de Archibeque, 'a soldier,' of certain real estate in Santa Fe, in the year 1701. Lastly there is the Inventory of the goods and chattels of the Captain Juan de Archibeque, a Frenchman, bearing date 1720. From this manuscript we gather that our man accompanied the expedition to the Arkansas which he had so strongly advocated, and that he, with some forty-three other Spaniards, was killed there by the Pawnee Indians on the 17th of August of the same year.

. . . . . .

"We further gather that Archibeque was twice married, and left two legitimate and two illegitimate children; that after leaving the military service he became a successful trader, extending his trading tours to Sonora, and sometimes buying directly at the City of Mexico. His estate, after settlement, yielded 6,118 pesos to the heirs, an amount quite respectable at the time. Upon a second visit to Santa Clara I found there at last the *Diligencia* matrimonial of L'Archeueque alias Archibeque. It bears date 1697, and his (first) wife was the widow of Thomas de Ytta, murdered in 1694 near Zacatecas by a mulatto. She herself was a native of Tezcuco, in the valley of Mexico."

Felipe de Tamaris, a soldier of the Santa Fe garrison, who had accompanied Villasur to the Platte, brought the news of the defeat of the Spaniards by the French and Pawnees, on the 6th of September, 1720. There were a few other survivors.

14 JOSEPH DE ATIENZA. *Villa Nueva de Santa Cruz.* April 14, 1722.

A petition for land. It was referred on the same day to Captain Alonzo Rael de Aguilar by Don Juan Domingo de Bustamante, governor and captain-general.

Captain Alonzo Rael de Aguilar was one of the *reconquistadores*; he was secretary of government and war.

The tract known as *"Cerrillos"* was granted to him by General De Vargas at the time of the first *entrada*, as appears from the following archives:

On the 20th of April, 1788, Josef Miguel de la Peña asked for a piece of land called "Los Cerrillos" which said tract "when this province was conquered belonged to Don Alonzo Rael de Aguilar, who was my wife, Maria Rael's grandfather, and having left it so many years unoccupied, and Don Alonzo having lost the right he had to it," possession was given to the applicant and the other heirs of Don Alonzo de Aguilar by Don Josef Antonio Ortiz under orders of the lieutenant-colonel and political governor, Don Fernando de la Concha; the boundaries of the land being on the north the Cañada Guīcu and lands of Los Bacas; on the south by the Cerros Altos; on the east by the road that goes to Galisteo. Mention is made of lands belonging to Don Cleto Miera y Pacheco. Josef Miguel de la Peña, for the sum of $450.00, in 1791, sold the property to Don Cleto de Miera. This property later belonged to Colonel Manuel Delgado, who was second in command in New Mexico under General de la Concha. Upon this property was a mine known as the "Mina del Toro."

The heirs in the year 1750 of the conquistador Alfonso Rael de Aguilar were: Eusebio de Aguilar; Juan Rael de Aguilar; Antonia Teresa Rael de Aguilar; Francisco Rael de Aguilar; and children of the deceased Alfonso Rael de Aguilar, and the children of Feliciano Rael de Aguilar. Don Diego de Vargas granted the Cerrillos tract to the elder Alfonso Rael de Aguilar. In the year 1696 the elder Rael de Aguilar retired from Los Cerrillos by the order of General de Vargas, where he had lived four years and built houses, the ruins of which were visible in 1750. In that year Juan Rael de Aguilar, one of the heirs, was in the city of Santa Fe, but he was then a resident of the city of Chihuahua, but was willing to return "as soon as your excellency shall deign to concede us the said grant."

The original grant to Alonso Rael de Aguilar, the secretary of government and war under De Vargas, was as follows:

"HIS EXCELLENCY THE GOVERNOR AND CAPTAIN-GENERAL:

"I, Ensign Alfonso Rael de Aguilar, a soldier and secretary of state and war of this province of New Mexico, by appointment of your excellency, before whom I appear and state: That considering that this said province of Mexico is now reduced and conquered, it having cost your excellency much watching, much care, and great expense, I enter a tract of land situated from this city of Santa Fe from four to five leagues, and called the Cerrillos tract, for which your excellency will please make me in the name of His Majesty a grant, as one of the conquering soldiers that have come with your excellency, which tract of land I ask, with its entrances, and exits, uses and customs, as well as the water, pasturage, and watering-places, as the same were enjoyed by the *former settlers* of the tract. I ask and pray in due humility that your excellency be pleased to concede and make me, in the name of His Majesty, a grant for said tract of land, as I am a poor married man, with children, and I trust that your excellency will grant me, as I have requested; and I declare in due form of law that this my petition and entry is not made in dissimulation, and as may be necessary, etc.   ALFONSO RAEL DE AGUILAR."

"At this fortified town and garrison aforementioned, of the city of Santa Fe, in the province of New Mexico, on the 18th day of the month of September, in the year 1692, before me, Diego de Vargas Zapata y Lujan Ponce de Leon, His Majesty's governor and captain general of this said province, and its domain and districts and castellan of the forces and garrisons therein, the foregoing petition was presented by the petitioner, who is a soldier at this garrison, and my secretary of state and war, and in consideration of his services and of the loyalty with which he has served, and the love he has borne His Majesty, I, the said governor and captain general do, in the name of His Majesty, make him a grant for the land, together with its

PAGE FROM OLDEST ARCHIVE IN OFFICE OF SURVEYOR-GENERAL
With Signature of Don Antonio Otermín, Governor and Captain-General of New Mexico

pasturage, waters, timber, watering-places, uses and customs, and the appurtenances, so that at his will he may, 'God, the father willing,' enjoy the same for himself and his heirs, as the will of our Lord, the King, in whose royal name, and in consideration of the merits and services of the party, I do make to him the said grant. In testimony whereof I signed this with two witnesses, the same being the captain and ensign of this garrison, and I returned to the party the said petition, and the granting decree thereon, in the presence of Sergeant Major Fernando de Chavez and Captain Antonio Jorge, residents of this said province, and participants in the said conquest.

"DIEGO DE VARGAS ZAPATA LUJAN PONCE DE LEON
"ROQUE MADRID
"JUAN DE DIOS LUZERO DE GODOY"

Don Juan Domingo de Bustamante had been exercising the functions of governor and captain-general a little over a month at the time this petition was presented. He was governor during two terms, the second ending in 1731. He was a great Indian campaigner and led all the campaigns during his rule. It was during his administration that the controversy arose between the Franciscans and the bishop of Durango. In this controversy Rael de Aguilar took side with the frayles, while General Juan Paez Hurtado, a companion in arms, was against them. Bustamante was tried on the charge of "illegal trade" and found guilty.

This archive proves conclusively that the *Estancia* of Los Cerrillos was occupied before the rebellion of 1680.

Diego Arias de Quiros, in addition to being an alcalde, was a captain. All of the prominent soldiers also occupied civil positions. In this way a great deal of complaint arose on the part of the Franciscan friars, although a search of all available records does not sustain the charge that the officers were brutal in their treatment of the Indians, although it is rather apparent that the officers made everything possible in a pecuniary way out of their positions, both civil and military.

F. Carlos Delgado in his *Informe* says that the alcaldes were creatures of the governor, each one appointed on condition that he make all he can and divide with the governor. It is certain that the Spaniards made the Indians pay quite a tax in the shape of cotton cloths, working in the fields, etc.

The father of Roque Madrid had a rancho near the Cerrillos. Captain Roque Madrid worked a prospect at Cerrillos for the purpose of obtaining lead for the guns of the Spanish soldiers.

It was also said that the governors sent to New Mexico were compelled to pay tribute to the viceroys to whom they owed their appointments. See letter of Fr. Suarez where he says: *"Pero, muy catolico Rey y Señor, como los que vienen son criados de los virreyes, o compran los officios, &c."*

In the beginning, subsequent to the conquest of Mexico by Hernando Cortes, it seems that all offices were given more as favors than as rewards for services to the crown.

General Juan Paez Hurtado had special charge of the colonists who came back with De Vargas in 1693. When charges were preferred against De Vargas, Hurtado was also accused. His arrest was ordered by Governor Cubero; he was charged with defrauding the colonists of half the royal allowance to each; after the death of De Vargas he served as governor *ad interim* until the arrival of Governor Cuervo y Valdes, in the summer of 1704. Governor Cuervo commissioned him as general. In 1715 he made a campaign against the Apaches. In 1716, when Governor Martinez was ordered to report to the viceroy at Mexico, Martinez tried to leave him in charge at Santa Fe as governor; he probably filled the office for a short period until Valverde assumed the office; he was lieutenant-general in 1724.

De Vargas's term of office expired in 1696, but he was still in office in that year; see archive No. 2.

Don Pedro Rodriguez Cubero took possession of the office of governor on the 4th of July, 1697. He had a commission as *juez de residencia*; De Vargas gave up the office unwillingly and Cubero became his enemy; the *cabildo* of Santa Fe were enemies of De Vargas because he kept his promises with the Indians and restored captives who were slaves and servants of the Spanish settlers and officers; he treated De Vargas very cruelly; found him guilty of charges of embezzlement. Cubero made a tour of the pueblos of the province. In 1703, Cubero learned that De Vargas had been exonerated and re-appointed and left the country without meeting De V., who was now Marqués de la Nava de Brazinas. He was afterwards made governor of Maracaibo and died in Mexico the year after he left Santa Fe.

THE SPANISH ARCHIVES OF NEW MEXICO 19

15 IGNACIO LOSANO to Joseph de Armijo. May 15, 1727. City of *Santa Fe*. Before Diego Arias de Quiros, Alcalde.
    Conveyance of a house and land.

16 ANTONIA and FRANCISCA MAESE to Alonzo Rael de Aguilar. June 10, 1727. City of *Santa Fe*.
    Conveyance of land. Before Diego Arias de Quiros, Alcalde. One of these grantees was the wife of Nicolas Ortiz Niño Ladron de Guevara, who was an owner in the Caja del Rio Grant.

17 MIGUEL DE ARCHIVEQUE.
    August 14, 1727. City of *Santa Fe*. Will. He was the son of Captain Juan de Archibeque.

18 LORENZO GRIEGO to Teresa Ansures. December 20, 1734. City of *Santa Fe*.
    Conveyance of land. Before Geronimo Xaramillo, Alcalde.

19 JUANA MARTIN to Juan de Apodaca. September 20, 1734. City of *Santa Fe*.
    Conveyance of land. Before Antonio de Uribarri, Alcalde.
    Antonio de Uribarri was also a captain. He took part in the troubles between the bishop of Durango and the Franciscans. He held the position of alcalde of Santa Fe for more than fifteen years. The alcalde mayor of Santa Fe at this time was Francisco Bueno de Bohorques y Corcuera, who was also a captain in the army. There seem to have been four alcaldes of Santa Fe at this time.

20 LAZARO DE ATIENSA versus ANTONIO MARTIN.
    Suit over land. September 30, 1735. Before Juan Esteban Garzia de Noriega, Alcalde. *Sitio del Ojo Caliente, Rio Arriba* county, New Mexico. Before Gervasio Cruzat y Gongora, Governor and Captain-General.
    Juan Estevan Garcia de Noriega was the son of Juan Garcia de Noriega, an officer under Cruzate and later with De Vargas.
    Don Gervasio Cruzat y Gongora held the office of governor five years, succeeding Don Juan Domingo de Bustamante in the year 1731. He took evidence for the bishop of Durango in his contest with the Franciscans. It is

certain that he was acting in 1731: see archive 317. He founded a mission of Jicarilla Apaches on the Rio Trampas, Taos county, in 1733. Fr. Juan Mirabal was the Franciscan who looked after this mission. Fr. Mirabal thought that inasmuch as the Jicarillas were Christians they had a right to make war on the Comanches, who were not.

21 JUANA DE LOS REYES PEREA to Francisco Angel. September 20, 1738. City of *Santa Fe*.

Conveyance of land. Before Captain Antonio Montoya, Alcalde. Antonio Montoya was a celebrated Indian fighter.

22 ANTONIO DE ULIBARRI to Francisco Xavier Angel. August 5, 1738. City of *Santa Fe*.

Conveyance of lands. Before Captain Antonio Montoya, Alcalde.

23 PASCUALA PADILLA to Agustin de Archibeque. May 17, 1739. City of *Santa Fe*.

Conveyance of lands. Before Antonio Montoya, Alcalde. Agustin de Archibeque was the son of Juan de Archiveque.

24 JUAN JOSE DE ARCHULETA. August 20, 1742. City of *Santa Fe*.

Grant made by Governor and Captain-General Don Gaspar Domingo de Mendoza. This tract of land lies about a mile below the City of *Santa Fe*.

Don Gaspar Domingo de Mendoza was appointed governor on May 12, 1737, but did not assume the duties of his office until the month of January, 1739. He continued in office until 1743. In 1740, some Frenchmen came into the province by way of Taos, two of whom remained at Santa Fe. One of these was named Louis Marie; he had some trouble with the authorities, and was shot in the plaza by order of Mendoza. There were nine of them in the party. Villaseñor says they settled near Alburquerque; this must be the settlement near Isleta, called *Canada* and later *Fuenclara* and *Limpia Concepcion*.

Among these Frenchmen were the Mallet brothers. They came from the French settlements on the Mississippi river. They followed up the Missouri river for a long distance, thinking that was the route. They found out from some *Aricara* Indians that they were mistaken and were shown by them the route. They arrived at Santa Fe July 22, 1739, and on the first of May, 1740, leaving two of them at Santa Fe; only three went back and these returned by way of the *Pawnee* villages; some of them returned by way of the Arkansas river and the Mississippi to New Orleans, it is stated.

The next Frenchman to come to Santa Fe was Baptiste LaLande, who came there in 1804. At least he told Major Zebulon Pike, in 1807, that he had been in Santa Fe three years.

During the administration of Don Joachim Codallos y Rabal, who succeeded Mendoza, thirty-three Frenchmen visited the Jicarillas and Comanches and sold them a lot of guns. Governor Codallos thought that some of those who had come in 1739 were in this party and that the French were hostile in their intentions.

25 JUAN ANTONIO ARCHULETA and LEONARDO GONZALES.

A grant of land. September 4, 1742. City of *Santa Fe*. Made by Don Gaspar Domingo de Mendoza, governor and captain-general. The land is situate near *Santa Fe*, close by a little hill called "*Serrito de Lara.*"

26 VICENTE DE ARMIJO.

Will. November 15, 1743. City of *Santa Fe*. Before Don Antonio de Ulibarri, Alcalde.

The full name of this "*re-conquistador*" was Vincente Duran de Armijo. In 1739, he made application to Governor Mendoza for a tract of land near the pueblo of *Nambé*. The petition recites several points of historical interest, and the disposition to guard the interests of the Indians is manifest in the act of possession, both of which are as follows:

"To His Excellency, the Governor and Captain-General:

"Vincente Duran de Armijo, resident of the *Villa de Santa Fe*, and settler and conqueror of the Kingdom of New Mexico, appears at your excellency's feet in the most approved manner the law allows, and states: That having experienced innumerable sufferings and hunger and nakedness, and other misfortunes we have undergone in this poor kingdom, on account of having lost our personal labor in our corn and wheat fields, with which we were to meet our obligations, owing to the scarcity of water in the river running through the city, which arises from the absence of rain for some time back, and our personal labor upon our grain crops being useless as they have all failed; and having been one of the settlers of this kingdom from the year '94, and always ready armed and equipped, at my own expense, to go upon any campaign or expedition whenever required as a loyal subject of His Majesty, whom may God preserve; This, sir, has always been [torn] having been in the army which has gone on said campaigns and expeditions against the hostile Indians who inhabit these parts of the kingdom at this time. Sir, I have by my exertions accumulated a little capital with a great risk to my life by making journeys to the outer country, and have become the owner of a certain amount of live stock which is not secure from the hostile attacks of the Indians, who on certain occasions inhabit the country where my stock is pastured; and I have had warning from two cows belonging to me which have been killed by the enemy during the present year.

"I have seen proper to register a piece of land which is a surplus beyond the lands of the friendly Indians of the pueblo of *Nambé*, without disturbing the pastures or waters upon which the herds of this royal garrison or the animals of the aforesaid Indians are pastured, nor any other person using said lands. It contains about six *fanegas* of wheat and two of corn, and its boundaries are as follows: on the north it is bounded by an *arroyo*; on the south by the lands of Bernardo de Sena; on the east by a mountain; on the west by lands of the aforementioned Indians of *Nambé*.

"This piece of land, in the name of the King, our sovereign, whom may God preserve — [torn] — four families whom I have emancipated — my children, that the piece of land in this city is not sufficient for all; and by granting us the aforesaid land we may receive some benefit from our labor, and my cattle will be secure from the enemy, to be with pastures and watering places, and that royal permission be given me in the name of His Majesty; and I swear that this, my petition is not made through malice, etc.   VINCENTE DURAN DE ARMIJO"

ROYAL POSSESSION

"In the City of Santa Fe, capital of the kingdom of New Mexico, on the twenty-fifth day of September, in the year one thousand seven hundred and thirty-nine, I, Don Gaspar Domingo de Mendoza, governor and captain-general of said Kingdom by his Majesty, whom may God preserve, having seen the above, considered it as presented, and having ascertained its contents, I ordered that possession be given to the petitioner of the land he solicits. It is not, however the land he mentions in his petition, the Indians of the adjoining pueblo having objected to his having the land he asks for; although I caused the Indians of said pueblo to appear before me, who before the petitioner, declared themselves pleased that the land should be given to him in the vicinity of their pueblo where no injury would result to them. Therefore, I order and direct the senior justice of the proper jurisdiction to proceed to place him in possession of said lands in the name of His Majesty, in order that he may settle upon, cultivate and improve them according to the royal decrees, for himself, children, heirs, successors and others having a better right thereto; establishing his boundaries with all the formalities required in the royal grants, so that by virtue of these formalities all difficulties may be prevented in the future. I so provided, signed and ordered with my attending witnesses, acting by appointment, in the absence of a royal or public notary, there being none in this Kingdom, and on this common paper, there being none which is stamped.

"DON GASPAR DOMINGO DE MENDOZA

"Witnesses:
"DIEGO DE UGARTE
"JOSEPH DE TERRUS"

"On the fifth day of the month of October of the present year, one thousand seven hundred and thirty-nine, I, the senior justice and war-captain of the new city of Santa Cruz and its districts, by virtue of the decree of his excellency the governor and captain-general, Don Gaspar Domingo de Mendoza, I proceeded to the pueblo of *Nambé* within my jurisdiction, taking with me five witnesses to act in that capacity, and three of whom were to act as instrumental and two as my attending witnesses, with whom I acted, and these being present with the parties, Vincente Duran de Armijo and the *Cacique* and old men, natives of the pueblo, with the governor and other authorities of the aforesaid pueblo of *Nambé*, I read to them the foregoing document presented by Vincente Duran de Armijo. I also read to them, in a clear and audible voice, the provisions made by the said governor and captain-general, where his excellency directs and orders that possession be given to him of the lands the petition asks for, but afterwards the Indians of the aforementioned pueblo, having made opposition on the ground that the granting of the land asked for by the petitioner would be a great injury to them, although it did not belong to the pueblo, they voluntarily agreed to give to the said Vincente Duran de Armijo a piece of land for himself, his children, heirs and successors from the lands of the pueblo, in the place of that he asked for, and which would be so much to their injury. In view of which his excellency provides that he shall not have the lands he asks for, but that which may be selected with the consent of the Indians, and I, the said senior justice, as aforesaid, all the natives of the aforesaid pueblo being present and informed of his excellency's order, and of all that had been agreed upon with the said Vincente in the presence of the said governor and captain-general, they stated that they would assign, and did assign, to the said Vincente Duran de Armijo a piece of land to the west of the said pueblo of *Nambé*, on the borders of their lands; that on the said western side a small portion is bounded by lands of the pueblo of *Pojoaque,* whose boundary is an *arroyo* which runs into the *Rio Nambé,* that is on the southern side of said river of *Nambé,* and on the east by a stone mound and a medium sized cedar, which is the boundary between the pueblo and the said Vincente; and on the north this little piece is bounded by said river and on the south by an *acequia,* which runs along the foot of some barren hills, the distance being cords of fifty varas each from the river aforesaid to the said *acequia*; and the large piece of land which they gave to the said Armijo, which is north of said river, contains seven hundred and forty varas in latitude, which is understood to be from east to west, and from north to south it contains five hundred and fifty varas; the boundaries of which are: on the north some stone mounds scattered along some barren hills, which form the boundary of the lands of General Juan Paez Hurtado, and on the south is bounded by the river of said pueblo; on the east the boundary is a cross, on the side of the main road and lands of the Indians of said town; and on the west lands of General Juan Paez Hurtado, which boundaries are marked by several mounds of stone, and on one of them is a holy cross, which is to serve as a boundary and division, of which two pieces of land I gave him royal possession. I took him by the hand and walked with him over said lands. He threw stones, pulled up grass, and cried aloud, saying long life to the King, in whose royal name I left him in quiet and peaceable possession; and he offered to cultivate and settle the same, as directed by royal decrees, under penalty of forfeiture, as directed by his Majesty in his royal orders; and in order that said possession and the consent and agreement had with the said Vincente Duran de Armijo by the aforesaid Indians be placed upon record, I certify that such has been the case, and I signed, with my undersigned attending witnesses, Antonio Trujillo, Tomas Madrid and Gregorio Garduño, being instrumental; the last having been selected by the *Cacique* and authorities of the pueblo at their request to sign for them the name of the aforesaid Indians, knowing not how to do so themselves; and as aforestated I so acted and signed with those in my attendance in the absence of a royal or public notary, there being none in this kingdom, and on this common paper, the stamp not being in use in these parts; to all of which I certify.

"JUAN GARCIA DE MORA, Acting Justice.

"Witnesses:
"NICOLAS ORTIZ
"FRANCO. GARDUÑO
"At the request of the natives of the Pueblo of *Nambé*.
"GREGORIO GARDUÑO"

Don Gaspar Ortiz, a prominent New Mexican, inherited this property from his grandfather, Gaspar Ortiz, who purchased it from Vincente Duran de Armijo. The elder Gaspar Ortiz lived upon the property from 1789 until 1824, when he died.

27 ANTONIO TAFOYA ALTAMIRANO.
Will, partition and division of property. February 18, 1844. Town of *El Paso del Rio del Norte*. The will is a copy certified by Alonzo Victores Rubin de Zelis, Alcalde of *El Paso*.

The partition was made upon the petition to Bernardo de Bustamante de Tagle before Francisco Ortiz, Alcalde.

28 INHABITANTS OF ABIQUIU and OJO CALIENTE.
Petition for permission to remove. Before Juan de Beytia, Alcalde, and Don Joachin Codallos y Rabal, Governor and Captain-General, 1748.

The settlers of *Ojo Caliente, Abiquiú*, and *Pueblo Quemado* asked to remove to places of greater security.

The inhabitants desired to remove on account of the Indian outrages of 1747. The Indians were the *Utes*. Ojo Caliente is about 6,250 feet above sea level; there are some fine hot medicinal springs there. Three great pueblo ruins are found there. They are *Houiri, Homayo,* and *Poseuingge*. The last named is near the baths (springs). The story of *"Montezuma"* comes from the legend of *Poseuingge*.

The modern plaza of *Abiquiú* stands on the very site of an ancient pueblo. The old pueblo, it is said, was peopled by *Genízaros*, Indian captives, whom the Spaniards had rescued from their captors. The ruins lie on the highest point of the present town. This pueblo is of pre-Spanish origin. Nobody dwelt there in the sixteenth or seventeenth centuries. This was not the pueblo occupied by the *Genízaros*. There were two settlements made at *Abiquiú* in the eighteenth century. The first was by the settlers who made this petition to the governor, as it was raided on the 12th of August, 1747, in which a number of settlers were killed and the rest compelled to leave it.

It was re-settled in 1754, and Fr. Juan José Toledo was the priest. The settlers continued to have trouble with the Utes and the Navajós. They left, but Governor Mendinueta compelled them to return to their homes in 1770. The mission at this place was called *Santo Tomas de Abiquiú*. In 1779, there were 851 people living here and in the immediate vicinity. In the year 1808, there were 122 Indians, 1,815 whites and half-breeds. So says Fr. Josef Benito Pereyro in his *Noticias de las Missiones,* etc., *Ms.* The name of the old pueblo, according to the Indians of San Juan was *Fe-jiu*. Some of the Indians called it *Jo-so-ge*. *Jo-so* is the name by which the *Tehuas* knew the *Moquis*.

The old pueblos near Ojo Caliente are probably of the same period as the old pueblo at *Abiquiú*. They certainly were not inhabited when the Spanish explorers in the sixteenth century went as far north as Taos (*Barba*).

General De Vargas passed by the ruins in 1694, but he is mistaken as to what they were, as they were not the ruins of old San Gabriel. See his *Relacion Sumaria de las Operaciones militares del Año de 1694, Ms.*, Washington, Library of Congress.

Don Joachin Codallos y Rabal was governor and captain-general of New Mexico from 1743 to 1749. During his administration 440 Moquis came to see him, asking protection and frayles. It is more than likely that a num-

THE SPANISH ARCHIVES OF NEW MEXICO   27

>ber of these Moquis were settled at *Abiquiú* in the pueblo of "*Genízaros*" and this accounts for the Tehua appellation given the pueblo of *Jo-so-ge*.

29 PEOPLE OF ALAMEDA.
>Relative to Joseph Montaño having come upon their lands. January 20, 1750. Before Miguel Lucero, Alcalde. Don Tomas Veles Cachupin, Governor and Captain-General.

30 SEBASTIAN DE VARGAS to Antonio Duran de Armijo. July 24, 1751. City of *Santa Fe*.
>Conveyance of lands. Before Manuel Gallegos, Alcalde.

31 JULIAN RAEL DE AGUILAR.
>Proceedings in the matter of a contested will. 1751. Before Don Tomas Veles Cachupin, Governor and Captain-General.

32 MANUEL MARTIN to Nicolas de Apodaca. June 7, 1751. At *San Francisco Xavier del Pueblo Quemado*. *Rio Arriba county*.
>Before Juan Joseph Sandoval, Alcalde. Conveyance of land.
>Juan Leon; Felipe Romero.

33 MARIA DE HERRERA, widow of Captain Antonio Martin, to Vicente Apodaca. April 5, 1753. *Santa Cruz del Ojo Caliente*.
>Donation of land. Before Juan Joseph Lobato, Alcalde. Antonio Pacheco; Gregorio Sandoval.

34 JOSE GABRIEL VITTON (BITON) to Tomas de Armijo. December 20, 1758. City of *Santa Fe*.
>Conveyance of land. Before Francisco Guerrero, Alcalde.
>This deed refers to the *Rio Chiquito*.

35 MARCIAL GONZALES to Francisco de Analla (Anaya). June 4, 1759. City of *Santa Fe*.
>Conveyance of land. Before Francisco Guerrero, Alcalde.

36 TOWN OF ABIQUIU.
>Order for its re-settlement. November 2, 1770. Made

28   THE SPANISH ARCHIVES OF NEW MEXICO

by Don Pedro Fermin de Mendinueta, Governor and Captain-General.

Refers to the re-settlement of *Abiquiú* by Governor Tomas Veles Cachupin.

37   ROSALIA DE GILTOMEY, widow of Juan Manuel Varela, to Isabel de Armijo, widow of Antonio de Sena. November 21, 1760. City of *Santa Fe*.

Conveyance of land. Before Francisco Guerrero, Alcalde.

38   PEDRO ANTONIO BUSTAMANTE Y TAGLE to Marcial Angel. July 26, 1762. City of *Santa Fe*.

Conveyance of land. Before Manuel Gallego, Alcalde.

39   MANUEL DE ARMIJO and JUAN DE LEDESMA.

Entry of a mine about one league south of the *Cerrillos* rancho and called *Nuestra Señora de Los Dolores* in the papers. Before Tomas Veles Cachupin, Governor and Captain-General.

40   JOSEPHA DE LA ASCENCION, widow of Hernando Martin. October 29, 1767.

Claim for lands donated by Mateo Martin in the *Pueblo Quemado*. Before Don Pedro Fermin de Mendinueta, Governor and Captain-General.

41   MARCELA TRUGILLO to Ines de Apodaca. October 30, 1767. City of *Santa Fe*.

Conveyance of land. Before Francisco Guerrero, Alcalde.

42   JOAQUIN DE ALDERETE.

Will. April 9, 1767. City of *Santa Fe*.

43   JOSE IGNACIO ALARID and GABRIEL QUINTANA. March 21, 1768. County of *Rio Arriba*.

Grant of land. Made by Don Pedro Fermin de Mendinueta, Captain-General. Possession given by Antonio Joseph Ortiz, Alcalde. Boundaries: North, Manuel Lucero; south, Joseph Baca; east and west, the boundaries held by the former owner, Geronimo Pacheco.

44   ANTONIO ARMIJO. May 18, 1769. County of *Santa Fe*.

Grant of land. Made by Don Pedro Fermin De Mendinueta, Governor and Captain-General. Four hundred varas square. Adjoining the City of *Santa Fe*. Possession given by Felipe Tafoya, Alcalde.

45 JUANA BENABIDES to Ignacio Alarid. March 23, 1772. County of *Santa Fe*.
Conveyance of land on the *Tesuque* river. Before Manuel Garcia Pareja, Alcalde.

46 CARNUEL TRACT.
Petition of persons of *Alburquerque* to settle upon the same. March 24, 1774. Denied. Before Don Pedro Fermin de Mendinueta, Governor and Captain-General, and a report made by Francisco Trebol Navarro, Alcalde.

47 MANUELA BRITO to Tomas Alire. August 28, 1774. City of *Santa Fe*.
Conveyance of land. Before Manuel Garcia Pareja, Alcalde.

48 GERTRUDIS ARMIJO, wife of MANUEL VIGIL. 1776.
Inventory of her effects. Before Don Pedro Fermin de Mendinueta, Captain-General and Manuel Vigil, Alcalde. County of *Taos*.

49 LAZARO ATENCIO.
Will. August 1, 1777. Before Manuel Garcia Pareja, Alcalde.

50 FRANCISCA TRUXILLO to Maria de Guadalupe de Archibeque. September 14, 1767. County of *Santa Fe*.
Conveyance of land. Before Francisco Guerrero, Alcalde.

51 HEIRS OF THE ALAMEDA TRACT vs. PEDRO BARELA. 1778. County of *Bernalillo*.
Opposition to sale of lands. Before Francisco Trebol Navarro, Acting Captain-General.

52 ANTONIO DE ARMENTA.
Land grant. 1789. County of *Bernalillo*. Made by Don Fernando de la Concha, Governor and Captain-General. Possession given by Antonio José Ortiz, Alcalde. Two hundred varas.

30 THE SPANISH ARCHIVES OF NEW MEXICO

53 INHABITANTS OF THE TOWN OF ALBURQUERQUE vs. ANTONIO DE SILBA. No date.

>Requiring him to give up a land grant which he has in his possession. Before Juan Gonzales Baz, Alcalde.

54 SALVADOR ARMIJO. September 22, 1803. County of *Santa Fe*.

>Inventory and partition of estate. Before Pedro Bautista Pino, Alcalde.

55 NEMESIO SALCEDO, Comandante. August 11, 1809.

>Permitting José Manuel Aragon to occupy land at *Laguna*.
>
>This is a letter from Nemesio Salcedo, the commandant general at Chihuahua, to the acting governor of New Mexico, dated August 11, 1809, stating that there are no grounds for granting the petition of José Manuel Aragon, who had asked that certain lands, belonging to the Indians of Laguna, which he had formerly used, be turned over to him; but in view of Aragon's being the alcalde of that district, having a large family, and being in need, Salcedo had decided that as long as Aragon should continue in the office of alcalde he might have designated for his use a piece of land large enough to enable him to raise crops needed by his family, but that he could not claim *title* to the land.

56 JUAN de AGUILAR. August 17, 1818.

>Question of boundaries with the Pueblo of the *Pecos*. Before Don Facundo Melgares, Governor. Vicente Villanueva, Alcalde.
>
>Pueblo of Pecos; measurements made from the church and the location of the latter with respect to the end of the pueblo at that time (1818) occupied by the Indians.
>
>In the same item is a report made to Governor Pedro Maria de Allande by José Vicente Ortiz, alcalde, in regard to the property of Francisco Garcia, dated at *Sebolletta*, June 16, 1818. County of Valencia.
>
>This is a petition of Juan de Aguilar to the governor of New Mexico, complaining that the alcalde of El Vado, Don Vincente Villanueva, had made certain measurements from the pueblo of Pecos in defiance of the accepted rules for such operations, in that he had begun them at the edge of the town, instead of at the cross in the cemetery, and with a cord one hundred *varas* in length instead of

only fifty, which alleged errors had resulted in extending the boundaries of the league of the Indians so as to embrace land belonging to the petitioner, and also lands belonging to other citizens. The petitioner asks the governor to decide the two questions raised by him as to the correct manner of making the measurements.

On August 19, 1818, Governor Melgares called upon the alcalde to report on the matter, which he did on the same day.

He says that no injury had resulted to anyone from the use of the hundred *vara* cord, because he had dampened it and stretched it out by two stakes, to offset what shrinkage it may have suffered while it had been coiled; that he had presented it to the petitioner, his son and others, who had again stretched it until they broke it; that with this cord he had made the measurement, with which they were satisfied; that the statement that other lands than those of the petitioner were embraced in the league was false; that if he had used a shorter cord it would have been to the injury of the Indians, on account of the irregular and broken character of the ground; etc., etc.

In regard to his beginning at the edge of the *pueblo* he states that he knew it was the custom (but not a fixed rule) to begin at the cross in the cemetery; that the reason for this was that in all the *pueblos*, except Pecos, the church was approximately in the center of the *pueblo*; that in addition to the *pueblo* of Pecos being long, the church was more than a hundred *varas* distant from one of its extremities, which extremity was opposite to the one then occupied by the Indians; that he had made two other measurements which were favorable to the citizens; etc.

No action appears to have been taken on this report by the governor.

57 JOSE ANTONIO ALARID.
Will, March 12, 1822. County of *Santa Fe*. Before Josef Salaises, Captain of the military company.

58 JOSE ANTONIO ALARID.
Grant, April 29, 1822. County of *Santa Fe*. Made by the *Ayuntamiento* of *Santa Fe*. At *Galisteo*. Possession given by Pedro Armendaris, Alcalde.

59 AGAPITO ALBA. April 26, 1823.
Petition for a piece of land. Forwarded by José Ignacio Rascon to the Governor of the Province.

60 JUAN ANTONIO ARMIJO; MATTIAS DURAN; ANTONIO LUXAN; RAFAEL ROIBAL; JOSE MARIA ROIBAL; JOSE MARTINEZ. March 3, 1825.
Grant. Made by the Territorial Deputation. *Hijuelas* made by Diego Padilla, Alcalde. No *hijuela* on file in favor of José Martinez. Land situate on the *Pecos* river, Land granted to the Sacristan, Diego Padilla, mentioned.

61 TOWN OF ABIQUIU. See Reported Grant.

62 PUEBLO OF THE PECOS.
Report concerning area of lands. By José Ramon Alarid. August 21, 1826.

63 JOSE RAMON ALARID.
Reports that Gregorio Arteaga, attorney of the half-breeds, refuses to go to *El Bado* to attend to the matter of the land called "*La Cuesta.*" Report made to Antonio Narbona, Governor, etc.

64 SEBOLETTA GRANT. 1827.
Question of partition of lands. Before Pedro Iturrieta, Alcalde, and José Antonio Chaves y Duran, Secretary of the *Ayuntamiento*. Salvador Ansures for his wife, Leogarda Chaves, through her father, José Antonio Chaves.

65 TOWN OF ABIQUIU. See Reported Grant.

66 RAMON ABREU.
Registration of a mine. October 29, 1832. Location — *Real de los Dolores*. County of *Santa Fe*. José Francisco Terrus and Ramon Abreu for themselves and others. Registration of a mine. June 5, 1832. Situate in the *Sierra de San Lazaro*, near the *Ojo del Oso*, county of *Santa Fe*.

67 JUAN BENAVIDES.
Question of mines. December 24, 1835. *Real de Dolores*, county of *Santa Fe*.

68 ANTONIO ARMIJO, et al.
Report of Commissioners on their petition for lands in the *Badito del Arroyo*; report is made to the Territorial Deputation, December 23, 1835.

Courtesy of Bureau of Ethnology

INSCRIPTION ON EL MORRO BY GENERAL DE VARGAS

Translation: "Here was the General Don Diego de Vargas, who conquered for our holy faith, and for the Royal Crown, all of New Mexico, at his [own] expense. Year of 1692."

THE SPANISH ARCHIVES OF NEW MEXICO   33

69 JOSE MANUEL ANGEL; MANUEL ANGEL; CARLOS TORRES; FRANCISCO CRESPIN; JULIAN GAYEGOS; DIEGO ANTONIO CRESPIN; RAFAEL CRESPIN; JOSE PABLO MONTOYA; ANTONIO BIGIL.
>Petition for lands at place called "*Arco del Arroyo de Galisteo.*" September 23, 1839. No action taken.

70 JUAN LORENZO ALIRE.
>Grant. October 12, 1844. Situate in "*Los Valles de Santa Gertrudis de lo de Mora.*" Made by Tomas Ortiz, Judge.

71 MARIA CONCEPCION ARMIJO. 1844.
>Question of lands, near *Los Corrales, Bernalillo* county.

72 JUAN NEPOMUCENO ALARID.
>Will. November 27, 1844. County of *Santa Fe.*

73 MARIA CONCEPCION ARMIJO, wife of Nicolas Sandoval. 1844.
>Question of lands, before Mariano Martinez, Governor, and Tomas Ortiz, Alcalde. *Los Corrales, Bernalillo* county. Item No. 71, *q. v.* With the estate of Juan Pino, deceased.

74 NASARIO MARTINEZ to Josefa Armijo. July 15, 1844. County of *Santa Fe.*
>Conveyance of land. Before Tomas Ortiz, Alcalde.

75 NASARIO AGUILAR.
>Grant. October 8, 1844. Situate in the "*valle de Santa Gertrudis de Mora.*" Made by Tomas Ortiz, Judge of 1st Instance. No. 70 *ante, q. v.*

76 FRANCISCO ROMERO DE PEDRAZA to Domingo de la Barreda. June 26, 1698. County of *Santa Fe.*
>Conveyance of lands. Before Diego Arias de Quiros, Alcalde. Testimonio.

77 ANA LUJAN to Diego de Veccia. September, 1701. County of *Santa Fe.*
>Conveyance of lands. Before Joseph Rodriguez, Alcalde.

78 CRISTOBAL JARAMILLO and JUAN BARELA JARAMILLO. February 26, 1704.

Question of lands with the Indians of *San Felipe*, county of *Bernalillo*. Before the Marqués de la Nava de Brazinas, Governor and Captain-General. Alfonso Rael de Aguilar.

Petition for a grant of lands to Spanish citizens at the place called *Angostura*, the lands at the time (1704) being occupied by Indians of the pueblo of San Felipe. The attorney for the Indians opposed the making of the grant because of *their loyalty to the crown during the uprisings of 1693 and 1696* and the grant was refused.

Petition by Cristobal Barela Jaramillo and Juan Barela Jaramillo, to the governor of New Mexico, asking that they be granted lands at Angostura, on the west side of the Rio Grande. Apparently the lands asked for were being used by the San Felipe Indians, as the petitioners ask that the lands belonging to those Indians be measured, and state that the Indians have more lands than the law allows, and that it is not fair that this should be permitted, while the petitioners are without lands.

They say in regard to the boundaries: "The said lands are on this side (of the river) and they adjoin the lands of Captain Don Fernando on the south side, and on the north side by the lands of said Indians, and on the east by the Del Norte river, and on the west by the tablelands."

This petition was presented to Governor De Vargas, at Bernalillo, on February 26, 1704, and he thereupon ordered that the chief alcaldes, Diego Montoya and Don Fernando Duran y Chaves, together with the attorney for the Indians, Don Alfonso Rael de Aguilar, should inspect the lands in question, and report to him as to what might be properly granted to the petitioners.

On February 29, 1704, the alcalde, Diego Montoya, and the attorney for the Indians, Alfonso Rael de Aguilar, went to Angostura to examine the lands, and the latter made a statement, in favor of the Indians and against the petitioners, which is set forth at length in the manuscript, and is signed by him. He alleges, among many other reasons for not making the grant, that the lands had been held by the natives of the *pueblo* since its foundation; that the petitioners had a great deal of live stock which would trespass on the Indians' lands; that the petitioners had a grant of lands on the other side of the river; that the Indians ought to be treated with consideration because of the loyalty they had displayed during the uprisings of 1693 and 1696, etc., etc.

This proceeding was not signed by Montoya, because of his having suffered a severe injury to his arm, by a fall; and it is stated that the alcalde, Don Fernando Duran y Chaves, did not participate in the proceedings because he was not at home.

No grant appears to have been made to the petitioners.

It is to be noted that this manuscript indicates that the town of Bernalillo was at that time on the west side of the Rio Grande.

79 JOSE FRESQUES and MARIA DE HERRERA, his wife, to Simon Baca. November 13, 1716. County of *Rio Arriba*.

    Conveyance of land. Before Juan Garcia de las Rivas, Alcalde.

80 FRANCISCO ALBERTO DE LA MORA to Simona de Bejar. November 14, 1716. County of *Santa Fe*.

    Conveyance of lands. Before Francisco Lorenzo de Cassados, Alcalde.

81 VALENTINA DE MONTES DE OCA to the woman called *La Benavides* because she is the widow of Nicolas Benavides. June 21, 1723. County of *Santa Fe*.

    Conveyance of land. Before Francisco Bueno de Bohorques y Corcuera, Alcalde.

82 ANTONIO BALLEJO.

    Will. June 7, 1727. County of *Santa Fe*.

83 DIEGO MANUEL BACA.

    Will. March 23, 1727. County of *Santa Fe*.

84 JOSEPH BASQUEZ.

    Grant. March 16, 1727. Made by Don Juan Domingo de Bustamante, Governor and Captain-General. Antonio Grusiaga, Secretary of War and Government.

    Grant revoked by Governor Cruzate. Rejected "Lo de Basquez" by court of private land claims.

85 JUAN DE LEON BRITO.
Grant. Originally made to his father by Don Diego de Vargas Zapata Lujan Ponce de Leon. Re-validated by Don Juan Domingo de Bustamante, Governor, August 27, 1738. *Testimonio.*

Another grant, made by Don Gaspar Domingo de Bustamante, August 20, 1742. Both of these grants are apparently small and close to *Santa Fe.* Antonio de Cruciaga; Antonio de Hulibarri; Gregorio Garduño; Joseph de Terrus. The following are given in full, illustrative of forms in use:

"Town of Santa Fe, August 5th, 1728, before his excellency, the governor and captain-general of this kingdom of New Mexico, it was presented by the party stated therein, to wit, Juan de Leon Brito, Mexican, and settler of the *ward of Analco,* in this town of Santa Fe: I appear before your excellency in the best form allowed me by law and say that I, having come into this kingdom, and a grant having been made to me of certain lands that formerly belonged to my father, may he rest in peace, by the General Don Diego de Vargas Zapata Lujan Ponce Leon, deceased, in the name of his majesty, consisting of one *sitio* of lands, and now I having settled on it, and because the said grant papers are not in my possession, I ask of your greatness to revalidate to me the said land, which lies at the other side [*banda*] of this town, its boundaries being, on the north the acequia from which Captain Bargas irrigates, and on the south another ditch of the same person, and on the east lands of Pedro Lopez, on the west the road leading to Pecos; for all of which I ask and beg your excellency, with the greatest veneration due, to concede to me said grant of said lands in the name of the King my master, for myself and my wife and my children and heirs, for I swear by God our Lord and the Holy Cross that this my statement is not made in bad faith, and in the necessary, etc.

"JUAN DE LEON BRITO."

The "*Britos*" were Tlascalan Indians. The "Analco" district surrounds the old chapel of San Miguel. "Analco" means, "the other side of the river."

"And it having been seen by his excellency he received it as presented, and in view of what the party states his excellency said that he ought and did command Sebastian de Bargas and Pedro Lopez, for the reason that these were the nearest neighbors to the lands petitioned for by this party that if they should have any right to the same they should bring it forward, with such instruments as they might have, in order to give to each one his due, and it not being of any injury to any third party representing a better claim that it should be adjudicated for and revalidated to him in the bona fide possession that he now enjoys. Thus it was decreed, commanded and signed by his excellency D. Juan Domingo Bustamante before me, the actual secretary of government and war, by order of his excellency the governor and captain-general.

"ANTTO. DE CRUSIAGA [rubric]
"Secretary of Government and War.

"In the said town, on the 17th day of the month of August, 1728, by virtue of the command in the above provision, Sebastian de Bargas was cited, who, having known of the registration of land sought by Juan de Leon Brito, he stated that he is not harmed, for the reason that it lies beyond his own lands, and because the ditches referred to form boundary lines only; in view of which he has no opposition to offer to the possession and ownership sought by the party, and he signed it with me, the actual secretary of government and war.

"SEBASTIAN DE BARGAS
"Before me: ANTONIO DE CRUCIAGA,
"Secretary of Government and War.

"Immediately thereafter, Pedro Lopez not being within the realm, his wife was cited to appear, and she offered the bill of sale made by Don Miguel de Coca to Josepha Lopez, daughter of the said Pedro Lopez, and from its contents it appears that this party is not harmed by the lands asked for by Juan de Leon Brito, for he only cites it as a boundary, on which she did not sign, because she did not know how. I signed it, to which I certify.

"At said town, on said month and year, his excellency the Governor and Captain-General of this kingdom of New Mexico, having seen the citations that preceded, and it appearing from them that no harm is occasioned to any third party by the grant of lands which Juan de Leon Brito asks to be revalidated to him anew, which he says were given to him by General Don Diego de Vargas, for the reason that he has no title papers, and in view of all this his excellency, in the name of his majesty, may God preserve him, makes and revalidates to him the grant, protecting him as he does in the possession that

he has acquired in good faith for himself and which he now acquires judicially, so that he may not be dispossessed of the same without first being proceeded against according to law, and in order that he, his heirs and successors, may enjoy the products of the same, and in order that he may be able to exchange, sell, and transfer as his own property and of his wife, except that he shall not convey it to prohibited persons; thus be decreed, ordered, and signed before me, the actual secretary of government and war. I certify. BUSTAMANTE
"ANTONIO DE CRUCIAGA
"Secretary of Government and War.

"This copy agrees with its original, which remains in the archives of this government, from which I made the same for the benefit of the party on this day, the 30th of August, 1728. It is true and faithful, corrected and compared and at its making the witnesses were Juan Joseph Moreño and Don Alfonso Rael de Aguilar, they being present. I make my customary signature in testimony of the truth. ANTONIO DE CRUCIAGA [rubric]
"Secretary of Government and War."

SECOND GRANT

"Santa Fe, August 18th, 1742. Let the alcalde mayor report if it is proper for the petitioner in this petition, in order to provide what may be convenient.
"MENDOZA"

"Juan de Leon Brito, resident of the town of Santa Fe, at the feet of the greatness of your excellency, in all form allowed to me by law, and which may to me belong, I say, sir, that whereas I am loaded with duties to which I must necessarily attend, and because I have not land sufficient, because that which I have is small, I have seen fit to have registered a tract of lands lying at the other side (banda) of the river where a cañada is formed, and its boundaries are the following: On the east it is bounded by the highway (camino real) that leads to Pecos, on the west it is bounded by another road that likewise goes to Pecos, on the south with lands of Luiz de Armenta, and on the north with lands of Captain Manuel Thenorio, which lands I ask for in the name of his Majesty, whom may God preserve, to be given to me as a grant, I petition your excellency with all due submission to concede them to me, for I am a poor man, and if they are granted to me that royal possession shall be given me, for I will

THE SPANISH ARCHIVES OF NEW MEXICO 39

receive grace and profit. I swear in all form that this petition is not done in bad faith.

"JUAN DE LEON BRITO"

"Having seen and examined the lands petitioned for by this party, I say that it is proper, because he has it registered, and they are recognized as lands of the King, my Lord, whom may God preserve, whereupon your excellency may do what shall be just, which shall be as in every case the best, and that it may so appear I signed it on June 19th, 1742.

"ANTONIO DE ULIBARRI [rubric]"

"In the town of Santa Fe, on the 20th of August, 1742, I, the lieutenant-colonel, governor, and captain-general of this kingdom of New Mexico, Don Gaspar Domingo de Mendoza, ought to command and did command, in view of the report of Captain Antonio de Ulibarri, alcalde mayor of said town, to place the petitioner in this petition in possession of the land that he asks for, so that in the name of his Majesty he may possess and cultivate the same; thus I provided, ordered, and signed with those of my attendants with whom I act, as customary on account of the actual conditions of this realm. It is valid.

"DON GASPAR DOMINGO DE MENDOZA [rubric]
"JOSEPH DE TERRUS
"JUAN PHE. DE RIVERA"

"In the town of Santa Fe, on the 20th day of the month of August, 1742, I, the captain, Antonio de Ulibarri, alcalde mayor of this town, in obedience to the order of his excellency, the Colonel Don Gaspar Domingo de Mendoza, governor and captain-general of this kingdom, I, the said alcalde mayor, went upon the lands that this party states, and I took him by the hand and walked with him over said lands. He plucked grass, cast stones, shouted, saying 'Long live the King, my Lord, Don Phillipe the Fifth, whom may God preserve,' the witnesses to the royal possession being Tomas de Sena and Cayetano Lovato. Thus I acted with the witnesses of my attendance for the lack of public or royal notary, for there are none in this kingdom, upon the actual paper, for there is none of the seal in these regions, to which I certify.

"ANTONIO DE ULIBARRI [rubric]
"Judge Commissioner.
"GREGORIO GARDUÑO."

86 PEDRO GOMEZ DE CHAVES to Bernabe Baca. March 26, 1732. County of *Bernalillo*.
    Conveyance. Before Juan Gonzales Bas.

87 BENTURA DE LA CANDELARIA to Salvador Barela. May 7, 1734. County of *Bernalillo*.
    Conveyance. Before Geronimo Jaramillo.

88 CRISTOBAL BACA.
    Will and inventory and partition of his estate. 1739. County of *Santa Fe*.

89 VALENTINA MONTES DE OCA to Juana de Benavides. June 9, 1739. County of *Santa Fe*.
    Conveyance. Before Antonio Montoya. Ante No. 81.

90 JUANA DE BENAVIDES and TOMASA DE BENAVIDES. June 11, 1739. County of *Santa Fe*.
    Exchange. Before Antonio Montoya, Alcalde.

91 JUAN DE BENAVIDES to Tomasa de Benavides. June 15, 1739. County of *Santa Fe*.
    Conveyance. Before Antonio Montoya, Alcalde.

92 BERNABE BACA vs. NICOLAS DE CHAVES. 1704.
    Reported case of Nicolas de Chaves, *q. v.*

93 ANTONIO MONTOYA to Juan de Benavides. November 23, 1744. County of *Santa Fe*.
    Conveyance of a piece of land above the Pueblo of *San Diego de Tesuque*. Before Antonio de Ulibarri, Alcalde.

94 JOSEPHA BACA.
    Will and inventory of estate. 1746. County of *Bernalillo*. At *Pajarito*.

95 MAGDALENA MARTIN, by her executor, Manuel Montoya, to Pedro Baptista. April 11, 1751.
    Conveyance of land in the county of *Rio Arriba*. Before Juan José Lobato, Alcalde.

96 ANTONIO DURAN to Salvador Barela. April 22, 1752. County of *Taos*.
    Conveyance. Before Juan Joseph Lobato. The donor

was the wife of Juan Antonio Giron and acquired the property by inheritance from her mother, Rosa Martin.

97 SEBASTIAN MARTIN to Salvador Barela. April 22, 1752. County of *Taos*.
Conveyance. Before Juan José Lobato, Alcalde.

98 DIEGO BASQUEZ BORREGO, of *Rio Abajo*.
Will and proceedings. *Santa Fe*, May 5, 1753. Before Don Tomas Veles Cachupin, Governor. Tomas de Alvear y Collado.

99 SEBASTIAN MARTIN to Salvador Barela and Francisco Barela. October 8, 1753. County of *Santa Fe*. *Pueblo Quemado*.
Conveyance. Before Juan José Sandoval, Alcalde.

100 MANUEL MARTIN to Tiburcio Barela. November 6, 1753. County of *Rio Arriba*.
Conveyance. Before Juan José Sandoval, Alcalde.

101 MANUEL BACA.
Will. May 6, 1755. No residence stated.

102 EUSEBIO LEYBA to Tomasa de Benavides. June 9, 1759. County of *Santa Fe*.
Conveyance. Before Francisco Guerrero. Manuel Bernardo Garvisu.

103 DIEGO BASQUEZ BORREGO.
Inventory of the estate of. Ante No. 98, *q. v.*

104 TOMASA BENAVIDES.
Inventory of estate of and partition of the same.

105 ANTONIO BACA vs. INHABITANTS OF RIO PUERCO.
The original settlers of Rio Puerco were Joaquin de Luna, district lieutenant, Joaquin Romero, Maria Rosalia Romero, Pedro Varela, Juan Pedro Sisneros, Diego Basques Borrego, Bernardo Ballejo, José de Luna, Antonio Lucero, Andres Manzanares, Francisco Lovato, Gaspar Gonzales, José Romero, Juan Ygnacio Romero, Antonio Martin, Juan Lorenzo Atencio, Antonio Martin, Pablo Martin, Matias Salazar, Miguel Romero, Juan

Diego Trujillo, Alejandro Espinosa, Mateo Salazar, Salvador Trujillo, Pedro Aguilar, Juan Gonzales, Francisco Borrego, José Miguel Logardo, Francisco Giron, Santiago Pais, Antonio Romero, Marcelina Francisco, Tomas Antonio Romero, Alonzo Gonzales, and Antonio Lucero. At the time that this petition was made the petitioners stated that there were grazing upon the tract about ten thousand head of sheep and cattle. One of the reasons for making of this grant was that the settlement would serve as a barrier to the Ute and Navajo tribes of Indians. The tract is described as follows: On the north the Tortugas creek; on the south the southern point of the mesa continguous to the Hondo creek; on the east the side of the mountain extending from Jemez to the Piedra Lumbre, looking toward the Jemez pueblo, and on the west the *"Arroyo de en Media."*

Captain Antonio Baca was granted a tract of land known as Nuestra Señora de la Luz de los Lagunitas del Rio Puerco previous to 1761; he was afterward dispossessed and the property was given to Joaquin Mestas. Baca commenced proceedings before Don Manuel Portillo Urrisola which were concluded in 1762 by Governor Veles Cachupin, who on July 20, 1762, re-granted the land to Antonio Baca. The questions involved were referred to Don Juan Ygnacio Garcia Villegas, counselor for the Royal Audience of Guadalajara, who decided in favor of Captain Baca. The grant was first made to Baca by Governor Marin del Valle. Baca states in his petition that he had always "without pay served his country in maintaining continual war with the Apaches, and that all provisions and expenses were supplied by himself."

106 JUAN TAFOYA and JOSEPH MORENO to Pablo Baca. October 2, 1763. County of *Santa Fe*.
Conveyance. Before Manuel Gallego, Alcalde.

107 JUAN JOSEPH DURAN, by his attorney CRISTOBAL DURAN to Joseph Baca. In *San Pedro de Chama*, August 9, 1764.
Conveyance. Before Manuel Garzia Pareja, Alcalde.

108 JOSE MARTIN to JOSE VACA. October 29, 1764. County of *Rio Arriba*.
Conveyance. Before Manuel Garzia Pareja, Alcalde.

THE SPANISH ARCHIVES OF NEW MEXICO 43

109 MARIA DE LA VEGA Y COCA. *Santa Fe*, May 17, 1764.
> Partition of lands of her estate at the *Cienega and Cañada of Guiqu*. Before Francisco Guerrero, Alcalde.

110 ANTONIO DE BEYTIA of *Abiquiú* December 30, 1765.
> Will. In this item, in the first paragraph, the testator says he is a resident of *"El Pueblo de San Antonio del Biquiu."* Later on he says, in dating the instrument,—*"este Pueblo de San Antonio del Guyquiu."* In the county of *Rio Arriba*.

111 GRANTEES OF THE NUESTRA SEÑORA DE LA LUZ Y SAN BLAS TRACT vs. THE GRANTEES OF THE ATRISCO TRACT. 1759.
> Question of boundary. Before Francisco Antonio Marin del Valle, Captain-General; also before Don Tomas Velez Cachupin, Captain-General; the last named proceedings were had in 1766.

112 PHELIPE TAFOYA and PHELIPE SANDOVAL to Joseph Baca. February 3, 1767.
> Conveyance of a rancho called *"Pueblo Quemado,"* about a league from the City of *Santa Fe*. Before Francisco Guerrero, Alcalde.

113 GRANTEES OF THE BELEN TRACT VS. SALE OF LAND BY PEDRO ITURRIETA to Fernando Chaves. 1767.
> Before Don Pedro Fermin de Mendinueta, Governor. Francisco Trebol Navarro; Manuel Garvisu; Manuel Zanez; Manuel Garvisu Zanez.
> The petition for the Belen Grant asked for a tract of land which in 1740 was uncultivated and unappropriated. It is described and "bounded on the east by the Sandia Mountains; on the west by the Rio Puerco; on the north on both sides of the river the boundary is the land of Nicolas de Chaves and those of the adjoining settlers of Our Lady of the Concepcion tract of Tomé, and on the south the place called Felipe Romero, in a direct line until it intersects the boundary above mentioned, from the east to the west." The first settlers were: Diego Torres de Salazar; Pedro Bigil; Miguel Salazar; Juana Teresa Romero; Lugarda Romero; Juan Antonio Salazar; Miguel Salazar; Pablo Salazar; Nicolas Salazar; Manuel Antonio Trugillo; Maria Torres; Salvador Torres; José

Antonio Torres; Ladeo Torres; Cayetano Cristobal Torres; Diego Torres; Barbara Romero; Gabriel Romero; Maria Vigil; José Trujillo; Francisco Martin; Nicolas Martiniano; Ygnacio Barrera; Juan Domingo Torres; José Romero; José Tenorio; Juan José de Sandoval; Francisco Trujillo; Francisco Hiron; Cristoval Naranjo; José Antonio Naranjo; Bartholomé Torres; Pedro Romero. The grant was made by Don Gaspar Domingo Mendoza, and possession was given by Don Nicolas de Chaves, alcalde mayor of Alburquerque.

The house of Felipe Romero was a ruin, this hacienda having been destroyed in the revolution of 1680.

114 BALTAZAR BACA.

Reported Claim No. 104.

Baltazar Baca was born in New Mexico and was, in 1769, a resident of the Plaza of Belen. He asked for a tract of land about three leagues from the pueblo of Laguna, and about a league and a half from the Encinol.

Being "descended from the conquerors of this province," Governor Mendinueta was induced to grant his request and he was placed in possession of the tract known as "San José del Encinol" by Don Antonio Sedillo, chief alcalde and war-captain of the pueblo of Laguna. In the act of possession it appears that there was "an outside ranch belonging to an Acoma Indian." He had two sons.

115 DOMINGO DE VENAVIDES.

Will. May 8, 1770. County of *Santa Fe*.

116 MARINA BACA vs. MIGUEL BACA. October 2, 1771.

Question of the possession of a house. County of *Santa Fe*. Before Don Pedro Fermin de Mendinueta, Governor.

117 JOSEPH BACA.

Will. *Pueblo Quemado*. Jurisdiction of *Santa Fe*. March 2, 1772.

118 LUGARDA TAFOYA to Marina de Jesus Baca. August 14, 1773. City of *Santa Fe*.

Before Manuel Garcia Pareja, Alcalde.

119 FRANCISCO GONZALES to Manuela Brito. July 12, 1774. City of *Santa Fe*.

Before Manuel Garcia Pareja, Alcalde.

THE SPANISH ARCHIVES OF NEW MEXICO   45

120 JOSEFA BUSTAMANTE to José Antonio Ortiz. February 13, 1784.
> Mortgage of rancho at *Tesuque*. Before Don Juan Bautista de Anza, Governor.

121 JUANA MARIA BACA, wife of MIGUEL BACA vs. DIEGO BORREGO. January 21, 1789. County of *Santa Fe*.
> Question of lands sold by Borrego in Cuyamungue. Before Don Fernando de la Concha, Governor, and Antonio Josef Ortiz, Alcalde, and Captain Manuel Delgado.

122 ISABEL BACA, Pueblo of *Isleta*, 1792.
> Investigation to determine whether she has any lands by inheritance in the *Pajarito* Tract. Report by Manuel de Arteaga, Alcalde, by order of Don Fernando de la Concha, Governor.

123 JOSEF MARIA BACA.
> Will. *Santa Fe,* November 3, 1799.

124 MARIA BARBARA BACA, widow of José Pablo Rael.
> Question of inheritance. *Santa Fe.* 1800. José Pablo Rael, deceased, was son of Nicolas Rael and Teodora Ortiz, both deceased. Will of Gertrudis Teodora Ortiz, *Santa Fe,* July 9, 1800. Cancelled by Chacon, Governor, before whom the proceedings were had. Joseph Miguel de la Peña; José Campo Redondo.

125 TOWN OF SAN MIGUEL DEL BADO.
> Reported Claim No. 119, *q. v.*

126 JOSE VARELA vs. EUSEBIO VARELA, his father. 1814.
> Protest against sale of lands at *Tomé*. Before Manrique, Governor. Bartolomé Baca; Pedro Bautista Pino.

127 JOSE ANTONIO BUSTOS vs. JOSE IGNACIO MADRID. 1826.
> Question of a piece of land at *Santa Cruz de la Cañada*. Many of the papers in this case appear to be missing. Proceedings before Colonel Antonio Narbona, Governor.

46   THE SPANISH ARCHIVES OF NEW MEXICO

128 TOMAS BERNAL, ANTONIO RAEL and JULIAN BERNAL, *El Paso*, June 19, 1820.
   Relating to the boundaries of town grant. Letter to Facundo Melgares, Governor.

129 JESUS BENAVIDES.
   Grant. 1820. 100 varas of land at *Galisteo*. Don Facundo Melgares, Governor.

130 ESTEVAN BACA. *Santa Fe*, February 10, 1821.
   Petition for lands for himself and others on the *Pecos* river. No final action taken. Before Don Facundo Melgares, Governor.
   From this it appears that in 1821 there were only eight or ten families of the Pecos pueblo still living.

131 FRAY MANUEL BELLIJO, of *Cochiti*, complains of the Alcalde, Juan Armijo, to Don Facundo Melgares, June 6, 1821.

132 LUIS BENAVIDES.
   Will. *Santa Fe,* March 4, 1822.

133 JOSE BACA.
   Grant of land at *Galisteo*. Possession given April 29, 1822, by Pedro Armendaris, Alcalde. By order of the *Ayuntamiento* of April 8, 1822, in which grants were made to nineteen persons. José Maria Baca, Secretary of the *Cabildo*.

134 MANUEL BACA and SANTIAGO ABREU.
   Petition for lands lying between the pueblos of *Santo Domingo* and *San Felipe*, February 14, 1824. Referred to the Provincial Deputation by the Jefe Politico and read on the 16th of the same month. Captain Bartolomé Baca, Jefe Politico.
   It was presented to the governor of New Mexico on February 14, 1824, and on the same day forwarded by him to the so-called Provincial Deputation, for the official action of that body. Some record of the making of a grant may be found in the "Journal, Provincial Deputation, 1822, 1824."

135 RAFAEL BENAVIDES, PEDRO LOBATO, JESUS BENAVIDES and JUAN NEPOMUCENO VIGIL and JOSE NESTOR ARMIJO.

Petition for lands on the other side of the *Pecos* river. Granted by the Territorial Deputation, March 3, 1825. Book 2 of the Acts of the Deputation, page 44.

This shows a grant of lands in 1825 to a Mexican citizen, within the boundaries of the Pecos pueblo.

136 JOSE FRANCISCO BACA.

Petition for land on this side of the *Pecos* river. Referred to the *Jefe Politico* on March 3, 1825, for action under Par. 5 of the session of preceding November. See page 44, as cited in No. 135 *supra*.

137 LUIS MARIA CABEZA DE BACA.

Reported Claim No. 20.

The following is a list of the family of Luis Maria Cabeza de Baca.

Luis was married the first time with Ana Maria Lopez, and their children were: Antonio, Juan Antonio, Rosa, José Domingo, Guadalupe, Miguel, and Ramon.

His second wife was Josefa Sanches, and their children were: Luis Maria, Prudencio, Mateo, Josefa 1st, and Luz.

His third wife was Encarnacion Lucero, and their children were: Juana Paula, Jesus Bacalro (Cañonero), Juan Felipe, Jesus 2nd (Carretero), Josefa 2d, Domingo, Manuel, Maria de Jesus, Luisa, and Luz.

1. Antonio Cabeza de Baca, the first son of Luis Maria Baca was married to Francisca Garvisu, and the issue was Juan Manuel.

2. Juan Antonio Cabeza de Baca, the second son of Luis Maria, was married with Josefa Gallegos and their children were, Jesus Maria, Francisco Tomas, Encarnacion, Cesaria, Domingo, José de Jesus, Quiriño, Josefa, Guadalupe, Alta Garcia, Trinidad, Nicolasa, and Tomas D.

3. Rosa, the third child, was married to Sebastian Salaz, and their children were, Francisco, Dolores, and Josefa.

4. Domingo, the fourth child, had no issue; died in infancy.

5. José, fifth child, was married to Dolores Gonzales, and their children were, Felipa, Antonio, Jesus Maria, Maria de Jesus, Francisco, Fernando, and Apolonia.

6. Guadalupe, sixth child, married Santiago Trujillo,

and their children were, Antonio, Maria, Andres, Feliciana, Juana, Santiago, and Ana Maria.

7. Miguel, seventh child, was married to Dolores Sanches, and their children were, Quirina, Diego, Rumualdo, Guadalupe, Paulina, Juan Pablo, and Martina.

8. Ramon, eighth child, married with Serafina Salaz, and their only child was Ignacio.

9. Luis Maria, ninth child, married Isabel Lopez, and their children were, Trinidad and Miguel. Miguel died without issue.

10. Prudencio, tenth child, was married the first time with Manuela Armijo, and their children were, Juan, Ignacio, Julian, and Apolonia.

His second wife was Josefa Flores, and his children were Valentin Escolastico, Gregorio, and Julian.

11. Mateo, eleventh child, was married to Guadalupe Montoya, and their children were, Luis Maria, Alejandro, Juan de Dios, and Martin.

12. Josefa 1st was married to Juan Luis Montoya, and their children were, Antonio and Donaciano.

13. Luz 1st, thirteenth child, had no issue; never was married.

14. Juana Paula, fourteenth child, was married to José Garcia; their children were, Juana Maria, Antonio, Francisco, Inez, Maria de los Angeles, and Crecencio.

15. Jesus C. de Baca, 1st (Cañonero), fifteenth child, was married to Ana Maria Gonzales, and their children were, Luis Maria, Guadalupe, Nestor, Francisco, Juliana, and Feliciano.

16. Juan Felipe, sixteenth child, was married to Tomasa Gonzales, and their children were, Juliana, Francisca, José, Rumualdo, Sotero, Apolona, Julian, Nazaria, Petra, and Leonor.

17. Jesus 2d, (Carretero), married Rafaela Martinez, and their children were, Encarnacion, José Esteban, Faustina, Toribio, Cosme, Julian, and Pedro.

18. Josefa 2d, married Luis de la O, and their children were, Ramos, José Maria, Zenobia, Nicolasa, Mariano, Flavio, Juan de Dios, and Refugio.

19. Domingo 2d, nineteenth child, was married to Rosalia Garcia, and their son was José.

20. Manuel.

21. Maria de Jesus, 21st child, was married to Francisco Martin (called Borreguito); had no children.

22. Luisa.

23. Luz 2nd, 23rd child, died without issue.

Courtesy of Bureau of Ethnology
INSCRIPTION ON EL MORRO BY CAPTAIN JUAN DE ULIBARRI
Re-conquistador under General De Vargas

THE SPANISH ARCHIVES OF NEW MEXICO 49

138 LUIS BENAVIDES.
: Petition for lands on the *Pecos* river. *Santa Fe,* March 8, 1825. No action taken.
: This is a petition for a grant at the pueblo of Pecos.

139 JOSE FRANCISCO BACA. March 14, 1826.
: Petition for lands on the *Pecos* river. Reported by the *Ayuntamiento* of *San Miguel del Bado,* on March 19, 1826. Teodosio Quintana, Secretary of the Deputation. Juan José Baca, 2nd Regidor; José Ramon Alarid, Alcalde Constitutional; Candelaria Flores, 3rd Regidor; Santiago Sandoval, 1st Regidor; José Miguel Sanches, Secretary of the *Ayuntamiento.*

140 CRISTOBAL BUSTOS vs. JOAQUIN PINO. 1827.
: Question of lands in the *Cebolleta* Grant. Before Antonio Narbona, Governor.

141 JUAN ESTEVAN BACA vs. ALCALDE OF COCHITI. 1827.
: *La Majada* Grant. Before *Supremo Tribunal de Justicia,* City of *Mexico.* Aguilar y Lopez, Secretary.
: The memorandum on the wrapper inclosing this document is entirely misleading. It says the document is a land suit by Juan Esteban Baca against the Indians of Cochiti. *It has nothing to do with a land suit.* It is a complaint by Baca against the *alcalde* of *Cochiti,* who had unjustly imprisoned and otherwise ill-treated him. The date is December 14, 1827. It was sent to the supreme tribunal of justice at Mexico, and by that court was ordered to be transmitted to the *jefe politico* (governor) of New Mexico, to be placed in the hands of a competent judge, who was to do justice to the complainant.
: The Majada Grant was confirmed by the court of private land claims and surveyed for over 54,000 acres. All that portion of the grant to the pueblo of Cochiti which lies east of the Rio Grande conflicts with the Majada, amounting possibly to 5,000 acres. The southern boundary of the Majada and the northern boundary of the Pueblo of Santo Domingo Grant for a distance of eight and one-half miles are coterminous. The grant was patented October 26, 1908.

142 TOMAS BACA, JOSE ANTONIO CASADOS and OTHERS.
: Report of Santiago Ulibarri, Judge, as to quality of

lands asked for by the persons named. Report is made to the Territorial Deputation. 1829. *San Miguel del Bado*.

143 TOMAS BACA, JOSE ANTONIO CASADOS and OTHERS.
Petition to the *Ayuntamiento* of *San Miguel del Bado* for lands. Referred, by Santiago Ulibarri, to the Territorial Deputation and also signed by José Antonio Casados, Secretary of the *Ayuntamiento*. *San Miguel del Bado*, April 27, 1829. Ante No. 142, *q. v.*

144 MARIA MIQUELA BACA.
Will and inventory. 1831. County of *Santa Fe*. Juan Garcia, Alcalde.

145 JESUS MARIA ALARID to José Francisco Baca. May 18, 1831. County of *Santa Fe*.
Conveyance of land in the rancho of the *Alamo*, formerly belonging to Diego Montoya. Before Pablo Montoya. There are no signatures to this document.

146 MICAELA BACA. (Maria Micaela Baca.)
Distribution of estate. 1832. Ante No. 144, *q. v.*

147 JUAN MANUEL BACA vs. JUAN ANTONIO ARMIJO. *Santa Fe*, April 28, 1832.
Question as to a tract of land. Before Juan Garcia, Alcalde.

148 MARIA DE LOS DOLORES SANDOVAL vs. JUAN GARCIA, Alcalde of the City of *Santa Fe*. 1834.
In suit of Manuel Bustamante vs. said Sandoval she complains of being unjustly deprived of her property, etc. Appealed to the *Suprema Corte de Justicia*, City of *Mexico*. Aguilar y Lopez, Clerk of the Supreme Court; Manuel de la Barrera, 1st Official; Don Francisco Sarracino, Governor.

149 TRINIDAD BARCELO vs. PABLO ORTIZ. *Santa Fe*, April 9, 1837.
Question as to a tract of land at *Pojoaque*. Albino Perez, Governor; J. M. Alarid, Secretary.

150 FOUR PAGES OF THE JOURNAL OF THE TERRITORIAL ASSEMBLY in which are recorded the Proceedings had in relation to the Beaubien and Miranda or Maxwell Grant.

The Maxwell Land Grant is situated in the northern part of New Mexico, in the county of Colfax; a portion is in the State of Colorado in Las Animas county. After the influx of settlers from the East, in the "seventies" and "eighties," the title of the grantees was bitterly contested.

In August, 1882, the government of the United States filed a bill in chancery in the United States circuit court in Colorado to cancel the patent which had been issued in 1879 for this property, embracing 1,714,000 acres. The case was litigated during a period of five years and was ultimately decided in favor of the company by the supreme court of the United States, which court, in two opinions, one on a motion for re-hearing, sustained the title of the company to the full extent of area as granted by the Mexican government. The government of the United States (the interior department and the department of justice) declined to accept the decision of the supreme court as final and instituted another suit in the courts of New Mexico to cancel the patent which had been made to the grantees, claiming that the lands in New Mexico, which formed a greater part of this property, were not affected by the decision of the nation's highest tribunal.

The Maxwell Company set up the decision of the supreme court as a defense to this suit; it was heard before Reeves, J., then presiding over the first judicial district of the Territory of New Mexico, and the plea of *res adjudicata* was sustained and the bill dismissed. An appeal was taken by the government to the territorial supreme court, where the decision of the lower court was affirmed.

The opinion of the New Mexican supreme court (an extract) follows:

"The United States brought suit in the circuit court for the United States for the District of Colorado, to set aside, vacate and cancel the patent assailed here. The bill in that case is grounded upon allegations of fraud committed by the patentees and others holding through or under them, by means of which the officers of the plaintiff were deceived into issuing and delivering the patent. Fraud in various ways was charged against the grantees under the patent, and the patent as an entirety was involved in this issue raised, heard and finally determined in the circuit and supreme courts of the United States.

"It is quite clear that had the United States succeeded in that suit, the decree would have affected the title to the lands embraced in the patent lying in New Mexico. Personal service was had upon the Maxwell Land Grant Company in that suit, and an appearance entered, and the suit after long delays, finally decided, declaring the patent valid for the lands covered by it wherever situated. The final judgment in this suit was intended to be, and we think was, conclusive upon the United States and all persons claiming through or under it, whether the lands covered by the patent were located in Colorado or New Mexico.

"The suit was instituted and contested through the courts to a final decision in the court of last resort solely, or mainly at least, upon the ground that such fraud had been committed by the original grantees and those claiming under them in locating the lands and extending the true boundaries thereof in such manner as to deceive the officers of the United States, and thereby caused them to issue the patent; that a court of equity would annul the patent. The court found that there was no fraud proven in the case, and that the patent was legal and valid, and free from taint of fraud.

"The issue directly involved in the controversy was that of fraud practiced upon the United States through its officers. The determination was against the truth of the facts alleged, and the United States, like any other suitor in a court of justice, is bound by the final judgment of courts of competent jurisdiction, when it elects to litigate any question of fact in the courts.

"The supreme court of the United States affirmed in distinct terms that there was no fraud committed in procuring the patent to be issued by the patentees, or those claiming under them; that the patent was legal and is the evidence of the legal ownership of all the lands embraced in it, or covered by it.

"It directly affirmed the non-existence of fraud, and having done so in a proper case, the courts of the country will not permit the plaintiff in any other suit, to contro-

THE SPANISH ARCHIVES OF NEW MEXICO 53

vert this judicially established fact, where the issue is between the same parties or their privies.

"The United States having exhausted its powers in a fruitless effort to cancel this patent, it becomes the duty of the courts and the people to abide the final judgment of the highest tribunal to which a controversy can be appealed, and to seek redress for meritorious grievances, if any exist, at the hands of a just and generous government."

In the argument of counsel, Frank Springer, Esq., of New Mexico, before the supreme court of the United States, in the case first brought in the circuit court of the United States for the District of Colorado, on the part of the Maxwell Company, accurately and learnedly discussed the motives which actuated the Mexican government in the making of these large grants of land. In the entire history of jurisprudence in the West no abler presentation of law and facts in any case was ever submitted by any member of the bar of the supreme court of the United States. In his oral argument, extended from the notes of the stenographer, Mr. Springer, among other things, in conclusion, said:

"During the course of this discussion, there has been frequent mention by counsel for the government of the large size of this grant, and their argument has abounded in allusions to 'principalities' and 'empires,' as if it were supposed that the principles of law are so flexible that they may be varied according to the subject matter, and that there may be one rule applicable to a small property, but another and different one to a great. It is a species of argument much affected in cases like this, but it seems to me an appeal far more befitting a jury trial than a grave discussion before this court.

"It is but a repetition of the popular clamor for which these Mexican grants have proved a fruitful subject, ever since the advancing civilization of the country has given them some value. Mexico has been denounced for making them, and no epithet is found too severe to characterize those who venture to claim their ownership. They are said to be monopolists, land pirates, and robbers. Even the tribunals, which seek by the force of judicial decision to keep the plighted faith of the nation by sustaining them when valid, are not secure from imputation of some improper motive.

"It is well enough, in this connection, to remember that times change, and people and conditions change with them. Whatever may be our notions now about the propriety of putting such large bodies of land into private ownership, we have no right to forget that these great grants upon the frontiers of Mexico were made under circumstances and motives of public policy totally different from those which now prevail. At that day the country was of no value to the Mexican people. It was not even reduced to possession by them. The greater part of it was occupied and over-run by hostile tribes of Indians, who were a constant menace to the outlying settlements. The frontiers of those settlements were continually harassed by their inroads. So that with the Navajos and Apaches on one side, the Utes on another, and the Plains Indians on another, the whole region was unsafe for the habitations of civilized men. Besides, it bordered on a territory of the United States on the north, and of Texas on the east, as to both of whom the Mexican people were suspicious and uneasy.

"It became, therefore, a part of the deliberate policy of the Mexican government to encircle these outlying provincial settlements with large grants of land, made to those adventurous spirits who were willing to lead forth colonies, extend the frontiers of civilization, and build up barriers against the inroads of their savage enemies, and the encroachments of their enterprising neighbors across the border. For this purpose, it gave the lands without stint, and without regard to quantity. As to any value in the land itself, they gave it no sort of consideration. A league then signified less than an acre now in the fertile and secure valleys of the Ohio or Mississippi. Measurements and descriptions were rude and carelessly made. It was never contemplated that they should be submitted to the tests by which scientific engineers would define the boundaries of a bonanza mine, or survey a lot on Broadway.

"The grantees of these lands paid for them, not in money, but in the service they then gave the state, and by the risks they took in maintaining a foothold upon them. And the same may be said of the early American pioneers who acquired them from their Mexican owners. I doubt if any of those who now bawl the loudest about the Maxwell Grant would have had either the sagacity to secure it as Maxwell did, or the courage to hold it through the perils of a quarter of a century of Indian warfare.

"When this portion of its territory came to be ceded

THE SPANISH ARCHIVES OF NEW MEXICO 55

to the United States, the Mexican government made it an express condition that its previous grants of land should be acknowledged and protected. It is a fact worthy of note, that notwithstanding the desperate condition of Mexico after the war; with her armies dispersed; her strongholds in our possession; and our flag flying over her capital; when the treaty of peace had been formulated, and was ratified by the United States senate, with only the general clauses for the protection of property rights which are usually quoted in the eighth and ninth articles, the Mexican government refused to ratify it until they had obtained a solemn guarantee from the commissioners of the United States, added in the form of a *protocol,* expressly stipulating that the grants of land in the ceded territory made prior to May 13, 1848, should be acknowledged by the American tribunals.

"And I say now, after the labors of the pioneers for half a century have made it safe and comfortable to live there, it lies not in the mouth of any man coming there amid the ease and luxury of a palace car, to say that Mexico had no right to make these grants, and the grantees no right to own them. The United States, so far as it depended upon its legislative and judicial departments, has never sought to evade the obligations imposed upon it by this treaty. It has desired to acknowledge and confirm the property rights derived from Mexico. Whether great or small, in every case where it is evident that the title would have been recognized or perfected by the Mexican authorities, it has, as this court has said, not sought to discover forfeitures, nor enforce rigorous conditions. It has not sought to defeat them by a rigid adhesion to strict rules, or the application of refined technicalities. It has endeavoured to act as a great nation, ready and anxious to perform its treaty stipulations, ungrudgingly and liberally, as the law and policy of nations enjoin. Its declared purpose, as long ago stated by this court, has been to authenticate titles, and to afford the solid guaranty to rights which ensue from their full acknowledgment by the supreme authority.

"To judge from the records of the *nisi prius* courts in many of the western states and territories during the past few years, an observer might well suppose that a United States patent, instead of being a settlement of title, is but the beginning of litigation; that instead of being a record proof of the final action of the government in discharge of its treaty obligations, as this court has said it shall be; instead of being the guaranty of peaceable and quiet enjoyment, it is but a delusion and a snare; a trap to catch confiding purchasers; and that its issue, even at the end of protracted controversies, is but the signal for fresh attack in the name of the government which gave it, with all its accompanying train of expense, delay, vexation, disaster, and ruin. It has become fashionable of late to attack United States patents. And so feeble has become the security they afford, and so little regard is shown for the sacred character which they were supposed to possess, that their holders are called upon to defend their validity in ruinous litigation, as often as any covetous intruder or restless demagogue can get near enough to the law officers of the government, to make them hear his loud resounding cry of fraud.

"Macauley has somewhere given a picture of the British public in one of its periodic attacks of morality, and I am not sure but it might equally apply to those paroxysms of virtue into which a portion of the American public occasionally works itself. At such times, the cry of fraud becomes epidemic throughout the land, and is echoed far and wide. It is taken up by every man who covets the possession of his neighbor. It is the cry of indolence against activity and energy; of envy against success; of the sluggard against the vigilant. It is the cry of every man who has slept away his opportunities, against those who were shrewd to think and bold to act when the time was ripe. It is the cry of every demagogue, who is looking for some popular wave upon which he may ride into public favor. And in the majority of such cases, as in the case before us, it is found after all to be little less than clamor — *vox, et praeterea nihil.*

"Furthermore, it is one of the oldest maxims of the law that it is for the public good that there be an end of suits. If this bill can be maintained, then no title, resting on a United States patent, is safe from disturbance, whenever its law officers, whether with good judgment or bad, whether from motives proper or improper, see fit to bring a suit. Nor can any man, so claiming, ever tell when his rights are finally adjudicated. Suppose the court should vacate this patent, on account of the errors alleged in the location of its boundaries; the court cannot tell us where the true boundaries are upon the ground. It cannot send corps of engineers to mark them by appropriate monuments in the field. It can not give us a new patent. We must go back to the land department for that."

Mr. Justice Miller: "Do you contend, Mr. Springer, that this court has not the power to reform this patent? Suppose the court should become satisfied that a patent has been issued for a certain number of sections of land in excess of the quantity authorized by law; could not the court by a decree declare that the patent should not include them? Or, if the proofs should show that this grant was limited to the summit of the Raton mountains on the north, and there were no other objection to such a decision, could not the court direct a decree to be made reforming the patent so that it should only include lands within that boundary?"

Mr. Springer: "Undoubtedly it might do either of the things your honor suggests. But the difficulty is it would settle nothing. If this grant had been laid off into townships, and sections, as public lands are, and the patent had been for certain of these sub-divisions, among which were some improperly included, the patent could be reformed so as to exclude these, and it would remain still a definite muniment of title for lands about whose boundaries or location there could be no further controversy. But Mexico did not survey or describe her lands in this way; when we undertake to locate a grant of land described by natural objects alone, so as to conform to our methods, we are compelled to mark the boundaries by monuments erected upon the ground, and by reference to the courses and distances preserved in the field notes, constituting a special survey which bears no relation to any other survey, except that it may at some point be connected with one of the known base lines or meridians. If the court should decree that the patent should be limited to such part of the tract which has been so surveyed as lies south of the summit of the Raton mountains, we are left without any definite or authoritative location of that line upon the ground. If the Raton summit were marked by a Chinese wall, or some other object so conspicuous and universally known that no two persons could have different opinions about it, it might thus have that degree of certainty on which such a decree could be based. But the precise position of that summit is one of the disputed facts of this case. There is conflicting testimony as to how far the Raton mountains extend, and whether the northern or the southern edge is the actual summit;

and this question would arise and have to be litigated afresh, every time such a patent was introduced in evidence. We would have the same old controversy with the government as to where the grant ends and the public lands begin. This could only be determined by a government survey, locating that line by scientific methods as the other lines are located. And when after another five years have been consumed in proceedings to that end, we succeed in securing another survey and another patent, some other attorney-general, having other and different theories upon these questions, may bring a bill to set aside that patent, on the ground that the land officers have been again mistaken. In fact, the relative provinces of these two great co-ordinate branches of the government would be reduced to this — if I may be pardoned a homely illustration — that the land department drives the stakes, and the courts follow after and pull them up.

"What is to be the end of all this? And what is to be the redress of these people whose property is for all practical purposes thus confiscated under the guise of equitable proceedings? Such a result would be revolting to every proper sentiment of public honor. It is unworthy of a great nation like this; and yet it is a picture not overdrawn, but is a legitimate deduction from the principles contended for by the government counsel in this case.

"It is a fact well known, both as a matter of public history, and from the record of cases that have come before this court, that the validity of these Mexican grants has been persistently denied by the American settlers who went into that country after the tide of emigration began to set that way. Squatters overran them in swarms, picking out the choicest spots without giving themselves the least concern about their titles. I venture to say that the inroads of these enterprising bands have given the grantees and their successors far more trouble than the depredations of the savage tribes with which they had originally to contend. They have fought these titles in every way, and in every place where contest was possible; in court and out; before the land tribunals, and the executive departments. Every stage of the proceedings looking to the final establishment of the title, and the location of the boundaries by the United States authorities, has been marked by controversies of some sort. Their opponents have generally found powerful aid from the land department, which has always been jealous of Mexican grants, and has never lost an opportunity to defeat or curtail them by application of the most strict and narrow rules of construction. As a general rule, the history of any of these grants has been that of one long contest between the owners, seeking recognition of their rights, on the one side, and the land officers of the United States, aided by trespassing settlers, on the other; in the course of which every weak spot in the title has been tested by numerous and vigilant adversaries. In the very nature of the case there could be no such thing as hasty or inadvertant action.

"In this case, forty years have elapsed since the Territory passed under the dominion of the United States; and more than a quarter of a century has been consumed in controversies and proceedings such as I have described. It would seem obvious, according to the plainest dictates of public policy, and in furtherance of that repose of titles which the peace and order of society demand, that when, after such protracted controversies, action is had by the government purporting to be final, it should be so in fact; and that not only the claimants, but also the public, should have the right to rely upon it as such. There ought to be some time, in the history of a title, when it will be safe to deal with it. There ought to be some time, during the life of a generation, in which a title, for the due acknowledgement of which the sacred honor of the nation is pledged, shall become settled, so far as the action of the government is concerned.

"There are some considerations higher than the merits or the equities of any particular case. There are some obligations which the government owes to itself and the public, which are of far greater importance than the possession of a few thousand, or a few hundred thousand acres of land. The faith and credit which are due to its public acts ought not to be lightly impugned. And when so solemn an instrument as a patent, signed by the highest officer of the nation, bearing upon its face the great seal of the United States, is duly and regularly given out as the evidence of title, and the acknowledgement by the supreme authority of the right of private property entitled to recognition by its treaties,— it ought to be as sacred, and as safe from attack, from any quarter, high or low, as the flag under which we live. The impeachment of the good name of the government, the destruction of confidence in the titles which it gives, and the disturbance of public credit and business which follows in their train, are public calamities, in comparison with which the interests involved in this suit, were they all that are claimed, pale into insignificance.

"Unfortunately it is not in the power of this court, or of any other tribunal, to afford my client any redress for the wrong it has suffered by the bringing of this most unfounded suit. The expenses of litigation, the colonization of its lands with fresh swarms of squatters, and the ruin of its business for a long period of years,— all these must be borne in silence. But if it shall in the end result in an effectual declaration by this court, of the principles which shall hereafter guide the officials of the United States as to the hundreds of other titles in the territory from which I come, then it will not have been entirely in vain."

Relative to the first cultivation of any of the lands upon the Maxwell Grant, the testimony of General Kit Carson has been preserved, who in 1857, giving testimony before the surveyor-general of New Mexico, said: "I have known the property since 1845. I passed there in 1844 with Lucien B. Maxwell and saw large fields of corn, beans, pumpkins, and a great deal of land cultivated, and several houses built on the Big Cimarron. I went there myself with Richard Owens in 1845; we built houses and I had fifteen acres under cultivation. I left in August of the same year for California. Lucien B. Maxwell settled on the Rayado, in 1849, and has been there up to this time: there are about 200 acres under cultivation, $15,000 in buildings, and about 15,000 head of stock on the grant. Maxwell is the son-in-law of Carlos Beaubien and he holds the land under the right of Beaubien."

The members of the Departmental Assembly at the time this grant was made were Felipe Sena, Antonio Sena, and Donaciano Vigil was the acting secretary. Don Juan Andrés Archuleta was the prefect. He, under orders from the Department Assembly and the governor, placed the grantees, Beaubien and Miranda, in possession on the 18th of April, 1844. The place called Rayado was settled just one year after the American occupation of New Mexico.

The charges which were made against Beaubien by Fr. Antonio José Martinez were declared to be false by the Departmental Assembly, as appears from a report to Governor Armijo, as follows:

THE SPANISH ARCHIVES OF NEW MEXICO 61

"MOST EXCELLENT SIR: In session today of this most excellent assembly, in consideration of your excellency's decree, has resolved upon the following opinion:

"This most excellent assembly being informed of the petition of Mr. Carlos Beaubien, in which he states for himself and in the name of his associate, Miranda, that in consequence of an order issued by the most excellent Governor Don Mariano Chavez, the free use and benefit of their possession was forbidden them, and that this was done on account of a petition made by the priest Martinez and the chiefs of the Pueblo of Taos, falsely stating that this land was granted to Don Carlos Bent and other foreigners, the aforesaid statement of the priest, Martinez and associates being untrue, this assembly believing that the order of suspension having been based upon that false statement, and in view of the documents which accredit the legitimate possession of Miranda and Beaubien, and their desires that their colony shall increase in prosperity and industry, for which purpose he has presented a long list of persons to whom they have offered land for cultivation, and who shall enjoy the same rights as the owners of the land; that the government having dictated the step for the sole purpose of ascertaining the truth; that the truth having been ascertained, and the right of the party established, is of the opinion that the aforesaid superior decree be declared null and void, and that Miranda and Beaubien be protected in their property, as having been asked for and obtained according to law. This is our opinion; but your excellency may determine what you may deem most proper.

"FELIPE SENA

"AGUSTIN DURAN
"ANTONIO SENA

"DONACIANO VIGIL, Secretary"

It is interesting and worthy of preservation that some of the greatest lawyers in the United States passed upon the title to this great estate. The concluding paragraph of an opinion delivered by one of America's greatest jurists is as follows:

"The one unanswerable, conclusive reply to all the objections raised, and to all that could be raised (unless indeed, Congress had been deceived by the fraud of the petitioners into the confirmation, which no one suggests) is that the United States are sovereign; that they owned the title to the tract in question, if the antecedent grant was void; that they had the undisputed, exclusive power to grant or withhold; to concede, with or without limitations, and that they have chosen to confirm without limitation; that, to the expression of their will, their own officers owe implicit obedience, and are without power to question or evade what is expressed by the law to be their duty. If it be necessary to quote authority in support of the proposition that the act of the sovereign, unlike the deed of an individual, can confirm and make valid a void grant or conveyance, the case of *Wilkinson v. Leland*, 2 Peters, 627, is directly to the point.

"I can find nothing in this case, under any aspect in which it can be viewed, to justify the land officers of the United States in refusing to survey this grant as confirmed by congress. With all the respect which I entertain for their opinions, I cannot doubt that they are (without the least intention of doing so) inflicting a grievous injustice on the purchasers by refusing to survey the grant unless restricted in the manner they propose. J. P. BENJAMIN

"Temple, 18th January, 1871."

In addition to the foregoing opinion others of like tenor were given by Thomas F. Bayard, William M. Evarts, Noah Davis, George T. Curtis, and George H. Williams.

151 SANTIAGO BONE and OTHERS.
Reported Claim No. 35 *q. v.*

152 FRANCISCO BACA y ORTIZ and SANTIAGO ABREU to Maria Gertrudis Barcelo. August 6, 1844. County of *Santa Fe*.
Conveyance. Before Tomas Ortiz, Alcalde.

153 CARLOS BEAUBIEN.
Petition in the name of the settlers of the *Poñil*. Santa Fe, June 8, 1844. No action taken.

On January 8, 1841, Charles Hipolyte Trotier-Beaubien and Guadalupe Miranda filed a petition with the governor of New Mexico, Manuel Armijo, asking for a grant of land in that portion of New Mexico now embraced within the limits of Colfax county and a part of Las Animas county, Colorado. The petition requested a tract of land "commencing below the junction of the Rayado and Red rivers, from thence in a direct line to the east to the first hills, from thence following the course of Red river in a northerly direction of Uña de Gato with Red river; from whence following along said hills to the east of the Uña Gato river to the summit of the tableland (mesa), from whence turning northwest, following said summit to the summit of the mountain which separates the waters of the rivers which run towards the east from those which run to the west, from thence following the summit of said mountain in a southerly direction to the first hill east of the Rayado river; from thence following along the brow of said hill to the place of beginning.''

On January 11th, the governor, in conformity with law, made the grant as requested. On February 22, 1843, possession was given by Cornelio Vigil, a justice of the peace of Taos. The following year Mariano Chavez, acting governor, suspended the grant, basing his action upon a complaint filed by the Rev. Antonio José Martinez, joined by the *principales* and chiefs of the pueblo of Taos who complained that the land in question, known as the "rincon del Rio Colorado" had previously been granted to the Indians by Carlos Bent, afterward appointed governor by General Kearny and killed in the revolution of January 19, 1847; they also charged that neither Beaubien nor Miranda were citizens of Mexico, but were foreigners.

Manuel Armijo having been again appointed governor, on the 18th of April, 1844, referred the matter to the Departmental Assembly, which body reversed the action of Governor Chavez and approved the grant to Beaubien and Miranda.

Guadalupe Miranda had been collector of customs for General Armijo. Carlos Beaubien was a very prominent man, and on September 22, 1846, when New Mexico's first officials were named by General S. W. Kearny, was appointed justice of the supreme court by that army officer.

The petition filed by the grantees is as follows:

"Most Excellent Sir: The undersigned, Mexican citizens and residents of this place, in the most approved manner required by law, state: That of all the departments of the Republic, with the exception of the Californias, New Mexico is one of the most backward in intelligence, industry, and manufactures, etc., and surely few others present the natural advantages to be found therein, not only on account of its abundance of water, forests, wood, and useful timber, but also on account of the fertility of the soil, containing within its bosom rich and precious metals, which up to this time are useless for the want of enterprising men who will convert to the advantage of other men all of which productions of nature are susceptible of being used for the benefit of society within the department, as well as in the entire Republic, if they were in the hands of individuals who would work and improve them. An old and true adage says that 'what is the business of all is the business of none;' therefore while the fertile lands in New Mexico, where, without contradiction, nature has proven herself more generous, are not reduced to private property, where it will be improved, it will be of no benefit to the department, which abounds in idle people, who, for the want of occupations, are a burden to the industrious portions of society, which with their labor they could contribute to its welfare and honestly comply with their obligations.

"Idleness, the mother of vice, is the cause of the increase of crimes which are daily being committed, notwithstanding the severity of the laws and their rigid execution. The towns are overrun with thieves and murderers, who, by this means alone, procure their subsistence. We think it a difficult task to reform the present generation, accustomed to idleness and hardened vice. But the rising one, receiving new impressions, will easily be guided by the principles of purer morality. The welfare of a nation consists in the possession of lands which produce all the necessaries of life without requiring those of other nations, and it cannot be denied that New Mexico possesses this great advantage, and only requires industrious hands to make it a happy residence. This is the age of progress and the march of intellect, and they are so rapid that we may expect, at a day not far distant, that they will reach even us.

"Under the above conviction we both request Your Excellency to be pleased to grant us a tract of land for the purpose of improving it, without injury to any third person, and the raising of sugar beets, which we believe will grow well and produce an abundant crop, and in time to establish manufactories of cotton and wool and raising stock of every description. [Description as worded in first part of note.]

"For the reasons above expressed, and being the heads of large families, we humbly pray Your Excellency to take our joint petition under consideration, and be

COAT OF ARMS OF GENERAL DE VARGAS

pleased to grant us the land petitioned for, by doing which we will both receive grace and justice.

"We swear it is not done in malice; we protest good faith, and whatever may be necessary, etc.

"GUADALUPE MIRANDA
"CARLOS BEAUBIEN

"Santa Fe, January 8, 1841."

Beaubien purchased the interest of Miranda, and in 1846 removed from Taos to the Cimarroncito, where he found Lucien B. Maxwell residing. Beaubien died in 1864. His daughter, Luz Beaubien, became the wife of Maxwell, who meanwhile had purchased the interests of all the heirs of his father-in-law. Maxwell, in turn, sold the property to an English syndicate, through the agency of Wilson Waddingham, D. H. Moffat, and J. B. Chaffee. Maxwell died at Fort Sumner, New Mexico, in comparative poverty, July 25, 1875.

Beaubien was a native of Canada and was descended from a long line of noble ancestors. The first representative of the name in Canada was Jules Trotier, born in 1590, at St. Malod'lye au Perche, France; who married Catherine Loyseau. His son, Antoine, Sieur des Ruisseaux, married Catherine Lefebone, by whom he had a son, Michael, Sieur de Beaubien, the first of the family to bear that name. He married Agnes Godfroy de Linctot, and after her death he married Therese Mouet de Moras. Louis Trotier, Sieur de Beaubien, son of the second marriage, married Marie Louise Robida Manseaux. They had a son, Paul Trotier, Sieur de Beaubien, who, October 3, 1795, married Louise Charlotte Adelaide Durocher, daughter of J. B. Durocher and Marguerite Boucher-Denoix. Charles Hipolyte Trotier, Sieur de Beaubien, was the first child of this marriage. He came to the United States, using the name of Beaubien, and arrived in New Mexico in 1823, along with a number of other French-Canadians. He settled in Taos, where he married Paula Lobato, the daughter of a prominent Mexican citizen. Of this marriage there were born: Narcisco, killed in the revolution of 1847; Luz, the wife of L. B. Maxwell; Leonar, the wife of V. Trujillo; Juanita, who married L. D. J. Clouthier; Teodora, the wife of Frederick Muller; Petrita, who married Jesus Gil Abreu; and Pablo, who married Rebecca Abreu.

154 MARIANO VARELA, LUIS AGUILAR and JUAN TOURNIER. 1845.
>Registration of a mine called *"El Santo Niño,"* at the *Real de Dolores.* City of *Santa Fe.*

155 ANTONIO FRESQUI to Francisco Lorenzo de Casados. *Santa Fe*, May 23, 1704.
>Conveyance. Before Antonio Montoya, Alcalde.

156 LORENZO DE CARABAJAL. *Alburquerque*, 1707.
>Petition for title to lands granted in 1706. Possession given by Martin Hurtado.

157 FRANCISCO JOSEPH DE CASADOS. *Santa Fe*, April 12, 1708.
>Petition for lands. Petition granted by the Marqués de la Peñuela and possession given by Juan Garcia de las Rivas. Small tract near the City of *Santa Fe.*
>Gaspar Gutierrez de los Rios, Secretary of Government and War. Cristoval de Gongora, Secretario del Cabildo.

158 JUAN DE RIBERA and MARIA GARCIA DE NORIEGA, his wife, to Francisco Lorenzo de Casados. *Santa Fe*, November 9, 1705.
>Conveyance. Before Diego Arias de Quiros, Alcalde.

159 MARTIN GARCIA to Clara de Chaves.
>Donation. *Santa Fe.* December 1, 1710. House and land in the City of *Santa Fe.* Before Juan de Ulibarri, Alcalde. Cristoval de Gongora.

160 DIEGO VELASCO and MARIA DE TAPIA, his wife, to Juan Ruiz Cordero.
>Conveyance. *Santa Fe,* November 16, 1711. Before Diego Arias Quiros, Alcalde.

161 MARIA DE CABRERA, widow of Joseph Luis de Valdes, to Ana Baldes, wife of Lazaro de Cordoba.
>Dower. *Pueblo Nuevo de Santa Cruz.* April 12, 1712. Before Felipe de Aratia.

THE SPANISH ARCHIVES OF NEW MEXICO 67

162 JUANA DE SOSSA CANELA, widow of Salvador Matias de Rivera to Miguel Carrillo. City of *Santa Fe*, August 17, 1713.
>Conveyance of land. Before Juan Paez Hurtado, Governor.
>This deed (1713) refers to the *Rio Chiquito* and to a church then being built; this is in all probability the church which stood on the site of the present cathedral.

163 JUAN RODELO to Francisco Lorenzo de Casados. *Santa Fe*, September 22, 1713.
>Conveyance. Before Juan Garzia de la Rivas.

164 IDEM.

165 JUAN DE LEON BRITO and MARIA GRANILLO, his wife, to Juana de la Cruz, widow of Joseph de la Virgen. *Santa Fe*, November 25, 1713.
>Conveyance. Before Juan Garsia de la Rivas.
>Refers to a house standing in 1713 in the *Barrio de Analco*, Santa Fe.

166 SEBASTIAN DE VARGAS to Miguel de Coca. *Santa Fe*, April 9, 1714.
>Donation of one vara in a mine. Before Francisco Joseph Tomas de Bohorques, Nicolas Ortiz Niño Ladron de Guevara, Joseph Manuel Giltomey.

167 CRISTOBAL CRESPIN.
>Grant on the River *Chama*. 1714 and 1715. The petition is for "*Las sobras de tierras de las q. tiene registrada el Alférez Salvor de Santiestevan y el Capitán Bartolome Lobato de lo q. cupiere en dhas sobras de sembradura de maiz y trigo en el Rio de Chama.*" Grant approved August 29, 1714. Possession given August 21, 1714, by Sebastian Martin, Alcalde.
>Re-validated November 25, 1715, by Governor Juan Ignacio Flores Mogollon, who originally made the grant. In these papers are mentioned persons to whom grants had been made by this governor about the same time, viz: Nicolas Griego, Bartolomé Lobato, Antonio de Salazar, Nicolas de Valverde, Salvador de Santiestevan, Roque de Pintto, Secretary of Government.

68   THE SPANISH ARCHIVES OF NEW MEXICO

168 JUAN DE LA MORA PINEDA to Juan Ruiz Cordero. *Santa Fe*, April 22, 1716.
>Conveyance. Before Juan Garzia de la Riva. House and land.

169 DIEGO ARIAS DE QUIROS.
>In the matter of a reservoir he was constructing in the City of *Santa Fe*, at the *Cienega*. This item, a *testimonio*, covers sixteen pages and contains much of historical interest.
>
>Further proceedings were had in the same matter in the following year, as appears from a document attached to the foregoing. Phelix Martinez, Governor and Captain-General; Miguel Thenorio de Alva, Secretary of War and Government; Diego Arias de Quiros, Alcalde.

170 JUANA MARTIN, wife of Phelipe de Aratia to Cristoval Crespin. *Santa Fe*, October 28, 1718.
>Conveyance. Before Don Francisco Joseph Bueno de Bohorques y Corcuera, Alcalde.

171 CRISTOVAL CRISPIN to Miguel Duran. *Santa Fe*, October 25, 1718.
>Conveyance. Before Don Francisco Joseph Bueno de Bohorques y Corcuera, Alcalde.

172 PEDRO LUCERO, CRISTOVAL GARCIA and VENTURA DE LA CANDELARIA.
>Question in regard to the sale of lands at *Alburquerque*, before Alonzo Rael de Aguilar, Teniente General of New Mexico. *Alburquerque*, April 3, 1722.

173 HERMENEJILDO SISNEROS, PHELIPE NERI SISNEROS and JUANA SISNEROS vs. JOSEF LUJAN and SEBASTIAN MARTIN. 1727.
>Question as to sale of lands in *Rio Arriba*. Before Juan Domingo de Bustamante, Governor and Captain-General. This grant was originally made to ANTONIO SISNEROS, father of the complainants.

174 INHABITANTS OF SANTA CRUZ vs. JUAN, ANTONIO and CRISTOVAL TAFOYA.
>Relative to pastures for stock; 1727. Before Juan Domingo de Bustamante, Governor and Captain-General.

Petition by certain citizens in regard to pasture lands in the Cañada de Santa Clara, which they had formerly used, but the use of which shortly before had been denied them by Juan de Tafoya, Antonio de Tafoya, and their father, Cristobal de Tafoya, who claimed that they had been granted the land for the use of their own herds.

This petition was presented to Governor Bustamante on December 9, 1727, and he ordered the chief alcalde of Santa Cruz de la Cañada to have the Tafoyas appear within three days after notification, and present their title or grant for examination.

Antonio appeared before the alcalde and stated that his brother was sick, and his father was at Jémez, but that he (Antonio) would go to Santa Fe to see the governor. It appears that on his failing to do this within the period fixed, the governor ordered the alcalde to send him in to Santa Fe. This was done, and the governor put him in the guardhouse under arrest, and subsequently ordered him to make reply within three days to the charges made by the citizens in their petition.

Tafoya asked that the petition be delivered to him in order that he might be able to answer the charges; and stated that he would also explain why he had failed to appear before the governor when first ordered so to do.

Here the proceedings abruptly end. It seems likely that these Tafoyas were the same persons who subsequently had disputes with the Indians of Santa Clara in regard to the same lands. These disputes were settled by Governor Tomas Velez in the year 1763, in favor of the Indians.

175 LEONOR MONTAÑO and MARIA ANTONIA DE CHAVES to Antonio de Chaves. *Santa Fe*, September 9, 1729.

Conveyance of a tract of land in *Atrisco*. Before Don Diego Arias de Quiros, Alcalde.

176 ANTE No. 175, *q. v.*

177 PEDRO CHAVES.

Inventory of the estate and partition of the same by Don Juan Paez Hurtado, Governor and Captain-General. 1736.

178 NICOLAS DE CHAVES.

This document is marked *"Escrituras de Dn. Nicolas de Chaves, en ocho fojas."*

JUANA DE SEDILLO, wife of Francisco Garcia to Antonio de Sedillo. *Alburquerque,* January 9, 1734.
    Conveyance of land. Before Geronimo Jaramillo, Alcalde.

DIEGO PADILLA to Diego Borrego. *Alburquerque,* January 7, 1734.
    Donation of land. Before Juan Gonzales Bas.

ANTONIO SEDILLO, son of Joaquin Sedillo, to Diego Borrego. *Alburquerque,* January 11, 1734.
    Conveyance of a tract of land below the pueblo of *Isleta*. Boundaries, north, the league of the pueblo of *Isleta*; south, a twin alamo called *"Alamo de Culebra"*; east, the *Rio Grande*; west, the *Puerco* ridge. In the conveyance it is set forth that this tract was granted to the father of the grantor by the crown. Before Juan Gonzales Bas.

    This grant was made to the petitioner, Don Antonio Sedillo, in the year 1769, whose petition stated "that at the time when this kingdom was governed by his excellency, Don Francisco Marin del Valle, I and other neighbors of mine presented a petition asking a grant of lands called *'Los Quelites,'* which was granted and given to us, and which we inhabited for four years, and it is now nearly three years since the same was abandoned on account of the great risk and the small forces we had for such a frontier. I therefore appeal to the Catholic zeal of your excellency, and humbly kneel down before your royal patronage, asking that your excellency concede to me a tract of land, which at the end of the aforementioned land grant I have registered, and which is called *'La Cañada de Los Apaches.'* Its boundary on the east is a hill called Cerro Colorado, which is the boundary of those of Atrisco; on the west the point of a table-land, which runs in said direction and which comes out of the said Cañada; on the north the grant of the settlers of the Rio Puerco; on the south the boundary of Mateo Pino. This I expect from the Christian zeal of your excellency, and if at any time the said place should become settled, I shall put no obstacle to their enjoying it, if they do not prejudice me in the possession of my part, which I so humbly ask for, and which I claim on account of having no land of my own whereby to maintain my large family, and because I am a poor man, and have been for over twenty years in the royal service, as a private soldier, corporal, sergeant, and on various occasions as a commanding judge and at present the chief alcalde of the pueblos of Acoma, Laguna and Zuñi, for all of which I pray your excellency, etc.   ANTONIO SEDILLO"

The grant was made by Governor Mendinueta and possession given by Don Carlos José Perez de Mirabal, in the presence of Captain Baltazar Baca and Manuel Torres, and the settlers of Atrisco and Rio Puerco, including Manuel Vaca, José Chaves, and Lieutenant Juan Bautista Montaño, and some *"Navajo Apaches."* The Joaquin Sedillo Grant was confirmed by the court of private land claims and surveyed for more than 22,600 acres.

The survey was of two tracts, of which No. 1 is claimed by the heirs of Francisco Javier Chaves, and this conflicts with the Lo de Padilla Grant.

Tract No. 2 is claimed by the Isleta Indians. It was patented November 15, 1909.

179 MARIA GONZALES to Juan Carrillo. *Santa Fe*, April 12, 1738.

Conveyance of lands.   Before Antonio Montoya, Alcalde.

180 GREGORIO CRESPIN.

Grant by Don Gaspar Domingo de Mendoza, Governor and Captain-General, Santa Fe, August 8, 1742. Boundaries: North, the lands of Captain Sebastian de Vargas; south, the road of *El Alamo*; east, the lands of Captain Juan Garcia; west, the lands of Juan Phelipe Rodriguez. Possession given by Don Antonio de Hulibarri, Alcalde.

To his excellency the governor and captain-general: I, Gregorio Crespin, inhabitant of the town of Santa Fe, placed at the feet of the greatness of your excellency in the best form that there may be allowed to me and say: That because I am loaded with obligations and that I do not have a piece of land for ploughing to discharge my said obligations I have known of a piece of land which is sitting on the other side of the river which are surplus lands of Captain Juan Garcia de las Rivas, and its boundaries are the following: On the east they adjoin with the lands of the said Captain Juan Garcia, on the west with lands of Juan Phelipe Rodriguez, on the north of Captain Sebastian de Vargas, and on the south with the alamo road (*camino del alamo*), which lands I ask the greatness of your excellency to give to me as a grant in the name of his majesty (whom may God preserve) and if you will grant them to me that royal possession be given to me, for I will receive grace, and I swear in due form that this petition is not done in bad faith, etc.

GREGORIO CRESPIN [rubric]

ORDER

In the town of Santa Fe, on the 8th day of the month of August, 1742, I, the Lieutenant-Colonel Don Gaspar Domingo de Mendosa, governor and captain-general of this kingdom of New Mexico, in view of the present petition I should and did command the alcalde mayor of this town, Antonio de Ulibarri, to go upon the tract of lands asked for by the petitioner and after examining them to give him in the name of his majesty (God preserve him) the grant he asks for himself, his children, and successors by better right, observing at its delivery the circumstances and necessary requirements such as are accustomed, and especially the one that no harm shall result to third party; thus I provided and ordered and signed with witnesses of my attendance for the lack of public or royal notary, there being none, and upon the present paper, there being none of the seal in said kingdom, to which I certify, etc.

DON GASPAR DOMINGO MENDOSA [rubric]

JOSEPH DE TERRUS
JOSEPH TRUXILLO

In the town of Santa Fe, on the 8th day of the month of August, 1742, I, the Captain Antonio de Ullibari, alcalde mayor and war captain of this town, before me appeared Gregorio Crespin, inhabitant of the said town, and showed me a grant of land made to him by the Lieutenant-Colonel Don Gaspar Domingo de Mendosa, and having seen it, I, the said alcalde mayor, went upon the lands stated in this grant, and being upon them and having examined them I took the said Gregorio Crespin by the hand and led him over the ground. He plucked grass, cast stones, shouted, saying: "Long live the King of Spain, my lord Don Phillip the fifth" (whom may God preserve) fixing for him the boundaries, which are: On the east with lands of Captain Miguel Garcia de las Rivas, on the west reaching up to the lands of Phelipe Pacheco, on the north the highway for wagons that goes from this town to the alamo (camino real de los carros que sale de esta villa para el alamo) on the south side an ancient ditch which forms the boundary of Juan Arguello; and at said act

of possession were present Phelipe Tafoya, Juan Antonio de Apodaca, Juan Arguello, Juan Antonio de Archuleta, whom I asked if they knew or have noticed whether any one had a right to these lands, and all answered that they did not know or have notice that any other person had a right to the same, but they had always believed it to belong to Captain Juan Garzia de las Rivas; thus they stated before me the said alcalde mayor, acting as judge commissioner; for the lack of public or royal notary for there are none in this kingdom; upon the present kind of paper, for there is none of the seal in these regions, to which I certify. ANTONIO DE ULIBARRI [rubric]
Witt.:
PHELIPE TAFOLLA; JUAN MANUEL CHIRINOS.

181 JUANA BACA to Joaquin Codallos y Rabal, Governor and Captain-General.
> A house and lot. *Santa Fe,* June 10, 1746. The governor bought this property in order to destroy it as it obstructed the approach to the new church.
> This archive contains certified copies of two deeds, made in 1714, which describe lands situate *"En la Calle Rl. q ba de la plaza a la Yglesia nueba q se esta fabricando;"* translated — On the main street which goes from the plaza to the *new church which is being built.* This shows that the church which De Vargas built at the time of the reconquest, or the church which stood in Santa Fe before 1680, mentioned in archives No. 8 and No. 169, and which was destroyed by the Indians in 1680, was on the plaza.

182 ANTONIO SISNEROS.
> Only four pages and there is no date and no signature as well.

183 ANTONIO CASADOS and LUIS QUINTANA. *Indios Genízaros* vs. . . . Barrera, Diego de Torres, and Antonio Salazar.
> Matters relative to lands at *Belen,* county of *Valencia.* This item consists of *testimonios* of the original papers which were sent to the Cónde de Fuenclara, Viceroy of *New Spain.* 1746.
> Some Indians claimed that lands at Belen were the property of an Indian pueblo and that the Spaniards were intruding upon them.

74   THE SPANISH ARCHIVES OF NEW MEXICO

184 NICOLAS DE CHAVES. Compromise with Bernabe Baca.
: Reported Claim No. 155, *q. v.*

185 JUANATILLA, a half-breed woman. 1747.
: Inventory and partition of her estate. Pueblo of *San Buenaventura de Cochiti*. Before Don Joaquin Codallos y Rabal, Governor and Captain-General.

186 PARTIDO DE CHAMA.
: Decree of Captain-General Tomas Velez Cachupin prohibiting the abandonment of said Partido. *Santa Fe,* August 1, 1749.
: This is a decree prohibiting the abandonment of the Chama district.

187 JUAN ROMERO to Joseph Cordova. *San Francisco Xavier del Pueblo Quemado*, January 12, 1750.
: Conveyance of land. Before Juan Joseph Sandoval, Alcalde.

188 PEDRO CORDOBA to Lazaro Cordoba. *Pueblo Quemado*, February 12, 1750.
: Conveyance of land. Before Juan Joseph Sandoval, Alcalde.

189 LAZARO DE CORDOBA to Antonio de Cordoba. *Puesto de Nuestra Señora de la Soledad del Rio Arriba. En la Villa Nueva de Santa Cruz.* September 1, 1750.
: Conveyance of lands. Before Juan Joseph Lobato, Alcalde.

190 MANUELA DE VEYTIA to Salvador Casillas. *Santa Fe*, March 2, 1751.
: Conveyance of house and lot. Before Joseph Bustamante y Tagle, Alcalde.

191 ANA MARIA DE CORDOVA.
: Will. *Pojoaque,* March 16, 1753. Before Hilario Archuleta, Alcalde.

192 JOSEPH RODRIGUEZ to Tomas Casillas. *Santa Fe*, May 8, 1753.
: Conveyance of land. Before Nicolas Ortiz, Alcalde.

193 JUANA GALVANA, a half-breed of *Zia*.
   Inventory and partition of her estate. Before Antonio Baca, Alcalde, 1753.

194 SEBASTIAN DE VARGAS to Gregorio Crespin. *Santa Fe*, November 7, 1755.
   Before Francisco Guerrero. Lands. 400 by 58 varas in area.

195 MARCIAL MARTIN, Executor of Sebastian Martin, deceased, to Francisco Chacon. *Santa Cruz de la Cañada*, December 14, 1763.
   Before Manuel Garcia Pareja, Alcalde.

196 QUITERIA CHAVES. Petition *sobre el repartimiento de unas tierras á sus hijos naturales en defecto de no tenerlos legitimos.* Alburquerque, 1764.
   Lands situate in *Atrisco*. Before Don Tomas Velez Cachupin, Governor and Captain-General.

197 MARIA CHAVES, widow of Sebastian Martin.
   Will. *Puesto de Nuestra Señora de la Soledad,* county of *Rio Arriba,* May 2, 1765. Before Manuel Garcia Pareja, Alcalde.

198 PETRONA DE CARDENAS.
   Will. *Santa Cruz de la Cañada.* February 15, 1767. Before Manuel Garcia Pareja, Alcalde.

199 ANTONIO and PEDRO CHAVES.
   Grant. Reported Claim No. 99.

200 IGNACIO CHAVES, et al.
   Reported Claim No. 96.

201 NICOLAS DE CHAVES.
   Reported Claim No. 155.
   This grant was made in 1768, January 20, to Ignacio, Tomas, Miguel, and Antonio Chaves, all residents of the valley of Atrisco, whose "fathers and grand-fathers were the conquerors of this province" and who were anxious "to follow in their foot-steps" according to the wording of the petition. They also had in mind treating the Navajos and Apaches "with love and Christian sincerity, endeavouring to attract them to a love of our Holy Faith"

and all of whom were to be present when possession was ordered given. The grant was made by Governor Mendinueta and possession was given by Captain Bartolomé Fernandez, who names with the Chaves Don Domingo de Luna as a grantee, who had applied for the property along with the others.

202 INHABITANTS OF CARNUEL.
Reported Claim No. 150.

203 CARRISAL.
Testimonio of proceedings relating to the re-settlement of the same. Manuel Antonio San Juan, Sargento Mayor y Capitan Justicia Mayor, *El Paso del Rio del Norte*.
The re-settlement of *Carrizal*; probably in the present State of Chihuahua, Mexico.

204 FRANCISCO ANTONIO CHAVES and BARTOLOME MONTOYA, for themselves and 12 others of Atrisco vs. DIEGO ANTONIO CHAVES. *Atrisco*, 1786.
Question of entrances, exits, etc. Before Don Juan Bautista de Anza, Governor and Captain-General. Manuel de Arteaga, Alcalde.

205 CEBOLLETA GRANT.
Reported Claim No. 46, *q. v.*

206 CEBOLLETA GRANT.
Reported Claim No. 46, *q. v.*

207 CEBOLLETA GRANT.
Reported Claim No. 46, *q. v.*
This was confirmed March 3, 1869, and was surveyed in 1876. Its entire southern boundary is coterminous with the northern boundary of the Paguate Purchase, which is the property of the pueblo of Laguna. The grant was patented in 1882. The question of the correct location of the Gavilan table-land has been a matter of dispute for years.

208 TERESA CORTES.
Question in regard to the possession of lands at Abiquiú. Before Alberto Mainez, Governor, in the year 1808, and apparently continued until 1824.

The *expediente* contains forty-six *fojas* and is incomplete.

On page 1 of leaf 2 is a reference to the pueblo of *Abiquiú* having been founded in 1754, by Governor Veles Cachupin.

209 JOSE ANTONIO CHAVES for himself and in the name of the heirs of ESTEVAN and BERNARDO PADILLA, all of *San Andrés de las Padillas*.

Title as to lands. Before Don José Manrique, Governor, 1809. Lorenzo Gutierrez, Alcalde.

210 CANON DEL JEMEZ.

Complaint of settlers vs. Blas Lopez. November 6, 1809. Before Don José Manrique, Governor. No action taken.

211 JOSE AGUSTIN DE LA PENA, and in the name of DOMINGO CHAVES, LUIS PADILLA and FRANCISCO PADILLA and of the HEIRS of CLEMENTE GUTIERRES vs. URSULA CHAVES.

Question as to lands, 1809. Before Don José Manrique, Governor.

212 BUENAVENTURA CHAVES.

Question of lands in the *Los Lunas* Tract. 1810. Before Don José Manrique, Governor.

Los Lunas; there are matters of some historical significance in this item.

213 ANTONIO CANJUEBE; half-breed of the Pueblo of *Santa Clara*. 1744 to 1817.

Petition in regard to a piece of land near the pueblo of *Santa Clara*. Before Don Joaquin Codallos y Rabal, Governor. Francisco de Roa y Carrillo; Phelipe Jacobo de Nuanes; Santiago de Roybal, Vicar and Ecclesiastical Judge; Antonio Duran de Armijo, Notary; Pedro Maria de Allande, Governor; Bernardo Bonavia, Commandante General, *Durango*.

This document is interesting rather than important. It relates to a dispute between the pueblo of Santa Clara and certain Indians of that *pueblo*, in regard to a strip of land within the boundaries of the grant. These Indians claimed that the land in dispute had been acquired by their grandfather, Roque Canjuebe, in exchange for other land nearer the *pueblo*; that this occurred in 1744, when their grandfather by permission of the Spanish government severed his tribal relations and became a Spanish citizen.

The dispute about the land arose in 1815, when the pueblo of Santa Clara objected to the Indians who claimed to be Spanish citizens remaining within the boundaries of the grant, and occupying lands there.

Governor Alberto Maynez decided in favor of the *pueblo*, and some of the Indians who claimed to be Spanish citizens and to have a right to the land in dispute, not only because it had belonged to their grandfather, but also because they had occupied it long enough to acquire title by prescription, made as many as three trips clear to Durango and back, to lay the matter before the commandant general. It was finally settled by their surrendering the land to the *pueblo,* and being permitted to take up their residence wherever they saw fit.

The arguments advanced by the litigants in support of their several contentions are quite interesting.

The pueblo of Santa Clara is referred to as *"El Pueblo de Santa Clara de los Caballeros."*

214 TOWN OF CEVILLETA.

Reported Claim No. 95.

Don Juan de Oñate gave the name to the pueblo. He found it a small place and called it "New Seville." It was a *Piro* pueblo. Oñate also mentions a pueblo sixteen miles north which would be about where Sabinal of today is located; there is an old ruin there, which was inhabited in Oñate's time.

The pueblo of Sevilleta was destroyed in wars with other tribes, according to Fr. Benavides, *Memorial,* p. 16. In the year 1626, it was re-settled and a church dedicated to San Luis Obispo, was built. This was the headquarters of a mission and was the most northerly at that time of the Piro settlements. In 1680, at the time of the driving out of the Spaniards, this was a very small place, and the inhabitants accompanied the Spaniards to El Paso. Vetancurt, *Cronica,* p. 310, says of the place: *"Y le habitan tres familias, hoy está asolado."* Alonzo de Garcia — *Autos presentados en Disculpa,* folio 45, says: *"Y habiendome llegado al Pueblo de Sevilleta donde hallé á los naturales de dicho pueblo quietos y pacificos al paracer, pues dejaron su pueblo, y me fueron siguiendo hasta el del Socorro, que unos, y otros con de nacion Piros."*

These Piros were not invited by the northern pueblos to participate in the uprising; see *Interrogatorios de varios Indios,* 1681, folio 125: *"Que cogio un mecate de palmilla, y marando en el unos nudos, que significaban los dias que faltaban, para la egecucion de la tracion, lo despacho por todos los pueblos hasta el de la Isleta sin que quedase en todo el reyno, mas que el de la nacion de los Piros."*

The Sevilleta Land Grant was made in 1819, with an area of 224,770 acres; the claim was approved by the surveyor-general in 1874. It was confirmed to Felipe Peralta et al. by the court of private land claims, the area being 261,187.90 acres.

215 MARIA DE LA LUZ CANDELARIA. *San José de las Huertas,* 1820.

Complaint against Francisco Miera in the matter of a tract of land at *San Francisco,* jurisdiction of *Las Huertas.* Before Don Facundo Melgares, Governor.

RANCHO DE CUBERO. Three loose papers relating to a rancho situate between the pueblos of *San Felipe* and *Santo Domingo.* Santiago Fernandez and José Alexandro Quintana, claimants. Before Don Facundo Melgares, Governor.

216 URSULA CHAVES, of *Las Padillas,* vs. JOAQUIN PINO.

Question of a rancho by the name of *"El Rito."* 1821. Before Don Facundo Melgares, Governor.

217 IDEM, *q. v.*

218 ANTONIO CHAVEZ, of *Belen.*

Petition for lands, 1825. The place called *"Arroyo de San Lorenzo."* Boundaries: North, the *Mesita del Alamillo;* south, *Rancho de Pablo Garcia;* east, *El Rio del Norte;* west, *el ojo de la Jara.* Before the Territorial Deputation. On March 3, 1825, this petition was granted by the deputation.

These papers contain a reference to the Socorro Grant, *q. v.*

219 INHABITANTS OF LA CAÑADA.

Permission given them to settle on lands near the pueblo of Picuriés, by the Territorial Deputation. May 2, 1829.

80 THE SPANISH ARCHIVES OF NEW MEXICO

220 SAMUEL CHAMBERS, a naturalized citizen.
> Petition to the Territorial Deputation asking permission to settle on the *Rio del Poñil*. Refused. November 10, 1830.

221 JOSE and RAMON TORRES.
> Question of lands with the Cura, Vincente Chaves. Sabinal, November 9, 1831. Letter to José Antonio Chaves, *Jefe Politico*. The lands are at the place called "*Bosque Redondo.*"

222 ANA MARIA DEL CASTILLO vs. MIGUEL SENA. *Santa Fe*, May 20, 1834.
> Claims a house and lot in the City of *Santa Fe*.

223 IGNACIO, FRANCISCO, JOAQUIN, JOSE and JOSE DE LA CRUZ CHAVES and MIGUEL ARCHULETA and NICANOR IDALGO.
> Petition for lands at *Galisteo*. January 29, 1842. Before Colonel J. Andrés Archuleta, Prefect. Granted.

224 GRANT within the limits of the present State of *Colorado*.

225 JUAN DE JESUS CORDOBA and JOSE MANUEL TRUJILLO of *San Pedro de Chamita*.
> A question as to water rights, 1843.

226 JOSE FRANCISCO BARELA to Juan Coquindo. *Valles de Santa Gertrudis de lo de Mora*. October 7, 1844.
> Validation of a conveyance of land. Before Tomas Ortiz, Alcalde.

227 LUIS CARBONO. Grant. *Valle de Santa Gertrudis de lo de Mora*, October 10, 1844.
> The tract is situate at the place known as "*La Cueva de los Pescadores.*" By order of the Prefect of the First District, Colonel Juan Andrés Archuleta, dated January 3, 1844. Before Captain Tomas Ortiz, Alcalde.

228 LA CIENEGA. City of *Santa Fe*. Years 1826 to 1845.
> Seven papers relating to this tract of land.

THE SPANISH ARCHIVES OF NEW MEXICO 81

229 TOWN OF CHAPERITO.
>File No. 7, office of Surveyor-General, *q. v.*

230 MANUEL VACA to Fernando Duran y Chaves. *Bernalillo*, May 5, 1701.
>Donation of a piece of land *"que es la cantidad que alcanzare un ttiro de piedra con la mano."*
>Before Joseph Rodriguez, Alcalde. *Testimonio* certified to by Joseph Rodriguez.
>The original grant to the lands at Bernalillo, after the re-conquest was made by General De Vargas, to Felipe Gutierrez; it had previously been granted to Gutierrez by Governor Cubero, December 3, 1701. The original petition applied for a tract of land situate on "this side of the Rio del Norte, in front of the house of Captain Diego Montoya, which is called the Ancon del Tejedor (Weavers' Bend), containing a league and a half in area." De Vargas re-validated the grant in 1704, and royal possession was not given until 1708 — by Martin Hurtado, alcalde and war-captain. In 1742 Don Gaspar Domingo de Mendoza required Antonio Ulibarri, chief alcalde of Alburquerque, to ascertain and report to him whether this tract had been occupied or abandoned, as a grant of the same had lately been made to the Captain Luis Garcia. Don Tomas C. de Baca testifying in this case, declares that at the time of the making of the grant the Rio Grande was to the east of the property.

231 JOSEPHA DOMINGUEZ, widow of Matias Martin. *Santa Fe*, 1710.
>Presents will of her deceased husband. Before Captain Phelix Martinez, Governor, and Captain Juan Paez Hurtado, Visitador General. This is a partition proceeding.

232 BENITO DOMINGUEZ. Grant. *Santa Fe*, 1715.
>Before Don Juan Ignacio Flores Mogollon, Governor. Tract situate near the City of *Santa Fe*.

233 DIMAS XIRON DE TEGEDA, husband of Ana Maria Dominguez.
>Claims dower from José Dominguez. 1716. *Santa Fe.*

234 CARLOS LOPEZ to Antonia Duran, widow of Pascual Trujillo. *Santa Fe*, October 15, 1716.
>Conveyance of land in *Pojoaque*. Before Juan Garsia de la Riva.

235 JUANA DOMINGUEZ. *Santa Fe.*
   Will. January 12, 1717. Before Salvador Montoya, Alcalde.

236 ROSA DURAN DE AMIJO vs. ANTONIO DE URRIBARRI. 1732.
   Claims to be heir to estate of his deceased wife, Maria de Chaves. City of *Santa Fe.*
   Before Don Gervasio Cruzat y Gongora, Governor and Captain General. Juan Antonio de Unanues.

   JUAN BACA. Part of inventory of estate. *Bernalillo*, 1727. Antonio de Gruciaga, Secretary of Government and of War.

237 JOSEPH DURAN. Grant. *Santa Fe*, August 18, 1743.
   Before Don Gaspar Domingo de Mendoza, Governor. Possession given by Antonio de Hulibarri, Alcalde. Land on the other side of the river in the City of *Santa Fe.*

238 LEONOR DOMINGUEZ, widow of Cristoval Xaramillo, to Nicolas Duran. *Alburquerque*, December 11, 1734.
   Conveyance of land before Juan Gonzales Bas.

   PEDRO LUZERO to Nicolas Duran. *Alburquerque*, August 10, 1735.
   Conveyance of land. Before Juan Gonzales Bas, "*las quales tubo por erencia de su difunto padre, Nicolas Lucero, quien las poseo por mersed que de ellas y otras mas se le yso en nombre de su Magd. como a originario fundador de esta villa.*" No. 1040 q. v.

239 ANTONIO DOMINGUEZ. Grant. *Santa Fe*, August 14, 1742.
   A piece of land on the other side of the river (meaning the *Rio Santa Fe.*)
   Before Don Gaspar Domingo de Mendoza, Governor.

240 ANTONIO DURAN DE ARMIJO.
   Inventory of the estate and other papers. *San Geronimo de Taos,* 1748.
   Maria Gertrudis Duran de Armijo, daughter of the above and Barbara Montoya, sole legatee.
   Barbara Montoya. Will. Dated *San Geronimo de*

Taos, January 18, 1745. Before Francisco Guerrero, Alcalde.

CRISTOBAL DE LA SERNA. Grant.
A rancho in the valley of *Taos* formerly held by Fernando de Chaves. Boundaries: *"por una parte el camino de en medio, y por la otra el Ojo Caliente y por el oriente una monojera antigua, y por la otra, la sierra."* Serna first asked for this grant in 1710 and it was made by the Marquis de la Penuela. In 1715 it was re-validated by Mogollon, governor, and possession was given by Juan de la Mora Pineda, alcalde. On November 24, 1724, the grant was presented by Diego Romero to General Juan Paez Hurtado, governor and visitador general, and by him approved. The paper in this item is a *testimonio*, made in 1743, by Francisco Guerrero, alcalde, and is witnessed by Juan Domingo Paez Hurtado and Joseph de Terrus. It appears that the approval above mentioned was intended to vest the title to the grant in the said Diego Romero, as will be seen by the proceedings had before the alcalde, Francisco Guerrero, in May, 1743. The words used in the approval by the captain-general are *"Diego Romero vesino de dicho pueblo presento esta mersed que vista y reconosida por mi la doi por bastante titulo en forma por visitador."*

ANDRES and FRANCISCO ROMERO, ANTONIO DE ATTENCIO and ANTONIO DURAN DE ARMIJO.
Petition for partition of the grant now called *"Rancho del Rio de las Trampas."* The partition was made on May 5, 1743, by Francisco Guerrero, Alcalde.

DIEGO ROMERO.
Petition to register a brand, 1714, 1715. Before Miguel Thenorio de Alba and Juan Paez Hurtado, Governor and Captain-General. Miguel Enriquez, Secretary of Government and War.

JUAN (A) and SEBASTIAN (A) de la Serna to Diego Romero. *Villa Nueva de Santa Cruz*, August 5, 1724.
Conveyance of the above grant. Before Cristoval Torres, Alcalde.

ANTONIO ATTIENSA and MARIA ROMERO, his

wife, to Antonio Duran de Armijo. *San Geronimo de Taos*, October 29, 1726.
> Conveyance of house and 405 varas of land in the valley of *Taos*. Before Francisco Guerrero, Alcalde.

BARBARA MONTOYA, Intestate, widow of Diego Romero and afterwards married to Antonio Duran de Armijo.
> Proceedings in the settlement of her estate. Before Francisco Guerrero, Alcalde. *Testimonio,* May 18, 1748. (Original.)
> Further proceedings were had in this matter before Juan Antonio Ordenal, Juez y Visitador, in the year 1749.
> Don Joaquin Codallos y Rabal, Governor; Antonio Martin, Alcalde; Phelipe Jacobo de Unanues; Juan Garsia de Mora; Gregorio de Garduño; Miguel Thenorio de Alva; Cristobal Torres, Alcalde; Antonio Duran de Armijo; Thomas de Alvear y Collado.

241 JUAN TRUXILLO and TOMAS DE TAPIA to Juan Duran. Pueblo of *Pojoaque*, April 19, 1751.
> Conveyance of house and land. Before Juan Joseph Lovato, *Procurador General*. Conveyance of 146 varas of land.

242 DOMINGO BENAVIDES to Antonio Dominguez. *Santa Fe*, October 24, 1751.
> Conveyance of house and land. Before José de Bustamante Tagle, Alcalde.

243 CHATALINA DURANA, widow of Bartolomé Garduño, intestate, *Santa Fe*, May 23, 1752.
> Inventory of her estate. Before José de Bustamante Tagle, Alcalde.

244 MANUELA BRITO to Antonio Dominguez. *Santa Fe*, July 10, 1764.
> Conveyance of house and land. Before Francisco Guerrero, Alcalde.

245 MARIA DE ARCHIBEQUE, widow of Francisco Jo-

seph de Casados, and Joseph Sanches to Salvador Duran. *Santa Fe*, November 15, 1764.
> Conveyance of a rancho on the other side of the river (Santa Fe). Before Francisco Guerrero, Alcalde.

246 MANUEL DURAN DE ARMIJO of *Alburquerque*.
> Will, inventory, and partition of his estate. 1764. Before Baltazar Griego, Alcalde. It seems that this man was also known as Manuel Armijo, Segundo.

247 JUAN JOSEPH DURAN vs. ANTONIA DE MEDINA, widow of Batolomé Truxillo. *Santa Fe*, 1767.
> Claims the interest of his wife in the estate of said Truxillo. Before Don Tomas Velez Cachupin, Governor and Captain-General.

BARTOLOME TRUXILLO. Resident of *Chama*. May 16, 1764.
> Will. Executed before Joseph Esquibel, Alcalde.

TERESA ERRERA (HERRERA), resident of *San Joseph de Chama*.
> Will. Executed before Francisco Sanches, Alcalde, September 16, 1759.

BARTOLOME TRUJILLO. 1752.
> Part of *testimonio* of grant to a rancho at *Santa Rosa de Abiquiú*. Before Don Tomas Velez Cachupin, Governor. Possession given by Juan Joseph Lobato, Alcalde. *Testimonio* certified to by the Governor, Don Tomas Velez Cachupin.

BARTOLOME TRUJILLO.
> *Testimonio* of petition to Captain-General Don Tomas Velez Cachupin, for re-validation of grant to a tract of land at *Abiquiú* which petition was granted October 7, 1752. *Testimonio* dated November 7, 1766.

ANTONIO FELIZ VALDES LA VANDERA. *Abogado en las Reales Audiencias*, Chihuahua.
> Decision, January 27, 1767. Antonio de Beitia, Alcalde; Juan Joseph Lovato, Alcalde; Phelipe Tafoya, Procurador de la *Villa de Santa Fe*; Francisco Antonio Zis-

neros; Juan Domingo Lobato; Geronimo Esquibel; Carlos Fernandes; Domingo Labadia; Joseph Esquibel, Alcalde; Manuel Garzia Pareja, Alcalde; Francisco Guerrero, Alcalde; Juan Bautista Vigil; Joseph Maldonado; Julian de Armijo; Antonio de Armenta; Mattheo de Peñaredonda.

248 GERTRUDES RODRIGUEZ to Salvador Duran. *Santa Fe*, May 8, 1768.
>Conveyance of land. Before Don Phelipe Tafoya, Alcalde.

249 NICOLAS APODACA to Juan José Duran. *Santa Fe*, April 20, 1776.
>Conveyance of land in grant at *Pojoaque*. Before Manuel Garsia Pareja, Alcalde.

250 JOSE DURAN Y CHAVES. Intestate. *San Carlos de Alameda*. 1783.
>Inventory and partition of estate. Before Nerio Antonio Montoya, Alcalde. Don Juan Bautista de Anza, Governor; Francisco Perez Serrano; Vincente Troncoso; José Marcelo (also written Marzelo) Gallego; Jacinto Gutierres.

251 MARIA DOMINGA vs. *JUAN LAUREANO*. Natives of the Pueblo of *Sandia*.
>Inheritance. 1792. Before Cleto Miera y Pacheco, Alcalde.

>JOSE JOAQUIN DE LISARRARAS Y GAMBOA.
>Of the *Real Audiencia de Guadalajara*. Official letter relating to a murder case.

252 MANUEL DELGADO. Intestate.
>Inventory and partition of his estate. *Santa Fe*, 1815. Before Alberto Mainez, Governor. Juan Rafael Ortiz; Marcos Delgado; José Francisco Baca; Fernando Delgado; Manuel Delgado; Antonio Ortiz; Ignacio Elias Gonzales.

253 AYUNTAMIENTO of the Pueblo of *San Lorenzo del Real de Dolores*. February 18, 1823.
>Letter to the Provincial Deputation, asking information in regard to area of lands.

254 AGUSTIN DURAN, FRANCISCO BACA Y ORTIZ and FRANCISCO BACA y PINO.
  Petition for lands. 1826. Papers incomplete. Teodosio Quintana, Secretary of the Territorial Deputation; José Francisco Baca, Alcalde; Antonio Narbona, Jefe Politico.

255 AGUSTIN DURAN and OTHERS.
  Petition for lands between the pueblos of *Santo Domingo* and *San Felipe*. 1831. Before the Territorial Deputation. No final action taken. Abreu, Secretary.

  Juan Antonio Cabeza de Baca, First Regidor
  José de Jesus Sanches, Second Regidor
  Angel Maria Antonio Gonzales, Third Regidor
  } *Ayuntamiento* of *Santa Fe*.

  José Martinez
  Ramon Aragon, First Regidor
  Antonio José Lusero, Second Regidor
  José Manuel Padilla, Fourth Regidor
  Diego Montoya, Procurador Sindico
  Antonio Saenz, Secretary
  } *Ayuntamiento* of *Sandia*.

  Petition by Agustin Duran and others, for lands lying between the pueblos of Santo Domingo and San Felipe.

  It was presented to the Territorial Deputation of New Mexico on April 14, 1831, and by that body was ordered to be reported upon by the constitutional town councils of Cochiti and Sandia.

  The town council of the former place reported that there was no objection to making the grant, notwithstanding the fact that the pueblos of Santo Domingo and San Felipe had a "Document" for the lands, dated in the year "sixty" (evidently 1760). They say that the Indians had sufficient lands within their pueblo grants, and had not cultivated the lands for which the petitioners were asking.

  The town council of Sandia reported, that in view of the fact that the Indians had a very old "document" by which the land had been granted to them, it could not see how they could be dispossessed, and moreover it stated that the Indians had cultivated some portions of the land.

  There is no evidence either in this archive or elsewhere which shows that any grant was made to the petitioners.

  The document referred to by the town councils of Cochiti and Sandia was probably the grant of 1770, made by Governor Pedro Fermin de Mendinueta to the pueblos of Santo Domingo and San Felipe. This grant was filed with the surveyor-general for New Mexico under the act of July 22, 1854, but was not confirmed by Congress. The claim, however, was finally presented to the court of private land claims, and by that court was confirmed on December 8, 1898. (See Reported No. 142, U. S. Surveyor-General's office.)

256 TERRITORIAL DEPUTATION.
Decree relating to lands. August 9, 1827. Location not given.

FRANCISCO ORTIZ, Lieutenant.
Certificate relating to titles to lands in the *Real de los Dolores*. July 3, 1839.

257 FELIPE SENA.
Letter to the Governor of the Department. *Santa Fe*, July 3, 1845. Relative to the colony at *Doña Ana*.

258 JUAN PAEZ HURTADO to Francisca de Eguijossa. *Santa Fe*, September 7, 1713.
Conveyance of house and land. Before Juan Garsia de la Riva, Alcalde.

259 VENTURA ESQUIBEL.
Petition for lands. 1734. Before Gervasio Cruzat y Gongora, Governor and Captain-General. Refused.

260 MARIA ROSA MARTIN to Salvador de Espinosa. *Santa Fe*, May 9, 1736.
Conveyance of land in *Chimayo*. Before Estevan Garsia de Noriega, Alcalde.

261 FRANCISCO and JUAN MANUEL DE HERRERA to Joseph Esquibel. *Villa Nueva de Santa Cruz*, April 14, 1751.
Conveyance of land. Before Juan Joseph Lovato, Alcalde.

262 ANTONIA DE LA SERNA to Joseph Esquibel. *Villa Nueva de Santa Cruz*, July 17, 1751.
Donation. House and lot. Before Juan Joseph Lovato, Alcalde.

263 JOSEFA SENA to Clemente Esquibel. *Santa Fe,* March 15, 1817.
> Conveyance of land. Before José Francisco Baca, Alcalde.

264 JUAN RAFAEL ESQUIBEL.
> Will. *Santa Fe,* December 21, 1819.

265 ANTONIO ALEJANDRO ESQUIBEL.
> Will. *Santa Fe,* December 21, 1820.

266 FRANCISCO TORRES to Clemente Esquibel. *Santa Fe,* May 25, 1824.
> Conveyance of land. Before José Ignacio Ortiz, Alcalde.

267 LUIS BENAVIDES vs. VICENTE BACA, Alcalde. *Santa Fe,* 1827.
> Complaint in regard to lands purchased from Maria Manuela del Carmen Rodriguez. Before Antonio Narbona, Governor (*Jefe Politico*).

268 JOSE ESTRADA.
> Grant. *Valle de Santa Getrudis de lo de Mora,* October 7, 1844. Before José Ortiz, *Juez de Primera Instancia.* Law of April 30, 1842. Articles 13 and 15 *q. v.*

269 PEDRO BUEN-AMIGO ESPERANZA. Petition. *Santa Fe,* February 12, 1839.
> Asks for land at *Shapellote* (Sapello?). No action taken. No. 1244, *q. v.*

270 PHELIPE DE ARRATIA to Lucas Flores. *Santa Fe,* November 23, 1700.
> Conveyance of a house and lot. Before Antonio de Aguilera Isasi, Alcalde.

271 MARTIN FERNANDEZ.
> Petition. Jurisdiction of *La Cañada.* Petition asks for *"sobras"* of the lands of Cristobal de la Serna and Cristoval Tafolla, on the *Trampas* river. No date and no action taken.

272 ANTONIO MONTOYA to Maria Fernandez de la Pedrera. *Santa Fe,* February 13, 1740.
> Conveyance of house and lot. Before Juan Paez Hur-

tado, Governor and Captain-General. Antonio Duran de Armijo. Baltazar Montoya. Antonio Montoya.

273 IGNACIO JARAMILLO to Gabriel Fragoso. *Santa Fe*, August 26, 1762.
Conveyance of house and lot in *Alburquerque*. Before Manuel Gallego, Alcalde. Lucas Moya. Ignacio Jaramillo. Pedro Tafoya.

274 MARCOS RODRIGUEZ to Juan Joseph Fernandes de Salasar and Juan Antonio Archuleta to the wife of the same.
Conveyance and donation of lands. *Santa Fe,* September 28, 1752. Before Manuel Gallego, Alcalde. Juan Antonio Ortiz. Pedro Antonio Tafoya.

275 FRANCISCO XAVIER FRAGOSO.
Will. *Santa Fe,* April 24, 1766. Before Lieutenant Tomas Alarid and Ensign Francisco Esquibel.

276 SALVADOR DE SANDOVAL to Carlos Fernandez. *Santa Fe*, August 27, 1767.
Conveyance of land. Before Francisco Guerrero, Alcalde. Francisco Xavier Fragoso. José Miguel de la Peña.

277 NUESTRA SENORA DE LA LUZ SAN FERNANDO Y SAN BLAS.
Partition of lands. 1772. By Bernabe Montaño y Cuellar, Alcalde. By order of Don Fermin de Mendinueta, Governor and Captain-General. *Testimonio* certified to by the Governor. *Atrisco* Grant, *q. v.*
Nuestra Señora le la Luz San Fernando y San Blas:
"We, Ensign Ramon Garcia Jurado and Antonio, and José and Bernabe Manuel and Juan Baptista and Pedro and Ramon Garcia Jurado, legitimate sons of José Montaño, all residents of the town of Alburquerque, appear before your Excellency and state that at the place called *Rio Puerco,* there is some public land hitherto unsettled, with little permanent water, and at the places we now occupy, we are crowded and needy, for however much we may labor in the field and in the cultivation of our lands, we are unable to support ourselves nor always obtain even sufficient for our daily maintenance, and we are obliged to go out among the nearest Indian pueblos to

work for them, sometimes weeding their fields, sometimes bringing firewood from the mountains for the small compensation of a few ears of corn with which they pay for this and other very laborious work. In consideration whereof and to the end that our suffering stock may pasture in some adequate place as in the said *Rio Puerco,* we therefore humbly pray that your excellency be pleased in the name of his Majesty (whom may God preserve) to make us a grant to the said lands, your excellency being pleased to bear in mind that our fathers and grandfathers have served his Majesty in the conquest and reconquest of this province, as is well known, as we also ourselves have done since we have been of age; participating in all the expeditions and campaigns that have been projected against the savage enemies, without up to this time having asked or having been given a piece of land and if we now ask it of your Excellency it is because necessity compels us, especially the necessity of pasturing our stock this winter, and on account of which necessity we fear, and without doubt it will so prove, that there will be a great mortality; and therefore in order to prevent this as well as on account of the benefit which will result from the increase of the sacred tithes to ourselves, the community, and the few additional persons who may join us, for we all carry with us arms and horses, although up to this time there has been no instance in which the enemy has come in by that route, it being for them very difficult as they run great risks of being caught, and the mountains which they inhabit being far distant.

"BERNABE MANUEL MONTAÑO"

The decree by Governor Tomas Velez Cachupin gave authority to Don Antonio Baca, alcalde of *Santa Ana, Zia, and Jemez,* to reconnoiter the country and make report to him, which was done, as appears from the report by the alcalde, November 2, 1753, dated at the pueblo of *Zia,* on the 25th day of November of the same year. The grant was made by Governor Cachupin and the alcalde Antonio Baca instructed to place them in possession under the royal protection. The governor named the place *Nuestra Señora de la Luz de San Fernando y San Blas.* The governor also advised the settlers "to preserve peace, Christian unity and friendly social intercourse, in which matter the chief Alcalde who now or may hereafter officiate in that jurisdiction, will exercise particular vigilance and care and they are urged also to attend Mass on the holy days, taking care also that the young and the Indians be taught the prayers and the Christian doctrine, which as Catholics, they ought to know.''

The settlement was placed under the jurisdiction of the chief alcalde of *Santa Ana, Zia,* and *Jemez.* The original settlers as appear from the account of juridical possession, were: Antonio Gurule, his wife and eighteen children, including domestics, making twenty; Juan Zamora, his wife and six children; José Castillo and wife; Pedro Montaño, wife and three children; Antonio Montaño, wife and three children; Agustin Gallegos, wife and three children; Feliciano Hurtado, wife and two children; José Montaño, wife and three children; José de Jesus Montaño; Bernabe Montaño and son; Marcos Baca, wife and six children and two servants; Juan Baptista Montaño, wife and three children, two servants; in all twelve families. The grant was confirmed on March 29, 1754, by Governor Cachupin; thereafter on the 18th day of January, 1759, Governor Francisco Antonio Marin del Valle compelled the settlers to appear before him and obligate themselves to carry out the provisions of the original grant, which they did, whereupon the grant was again made to these parties, and their successors. Thereafter in 1769, owing to some erasures in the grant papers made by Juan Baptista Montaño, he was reprimanded with great severity by Don Pedro Fermin de Mendinueta for having tampered with the document.

Owing to the constant raids of the Navajós and Apaches after having cultivated the land for upwards of twenty years, the grantees were compelled to abandon it and it was not until the later seventies that the property was again occupied by the heirs of the original grantees.

Pedro Baca, a son of one of the original grantees, was killed at *San Blas* by the Navajós.

278 JOSEPHA ARMIJO by her husband Roque Lobato and Joseph de Dimas to Carlos Fernandez. *Santa Fe,* August 22, 1770.

Conveyance of house and lands. Before Phelipe Tafoya, Alcalde. Antonio Joseph Tafoya. Joseph Miguel Tafoya.

279 JULIANA FERNANDEZ.

Will. *Santa Fe,* May 21, 1785. Before José Maldonado, Teniente.

THE SPANISH ARCHIVES OF NEW MEXICO 93

280 JUAN ANTONIO FERNANDEZ. Intestate.
>Inventory and partition of his estate. *Santa Fe*, 1784. Before Antonio Ortiz, Alcalde. Juan Bautista de Anza, Governor and Captain-General. Francisco Perez Serrano; Julian de Armijo; Vincente Troncoso; Fr. José de Burgos; Vincente Armijo.

281 DOMINGO FERNANDEZ, SANTIAGO FERNANDEZ, JUAN DE ABREGO, BUENAVENTURA ESQUIBEL, SANTIAGO RODRIGUEZ for themselves and the other heirs of Bartolomé Fernandez.
>Petition for lands, 1815. Before Alberto Mainez, Governor. The land called for was then known as the *Rancho de Cuberos* and was originally granted to Bartolomé Fernandez and Josef Quintana by Don Manuel Portillo Urrisola, Governor and Captain-General. It was located between the pueblos of *Santo Domingo* and *San Felipe*. The petition was granted by Governor Maynez. José Alejandro Quintana was given one-half of the rancho and according to this item sold his one-half to the Indians of *San Felipe* in 1818.
>
>This is a lengthy manuscript in regard to a dispute between Domingo Fernandez et al. and José Alejandro Quintana, in regard to the interest claimed by the latter in the Santa Rosa de Cubero Tract, on the west side of the Rio Grande, between the pueblos of Santo Domingo and San Felipe. The dispute arose in 1819, and the allegations of the contending parties disclose a pretty full history of the grant, which is said to have been made originally about 1761 or 1762 — during the administration of Governor Manuel Portillo Urrisola. It is not necessary to set forth the details of the contents of this archive 281, as a complete translation into English is on file in the surveyor-general's office, in suit 267, in the former U. S. court of private land claims records.
>
>The important feature of it is that on pages 34 to 37 of the original there is a deed made by José Alejandro Quintana at Bernalillo on June 18, 1818, to the Indians of San Felipe, for his interest (one-half) in this grant. This deed shows that Quintana owned the southern half of the tract, the northern half belonging to the heirs of Bartolomé Fernandez.
>
>The boundaries of the grant were "on the north by the Santo Domingo league, on the south by the San Felipe

league, on the east by the Del Norte river; and on the west by the table-land of Las Casitas, which they call that of Cubero and Los Apaches.

This grant was confirmed by the court of private land claims on December 20, 1898, and has been surveyed.

BARTOLOME FERNANDEZ appears in the *La Majada* Grant, *q. v.*

Domingo Fernandez; José Gutierrez, Alcalde; Francisco Ignacio de Madariaga, Asesór; Fr. Francisco de Hozio, Cura of Santa Fe; José Petronilo Gutierrez, Alcalde; Juan de Abrego; Melgares, Governor.

282 DOMINGO FERNANDEZ. Grant.

Reported Claim No. 19, *q. v.*

283 DOMINGO FERNANDEZ and OTHERS.

Petition for lands in the place commonly called *Pueblo de Pecos.* 1823-24.

Before Bartolomé Baca, Governor and *Jefe Politico.* Read in session of February 16, 1824, of the Territorial Deputation. Not approved.

Domingo Fernandez was the original petitioner to the Spanish government for the grant known as the Eaton or San Cristobal, situate in Santa Fe county, N. M. He states that he was a "son and descendant of the conquerors and pacifiers of this Kingdom of New Mexico." His petition for the grant, which he registered as "El Pueblo de San Cristobal," is unique in its phraseology and recites a number of facts of historical interest. His petition was filed with the governor, April 26, 1822, at which time he says "the ruins of the pueblo may be seen and the walls of a sacred temple in a dilapidated condition and almost entirely razed to the ground, which calls my attention speaking with ingenuity, as upon seeing that sacred place where upon so many occasions the sacred and awful sacrifice of the mass has been offered, and where the most august sacrament was consecrated; considering that it is more than one hundred years since the natives who inhabited it have abandoned it, and it appears that Divine Omnipotence each day endeavours to make known to us that it sustains the foundations of this holy place, which is suffering under the disgrace of being a habitation for beasts, a stable for sheep and a manger for cows and calves, and, in a word, a lodging for brutes. His Divine Majesty knows that by the sole efforts of His great power and inscrutable providence he has moved my spirit for so great a purpose, and that it may not possibly be thought that I solicit said land through avarice, let the proof be made, let permission be given to me to commence repairing it, which I promise to do as my curtailed means will allow, and I will be careful to give notice to our most illustrious bishop, in order that ceremonies may be performed therein, although the pastoral letter granted us that privilege, this being the principal object I have in view in my petition."

The citizens of Santa Fe who were to assist Fernandez in this laudable enterprise and who were to receive land were of "good behaviour and sound habits, according to my sound judgment" as follows: Francisco Fernandez, Antonio Sena, Juan de Jesus Rivera, Miguel Rivera, José Maria Rivera, Ignacio Ortega, José Ortiz, Miguel Lobato, Pablo Ortiz, Florentino Ortiz, José Trugillo, Mariano Baca, Miguel Rodriguez, and José de Jesus Chaves, each with the appellation of "Don."

The matter was referred to a committee by Don Pedro Armendaris, president of the illustrious corporation of Santa Fe, who visited the locality and reported that "if the petitioners labor with all such perseverance as it is seen those (the Indians) did, they will be rewarded for their labor if they are aided by God our father with water from heaven to fill their tank, as, in truth, from the existing springs they will reap very little benefit." The grant was made to Fernandez. He did not secure possession, however and five years later filed another petition in which he states among others that from information received from a native of Pojoaque, named Ramon (Indian), in the presence of two witnesses "that the water on the land is abundant and that it is covered up; also that the ornaments and sacred vessels are buried, which he promised to show me and discover, together with the water." The "ornaments" referred to are those which were taken by the Indians at the time of the rebellion in 1680. He received the same information in reference to the ornaments from Francisco, the "White-eyed," without having been rewarded or requested, or compelled.

A favorable report was made by two aldermen of the City of Santa Fe, July 26, 1827, Don Rafael Sarracino and Don Miguel Baca, who with the lieutenant of Galisteo, Don Julian Lucero, had reported on the property in 1822. On August 21, 1827, the grant was made to Domingo Fernandez and thirty men, and possession was given by the first appointed constitutional alcalde, Don José Maria Martinez, who "having taken Fernandez by the hand, he entered and walked over the said land, he pulled up weeds, and uttered loud exclamations of joy and pleasure, scattered hand-fulls of earth, broke off branches from the trees and said 'Long life to our present President, Don Guadalupe Victoria! Long life to the Mexican Nation!' "

The persons who had agreed to participate in the glorious work outlined by Fernandez in his several petitions failed to appear when the time for performance had arrived, in consequence of which two years later Fernandez again asked the political chief of New Mexico for "la justicia."

On the same day the political chief, Chaves, issued an order compelling the "settlers" to comply and in the event of their failure other "industrious individuals" were to be substituted.

On January 20, 1851, Fernandez sold the property to E. W. Eaton and A. W. Raynolds. Eaton afterwards acquired the title of Raynolds under a sheriff's sale and by quit-claim from Raynolds.

The property today belongs to Benjamin F. Pankey.

The grant, as appears from the original title papers, was made according to the provisions of the royal edict of January 4, 1813, and also bears the approval of the Provincial Deputation, authorized by the government of Mexico after the change from Spanish sovereignty.

284 DOMINGO FERNANDEZ.

Petition for vacant lands on the *Pecos river*. *Santa Fe*, March, 1825. Lands granted by the Territorial Deputation, but no possession given. Captain Bartolomé Baca, Governor. Vigil, Secretary.

285 DOMINGO FERNANDEZ and OTHERS.

Same subject as *ante*, No. 284. No final action taken. 1828.

286 DOMINGO FERNANDEZ and JUAN ANTONIO ARMIJO. 1828.

In regard to lands in *"El Canyon."* No. 284-285, *q. v.*

287 RAFAEL FERNANDEZ and OTHERS.

Lands on the Pecos. No. 284-5-6, *q. v.* File No. 71 office of the Surveyor-General, *q. v.*

Facsimile of Signature of Don Juan Domingo de Bustamante, Governor and Captain-General, 1722-1731.

Facsimile of Signature of General Juan Paez Hurtado, Governor and Captain-General, 1704-5, 1717.

Facsimile of Signature of Don Gervacio Cruzat y Gongora, Governor and Captain-General, 1731-6.

Facsimile of Don Gaspar Domingo de Mendoza, Governor and Captain-General, 1739-1743.

288 DOMINGO FERNANDEZ, et al.
    Lands on the *Pecos.* No. 284-5-6 *q. v.* 1829. Territorial Deputation refused to confirm.
    This is a petition from two Indians of the pueblo of Pecos to the effect that they had been robbed of their lands five years before and asking for relief.

289 MELCHORA de los REYES and SEBASTIANA de MONDRAGON to Francisco Garsia. *Santa Fe,* October 2, 1700.
    Conveyance of house and lands. No signatures to this item.

    THOMAS PALOMINO to Cristoval Truxillo. *Santa Fe,* June 14, 1700.
    Conveyance of land. Before Antonio de Aguilera y Isasi, Alcalde. Tomas Palomino, Antonio Duran de Armijo, Miguel Ladron de Guevarra.

290 DIEGO de VECTIA (BEITIA) to Martin Garzia. *Santa Fe,* February 6, 1702.
    Conveyance of land. Before Joseph Rodriguez, Alcalde.

291 MARIA GARSIA de NORIEGA.
    Grant to a piece of land in *Santa Fe.* May 1, 1702. Don Pedro Rodriguez de Cubero, Governor and Captain-General. Antonio Aguilera Isasi, Alcalde; Cristoval de Gongora, Secretary of the Cabildo; Pedro de Morales, Secretary of Government and War.

292 FRANCISCO de la MORA to DIEGO GONZALES. *Santa Fe,* December 12, before Joseph Rodriguez, Alcalde.
    Conveyance of rancho and lands granted in 1699 by Cubero, Governor, to the grantor. Situate in the jurisdiction of *Villa Nueva de Santa Cruz.* Francisco de la Mora, Antonio Lucero de Godoy, Domingo de la Barreda.

293 TOMAS JIRON de XEDA for himself and for his wife, Ana Dominguez and Dimas and Maria Xiron, his children, to Isabel Gonzales. *Santa Fe,* December 4, 1703.
    Conveyance of a rancho which formerly belonged to Alonzo del Rio. Before Lorenzo de Madrid, Alcalde. See below; this name should be Texeda. Cristobal de Gon-

gora, Secretary of the Cabildo; Juan Manuel Chiriños; Ignacio de Aragon.

TOMAS XIRON DE TEXEDA to Juan de Archuleta. *Santa Cruz*, February 12, 1698.
> Before Roque Madrid, Alcalde. Conveyance of a rancho. Joseph Antonio de Giltomey, Miguel Ladron de Guebara.

MANUEL BALLEJO to Juan de Archuleta. *Santa Cruz*, November 11, 1697.
> Before Miguel Ladron de Guebara, Alcalde. Conveyance of a rancho. Miguel de Quintana, Joseph de Atienza.

294 MARIA and JUANA GRIEGO vs. DIEGO ARIAS DE QUIROS. 1703.
> Suit in the matter of a piece of land in *Santa Fe*. Before El Marqués de la Naba de Brazinas. There are three signatures of this governor in this archive. Alfonzo Rael de Aguilar, Secretary, etc.
> This is the earliest reference to the old palace at Santa Fe as the "*Palacio Real.*"

295 ANTONIO BAS GONZALES vs. DIEGO ARIAS DE QUIROS. *Santa Fe*, August 4, 1704.
> Question of lands. Before Don Francisco Cuerbo y Valdes, Governor and Captain-General Juan Paez Hurtado. Alfonzo Rael de Aguilar, Secretary of Government and of War.

296 PEDRO DE ABILA to Diego Gonzales. *Santa Fe*, April 4, 1701.
> Conveyance of a *fanega* of land in *San Cristobal*. Before Joseph Rodriguez, Alcalde, *Testimonio*.

297 FRANCISCO GARSIA. Grant. *San Francisco Xavier del Bosque Grande*, February 5, 1706.
> A tract of land called a "*Joya.*" Possession given by Martin Hurtado, Alcalde, in the name of the King. Possibly this tract is in the present county of Rio Arriba.

298 DIEGO DE BEYTIA to José Manuel Giltomey. *Santa Fe*, April 30, 1708.
> Conveyance of a lot in *Santa Fe*. Before Juan Garzia de la Rivas, Alcalde. Bartolomé Sanches.

This shows that the main street of Santa Fe was known by the name of *San Francisco* in 1708.

299 JUAN GARCIA DE NORIEGA.
Grant. A piece of land below *Santa Fe*. Before the Marqués de la Penuela, *Santa Fe*, August 13, 1708. Possession given by Juan Garsia de la Rivas, Alcalde. Cristobal de Gongora, Secretary of the Cabildo; Gaspar Gutierres de los Rios, Secretary of Government and War.

300 FRANCISCO XAVIER DE BENAVIDES to Juan Garcia de Noriega. *Santa Fe*, August 20, 1711.
Conveyance of land. Before Alfonzo Rael de Aguilar, Alcalde. Miguel de Sandoval Martinez.

301 NICOLAS, JOSEFA, MARIA and PEDRO GRIEGO vs. JOSEPHA LUXAN. *Santa Fe*, 1712.
Question of lands. Before Alfonzo Rael de Aguilar, Alcalde. Miguel de Sandobal Martinez.

302 FRANCISCO MONTES Y VIGIL to Juan Gonzales. *Santa Fe*, July 18, 1712.
Conveyance of a tract of land called *"Alameda"* granted to the grantor by the Marqués de la Penuela in 1710. Before Alfonzo Rael de Aguilar, Alcalde. Francisco Montes y Vigil; Antonio Duran de Armijo; Juan Gonzales; Cristobal de Gongora. No. 1029.

The Town of Alameda Grant was first surveyed in 1871 and had an area of more than 106,000 acres. The title was confirmed by the court of private land claims and under a new survey the area was reduced to about 89,000 acres. There is a conflict with the grant to the pueblo of Sandia, as to that which lies east of the Rio Grande. No patent has been issued.

303 JACINTO SANCHEZ to Juan Garcia de la Rivas. *Santa Fe*, May 9, 1713.
Conveyance of a house and land in *Santa Fe*. Before Juan Paez Hurtado, Alcalde. Diego Velasquez, Antonio Duran de Armijo.

304 JOSEPH BLASQUEZ (VELASQUEZ?) to Joseph Manuel Giltomey, *Santa Fe*, September 25, 1713.
Conveyance of a house and lot in *Santa Fe*. Before Juan Garcia de la Rivas, Alcalde. Diego Velasquez. The sig-

natures of this man in this item and that of No. 303 differ materially.

305 ANTONIO GODINES, of *Santa Fe.*
 Will. April 19, 1713. Before Juan Paez Hurtado, Alcalde. Joseph Maria Giltomey, Pedro de Roxas.

306 ALEJO GUTIERRES and BENTURA DE LA CANDELARIA. *Alburquerque,* August 15, 1715.
 Division of property. Before Luiz Garcia, Alcalde. Antonio de Silva, Baltazar Romero.

307 BALTAZAR ROMERO to Alejo Gutierrez. *Santa Fe,* March 11, 1715.
 Conveyance of house and lands in *Alburquerque.* Before Diego Arias de Quiros, Alcalde. Antonio Albarez Castrillon, Joseph Maria Giltomey.

308 A TESTIMONIO of No. 307.
 Felipe Tamaris. See No. 13.

309 FRANCISCA ANTONIA DE GUEJOSA.
 Reported Claim No. 109, *q. v.*

310 ANTONIO GALLEGOS, of *Bernalillo.* Intestate. 1715.
 Inventory and partition of his estate. Before Juan Ignacio Flores Mogollon, Governor and Captain-General. Roque de Pintto, Secretary of Government and War. Diego Montoya, Antonio Montoya.

311 CRISTOVAL TAFOYA vs. ISABEL GONZALES. Jurisdiction of *La Cañada.* 1715.
 Suit for lands. Before Juan Flores Mogollon, Governor and Captain-General. Joseph Truxillo, Alcalde. Juan de Atienza, Joseph de Atienza. Antonio de Balberde Cossio, General. Pedro de Villasur, Joseph Balentin de Aganza.

312 JACINTO SANCHES to Petrona Gomez. *Santa Fe,* November 9, 1716.
 Conveyance of lot in *Santa Fe.* Before Francisco Lorenzo de Cassados, Alcalde. Francisco Joseph Cassados.

313 JUAN RICO DE BROJAS and MARIA GUTIERRES to Juan Garcia de la Rivas. *Santa Fe,* July 10, 1716.

Conveyance of land near *Santa Fe*. Before Lorenzo de Cassados, Alcalde. Juan Manuel Chirinos, Salvador Montoya, Antonio Duran de Armijo.

314 FRANCISCO GARSIA.
Before Phelix Martinez, Governor and Captain-General.

315 ANTONIO GUTIERREZ.
Grant. Land near *Alburquerque*. Approved November 5, 1716. By Phelix Martinez, Governor and Captain-General.

316 JUAN GONZALES BAS vs. JERONIMO DE ORTEGA. 1731.
Question of lands above *Alburquerque*. Before Gervasio Cruzat y Gongora, Governor and Captain-General. Gaspar Bitton, Juan Antonio de Vnaues.

317 JUAN ESTEVAN GARZIA vs. JUAN LUJAN.
Question of lands at *Villa Nueva de Santa Cruz*. 1731. Before Gervasio Cruzat y Gongora, Governor and Captain-General. Land was sold to Juan Lorenzo Valdes. Gaspar Bitton, Juan Antonio Vnanues.

318 This is a continuation of the foregoing Item, with the same signatures.

319 DIEGO GALLEGOS.
Petition for lands. September, 1731. Before Gervasio Cruzat y Gongora. Not granted.

320 JUAN ESTEVAN GARZIA DE NORIEGA.
Grant. *Villa de Santa Cruz*, 1735. A tract of land above the *Pueblo Colorado*. Approved by Juan Paez Hurtado, Governor and Captain-General. Revoked by Cruzat y Gongora, Governor. No date. Diego Torres, Alcalde. Miguel Martin Serrano, Joseph Terrus, Juan Joseph de la Serda, Diego de Vgarte. Antonio de Ulibarri, Colindante.

321 FRANCISCO XAVIER DE MIRANDA to Francisco Antonio Gonzales, *Alburquerque*, March 25, 1735.
Conveyance of a tract of land in *Atrisco*. Before Geronimo Xaramillo, Alcalde. Bernardo Ballejos.

322 MANUELA GARCIA DE LAS RIBAS, ISABEL MONTOYA and FRANCISCO QUINTANA.
>Grant. 1735. Tract of land situate opposite the old town of *Abiquiú*. Approved by Juan Paez Hurtado, Governor, and possession given by Juan Estevan Garsia de Noriega, Alcalde. Called in for record, by Governor Cruzat y Gongora. No date. Antonio Montoya. Juan Lorenzo Baldez, Antonio de Uribarri.

323 MANUELA LUSERO to Lazaro Garsia. *Alburquerque*, April 23, 1735.
>Conveyance of house and land. Before Geronimo Xaramillo, Alcalde. Francisco Antonio Gonzales.

324 JUAN ANGEL GONZALES and ANTONIA DE CHAVES to Diego Gonzales. *Santa Cruz de la Cañada*, May 10, 1736.
>Conveyance of land. Before Juan Estevan Garsia de Noriega, Alcalde. Miguel de Quinttana, Tomas Nuñes de Aro.

325 ANTONIO GARSIA and THEODORA GONZALES to Diego Gonzales. *Villa Nueva de Santa Cruz*, May 17, 1736.
>Conveyance of a tract of land in the *Cañada*. Before Juan Estevan Garsia de Noriega, Alcalde. Alonso Rael de Aguilar, Antonio Felix Sanchez, Miguel de Quinttana.

326 JOSEPH GONZALES, of *Alameda*. Intestate.
>Inventory of his property. Before Juan Gonzales Bas, Alcalde. 1738. Alexandro Gonzales, Isidro Sanches.

327 JOSEPH DE HERRERA to Alonzo Griego. *Santa Fe*, February 26, 1738.
>Conveyance of lands. Before Antonio Montoya, Alcalde. Juan Manuel Chirinos, Joseph Tamari (Tamaris?).

328 MARIA TAFOYA to Lazaro Garcia de Noriega. *Santa Fe*, April 26, 1739.
>Conveyance of house and lands. Before Antonio Montoya, Alcalde. Gregorio Garduño, Baltazar Montoya.

329 JUAN GARCIA DE LA MORA to Joseph Garcia. *Santa Fe*, July 27, 1739.

Conveyance of house and lands. Before Antonio Montoya, Alcalde. Gregorio Garduño, Baltazar Montoya.

330 JOSEPH GARSIA to Manuel Sans de Garvisu. *Santa Fe*, September 26, 1739.
House and lands in *Santa Fe*. Before Antonio Montoya, Alcalde.

331 JOSE GARCIA to Juan Gavaldon. *Santa Fe*, September 9, 1739.
Conveyance of house and lands in *Santa Fe*. Before Antonio Montoya, Alcalde. Joseph de Terrus, Baltazar Montoya.

332 SALVADOR GONZALES.
Grant. Reported Claim No. 82, *q. v.*

333 FRANCISCO GUTIERRES vs. GREGORIO DE GONGORA.
Question as to land. Before Don Ignacio Codallos y Rabal, Governor and Captain-General, 1744. Jurisdiction of *Bernalillo*. Francisco de Roa y Carrillo, Fray Manuel Zambrano, Felipe de Silba, Antonio Aramburu, Joseph Roma de Vera, Alfonzo Rael de Aguilar.

334 FRANCISCO DE ROA Y CARRILLO to Francisco Guerrero. *Santa Fe*, July 17, 1744.
Donation of half a mine called "*Nuestra Señora del Pilar de Zaragoza.*" Three leagues from the pueblo of *Picuriés*. Antonio de Hulibarri, Alcalde. Sebastian de Apodaca, Joseph Roma de Vera.

335 JOSEPH DE TERRUS.
Entry of a mine. 1744. Before Joaquin Codallos y Rabal, Governor and Captain-General. Situate two leagues from *Picuriés* and called "*Santa Rosa de Lima.*"

JOSEPH DE TERRUS to Francisco de Roa y Carrillo and Francisco Guerrero.
Donation of the above. Antonio de Hulibarri, Alcalde. Francisco de Roa y Carrillo, Sebastian de Apodaca, Joseph de Roma de Vera.

336 HEIRS OF SEBASTIAN GONZALES. 1744.
Partition of lands. The heirs were the children of the above and GERONIMO de ORTEGA, and were eleven

in number. The lands were near *Santa Fe*. Partition made by Antonio de Hulibarri, Alcalde. ANTONIO de ORTEGA for himself and other heirs to ROSA de ARCHIBEQUE, widow of said GERONIMO de ORTEGA. 1750. Donation of a piece of land. Before Joseph de Bustamante Tagle, Alcalde. In 1760 further proceedings were had in this matter at the instance of the said widow, Rosa de Archibeque. Lucas Miguel de Moya, Joseph Maldonado, Carlos Fernandez, Francisco Guerrero, Alcalde, Thoribio Hortiz (Ortiz), Juan Antonio Hortiz (Ortiz), Juan Phelipe Rivera, Fray Joseph de Urquijo, Sebastian de Apodaca, Juan Francisco Arroniz, Nicolas Rael de Aguilar, Lucas Moya, Phelipe Tafoya, Antonio Joseph Ortiz, Joseph Reaño. Bartolomé Marques, *Mayor domo de Fabrica*. Francisco Antonio Marin del Valle, Governor and Captain-General. Bernardo de Miera y Pacheco. The last named came to New Mexico from Chihuahua in 1744. In 1768 together with Pedro Padilla of San Andrés (jurisdiction of Isleta) he was given a grant of land on the Rio Puerco. P. L. C. No. 98. Possession was given by Captain Francisco Trebol Navarro at the "Cañada de los Alamos."

Sebastian Gonzales was the father of Sebastiana Gonzales. The following is certificate of his death and burial:

"On the eleventh day of the month of June, seventeen hundred and twenty-six, died Sebastian Gonzales, married to Luisa Ortiz. His age was sixty years, he received the holy sacraments, and his body is interred in the Chapel of Our Lady; and that it may so appear, I sign on said day, month, and year. Ut supra.

"FRAY JOSEPH ANTTO. GUERRERO [rubric]"

337 MARIA GRIEGO. Grant. *Santa Fe*, January 16, 1695.

Petition for a piece of land a quarter of a league from the town. Approved by Don Diego de Vargas Zapata Lujan Ponce de Leon, Governor and Captain-General. Possession given on January 26, 1698, by Antonio Aguilera Isasi, Alcalde.

PEDRO ANTONIO TRUJILLO AND VALENTINA PACHECO. *Santa Fe*, 1745.

Compromise in the matter of the disposition of the estate of the above. Before Juan Antonio de Hulibarri, Alcalde. Alphonso Rael de Aguilar, Secretary of Government and War. Miguel Tenorio de Alba, Secretary of

Cabildo. Antonio Aramburu, Joseph Roma de Vera, Antonio Rodriguez, Antonio Felix Sanchez, Joaquin Codallos y Rabal, Gregorio Garduño, Francisco Rodriguez, Joseph Miguel Garduño.

338 GREGORIO GUTIERREZ, of *Alburquerque*, vs. MARIA SILVA, 1745.
Petition for ejectment. Before Don Joachin Codallos y Rabal, Governor and Captain-General. Lands in *Fuenclara*. Possession by Joseph Baca, Alcalde. Bernardo Ballejos, Marcial Rael de Aguilar.

339 JUAN MANUEL GAVALDON.
Will. *Santa Fe.* July 14, 1745. Before Juan Antonio de Hulibarri, Alcalde. Antonio Felix Sanchez, Gregorio Garduño.

340 LUIS GARZIA, of *Alburquerque*. 1746.
Petitions that the lands given to himself and his brothers, Vicente and Alonzo, by Captain General Marqués de la Penuela be given to him alone. Granted by Don Joachin Codallos y Rabal, Governor and Captain-General in the same year. Ramon Garzia Jurado, Phelipe Jacobo de Vnaues, Phelipe Barela, Geronimo Jaramillo, Miguel de Alire. Juan Moya, Alcalde. José Leon Oneto Escobedo, Antonio Gorole (Gurule).

341 LUIS GARCIA, of *San Antonio*, Jurisdiction of *Alburquerque*.
Inventory of estate. Before Bernardo Antonio Bustamante Tagle, Alcalde and *Teniente General este Reino y Justicia Mayor.* Ramon Garzia Jurado.

342 LUIS GARCIA DE NORIEGA, of *Alburquerque*. 1747.
Proceedings in the matter of the partition of his estate. Before Don Joachin Codallos y Rabal, Governor and Captain-General. Will. No. 341, *q. v.* Joseph Baca, Alcalde, Ramon Garzia Jurado, Miguel Montoya, Phelipe Romero, Fray Juan Joseph Toledo, Miguel de Alire, Bentura Romero, Domingo de Luna, Joseph Tenorio, Pedro Romero, Fray Joseph Irigoyen, Joachin Marin.

343 LUIS GARCIA.
Proceedings in the matter of the settlement of his estate. 1747. Before Don Joachin Codallos y Rabal, Governor and Captain-General. Nos. 341, 342, 414 and 1221, *q. v.*

BARBARA GARCIA JURADO, widow of Luis Garcia de Noriega.
> Power of attorney to her father, Ramon Garcia Jurado. In the matter of a suit brought by ROSALIA GARCIA de NORIEGA against the estate of Luis Garcia. *Testimonio.*
>
> ROSALIA GARCIA de Noriega was the daughter of Luis Garcia by his first wife. Her husband was Don Salvador Martinez. Joseph Romo de Vera, Ramon Garcia Jurado, Lucas Miguel de Moya, Felipe Jacobo de Vnanues, Phelipe Tafoya, Joseph Garsia.

344 MARIA DE LA CANDELARIA GONZALES.
> Will. *Santa Fe,* 1750. Before Joseph de Bustamante Tagle, Alcalde. Lucas Moya, Tomas Casillas.

345 ANTONIO DOMINGUEZ to Phelipe Garduño. *Santa Fe,* April 20, 1750.
> Conveyance of land. Before José Bustamante Tagle, Alcalde. Joachin Martin, Phelipe Tafoya.

346 HEIRS OF MICAELA BASQUEZ (VASQUEZ?), widow of Francisco Gonzales de la Cruz. *Santa Fe,* April 24, 1750.
> Partition of estate. By Joseph de Bustamante Tagle, Alcalde. Lucas Miguel de Moya. Phelipe Tafoya.

347 JUAN ESTEVAN GARSIA DE NORIEGA, by Phelipe Tafoya.
> Petition for a rancho said to have been abandoned at *Casa Colorada,* called "Santa Barbara." Before Don Tomas Velez Cachupin, Governor and Captain-General, 1751. Report of the Alcalde, Juan Joseph Lovato, of statement of Rosalia de Beytia, widow of Juan Antonio Lujan, as to the reason of the abandonment. Juan Domingo Lovato, Antonio Martin.

348 FELIPE NERIO SISNEROS to Manuel Gallegos. *Santa Fe,* June 5, 1751.
> Conveyance of house and land. Before Joseph Bustamante Tagle, Alcalde. Torrivio Ortiz, Antonio de Hulibarri.

349 ANTONIO TAFOLIA to Luis Fuera (Grazioso). *Santa Fe,* October 10, 1751.

Conveyance of house and land. Before Joseph de Bustamante Tagle, Alcalde. Sebastian (Fresqui) de Apodaca.

350 JOACHIN MARTINES to Francisco Garcia. *Santa Fe*, April 5, 1752.
   Conveyance of house and lands. Before Manuel Gallegos, Alcalde. Lucas Moya, Pedro Tafoya.

351 MARIA DIEGA GARDUNO, Intestate. *Santa Fe*, 1752.
   Inventory and partition of her estate. By Joseph Bustamante Tagle, Alcalde. Juan de Gabaldon, Pedro Tafoya. No. 350 *q. v.*

352 JUAN GABALDON. Grant.
   This grant was made in the year 1752 to Juan de Gabaldon by Governor Tomas Velez Cachupin. The petitioners agreed to erect a reservoir in the Tesuque river owing to objections made by the corporal, Juan de Benavides, who owned land near the pueblo of Tesuque.
   When this grant was confirmed by the court of private land claims and a new survey made it was found that a small conflict with the grant to the pueblo of Tesuque was made.

353 JUAN GARSIA DE LOS REYES.
   Will. *San Buenaventura de Chimayo*, August 18, 1752. Before Juan Joseph Sandoval, Alcalde. Nicolas Leal, Salvador Varela.

354 MARIA DE HERRERA, widow of Antonio Martin, to Diego Gomez. *Ojo Caliente*, April 5, 1753.
   Conveyance of land. Before Juan Joseph Lobato. Alcalde. José Martin, Bisente Apodaca, Francisco Zaes.

355 NICOLAS GARCIA.
   Will and partition of estate, by Nicolas Ortiz, Alcalde. *Santa Fe*, 1754. Francisco Guerrero, Phelipe Romero, Juan Antonio Ortiz, Joseph Maldonado, Thoribio Ortiz, Joseph Miguel de la Peña.

356 JOSEPH GARDUNO to Juan Gallego. *Santa Fe*, July 23, 1755.
   Conveyance of land. Before Francisco Guerrero, Alcalde. Joseph Miguel Garduño, Julian de Armijo.

JUAN TOMASA GALLEGO of *Corral de Piedra*, to Clemente Esquibel. January 20, 1811.
Conveyance of house and lands. Before José Miguel Tafoya, Alcalde. By endorsement. Antonio Tafolla.

357 LUIS DE ARMENTA to Cristobal Gamboa. *Santa Fe*, June 20, 1759.
Before Francisco Guerrero, Alcalde. Lucas Moya, Manuel Bernardo Garvisu.

Luis de Armenta was given a tract of land near the City of Santa Fe. The grant was made by Governor Cruzat y Gongora. In the act of possession mention is made by Antonio de Uribarri of "the house of *Sebastian de Vargas* along the hill" on the road from Santa Fe to Pecos.

To His Excellency the Governor and Captain-General:

I, Nicolas Armenta, lieutenant of the pueblo of Our Lady of Angels of Pecos, before your excellency, through the medium of this petition, in the best form allowed me by law, appear and say that whereas there exists in this superior archive of the government a grant of land of my deceased father (may he rest in peace), his name being Luis de Armenta, and the said possession was given by Captain Don Antonio de Ullibari, while he was alcalde mayor of this town of Santa Fe, in the time when the governor of this kingdom was Don Gerbacio Cruzat y Gongora, I therefore ask your excellency, if you should find it just, to have done to me what I have petitioned, for which reason I ask and pray your excellency most submissively to be pleased to command and do as I have petitioned; for in doing so I shall receive grace with justice, which I ask; and I swear in due form that this my petition is not done in bad faith in the necessary, etc.

NICOLAS ARMENTA [rubric]

Town of Santa Fe, May 26th, 1783, received as presented; and in view of what the petitioner asks, I should and do command that the testimonio which he prays for shall be given to him, which is in the following tenor: "To his excellency the governor and captain-general, I, Luis de Armenta, resident of this town of Santa Fe, appear before your excellency in the best form allowed me by law and say that in conformity with the royal ordinances of his majesty I register a piece of unoccupied lands, in which probably there can be ploughed two fanegas, lying on the left hand of the road leading to the pueblo of

Pecos, and it adjoins with the alto of the arroyo de los Chamisos, because it is royal domain and the said lands lying almost in the woods (monte), for which reason until the present day it is not known that they have had any owner nor that any person who might have a right has registered them. And because I am under the obligations of wife and children, and I have no farming lands for their maintenance, may the great justification of your excellency be pleased to make me a grant of the said lands in the name of his majesty and command that the alcalde mayor of this town give me the possession of the same and the personal use in the name of his majesty. For all of which I ask and pray of your excellency to be pleased to grant me the said lands accordingly and as I have asked for them, which is just; and I swear in form and in the necessary. LUIS DE ARMENTA"

"In the town of Santa Fe, on the 11th day of the month of September, 1732, it having been seen by me, the Colonel Don Gerbacio Cruzat y Gongora, governor and captain-general of this kingdom of New Mexico and its provinces, I received it as presented for what it may be worth in law. In view of what the petitioner asks, I made him a grant in the name of his majesty of one fanega for farming at the place he cites, without prejudice to third party who may have better claim, and that he be placed in possession in the land embraced by the said fanega of farming land by Captain Antonio de Ulibarri, alcalde mayor of the said town who will place the boundaries that belong to it according to what has been granted. Thus I provided, ordered, and signed with the witnesses of my attendance for the lack of public or royal notary, for there are none in this kingdom, and it is done upon the present common paper, because there is none of the seal in these regions.

"DON GERVACIO CRUZAT Y GONGORA

"Att. Witt.:
"GASPAR BITTON.
"JUAN ANTONIO DE UNANUE."

"In the town of Santa Fe, on the 19th day of the month of April, 1733, I, the Captain Antonio de Ulibarri, alcalde mayor and war captain of this said town, in obedience to what has been decreed by his excellency the Colonel Don Gervacio Cruzat y Gongora and captain-general of this kingdom, I went upon the lands asked for in his petition by Luis de Armenta, and being upon it I gave him the royal possession, with all the customary

formalities, fixing to him for boundaries of the fanega for planting corn by the road that leads to Pecos, which road starts from the house of Sebastian de Vargas, with the hill (lomas) the first cross to another cross that it makes on crossing another small hill (lomita), and to its size on the east, where there are two other crosses; and that it may so appear, I signed it with my attending witnesses for the lack of public or royal notary, for there are none in this kingdom. ANTONIO DE ULLIBARI
"Judge Commissioner.

"Wit.:
"DIMAS GIRON.
"PHELIPE TAMARIS."

"And for the effect that may be proper, I certify that it is the same to be found in the book of government which he cites, which I authorize and sign, I, the under-signed colonel of cavalry, political and military governor of this province, with the witnesses of my attendance for the lack of public or royal notary, for there are none in all this government; to which I certify.
"JUAN BAUTISTA DE ANZA [rubric]

"Att. witt.:
"VIZTE. TRONCOSO.
"FRANCO. PEREZ SERRANO."

358 JUAN GALLEGOS.

Will and partition of his property. 1760. Before Francisco Guerrero, Alcalde.

The will bears the signature of Fray Juan Joseph Toledo, and is dated at *Tomé*, November, 1760. Bartolomé Frnz. (Fernandez); Maria Butierrez (Gutierrez); Antonio Lucero, el Soldado.

In the papers in the Ojo de San Miguel Tract the petition of Don Bartolomé Fernandez recites:

"I, Bartolomé Fernandez de la Pedrera, brevet ensign of this royal garrison of the Villa de Santa Fe, appear before your excellency and state, sir, in consideration of the many and great services that my deceased grandfather, Captain Martin Hurtado, founder of the Villa of Alburquerque, and ensign of the line of this said garrison, pacificator of this province, rendered, and also those rendered by my deceased father, also pacificator and ensign of the line in the mounted company of the royal garrison of El Paso, as well as those rendered by my brother, who served his majesty and in whose service he died, and as well as those rendered by myself, I have registered and apply for a tract of vacant and unsettled land upon the water shed of the Navajo province."

The tract was called the Ojo de San Miguel and was granted to him by Governor Don Pedro Fermin de Mendinueta in September, 1767.

In 1873, Don Lorenzo Baca, ninety-seven years of age, a resident of Taos, says that Bartolomé Fernandez de la Pedrera was his great-grandfather on the maternal side; that his grandfather was Juan Antonio Fernandez, his father's name was José Baca, and his mother's Maria Rosa de Fernandez, the daughter of Don Juan Antonio Fernandez; that, when a young boy he had herded sheep and cattle upon this tract which was west of the Puerco river, Chaco Mesa. He states that they had to leave on account of the hostilities of the Navajos except when the Indians became quiet, coming to Santa Fe and receiving presents from the king.

359 MANUEL GARCIA PAREJAS, of *Rio Arriba*.
Will. April 15, 1763. Before Carlos Fernandez, Alcalde. Joachin Garzia de Noriega; Antonio Joseph Garcia de la Mora.

360 LEONARDO GONZALES to Rosalia Gonzales, his daughter. Donation.
House and land in *Santa Fe*. September 10, 1764. Vincente Armijo; Lucas Moya.

361 JUAN ALONZO MONDRAGON to Francisco Gonzales. *Villa Nueva de Santa Cruz*, November 13, 1764.
Conveyance of house and lands. Before Joseph Esquibel, Alcalde. Juan Luis Cano Saenz; Joseph Antonio Lopez.

362 JOSEPH MARCELO GALLEGOS vs. PEDRO ITURRIETA, of *Belen*. 1765.
Question of lands. Before Don Tomas Velez Cachupin, Governor and Captain-General. No final decision.
Ignacio Cornelio Figueroa; Isidro Trujillo; Carlos Fernandez; Juan de la Cruz Holguin; Juan Francisco Baca; Santiago Truiyo; Santiago Trugiyo; Joseph Maldonado; Miguel Lusero; Toribio Garzia Jurado; Juan Manuel Padia.

363 MANUEL GALLEGOS, of *Santa Fe*. Intestate.
Inventory of his estate. 1765. Before Nicolas Ortiz, Lieu-

tenant-Governor. Joseph Miguel Garduño; Bernardo de Zena; Pedro Tafoya; Fray Andrés Garcia.

364 BERNARDO DE BUSTAMANTE to Juan Francisco Gonzales. *Santa Fe*, May 2, 1767. Before Francisco Guerrero, Alcalde.
> Conveyance of lands. Juan Estevan Baca; Juan Francisco Niño Ladron de Guevara.

365 ANTONIA DURAN DE CHAVES and AGUSTINA, FRANCISCA and VICENTE, her grand-children to Pedro Antonio Gonzales. *Santa Fe*, November 28, 1767.
> Conveyance of lands. Before Francisco Guerrero, Alcalde. Miguel de Alire; José Miguel Tafoya; Lucas Moya.

366 RAMON GARCIA. *Santa Fe*, June 14, 1768.
> Will. Before Thomas Madrid, Lieutenant. Joseph Maldonado; Juan Antonio Alari.

367 VICENTE ARMIJO, of *Alburquerque*, and MARIA JOSEPHA LOPEZ, of *Santa Fe*, to Francisco Garcia. *Santa Fe*, April 18, 1769.
> Conveyance of land. Before Phelipe Tafoya, Alcalde. Joachin Lain; Joseph Miguel Tafoya.

368 CRISTOBAL GALLEGO, Minor Heirs of, vs. JUAN ROQUE GALLEGO. Question of lands.
> Before Francisco Trebol Navarro, Alcalde. Lands situate at *Bernalillo*. Judgment versus the Plaintiffs by Don Pedro Fermin de Mendinueta, Governor and Captain-General, July 24, 1770. Manuel Zainz Garvisu; Joseph Ibanez Corvera; Antonio Baca; Mattheo de Peñarredonda.

369 MANUEL MARTIN to Salvador Garcia. *Nuestra Señora de la Soledad*, August 6, 1763.
> Conveyance of lands. Before Carlos Fernandez, Alcalde. Copy. Certified by José Manuel Martinez, Secretary. No date.

370 VICENTE DE SENA to Maria Antonia Gabaldon, alias *La Lusera*. *Santa Fe*, November 2, 1768.
> Conveyance of house and lands. Before Phelipe Tafoya, Alcalde. Anacleto Miera; Joseph Miguel Tafoya.

THE SPANISH ARCHIVES OF NEW MEXICO 113

371 CLEMENTE GUTIERREZ.
>Inventory of his estate. 1785. Partition of the same. Before Don Juan Bautista de Anza, Governor.
>Pajarito Grant, Reported No. 157, *q. v.*
>Joseph Mariano de la Peña; Francisco Perez Serrano; Antonio Villegas Ruiz; Vincente Troncoso; Cristobal Larrañaga; Lorenzo Gutierrez; Francisco Antonio Garcia; Manuel de Arteaga; Antonio Baca; Manuel Alari.
>Will of Clemente Gutierres made by his attorney, Josef Mariano de la Peña, his son-in-law. *Pajarito*, May 20, 1785.

372 JOSE ANTONIO GRIEGO.
>Will and partition of his estate. 1785. Before Don Juan Bautista de Anza, Governor. Property located in *Santa Fe*. José Maldonado; José Miguel de la Peña; Juan de Dios Peña; Bernardo Bustamante; Juan Miguel Garduño.

373 EDUARDA RITA GARDUNO. *Santa Fe*, May 5, 1785.
>Before José Maldonado, Lieutenant. Diego Antonio de la Peña; Juan Miguel Trugillo.

374 FERNANDO DE LA CONCHA to Josefa Griego. Donation. *Santa Fe*, September 20, 1791.
>House in *Santa Fe*. Before Antonio Josef Ortiz, Alcalde. Maria de los Dolores Montoya; Josef Garcia Griego; Don Fernando de la Concha, Governor and Captain-General; Manuel Delgado, Captain; Vincente Troncoso, Lieutenant; Pablo Sandoval; Fray Francisco de Hosio (Ocio); Juan Ortiz, Lieutenant; Joseph Rafael Sarracino, Postmaster.

375 FRANCISCO and ANTONIO GARCIA.
>Grant. Year 1798. Reported Claim No. 25.

376 MIGUEL GALLEGO. *Santa Fe*, 1799.
>Settlement of his estate. Before Antonio Arze. José Campo; Fray Francisco de Hosio; Francisco Montoya; José Campo Redondo; Juan de Dios Peña;; Martin de Irigoyen; Santiago Silva; Jesus Lusero; Juan de Abrego.

377 JULIAN BEJIL (VIGIL) to Juan Cristobal Garciá. *Alameda*, April 20, 1806.
>Conveyance of house and lands. Before Don Cleto Miera y Pacheco, Alcalde. José Gutierrez; Mariano Perea.

378 JOSE GARCIA DE LA MORA.

Grant. 1807. File No. 783, *Vallecito* Grant. Surveyor-General's office.

Vallecito was settled in 1824 with fifty-two settlers. The place is about twenty-five miles from Abiquiú. The place was abandoned in 1844 owing to the war with the Utes; the settlers returned in 1846. General José Maria Chaves was an officer in this campaign against the Utes. He had been a lieutenant under the Spanish government; under the Mexican government he was made a captain of a squadron of militia, auxilliary to the regular garrison, and was also military inspector of the frontier district of Abiquiú, El Rito, and Ojo Caliente. He frequently commanded the Mexican military forces in campaigns against the Utes and Navajos. Under the American government he was prefect of Rio Arriba three times and during the Civil War and afterward was brigadier general of militia of the district of northern New Mexico; he was seven times a member of the Territorial Legislature; during the Mexican regime he was alcalde for the district of Abiquiú, a judicial position about equal to a county judge.

General Chavez was born in New Mexico, September 25, 1801, and with his parents removed to Abiquiú when he was three years of age. He died at the age of 101 years.

379 ANTONIO GARCIA vs. BARBARA BERNAL.

Letter of Cleto Miera y Pacheco, Alcalde, November 2, 1808. Addressed to Don José Manrique, Acting Governor.

380 VALLECTIO DE XEMES.

Grant. Question of boundaries. Before Don José Manrique, Governor. 1808. Ignacio Sanchez Vergara, Alcalde; Josef Tapia, Juez Commissionado; Thorivio Gonzales; Miguel Montoya; Pablo Montoya.

Town of Vallecito or *Santo Toribio de Jemez Grant.*

This claim was rejected by the court of private land claims. It was supposed to lie just north of the grant to the pueblo of Jemez.

381 LUCIANO GARCIA vs. ESTATE OF ANACLETO MIERA. 1815.

Before Maynez, Governor. For the recovery of purchase money of a house in *San José de las Huertas. Bernalillo* county. Juan José Gutierres, Alcalde; Josef Mariano de la Peña, Alcalde; José Marcos Baca.

382 XAVIER GARCIA, et al.

The *Socorro* Tract. Reported Claim No. 107.

The present city of Socorro is built upon the site of a Piro pueblo, named Pil-a-bo. The Franciscan mission was founded there in 1626; had a church and a convent, which was dedicated to the "Virgen del Socorro" — Virgin of Relief. The pueblo and all were abandoned in 1680, the greater portion of the people following the Spaniards to Paso del Norte. The dedication to the Virgin of Relief was made in honor of Juan de Oñate, who secured large quantities of provisions from the pueblo of Teypama, just across the Rio Grande from this point. The church was still standing in 1692, when De Vargas came up the valley; the roof had been burned. See Escalante — *Relacion*, p. 137. In 1725 the ruins of the pueblo could be plainly seen. Rivera, *Diario y Derrotero*.

There are a great many ruins of ancient pueblos in the vicinity of the present town of Socorro. There is a ruin at El Barro, three miles north of the town, and also at the Hot Springs, close to the mountain, three miles west. Those at the Hot Springs are almost obliterated; they stand on two bare promontories or small knolls, separated by an arroyo or gulch. There is to be found opposite to the promontory of El Barro, in the Arroyo de la Parida, the ruin of a large pueblo, which consisted of at least three edifices. This pueblo was built of adobe and in all probability was two or three stories in height.

This grant was claimed to contain 843,259 acres and was filed with the court of private land claims by Eutimio Montoya, of San Antonio, New Mexico. The claim was rejected by the court.

383 MARIA VICTORIA GUTIERREZ vs. PEDRO MIGUEL GUTIERREZ. 1820.

Before Facundo Melgares, Governor. Question of lands. *Bernalillo* county. José Francisco Ortiz, Alcalde; Pedro Miguel Gutierrez; Santiago Moya; Juan Isidro Gutierrez; Pedro Armendariz; Pedro Bautista Pino; José Petronilo Gutierrez; Joaquin de Luna; José Gutierres; Pedro José Perea.

Controversy between Maria Victoria Gutierrez and her brother, Pedro Miguel Gutierrez, in regard to the ownership of a ranch, the location of which is not accurately stated, but which apparently was at or near the place called Angostura, some miles north of the town of Bernalillo, and in the neighborhood of the junction of the Santa Ana (or Jemez) river with the Rio Grande.

In connection with this controversy one of the parties thereto filed a certified copy of a number of documents. which might possibly at some time be useful to the Indians of Santa Ana or San Felipe — probably the former.

This certified copy begins on p. 1, of leaf 22, and ends on p. 1, of leaf 27. It is authenticated by Facundo Melgares, then governor of New Mexico, on May 13, 1820, and includes the following documents:

(1) Deed of August 4, 1790, by Juan Candelaria, a San Felipe Indian, to José Miguel Garcia, a Spanish citizen of Bernalillo, for a piece of land at Angostura, acquired by purchase by Candelaria. The consideration was sixty *pesos*. The extent of the land from east to west was eighty-seven and three-fourths *varas,* bounded "on the north by the embankment of the Santa Ana irrigating ditch, and on the south by the edge of the old river."

(2) Statement of August 13, 1819, by José Mariano de la Peña, chief alcalde of Alburquerque, to the effect that while acting under commission from Governor Facundo Melgares, in carrying out the orders of the royal *audiencia* of the district dated March 27, 1818, the party named in the preceding writing (la antecedente escritura) having appeared before him, "his sale and the fourth part of his purchase" (whatever that may mean) were restored to him.

The language used in the original is somewhat vague, and the explanation of the reason for returning the land to the party is not so clear that I may not be in error in my interpretation of it, but, without giving to it more critical study than its apparently slight importance seems to justify at present, I understand it to mean this:—
That the land which had been sold subsequently was discovered to be a part of land which the *pueblo* of San Felipe was compelled to surrender to the *pueblo* of Santa Ana in obedience to a decision of the royal *audiencia,* and that the former *pueblo* then returned to the vendor certain lands of equal area which formed a part of certain lands which it owned by purchase at Algodones.

The San Felipe people were to recognize as their boundary the old edge of the river, which boundary they had disputed with those of Santa Ana.

THE SPANISH ARCHIVES OF NEW MEXICO 117

It is further stated that *"this document"* is to remain in full force and effect as a purchase from the community of San Felipe.

Among the signers of this statement was Ignacio Maria Sanchez Vergara, the protector of the Indians.

(3) Deed made at San José de las Huertas, on November 2, 1801, by Candelaria, a native of the *pueblo* of San Felipe, to José Garcia de Noriega, for a piece of land 230 *varas* long, and 71 *varas* wide, had by purchase by said Candelaria at Angostura.

The boundaries are stated to be, "on the north by the vendor himself, and on the south by the land of the purchaser himself, and on the east it is bounded by lands of Bautista, and on the west it is bounded by lands of Miguelito."

(4) Deed made at San José de las Huertas, on November 10, 1801, by Juan Rosalia, a native of the *pueblo* of San Felipe, to José Garcia de Noriega, for a piece of land acquired by purchase by said Juan Rosalia at Angostura.

The boundaries are, "on the north by lands of Candelaria, on the south by lands of Bautista, on the east it is bounded by lands of Perucho, on the west by lands of Bautista," and its extent is stated to be 350 *varas* by 37 *varas*.

(5) Statement by José Mariano de la Peña, dated August 13, 1819, to the effect that while acting under commission from Governor Facundo Melgares, in carrying out the orders of the royal *audiencia* of the district, dated March 27, 1818, the party named in the preceding writing having appeared before him "his sale" etc., was restored to him.

The reasons given for this action are the same as those set forth in the document designated as (2) herein, and it is stated that this present document is signed by Ignacio Maria Sanchez Vergara, the protector of the Indians.

(6) Deed made at San José de las Huertas, on September 10, 1803, by Candelaria, a native of the *pueblo* of San Felipe, to José Garcia de Noriega, for a piece of land 703 *varas* long, by 203 *varas* wide, at Angostura.

In recording the boundaries of the land no mention is made of an eastern boundary, and one word which has been changed, another which is probably erroneous, and an omission of one or more words in another place, render the boundaries extremely doubtful. It is impossible to make a satisfactory translation of them. The following will give some idea of the condition of the original:

"And its boundaries are on the north it is bounded by the same Indians of the *pueblo* of Santo domino (Domingo?) and on the south it is bounded by house (this word *casa* has been altered from something else) lands of the said *pueblo,* and on the west it is bounded by the (some word or words probably omitted here) *probios* (no such word in Spanish) Indians.

(7) Deed made at Bernalillo on December 4, 1815, by José Riaño, a native of the *pueblo* of San Felipe, to José Miguel Garcia, for a piece of land at Angostura, which is 323 and two and one half fourth *varas* long, and 94 and one and one half fourths *varas* wide.

The boundaries were, "on the north by lands of the *pueblo* of San Felipe, on the south by lands of the same *pueblo,* on the east by lands of the purchaser himself, and on the west by lands also of the same *pueblo."*

The statement is made that the land was sold by the consent of the whole *pueblo.*

(8) Statement by José Mariano de la Peña, chief alcalde of Alburquerque, dated August 13, 1819, to the effect that while acting under commission from Governor Facundo Melgares, in carrying out the orders of the royal *audiencia* of the district, dated March 27, 1818, the party named in the preceding writing having appeared before him "his sale," etc., was returned to him.

The reasons given for this action are the same as those set forth in the document designated as (2) herein, and it is stated that this present document is signed by Ignacio Maria Sanchez Vergara, the protector of Indians.

The above statement is made by W. M. Tipton.

384 TORIBIO GURULE vs. CRISTOBAL GONZALES.

Question of lands. County of *Bernalillo.* 1821. Before Don Facundo Melgares, Governor. José Miguel Aragon, Alcalde; Feliz Pino; Manuel Trujillo; Antonio Trujillo; Gregorio Ortiz; Tomas Antonio Bercera; Antonio Ruiz; Juan Luiz Trujillo; Vincente Ferrer Duran; Antonio Armijo.

385 JUAN GARCIA. Petition. 1821.

Before Don Facundo Melgares, Governor. Lands in *San Antonio de Carnue.* Not granted.

386 TOMAS ANTONIO GALLEGOS vs. PEDRO GALLEGOS. 1822.

THE SPANISH ARCHIVES OF NEW MEXICO 119

Before Armendariz, Alcalde. Question of inheritance. Plaintiff claims lands. Baltazar Perea, Alcalde; Marcial Torres; José Maria Gutierrez; Francisco Trujillo; Pedro Bautista Pino.

387 FRANCISCO GARCIA; DOMINGO GALLEGO, Primero; FRANCISCO JURADO; PASCUAL ARCHULETA; CRISTOBAL MARTIN; FRANCISCO GALLEGO; ANTONIO JOSE GARCIA; JULIAN GALLEGO; TOMAS MESTAS; MANUEL GALLEGO; RAMO GALLEGO; JUAN MADRIL; SALVADOR XARAMIO; MARCIAL ARCHULETA; DOMINGO GALLEGO, Segundo.

Petition for lands. Year 1824. Before Don Bartolomé Baca, Governor. Petition granted and petitioners put in possession of lands at *Cañones de Reaño* by Francisco Truxillo, Alcalde. *Rio Arriba* county.

Colonel Bartolomé Baca, at one time governor or political chief of New Mexico, and Don Antonio José Otero, appointed circuit judge by General S. W. Kearny, were among the first owners and settlers of the place known as Manzano, of which there were in all one hundred and sixty; the petition for the lands taken up by these was presented to the corporation or ayuntamiento of Tomé, September 22, 1829, and it is rather remarkable that no reference is made in any of the papers to the existence of the celebrated apple trees of that place. The petition recites that "not having the deed of possession to the said town in which they have settled, and the site of said town being known to be owned by no one, we request your excellency to be pleased to grant us the possession thereof, giving us the land which we are now occupying; giving us as boundaries from north to south, from Torreon to the old Mission of Abó, and from east to west, from the Mesa de los Jumanos to the mountain; all of which is to be for pasture grounds and other common purposes, cross roads and other uses necesary for every town established upon all the solid basis of common and private property and inhabited by the same; requesting further, as a condition for any of the above mentioned individuals, or any others to be admitted in the future without injury to the former, to the new town of Manzano, to acquire legal property therein, that he shall construct a regular terraced house of adobe in the plaza where the chapel is to be constructed, (for which permission has been granted us), and he shall bring with him his property of every description, contribute to all community labor, procure the increase and prosperity of the town, defending with arms the firesides of his town to the fullest extent against any domestic or foreign enemy; and finally, that the person who will not reside in said town with the family belonging to him, and who shall remove to another settlement, shall lose all right he may have acquired to his property.

"Tomé, September 22, 1829. Jose Manuel Trujillo."

This petition was referred to the Territorial Deputation by the president of the ayuntamiento, Don Jacinto Sanchez, with the statement that "the only objection found being in regard to the arable land therein situated belonging to the retired Lieutenant-Colonel Bartolomé Baca, who will be satisfied with the land which, as a new settler, he may acquire, together with that which he has purchased from other settlers, promising that although he will not establish his residence there, he will cultivate and improve the lands which may be recognized as his."

A "league" of land in each direction was granted by the Territorial Deputation, of which José Antonio Chavez was president, and Roman Abreú, secretary; when possession was given, the center was named as being at *"El Alto del Pino de la Virgen,"* which was situate in the middle of the cultivated fields.

388 JOSE MARIA GALLEGO.

Petition for lands *"sobrantes"* of the *Pecos*. 1825. Before Bartolomé Baca, Governor. J. B. Vigil, Secretary, of Territorial Deputation.

389 JUAN EUSEBIO GARCIA de la MORA. County of *Taos*.

Petition. 1826. Question of lands against Felipe Gonzales. Before Don Antonio Narbona, Governor. Juan Antonio Martin, Alcalde.

This is a dispute between Juan Eusebio de la Mora and Felipe Gonzalez, in regard to a piece of land at or near Taos.

There are six papers in this archive, but they are disconnected, and insufficient to give a perfect understanding of the case.

The controversy between Garcia and Gonzalez arose in 1826, but the incipiency of the trouble appears to have been not less than ten, and possibly more, years prior to that time. Garcia claimed that Gonzalez had promised him 100 varas of land in the tract, and insinuates that Gonzalez knew that he was improperly holding the land under a false claim of being an heir of the former owner. Gonzalez denies that he had promised any land to Garcia, and asserts that such promise was made by some people named Sanchez who were living on the tract.

The information contained in this archive is fragmentary, but may be of use in connection with other sources of knowledge.

There is a certified copy of *certain clauses* of the will of Francisca Pacheco. The will was dated June 8, 1802; the certified copy is by Antonio Narbona, then governor of New Mexico, and is dated May 18, 1826. In this will she names as her only heirs her brother José, and her sisters Barbara and Margarita. As executors of the will she names her brother José Pacheco and her nephew Joaquin Sanchez. In referring to the property she owned she said, "I declare that I have at Taos one hundred and fifty varas of land."

Among the papers in this archive 389 is a copy of a copy, not certified, at least if it was ever certified the certificate must have been upon the lower half of the first page of the second leaf, which is now missing. It appears from this paper that in certain proceedings had in the year 1815, it was shown that Joaquin and José Sanchez had sold certain lands to the Indians of the *pueblo* of Taos, Joaquin at that time stating to the Indians that there were no other heirs to the property; that subsequently three other persons appeared claiming to be heirs; that upon an investigation of the matter, under orders from Governor Alberto Maynez, by Felipe Sandoval, the protector of the Indians, the Indians surrendered three portions of the land claimed by the newly discovered heirs, and were paid back the money which they had paid for those portions — the land of the vendors, which amounted to 2,840 *varas*, from the boundary of their league to the north side, where the protector of Indians made them place landmarks "at the boundary which the grant of Captain Sebastian Martin cites."

In his petition of April 25, 1826, Garcia states that he is a son of Teodora Gallego, who claimed that she had an interest in certain lands which had been illegally sold to the Indians of Taos by Joaquin Sanchez, then deceased. This interest apparently was claimed by her because of her being an heir of Francisca Pacheco.

Apparently these lands were a part of a grant made to Antonio Martin. Referring to them, the petitioner, Garcia, says, "and sold to the Indians of the pueblo of Taos as the instrument which said Sanchez made those Indians states, and it states the grant to be donated to Antonio Martin who donated to Isabel Pacheco and to Francisca Pacheco as appears by the document and compromise which the alcalde Pedro Martin made to the children of Diego Rafael and to the Sanchez who are those who are on the tract and property of Francisca Pacheco."

390 MIGUEL GARCIA.
Petition, 1827. Before Manuel Armijo, Governor. Asks for a document of partition of lands of the *Romeros* in *Taos*. Manuel Martinez, Alcalde.

391 JOSE DOMINGO GARCIA et al. 1828.
Petition for lands near *Alburquerque*. Before Manuel Armijo, Governor. Refused because covered by grant of lands to Los Griegos. Ambrosio Armijo, Alcalde.

392 MIGUEL GARCIA, JULIAN GORDON, JOSE MANUEL COPAS. 1829.
Report of the committee of the Territorial Deputation against making them a grant of lands in *Taos*. Francisco Sarracino; Cabeza de Baca; Baca y Terrus.

393 SALVADOR XIRON. (GIRON). 1829.
Petition claiming possession of land in *Santa Ana del Sabinal*. Before Juan Geronimo Torres, Alcalde.

394 MARIA DE LA LUZ GALLEGOS, widow of Ignacio Madrid.
Will. *Santa Fe,* May 18, 1830. Before Ignacio Ortiz, Alcalde.

395 JOSE VICTOR GARCIA vs. JUAN RAFAEL ORTIZ.
Question of land at *Pojoaque*. 1831-2. Before Vincente Martinez, Alcalde. Juan Vigil; Domingo Fernandez; Juan Trugillo; Mateo Sandoval;; Juan Antonio Armijo; Vincente Martinez; Roman Abreu; Juan Bautista Vigil, Alcalde.

396 RAFAEL GONZALES.
Report on petition for land. 1832 Claim of José D. Fernandez et al. File No. 71, Surveyor-General's office, *q. v.*

397 JULIAN GARDUNO, JOSE MARIA BENAVIDES, ROMAN SISNEROS vs. ANTONIO ARMIJO.
> Question of land at *Real de los Dolores*...1835. Before Manuel Doroteo Pino, Alcalde. Juan Benavides.

398 LUIS GRIEGO. FRANCISCO PROVENCIO. JUAN SILBA. JOSE SILBA. FLORENCIO LA GARZA. VICENTE ROIBAL. BENITO VARELA. MARCELINO ORTIZ.
> Petition for lands at *Galisteo*. 1843. Before the *Ayuntamiento* of *Santa Fe*. Possession given by Antonio Sena, Alcalde. J. A. Archuleta, Prefect. Archive No. 802 has been transferred to this one.

399 MARIA DE LOS REYES GUTIERRES.
> Will. *Puesto de la Cienega*, May 9, 1843. Fernando Ortiz y Delgado. Rafael Romero.

400 TOMAS DE HERRERA Y SANDOVAL.
> Petition for land. 1695. Before Don Diego de Vargas, Zapata Lujan Ponce de Leon, Governor and Captain-General. Possession given by Roque Madrid, Alcalde. Half a fanega, near *Chimayo*.

401 TERESA DE HERRERA Y SANDOVAL vs. MARIA DE LEYBA Y MENDOZA. 1706.
> Question of a piece of land at *Santa Cruz*. Before Francisco de Ribera, Alcalde. Roque Madrid, Alcalde; Juan de Medina Ortiz; Joseph de Atienza; Juan de Atienza.

402 ANA MAGDALENA HERNANDEZ vs. TOMAS DE HERRERA. 1712.
> Question of lands at *Santa Cruz*. Before the Marqués de la Penuela, Governor and Captain-General. Juan Paez Hurtado, Ten'te General; Roque Madrid, Alcalde.

403 VICENTE FERRER DE ARMIJO to Juan Paez Hurtado. *Santa Fe*, December 4, 1713.
> Conveyance of house and lands. Before Juan Garcia de la Riva, Alcalde. Antonio Duran de Armijo; Joseph Maria Giltomey.

404 MARIA DE PALACIOS Y BOLIVAR to Juan Paez Hurtado. *Santa Fe*, January 13, 1716.
    Conveyance of a house and lot. Before Juan Garcia de la Riva. Alphonso Rael de Aguilar (Abbreviated sig.); Joseph Maria Giltomey.

405 MARIA HURTADO.
    Will. *Santa Fe*, December 28, 1725. Before Miguel Joseph de la Vega y Coca, Alcalde. Juan Manuel Chirinos; Tomas de Sena.

406 JUAN MANUEL DE HERRERA.
    Will. *Villa Nueva de Santa Cruz*, June 12, 1753. Before Juan Joseph Lovato, Alcalde. Francisco Valdes y Bustos; Pablo Truxillo.

407 JOSEPH GARDUNO to Joseph de Herrera. *Santa Fe*, June 16, 1784.
    Conveyance of a house and lot. Before Nicolas Ortiz, Alcalde. Juan Antonio Hortiz (Ortiz); Nicolas Rael; Juan Joseph de Icuza y Elisondo.

408 ANTONIO GONZALES to Juan Bautista de Herrera. *Santa Fe*, April 8, 1755.
    Conveyance of land. Before Francisco Guerrero, Alcalde. Manuel Begil (Vigil); Juan Antonio Ortiz.

409 BARTOLA HURTADO, widow of Joseph Bustamante. *Santa Fe*, May 13, 1762.
    Will and inventory of estate. Before Manuel Gallego, Alcalde. Tomas de Armijo; Joseph Miguel Garduño; Pedro Tafoya; Nicolas Ortiz.

410 JOHN HEATH.
    Petition for lands at the Bracito. 1823. Copy of proceedings.
    The claim of John Heath was not confirmed by the court of private land claims. The Bracito Tract was first settled by Don Juan Antonio Garcia de Noriega, a resident of El Paso; he was a lieutenant of dragoons of that town. In 1805 he constructed an irrigation ditch on the Bracito Tract, which lies just south of Mesilla Park, New Mexico. In the year 1816 in the valley of the Rio Grande, between Rincon and El Paso there was a great visitation of locusts which destroyed all the cultivated

fields. He was advised to make a settlement of this locality by the Lieutenant-Colonel Don Alberto Maynes. Don Juan lived amicably with the Apaches in this locality, as he says: "The Chiefs of the Apaches have told me that next year they desire to have their lands planted, and if said settlement is established, aided by the citizens of the town of El Paso and the new settlers, I will plant their lands so as to keep them more quiet."

In 1805, upon a similar petition from Garcia de Noriega, it was denied by Alencaster, then governor of New Mexico. Don Juan died at his ranch of Bracito in the year 1828.

Juan Maria Ponce Leon, political chief of the Bravos district, in March, 1849, certified "that D. Juan almost at his own expense kept the Apaches at peace, and rendered other useful services to travellers and even to the entire nation, until the savages by their insurrections and hostilities forced him to withdraw from said place; the land itself proves that it has been cultivated, as it is crossed by acequias; some of the land is irrigated and the ruins of the house still exist.

"I also know, not remembering the year, that an INDIVIDUAL OF THE UNITED STATES, named John Gid (Heath) asked for and received a GRANT OF LAND at the same place from the Mexican authorities, respecting those of Don Juan Garcia: THIS HE AFFIRMS, having been one of the Commissioners in the measurement of the land asked for, and at the request of the party interested."

It is quite interesting to know that the claim of John Heath (Juan Gid) to a grant of land at this place failed because his descendants did not know from what source the grant had been obtained; it came from the governor of Durango, and not from the New Mexican authorities.

In the testimony taken before the surveyor-general of New Mexico, Pelham, it also appears that at the time of the occupation of the city of El Paso by the American troops under General A. W. Doniphan, the town hall of El Paso was made headquarters by Doniphan, at which place all of the archives were kept. This is sworn to by Don Juan José Sanchez, who also says:

"I was first justice at that time, and that as such Captain Waldo, doctor of medicine, and belonging to the said army, informed him that the soldiers were entirely destroying the archives, and that for that reason he went there immediately, with several others, and collected the few public papers they had left, the greater portion having been already burned and thrown in the street, and even some time after there were important papers found scattered in the streets."

The title to this Bracito Tract in a proceeding before Horace Mower, justice of the supreme court of New Mexico, was finally adjudicated, by which Hugh Stevenson, successor in interest to the original grantee, received a two-thirds interest in the grant. The grant was originally made by Don José Ordas, lieutenant-governor of that jurisdiction.

411 ISABEL JORGE DE BERA.
Grant. 1696. City of *Santa Fe*. Half a fanega.
May 5, 1699; refers to the *Rio Chiquito* and to the *Rio Grande*, the latter being the present Santa Fe river. The *Rio Chiquito* was a small stream which had its rise at a large spring in what is now known as the Bishop's Garden and other springs located on the site of the convent of the Sisters of Loreto. Its course was down what is now known as Water street, Santa Fe, and joined with the Rio Santa Fe about opposite the site of the Guadalupe Church.

JOSEFA DURAN, widow of Faustin Griego.
Grant. City of *Santa Fe*. 1696. About half a fanega.

MICAELA DE VELASCO to José Blasquez. *Santa Fe*, October 15, 1708.
Conveyance of house and lot.

ISABEL JORGE DE BERA to Micaela de Velasco. *Santa Fe*, June 28, 1797.
Conveyance of house and lands.
On leaf 7, December 22, 1706, reference is also made to the "*Camino real que va al Alamo*"; this was to the south and the *Alamo* was a ranch or hacienda belonging to José Riaño, in these days called "Pino's Ranch."

LORENZO MADRID to Antonio Rael de Aguilar. *Santa Fe*, December 22, 1706.
Conveyance of house and lands.

JUANA DE CARRAS vs. ANTONIA SEDANO, wife of Juan Lorenzo de Medina. 1713.
Question of lands. Juana de Carras acts in the name of her absent husband, José Blasquez, and the land in ques-

tion is the same sold to him by Micaela de Velasco who was the widow of Miguel Garcia de la Riva.

Don Diego de Vargas Zapata Lujan Ponce de Leon, Governor and Captain General. Domingo de la Barreda, Secretary of Government and War. Antonio de Aguilera Isasi, Alcalde. Miguel Tenorio de Alva; Joseph Manuel Giltomey; Xpttobal de Gongora; Diego Arias de Quiros, Alcalde; Roque de Pintto, Secretary of Government and War; Juan Paez Hurtado; Lorenzo de Madrid; Francisco Romero de Pedrassa; Juan Garcia de la Rivas; Antonio Duran de Armijo; Antonia Sedano.

412 URSULA RAMOS to Antonia Xiron, wife of Francisco Vigil. *Santa Cruz de la Cañada.* August 23, 1736.

Conveyance of house and land. Acquired by the vendor from Diego Martin, with guarantee of Juan de Dios Martinez de Sandoval, March 21, 1713. Before Juan Estevan Garcia de Noriega, Alcalde. Antonio Trujillo; Miguel de Quinttana.

413 ROQUE JACINTO JARAMILLO and JUAN MANUEL DE HERRERA.

Grant. Situate on the *Rio del Oso*, county of *Rio Arriba*. 1746. Re-validation by Don Joachin Codallos y Rabal, Governor. Possession given by Juan de Beytia, Alcalde. No boundaries are set out either in the proceedings or in the possession. The original grant was made to the above named and to others, by Don Juan Domingo de Bustamante, governor and captain-general. The boundaries given in the petition are: North, lands of the Alférez Torres; south, lands of Juan de Tafoya; east, lands of Juan de Mestas, and west, the entrance of the canyon of the Sierra..

Vincente Ginzo Ron y Thobar; Francisco Gomez del Castillo; Phelipe Jacobo de Vnuanue; Juan de Beytia, Alcalde; Joseph Romo de Vera; Juan Lorenzo Baldes.

Cristobal de Torres Grant, *q. v.*

414 RAMON GARCIA JURADO and SALVADOR MARTINEZ, of *Alburquerque.* May 21, 1746.

Before Don Joachin Cadallos y Rabal, Governor. Petition in the matter of the partition of the estate of Josefa Valverde. Agreement as to the division of lands of the Ranchos. San Francisco de Sandia; San Joseph de los Corrales; San Antonio.

Josepha Valverde was the widow of Captain Luis Garcia, and Salvador Martinez claimed his part as husband of Rosalia Garcia.

The agreement was approved by Codallos y Rabal on the date *supra*.

415 JOSEPH DE MEDINA to Juana de Xaramillo. *Santa Cruz*, October 1, 1753.

Conveyance of two tracts of land. Before Juan Joseph Lobato, Alcalde. Juan Domingo Lobato; Antonio Martin.

Medina or Black Mesa Grant, R. No. 56, was confirmed by the court of private land claims and surveyed for more than 19,000 acres. A portion of its south boundary adjoins the San Juan Pueblo Grant. It was patented December 9, 1907.

416 RAMON GARCIA JURADO and BROTHERS.

Grant. 1753. Reported Claim No. 49, *q. v.*

417 JUAN ESTEVAN JUANJUEVE (or JUAJUEVE).

Will. *San Antonio. Jurisdiction of Villa Nueva de Santa Cruz.* April 2, 1764. Before Manuel Garcia Pareja, Alcalde. Francisco Sanches; Alletano Atencio.

418 LUIS XARAMILLO.

Will. December 27, 1784. Before Thomas Madrid, Teniente. Diego Antonio Margue; Joseph Maldonado.

419 CATALINA JURADA.

Will. *Puesto de Nuestra Señora de Guadalupe,* January 31, 1767. Before Manuel Garcia Pareja, Alcalde. Pedro Antonio Martin; Juan Joseph Bustos.

420 JOSEPH and XAVIER JARAMILLO. *Fuenclara,* 1768.

Petition for land. Before Don Pedro Fermin de Mendinueta, Governor and Captain-General. Francisco Trebol Navarro; Joseph Hurtado de Mendosa; Manuel Zeinos; Antonio Moreto; Mattheo de Peñarredonda.

421 LUIS JARAMILLO.

Grant. Reported Claim No. 108.

Luis Jaramillo, in 1769 had been thirty-six years a soldier and corporal of the garrison at Santa Fe. He asked the governor, Mendinueta, for lands on the Rio Puerco, adjoining those of Captain Antonio Baca; all of the settlers of Nuestra Señora de La Luz, San Fernando, and

Don Fernando de Alencastre Norona y Silva
Duke of Linares, Viceroy of Mexico 1711-16

San Blas del Rio Puerco protested. This availed them nothing, however, as Jaramillo was put in possession and the governor in discussing some of the things done by the settlers in times past, says: "they stupidly and maliciously altered the *testimonio* of the grant and the act of possession wherever 'leagues' were mentioned, as appears from the original," and on account of the expression made by Juan Bautista Montaño, before the above mentioned alcalde (Trebol Navarro), when executing the act of possession given to the residents of Atrisco, that those alterations were made by my predecessor aforesaid, I order that a writ be issued, commanding the said Montaño to appear before me in this, my tribunal, it being incredible that my predecessor could have done so, as well because said *testimonio* has always remained in the possession of said settlers, was made in the time of my predecessor, Francisco Antonio Marin del Valle, for if he had altered the testimonio he would have also altered the original, and in case he desired to extend the boundaries he would have done so in due form and not by destroying the document, which I direct remain on file in this office that the fact may at all times appear."

422 JUAN LUSERO DE GODOY.

Grant. Land near *Santa Fe*. 1693. Before Diego de Vargas Zapata Lujan Ponce de Leon, Governor and Captain-General. Re-validated in the year 1695.

Alfonzo Rael de Aguilar. Also written "Alphonso" in this same document.

"To his excellency the governor and captain-general, I, the adjutant, Antonio Lusero de Godoy, alderman of this town of Santa Fe, and inhabitant of these provinces of New Mexico, native of the same, appear before your excellency in the best form allowed me by law and say that in order to better continue in the community of this said town and in the royal service of his majesty, I need a tract for a house at the place where at present day I have a shanty standing in which I live, situate in the direction of the road to the pueblo of Tesuque, upon some low hills (lomas vajas) that are there together with the lands that surround them which on the north adjoin with a dry gulch (arroyo seco) that comes down from the mountains (sierra), and on the east they adjoin with the trail (vereda) that leads to the pueblo of Tesuque, and on the west with lands of the Sergeant Major Juan Lusero de Godoy, my father, and on the side of the river which is to the south with lands of Alonso Maese and of Juan Gonzales Lobon, upon all of which land there probably may be embraced about one-half fanega of corn and two of wheat, for in order that I may go there with my numerous family, it is a very [illegible, one word] portion of land I ask your excellency to be pleased to remember my services that I have rendered to his majesty, for since the time of the first entry made into this kingdom by General Don Diego de Vargas, I was the one to guide the fifty soldiers of the re-inforcements that his majesty gave him for making the conquest, and during the conquest I remained near to the person of the said general, as likewise in the entry with the families. I was one of those who, not stopping to consider the danger of the winter, conveyed my family of my wife and children, they being exposed to many discomforts such as are experienced in this kingdom and during all the conquests I always accompanied the said general at my own expense [one word illegible] as is public and notorious, and that I have not had any reward; and since your excellency represented the king our lord, that you be pleased to attend to my services, and as the royal agent of him and having as you do all his authority, that you grant to me in his royal name what I ask, accepting my statement as true, which I swear to God, and by the sign of the holy cross, that it is as I have stated and only for the purpose of obtaining justice which I ask, and I implore the royal help of your excellency. ANTONIO LUCERO DE GODOY''

PRESENTATION

"In this town of Santa Fe, on the 30th day of the month of July, 1697, before me, Don Pedro Rodrigues Cubero, governor and captain-general of this kingdom and provinces of New Mexico, commander of its forces and garrisons, governor-elect and captain-general of the provinces of Macaibo, Merida, and La Gritta, proprietary commander of the castle of San Salvador at Punta of the city of Havana, for his majesty, the party stated, presented it. Order. And I having seen it, accept it as presented for what it may be worth in law, and in view of the services that he states to have rendered to his majesty in this said kingdom, I at once made him the grant that the petitioner asks of the lands stated in the name of his majesty, without prejudice to third parties who may have a better claim, which said lands and grants I give to the said Antonio Lucero in order that he may enjoy, settle, cultivate, and possess, his wife, children, and heirs, and

I command that this petition and grant made in favor of said Antonio Lucero the said party do take and present it before the cabildo, justices, and aldermen of this said town, in order that they in their archive a record may be made (*se tome razon*) that it may appear at all times, when that being done they shall return it in order that a title in due form may be issued to him, and that it may so appear I signed it with the undersigned secretary of government and war. PEDRO RODRIGUES CUBERO
"Before me: DON ALONSO RAEL DE AGUILAR,
"Secretary of Government and War."

"Immediately thereafter on said day, month, and year, in pursuance of what was provided by his excellency, the governor and captain-general, the cabildo, justices, and aldermen received it as presented for what it may be worth in law, and that it may so appear we signed it with the secretary of the cabildo on the date as above.

"It agrees with the original that remains in the archive of government and war of this said town, and it is true and certain according to the same; and at its correction and comparing were present Cristobal de Gongora and Juan Antonio Ramos, and I, said secretary of cabildo, make my sign and customary rubric in testimony of the truth. MIGUEL TENORIO DE ALVA [rubric]
"Secretary of Cabildo"

Among other things it appears in this archive that General De Vargas, in 1693, made his camp on the edge of a forest (*monte*) known as "*Cuma*."

423 ANTONIO LUCERO DE GODOY.

Grant. Land near *Santa Fe*, 1697. By Don Pedro Rodriguez Cubero, Governor and Captain-General. *Testimonio* certified to by Miguel Tenorio de Alva, Secretary of the Council.

Antonio Lucero de Godoy says that he is the man who, at the time of the first expedition of De Vargas (1692), guided the soldiers which the king had given De Vargas and that he also accompanied the expedition which brought the settlers from Mexico.

ANTONIO MARTINEZ or LUCERO DE GODOY.

Originally as surveyed this grant conflicted with the grant to the Taos Pueblo; the title was confirmed by the court of private land claims and under the decree and survey the conflict was eliminated. The grant contains 61,000 acres and was patented May 8, 1896.

132   THE SPANISH ARCHIVES OF NEW MEXICO

424   JOSE CASTELLANOS to Bartolomé Lobato. *Santa Fe, August* 8, 1701.
>   Conveyance of house and land. Before Joseph Rodriguez, Alcalde. *Testimonio* certified to by the Alcalde.
>   This also mentions the *Rio Chiquito*.

425   JUANA DOMINGUEZ to Bartolomé Lobato. *Santa Fe*, August 14, 1701.
>   Conveyance of house and garden. Before Joseph Rodriguez, Alcalde. Lorenzo de Madrid, Joseph de Quintana.
>   Says there is no notary within 270 leagues; refers also to the *Rio Chiquito*.

426   JUAN GONZALES to José Lopez. *Bernalillo*, November 14, 1704.
>   Donation of land. Before Diego Montoya, Alcalde. Juan de Uribarri, Baltazar Mata.

427   RAMON GARCIA JURADO to Bartolomé Lobato. *Santa Cruz*, May 7, 1707.
>   Conveyance of land. Before Alphonso Rael de Aguilar, Alcalde. Xpttobal de Gongora, Antonio Duran de Armijo.
>   A deed for a piece of land at *Santa Cruz de La Cañada*, the boundaries being "on the north side by the river of said town (*Villa*) on that of the south by the said town." This shows that when the *Villa Nueva de Santa Cruz* was reëstablished by De Vargas in 1695, the same was on the *south side*; the present town of Santa Cruz is located on the *north* side of the river.

428   SEBASTIAN DE VARGAS to Antonia de Leyba. *Santa Fe*, August 25, 1710.
>   Donation of house, lot and lands. Before Diego Arias de Quiros, Alcalde. Xpttobal de Gongora, Antonio Duran de Armijo.

429   JUAN DE TORRES to Juan Lopez. *Santa Fe*, July 6, 1712.
>   Conveyance of house and lot. Before Diego Arias de Quiros, Alcalde. Pedro de Montesdoca, Joseph Manuel Giltomey.

430 DIEGO MARTIN to Juana Lujan. *Santa Cruz*, April 27, 1713.
> Conveyance of lands. Before Jacinto Sanches, Alcalde.

431 JUAN GARCIA DE NORIEGA to Josefa Lujan. *Santa Fe*, August 5, 1713.
> Conveyance of land. Before Juan Paez Hurtado, Alcalde. Juan Phelipe de Ribera, Pedro de Roxas.

431 ANTONIA BARELA DE LOSADA.
> Will. *Santa Fe*, June, 1712. Before Alphonso Rael de Aguilar, Alcalde. Juan de la Mora Pineda, Vsebio de Aguilar.

433 BARTOLOME LOBATO.
> Grant. Situate on the *Rio de Chama*. 1714. Granted by Don Juan Ignacio Flores Mogollon, Governor and Captain-General. Possession given by Sebastian Martin, Alcalde. Re-validated in 1715 by Phelix Martinez, Governor; Miguel Thenorio de Alva, Secretary of Government and War. Roque de Pintto, Secretary of Government and War. Francisco de Carmona, Miguel de Quinttana.

434 ALEJO GUTIERRES to Antonio Lopez. *Santa Fe*, June 13, 1715.
> Conveyance of house and land. Before Juan Garcia de la Riva, Alcalde. Gabriel de Cabrera, Juan Manuel Chirinos.

MARIA GUTIERRES to Alejo Gutierres. *Santa Fe*, August 7, 1712.
> Donation of the above land. Before Alphonso Rael de Aguilar, Alcalde. Miguel de Sandoval Martinez.

435 BARTOLOME LOBATO.
> Re-validation of grant on the *Chama* by Governor Mogollon. No. 433, *q. v.*

436 BARTOLOME LOBATO.
> With No. 433, No. 435, *q. v.*

437 BARTOLOME LOBATO. SALVADOR DE SANTIESTEVAN. ANTONIO TRUXILLO. ANTONIO DE

SALAZAR. XPTOBAL CRESPIN. NICOLAS GRIEGO. NICOLAS BALBERDE. JUAN DE MESTAS.

Petition in regard to the calling in of their grants. Before Juan Paez Hurtado, Visitador General. Nos. 433, 435, 436, *q. v.*

The grant to Antonio Trujillo is as follows:

"To the Governor and Captain General:

"Antonio Trujillo, resident of the new town of Santa Cruz, appears before your excellency in the manner most approved in law and convenient to me, and states that: I register a tract of land, which is wild and unsettled, on the opposite side of the Del Norte river, which I received as a grant in the name of his Majesty, from General Don Juan Flores Mogollon, and was placed in possession thereof by Captain Sebastian Martin, at that time senior justice of said town, and upon which I made a ditch and plowed up a field, an examination of which was made on the 9th instant by Don Juan Paez Hurtado, lieutenant general of this kingdom; and its boundaries are, on the east a hill which joins the Del Norte river; on the west an angostura or narrow, which forms a table-land, with the Chama river; and on the north said table-land, and on the south the Chama river. Said lands your excellency will be pleased to regrant me anew, in the name of his Majesty, for myself, my children, heirs, and successors, together with entrances and outlets, pastures, water and watering-places, rights, interests, customs, and appurtenances, thereunto belonging; directing royal possession to be given to me, compelling them to settle them within the time prescribed by law, in view of all which and whatever more I may set forth and may do in my own favor, and which I here express.

"I pray and request your excellency, with the most sincere expression of submission, to be pleased to do and determine as I have requested; and by so doing I will receive grace and favor with justice. I swear that this my petition is not made through malice. I implore royal aid and whatever may be necessary, etc.

"ANTONIO TRUJILLO."

"And seen by Don Juan Domingo de Bustamante, governor and captain-general of this kingdom. He considered it as presented, and I grant to the person therein mentioned the grant of land he asks me for, in the name of his Majesty, for himself, his children and heirs, without injury to any third parties who may show a better title; and I direct the senior justice of the new town of Santa Cruz to proceed to place him in possession of the aforesaid lands, and in order that it may be a matter of record I have signed it at this city of Santa Fe, on the 8th day of the month of June, one thousand seven hundred and twenty-four. JUAN DOMINGO DE BUSTAMANTE.''

"At this place of Yunque, on the 20th day of the month of June, in the year one thousand seven hundred and twenty, I, the reformed Ensign Cristobal Torres, chief justice and war captain of the new city of Santa Cruz and its jurisdiction, proceed to give royal possession to Antonio Trujillo, as I am directed to do by his excellency; and having arrived and examined the tract of land referred to in his petition, I took him by the hand and walked with him over the land. He threw stones, pulled up grass, and cried out in a loud voice, as if the land was his, and in proof of possession which I gave him in the name of the king, our sovereign, (whom may God preserve,) and which he received quietly and peaceably, Domingo Montes Vigil and Diego Martin being instrumental witnesses, and with the boundaries mentioned in his petition; and possession was given to him with the condition that he should settle it within the term prescribed by law. And in order that it may so appear, I signed as acting judge, with the undersigned as attending witnesses, on said day ut supra.

"CRISTOBAL TORRES.

"Attending:
"MIGUEL A. QUINTANA."

It will be seen that the place called *Yunque*, the site of Oñate's capital, was inhabited one hundred and sixteen years after the capital was removed to Santa Fe.

438 XPTOBAL CRESPIN to Miguel Lujan. *Santa Fe*, October 25, 1718.

> Conveyance of a house and lot. Before Francisco Bueno de Bohorques y Corcuera, Alcalde. Diego Arias de Quiros, Juan Manuel Chiriños.

439 JOSEPHA SEDANO to Cayetano Lobato. *Santa Fe*, March 20, 1722.

> Conveyance of a house and lands. Before Francisco Bueno de Bohorques y Corcuera, Alcalde. Pedro Lopes Gallardo, Gregorio Garduño.

440 MIGUEL DE LA BEGA Y COCA and MARIA MONTOYA to Maria Josepha Lopes. April 17, 1727.

Conveyance of house and lands. Before Diego Arias de Quiros, Alcalde. Manuel Thenorio de Alva, Juan Manuel Chirinos.

441 JOSEPH DE LEYBA.

Land situate near *Santa Fe*. Made by Bustamante, Governor. Possession given by Diego Arias de Quiros, Alcalde. Juan Manuel Chiriños, Juan Joseph Lobato.

The boundaries to this grant were: on the east by the San Marcos road, on the south by an arroyo called Cuesta del Orégano, on the west by land of Juan Garcia de la Rivas, and on the north by the lands of the Captain Sebastian de Vargas.

Juan Garcia de las Rivas was the son of the Captain Miguel Garcia, who was the owner of the sitio of the old pueblo of the Cienega. The Cuesta del Orégano was south and east of the Ojo del Coyote. The grant was held by the court of private land claims to have been an imperfect one; made as it was in 1728, it fell under the requirements of the Royal Ordinance of 1754, which provided that all grants made subsequent to 1700, unless already confirmed by royal order of the king or his viceroys, or presidents of the Audiencias of the several districts embracing the lands granted, should apply for such confirmation as a prerequisite to validity.

José de Leyba had a son, Simon de Leyba, who likewise had a son, Salvador Antonio, who had a son, Juan Angel Leyba, who had a son, Salvador Leyba; having been kicked by a mule, and fearing death, made his will and in this instrument, it is recited that this grant had been made to his father Joseph by the king. Juan Angel Leyba was killed by the Navajos near the Coyote Spring.

The sitio of the old pueblo of the Cienega was granted by General de Vargas to Bernabe Jorge; one of the boundaries of this old pueblo was the Peñasco Blanco de las Golondrinas. The word "Orégano" means marjoram.

Upon this tract of land are located the celebrated turquoise mines — the Chalchuitl of the Pueblo Indians.

In the testimony relative to the boundaries of this grant an interesting deed, made in 1701, was introduced in evidence: containing as the deed does, certain terms, dealing with matters of taxation, fees, etc., the deed is given in full:

"At the Villa of Santa Fe on the twelfth day of March,

one thousand seven hundred and four, before me Captain Juan Paez Hurtado, war lieutenant and captain-general of this Kingdom, acting as Juez Receptor with two attending witnesses, appeared Miguel Garcia de la Riba, resident of this city, and said that he was giving and gave in royal sale, the sitio of the old Pueblo of Zienega, in favor of his son, Juan Garcia de la Riba, for the price of one hundred dollars of the money of the country, that said Miguel Garcia de la Riba had by sale from Joseph Castellanos and that its boundaries are on the north the watershed of La Zieneguilla, on the East the Peñasco Blanco (White Rock) de las Golondrinas, on the South the Cañada of Juana Lopez, on the West Las Boquillas, and renounces the laws of NON NUMERATA PECUNIA and those of the DUBUS RES DE VENDI and AUTENTICA PRE FIDE JUROBUS so that as his own property, the said grant of the old Pueblo of Zienega, he can exchange and transfer it or use the same at his own pleasure, and empowering the court of His Majesty with all rigor of law to compel him to comply with the provisions contained in this document, and that if at any time he should bring suit, the said Miguel Garcia de la Riba, he shall not be heard in Court nor out of it, and as a guaranty he pledges his person and personal and real property he may now have or might have; and the said Miguel Garcia de la Riba further states that of the remainder he makes, grants, gives and donates pure and perfect which the law calls INTERVIVOS: To have and to Hold he so executed and signed the same the said grantee, Miguel Garcia de la Riba, together with myself and my assisting witnesses who were Mateo Trujillo and José Franco de la Barreda, both citizens [torn] of this city, and of [torn] the party I delivered this orig. [torn] in the power of the purchaser [torn] on ordinary blank paper [torn] there being no sealed paper [torn] parts.

"MGL GARCIA DE LA RIBA

"Testigo de Asistencia
  "JOSE FRANCO DE LA BARREDA
"Ante mi como Juez Receptor Testigo de Asistencia
  "JUAN PAEZ HURTADO MATEO TRUGILLO"

The *Non Numerata Pecunia* meant: Not in Ready Money.

442 LUIS LOPES.

Will. *Cañada*, October 27, 1728. Before Diego Arias de Quiros, Alcalde. Juan Joseph Lobato, Juan Manuel Chiriños.

138   THE SPANISH ARCHIVES OF NEW MEXICO

443 NICOLASA MONTOYA by her husband BARTOLOME GUTIERRES to Maria Josepha Lopez. *Santa Fe*, February 15, 1729. Conveyance of land.
>Before Diego Arias de Quiros, Alcalde.

444 JUAN LUJAN to Agustin Lobato. *Santa Fe*, August 16, 1738.
>Before Antonio Montoya Alcalde. Conveyance of land. Juan Manuel Chiriños.
>A description of land lying "between the big river and the little" — "*entre el Rio Grande y el chico*," meaning the Rio Santa Fe and the Rio Chiquito.

445 JUAN CAYETANO LOBATO.
>Piece of land on the other side of the *Santa Fe* river. Don Gaspar Domingo de Mendoza, Governor and Captain-General. Antonio de Hulibarri, Alcalde. Gregorio Garduño.

446 FELIPE RODRIGUEZ to Manuel Lopez (Lohpes). 1751.
>Conveyance of land in *Santa Fe*, called *Buena Vista*. Manuel Gallegos, Alcalde. Pedro Tafoya, Lucas Miguel de Moya.

447 ISIDRO MARTIN to Geronimo Lopez. 1753.
>Conveyance; land in *Santa Fe*. Manuel Gallegos, Alcalde. Pedro Tafoya, Lucas Moya.

448 MARCOS RODRIGUEZ to Joseph Losano. *Santa Fe*, 1762.
>Conveyance of land. Manuel Gallego, Alcalde. Juan Antonio Orttis, Pedro Antonio Tafoya.

449 JUAN MANUEL SANDOBAL to Juan José Luxan. *Santa Fe*, 1764.
>Conveyance of land. Francisco Guerrero, Alcalde. Diego Antonio Marquez, Thomas Casillas, Francisco Xavier Fragoso.

450 BARTOLOME TRUXILLO to Joseph and Antonio Lucretio Martin. *Abiquiú*, 1764.
>A tract of land; part of a grant to vendor. Juan Pablo Martin, Alcalde. Joseph Gomes, Antonio Gomes.

451 JOSE LOSANO vs. JUAN DE URIOSTI. *Santa Fe*, 1764.
> Questions as to boundaries of a piece of land donated to the grandfather of complainant, Miguel de la Cruz, by Sebastian de Vargas, Armero. Francisco Guerrero, Alcalde. Antonio Dominguez, Vicente Sena.

452 MARIA MANUELA, widow of Juan Losano.
> Will. *Santa Fe*, 1765. Francisco Guerrero, Alcalde. Joseph Mares, Joseph Miguel Garduño.

453 FRANCISCO LOBATO to Agustin Lovato. *Santa Fe*, 1765.
> House and lot. Francisco Guerrero, Alcalde. Lucas Moya, Juan Francisco Niño Ladron de Guebara.
> Describes a piece of land between the *Rio Chiquito* and the *Rio Grande*, in Santa Fe.

454 MIGUEL LUCERO, Alcalde-mayor of *Alburquerque*.
> Will. 1768. Also inventory and partition proceedings. Juan Cristobal Sanches, Alcalde. Bartolomé Olguin, Tomas Veles Cachupin, Governor. Felipe Silba, Juan Francisco Baca, Carlos Fernandez, Joseph Maldonado.

455 ANTONIO ORTEGA to Geronimo Lopez. *Santa Fe*, 1768.
> Conveyance of land. Phelipe Tafoya, Alcalde. Joseph Miguel Tafoya, Lucas Moya.

456 MANUELA BRITO to Simon de Leiba. *Santa Fe*, 1769.
> House and lot. Phelipe Tafoya, Alcalde. Joachin Lain. In 1767 Don Felipe Tafoya was an alcalde at Santa Fe; he states, in a petition signed by him as attorney for Don Diego Antonio Chavez and Don Pedro Chavez, that he is the legitimate son of Antonio Tafoya, formerly ensign of the Santa Fe garrison and one who reconquered the country with Diego De Vargas, and that his father served in the royal armies until 1747, when he lost his eye-sight; that he also had served ten years; that he had asked for the Chavezes and himself a piece of land in. the Rio Puerco country which had been refused by Don Tomas Velez Cachupin, at the time governor. This governor, on December 3, 1766, addressing himself to the petition which Tafoya had filed says: "If these parties have not had

any land or grant whereon to pasture their animals, they might have joined the new settlements of San Miguel de Laredo and that of San Gabriel de las Nutrias . . . But these parties doubtless experienced fear, as the said places were on the frontier and as they lacked courage for their establishment, and they have registered the tract they mention because it is in the *peaceful region of the Navajo country*. They may occupy the same while the natives (Navajos) do not object." They were enjoined to treat these "Apache Navajos" "with the greatest love and kindness, to win them over and treat them well, so as to keep them in amity with us, and so that in the course of time, and showing them good examples and Christian conduct, they may be brought to the holy Catholic faith."

Captain Bartolomé Fernandez says of the Navajos in that section of the country: "Owing to their dread of the Utes, the Apaches (Navajos) make their houses on the highest and roughest parts of the Mesas."

457 GERONIMO LOPEZ.
Will, *Santa Fe*. No date. Phelipe Tafoya, Alcalde. Joseph Armenta.

458 ISABEL LUJAN.
Will, *Santa Fe*, 1771. Manuel Garcia Pareja, Alcalde. Antonio de Armenta.

459 JUANA DE OJEDA BENAVIDES to Francisco Lujan. 1772.
Donation of a tract of land on the *Tesuque* river. Manuel Garcia Pareja, Alcalde. Joseph de Armenta.

460 ANTONIO JOSEPH LOPEZ and MATHIAS THENORIO DE ALBA vs. MIGUEL THENORIO DE ALBA. 1772.
Question of lands at the *Cienega*. Don Pedro Fermin de Mendinueta, Governor. Antonio Moreto, Mateo de Peñarredona.

461 MARIANA DE LA PAZ to Joseph Manuel Lovato. *Santa Fe*, 1769.
Conveyance; house and lot. Phelipe Tafoya, Alcalde. Joseph Miguel Tafoya.

462 ANTONIO DE LUNA. Intestate. 1786.
Proceedings in the matter of his estate. Don Juan Bautista de Anza, Governor. Vicente Troncoso. Manuel de Arteaga, Alcalde. Juan Francisco Baca, Juan Miguel Albares del Castillo. Don Tomas Veles Cachupin, Governor. Antonio Villegas Ruiz, Francisco Perez Serrano, Manuel de Arteaga, Miguel Gabaldon, Cristobal de Larrañaga, Manuel Antonio Lorenz, Bautista Montaño. Antonio José Ortiz, Alcalde.

Bonifacio Jollanga (Joyanaga) to Domingo de Luna. Alburquerque, 1747. A piece of land in the *San Clemente* Tract. Joseph Baca, Alcalde. Joseph Gallego, Isidro Sanches.

Antonio Gallego, alias *El Collote*, to Domingo de Luna. Land in the *San Clemente* Tract. 1748. Joseph Baca, Alcalde. Isidro Sanchez, Manuel Carillo.

Bonifacio Jollanga (Joyanga) to Domingo de Luna. 1748. Land in the *San Clemente* Tract. 1748. Joseph Baca, Alcalde. Isidro Sanches. Reported Claim No. 67, q. v. Ana de Sandoval y Manzanares, or LOS LUNAS Tract.

Domingo de Luna was lieutenant of the militia company at the town of Tomé, in 1766. De Luna sold to Don Pedro Martin Serrano all his right to what is known as the Piedra Lumbre Tract. Governor Tomas Veles Cachupin granted the tract to Serrano, he being a descendant of the first settlers of the Province. It appears in the granting papers that the Indians of the *pueblo of Abiquiú* were requested to be present at the time possession was given to Lieutenant Pedro Martin Serrano, who was a lieutenant of militia of the district of Chama.

In the year 1716, Ana De Sandoval y Manzanares asked for this tract, petitioning Governor Phelix Martinez to that effect and stating that "when the Marquis de la Nava Brazinas, whom may God keep in Glory, was governor and captain-general of this province, brought us hither in the year ninety-two for its settlement" he had promised to give to each one of the "native citizens of this province who might come to settle and pacify the same, the tracts of land and fields, and stockraising ranches that we abandoned in the year eighty on account of the powerful insurrection." She was the widow of Blas de la Candelaria and asked for the place called "San Clemente, which I inherited from my father, deceased, Mateo de Sandoval y Manzanares."

The grant was made and she was placed in possession by Don Antonio Gutierrez, chief alcalde and war-captain of the Villa de Alburquerque, in the presence of Don Antonio de Chaves and Baltazar Romero; possession was given actually to Felix de la Candelaria, son of his mother, the petitioner; the land was bounded on the east by the Rio del Norte, on the west by the Rio Puerco; on the south by the house of Tomé Dominguez, and on the north by a ruin that is a little above the pueblo of San Clemente.

Those who returned with De Vargas were required to claim and occupy the possessions which had been abandoned in 1680 and to obtain from the government a recognition of the renewal of title before possession could be given.

463 FRANCISCO VIGIL to Bernardo Lucero. 1793.
Land in *Las Trampas* Tract.

464 CAPTAIN DIEGO DE TORRES, BARTOLOME TRUJILLO, ANTONIO DE SALAZAR, MANUEL VALERIO, and MANUEL MARTIN, legal representatives of Cristobal de Torres.
Petition relative to a tract of land of the estate of the said Cristobal de Torres, in *Chama*. Incomplete.

465 FRAY JOSEPH MEDRANO to Maria Dolores and Mariano, two children he had raised.
Land in *Alameda*. Antonio de Armenta, Alcalde; Benito Lucero.

GERTRUDIS CASTELA, or Juana Gertrudis Castela vs. Miguel Baca and Juan Antonio Baca. 1794-5. Question of lands at *Alameda*. Nerio Antonio Montoya, Alcalde; Antonio José Ortiz, Alcalde; Fernando Chacón, Governor; Tomas Manuel Montoya; Antonio de Armenta, Alcalde.

466 ANTONIO DE LUNA. 1811.
Question of land with Ventura Chaves. Papers incomplete. 1816. Further proceedings in the same matter. Manrique, Governor; Allande, Governor; José Antonio Chaves; Francisco Ortiz.

San Clemente Tract. Ana de Manzanares de Sandoval. Reported Claim No. 67.

According to the first survey of the San Clemente Grant, made in 1878, the grant contained more than 89,-

000 acres. It was confirmed by the court of private land claims and under another survey contained an area of about 37,000 acres. The last survey adjoins on the east the western boundary of the property commonly called "Lo de Padilla," which is claimed by the Indians of the pueblo of Isleta. The San Clemente was patented November 15, 1909.

467 BERNARDO LUCERO vs. MAURILO BARGAS. 1820.

Question of land in *Las Trampas de Taos*. Facundo Melgares, Governor; Marcos Garcia, Alcalde; Juan de Dios Peña; Antonio José Ortiz, Alcalde.

FRANCISCO VIGIL to Bernardo Lucero. 1793. Land in *Rancho de Las Trampas*. *Testimonio* certified by Juan de Dios Peña, Alcalde.

468 BERNARDO LUCERO. 1820.

No. 467, *q. v.* No. 467 also for signatures of the members of the *Ayuntamiento de Taos*, *q. v.*

469 ANTONIO ANALLA and JOSE SANDOVAL to Juan José Lujan. 1827.

Land in the *Cañon* of the *Santa Fe* river granted to Santiago Ramirez. Juan Vigil, Alcalde; Luis Benavides; Juan Diego Sena.
Santiago Ramirez was a brother of José Serafin Ramirez, whose full name was José Serafin Ramirez y Casanova. He was a native of Chihuahua.

470 JUAN LUCERO.

Will, *Santa Fe*, 1827. Joseph Maria Martinez, Alcalde. José Vitervo Ortiz, Domingo Fernandez.

471 MARIA FRANCISCA LOVATO.

Will, *Santa Fe*, 1830. José Ignacio Ortiz, Alcalde. Bentura Montoya, Victorino Padilla.

472 JOHN S. LANGHAM vs. the *Ayuntamiento* of *Santa Fe*. 1837.

In regard to fencing the *Cienega*. Albino Perez, Governor. J. M. Alarid, Secretary. Juan Garcia, Alcalde.

473 ANTONIO LERUD (Antoine Leroux). 1844.

Grant. Land in *Los Valles de Santa Getrudis de lo de Mora*. Law of April 30, 1842. Articles 13 and 15, *q. v.*

Tomas Ortiz, Alcalde. Mauricio Duran, Miguel Antonio Lobato.

Antoine Leroux was the grantee of a grant of that name. All of the grant to the pueblo of Picuriés is included within the limits of this grant. There is no conflict with the survey of the Taos Pueblo Grant which lies only a short distance to the east.

In 1905-1907 another survey was made and the new survey makes a conflict with the Taos Grant while not interfering with the Picuriés.

474 CARMEN LEYBA to Antonio Sena. *Santa Fe*, 1844.
House and lot. Tomas Ortiz, Alcalde.

475 ANTONIO SANCHEZ, alias *el Chopo* vs. JULIAN LUCERO. 1844.
Question of lands in *Rio Arriba* county. Diego Lucero, Juez de Paz, José Sanchez. Santiago Flores, Judge of 1st Instance.

476 ROQUE MADRID.
Grant. 1693. Land at *Pueblo Quemado*, at or near Santa Fe. Don Diego de Vargas Zapata Lujan Ponce de Leon, Governor. (Seal.) Antonio Balverde Cossio, Secretary.

Refers to a tract of land near Santa Fe, one of the boundaries of which was the "Pueblo Quemado"; another the "Ojo fresco."

The coat of arms of General De Vargas is stamped on this archive.

477 DOMINGO MARTIN.
Grant. *Santa Fe*, 1695. Don Diego de Vargas Zapata Lujan Ponce de Leon, Governor.

478 LUIS MAESE.
Grant. *Santa Fe*, 1695. Don Diego de Vargas Zapata Lujan Ponce de Leon, Governor.

A tract of land in Santa Fe "*el qual sitio esta en esta Villa en el pueblo quemado, con solar de casa y huerta y media fanega de sembradura asta el arroio.*"

479 DOMINGO MARTIN and ANA LUJAN. *Santa Fe*, 1705.
Compromise in the matter of a grant made to them by Governor de Vargas. Francisco Romero de Pedraza, Al-

THE SPANISH ARCHIVES OF NEW MEXICO   145

  calde. Joseph de Atienza Alcala y Escobar. Joseph de Contreras.

480 ALEXO MARTIN and his wife Maria de la Roche to José Castellanos. *Santa Fe*, 1701.
  House and land. *Testimonio* certified by Xptobal de Gongora, Clerk of the Cabildo.

481 ANTONIO MONTOYA vs. SALVADOR MATHIAS DE RIBERA.
  Question of lands. *Santa Fe*, 1704. El Marqués de la Naba de Brazinas, Lorenzo de Madrid, Joseph Manuel Giltomey, Antonio de Aguilera Isasi, Alphonso Rael de Aguilar. Juan Paez Hurtado, Alcalde. Xpttobal de Arellano, Antonio Lucero de Godoy, Xpttobal de Gongora.

482 RAMON GARCIA JURADO to Captain Felix Martinez. *Santa Fe*, 1706.
  House and land. Diego Arias de Quiros, Alcalde. Juan de Ulibarri, Alphonsso Rael de Aguilar.

483 FELIX MARTINEZ to Diego de Bectia. *Santa Fe*, 1706.
  House and land. Diego Arias de Quiros, Alcalde. Antonio Duran de Armijo, Xpttobal de Gongora.

ANA LUJAN. *Santa Fe*, 1700.
  Re-validation of her grant. Pedro Rodriguez Cubero, Governor. Domingo de la Barreda, Secretary. Ana Lujan to Diego de Vectia, *Santa Fe*, 1701. House and land. *Testimonio*. Certified to by Joseph Rodriguez, Alcalde.
  Diego de Vectia to Francisco Rico. *Santa Fe*, 1703. House and land. Lorenzo de Madrid, Alcalde. Xpttobal de Gongora, Juan de Chabes.
  Diego de Vectia to Martin Garcia, *Santa Fe*, 1702.
  Land. *Testimonio*; Certified by Joseph Rodriguez, Alcalde. Martin Garcia. 1702. Conveys to Maria de la Encarnacion. Francisco Rico to Captain Felix Martinez. *Santa Fe*, 1705. House and land. Juan de Ulibarri, Alcalde. Francisco Belarde, Matheo de la Peña.

484 JOSEPHA LUJAN to Sebastian Martin, 1707.
  Rancho above *San Juan de los Caballeros*. Granted to her deceased husband by the Marqués de la Naba Brazinas. Alphonso Rael de Aguilar, Alcalde.

146 THE SPANISH ARCHIVES OF NEW MEXICO

485 ROQUE MADRID vs. SYLVESTRE PACHECO. *Santa Fe*, 1708.
> No action taken. Rubric of the Marqués de la Penuela.

486 ROQUE MADRID vs. SYLVESTRE PACHECO. *Santa Fe*, 1708.
> No final action. Joseph Chacón Medina Villaseñor, Marqués de la Penuela. Gaspar Gutierres de los Rios, Secretary.

487 SILVESTRE PACHECO to Antonio Montoya. *Santa Fe*, 1708.
> Land about a league down the river (Rio Santa Fe). Ignacio de Roibal, Alcalde. Alphonso Rael de Aguilar, Francisco Ignacio Gomez Robledo.
> Describes a tract of land about one league down the river from Santa Fe and which extended from a *cottonwood tree* to the *Pueblo Quemado*.

488 ROQUE MADRID vs. SYLVESTRE PACHECO. *Santa Fe*, 1708.
> Compromise. Ignacio de Roibal, Alcalde. Antonio Montoya.

489 MAGDALENA DE OGAMA to Salvador Montoya. *Santa Fe*, 1711.
> Land. Diego Arias de Quiros, Alcalde.
> Describes a piece of land on the west side of the *principal plaza* at Santa Fe, which land, on the *north side*, adjoined the *main ditch which ran along the edge of this fortress and castle*.

490 FRANCISCO MARTIN vs. CRISTOVAL MARTIN, 1711-1712.
> Question of lands in *Rio Arriba*. El Marqués de la Penuèla, Miguel Thenorio de Alva, Manuel Ramon Ipalenzia, Xpttobal de Gongora. Juan de Ulibarri, Alcalde. Juan de Atienza, José Manuel Giltomey, Francisco Montes y Vigil, Francisco de Rivera (Derrivera), Miguel de Dias (Dios). Roque Madrid, Alcalde. Juan Paez Hurtado, Teniente de Gobierno and Captain-General. Juan Ignacio Flores Mogollon, Governor. Roque de Pintto, Secretary of Government and War.

491 ANTONIA DE MORAGA vs. JUANA DE SOSA CANELA. *Santa Fe*, 1713.
>Question of a piece of land in the *Cienega*. Juan Ignacio Flores Mogollon, Governor; Roque de Pintto, Secretary; Antonio Duran de Armijo; Roque Madrid; Pedro Rodriguez Cubero, Governor; Juan Paez Hurtado, Alcalde; Tomas Jiron de Texeda; Xpttobal de Arellano; Domingo de la Barreda, Secretary.
>
>Don Diego de Vargas Zapata Lujan Ponce de Leon, Governor. Miguel de Quintana. Two signatures; difference in them; *q. v.*
>
>In the depositions of two witnesses reference is made to the "church which is now (1713) being built in Santa Fe."

492 MATEO DE ORTEGA to Manuel Martin. *Santa Fe*, 1712.
>Land at *Chimayo*. Manuel Albares Castrillon, Xpttobal de Gongora, Diego Arias de Quiros, Alcalde.

493 GONZALO JOSEPH HOYO DE MENDOZA. Francisco Bueno de Bohorques. Alphonso Rael de Aguilar.
>Registration of a mine in *Rio Arriba*. 1713. Don Juan Ignacio Flores Mogollon, Governor.

494 CLEMENTE MONTOYA.
>Will. *Santa Cruz de la Cañada..* 1753. *Testimonio.* Certified by Juan Joseph Sandoval, Alcalde.

495 FRANCISCA DE MISQUIA.
>Will. *Santa Fe*, 1714. Francisco Joseph Bueno de Bohorques, Alcalde. Miguel de Sandobal Martinez, Juan Manuel Chirinos.

496 ANTONIA DE MORAGA vs. XPTTOBAL and FRANCISCO MARTIN.
>Question of boundaries of land at *Chimayo*. Ignacio de Roybal, Alcalde; Francisco de Ribera; Francisco de la Mora; Mogollon, Governor.

497 FRANCISCO DE ANAYA ALMAZAN.
>Grant, 1693. Reported Claim No. 115, *q. v.*

498 ANTONIO GODINES to Pedro Montes de Oca.
>House and lot. Francisco Joseph Bueno de Bohorques,

Alcalde; Juan de la Mora Pineda; Diego Marqués de Ayala.

Description of a house on the main street of Santa Fe as follows: *"En la Calle Real que ba de la plaza a la Yglesia nueba q se esta fabricando."*

499 FRANCISCO MONTES Y VIGIL and wife to Maria Vigil, et al, 1715.

Donation of cattle. Alphonso Rael de Aguilar, Antonio Duran de Armijo, Juan de la Mora Pineda.

The translation appearing below appeared first in the *Land of Sunshine*, vol. viii, no. 3, February, 1898, at the time edited by Dr. Charles F. Lummis:

"Letter from Fr. Antonio Duran de Armijo

"Sir Governor and Captain General — My Lord:

"I report to your Lordship how this day and date seven Cumanches entered this Pueblo; among them the Captain Panfilo. They tell me they have come in quest of tobacco; that their village is composed of a hundred lodges, pitched on the Jicarilla river, where they are tanning (buffalo) hides, so as to come in and barter as soon as the snow shall decrease in the mountains. This is what they tell me. There is nothing else to report to your Lordship, whom our Lord Preserve for many years. Taos, Feb. 27, 1748. I kiss the hand of Your Lordship. Your humble servant.   ANTONIO DURAN DE ARMIJO.

"Since the above was written one Cumanche of the seven who have come, has related to me in the house of Alonzito that 33 Frenchmen have come to their village and sold them plenty of muskets in exchange for mules; that as soon as this trade was made, the Frenchmen departed for their own country, and that only two remain in the village to come in with the Cumanches when they come hither to barter."

"Opinion of the Governor

"Most Excellent Sir:—By the testimony subjoined, which is from the original letter containing it, which the sovereignty of your excellency will please to see, it appears that forty leagues distant, more or less, (according to some settlers) from the Pueblo of San Geronimo de Taos, there are pitched a hundred lodges of the hostile Gentiles, of the Cumanche nation; and that seven of these Indians arrived at the above mentioned Pueblo (Taos) with the news that 33 Frenchmen were, some days before, on the said Jicarilla river, where are the aforesaid one hundred lodges; which Frenchmen sold to the aforesaid Cumanches plenty of muskets in exchange for mules. And soon as this barter was effected, said Frenchmen departed for their own country, only two of them remaining in the village of the Cumanches to come in with them to trade in the Pueblo of Taos; as these hostile savages have done on other occasions. And since it is to be feared that if these Frenchmen insinuate themselves into this Kingdom they may cause some uprising — as was attempted by a Frenchman named Luis Maria, who with eight of his own nation entered this Kingdom in the former year of 1742, coming by the same route of the Jicarilla to the Pueblo of Taos and for it was shot in the public square in this Capitol town of Santa Fe, in virtue of sentence by the superior government of this New Spain; and in the said year, seven of these nine Frenchmen returned to their country by a different route from that by which they came here; and it is very natural that, remaining several months in this Kingdom, they should learn the 'lay of the land' and its circumstances. One of them, named Juan de Alari, has remained in this said town, is married and has children, comporting himself honorably as a man of substance.

"Likewise I give account to Your Excellency that in the month of June, of the year 1744, a Frenchman by the name of Santiago Velo, penetrated this Kingdom and arrived at the Pueblo of Our Lady of the Porciuncula of Pecos. As soon as I received the news, I despatched the sargent and two soldiers to bring him to me in this Town (Santa Fe), where I took his declaration. And without the knowledge of any person I forwarded that declaration To The Most Excellent Sir Count of Fuenclara, your excellency's predecessor (as viceroy of Mexico) along with the judicial procedures duly had thereon. Of this Frenchman's whereabouts I have had no further information, save what was given me by the Captain of the Royal Garrison at El Paso, on the Rio del Norte (Rio Grande), whose receipt I hold, acknowledging have sent him to the Governor of New Biscay.

"Most Excellent Sir: — By the zeal which assists me in the service of their Majesties (the King and Queen of Spain) and for the tranquility, peace and well being of the poor dwellers in this said Kingdom (let me say). Noting that it is wholly surrounded by various nations of hostile savages, who harrass it; and particularly how numerous and warlike are the Cumanches, whose regular entrances to this Kingdom are by way of the Jicarilla river — and that on these two occasions the French have likewise penetrated by the same route, this last time joining the Gentile Cumanches on the aforesaid Jicarilla river — there is reason to fear some conspiracy. This would be irreparable, by the slight military forces that are in this said Kingdom for its defense. Particularly as the said Gentile Cumanches now find themselves with fire-arms, which the French have sold them, as hereinbefore set forth. I remind your Excellencies high comprehension that in the by-gone year, 1720, when Don Antonio Valverde was governor of this Kingdom he ordered, under superior mandate of his Lordship, the then viceroy of this New Spain, that a force of soldiers, settlers and Indians should go to reconnoitre where the French were located. But the French ambushed our said force and killed more than thirty of them, soldiers, settlers and Indians, besides wounding several who reached this said town. For which reason, and many others which I omit, that I may not weary your Excellency's attention, I deem it very fitting and necessary that your Excellency's greatness order the establishment of a garrison with the endowment of fifty mounted soldiers, including captain and subaltern officers at a point called the Jicarilla, distant from the said Pueblo of Taos twenty leagues. This location is very convenient, as to lands, water, pasturage and timber. Here were located, in times past, the Indians of the Jicarilla nation (a branch of the Apaches), who were numerous and had houses, palisade huts and other shelters. Thence the Gentile Cumanches despoiled them, killing most of them; the few that remained of said Jicarillas have sheltered and maintained themselves in peace nearby the Pueblos of Taos and Pecos, with their families. Said site of the Jicarilla is the pass (or defile); literally 'throat' (for shutting of the aforesaid populous nation of Cumanches — and the French, if they tried to make any entrance to this said Kingdom.

"Furthermore, I notify your Excellency of the happenings in the Pueblo of Our Lady of the Porciuncula of Pecos, on the twenty-first of January last past. Which whole affair is established by the accompanying deposition of the Rev. Fr. Lorenzo Antonio Estremera, an eye-witness of it all, which I forward. In view of which, your Excellency will please approve the action taken by me in said engagement, or give such orders as shall be in your Excellency's pleasure. This is how it has seemed to me; especially, as I have said, to represent to your Excellency its expediency. This is my duty, that the sovereign will of your Excellency may determine with your great equity, as shall seem best to you, which will be, as always, the best way.

"Villa de Santa Fe, New Mexico, March 4, 1748.
"DON JOAQUIN CODALLOS Y RABAL"

This copy agrees with the original deposition, letter and opinion which I, the Colonel Don Joaquin Codallos y Rabal, governor and captain-general of this kingdom of New Mexico, have forwarded to the superior government of this New Spain. The witnesses who saw it drawn, corrected and compared were Sebastian de Apodaca, Lucas Miguel de Moia, and Domingo Valdez; and that it be certain, I have signed it in this Villa de Santa Fe, March 6th, 1748; acting as actuary with the witnesses of my staff, for want of a notary public or royal notary — whereof there is not one in this kingdom. I pledge my faith.

In witness of the truth I have signed it with my accustomed signature. JOAQUIN CODALLOS Y RABAL
Witness FELIPE JACOBO UNANUE
Witness MIGUEL DE ALIRE

500 ANTONIO MONTOYA.

Petition for lands between *Santo Domingo* and *San Felipe*. 1716. No final action.

Captain Felix Martinez, Governor. Joseph de Quintana.

Petition by Antonio Montoya for lands which were the surplusage of the lands of the pueblos of Santo Domingo and San Felipe, "on the other side of the Rio del Norte."

This petition was presented, on March 18, 1716, to Governor Felix Martinez, who ordered Manuel Baca, chief alcalde of the *pueblos* of San Felipe, Santo Domingo, and Cochiti, to examine the lands asked for, to inform the Indians of San Felipe and Santo Domingo in regard to the petition made by Montoya, and to report what they had to say about the matter.

The alcalde reported that the Indians said that they wanted their league measured so that they might know what belonged to them. Here the proceeding ends abruptly.

501 FRANCISCO MARTIN.
Grant. 1716. Land at *Chimayo*. Xptobal Martin and Felipe Moraga, *q. v.* Pedro Rodriguez Cubero, Governor; Alonsso Barela; Don Juan Ignacio Flores Mogollon, Governor; Francisco Ribera; Sebastian Martin; Roque Madrid; Pedro de Morales, Secretary; Miguel de Quintana; Joseph Manuel Giltomey; Xtobal Torres; Salvador Martinez.

502 LORENZO MADRID.
Will, *Santa Fe*, 1716. Juan Garsia de la Riva, Alcalde; Manuel Chiriños.

503 ANTONIO MARTINEZ.
Grant. 1716. Reported Claim No. 116, *q. v.*

504 XPTOBAL MARTIN vs. FRANCISCO MARTIN, 1717.
Land at *Chimayo*. Felipe Moraga, *q. v.* Juan Paez Hurtado, Captain-General; Juan Garsia de la Rivas, Alcalde; Miguel Thenorio de Alba, Sec.; Juan de Atiensa; Francisco de la Mora.

505 JUANA DE ARGUELLO to Josepha Martin. *Santa Fe*, 1718.
Donation of land. Francisco Bueno de Bohorques y Corcuera, Alcalde.

506 DIEGO ARIAS DE QUIROS to Francisco de Mestas, 1720.
Donation of land in *Cuyamungue*. Francisco Joseph Bueno de Bohorquez y Corcuera, Alcalde.

507 ANTONIO MARTIN.
Land at *Alburquerque*. Possession not given. Don Juan Domingo de Bustamante, Governor. Manuel de Cruciaga, Secretary.

508 JOSEPH DE QUINTANA, with consent of Josepha Sedano, to Juan Lorenzo de Medina. *Santa Fe*, 1722.
Land. Francisco Bueno Bohorques y Corcuera, Alcalde. Tomas Xiron de Tegeda; Joseph de Quintana.
JOSEPH SEDANO. *Santa Fe*, 1721. Protest against above conveyance. Francisco Bueno de Bohorques y Corcuera, Alcalde. Juan Manuel Chiriños.

THE SPANISH ARCHIVES OF NEW MEXICO 153

509 MIGUEL MARTIN and JOSEPH DE ATIENZA.
>Compromise as to boundaries of lands in the *Cañada de Santa Cruz*. 1722. Alphonso Rael de Aguilar; Miguel de Quintana.

510 DIMAS XIRON DE TEXEDA and Maria Domingues, his wife, to Sebastian Martin. 1723.
>A tract of land in the jurisdiction of *Taos*. Francisco Bueno de Bohorquez y Corcuera, Alcalde. Juan Rael de Aguilar; Juan Joseph Moreno.

511 ANDRES MONTOYA to Josepha Montoya. *Santa Fe*, 1725.
>Donation of land. Miguel Joseph de la Bega y Coca, Alcalde. Juan Joseph Lobato; Juan Manuel Chiriños.

512 SALVADOR MONTOYA.
>Will. *Santa Fe*. 1727. Diego Arias de Quiros, Alcalde. Juan Manuel Chiriños; Miguel de Sandobal.

513 DIEGO MARQUES.
>Will. *Villa Nueva de Santa Cruz*. 1729.
>Joseph Miguel Marques de Ayala; Dimas Giron de Tegeda; Juan Domingo de Bustamante, Governor; Fray Manuel de Sopeña; Antonio de Gruciaga.

514 MARIA DE MOYA to Getrudis Montes y Vigil. *Santa Fe*, 1729.
>House and land. Diego Arias de Quiros, Alcalde. Juan Manuel Chiriños.

515 CRISTOBAL MARTIN vs. FRANCISCO MARTIN. 1731.
>Question of boundaries of land at *Santa Cruz*. Felipe Moraga, *q. v.* Gervasio Cruzat y Gongora, Governor. Miguel de Quintana; Juan Antonio de Vnuane.

516 JUANA DE ANALLA to José Montaño. *Alburquerque*, 1731.
>Land. Juan Gonzales Bas, Alcalde. Joseph de Quintana.

517 JOSEPH FRANCISCO MONTOYA vs. BALTAZAR ROMERO. 1733.
>Question of a tract of land at *Pajarito*. His grandfather, Miguel Garcia de la Ribas, registered the *Pajarito* Tract.

154 THE SPANISH ARCHIVES OF NEW MEXICO

Gervasio Cruzat y Gongora, Governor. Juan Antonio de Vnanue; Isidro Sanches; Gaspar Bitton; Juan Gonzales Bas, Alcalde; Pedro de Chabes, Alcalde.

518 GERONIMO and IGNACIO MARTIN, Juan de Gamboa and Pascual and Tomas de Manzanares, all of *Chama.*

Grant. Land above *Abiquiú*. Juan Paez Hurtado, Acting Governor. 1735. Diego de Vgartte.

This grant was revoked by Gervasio Cruzat y Gongora, Governor.

519 JACINTO MARTIN and JOSEPH GARCIA.

Grant. 1735. Land in a place called *Cieneguilla* in the county of *Taos.* Juan Paez Hurtado, Acting Governor. Revoked by Governor Cruzat y Gongora.

520 VENTURA DE MESTAS vs. Antonio de Beitia. 1736.

Question of lands at the mouth of the *Ojo Caliente.* Gervasio Cruzat y Gongora, Governor. Gaspar Bitton.

It appears that Antonio Martin also had a grant at this place.

On the first page we find *"Por la parte del sur con el paso del rrio que llaman el bado."* Shows that the use of the word *"paso"* is identical with that used in the name of the city of El Paso del Rio del Norte, meaning *"ford"* or *"crossing."*

521 REPORT on the condition of the property of Felix Martinez, Governor, deceased. Antonio Montoya, Alcalde. Item No. 1105, *q. v.*

522 DIEGO ARIAS DE QUIROS to Francisco Xavier de Mestas.

Donation of land in *Cuyamungue.* 1738. Antonio Montoya, Alcalde. Joseph de Riaño.

523 CRISTOBAL MARTIN vs. Francisco Martin. 1738.

Question of lands. No. 515, *q. v.* Henrique de Olavide y Michelena, Governor. Pedro Joseph de Leon; Gervasio Cruzat y Gongora, Governor; Balthazar Montoya; Miguel de Quintana.

524 GERONIMO MARTIN. 1739.

Revocation of grant made to him at *Villa Nueva de Santa*

THE SPANISH ARCHIVES OF NEW MEXICO 155

Cruz by Juan Paez Hurtado, Acting Governor. Revocation by Cruzat y Gongora, Governor.

In his paper the governor says: "*por quanto mande recojer por siertos motivos que para ello tube, las mersedes de tierras que dio el Theniente General Don Juan Paez Hurtado, en el tiempo que yo estava hasiendo la visita,*" etc.

525 ANTONIA DOMINGUEZ MENDOZA to Maria Madalena Medina. 1740.

Land in *Santa Fe*. Antonio Montoya, Alcalde. Baltazar Montoya.

526 ANDRÉS MONTOYA. *Cieneguilla.* 1740.

Will. Juan Paez Hurtado, Alcalde. Joseph Miguel de la Peña; Gregorio Garduño; Juan Orttis.

527 CATARINA MAESE.

Grant. 1742. Land on the other side of the *Santa Fe* river. Gaspar Domingo de Mendoza, Governor. Gregorio Garduño.

528 ANTONIO MONTOYA. *Villa Nueva de Santa Cruz.*

Will. 1749. Juan Joseph Sandoval, Alcalde. Salbador Barela.

With this also are:

Bartolomé Lovato. Petition. 1703. Claim for an Apache woman from Captain Xptobal de Arellano. El Marqués de la Naba Brazinas, Governor.

529 JACINTO MARTIN   Juan Francisco Martin.
    Phelipe Bustamante   Antonio Martin

Relative to the settlement of lands near the pueblo of the *Picuriés*. 1744. Joachin Codallos y Rabal, Governor.

530 MARGARITA MARTIN. *Villa Nueva de Santa Cruz.* 1744.

Inventory and partition of her estate.
Joachin Codallos y Rabal, Governor. Francisco de Roa y Carrillo; Juan Garcia de la Mora; Joseph Antonio de la Thorre; Carlos Fernandez; Francisco Ortiz, Alcalde; Juan Joseph Pacheco; Francisco Orttiz, Alcalde.

531 FRAY JUAN MIGUEL MENCHERO. 1748.

Petition relating to confiscated property of criminal Indians. Joachin Codallos y Rabal, Governor.

Petition by Father Juan Miguel Menchero, asking that certain property, which had been confiscated from persons guilty of various crimes, should be turned over to him (after the payment of the necessary fees incident to the legal proceedings), to be applied to the reëstablishment of the then deserted pueblo of Sandia.

Governor Codallos y Rabal on April 19, 1748, decided that he did not have authority to grant the petition, but advised the priest to apply to the viceroy, to whom the decision of the disposition of the confiscated property belonged.

The only important thing in the document is that the *pueblo* of Sandia had been deserted, and was then being reëstablished, with a view to gathering together the Moqui Indians, who were scattered about among the different pueblos of the kingdom.

In this it appears that the pueblo of Sandia had been deserted and in (1748) was being reëstablished. It also shows that certain property of the Indians of Cochití, Tesuque, and San Juan had been confiscated because the owners had been guilty of *lese majeste* and other crimes.

532 SALVADOR MARTINEZ. 1748. Petition.

Complains of having been dispossessed of his property, houses and lands, at the "*Vega of Sandia*," by the priests. Joachin Codallos y Rabal, Governor. Fray Juan Miguel de Menchero; Phelipe Jacobo Vnanue; Miguel de Alire; Fray Joseph Juan Hernandez.

Petition of Salvador Martinez to have restored to him certain lands, houses, etc., which he alleged had been given to the Indians who were brought from Moqui to Sandia in 1742, by the friars Carlos Delgado and Pedro Pino.

The petition was denied by Governor Codallos on July 13, 1748, apparently for the reason that the petitioner had not made any protest at the time he alleged his property was given to the Indians, and also because he had suffered no real injury, having more desirable property elsewhere.

This indicates that the Indians were brought from Moqui to the neighborhood of the deserted pueblo of Sandia in 1742 under the direction of the frayles, Carlos Delgado and Pedro Pino; also shows that this region was exposed to raids from the Faraon Apaches.

533 VENTURA DE MESTAS, *Villa Nueva de Santa Cruz*. 1748. Vs. Juan Antonio Lujan, Manuela Beytia and Salvador de Torres.

Joachin Codallos y Rabal, Governor. Juan de Beytia, Alcalde. Vincente Ginzo Ron y Thobar; Joseph Romo de Vera; Antonio de Armenta; Leonardo de la Cruz; Francisco Gomez del Castillo.

534 ANTONIO MARTIN. *Chimayo.* 1748.
Question of lands with Martin Fernandez. *"vecino de tan sumamente mal corazon.* Joachin Codallos y Rabal, Governor. Vincente Ginzo Ron y Thobar; Juan de Beytia, Alcalde; Martin Balerio; Francisco Gomez del Castillo.

535 LORENZO MARTIN, of *El Paso del Norte*, to Francisco Martin, 1749.
Land in *Chimayo.* Juan Joseph Sandoval, Alcalde. Martin Valerio.

536 ROSA MARTINA FERNANDEZ. *Villa Nueva de Santa Cruz.* 1750.
Will. Juan Joseph Sandoval, Alcalde. Salvador Varela; Alonzo Sandoval.

537 ANTONIO de SALAZAR to Pedro Martin. 1750.
House and land in *"Corral de Piedra."* Juan Joseph Lobato, Procurador General. Juan Joseph Jaques; Juan Domingo Lovato.

538 MANUEL de la ROSA to Pedro Martin. 1751.
Land in *Abiquiú.* Juan Joseph Lovato, Procurador General. Juan Domingo Lovato; Juan Trujillo.

539 MANUEL BACA to Josefa Montoya. 1751.
Land in *"Cañada de Guicu. ques el lindero un alamo grande de o gare donda y por lo que mira de norte a sur lo que resa la merced o venta real del Puesto de la Cieneguilla."* Manuel Gallegos, Alcalde. Pedro Tafoya.

540 ANTONIO MARTIN vs. Martin Valerio. *Chimayo.* 1751.
Question of boundaries. Juan Joseph Lobato, Alcalde. Juan Andrés de Avalos.

541 CRISTOBAL AMESTAS (Mestas) for himself and his father, Mateo Mestas, and his brothers vs. Ventura de Mestas. Jurisdiction de la *Cañada.* 1752.
Question of lands. Tomas Veles Cachupin, Governor. Nicolas de Orttiz.

542 CASILDA DE MESTAS and JUAN PEDRO SISneros to Ventura de Mestas. 1754.
> "*Una parte considerable de tierra*" on the *Chama* river, above the *Rio del Oso*. Juan Joseph Lovato, Alcalde. Juan Domingo Lovato; Francisco Baldes y Bustos.

543 CRISTOBAL MARTIN to Marcos Martin. *Villa Nueva de Santa Cruz.* 1753.
> Land. Juan Joseph Lovato, Alcalde. Miguel Salazar.

544 MARIA DE HERRERA to Manuel Dias del Castillo (alias Mora). *Santa Cruz del Ojo Caliente.* 1753.
> Lands. Juan Joseph Lobato, Alcalde. José Martin.

545 BARTOLOMÉ TRUGILLO to Manuel Martin. *Abiquiú.* 1753.
> Land. Juan Joseph Lovato, Alcalde. Antonio Martin.

546 MIGUEL MARTIN SERRANO. *San Antonio. Rio Arriba* County(?).
> Will. 1752. Hilario Archuleta, Alcalde. Francisco Gomez del Castillo; Juan Gomez del Castillo.

547 DOMINGO DE HERRERA and Gertrude Xaramillo, his wife, to Joseph de Medina. *Villa Nueva de Santa Cruz.* 1753.
> Juan Joseph Lovato, Alcalde. Antonio Martin.

548 GREGORIO LOBATO to Bartolomé Marquez. 1754.
> Land in *Santa Fe.* Nicolas Orttiz, Alcalde. Juan Antonio Ortiz.

549 JOSEPH and JUAN HURTADO to Diego Marquez. 1754.
> House and land in *Santa Fe.* Nicolas Orttiz, Alcalde. Joseph Maldonado.

550 JOSEPH RINCON to Bartolomé Marques. *Santa Fe,* 1755.
> Land on the other side of the *Rio Santa Fe.*

> FRANCISCO RAEL DE AGUILAR to the same. Same date.
>> Land adjoining the above. Francisco Guerrero, Alcalde. Manuel Vigil; Estevan Rodriguez.

551 IGNACIO DE ROYBAL to Juan Miñon. *Santa Fe.* 1755.
>Donation. Land. *Testimonio.* Certified by Francisco Guerrero, Alcalde. Antonio Guerrero; Manuel Vigil.

552 JUAN JOSEPH MORENO.
>Will. *Santa Fe.* 1756. Francisco Marin del Valle, Governor. Miguel de Alire; Francisco Xavier Fragoso.
>The preamble of this instrument is very interesting.

553 BARTOLOMÉ FERNANDEZ to Isidro Martin. *Santa Fe.* 1757.
>Land. Francisco Guerrero, Alcalde. Manuel Bernardo Garvisu; Phelipe Sandoval Fernandez.

554 JUAN FRANCISCO MOYA to Lucas Moya. *Santa Fe.* 1758.
>House and land. Francisco Guerrero, Alcalde. Manuel Bernardo Garvisu; Antonio Guerrero.

555 ANTONIO MONTOYA to Urbano Montoya. *Santa Fe.* 1759.
>Lands at a place called *Los Palacios.* Francisco Guerrero, Alcalde.

556 CRISTOBAL MARTIN to José Maldonado. *Santa Fe.* 1761.
>House and land on the other side of the *Rio Santa Fe.* Francisco Guerrero, Alcalde. José Miguel de la Peña; Lucas Moya.

557 JOAQUIN MESTAS.
>Petition to be permitted to remain for a certain time on land occupied by him at *Lagunitas del Rio Puerco.* 1762. Tomas Veles Cachupin, Governor. Reported Claims Nos. 97 and 101, *q. v.*
>At Santa Teresa de Jesús, Feb. 8, 1768, Captain Bartolomé Fernandez, chief alcalde, placed Joaquin Mestas in possession of a tract of land, under a grant from Governor Mendinueta, *upon which no Apaches were living,* in the presence of Miguel and Santiago Montoya; the Chaco Mesa was the western boundary; in measuring this land the alcalde used a "cordel, one hundred Castillian varas long." The grantees were cautioned by the governor to occasion no injury to the "Apaches of the Navajo coun-

try," and to treat them with "love, fidelity and kindness, endeavouring earnestly to bring them to the pale of our mother, the church," with the penalty that if such treatment was not given the Indians the grant would be forfeited. Mestas recites that he had a former grant from Governor Marin del Valle, upon the Rio Puerco, and had been dispossessed by Governor Cachupin who gave the property to Captain Antonio Baca.

558 SEBASTIAN MARTIN vs. Manuel Martin. *Villa Nueva de Santa Cruz.* 1763.
    Question as to the validity of donation of lands. Juan Paez Hurtado, Governor; Tomas Veles Cachupin, Governor; Antonio de Beitia, Juez Commissionado; Carlos Fernandez; Manuel Antonio Lorenz; Joseph Garcia de Mora; Matheo de Peñarredonda.

559 GETRUDIS MARTIN. Intestate. *Santa Cruz de la Cañada.* 1763.
    Inventory and partition of her estate. Cristobal Madrid, son of the deceased; Juan Sanches; Francisco Antonio Zisneros; Carlos Fernandez, Alcalde Mayor.

560 XPTOBAL MADRID. *Santa Fe.* 1765.
    Will. Tomas Madrid, Lieutenant. Francisco Esquibel, Alférez.

561 GERONIMO MARTIN to José Martin. *Abiquiú.* 1764.
    Rancho; boundaries: *Por el oriente con el lindero de los Indios: Por el sur, donde rezare la merced de dicho sitio; por el poniente la orilla del estero en lo que mira a labor; el bordo del estero con la mojonera de Marcelino, y el camino a libre al pie del cerrito, que esta al sur para entrar y sali el bosque pleyto de los Frijoles y la casa de Marcelino — por la derecera de la punta de la Mesa Alta; al poniente; por el norte el Rio de Chama;* sold for $1,668. Manuel Garcia Pareja, Alcalde. Lorenzo Baldes; Santiago Martin.

562 JOSEPH BACA to Joaquin Mestas. *San Pedro de Chama.* 1784.
    House and lands. Manuel Garcia Pareja, Alcalde. Joseph Lujan.

Don Baltazar de Zuñiga, Marqués de Valero
Duke of Arion, Viceroy of Mexico, 1716-22

THE SPANISH ARCHIVES OF NEW MEXICO   161

563 MIGUEL DE HERRERA to Simon Martin. *Villa Nueva de Santa Cruz.* 1784.
　　House and land. Manuel Garcia Pareja, Alcalde. Joseph Lujan.

564 MATEO MESTAS.
　　Will. *Santa Cruz de la Cañada.* 1764. Joseph Esquibel, Alcalde. Luis Cano Saenz.

565 FRANCISCO MARTIN.
　　Will. *San Antonio del Embudo.* 1784. Francisco Antonio Zisneros, Alcalde. Cristobal Lorenzo Lobato; Julian Martin.

566 JUAN ANTONIO FRESQUIS to ANTONIO MARTIN. *San Antonio del Embudo.* 1765.
　　Land on *El Rio del Norte.* Manuel Garcia Pareja, Alcalde. Manuel Zamora.

567 NICOLAS MARES.
　　Will. *Santa Fe.* 1766. Thomas Madrid, Teniente. Juan Cayetano Nvuane.

568 JUAN PABLO MARTIN.
　　Grant. *Polvadera,* Rio Arriba county. 1766. Reported Claim No. 131, *q. v.*

569 JOSEPHA MONTOYA.
　　Will. 1766. *Santa Fe.* Francisco Guerrero, Alcalde. Francisco Xavier Fragoso; Juan Francisco Niño Ladron de Guebara.

570 QUITERIA PACHECO to Antonio Madrid. *Santa Fe.* 1766.
　　Francisco Guerrero, Alcalde. Ignacio Xaramillo; Santiago Frnz (Fernandez).

571 MIGUEL and SANTIAGO MONTOYA vs. Juan Pablo Martin. 1766.
　　In the matter of the *Polvadera* Tract. Tomas Veles Cachupin, Governor; Joseph Maldonado; Gaspar Domingo de Mendoza, Governor; Pedro Martin Serrano; Lucas Manuel de Alcala; Joseph Miguel de la Peña; Carlos Fernandez; Joseph Terrus; Antonio de Herrera; Phelipe

Tafoya, Procurador; Juan Antonio Ortiz; Domingo Labadia.

In the year 1767, Miguel and Santiago Montoya were residents of Alburquerque; they were grandsons of the great Captain Antonio Montoya, who came with De Vargas, who, with his two sons, Miguel Montoya and Juan Manuel Montoya, lived at Santa Rosa de Abiquiú until the place was abandoned. On the lands of the elder Montoyas, at Abiquiú, Governor Tomas Veles Cachupin founded the pueblo of Santo Tomas de Abiquiú, and promised Miguel Montoya, father of Miguel Montoya, to give him in lieu thereof a tract of land in some other part of the province; this he did not do, and the son, Miguel, and his cousin, Santiago, "finding themselves with the large families of their widowed mothers on hand," residing at Atrisco (near Alburquerque), asked for a tract of land on the Rio Puerco. This tract was denied them, as it was already occupied by Antonio Baca and Salvador Jaramillo; in the month of October, 1766, Governor Cachupin "in lieu of the ranch they refer to at Abiquiú, where the Indian mission of Santo Tomas was established and settled, the same having been found uninhabited," granted the Montoyas a tract on the Rio Puerco, "bounded on the south by lands of José Garcia, on the north the place where Joaquin Mestas is located, on the east the Rio Puerco and on the west the brow of a hill." Possession was given in the presence of the Indians of the pueblo of Zia (adjoining owners). The testimonios were deposited in the archives February 14, 1767, approved by the governor.

572 JUAN FRANCISCO MARTIN.
Will. Fragment. 1787. Manuel Garcia Pareja, Alcalde. Antonio Joseph Lovato.

573 JUAN BAUTISTA MONTANO.
Petition. *San Fernando del Rio Puerco*. 1767. Asking for lands *"sobras"* of Antonio Baca and Salvador Xaramillo. Not granted. Don Pedro Fermin de Mendinueta, Governor. Antonio Moreto; Mateo de Peñarredonda; Antonio Baca. File No. 105, office of S. G., *q. v.*

574 FELIPE DE SANDOVAL to Antonio Nerio Montoya. 1767.
Reported Claim No. 118, *q. v.*

THE SPANISH ARCHIVES OF NEW MEXICO 163

575 LUCAS DE MOYA to Manuel Moya. *Santa Fe.* 1767.
Land down the river.

576 SANTIAGO and MIGUEL MONTOYA.
Grant. 1767. Reported Claim No. 100, *q. v.*

577 VICENTE DE SENA to Joseph Maldonado. *Santa Fe.* 1767.
Land at *Buena Vista.* Francisco Guerrero, Alcalde. Antonio Dominguez.

578 JUANA DE OJEDA and JUAN DE BENAVIDES to Vicente Martinez, *Santa Fe*, 1767.
House and lands. Francisco Guerrero, Alcalde. Francisco Xavier Fragoso.

579 MEMORIA del Soldado, Cristobal Madrid, "*donde declara los bienes que tiene por hallarse para dar quenta al criador.*"
Thomas Madrid, Teniente; Phelipe Sandoval; Miguel Tenorio; Diego Antonio de la Peña.

580 JUANA TERESA, JULIANA and JUANA GETRUDIS FLORES to Bartolomé Marques. *Santa Fe.* 1767.
Lands. Francisco Guerrero, Alcalde. Nicolas Ortiz.

581 JOAQUIN MESTAS. 1788.
Grant. Reported Claim No. 97, *q. v.*

582 BERNARDO DE MIERA Y PACHECO and Pedro Padilla.
Grant. 1768. Reported Claim No. 98, *q. v.*

583 NERIO ANTONIO MONTOYA.
Grant. 1768. Reported Claim No. 11, *q. v.*

584 PAULIN MONTOYA and Five others.
Grant. 1768. File No. 185, *q. v.*

585 MATEO GUTIERREZ to Tomas Madrid. *Santa Fe.* 1768.
House and land. Phelipe Tafoya, Alcalde. Juan Miguel Tafoya; Joachin Lain.

164 THE SPANISH ARCHIVES OF NEW MEXICO

586 BERNARDINO DE SENA MAESE to Joseph Maese. 1768.
> House and lands. Phelipe Tafoya; Anacleto Miera; Joachin Lain.

587 MARIA MARTIN. Will. *Santa Fe*, 1768.
> Phelipe Tafoya, Alcalde; Lucas Moya; Santiago Fernandez; Manuel Fernandez.

588 JUAN DE ATENCIO to Manuel Manzanares. *San Pedro de Chama.* 1769.
> House and lot. Antonio Joseph Ortiz, Alcalde. Juan Domingo Lobato; Joseph Garcia de la Mora.

589 ANDRES MANZANARES to Manuel Manzanares. *Pojoaque.* 1769.
> House and lot in *Chama.* Antonio Joseph Ortiz, Alcalde. Manuel de Arteaga.

590 MONICA TOMASA MARTIN.
> Intestate. *Valle de San Geronimo de Taos.* 1770. It appears that a will was made in 1768. It is on file with these papers. Inventory and partition of her estate. Antonio Armijo, Alcalde. Pedro Fermin de Mendinueta, Governor. Antonio Solano; Domingo Benavides, Alcalde; Salvador Rivera; Nicolas Leal.

591 ANTONIO DE ARMENTA to Isidro Maese. *Santa Fe*, 1771.
> Land. Manuel Garcia Pareja, Alcalde. Joseph Armenta.

592 MARCIAL MARTIN SANGIL, of *Santo Domingo de Cundiyo*, vs. MARCIAL MARTIN.
> Question of land under a grant had by purchase by the complainant's father from Phelipe Moraga. 1771. Cristobal Montes Vigil, Alcalde. Mateo de Peñarredonda; Juan Francisco Mascareñas; Domingo Labadia; Pedro Fermin de Mendinueta; Antonio Moreto; Juan de Arteaga; Joseph de Medina.

593 ANACLETO DE MIERA Y PACHECO and Maria Catarina Pino.
> Petition. 1786. Asking that the property of Antonio de Luna, deceased, and said Maria Catarina de Pino be placed in their custody.

593 MANUEL DE ARMIJO and Juan de Ledesma to José Mares. *Santa Fe.* 1764.
    Donation of share in mine. Francisco Guerrero, Alcalde. Antonio de Armenta.

594 VICENTE MARTIN. Will. 1774. *Santa Fe.*
    Manuel Garcia Pareja, Alcalde. Antonio Armijo.

595 TOMAS MADRID. Will. *Santa Fe,* 1781.
    José Maldonado. Antonio Guerrero.

596 JOSEPHA MESTAS. *Pojoaque.* Will. 1785.
    Also partition of her estate. José Campo Redondo. Anza, Governor.

597 ANACLETO MIERA Y PACHECO and Maria Catarina Pino.
    Petition. 1788. Asking that the property of the minor children of Antonio de Luna and said Maria Catarina be placed in their custody. Juan Bautista de Anza, Governor. Josef Andrés Calles. Copy of No. 593.

598 JOSÉ MALDONADO. Will. 1789. *Santa Fe.*
    Also inventory and partition of his estate. Antonio Guerrero, Alférez. José Sandobal; Fernando de la Concha, Governor; José Rafael Sarracino, Administrador de Correos; Cristobal Maria Larrañaga; Nicolas Antonio de Henestrosa; Manuel Delgado, of Chihuahua; Cleto Miera; Antonio José Ortiz, Alcalde; Vincente Troncoso, Teniente; Fernando Lamelas.

599 CLEMENTE GUTIERRES to Viviana Martin. *San Isidro de los Corrales.* 1784-1793.
    Lands in Alameda. Nerio Antonio Montoya, Alcalde; Fernando de la Concha, Governor; Juan Gabriel de Lago; Fernando de Lamelas.

600 JUAN FRANCISCO MARTIN.
    Will. *San Antonio del Embudo.* Incomplete. Four pages and no signature.

601 FRANCISCO XAVIER DE MIRANDA. *Alburquerque.* No date.
    Asking that Juan Montaño be ordered to give him a deed. Antonio Gurule is mentioned as "*Colindante.*"

602 MARIA MICHAELA MAESE. *Santa Fe.* No date.
Asking that land granted to her deceased husband, Martin Padilla, in the *Partido del Bado,* be confirmed to her.
The land granted was 150 *"caisadas."*

603 PAULIN MONTOYA vs. Miguel Ortiz. *Sitio de la Majada.* 1800.
Trespass, etc. Josef Miguel de la Peña; Fernando Chacon, Governor; José Campo Redondo; Francisco Montoya. *La Majada* Tract.

604 MANUEL MARES.
Will. *Santa Fe.* 1804. Juan de Dios Peña, Alférez; Fernando Chacón, Governor; José Campo Redondo.

605 MIGUEL MIRABAL, of *Las Huertas.* 1808.
Petition relating to inheritance of land under the will of his great grandfather. Land in *Alameda.*

Cleto Miera y Pacheco; Eusebio Rael; Domingo Labadia; José Garcia, Alcalde; José Garcia de la Mora, Alcalde; Ignacio Sanchez Vergara; José Gutierrez; Nicolas Salazar; Manrique, Governor; Juan José Santillanes; Feliz Pino; Alencaster, Governor.

The Alameda Tract was granted to Captain Francisco Montes Vigil January 27, 1710, by Admiral Joseph Chacón, Marqués de la Penuela. Montes Vigil came to New Mexico "among the collection of families made in the City of Our Lady of Zacatecas, my native place, by General Juan Paez Hurtado." Montes Vigil participated in all of the battles of the re-conquest. The boundaries of the tract as described in the decree of royal possession, are, on the north a ruin of an old pueblo, of two that there are, is the more distant one from the Alameda tract; and on the south a small hill, which is the boundary of Luis Garcia; on the east the Rio del Norte, and on the west plains and hills for entrances and exits. Possession was given in the presence of Martin Hurtado, son of the General Juan Paez Hurtado, Luis Garcia and José de Quintana. Hurtado at the time was war chief and alcalde of Alburquerque.

606 JUAN MANUEL MARTIN and his brothers, heirs of Antonio Sisneros, their grandfather, and Pedro Martin, their father.
Agreement with their mother, Maria Manuela Sisneros.

Abiquiú. 1809. Question as to lands. Manuel Garcia, Alcalde. José Miguel Tenorio.

607 MARIA MARQUES DE AYALA. *Pojoaque.* 1811.
Question of title to *Rancho de Cuyamungue,* sold under mortgage, and bought by Juan Rafael Ortiz. Manuel Garcia de la Mora, Alcalde. Manrique, Governor. Tomas de Herrera.

608 JOSE MONTOYA. *Cañon de Jemez.* 1810.
Petition for land. Referred to the Governor with favorable recommendation. Ignacio Sanchez Vergara, Alcalde.

The names of the settlers of the *Cañon de Jemes* are found in this item.

The first settlers of the tract known as the Cañon de San Diego were Francisco and Antonio Garcia, brothers, who were interpreters of the Navajo nation, Miguel Garcia, Joaquin Montoya, Salvador Garcia, José Manuel Garcia, Juan José Gutierres, Juan de Aguilar, Blas Nepomuceno Garcia, Bartolomé Montoya, José Montoya, Tomas Montoya, Juan Domingo Martin, José Gonzales, Salvador Lopez, Antonio Abad Garcia, Miguel Gallegos, Marcos Apodaca, José Miguel Duran, and José Maria Jaramillo, who applied for a quantity of uncultivated land in the Cañon de San Diego, adjoining lands belonging to the Indians of Jemez. Their petition was filed in 1798, and asked for lands from east to west to the middle arroyo called Los Torreones, and from north to south to the Vallecito de la Cueva, which is in front of the water fall and in a transverse line from the middle arroyo to the Rito de la Jara. They also protested that they would not injure the Indians with their persons nor their stock, stating that the few trees which the Indians had set out were planted on lands which did not belong to them.

The grant was made by Don Fernando Chacón, knight of the order of Santiago, lieutenant-colonel of the royal armies, and political and military governor of the province. Possession was given March 14, 1798, in the presence of the natives of the pueblo of Jemez, who had been summoned by the chief justice of that pueblo, Don Antonio de Armenta.

609 MARIA VIVIANA MARTIN. *Alameda.* 1812.
Petition. Asks that her son-in-law, Vincente Montaño, be ordered to return to her the title deeds to lands in *Alameda.* Incomplete. Manrique, Governor. Lorenzo

168   THE SPANISH ARCHIVES OF NEW MEXICO

Gutierrez.   Josef Mariano de la Peña, Alcalde.   No. 599, q. v.

610 JUANA BARBARA MONTANO. *Cochiti.* 1813. Vs. Vicente Montaño, her father.
Complaint that he sold land belonging to herself and her brothers without their consent, to Miguel Hurtado. Finally settled in favor of purchaser, Miguel Geronimo Hurtado, Manrique, Governor. Herrera (Mariano de) *Auditor de Guerra,* Chihuahua. Cleto Miera y Pacheco.

611 ANTONIO XAVIER MADRID.
Will. *Santa Fe.* 1813. Miguel Portillo, Alférez. Josef Francisco Griego; Josef Larrañaga.

612 PEDRO MARTIN. *Abiquiú.* 1806.
Proceedings in the matter of the settlement of his estate. Maria Manuela Sisneros; Joseph Anastacio Hernandez; Manrique, Governor; Manuel Garcia de la Mora, Alcalde; Juan de Terrus Luzero; Pedro Ignacio Gallego.

613 MARCIAL MONTOYA and Pablo Antonio Romero. *Abiquiú.* 1814.
Petition for themselves and sixty others for lands on the *Brazos del Rio de Chama.* Referred to the Governor. Pedro Ignacio Gallego, Alcalde.

614 DIEGO ANTONIO MARTIN. *Santa Cruz de la Cañada.* 1819.
Damages by a ditch. Facundo Melgares, Governor. Juan Francisco Ortiz, Alcalde.

615 MANUEL MARTIN and Pablo Romero. 1820.
Petition for the *Tierra Amarilla* Tract. Facundo Melgares, Governor. José Garcia de la Mora.

616 MARIA NIEVES MIRAVAL.
Grant. 1822. Land in *Galisteo.* Pedro Armendariz, Alcalde. José Maria Baca, Secretary.

617 PABLO MONTOYA vs. Francisco Xavier Mares. 1822-23.
Lands in the *Majada* Tract. Incomplete. Antonio Vizcarra, Governor. José Francisco Baca, Alcalde.

618 PABLO MONTOYA. *Cienega.* 1824.
> Petition to the Territorial Deputation for lands on the *Rio Colorado del Rincon de la Cinta á la Trinchera.* Granted by the Deputation on November 19, 1824. Juan Bautista Vigil, Secretary. Bartolomé Baca, *Jefe Superior Politico.*

619 JOSÉ ANTONIO MARTIN. *Bosque Grande.* 1824.
> Petition relative to lands. No action taken.

620 JOSÉ IGNACIO MADRID and the other heirs of Roque Madrid vs. Matias Ortiz. *Santa Cruz de la Cañada.* 1824.
> Question of lands. No final action. Bartolomé Baca, *Jefe Politico.* Mariano Chaves, Alcalde.

621 JOSÉ ANTONIO MARTIN, alias *"El Renegado,"* vs. José Manuel Sanchez. *Bosque Grande,* Jurisdiction de *San Juan.* 1821-1828.
> Question of lands. Tomas de Herrera, Alcalde; Diego Antonio Lucero, Alcalde; Tomas de Herrera, Alcalde; Manuel Armijo, Governor; Juan de Jesus Martin, Alcalde; Antonio Narbona, Governor; Diego Sisneros, Alcalde; Josef Antonio Martinez; Juan Andrés Archuleta.

622 BERNARDO MARTINEZ. *Los Corrales.* 1828.
> Petition for land near the Sandias. Not granted. Baltazar Baca, Alcalde.
> Baltazar Baca had a grant called the *"Encinol,"* reported No. 104.
> This grant was rejected by the court of private land claims. There was a preliminary survey under the act of 1854, and this conflicted with the Laguna Pueblo Grant. Persons who claimed under the former grant title are now endeavoring to assert title by possession against the Indians of Laguna as to the part which conflicted with the Paguate Purchase.

623 MARIANO MONTOYA, Indian of *Sandia,* in the name of the Pueblo, vs. Eusebio Rael. 1826.
> Title to land.

624 BERNARDO MADRID vs. José Antonio Bustos. *Santa Cruz de la Cañada.* 1826.
> Lands. Apolinario Lopez, Alcalde.

625 JUAN DE JESUS MARTINEZ, Alcalde del *Pueblo de San Lorenzo de Picuriés*. 1829.

In the name of the pueblo protests against cession of lands adjoining the pueblo. Juan Antonio Lobato, *Presidente del Ayuntamiento de Taos*. Santiago Martinez, Secretary.

626 MARIA GETRUDIS MONTOYA.

Will. *Agua Fria*. 1820. José Ignacio Ortiz, Alcalde. J. M. Alarid; José Ortiz.

627 PABLO MONTOYA. *Cieneguilla*. 1831-1832.

This is a very voluminous *expediente* relating to the title of Montoya to this tract. Reported Claim No. 115, *q. v.*

628 JOSÉ VICTORINO MONTES VIGIL. Taos. 1836.

Claim to land at place called Rio Lucero, as heir under the first settlers. The grant was made to his great-grandfather, Pedro Montes Vigil. Albino Perez, Governor; Rafael de Luna, Alcalde; Santiago Martinez, Alcalde; Anttonio J. Orttiz, Alcalde.

On July 5, 1836, José Vitorino Montes Vigil directed a petition to the second alcalde of Taos, stating that he had learned that there was a piece of land on the Lucero river which had belonged to his great-grandfather, Pedro Montes Vigil, as was stated in the grant; that the petitioner was the lawful owner of the land in question, and that he desired that the alcalde should investigate the legality of his claim, and place him in possession of the land.

On July 9, 1836, the alcalde, Santiago Martinez, returned the petition, stating that it should be presented on paper of the third stamp, and should be accompanied by proofs of his heirship, and by other pertinent documents.

On August 4, 1836, the petitioner presented a second petition, on the proper paper, which was followed by a statement by Joaquin Montes Vigil to the effect that he had an equal right in the property, and he joined in the petition made by José Vitorino Montes Vigil.

On August 6, 1836, the alcalde referred the petition to the *ayuntamiento* of Taos, stating that the matter in question was within the jurisdiction of that body.

On August 13, 1836, a petition signed by fourteen persons from the ranchos of the tract of *Los Estiercoles*, from the town of San Fernando, and the *pueblo* of Taos, was presented to the *ayuntamiento* of Taos. This petition was in opposition to the one presented by José Vitorino Montes Vigil. It states that the latter petition was presented by Vitorino Vigil, a citizen of Paso del Norte, by Rafael and Joaquin Vigil, residents of Cieneguilla, and by other persons, not named, who claimed to be descendants of the deceased Pedro Vigil; that these persons wanted to cultivate land along the margins of the Lucero river, where that stream emerged from the mountain; that the cultivation of said lands would result in great injury to the persons already settled in the vicinity, and who for years had depended upon the waters of the Lucero river for the irrigation of their lands.

They ask that the persons claiming the lands in question be required to present proofs of their genealogy, to show the last will of the original grantee, with the institution of heirs, etc. In support of their contention they allege that the claim of the petitioners to land on the Lucero river is combated by the decree of 1813, promulgated by the king of Spain, and still in force in the Mexican Republic, as well as by the laws of prescription, acknowledged and observed throughout the world.

On August 28, 1836, a report was made to the *ayuntamiento* of Taos by a committee of three persons, perhaps members of that body, which report was not favorable to the claim made by the Vigils, and which declared that the people of the *pueblo* of Los Estiercoles and Fernando de Taos were the legal owners of the waters of the Lucero river.

Subsequently, from September 9, 1836, to January 19, 1837, on four occasions, José Vitorino Montes Vigil presented petitions to the jefe politico (governor) of New Mexico, complaining that his petitions to the authorities at Taos had not received the attention to which they were entitled.

There are a number of statements by the *alcalde* of Taos and others in regard to various features of the case.

The question at issue between the parties, so far as is disclosed by this archive, was never passed upon by the jefe politico, who at that time was Albino Perez, who subsequently was murdered (August 10, 1837) by the Indians of Santo Domingo.

629 GUADALUPE MIRANDA.

Report recommending that the spring known as *San Marcos* be granted to him. No signatures.

Guadalupe Miranda was secretary of New Mexico from

April 9, 1839, to October, 1843. After the occupation of the Territory by the Americans in 1846 he declined becoming an American citizen and in 1853 was appointed commissioner-general of Mexico to induce Mexicans in New Mexico to locate and colonize lands south of the Rio Grande. As such he succeeded the Fr. Ramon Ortiz of El Paso. Miranda delivered possession of the lands to the colony at Mesilla. At the time of the making of the grant to the settlers, there were present, among others, Domingo Cubero, José Manuel Sanchez Baca, Cesario Duran, Blas Duran, Francisco Rojas, Valentin Maese, Mauricio Sanchez, Eugenio Moreno, Vincente Lucero, and Martin Trujillo.

On April 24, 1851, the dividing line between New Mexico and Mexico — 32 degrees and 22 minutes north latitude — was fixed as being "the point at which said river (Bravo or Grande del Norte) intersects the southern line of New Mexico," it being understood that the distance from this point from which the river now runs, in the direction of the same parallel is two hundred and nineteen and four-tenths meters, consequently to the east of said point.

There were present on this day, Don Juan José Sanchez, political chief of the Brazos district of the State of Chihuahua, Brevet Captain Abraham Buford, commander of Company H, 1st U. S. Dragoons, and Colonel Charles F. Tappan, aide-de-camp to James S. Calhoun, governor of New Mexico. General Juan Maria Ponce de Leon was also present. Important settlements in this locality at this time were Mesilla, Amoles, Paso del Norte, Senecú, Ysleta, Socorro, and San Elezario. At the time that Miranda acted Mesilla was in the State of Chihuahua, that portion being afterwards acquired by the United States under the Gadsden Purchase. There were about 1,500 people at Mesilla at the time. Don José Joaquin de Herrera was president and Don Mariano Otero, secretary of state of Mexico at the time.

630 TOWN OF MORA. 1842.

Distribution of land. Grant to José Manuel Cordova, *q. v.* File No. 35.

631 MIGUEL MASCARENAS.

Grant. 1844. *Valles de Santa Getrudis de lo de Mora.* Law of April 30, 1842, *q. v.* Arts. 13-15. Tomas Ortiz, Alcalde. Miguel Antonio Lobato.

632 MIGUEL MASCARENAS.

Grant. *Valles de Santa Getrudis de lo de Mora.* Tomas Ortiz, Alcalde. Mauricio Duran.

On the 20th of October, one thousand eight hundred and thirty-five, I, Manuel Antonio Sanchez, constitutional justice of the jurisdiction of San José de Las Trampas, with my attending witnesses, with whom I act by appointment, in compliance with the superior decree of Don Albino Perez, political chief of the Territory, dated the 28th day of September last past, I proceeded to the place called Lo de Mora, within the jurisdiction under my charge, for the purpose of distributing this public land, as is provided in the aforementioned superior decree, and being there, and the settlers interested, amounting to seventy-six citizens, being there also, the lower valley was called *"Valle de Santa Gertrudes"* and the upper one *"Valle de San Antonio,"* and in the name of the Mexican Nation, and of this municipality, the town-site was marked out in both valleys, the one at *Santa Gertrudes* being two hundred varas from north to south, and one hundred and fifty varas from east to west, leaving thirty varas outside for drippage and a common road, and the meadow for the benefit of all, with its entrances and exits free. The site of the town of *San Antonio* contains two thousand varas from north to south, and one hundred and fifty varas from east to west, leaving the meadow for the benefit of all settlers, with the following entrances and exits. On the north the cañon of the *Cumanches;* on the south the *Rio de Las Casas,* and in the direction of the *Cebolla.* Thereupon I proceeded to distribute the land suitable to cultivation, and drawing the line from east to west, on the south side of the valley of *Santa Gertrudes,* there were measured four thousand one hundred varas of land, and on the north, in the direction of *Tulquillo,* there were measured one thousand seven hundred varas of land, which were distributed among the settlers in the order in which they are arranged on the list.

On the subsequent day we proceeded to the valley of *San Antonio,* and being there, we drew the line from the edge of the *Cienega* towards the west, another was measured and distributed according to the list aforementioned; two thousand eight hundred varas of land in the valley; five hundred and sixty varas at the *Lagunita;* and two hundred and fifty varas of land opposite the town, toward the southwest thereof, as will appear by the aforementioned list; the general boundaries of this tract, being for the benefit of the grantees and for common pasturage; on the north, the *Ocaté* river; on the south to where the *Sapello* empties; on the east the *Aguage de la Yegua*, and on the west, the *Estillero*, and as having taken possession thereof quietly and peacefully, and without opposition from any person whatsoever, the grantees, in token of joy, pulled up weeds, threw stones, scattered handsfull of earth, and performed other acts of possession, giving thanks to God and to the Nation.

. . . . .

        MANUEL ANTONIO SANCHEZ
Instrumental: TEODOCIO QUINTANA.
      NESTOR ARMIJO.
Attending witnesses: ALBINO CHACON.
      RAFAEL PAEZ.

The original settlers as appears in this instrument were as follows:

Valle de Santa Gertrudis:

José Tapia, 100 varas; Carmen Arce, 150 varas; Juan Lorenzo Aliso, 200 varas; Juan Antonio Garcia, 150 varas; Carlos Nieto, 200 varas; Mateo Ringinel, 200 varas; Manuel Suhazo, 100 varas; Geronimo Martin, 100 varas; Francisco Sandoval, 100 varas; Francisco Lore, 100 varas; Francisco Conen, 200 varas; José Mestas, 100 varas; Ramon Archuleta, 100 varas; Antonio Aban Trujillo, 100 varas; Juan de Jesus Cruz, 100 varas; Maria Dolores Romero, 200 varas; Faustin Mestas, 100 varas; Maria Dolores Sanches, 200 varas; José Miguel Pacheco, 100 varas; Yldefonzo Pacheco, 100 varas; Manuel Sanches, 100 varas; Juan Trujillo, 200 varas; Felipe Carbajal, 100 varas; José Maria Garcia, 100 varas; Miguel Garcia, 100 varas; Gabriel Lujan, 100 varas; Manuel Arguello, 100 varas; Ygnacio Gonzales, 200 varas; José Guadalupe Ortega, 100 varas, Felipe Arguello, 100 varas; Manel Gregorio Martin, 100 varas; Juan Cristobal Trujillo, 100 varas; north bank looking toward Tulquillo, measured from east to west: Tomas Encarnacion Garcia, 150 varas; Carlos Salazar, 150 varas; Francisco Arguello, 100 varas; Francisco Sena, 100 varas; José Ygnacio Madrid, 100 varas; Miguel Paez, 100 varas; Miguel Mascarenas, 200 varas; Cecilio Montano, 50 varas; Cruz Medina, 100 varas; Bernardo Martin, 100 varas; Miguel Arguello, 150 varas; Ramon Amado, 150 varas; Pedro Aragon, 150 varas; Estevan Valdez, 100 varas.

Valle de San Antonio: "*Banda del Sur medida de Oriente a Poniente:*"

Manuel Sanchez, 100 varas; Juan Ygnacio Sanches, 100 varas; Francisco Sarracino, 100 varas; Albino Chacón, 100 varas; Damacio Chacon, 100 varas; Teodocio Quintana, 100 varas; José Garcia, 100 varas; Rafael Paez, 100 varas; Nepomuceno Gurule, 100 varas; José Vigil, 100 varas; Nestor Armijo, 300 varas; Andres Ornelas, 100 varas; Mateo Montoya, 100 varas; Juan de la Cruz Trujillo, 100 varas; Juan de Jesus Lujan, 100 varas; Francisco Trujillo, 100 varas; Andres Trujillo, 100 varas; Juan Andres Archuleta, 100 varas; Ramon Abreu, 100 varas; Jesus Maria Alarid, 100 varas; Vincente Sanches, 100 varas; Mateo Sandoval, 100 varas; Juan Lopez, 100 varas; Pedro Chacon, 100 varas; Miguel Antonio Mascarenas, 100 varas; Antonio Arguello, 100 varas.

Lagunita de San Antonio, medida de Oriente a Poniente
José Silva, 280 varas; Juan José Vigil, 280 varas.

Frente a la Plaza de San Antonio punto al Serrito que divide a la Lagunita:
Miguel Olguin, 250 varas.

633 FELIPE MONTOYA.
Grant. *Valles de Santa Getrudis de lo de Mora.* 1844. Under law of April 30, 1844. Articles 13-15. Tomas Ortiz, Alcalde; Mauricio Duran; Miguel Antonio Lobato.

634 MARGARITA MARTINEZ vs. Miguel Benavides. *Real de San Francisco del Tuerto.* 1845. Mining suit.
Testimonio. José Baca, Alcalde.

635 ASAMBLEA DEPARTAMENTAL DE NUEVO MEXICO. 1845.
Relating to Grant called *Manuelita*. Felipe Sena. Tomas Ortiz, Secretary.

636 CHAFFIE MARTINET. *Santa Fe.* 1846.
Mining suit. Trinidad Barcelo, Alcalde. Benito Antonio Larragoite; Jorge Ramirez; Antonio Apodaca; José Miguel Romero, Alcalde; Diego Sisneros.

637 JUAN JOSÉ MONTOYA and seven others.
Petition for lands. *Las Vegas.* 1846. Juan de Dios Maese, Alcalde. No final action.

638 XPTOBAL NIETO. *Santa* Fe, 1700.
>Re-validation of his grant. *Testimonio.* Certified by Antonio de Aguilera Isasi, Alcalde.

639 JOSEF MANUEL GILTOMEY to Simon Nieto. *Santa Fe*, 1707.
>Land in *Santa Fe.* Antonio Montoya, Alcalde. Xptobal de Gongora.

640 SEBASTIAN DE VARGAS to Maria de Naba. *Santa Fe*, 1710.
>Land. Diego Arias de Quiros, Alcalde. Xptobal de Gongora.

641 JOSEF FRESQUI and Maria de Herrera, his wife, to Tomas Nuñes. *Santa Cruz de la Cañada.* 1716.
>Land. Juan Garcia de la Rivas, Alcalde. Juan Manuel Chirinos.

642 SIMON NIETO to Juan Garcia de Noriega. *Santa Fe.* 1728.
>Land. Diego Arias de Quiros, Alcalde. Juan Manuel Chiriños.

643 QUESTION OF LANDS. 1752.
>Tomas Velez Cachupin, Governor; Nicolas Ortiz; Tomas de Alvear; Francisco Sisneros.
>Dispute between José Antonio Naranjo and Diego Torres in regard to the amount which the former paid to the latter for a house, which Naranjo on complaint of the Indians of San Juan, had been ordered to give up by Governor Velez Cachupin.
>It seems that the house in question was on lands of the Indians of San Juan; that Torres sold it to Naranjo; that the Indians made some complaint about it, the nature of which does not appear; that Governor Velez ordered Naranjo to get out of the house; that he obeyed the order in the month of March, 1753, and a few months later asked the governor to compel Torres to return to him the fifty pesos he had paid for the house; that Torres made a statement before the governor to the effect that the price was only 10 or 12 pesos; which was paid in 5 or 6 goats; that Naranjo produced two witnesses whose testimony was conflicting; that the governor, in view of the conflicting testimony and the slight importance of the case, or-

dered Torres to return to Naranjo the five or six goats, and he further imposed perpetual silence upon both parties, under penalty of a fine in case either should again bring the matter up.

There is nothing in the document to show the location of the house with respect to the *pueblo* of San Juan.

644 FRANCISCO NIETO to Jacinto Perea. *Santa Fe.* 1765.

One-half of the land in the *Pueblo Quemado* purchased of Andres Montoya, of Cieneguilla. Francisco Guerrero, Alcalde. Antonio Guerrero.

645 SETTLERS of SAN GABRIEL de LAS NUTRIAS. 1771.

Abandonment of the settlement. Don Pedro Fermin de Mendinueta, Governor. Antonio Moreto.

646 FRANCISCO TREBOL NAVARRO.

Will. *Santa Fe.* 1785. José Maldonado. Cleto Miera.

Reference is made to the military chapel *Capilla Castrense* at Santa Fe; also mentions the alférez, Don Alberto Mainez, later a governor of New Mexico; also to Don Pedro Fermin de Mendinueta, former governor of the Province, as residing at *Elizondo, in the Valley of Bastas, Province of Navarre.*

647 NICOLAS ORTIZ NINO LADRON DE GUEBARA. *Santa Fe.* 1742.

Will. Francisco Guerrero, Alcalde. Antonio Ulibarri.

There were many valiant cavaliers accompanying the conquistador, Captain-General Diego de Vargas Zapata Lujan Ponce de Leon, to the kingdom of New Mexico in the year 1693, not the least of whom was Captain Nicolas Ortiz Niño Ladron de Guevara. He was a most adventurous spirit, whom a restless love of enterprise induced to join the expedition under the great Spanish captain.

An ancestor of Don Nicolas Ortiz Niño Ladron de Guevarra had won the favor of the king by capturing from the Moors the city of Guevara, by which exploit he secured from his royal master the addition to his name "Niño Ladron de Guevara."

When the expedition under de Vargas left El Paso, having in view the reconquest of New Mexico, Captain Nicolas Ortiz Niño Ladron de Guevara accompanied it along with his family. His wife was Maria Anna Garcia Coronado; the oldest son bore the same name as the father. This son married Doña Juana Baca, and of the marriage there were three children, Nicolas Ortiz Niño Ladron Guevara, third, Francisco and Toribio Ortiz Niño Ladron de Guevara. The eldest married Doña Gertrudis Paez Hurtado, of which marriage there were two children, Juan Antonio and Antonio José. The last named married Doña Rosa de Bustamante, the daughter of Don Pedro de Bustamante, governor of the Province of New Mexico, of which union there were five children, among them a daughter, Ana Gertrudis Ortiz Niño Ladron de Guevara, who became the wife of Juan Domingo Baca. There were twelve children of this marriage, one of whom, Ana Maria, married Pedro Bautista Pino in the latter part of the eighteenth century.

648 FRANCISCO ORTIZ NINO LADRON DE GUEBARA. *Santa Fe.* 1749.
    Will. Antonio de Ulibarri, Alcalde. Sebastian de Apodaca.

649 BARTOLOMÉ OLGUIN and Others. 1751.
    Petition for lands near the pueblo of the *Picuriés*. Not granted. Tomas Velez Cachupin, governor. Manuel Saenz de Garvisu, Secretary.

650 TOWN OF OJO CALIENTE. Re-settlement. 1753.
    Bernardo de Bustamante y Tagle, Alcalde. Pablo Francisco de Villapando; Blas Martin Serrano.
    Re-settlement of Ojo Caliente.

651 ANTONIO DE ORTEGA to Tomas de Ortega. *Santa Fe.* 1758.
    Land. Francisco Guerrero, Alcalde. Carlos Joseph Perez Mirabal.

652 TORIBIO ORTIZ and MIGUEL DE ALIRE. *Santa Fe.* 1758.
    Petition. *Rancho in La Cienega.* Asking that it be partitioned among the heirs under the will of Miguel de la Vega y Coca. Proceedings, etc. *Testimonio.* Certified by Francisco Guerrero, Alcalde.
    Nicolas Ortiz to Manuel Gallegos. *Santa Fe.* 1758. His share in said rancho in *La Cienega.*

Francisco Guerrero, Alcalde. Manuel Bernardo Garvisu.

653 ANTONIO XIRON to Tomas de Ortega. *Santa Fe.* 1767.

Land. Francisco Guerrero, Alcalde. Nicolas Ortiz.

654 MANUEL OLGUIN. Will.

Inventory and partition of his estate. *Santa Fe.* 1767. Vicente de Sena, Alcalde. Joseph Garcia Jurado; Francisco Lobera; Eugenio Perea.

655 TOWN OF OJO CALIENTE.

Re-settlement. 1768-1769. Manuel Garcia Pareja, Alcalde. Tomas Velez Cachupin, Governor.

The names of many settlers are given in this item.

The site of the ancient pueblos near the Ojo Caliente was re-settled during the rule of Governor Tomas Velez Cachupin. There were fifty-three families and the boundaries of the tract as granted were "from the Cañada de Los Cumanches to the tower (*Torreon*) of José Baca, deceased, with a small difference just below, its boundaries being on the north the Cañada de Los Comanches; on the south a landmark which I ordered to be constructed of stone and mortar with a holy cross of cedar placed in the center, just below the said tower of José Baca; on the east the foot of the hill; and on the west the foot of the other hills on the opposite side of the river. The leaders of this settlement were the sergeant Luis Duran and the district lieutenant, Gregorio Martin.

A *torreon* (tower) was a sort of fortification used for purposes of defense and look-out against the hostile Indians.

656 TOWN OF OJO CALIENTE.

Re-settlement. 1769. Don Pedro Fermin de Mendinueta, Governor. Names of many of the settlers are given.

657 LUCIA ORTEGA vs. Roque Lobato. *Santa Fe.* 1769.

Question of lands. Don Pedro Fermin de Mendinueta, Governor.

658 ANTONIO DE JESUS LUCERO to Francisco Ortega. *Santa Fe*, 1776.

Land. Manuel Garcia Pareja, Alcalde. Simon de Armenta.

180 THE SPANISH ARCHIVES OF NEW MEXICO

659 ANTONIO ORTEGA.
> Will. *Santa Fe.* 1781. José Maldonado, Alférez. Juan de Abrego.

660 FRANCISCO DE ORTEGA.
> Will. *Santa Fe.* 1782. Manuel de la Azuela, Captain. Salvador Tenorio.

661 ANTONIO ORTEGA.
> Will. Inventory and partition of his estate. *Santa Fe.* 1785. José Maldonado, Teniente. Juan Bautista de Anza, Governor. José Miguel Maldonado; José Andres Calles.

662 JOSEFA BUSTAMANTE to Antonio Josef Ortiz. *Santa Fe*, 1784.
> House and land. Juan Bautista de Anza, Governor. Antonio José Ortiz; Francisco Perez Serrano; Bernardo de Miera y Pacheco.

663 BARTOLOMÉ FERNANDEZ to Miguel Ortiz. 1785.
> Land in the *Majada* Tract. José Maldonado, Teniente. José Miguel Maldonado. *La Majada* Claim, q. v.

664 TOWN OF OJO CALIENTE.
> Grant. 1793. Reported Claim No. 77, q. v.

665 CARMEN PEREA, deceased, by her administrator, Manuel Delgado, to José Maria Vivian de Ortega. *Santa Fe*, 1804.
> Land. José Maria Vivian de Ortega to Maria Feliciana Padilla, *Santa Fe*, 1805. Conveyance of the above land.

666 FELICIANA PAULA ORTIZ Y BUSTAMANTE.
> Will. *Santa Fe.* 1815. Matias Ortiz, Alcalde. José Campo Redondo. Cristobal Maria Lariñaga, Secretary.

667 MATIAS ORTIZ. *Pojoaque.* No date.
> Complaint against Tomas Sena, Alcalde.

668 INDIANS OF LAGUNA vs. Joaquin Pino.
> Protest against his occupation of land in the *Rillito* (*Riyito*) Tract. 1815. Joseph Vicente Ortiz, Alcalde. Pedro Maria de Allande, Governor.
> The various grounds on which the protest was based are unimportant in view of the fact that Governor Pedro Maria de Allande, on October 16, 1816, after a hearing at

which the alcalde, twelve Indians from Laguna, and Don Joaquin Pino were present, decided in favor of Pino.

Certain services required, free of charge of the Pueblo Indians are recited in the following statement, which is preserved here on that account.

"Don José Manuel Aragon, chief justice and war captain of these pueblos of Acoma, Laguna, settlement of Ceboletta, and its districts:

"In view of the resignation I have tendered of the office I have held on this frontier for the period of over twenty years, José Alarigua, governor of this Pueblo of San José de la Laguna, and the chiefs thereof, together with their interpreter, Antonio Herrera, appeared before me, asking me to leave them a statement of the government and orders given by the honorable governors of this province, urgently requesting me to see if by this means they could be relieved from the disorders and grievances the pueblo formerly suffered in the changes of justices and ministers, and providing against a recurrence of the same thing in the future; and, in compliance with this just demand, I have executed on this paper this declaratory statement, saying as I do say, that being present at the general visits made to this Pueblo by Governors Don Fernando Chacon, Don Joaquin del Real Alencaster, Don Alberto Maynes, and Don José Manrique, authorizing these Indians to extend their fields beyond the league granted to them by the King as far as they could plant, for the actual support and maintenance of their families. The pueblo being situated in such a locality as not to afford them a sufficient quantity of arable land within the league allowed by the King, and this pueblo having formerly suffered this scarcity of land for cultivation when this province was governed by Don Tomas Velez Cachupin, these Indians purchased the Rancho called *Paguati*, situated to the north and adjoining the site of Cebolleta, distant three leagues from this pueblo. This rancho was formerly granted to Pascual Pajarito, Vicente Pajarito, Antonio Paguati, and Miguel Magnino, and having possessed it for thirty years, they sold it to the Pueblo; and certain citizens having petitioned and asked for permission to settle there they have not been allowed to do so by the Superior Government, as it was a purchase made by the Indians, who held a deed authorized by the former alcalde of this pueblo, Don Antonio Sedillo.

"In regard to the land towards the east, they have been allowed to plant on the rancho known as El Rito, and therefore also the Cañada de Los Gigantes to the Ojo del Chamiso, together with the Rancho commonly called San Juan, for pasture lands for their animals, the frontier being so much exposed that they cannot risk them in any other direction. On the west they have the site known as Cubero, where they have fields under cultivation and an acequia of their own, and they irrigate with the same water that passes through this Pueblo; and in the same westerly direction, distant a mile from said Pueblo, is the rancho called Santa Ana, where they hold lands for cultivation in common, as far as the alcalde is concerned, who is to reside in this pueblo, he is forbidden by superior orders from availing himself of the labor of the Indians for any purpose except by paying them the just value of their labor; neither can he compel them to serve on escorts for private individuals unless required by the government to treat upon subjects connected with the royal service.

"As far as the officiating minister (priest) is concerned, he is placed upon the same terms as the alcalde, without any authority to tax the pueblo or any Indian with services excepting a sexton to ring the bell and the feed of a horse, which is to be furnished by the pueblo in case it should be necessary for him to hear confession.

"This is the method established by the government for the good administration of these Pueblos, and having no private malice to accomplish, and at the request of the Indians of the Pueblo of Laguna, I leave this statement, which I signed on the 25th day of March, 1813.
"MANUEL ARAGON

"Santa Fe, August 28, 1826.
"Approved so far as this government is concerned and legal and formal in its contents. NARBONA."

Colonel Narbona was governor at this time.
On the margin of the above instrument (grant) appear the following notations:

"This document is to remain in the hands of Don Juan Miguel Cacique and at his death in the hands of his two daughters, Catarina and Josefa, who have the same right and interest in the site together with Don Vincente Romero, included in the same interest. [Rubric.]

"The site of Cubero, mentioned in this document, and the water running through it, is the only water these Indians have the use of, as this proceeds from the Ojo del Gallo; therefore if the said spring is settled upon, these poor Indians would perish, as it is the same water which reaches to the pueblo and these Indians are entitled to it, being old settlers in good faith for more than one hundred years. [Rubric.]

"In this year one thousand eight hundred and twenty, Don Ignacio Sanchez Vergara, Protector General of the Indians, of this Province of New Mexico, executed a document alike to the instrument authorized by Don Antonio Sedillo, in the year one thousand seven hundred and sixty-nine; and for not stating three boundaries which said Protector did not mention in his document, the parties mentioned in said document requested me to make a copy thereof, stating the boundaries to which the rancho of Paguati is entitled, which document is of the tenor following:

"For this Pueblo of Jemes, on the first day of June, in the year one thousand eight hundred and twenty, a document authorized by the former alcalde of the pueblo of Laguna was presented to me by Lorenzo and Alonzo, Santiago, Alonzo, segundo, Toribio and Rita, native Indians of said pueblo, requesting me to take charge of the interests they represented in the rancho called Paguati; and having registered it, I find that Don Antonio Sedillo, the said alcalde at that time, took cognizance of a suit brought by Juan Paguati and Pascual Pajarito, both residents of said pueblo, and it was ordered that each one should quietly remain upon his own property, without disturbing the other.

"Such being the case, and as Protector of the Indians for the Royal Audience of Guadalajara, to whom alone it is proper for the Indians to refer matters of a common or private nature, if they are in any way aggrieved, or if they have not a sufficient amount of land with that the law allows them, or that they may have legally acquired, and by virtue of the ancient possession of said lands to which the said natives refer, called the rancho of Paguati, acquired by a legal title, and that the new settlement of Cebolleta, granted by Governor Don Fernando Chacón to certain citizens, and possession given by the alcalde, Don José Manuel Aragon, with the formalities required by the laws of possession and settlement, the boundaries having been marked out.

"The aforesaid rancho and its boundaries in the direction of Cebolleta remained free with its ancient appurtenances as far as the table land of El Gabilan, to the south of La Cuesta, on the west to the Rito del San José, and on the east to the Cañoncito del Cajo.

"The new settlers of Cebolleta were satisfied with their boundaries at the table land of El Gabilan, adjoining the holders in good faith.

"The want of land by these Indians is to be taken into consideration, and that the tract of Paguati is the only one that in a measure aids them with the scant produce in their misery; and although at the commencement they had more land extending as far as El Rito, they were restricted by Don Joaquin Pino to a tract of waste land, he having deprived them of the said land by virtue of a right to it held by his late father, whom he represents, but which land had been abandoned for more than thirty years. Nevertheless, his title was recognized, and they are so much reduced that the only aid they receive is from Paguati, where the principal owners cultivate the soil in common with the pueblo, and those who have no lands to cultivate for their support are in a measure relieved.

"All of which has been well premeditated and considered, and will be shown whenever an effort is made to injure them by depriving them of the ancient possession of Paguati. There is no doubt that, presenting themselves in person or through their protector to the Superior Audience, they will be allowed to remain in peace, in the enjoyment of what is unquestionably theirs.

"In testimony whereof, and in compliance with the duties so repeatedly enjoined upon me by the royal laws of the Recopilacion of the Indies, I executed this document for their protection, as Protector of the Indians, who are so highly recommended to me by the attorney, protector-general of the Indians, and for its due authenticity, I signed on this said day, month and year.

"I signed this as a witness to the truth of the statement made by the Protector.   EUSEBIO ARAGON

"This document is approved, etc.   NARBONA"

Laguna Pueblo Tracts called the Laguna Purchases. Reported No. 30; File No. 68.

This covers five ranches called Paguate, El Rito, Gigante, San Juan and Santa Ana, all near the pueblo of Laguna. The claim was confirmed by Congress, June 21, 1860. It was patented September 22, 1884.

Some Navajos wanted to leave *Encinal, San José, and Cubero*, where they had lands planted, to go to *"Chelli"* to join their companions for fear of the *Cumanches*. They asked the governor (Allande) to give them a paper which would prohibit the Spaniards from taking their lands while they were absent and to notify them at Laguna in the event he heard of the Cumanches coming into the country, so that they would receive word from Laguna in time to make their escape.

669 IGNACIO ORTIZ. *Santa Fe*, 1824.
Petition for lands between the pueblos of *Santo Domingo* and *San Felipe*. Referred to Provincial Deputation. Bartolomé Baca, *Jefe Politico*.

670 JOSÉ IGNACIO ORTIZ. *Santa Fe*. 1824.
Grant. Small piece of land. Possession by Santiago Abreu, Alcalde. Bartolomé Baca, *Jefe Politico*. Ramon Abreu, Secretary.

671 ANDRES ORTEGA. *Alburquerque*.
Petition for lands. 1825. Referred to the Provincial Deputation. Bartolomé Baca, *Jefe Politico*.

672 JUAN RAFAEL ORTIZ. *Santa Fe*.
Petition for land in *Santa Fe*. 1831. Refused by Territorial Deputation. Abreu, Secretary Territorial Deputation. Pablo Montoya, *Ayuntamiento*. Domingo Fernandez, *Ayuntamiento*. Teodosio Quintana, Secretary *pro tem* of *Ayuntamiento*.

673 JUAN RAFAEL ORTIZ. Petition. *Santa Fe*, 1833.
Same as No. 672. No final action. Mateo Sandoval, *Sindico*.

674 JOSÉ FRANCISCO ORTIZ and Ignacio Cano. 1833.
Reported Claim No. 43, *q. v.* Ortiz Mine Grant.
In 1833 about 69,458 acres in Santa Fe county, N. M., were granted to José Francisco Ortiz and Ignacio Cano. This property was known as the Ortiz Mine Grant. It conflicts with the grant known as the Mesita de Juana Lopez, upon which latter are located the coal mines in the vicinity of Madrid. In 1836, Ignacio Cano conveyed to Ortiz all his interest in the grant. Ortiz died in 1848, leaving the property to his widow, Maria Inez Montoya, who, in 1853, conveyed the property to John Greiner. In

1854, August 19, Greiner sold the property to Charles E. Sherman and associates, who in turn disposed of it to the New Mexico Mining Company. This grant was confirmed by Congress in 1861. Upon this property are situate valuable gold mining properties.

675 SANTA FE. AYUNTAMIENTO.

Two pages of the proceedings, 1836. Names of members: Agustin Duran; Felipe Sena; José Maria Alarid; Antonio Maria Ortiz; Gaspar Brito; Antonio Sena; José Francisco Baca y Terrus; Jesus Romero; Domingo Fernandez, Secretary.

676 JUAN OTERO.

Grant. 1845. Reported Claim No. 106, q. v.

677 ANTONIO JOSÉ DE OTERO. 1846. Grant. "*Ojo de la Cabra.*"

Letter of Miguel Altamirano of the *Superior Tribunal de Justicia del Departamento de Chihuahua*. Archive No. 676 and Reported Claim No. 106, q. v.

This claim was rejected by the court of private land claims.

Proceedings in the matter of the Ojo de la Cabra ranch claimed by Antonio José de Otero, of which ranch he claimed he had been unjustly dispossessed. It appears that the matter had reached the superior tribunal of justice of the department of Chihuahua, and that tribunal wrote to the governor of New Mexico inquiring whether the general laws of February 28 and March 2, 1843, in regard to superior tribunals, were in force in his department, and whether in compliance with articles 2 and 25 thereof the tribunal of second instance had been created, or the Assembly (asamblea) in exercise of its constitutional powers had created the tribunal in some other manner which it considered better.

On April 16, 1846, Governor Manuel Armijo wrote to the president of the Assembly, requesting him to lay the matter before that body for its official action.

There is nothing in this archive to show that the Assembly took any action on the matter.

The Ojo de la Cabra is situated within the boundaries of the grant to the pueblo of Isleta, at a distance of about 10 or 11 miles east of the Rio Grande.

A claim covering this tract was filed with the surveyor-general on January 29, 1875, under the Act of July 22, 1854, but the claim was never acted upon by Congress.

After the creation of the U. S. court of private land claims, a petition was filed therein, on March 2, 1893, asking the confirmation of the grant, but it was rejected on November 30, 1896. An appeal was taken to the supreme court of the United States, and that court, on January 18, 1899, dismissed the appeal.

678 SEBASTIAN DE SALAS to Tomas de Herrera. *Santa Fe*, 1703.

Lands in *Santa Cruz*. Antonio de Montoya, Alcalde. Xptobal de Montoya.

TOMAS DE PALOMINO to Thomas de Herrera. *Villa Nueva de Santa Cruz.* 1700.

Land. Roque Madrid, Alcalde. Miguel Ladron de Guebarra.

JUAN DE PAZ BUSTILLOS to Tomas de Herrera. *Santa Fe.*

ANTONIO AGUILERA ISASI, alcalde.

Land in *Santa Cruz*. Confirmation of the three foregoing conveyances by Juan de Ulibarri, Juez Visitador. *Villa Nueva de Santa Cruz*, 1709.

679 SEBASTIAN DE MONDRAGON to Silvestre Pacheco. *Santa Fe.* 1708.

Land. Juan Garcia de la Rivas, Alcalde. Francisco Lorenzo de Casado.

Silvestre Pacheco to Nicolas Ortiz. *Santa Fe*, 1708. The above property. Juan Garcia de la Rivas, Alcalde.

680 MARIA DE PEREA. *Santa Fe.* 1715.

Will. Diego Arias de Quiros, Alcalde.
This refers to the parish church of Santa Fe.

681 DIEGO DE PADILLA. Grant. 1718.

Reported Claim No. 146. *El Tajo* Grant, *q. v.*

This claim was filed in the court of private land claims, confirmed and surveyed for nearly 52,000 acres. It lies east of the Rio Grande and the northern boundary is that of the south boundary of the grant to the Isleta pueblo. It was always supposed that this property belonged to the Indians of Isleta, but it has recently been ascertained that numbers of persons living within its boundaries have rights by purchase from the Indians many years ago. The original grantee was Diego Padilla, whose heirs sold to the Indians of Isleta about the middle of the eighteenth century. It was patented April 9, 1908. See archive 684.

682 JOSEPHA SEDANO to Juan de la Mora Pineda. *Santa Fe*, 1722.
>House and land. Francisco Bueno de Bohorques y Corcuera, Alcalde.
>Refers to the *"Rio Grande de dicha Villa"* and to the *"Rio Chiquito de dha Villa,"* Santa Fe.

683 ANTONIO BERNAL of *La Cañada* to Antonio Pacheco. 1729.
>Land in *Santa Fe*. Miguel Joseph de la Vega, Alcalde.

684 DIEGO DE PADILLA vs. Indians of *Isleta*. 1733.
>Question of pasturage. Gervasio Cruzat y Gongora, Governor. Juan Gonzales Bas, Alcalde.
>Dispute between Diego de Padilla and the Indians of Isleta in regard to the former's flocks trespassing on the planting lands of the latter, and also in regard to the destruction of poles, forming a corral belonging to Padilla by the said Indians. Year 1733.
>The decision, by Governor Cruzat y Gongora, was favorable to the Indians.

685 DIEGO PADILLA. Will.
>Inventory and partition of his estate. *Alburquerque*. 1736. Eurique de Olavide y Michelena, Governor. Pedro Joseph de Leon; Bernardo de Bustamante.

686 JUAN PACHECO vs. ANTONIO MARTIN.
>Question of inheritance of his wife, *Santa Cruz*, 1736. Juan Estevan Garcia de Noriega, Alcalde. Joseph Garcia de Noriega; Juan Felipe Rivera. Gervasio Cruzat y Gongora, Governor.

687 JUAN JOSEPH PACHECO vs. Sebastian Martin.
>Question of right to build on certain land. *Santa Cruz de la Cañada*. Juan Estevan Garcia de Noriega, Alcalde. Tomas Veles Cachupin, Governor. Francisco Valdes y Bustos.

688 NUESTRA SENORA de la LUZ SAN FERNANDO y SAN BLAS.
    Grant on *Rio Puerco* to twelve families of Alburquerque. 1753-1759. The names of these twelve families are given in the grant. See conditions imposed as to pasturage in common. Tomas Veles Cachupin, Governor. Antonio Baca, Alcalde. Antonio Marin del Valle. Phelipe Tafoya, Procurador.

689 JUAN ANTONIO de ARCHULETA to Marcos Pacheco. *Santa Fe*, 1755.
    Land on the other side of the Santa Fe river. Francisco Guerrero, Alcalde.

690 SEBASTIAN MARTIN to Heirs of Juan Pacheco. *Nuestra Señora de la Soledad del Rio Arriba.* 1763.
    House and lot, etc. Carlos Fernandez, Alcalde. Pablo Francisco de Villapando.

691 TOWN OF EL PASO del RIO del NORTE and Town of *San Lorenzo*.
    Question as to right to use timber, etc. 1765. Pedro de la Puente, *Justicia Mayor de El Paso*. Juan Antonio Calderon; Tomas Veles Cachupin, Governor; Lorenzo Antonio Quaron; Carlos Fernandez.

692 SAN FERNANDO del RIO PUERCO. 1767.
    Complaint of raids of Apaches. Don Pedro Fermin de Mendinueta, Governor. Bartolomé Fernandez.

693 JUAN ANTONIO de ARCHULETA to Francisco Padilla. *Santa Fe*, 1767.
    Francisco Guerrero, Alcalde.

694 TOWN OF ATRISCO, 1768.
    Reported Claim No. 145, *q. v.*

695 FRANCISCO PADILLA. *Isleta.* 1768.
    Relating to the sale of one-seventh of the *Diego Padilla* Grant to Clemente Gutierrez. Don Pedro Fermin de Mendinueta, Governor. Francisco Trebol Navarro, Alcalde.

190 THE SPANISH ARCHIVES OF NEW MEXICO

696 JOSEPH PACHECO, *Santa Fe*, 1771, vs. Juan de Alari.

    Question of boundaries. Don Pedro Fermin de Mendinueta, Governor. Juan Antonio Alari.

697 EUGENIO PEREA, *Bernalillo*, vs. Roque Gallego, 1785.

    Question of land. This is a very voluminous document — about 75 pages.

698 JUAN PADILLA.

    Petition and proceedings in the partition of estate of Sebastian Martin and Maria Lujan, deceased. 1772. Pedro Fermin de Mendinueta, Governor. Salvador Garcia de Noriega, Alcalde. Sebastian Martin Grant, reported, *q. v.*

    The Sebastian Martin Land Grant was originally made in 1711, by the governor and captain-general of New Mexico, to Captain Sebastian Martin, one of the most prominent men of his day; the grant embraced the valley of the Rio Grande on both sides of the river from the boundary of the grant to the pueblo of San Juan on the south to the end of La Joya on the north and to the east as far as Las Trampas. The settlements of Plaza del Alcalde, Los Luceros, La Villita, and La Joya, are all within the original grant. The grant contained over 40,000 acres. The Indians of San Juan claim that Captain Sebastian Martin gave them a piece of the land in the valley in payment for services in constructing the first great irrigation ditch on the east side of the Rio Grande.

    The documents in the Sebastian Martin Grant show that, in 1703, the original grantee, in company with others, registered a tract of land in what is now Rio Arriba county, the original petition being lost. It seems that Captain Martin, alone of those originally asking for the tract, cultivated or remained upon any part of it. He petitioned the Marqués de la Penuela, asking that the grant be made to him alone, as the others had forfeited any right which they might otherwise have had. There is no date to the petition, which is as follows:

    "Captain Sebastian Martin, resident of the jurisdiction of the Villa de Santa Cruz, appears before the greatness of your excellency with profound submission, and in the most approved manner the law allows me, and states, that whereas in the year 1703 Antonio Martin and myself registered and denounced for both of us a vacant, uncultivated, and unoccupied tract of land in Rio Arriba [torn] a short distance from the pueblo of San Juan [torn] present year, which many years ago was registered by Joseph Garcia Jurado, Sebastian de Vargas, and Sebastian de Polonia, who never occupied it, for which reason they lost all rights and title to it as His Majesty (whom may God preserve) has ordered and directed in his royal laws, which registration and denouncement was made by us before the Marqués de la Nava de Brazinas, governor and captain-general of this kingdom, who by virtue thereof was pleased to confer the grant upon us in the name of His Majesty, declaring the first parties without any right according to the royal laws, in order that they should never lay any claim to said tract, and therefore royal possession was given to me by the sergeant major, Juan de Ullibari, by virtue of a commission given to him for that purpose by General Don Francisco Cuervo y Valdes, which I took quietly and peaceably without any opposition whatever; and myself, as well as five of my brothers, have resided upon and possessed the same from that time. I have broken up lands, opened a main ditch from the Rio del Norte for irrigating the land, built a house with four rooms, and two strong towers for defense against the enemy in case of an invasion, being on the frontier; and the portion belonging to Antonio Zisneros was bought by me at royal sale from Josefa Lujan, widow of the said Antonio Zisneros, which sale was effected and took place before the Captain Antonio Montoya, who at that time was judge of first instance; and, whereas, all the said instruments, deeds, and titles belonging to said tract and lands have been lost and I have not been able to find them although I have diligently sought for them, and although the laws would protect me in holding them, being in possession in good faith, in case I have not registered them, however justice intervening, your excellency will be pleased in view of what I have stated, to grant to me, in the name of his Majesty, the said tract and arable land, also for raising cattle and horses, with waters, pastures, woodland, and watering places, in the manner in which said royal possession was given to me, and to the boundary signed and measured by Lieutenant-General Juan Paez Hurtado, who ran the line from the said pueblo of San Juan to where he ordered a cross to be placed as proof of a boundary, and the others up the river to the cañon which reaches to El Embudo, and on the east to the river, which leads from Chimayo to the Pueblo of Picuriés, and on the west to a table land on the other side of the Rio del Norte; all of which was given to me in royal possession by the said sergeant-major as above stated.

. . . .

"SEBASTIAN MARTIN"

"In the capital city of this kingdom and province of New Mexico, on the twenty-third day of the month of May, in the year one thousand seven hundred and twelve, the foregoing petition was presented before me, Admiral Don Joseph Chacón Medina Salazar y Villaseñor, gentleman of the Order of Santiago, Marqués de la Penuela, governor and captain-general of the said kingdom, its provinces, and Castellan of its forces and garrisons by His Majesty, the contents whereof having been seen by me, I consider it presented as the law requires; and in consideration of its contents and the reasons upon which he bases his petition, I confer upon him the new grant as he has held, enjoyed, and possessed it, as appears by his petition, and of which I declare him to be the lawful owner, notwithstanding any right which any of said citizens may claim to said lands, who now, or hereafter shall be heard in court or out of court; and I pray and enjoin upon my successors to protect him in the rights he is so justly entitled to, as during the time of my government, I have known him to be the lawful owner thereof, as is well known, declaring, as I do declare, without any legal right, any person who, with evil intentions, shall denounce said land, or who shall enter suit against the petitioner for any private end or any sinister motive, against the said Sebastian Martin; and by virtue thereof I hereby revalidate and confirm this grant, as he requests, in order that he may enjoy the same for himself, his heirs and successors, without injury to his person, declaring, as I do declare, as null and void, any other instrument (with which an adverse claim might be set up against him) the said Sebastian Martin having occupied the land as his Majesty directs, and having remained there at the immediate risk of losing his life by the hands of the common enemy, said tract being situate on the frontier, where he has persisted in remaining up to this day; and I direct my secretary of government and war, Sergeant Cristobal de Gongora, to

Facsimile of Signature of Don Domingo Jironza Petriz de Cruzate, Governor and Captain-General, 1683-6, 1689-91.

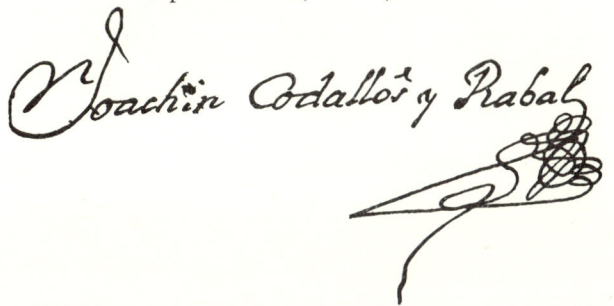

Facsimile of Signature of Don Joaquin Codallos y Rabal, Governor and Captain-General, 1744, 1749.

Facsimile of Signature of General Felix Martinez, Governor and Captain-General, 1715-1717.

Facsimile of Signature of Don Juan Ignacio Flores Mogollon, Governor and Captain-General, 1712-1715.

Facsimile of Signature of Don Pedro Rodriguez Cubero, Governor and Captain-General, 1697-1703.

proceed to said tract of land and leave the said Sebastian Martin in quiet and peaceable possession, assigning him the boundaries he asks for.

. . . .

"EL MARQUÉS DE LA PENUELA
"Before me:
"XPTTOBAL DE GONGORA,
"Secretary of Government and War."

The original of this document is very much worn and in places the writing is almost entirely obliterated.

It bears the seal of the governor's coat of arms. A portion of this land was given to the town of Las Trampas by the original grantee, Captain Martin.

699 JOSE DE LA PENA. *Santo Domingo.* No date.

Petition for lands between the pueblos of *Santo Domingo* and *San Felipe.* No action.

700 HEIRS OF PINO vs. HEIRS of GUTIERRES. *Chihuahua,* 1909.

Letter of Francisco del Valle, of the Real Audiencia.

701 JOSÉ UVALDO PINO.

Petition. 1811. For lands in *"El Sausal."* Valencia county. Manrique, Governor. José Antonio Chaves, Alcalde.

702 JOSÉ ANTONIO PADILLA.

Petition, 1814. *Sevilleta.* Ejectment. Manrique, Governor. José Antonio Chaves, Alcalde.

703 JUAN DE DIOS PENA, Francisco Ortiz and Juan Bautista Aguilar.

Petition for lands on the *Pecos. Santa Fe,* 1814. Manrique Governor. No final action.

"To the lieutenant colonel and acting governor, Juan de Dios Peña, a retired ensign of this royal garrison, for himself and in the name of Don Francisco Ortiz, 2d, and Don Juan de Aguilar, residents of this capital, appear before your excellency with the greatest attention and due respect that by law is conferred, and saith: Sir, that having large families and owners of some stock, and not owning sufficient pasture ground for our animals, nor sufficient tillable land for the very necessary maintenance of ourselves and families, we have recorded a tract of land at this time, wild and unsettled, which is situate in the vicinity of the Pecos Pueblo, to the west, beyond the limits of the Pueblo, as is well known by the protector of the Indians and the alcalde of that jurisdiction, both of whom are aware that our petition is not in prejudice to a third person nor to the Indians of that district, for which reason we present this petition that if your excellency may deem it proper, and being your pleasure, respectfully ask that you will grant the same to us in the name of H. M., (whom may God preserve,) (de S. M. Q. D. G.) obligating ourselves to settle and cultivate the same with the greatest possible exertions, and will keep arms, horses, horse equipage, and all other necessaries for our protection and the defense of the country. Therefore we respectfully ask and request your excellency to be pleased to order to be done as we petition, that in so doing we will receive the mercy and grace we petition for.

"JUAN DE DIOS PEÑA

"Santa Fe, March 28, 1815."

"Santa Fe, March 27, 1815.

"Let the Protector of the Indians report.

"MAYNES"

"In exact compliance to instructions from H. E., and in view of the solicitude of the petitioners of the said tract of land I answer: Sir that the said tract of land is independent of the league and labor of the natives of that pueblo, at regular distance and entirely separated from the possession of said pueblo, nor is it in injury to a third person. Your excellency can, therefore, accede and concede the grant, it being your pleasure to do so, because the wish of the king is that the desert tracts and places shall be settled, permanent settlers having arms, horses, horse equipage, and all other necessaries for their defense as they promise to keep. In which view you may grant their petition, or as you may please to determine which will be best. FELIPE SANDOVAL.

"Santa Fe, March 28, 1815."

"The first alcalde of this capital will make a report of what he knows of himself or by the reports of others relative to their petition. MAYNES"

"Santa Fe, March 28, 1815.

"TO THE GOVERNOR OF THIS PROVINCE:

In view of the protector's report, I would say: Sir, that everything therein set forth is true, and your excellency may determine as you may deem proper, for the petition presented by the parties does not injure any person. MATIAS ORTIZ"

"Santa Fe, March 29, 1815.

"The first alcalde, Don Matias Ortiz, being acquainted with the order of the establishment, will comply with the petition, who will measure the pieces (suertes) of tillable land, limiting the grants solely to the land they plough and plant, with the obligation that they shall enclose the same to prevent the recovery of damages, because the ground must be common and public pastures for the Indians and citizens that have a right therein.

"MAYNES"

"Santa Fe, June 30, 1815.

"In due compliance with the decree of the governor of this province, Don Alberto Maynes, under date of the 29th of March, one thousand eight hundred and fifteen, I, Don Matias Ortiz, first alcalde of the town of Santa Fe and its jurisdiction, proceeded to put in possession Don Juan de Dios Peña, retired ensign, as principal petitioner of this grant, and, at the same time, Don Francisco Ortiz and Don Juan de Aguilar, as companions of said ensign; and, having arrived at the Pueblo of Pecos, I measured the league commencing at the cross of the cemetery up the river and having measured the entire league of the Indians on the residue, I took Juan de Dios by the hand, and at the same time his companions as partners in the said possession, and conducted them over the ground, placing them in legal possession, together with other individuals who entered in the same possession; whereupon I delivered the same to them in the name of his Majesty, (whom may God preserve); they pulled up grass, threw stones, and cried out, saying long live the King of Spain, my lord, Don Fernando Seventh, by the grace of God; I then proceeded to deliver to each individual the pieces (suertes)of land that he was entitled to, giving them to understand that this grant protected them in the possession of the (suertes) land that I had delivered to them, as also to lots for houses and building pens on, and that the other land should remain common pasture ground and watering places; whereupon they received possession without any opposition. I directed them at the same time that their houses should be built close together for their own defense; that they should enclose their fields, in order not to claim damages; and, also, that they must cultivate

their lands for the term of five years, in order to acquire a good title thereto, and be able to sell the same to any other person; and, further, that any person who should abandon the land and not cultivate the same for one year, the land should be taken from him and given to another; and therefore thus I approved, ordered, and signed, with the witness in my presence, with whom I acted in the absence of a royal notary public, there being none of any class in this government: to all of which I hereby certify.
"Matias Ortiz

"Witnesses:
"José Silva
"Ygnacio Ortiz."

704 JOSÉ MARTIN PADILLA. *Santa Fe*, no date.
Inventory of his property, etc. No. 705, *q. v.*

705 JOSÉ MARTIN PADILLA, *Santa Fe*, 1818.
Inventory of his estate. Fernando Delgado, Alférez.

706 JOSÉ MIGUEL PEREZ. *Abiquiú.* 1818.
Registration of a mine.

707 JUAN ESTEVAN PINO vs. José Apodaca. *Santa Fe,* 1819.
Sale of a house in Santa Fe. José Francisco Ortiz, Alcalde. Facundo Melgares, Governor.

708 JUAN ESTEVAN PINO, 1824.
Protest of people of *San Miguel del Bado* against grant to him on their lands. Referred to the Territorial Deputation. Blas Baca, *Sindico Procurador.*

709 MARIA MANUELA PEREA vs. José Garcia de la Mora, Alcalde. Abiquiú. 1824.
Question of lands bought from the Indians of *Abiquiú.* Bartolomé Baca, Governor.

710 PEDRO JOSÉ PEREA.
Grant on the *Pecos,* 1825. Made by the Territorial Deputation. Antonio Chaves. Grant made at same time. Bartolomé Baca, Governor. Juan Bautista Vigil, Secretary.

711 GEORGE R. PRATT, *Santa Fe.* 1833.
Petition to erect a saw-mill and tannery in Santa Fe

cañon. No action taken because of ignorance as to whether the place asked for was on land of Juan José Lujan.

Reported Claim of Santiago Ramirez, *q. v.* This land is below Monument Rock in Santa Fe cañon. Abreu, Governor. Santiago Abreu, President of the Ayuntamiento.

712 DIEGO PADILLA.
Will, *Santa Fe*, 1833. Antonio Sena, Alcalde.

713 JUAN ESTEVAN PINO vs. *Ayuntamiento* de Santa Fe. 1837-36.
Question of land in said city. Albino Perez, Governor. Agustin Duran, Alcalde. Francisco Ortiz y Delgado, Alcalde.

Refers to Don Juan Rafael Ortiz as being *Jefe Politico Interino* on December 10, 1836.

714 NICOLASA PEREA vs. Juan Cristobal Armijo. *Bernalillo.* 1844.
Question of lands. Tomas Ortiz, Alcalde.

715 MARIA ANTONIA PADILLA to Rafael Padilla. *Santa Fe*, 1844.
House and land. Tomas Ortiz, Alcalde.

716 JUAN GRIEGO and JULIANA SAIS, his wife and Francisco Sais to Diego Arias de Quiros, *Santa Fe.* 1718.
House and land. Francisco Joseph Bueno de Bohorques y Corcuera, Alcalde.

Juan Griego received a concession of lands just outside the city of Alburquerque in 1708, as appears from the record of deeds on file in Bernalillo county, New Mexico, as follows:

"Let it be notorious and know all who may see this letter of testimony, that before me, Captain Joseph Ignacio de la Plaza, appeared Juan Griego and exhibited to me a grant title which he has in his favor, made to the Sergeant Cristobal de Gongora, which was somewhat torn but free from any other suspicion, and its contents very complete, and he asked me to make a literal copy of it,

the original to remain in the archives under my charge, and it is as follows:
[On margin] "Petition of Juan Griego.

"The Sergeant Cristoval de Gongora appeared before your excellency, Señor governor and captain-general, asking that all the privileges allowed by law be given me, and I say that being in this kingdom, burdened with a family, and not having a piece of land to cultivate as a settler of this kingdom, for this reason I register a rancho uncultivated and unoccupied, which ruin was owned by Luis de Carabajal, formerly in the town of Alburquerque, between a rancho of Captain Diego Montoya and the house of Captain Baltazar Romero, and on the north it is bounded by lands of the said Captain Montoya, on the south by lands of Francisco Lucero, on the east by [Note: Here follow one or two words which I cannot make out.] mountain range, and on the west by the Rio del Norte, which rancho and agricultural lands are a little less than a quarter of a league in width, in order that I may be able to raise crops and some stock, with entrances and exits, free pastures and watering places, uses and customs, that your excellency will be pleased said . . . grant in the name of His Majesty, directing Captain Martin Hurtado, alcalde mayor of that jurisdiction, to give real possesion to the said Captain Baltazar Romero in my stead, and also granting me the favor to allow me a long term for its settlement, in order that within such term [Note: Here follows three words which I cannot decipher.] said tract, wherefore of your excellency I beg and pray that you will be pleased to admit this petition granting me that which I ask, as it is just, and I swear by God our Lord and the Holy Cross that I do not act in bad faith, and that which is necessary, &c.

"CRISTOVAL GONGORA

[On margin:] "Presentation.

"In the town of Santa Fe, capital of this kingdom and provinces of New Mexico, on the twelfth day of the month of December, of the year one thousand seven hundred and eight, before me, Admiral Don Joseph Chacón Medina Zalasar Villaseñor, Caballero de la Orden de Santiago, Marqués de la Penuela, governor and captain-general of the said kingdom and provinces of New Mexico, castellan of the forces and garrison of His Majesty:
[On margin:] "Decree.

"IT WAS PRESENTED by the person named in it, and

having examined it, I admitted it, with all the privileges allowed by law; and being advised of the justness of his petition I make him the grant of the said tract he asks for, and I make it in the name of His Majesty, in order that, as his own, he may enjoy it for himself and his heirs, without prejudice to any third party who may have a better right, and this decree shall serve as a special title for him; and I order the alcalde mayor of San Felipe de Alburquerque to give royal possession in the form and manner asked by the petitioner and without omitting a single point of that which I order. And in order that it may so appear thus I provided, ordered and signed, with the undersigned secretary of government and war on the said day at supra.

"EL MARQUES DE LA PENUELA

"By Order of the governor and captain-general:

"ALFONSO RAEL DE AGUILAR,

"Secretary of Government and War.

[On margin:] "Royal possession.

"I, Martin Hurtado, alcalde mayor and war captain of the town of San Felipe de Alburquerque, being informed as to the contents of the order as above issued by the Marqués, governor and captain-general of this kingdom of New Mexico, not discovering any better right, proceeded to give possession to the said Captain Baltazar Romero, in the form and manner contained in the petition of the petitioner, the boundaries being those set forth in his petition, this possession being the most sufficient security that he may enjoy them as his own, and I grant it in the name of His Majesty, the pastures, waters, watering places, entrances and exits free, as he asks, and, in order that it may so appear, I signed it, with assisting witnesses, acting by delegated authority (*receptoria*), in the absence of a notary public or royal, of which there is none within two hundred leagues of this kingdom, and it is done on the tenth day of January, one thousand seven hundred and nine, in this town of Alburquerque.

"Before me, Juez receptor, MARTIN HURTADO.

"Assisting witness, FRANCISCO DE LA CANDELARIA.

"Assisting witness, JUAN DE LA MORA PINEDA.

"It agrees with the original, whence I, the Ensign, Joseph Ignacio de la Plaza, directed it to be taken literally from its original, to which I refer. It is certain and true, corrected and compared, and there were present to see it corrected and compared Captain Antonio de

200 THE SPANISH ARCHIVES OF NEW MEXICO

Chaves and Antonio de Luna, residents of this town of Alburquerque, where it is made, on the nineteenth day of the month of May, one thousand seven hundred and twenty-six.

"In testimony of truth I set my hand and rubric.
"Martin Hurtado" [rubric]

717 DOMINGO DE BALDES and ANA MARIA MARQUES, his wife to Diego Arias de Quiros. *Santa Fe*, 1720.

Francisco Joseph Bueno de Bohorques y Corcuera, Alcalde.

718 PEOPLE of PUEBLO QUEMADO.

Petition, 1749. To be permitted to return to said place and cultivate their lands having been driven away on preceding years by Indians. Joachin Codallos y Rabal, Governor.

719 LOS QUELITES.

Grant, 1761. Reported Claim, *q. v.* Francisco Antonio Marin del Valle, Governor. Miguel Lucero, Alcalde. The names of the grantees are fully set out in this grant.

Mentions an attack made on the frontier of "*San Geronimo de los Thaos*" by the Cumanches on August 4, 1760.

720 LOS QUELITES. 1765.

Revocation of Grant to certain parties of the first settlers. Tomas Veles Cachupin, Governor.

721 JUAN MARTIN to Manuel Quintana. *Pojoaque*. 1769.

Land in *Cañada de Santa Cruz*. Antonio Joseph Ortiz, Antonio Joseph Ortiz, Alcalde.

722 ISIDRO MARTIN to Leonicio Quintana. *Pojoaque*. 1769.

Land in *Cañada de Santa Cruz*. Antonio Joseph Ortiz, Alcalde.

723 JOSE QUINTANA vs. Gregorio Garcia. 1775.

Question of sale of rancho in *Santa Cruz*. Don Pedro Fermin de Mendinueta, Governor. Salvador Garcia de Noriega.

THE SPANISH ARCHIVES OF NEW MEXICO 201

724 JUAN SEGURA to Miguel Quintana. *Santa Fe*, 1827.
Land in *Cañada del Tio Leonardo*. *Testimonio*. Domingo Fernandez, Secretario del Cabildo.

725 TEODOSIO QUINTANA.
Report of Committee of Ayuntamiento in regard to giving him permission to build a portal to his house.

726 MARIA DE LOS ANGELES QUINTANA and José Pablo Griego to Gaspar Ortiz. *Santa Fe*. 1844.
Land. Tomas Ortiz, Alcalde.
Mentions the *"Camino Real de Cuma."* For *"Cuma"* see No. 423 (Lucero de Godoy), leaf 3.

727 ANTONIO ORTIZ.
Grant, 1819. Reported Claim No. 42, *q. v.*

728 CLARA RUIZ DE CACERES vs. Pedro Barela de Losada. *San Lorenzo de la Toma del Rio del Norte*. 1682.
Question of lands. Antonio de Otermín, Governor. Juan Lucero de Godoy, Alcalde.
This is the oldest of the archives in the office of the surveyor-general. It bears the signatures, among others of Don Antonio de Otermín, Nicolas Luzero de Godoy, and Simon de Molina. The petition is addressed to the governor, dated July 12, 1682, and is as follows:
"Clara Ruiz de Caceres, widow, a resident of the Provinces of New Mexico and handmaid (*asistenta*) in this military camp of San Lorenzo, appears before Your Excellency in the most ample form of law, waiving no rights guaranteed to me favorable to my cause, and state: That about one year ago the sergeant major, Sebastian de Herrera gave me a hut (rancho) built by him and his son-in-law, Nicolas Luzero, a hut for me to live in and for me as I have lived and taken care of it and fixed it up as my own.
"And now, without my being at my house (*cassa*) came the Adjutant, Pedro Barela de Posada and went into my hut and put all of my household goods outside, throwing them out on the commons, without considering that they might be stolen in my absence.
"For all of which I ask and pray that Your Excellency be pleased to order said Pedro Barela to get out of the said hut and leave it to me as it was given to me by the

said Sebastian de Herrera for me, which necessarily he must declare and Your Excellency will deign to protect me as a poor widow who has no one to even cut a stick with which to build another.

"I swear before God and by this cross that this, my petition, is not made in malice, but in search of justice which I hope to receive from the Catholic breast of Your Excellency.

"Imploring the Royal aid in that which is necesary, etc.
"CLARA RUIZ"

"Presented by the Petitioner on the 12th day of July, in the year 1682 and examined by His Excellency who commands that the *alcalde ordinario*, Juan Lucero de Godoy, shall go to the hut from where the petitioner says she was ejected and leave her in possession as she had been. And if the adjutant, Pedro Barela, should have any charges to make by way of justification, to hear them according to law, that the place may be given to the one entitled to it.

"I have so ordered, decreed and signed.
"ANTONIO DE OTERMIN [rubric]

"Before me the present special secretary of government and war.   LUIS GRANILLO (rubric)
"Special Sec. of Gov. and War."

The writ was served on July 12, 1682, by Juan Lucero de Godoy, *alcalde ordinario*; Pedro Barela de Posada claimed that the hut was his and his brother-in-law's, Nicolas Lucero de Godoy; that Sebastian de Herrera had helped to build it. He agreed to obey the writ pending investigation of his own charges and claims; that he had notified Clara Ruiz to vacate and had sent the notification by José de Arvisu and she had not done so; that he put the goods out under a cottonwood tree and had had them guarded until Clara Ruiz returned; she denied having been notified; and José de Arvisu gave as an excuse that it "had departed from his memory."

This is signed by Juan Lucero de Godoy with his rubric. The signatures of Pedro Barela de Posada, Antonio Lucero de Godoy, and Sebastian Gonzales also appear here. Sebastian de Herrera also made a statement before the *alcalde ordinario*; he denied that the hut was built for her; that the hut had been loaned to her by him; says he is forty-four years of age; this part of the proceeding is signed by Sebastian de Herrera, Pedro Barela de Posada, Simon de Molina, with their rubrics.

Nicolas Lucero de Godoy, 26 years of age, said that he built the hut along with his father-in-law, the sergeant major, Sebastian de Herrera; that the hut was loaned to Clara Ruiz while they went to San Lorenzo to spend Holy Week.

"At the Town of San Lorenzo, of the Dam of the *River Del Norte*, on the 18th day of July, 1682, in the prosecution of this cause, the said *alcalde ordinario* [torn] witnesses read and made notorious the declaration of the sergeant major, Sebastian de Herrera, and of the adjutant, Nicolas Luzero, to Clara Ruiz de Caceres, in her proper person; that if she has any allegations to make or other witnesses to be heard, they will be received and examined.

"She said that having heard and understood them (the declarations) she then and there desired and withdrew from the suit (pleito) and demand she has for the hut and that in supposition that what the said Sebastian de Herrera and Nicolas Luzero state in their declaration is sufficient reason that said Pedro Barela should live in said hut, then what can she say? Inasmuch as they are the owners and the ones who built it, and this she gave as her answer; and I said alcalde signed it with these witnesses and she said that she did not know how to sign.

"JUAN LUZERO DE GODOY [Rubric]
"ANTONIO LUZERO DE GODOY [Rubric]
"MATHIAS LUZERO [Rubric]"

729 DOMINGO MARTIN SERRANO to Sebastian Rodriguez. *Santa Fe*, 1697.
>Land. Diego Arias de Quiros, Alcalde. Joseph de Contreras, Antonio de Aguilera Issasi.

730 *TESTIMONIO* of the above; not signed.

731 JUAN RODELO.
>Will, Santa Fe, 1716. Juan Garcia de las Rivas, Alcalde.

732 JOSE CASTELLANOS to Miguel Garcia de las Rivas. *Santa Fe*, 1701. *El Sitio del Pueblo Viejo de la Cienega.*
>*Testimonio.* Joseph Rodriguez, Alcalde.

733 ALFONZO RAEL DE AGUILAR.
>Grant, 1704. Reported Claim No. 81, *q. v.*

734 PEDRO FELIPE RODRIGUEZ.
   Will, *Santa Fe*, 1784.   José Maldonado, Teniente.

735 JUAN DE MESTAS to Ignacio Roibal. *Santa Fe.* 1705.
   Land on *Cuyamungue* river, adjoining *Rancho Jacona*. Diego Arias de Quiros, Alcalde. Antonio Albares de Castrillon.

   Juan de Mestas Grant, Reported No. 80, was filed in the office of the surveyor-general and was surveyed for an area of more than 1,600 acres, all of which was within the limits of the Pojoaque Grant. The court of private land claims dismissed the claim.

   One of the oldest grants is the one made to Juan de Mestas, being the land mentioned in this archive. The grant was made by Don Pedro Rodriguez Cubero, the successor of General De Vargas; the land originally applied for is described in the petition as "extending from the house erected by Don Jacinto Palaes (Captain) toward the river-side, below the Pueblo of Pojoaque, and to a bluff and hollow formed thereby, which are the boundaries, and on the south side to the hills, and on the north side to the same." Possession was given by the sergeant major, Francisco de Analla Almazan, and the maestre de campo, Roque Madrid. The land extended toward the old pueblo of Jacona.

   Town of Jacona Grant, Reported No. 92, was confirmed by the court of private land claims and under the survey contains 6, 952 acres. Of this there is a conflict with the grant to the pueblo of San Ildefonzo amounting to 902 acres and nearly 2,776 acres of a conflict with the grant to the pueblo of Pojoaque, and more than 1163 acres conflict with the grant to the pueblo of Tesuque. The grant was patented November 15, 1909.

736 DIEGO MARTIN by his attorney, Juan de Dios Martin de Sandobal, to Ursula Ramos. *Villa Nueva de Santa Cruz.* 1710.
   Land. Juan de Uribarri, Alcalde.

737 DIEGO DE VELASCO to Juan de los Rios. *Santa Fe*, 1712.
   Land. Diego Arias de Quiros, Alcalde.

738 JUAN DE APODACA to Lorenzo Rodriguez. *Santa Fe,* 1712.
    Land. Diego Arias de Quiros, Alcalde. Joseph Maria Giltomey.

739 ALPHONZO RAEL DE AGUILAR.
    Grant. Mine. 1713. Juan Ignacio Flores Mogollon, Governor.

740 JUAN ALONZO DE MONDRAGON and Sebastiana Truxillo to Santiago Romero. *Villa Nueva de Santa Cruz.* 1713.
    Land. Juan Garcia de la Ribas, Alcalde.

741 FRANCISCO XAVIER ROMERO. Grant. 1716.
    Land in the *Cañada de Santa Cruz.* Re-validated by Phelix Martinez, Governor.

742 ANDRÉS DE LA PAZ and Francisca Antonia Guijosa to Santiago Romero.
    House and lands in *Cañada de Santa Cruz.* Francisco Joseph Bueno de Bohorques y Corcuera, Alcalde. Joseph Manuel Giltomey.
    Shows that *Santa Cruz de la Cañada* was on the south side of the river in 1720.

743 ANTONIO DE ABEYTIA to Francisco Rendon. *Santa Fe,* 1721.
    House and land. Francisco Joseph Bueno de Bohorquez y Corcuera, Alcalde.

744 DIEGO DURAN to ALONZO RAEL DE AGUILAR. *Santa Fe,* 1721.
    House and land. Bohorquez, Alcalde.

745 IGNACIO DE ROIBAL vs. Juan de Mestas. *Villa Nueva de Santa Cruz.* 1721.
    Question of boundaries. Don Juan Domingo de Bustamante, Governor.

746 FRANCISCO SAIS to Alonzo Rael de Aguilar. *Santa Fe,* 1721.
    Land. Diego Arias de Quiros, Alcalde. Miguel de Sandoval Martinez.

747 MARIA GUTIERRES to Francisco Rendon. *Santa Fe*, 1728.
 Land. Diego Arias de Quiros.

748 FRANCISCO JOSEPH CASADOS and Maria de Archiveque, his wife, to José Riaño. *Santa Fe*, 1729.
 House and land. Diego Arias de Quiros, Alcalde. Dimas Jiron.

749 MANUEL CASILLAS to Juan Phelipe de Ribera. *Santa Fe*, 1731.
 House and land.

750 BALTAZAR ROMERO to Juan José Romero. 1752.
 Reported Claim No. 109, *q. v.* Francisca Antonia Gijosa.

751 CRISTOVAL XARAMILLO. *Alburquerque*, 1736, to Matias Romero.
 Land. Geronimo Xaramillo, Alcalde. Isidro Sanches.

752 DIEGO DE TORRES and Maria Martin, his wife, of *Chama*, to Nicolas Romero. *Villa Nueva de Santa Cruz*. 1736.
 Juan Estevan Garcia de Noriega, Alcalde.

753 FRANCISCO MARTIN and Casilda de Contreras, his wife, of *Embudo*, to Juana Maria Romero. *Villa Nueva de Santa Cruz*, 1736.
 Land in rancho called "*Chico Payemo.*" Juan Estevan Garcia de Noriega, Alcalde.

754 DIMAS GIRON DE TEGEDA and Ignacio Roibal vs. Juan Rodriguez. 1736.
 Question of lands in *Rio Arriba*. Gervasio Cruzat y Gongora, Governor.

755 MARIA DE SAN JOSEPH. *San Geronimo de Taos*. 1735.
 Division of her property. Gervasio Cruzat y Gongora, Governor. Francisco Guerrero, Alcalde.

756 JUAN RODRIGUEZ.
 Will, inventory, and partition of his estate. *Santa Fe*,

THE SPANISH ARCHIVES OF NEW MEXICO 207

1738. Henrique de Olavide y Michelena, Governor. Antonio Montoya, Alcalde.

757 MARCIAL GARCIA of *Alburquerque* to Melchor Rodriguez. *Santa Fe.* 1738.
Land in Santa Fe. Antonio Montoya, Alcalde.

758 JOSEPH DE RIANO vs. Juan Lucero. *Santa Fe*, 1732.
Question of entrances and exits in *Santa Fe*. Gervasio Cruzat y Gongora, Governor. Juan Lucero de Godoy.

On page 2 or leaf 16 of this manuscript it appears that at one time there was a *church* on the *north side of the plaza,* either immediately adjoining or within a very few varas of the Palace of the Governors. This is the church referred to in archives No. 8 and No. 169, and *it was in this church in all probability that the body of Don Diego de Vargas was interred.* See his will.

759 DIEGO ROMERO.
Will, *Taos*, 1742. Francisco Guerrero, Alcalde. Reported Claim No. 158, *q. v.* Cristobal de la Serna, of *Los Ranchos de Taos.*

760 ANDRES ROMERO, Francisco Romero, Antonio de Atencio, Antonio Duran de Armijo.
Petition for partition of lands of the estate of Diego Romero. *San Geronimo de Taos*, 1743. Rancho called "*Rio de Las Trampas.*" Francisco Guerrero, Alcalde. Reported Claim No. 158, *q. v.* Archive No. 759

761 FRANCISCO MAGRINAN. *Santa Fe*, 1744.
Registration of a mine. Situate three leagues from the pueblo of *Picuriés*. Joachin Codallos y Rabal, Governor. Joseph de Terrus; Francisco de Roa y Carrillo; Joseph Romo de Vera.

762 JOSÉ RIANO. *Santa Fe*, 1744.
Proceedings in the settlement of his estate. Joachin Codallos y Rabal, Governor; Antonio Aramburu; Antonio Hulibarri, Alcalde.

763 FRANCISCO ORTIZ. *Santa Fe*, 1744.
Registration of a mine near the pueblo of the *Picuriés*. Donation of the same to Francisco Roa y Carillo. Joachin Codallos y Rabal, Governor.

764 FRANCISCO GUERRERO. *Santa Fe*, 1744.
   Registration of a mine near the pueblo of the *Picuriés*. Donation of the same to Francisco Roa y Carillo. Codallos y Rabal, Governor.

765 ALFONZO RAEL DE AGUILAR. Will. *Santa Fe*, 1745.
   Antonio Ulibarri, Alcalde.
   Alfonzo Rael de Aguilar or Pueblo of Cuyamungue Grant. Reported No. 81. This grant was approved by the surveyor-general for about 6 acres, all of the land being within the limits of the Pueblo of Pojoaque Grant. The court of private land claims rejected the grant. This is not the Bernardo de Sena Grant which was confirmed by the court of private land claims.

766 MANUEL MONTOYA and Pedro de Holiba to Juan de Dios Romero. *San Francisco Xavier del Pueblo Quemado, Partido de Chimayo*. 1750.
   Land. Juan Joseph Sandoval, Alcalde.

767 SEBASTIAN MARTIN to Manuel Ramos Barela. *San Xavier del Pueblo Quemado*. Partido de Chimayo, 1750.
   Land. Juan Joseph Sandoval, Alcalde.

768 MANUEL RAMOS.
   Will, *Pueblo Quemado*, 1750. Juan Joseph Sandoval, Alcalde.

769 HEIRS of ALPHONSO RAEL DE AGUILAR, *Santa Fe*, 1750.
   Petition for possession of Grant made to him. Petition refused. Tomas Veles Cachupin, Governor. Juan Antonio Gonzales del Peral. Joseph de Bustamante de Tagle.

770 JOSEPH RIANO, *Santa Fe*, 1753, to Nicolas Ortiz.
   Land.

771 JUAN DE DIOS ROMERO.
   Grant. Nicolas Romero, Julian Romero, Miguel Despinosa, Ventura Despinosa, Xavier Romero, Cristobal Martin, Bernardo Romero, Salvador Espinosa, Tadeo Es-

pinosa, Domingo Romero, Francisco Vernal, Joseph Manuel Gonzales, Juan Luis Romero.

Grant made by Tomas Veles Cachupin, Governor. Possession given by Juan Joseph Lobato, Alcalde, 1754. One hundred and fifty varas were given to each settler and one league of *"egido"* to them all in addition to house and lot and garden in the town. The boundaries of the *"egido"* are: East: *la toma de la acequia de el rio del Pueblo Quemado*; west: *el camino real que para Picuriés*; north: *las corrientes del rio de las Truchas*; south: *el alto inmediato al referido Rio Pueblo Quemado*. Name of the town; Nuestra Señora del Rosario San Fernando y Santiago.

772 PEDRO TAFOYA to Salvador Matias de Rivera. 1755. *Santa Fe.*

House and lot. Francisco Guerrero, Alcalde.

773 JUAN JOSEPH MORENO. Grant. 1754.

Land in *Santa Cruz*. Made by Joachin Codallos y Rabal, Governor. Possession given by Manuel Sanz de Garvisu, Alcalde.

JUAN JOSEPH MORENO and Juana, his wife, to Santiago Roibal. Vicario y Juez Eclesiastico.

Donation, Santa Fe, 1755. The land included in the above grant. Francisco Antonio Marin del Valle, Governor. Juan Francisco de Arroniz; Antonio Aramburu; Manuel Sanz de Garvisu; Phelipe Jacobo de Vuanue.

774 MANUELA RAEL DE AGUILAR.

Will, *San Antonio*, 1758. Also proceedings in the partition of her estate. Francisco Antonio Marin del Valle, Governor.

775 GREGORIO CRESPIN to Antonio Rivera. *Santa Fe,* 1762.

House and land. Manuel Gallego, Alcalde.

776 JUANA ROMERO.

Will, *Cieneguilla*, 1762. Manuel Gallego, Alcalde.

777 BLAS LOVATO to Tomas Roibal. *Santa Fe.* 1764.

House and lot. Francisco Guerrero, Alcalde.

778 FRANCISCO XAVIER ROMERO, son of Diego Romero.
> Question of boundaries with Andrés Romero. Private Land Claim No. 158, *q. v. Cristobal de la Serna* Grant.

779 FRANCISCO XAVIER RODRIGUEZ.
> Will, 1764. *Santa Fe.* Tomas Madrid, teniente.

780 SAN GAVRIEL DE LAS NUTRIAS.
> Grant, 1765. On Rio Grande near *Belen*. Made by Tomas Veles Cachupin, Governor. Originally to 30 families, the names of which are given in the grant No. 645 and 781, *q. v.*

781 FRANCISCO ROMERO, alias "*Talache Coyote.*" Intestate. *Taos.* 1765.
> Inventory of his estate. Tomas Veles Cachupin, Governor. Reported Claim No. 158, *q. v.* Grant to Cristobal de la Serna.

782 JOSEPH MIGUEL DE LA PENA to Nicolas Rael de Aguilar. *Santa Fe.* 1765.
> House and land. Francisco Guerrero, Alcalde.

783 MARIA ROMERO. *Embudo.* 1766. vs. Maria Antonia Villapando.
> Question of land. Felipe Tafoya, *Procurador*; Tomas Veles Cachupin, Governor.

784 TORIBIO DE ORTIZ to Manuel Rodriguez. *Santa Fe.* 1766.
> House and land. Francisco Guerrero, Alcalde. Juan Francisco Niño Ladron de Guebara, Francisco Estevan Tafoya.

785 JUAN DE LEDESMA to Vicente Rodriguez. *Santa Fe.* 1767.
> House and land. Francisco Guerrero, Alcalde, Francisco Xavier Fragoso.

786 MARIA ROSALIA ROMERO vs. Pablo Salazar. 1768.
> Question of boundaries of contiguous ranches in *Sandia*. Pedro Fermin de Mindinueta, Governor. Domingo de Luna.

THE SPANISH ARCHIVES OF NEW MEXICO 211

787 JUAN ANTONIO RODRIGUEZ to Isidro Rodriguez. *Santa Fe*, 1768.
    House and lot. Phelipe Tafoya, Alcalde. Lucas Moya, Antonio de Armenta, Joseph Garcia de la Mora.

788 JOSEPH MIGUEL DE RIVERA. *Santa Fe*, 1769.
    Phelipe Tafoya, Alcalde. Joachin Lain.

789 MARIA MESTAS to Juan Bautista Romero. 1769.
    Land in *Cuyamungue*. Antonio Josef Ortiz, Alcalde. Manuel de Arteaga.

790 JUANA ROIBAL.
    Will, *Santa Fe*, 1770. Phelipe Tafoya, Alcalde. Antonio Joseph Garcia de la Mora.

791 SAN GABRIEL DE LAS NUTRIAS.
    Grant, 1771. Commission to settle to sixteen families. Pedro Fermin de Mendinueta, Governor; Joseph Garcia de Noriega, Alcalde; Antonio Duran; Joseph Gonzales Serna. No. 645 and 780, *q. v.*

792 MIGUEL ROMERO. Will.
    Inventory and partition of his estate. *Cochiti*, 1771. Nerio Antonio Montoya, Alcalde; Pedro Antonio Trujillo; Manuel Garcia Pareja, Alcalde; Andrés Montoya; Joseph Miguel de la Peña; Antonio Moreto.

793 MARIA MANUELA OLGUIN vs. Maria Estela Palomino Rendon. 1770. *Santa Fe*.
    Question of inheritance of the two children of plaintiff, grandsons of Joseph Miguel Tafoya, deceased, who is the husband of defendant. Pedro Fermin de Mendinueta, Governor. Santiago Roibal, Juez Eclesiastico, Salvador Ribera, Joseph Miguel de la Peña.

794 JUAN ANTONIO ARCHULETA to Vicente Rodriguez, *Santa Fe*, 1771.
    Land. Manuel Garcia Pareja, Alcalde. Antonio de Armenta, Antonio Joseph de la Mora.

795 TORIBIO ORTIZ to Manuel Rodriguez. *Santa Fe*, 1772.
    Land. Manuel Garcia Pareja, Alcalde. Joseph de Armenta.

796 SALVADOR DE ARCHULETA to Vicente Rodriguez. *Santa Fe*, 1772.
    Land. Manuel Garcia Pareja, Alcalde. Simon de Armenta.

797 MARCOS RODRIGUEZ.
    Will, *Santa Fe*, 1772. Manuel Garcia Pareja, Antonio de Armenta.

798 JUAN ANTONIO GURULE to Domingo Romero. 1775.
    Land in the *Cieneguilla* which he inherited from his wife, Maria Montoya. Manuel Garcia Pareja, Alcalde. Joseph de Armenta. Reported Claim—The *Cieneguilla* Tract, q. v.

    Domingo Romero was the grantee of the *Mesita de Juana Lopez* along with Miguel Ortiz and Manuel Ortiz, his half brothers—the grant was made by Governor Juan Bautista de Anza, 1782. Madrid coal mines are on this property.

799 MIGUEL ROMERO. *Cañada de Cochiti.* 1775.
    Inventory and partition of his estate. Pedro Fermin de Mendinueta, Governor. Juan Antonio Lujan, Tomas de Sena, Miguel Ortiz, Domingo Labadia.

800 MANUELA ROIBAL.
    Will, *Santa Fe*, 1778. Joseph Miguel de la Peña, Antonio Serrano.

801 GRANT OF LAND on *Rio Colorado* to 50 Families. 1842.
    Correspondence on this subject between J. Andrés Archuleta, prefect of the first district, and Guadalupe Miranda, *secretario de Gobierno*. Question as to the right of the prefect to grant lands for agricultural purposes. Reported Claim No. 93.

    In the year 1836, the ayuntamiento of Taos made this grant to Antonio Elias Armenta, José Victor Sanches and José Manuel Sanchez. Don Antonio José Ortiz, Don Santiago Martinez and Juan Antonio Lobato were members of the ayuntamiento as was also Dr. David Waldo, an American citizen. This property is known as the Canyon del Rio Colorado; the grant was made under powers given to alcaldes and ayuntamientos known as the "Siete Leyes;" according to Don Donanciano Vigil this law was repealed in 1838.

In 1829, being a sergeant of the Santa Fe Company, Vigil accompanied a body of 200 soldiers on a campaign against the Utes and was at the little town of Rio Colorado which at that time had about fifty families. The houses were all equipped with "loop-holed" battlements for the purpose of safety in fighting off Indians. In 1845 Captain Pablo Dominguez was sent from Santa Fe into this part of the country on a campaign against the Cheyenne (Panana, Dominguez calls them) Indians who had been raiding in that country killing shepherds.

802 VICENTE ROIBAL and MARCELINO ORTIZ.
Archive No. 398, q. v.

803 MARIA LUISA RIBERA.
Will. *Santa Fe,* 1823. Manuel Baca, Sargento.

804 JOSE GUADALUPE ROMERO and IGNACIO BACA.
Petition, *Santa Fe,* 1824.
Asks for land. No action taken.

805 PABLO ROMERO and others.
Petition. 1824. Land on the Chama river. Referred by Truxillo, president of the jurisdiction of *Abiquiú,* to Bartolomé Baca, jefe politico.

806 MIGUEL RIVERA. No. 807, q. v.

807 MIGUEL RIVERA and six others.
Grant. Land on the *Pecos.* Made by *Diputacion Provincial* on March 3, 1825. Boundaries: East: The *Arroyo que baja de la sierra y pija al rio; y por abajo la bareda que baja del Tecolote y Casita que le llaman de la Guadalupe; por el oriente queda tambien la sierra, y al poniente el citado rio.*"

808 MIGUEL RIVERA vs. Diego Padilla. *Santa Fe,* 1825.
Petition to *Diputacion Territorial.* No action taken. Land in *San Miguel.*

809 MANUEL RIVERA.
Petition for land in the *Arroyo Hondo. Santa Fe.* No final action taken. 1827.

Quintana, Secretary of the Territorial Deputation. José Francisco Baca, Governor. Juan José Lujan, Sindico Procurador. Vincente Baca, of the Ayuntamiento. Domingo Fernandez, Secretary of the Ayuntamiento.

Domingo Fernandez, who appears in this archive, in his testimony before the surveyor-general of New Mexico, says that he was the collector of rents and tithes of the religious society known as "Nuestra Señora de la Luz." It has been claimed that the society, known as the "Penitentes," had its origin in New Mexico with that of Nuestra Señora de la Luz; this is not correct. The last named society became the owner by purchase of what is known as the "Lamy Grant" or rancho. Domingo Fernandez gives us the names of the vicarios of the Catholic church in New Mexico from the time of the establishment of Mexican sovereignty down to the administration of Archbishop Juan B. Lamy; they were, prior to 1820. Rt. Rev. Francisco Ygnacio de Madariaga. The "chief brother" of the Society of Nuestra Señora de la Luz at that time was Don Fernando Chacón. Rt. Rev. Juan Tomas Terrazas succeeded Madariaga, and he in turn was succeeded by Rt. Rev. Juan Felipe Ortiz. The society applied to Governor Facundo Melgares for an order upon all "persons indebted to such society" to pay forthwith. This petition was referred to the constitutional justice of Santa Fe, Don Juan Estevan Pino, who compelled Fernandez to give a list of all those who were so indebted; this was done, and it appeared that Carlos de Herrera had, in his lifetime, 500 sheep belonging to the "society," which he had lost, and in payment of the debt he left by will a farm called "El Cañon." Fernandez stated that this farm had been secured by Herrera from Diego Antonio Baca, who had acquired it from the government in exchange for a house and lot in Santa Fe, which was used for building a barracks for the soldiers.

Domingo Fernandez was born in the City of Santa Fe in 1786. He was a member of the ayuntamiento of Santa Fe for a number of years; was chief alcalde, and under the government of the United States during the Military Occupation period, was circuit attorney of the first district.

810 JOSÉ RODRIGUEZ. *Santa Fe*, 1827. *Juicio de Apeo*.
Rodriguez lost his title deeds and asked the court to es-

THE SPANISH ARCHIVES OF NEW MEXICO 215

tablish them by reference to the titles of his *colindantes,* which was done.

811 RAFAEL FERNANDEZ and Miguel Gonzales.
Petition for lands. 1829. Report of committee on memorial of Mariano Rodriguez, protesting against granting said lands. José D. Fernandez *et al.,* File 71, *q. v.*

812 REPORT of Committee appointed by the Territorial Deputation to give opinion in the matter of the refusal of the Deputation to grant lands to José Guadalupe Romero and Manuel Bustamante, and later to grant the same to other persons.
On the question as to the power of the Deputation to grant the lands the Committee says: *"no queda duda de que estubo en las atribuciones de la Exma. Diputacion, á donar el precitado terreno á las que actualmente lo poseen."*

813 DOLORES JALLONO, Ignacio Ladron de Guevara, and Marcelino Abreu to Antonio Roubidoux. *Santa Fe.* 1834.
Mine in the *Cerro del Oro.* Santiago Abreu, Alcalde.

814 JOSE DOLORES ROMERO vs. Manuel Romero, *Santa Fe.* 1844.
In the matter of a house sold without the consent of the plaintiff and his brothers and sisters by his mother, etc. José Francisco Baca y Terrus, Alcalde.

815 THIS ARCHIVE contains three papers which are apparently rough copies of documents in as many different suits. They are not signed and bear the date of 1846. Reference is made in them to the *Las Huertas Grant.* Reference is also made to Jorge Ramirez and to José Maria Mier.

816 CORPORATION of the City of *Santa Fe.* 1692.
Testimonio of a Petition asking for extension of lands. Incomplete.
Further on is given the opinion of the supreme court of the United States in the *"Santa Fe Grant"* case. When

this claim of the City of Santa Fe was heard in the court of private land claims, Associate Justice Murray dissented, his judgment as to the law afterward becoming the law of the court in similar cases. For historical reasons the dissenting opinion is given in full.

"The city of Santa Fe, claiming, as the successor of the ancient town formerly known as *La Villa Real de San Francisco de Santa Fe*, filed its petition in this court, asking for a confirmation to it of four square leagues of land in trust for the use and benefit of all the inhabitants and occupants thereof. This cause was heard, together with a number of others, in which the petitioners pray for a confirmation of Spanish grants to them for land within the four square leagues claimed by the city. It was not claimed that a grant was, in fact, made to the pueblo for any quantity of land, or that four square leagues, or any other quantity, was ever surveyed or set apart to it; but counsel insists that on the settlement of the pueblo the title to four square leagues passed to it by operation of law and that all subsequent grants made by authority of the sovereign to private parties within the four leagues are null and void, and a majority of my brother judges so hold.

"The rights of the petitioner must be determined by the law in force at the date of the supposed grant. The *cédula* of King Phillip II, issued in the year 1511, provided for the settlement of new towns, or pueblos, but there is no mention of four leagues or any other specific quantity of land to be granted. The quantity to be granted was left entirely to the discretion of the governor or viceroy. (*Hall's Mexican Law*, pp. 17 and 18.) In the case of *Juan Sandoval et al. vs. The United States*, decided at the present term of this court, the grant for the purpose of establishing a pueblo was made by the governor to fifty-one persons, and the land granted was about 315,000 acres.

"Now, if this law was in force when the ancient pueblo of Santa Fe was settled, the court might presume that a corporation existed, but I can not see how it would be possible to determine the quantity of land (if any) that such corporation would be entitled to.

"It is alleged in the petition that the 'pueblo was in existence prior to 1680, and that prior to that date said town or villa contained a population exceeding thirty-five families in number, and that there was not any city or village of Spaniards situated within five leagues of said town or *villa.*' From the foregoing statements I infer that the organization of the ancient pueblo is claimed under the provisions of the law of Spain in relation to the settlement of new towns and pueblos by contractors, who might undertake to settle not less than thirty families. This law provides that if the contractor complied with the law in such cases that there shall be granted to him four square leagues of land, etc. The land is granted to the contractor, and not to the town or pueblo. A town might be established by a contractor with ten families, but in that event only one-third of four square leagues was to be granted.

"The lands where thirty families were settled were divided as follows: 'The tract or territory granted by agreement to the founder of a settlement shall be distributed in the following manner. They shall, in the first place, lay out what shall be necessary for the site of the town and sufficient liberties (*exidas*) and abundant pasture for the cattle to be owned by the inhabitants, and as much besides for that which shall belong to the town (*propios*). The balance of the tract shall be divided into four parts, one to be selected by the person obligated to form the settlement, and the remaining three parts to be divided in equal portions among the settlers. These lots shall be distributed among the settlers by lots, beginning with those adjoining the main square, and the remainder shall be reserved to us, to give as rewards to new settlers or otherwise, according to our will, and we command that a plan of the settlement be made out.' (See *White's Recop.,* 2 vol., p. 46.)

"The law in relation to the settlement of pueblos by contractors, and the allotment of lands among the settlers and the towns is in *2d White,* from page 44 to 47. There is no evidence in this cause tending to show that any allotments of land were ever made among the settlers by the town council or any authority, or that the town was settled by ten or thirty families, or by the Government.

"Chief Justice Reed, speaking for a majority of the court in this cause, said: 'Pueblos or towns were established either by direct action of the Government or by promoters or contractors who undertook to settle not less than thirty families. When the establishment was made directly by the Government no express grant of land was made, but the appropriation of a quantity sufficient for the purpose of the towns was by general custom or by operation of general laws. The city of Santa Fe appears to have been established in that manner.'

"The law of Spain in force in relation to the settlement of new towns and pueblos by the Government in New Spain prior to 1789 left the question of the quantity of land to be granted wholly in the discretion of the governor or viceroy.

"Nothing whatever is to be found in the law in regard to any town or pueblo so established being entitled to four square leagues or any other quantity of land by operation of law. (*White's Recop.*, vol. 2. pp. 47, 48, 49, 50, and 51.) So if the ancient pueblo of Santa Fe was established by the Government as early as 1693, as stated in the opinion of the court, I do not see on what ground the court could presume a grant to it by operation of law to any specific quantity of land. The authorities referred to by the court as sustaining the position assumed by it in relation to towns and pueblos being entitled to four square leagues of land when recognized by the Government have no sort of application to towns and pueblos established by the Government prior to 1789.

"The Republic of Mexico adopted the laws of Spain in relation to towns and pueblos, and the rights of towns and pueblos established by Mexico have been adjudicated by the supreme court of the United States in a number of cases growing out of the act of March 3, 1851, for the settlement of private land claims in California. In the case of *Brownsville vs. Cavazos* (100 U. S., p. 138), Mr. Justice Field said: 'Previous to the revolution which separated Texas from the Republic of Mexico, Brownsville constituted a portion of Matamoras, which was recognized as a town in 1826 by a decree of the congress of Tamaulipas, one of the states of Mexico. By the laws of Mexico in force at that time, pueblos or towns, when recognized as such by public authorities, became entitled for their use and benefit, and the use and benefit of their inhabitants, to certain lands embracing the site of such pueblos or towns and adjoining territory to the extent of four square leagues. This right was held by the cities and towns of Spain for a long period before her conquests in America, and was recognized in her laws and ordinances for the

THE SPANISH ARCHIVES OF NEW MEXICO 219

government of her colonies here.' (*Laws of the Indies, White's Recop.*, vol. 2, pp. 44; *Townsend vs. Greely*, 5 Wall., p. 326; *Gresar vs McDowell*, 6 Wall., p. 363.)

"The law referred to by the learned judge, on page 44 of *White's Recop.*, provides for the settlement of pueblos and towns by contractors, with not less than thirty heads of families, hereinbefore referred to, and does not apply to pueblos and towns established by the Government prior to the royal instruction of 1789. In the case of *Townsend vs. Greely, supra*, Mr. Justice Field delivered the unanimous opinion of the supreme court of the United States, and explains what is meant in the case of *Brownsville vs. Cavazos* by the laws of Mexico in force in 1826, which gave to pueblos and towns certain right to four square leagues of land. The learned judge said: 'The royal instructions of 1789 for the establishment of the town of Pitic, in the province of Sonora, were applicable to all new towns which should be established within the district under the commandant-general, and that included California.' (It also included New Mexico and the State of Tamaulipas.) 'They gave special directions for the establishment and government of the new pueblos, declared that there should be assigned to them four square leagues of land, and provided for the distribution of the building and farming lost to settlers, the laying out of pasture lands and lands from which a revenue was to be derived, and for the appropriation of the residue to the use of the inhabitants.' These royal instructions did not attempt to confer any right to lands on pueblos or towns then in existence. But if the town of Santa Fe had a grant to the four square leagues claimed, the undisputed facts of this case show that all the land granted to other parties by the Spanish Government within the limits of the four leagues should be excluded from the decree. As before stated, no allotments of lands were ever made to the settlers. The four leagues were never surveyed or set apart to the town. The legal title, with full power to dispose of the land, remained in the sovereign. (*Townsend vs. Greely*, 5 Wall., 326-338; *Alexander vs. Rowlett*, 13 Wall., 388; *U. S. vs. Pico*, 5 Wall., 540; *Hurt vs. Burnett*, 15 California, 530, 20 *id.*, 480; *Pueblo Case*, 4 Sawyer, 566; *Brownsville vs. Cavazos*, 100 U. S., 138; *Grisar vs. McDowell*, 6 Wall., 379; *Hall's Mexican Law*, Sec. 122, p. 53.)

"It was the policy of the Spanish Government to encourage the settlement of new towns and pueblos by giving to them, and the inhabitants thereof, certain rights and easements to large quantities of land outside of the small lots to be assigned to the settlers and to which they obtained a fee simple title by four years' use and occupation. It must, however, have been well understood by the authorities of such towns and pueblos and the inhabitants thereof that the Government reserved the right to sell or otherwise dispose of such lands, except the small allotments to the inhabitants and the necessary ground for plaza, streets, corporation buildings, etc. In 1808, a general law was promulgated, which provided that all the unoccupied town or pueblo land should either be sold, mortgaged, or set apart to soldiers as pensions.

"No question was ever made as to the power of the Government to dispose of such land. (*Hall's Mexican Law*, Secs. 94, 95, 96, 97, 98, and 99.)

"Mexico succeeded to the rights of the Spanish Government in all such town or pueblo land, and provided for a sale of the same in 1856. (*Hall's Mexican Law*, Sec. 140, p. 56.) The right of the Republic of Mexico to so dispose of such land has not been questioned, so far as I know. In the case of *Grisar vs. McDowell*, supra, in speaking of the rights of the city of San Francisco to the four square leagues claimed, Mr. Justice Field said: 'Until the lands were assigned and measured off, the right or claim of the pueblo was an imperfect one. It was a right which the Government might refuse to recognize at all, or might recognize in a qualified form; it might be burdened with conditions, and it might be restricted to less limits than four square leagues, which was the usual quantity assigned. Even after assignment the interest acquired by the pueblo was far from being an indefeasible estate, such as is known to our laws. The purpose to be accomplished by the creation of pueblos did not require their possession of the fee. The interest, as we had occasion to observe in the case already cited, amounted to little more than a restricted and qualified right to alienate portions of the land to its inhabitants for building or cultivation, and to use the remainder for commons and for pasture lands, or as a source of revenue, or for other public purposes. And this limited right of disposition and use was, in all particulars, subject to the control of the Government of the country.'

THE SPANISH ARCHIVES OF NEW MEXICO 221

"There is no occasion in this case to indulge in any presumption as to the power or authority of the Spanish government of New Mexico to make grants to the public lands subsequent to 1754. Article 12 of the royal regulations, issued October 15th, 1754, expressly confers power on the governors of the distant provinces to approve grants to land. (*White's Recop.,* vol. 2, p. 66.)

"The grants introduced as evidence in this cause, to land within the four square leagues claimed by the city, are from the archives of the surveyor-general's office and seem to be in all respects regular. The archive evidence further shows that the grantees were put in juridical possession of the land granted by the proper officer without objection or injury to third parties, and in some cases the proof shows that valuable improvements have been made on the land; with continued possession of nearly one hundred years there never was at any time objection made by the town authorities, either to the making of the grants or possession under them.

"One of the exhibits in evidence shows that the town council of Santa Fe petitioned the governor for a grant of land now within the city limits, and that a grant was made by the governor to it for the land asked for.

"The ancient pueblo is estopped under the facts in this case from setting up claim to the lands granted by the governors of New Mexico to individuals within the four square leagues. (*Henshaw vs. Bissell,* 18th Wall., 255; 93 U. S., 326; 100 U. S., 598; 102 U. S., 68; 13 How., 307), and the present city of Santa Fe, as its successor, is also estopped.

"But it is quite clear, from the exhibits in evidence, that the corporate authorities of the ancient town or pueblo did not claim any right to four leagues of land by virtue of a grant or supposed grant to it, and it is equally clear that the officials of the Spanish Government who had authority to dispose of the public domain did not understand that the pueblo was entitled to any such quantity of land. Under the provisions of the act of March 3, 1851, in relation to the settlement of private land claims in California, the board of commissioners, by the 14th section of the act, was authorized, when the existence of a city, town, or village, was shown to be in existence on the 7th day of July, 1846, to presume, prima facie, a grant to such town, city, or village. The board was also authorized to take jurisdiction of any claim to land, whether legal or equitable, and to confirm such claim, etc. (9 *Statutes,* pp. 630-631.) It was under the provisions of that act that the city of San Francisco, as a successor to a pueblo, presented her claim for four square leagues to said board for confirmation. The pueblo under which the city claimed was a Mexican town settled in 1835, and under the royal instruction of 1789 had some rights in the quantity of land claimed. The real question in the case, out of which so much litigation arose, was in regard to the pueblo's title to the land at the date of the change of flag. It was conceded that the act was broad enough to authorize the board of commissioners to convert any sort of a claim or easement to land into a legal estate. But inasmuch as the United States had appropriated a portion of the land claimed by the city prior to March 3, 1851, it became important to ascertain the pueblo right to the land under the law of Mexico and the treaty of *Guadalupe Hidalgo.* The board of commissioners confirmed to the city the greater portion of the land claimed for the use and benefit of the inhabitants of the city, and the district court approved the decree of the commissioners. This decree vested in the city the legal title to the land claimed for the use and benefit of the inhabitants. Before the cause was finally disposed of in the district court, congress passed an act transferring the record and proceedings to the circuit court for the district of California. The circuit court modified the decree of the district court by excluding from it all lands disposed of by former governments or appropriated by the United States. (4 *Sawyer,* pp. 566-7.)

"In 1855, the common council of the city of San Francisco passed what is called the *Van Ness* ordinance, which provided for an adjustment of the claims of the inhabitants and the city to the lands which had been confirmed. This ordinance was subsequently ratified by the legislature of the State. But notwithstanding the holding of the board of commissioners and the district and circuit court and the action of the common council, congress on the 8th day of March, 1866 (while said pueblo case was still pending in the court), passed a special act to quiet the title to the land claimed by the city of San Francisco, imposing certain conditions and limitations. (*Statutes* 1865-6, p. 4.)

"After the passage of this act the question of the character of the city's title at the date of the treaty came before the supreme court of the United States in the case of *Grisar vs. McDowell*, 6 Wall., 363.

"The plaintiff in the case claimed as seized in fee, under the title from the city of San Francisco; the defendant claimed possession as an officer of the United States, setting up that the property was public property of the United States reserved for military purposes. Mr. Justice Field, who decided the pueblo case (4 *Sawyer*, 566-7), delivered the opinion of the court, and discussed with great ability all the questions growing out of or connected with the claims of the city to the land in controversy.

"It was again held by the court that the legal title to the land claimed by the defendant passed to the United States from Mexico under the treaty of 1848, and was a part of the public domain of the United States, and having been appropriated by the United States and reserved by the act of 1865-6, never had been the property of the city. The law of nations and the terms of the treaty of 1848, make it the duty of the government to secure to the citizens or corporation in the ceded territory such rights to private property as they possessed under the laws of Spain or Mexico at the date of the treaty. Our governments may grant additional rights, but the citizens have no right to demand more.

"The act of March 3d, 1851, authorized the board of commissioners to confirm to pueblos and towns, for the benefit of the inhabitants thereof, mere easements and usufructuary rights to land granted to them by the government of Spain or Mexico, and by such decree of confirmation they acquired the legal title to the land with full power to sell and dispose of the same. This, congress in its sovereign capacity and absolute control over the public domain had a right to do. (*Pollard Lesser vs. Polk*, 2 Howard, p. 603.)

"Subdivision one of section 13 of the act of March 3d, 1891, is as follows: 'No claim shall be allowed that shall not appear to be upon title lawfully and regularly derived from the government of Spain or Mexico, or from any State of the Republic of Mexico having lawful authority to make grants to land, and one if not then complete and perfect at the date of the acquisition of the territory by the United States, the claimant would have had a lawful right to make perfect had the territory not been acquired by the United States.' It will be seen that this court can not confirm any imperfect or incomplete title which the claimant would not be entitled to have made perfect had the United States not acquired the territory. Now, as I have shown, the supreme court of the United States has repeatedly held that the title acquired to four square leagues of land by a grant to a pueblo or town is an imperfect one. It follows necessarily that this court has no power to confirm such a title. It is true the right or easement in the land acquired by a pueblo or town may be conferred by a perfect grant to such right or easement, but under the law the right may be terminated at the will of the sovereign, and such right terminated at the date of the transfer of sovereignty, as was held by this court in the case of pueblos *Zia, Santa Anna,* and *Jemez vs. The United States,* decided at a former term. For some reason congress did not confer power on this court to convert, by decree of confirmation, easements and usufructuary rights given by the Spanish and Mexican governments to pueblos and towns in large tracts of land to be used for the benefit of such pueblos and towns and the inhabitants thereof during the pleasure of the sovereign, into indefeasible estates. There is one other question in the cause which seems to me conclusive against the claim made in the petition to four square leagues of land. The laws of Spain and Mexico granting lands to new pueblos and towns settled by Spaniards do not apply to Indian pueblos and towns nor to old pueblos or towns taken possession of by Spaniards. The law prohibits Spaniards from in any way interfering with the lands, towns, or pueblos occupied by Indians. (*White's Recop.,* vol. 2, pp. 44, 45, and 54.)

"History informs that 'When the Spaniards first visited Santa Fe in the year 1542 (?) it was a populous Indian pueblo. It is not known when the Spaniards took possession of it, but it has been the capital of New Mexico since the year 1640.

" 'It was recaptured by the Indians in 1680, the principal buildings burned, and the whites driven out. The town was recaptured by the Spaniards in the year 1694.' (*The American Cyclopedia,* vol. 15, p. 619.)

"The court confirmed the supposed grant to all the lots within the said four square leagues of land, now held in

Facsimile of Signature of Captain Roque Madrid, re-conquistador.

Facsimile of Signature of Don Nicolas Ortiz Niño Ladron de Guevara, re-conquistador.

Facsimile of the Signature of Captain Alphonsso Rael de Aguilar, re-conquistador.

Facsimile of Signature of Captain Don Juan de Ulibarri, re-conquistador.

Facsimile of Signature of General Don Diego de Vargas Zapata Lujan Ponce de Leon, Governor and Captain-General, 1691-1697, 1703-4.

severalty, to the respective lot holders thereof, holding said lots in privity with said Santa Fe pueblo grant, without reference to the date of the claim under which they might hold. No assignment of lots was ever made by the city or pueblo to anyone. The lot claimants under the city are not parties to the suit, and no decree should be entered in their favor.

"A decree should be ordered conferring to the city the land granted to it by the governor of New Mexico, and the plaza, streets, alleys, and other property held by the corporation for public purposes, and the petition should be dismissed as to all other claims. The court should examine the grants and evidence filed in support of claims to land within the four square leagues which are submitted with this case, and if such grants are genuine, and the claimants have such an interest as entitles them to prosecute the suit, such grants should be confirmed.

"W. W. MURRAY,
"Associate Justice."

The supreme court of the United States, speaking through Mr. Justice White, declares that the origin of the town or city of Santa Fe is obscure, "but the record (*United States vs. Santa Fe*, 165 U. S., 676), indicates that as early as 1543 the settlement was made by deserters from the Spanish military force under Coronado, who refused to accompany their commander on his return to Mexico, and settled at Santa Fe.'"

There is not a line of documentary proof in existence which by any possible stretch of the imagination can justify a statement of this sort, coming from the highest judicial tribunal in the United States.

The Spanish City of Santa Fe was not settled until 1605, when it was made the capital of New Mexico by Don Juan de Oñate, governor and captain-general of the Province of New Mexico.

When the court of private land claims was created a petition was filed, under the act of March 3, 1891, creating that court, setting out the existence of the Villa de Santa Fe. In this petition it was declared that prior to the insurrection of 1680, the Villa had received a pueblo grant of four square leagues, the central point of which was in the center of the plaza of the City of Santa Fe; that such grant had been made by the king of Spain; that juridical possession was given thereunder and that such facts were evidenced by a valid *testimonio*; that the archives and records of the Villa were destroyed in the Pueblo Rebellion of 1680 and on that account could not be produced. The petition concluded with a prayer for confirmation to the city "in trust for the use and benefit of the inhabitants thereof, and of such grantees and assignees of parts of the said lands as have derived, or may hereafter acquire by due assignments, allotments, and titles in severalty to said parts respectively." A demurrer to this petition was filed, giving as grounds that no cause of action had been stated and that it failed to disclose the fact that there were many adverse claimants, under Spanish grants, to the land sued for, and that such claimants were necessary parties defendant. Thereafter seventeen persons appeared, alleging that they were the holders of Spanish titles to land within the area claimed and that their interests were adverse to the city. An amended petition was filed and these seventeen persons were made defendants.

The United States government, in its answer, denied the facts as alleged relative to the foundation and organization of the Villa de Santa Fe; it denied also that the Spanish Villa had received title to or was by operation of the Spanish law entitled to claim the four square leagues of land; the answer averred that title to a large portion of the land embraced within the four square leagues was claimed under Spanish grants by others than the plaintiff, the validity of which claims, however, were not admitted, and that other portions of the four square leagues were in control, occupancy, and possession of the United States for a military post, known as Fort Marcy, for a building known as the "Federal Building," and for an establishment known as the Indian Industrial School, and that another portion was in possession of the Territorial executive officers under the authority of the United States.

At the hearing before the court of private land claims, the proof established the settlement and organization of the City of Santa Fe. The various grants referred to in the answer of the several defendants were offered in evidence and testimony adduced tending to show that they covered territory embraced within the claim to the four leagues, and were, therefore, adverse to the claims of the city.

There was no evidence introduced showing that La Villa de Santa Fe, in any of its forms of organization under the Spanish government, or that the City of Santa Fe itself, had ever possessed the four square leagues to which it asserted title, or that any lot-holder in the city claimed to own or hold by virtue of any title derived under the supposed right of the city. There was an entire absence of proof showing that any right by possession or otherwise within the area claimed was held under or by virtue of the implied grant of four square leagues upon which the city relied. On the contrary there was proof that in 1715 the city of Santa Fe petitioned for a grant of a tract of swamp land situate within the boundaries of the four square leagues.

The decision of the court of private land claims was favorable to the contention of the City of Santa Fe. The United States appealed to the supreme court of the United States, where the decree of the court of private land claims was reversed and the cause remanded with instructions to dismiss the petition. The supreme court held that "Under the act of March 3, 1891, it must appear, in order to the confirmation of a grant by the court of private land claims, not only that the title was lawfully and regularly derived, but that, if the grant were not complete and perfect, the claimant could by right and not by grace, have demanded that it should be made perfect by the former government, had the territory not been acquired by the United States.

"Although the act of 1891, in section 11, authorized a town presenting a claim for a grant to represent the claim of lot-holders to lots within the town, this provision does not override the general requirements of the statute as to the nature of the claim to title which the court is authorized to confirm. The difference between the act of 1891 and the California act of 1851 . . . accentuates the intention of congress to confine the authority conferred by the later act to narrower limits than those fixed by the act of 1851. The act of 1851 authorized the adjudication of claims to land by virtue of any 'right' or 'title' derived from the Spanish government, and conferred the power in express language on the board and court to *presume a grant in favor of a town*. The act of 1891 not only entirely omits authority to invoke this presumption, but, as we have seen, excludes by express terms any claim, the completion of which depended upon the mere grace or favor of the government of Spain or Mexico, and of the United States as the successor to the rights of those governments.

. . . .

"The petition is framed upon the theory merely of a right to four square leagues, vested in the city by operation of law, and as the record contains no proof whatever as to the possessory claims of lot-holders in the city of Santa Fe, or as to the actual possession enjoyed by that city of public places, these latter rights, if any, as well as the asserted title of the city to the swamp tract to which reference has been made in the course of this opinion, are not to be controlled by the rejection now made of the pretensions of the city to a title to the four square leagues tract asserted to have been acquired by operation of Spanish laws."

The claim of the City of Santa Fe having thus been decided adversely by the highest tribunal in the United States, the Congress of the United States, afterward, with certain provisions protecting the rights of the government to certain areas occupied by it, passed an act by which a grant was made to the City of Santa Fe — the lot-holders — and deeds were subsequently made by the city to those holding possession of the tracts and lots within the area granted by the government.

Hall, *Mexican Law*, p. 51, on the Limits of Pueblos, says: "There never existed any general law fixing four square leagues as the extent of pueblos or towns. That extent of land was assigned to pueblos founded by contractors for Spaniards, by law 6, title 5, book 4, of the Laws of the Indies. Those formed by the government independent of contractors, were only limited by the discretion of the governors of the provinces, and viceroys, subject to the approval or disapproval by the King. There are numerous pueblos in Mexico which have less and many that have more than four square leagues."

817 VILLA NUEVA DE SANTA CRUZ. 1696.

Settlement of nineteen families in said place by order of Don Diego de Vargas Zapata Lujan Ponce de Leon.

Santa Cruz was re-settled April 12, 1695. The Indians who had moved thither from Galisteo were deprived of their houses and lands and a grant made to the Spaniards.

At the time of the re-conquest, before a definitive title

to the public lands passed against the crown, the acts of the colonial officers required royal confirmation. However, this system must have been modified, for on November 24, 1735, we find a royal cédula wherein it requires that all grants be referred to him specially for confirmation; thus indicating that before that time some other royal official had that power.

The royal instructions of 1754, October 15, among other things recited that "the holders of land sold or adjusted by the several deputies from the year 1700 up to the present time, shall not be molested, interfered with, nor denounced, now, nor at any time, if it appears they have been confirmed by my royal person, or by the viceroys and presidents of the Audiencias of the several districts in the time when this requirement was in force; but those who hold them without this necessary requisite shall apply for the confirmation thereof to the Audiencias in their district and to the other officers to whom the power is given by these new instructions, who, in view of the proceedings had by the deputies, in their order in regard to the survey and valuation of such lands and of the title issued by them, shall examine as to whether the sale or composition is made without fraud or collusion and at appropriate and equitable prices, with the presence and hearing of the Attorneys General, so that, with attention to everything, and if it appears that the price of the sale and composition and the corresponding half annata tax have been paid into the royal depositories, and after performing whatever pecuniary service appears necessary, they may issue to them in my royal name the confirmation of their royal titles with which they will be established in the possession and dominion of such lands, waters, or wild lands, and neither the holders nor their general or individual successors shall at any time be molested therein."

818 VILLA NUEVA DE SANTA CRUZ. 1696.

Petition of Inhabitants in regard to change of place on account of poisonous herbs which kill their stock. Don Diego De Vargar Bapata Lujan Ponce de Leon, Governor. Martin Urioste; Alphonso Rael de Aguilar; Domingo de la Barreda, Secretary of Government and War.

This grant was confirmed by the court of private land claims and surveyed for an area of more than 4,500 acres. It lies south of the grant to the pueblo of San Juan.

819 ANTONIO DE SILVA. Grant. 1699. Land in *Santa Cruz*.
>Re-validation made by Pedro Rodriguez Cubero of the same made by his predecessor, Don Diego de Vargas, Governor. *Testimonio* certified by Antonio Aguilera Isassi, Alcalde.

820 TOMAS PALOMINO to Antonio de Silva. *Santa Fe*. 1699.
>Exchange of lands. *Testimonio*. Certified by Antonio Aguilera Isassi, Alcalde.

821 BARTOLOME LOVATO to Pedro de Sandoval. *Santa Fe*. 1701.
>House and lands. Joseph Rodriguez, Alcalde. Diego de Belasco.

822 JACINTO SANCHEZ. Grant. 1703-1704.
>Lands near the pueblo of *Cochiti*. El Marqués de la Nava y Brazinas, Governor. Annulled. *Majada* Tract, q. v.
>
>Petition by Jacinto Sanchez, asking for a grant of a tract of land opposite the pueblo of Cochiti, which tract had belonged to Cristobal Fontes before the revolution (1680) and of which subsequently a grant had been made to Sanchez by Don Pedro Rodriguez Cubero, which grant Sanchez had lost.
>
>The grant asked for was made by the Marqués de la Nava de Brazinas (Diego de Vargas), on December 23, 1703, and the chief alcalde, Manuel Baca, was ordered to give the possession.
>
>Subsequently, after the receipt of a letter from the Reverend Father Juan Alvarez, setting forth the request of the Indians of Cochiti that the grant which had been made should be recalled, the governor made an additional order to the effect that the grant made to Sanchez should be understood as applying only to what had legally been the tract owned by Fontes, and that in giving the possession of the tract no injury should be done to the Indians.
>
>This document does not contain any evidence of the giving of possession.
>
>The governor's additional decree is dated January 11, 1704.

THE SPANISH ARCHIVES OF NEW MEXICO 231

823 LORENZO DE MADRID. 1704-05.
> Question of lands with the convent of *San Juan*. El Marqués de la Nava de Brazinas. Pedro Rodriguez de Cubero.
> It is stated that the Marqués de la Naba de Brazinas died on April 8, 1704; that twenty-one frayles (Religious) gave up their lives in the revolution of 1680 and five in that of 1696.

824 BARTOLOME SANCHEZ.
> Grant. Land on the *Chama* near *Santa Clara*. *Santa Fe*. 1707. Made by Francisco Cubero y Valdes, Governor. Possession given by Juan Roque Gutierres, Alcalde.
> **Bartolomé Sanches Grant. R. No. 264.**
> This grant was confirmed by the court of private land claims and according to the survey has an area of 4,400 acres. It lies along the western and southern sides of the San Juan Pueblo Grant, west of the Rio Grande; its south boundary is the grant to the pueblo of Santa Clara.

825 ANDRÉS MONTOYA and Antonia Lucero de Godoy, his wife, to Bernardino de Sena. Santa Fe, 1710.
> Land on the other side of the *Rio de Santa Fe*. Diego Arias de Quiros, Alcalde. Manuel de Servantes.

826 SEBASTIAN DE MONDRAGON to Bernardino de Sena. *Santa Fe*. 1710.
> Donation. Land. Diego Arias de Quiros, Alcalde. Manuel de Servantes. Xptobal de Gongora, Secretario de Cabildo.

827 BARTOLOME SANCHEZ.
> Re-validation of a grant on the *Chama*. El Marqués de la Peñuela, Governor. No. 824, *q. v.*

828 PASCUAL TRUXILLO to Pedro Sanchez. *Santa Fe*. 1713.
> Rancho in the *Cañada*. Jacinto Sanches, Alcalde. Juan de Atienza Alcala; Francisco de la Mora.
> "Pedro Sanchez, a native of this kingdom, and a resident of the town of Santa Cruz, in the most approved manner prescribed by law, and most convenient to myself, appear before your excellency, representing that, whereas I have to support twelve children and three orphan nephews who are without father or mother, three

female servants, and, with my wife, will make, in all, the number of twenty persons, and having a piece of land acquired by purchase, which is so small that I am compelled to borrow lands from my other immediate neighbors in order to extend my crops every year, and even in this manner I cannot support myself, nor can I maintain on said land a few sheep and four cows and some mares and horses, all of which are necessary to the support of so large a family, and which are poor for the want of pasture, and suffer a great many wants, and in order to supply them I have deemed proper to register and do register a piece of land on the other side of the river Del Norte, uncultivated and abandoned, and as such, unoccupied, there being no one having any claim thereto; the boundaries being on the north the lands enjoyed by right by the Indians of the pueblo of San Ildefonso, on the south the lands of Captain Andrés Montoya, on the east the Del Norte river, and on the west the Rocky Mountains; and, imploring the royal aid of your excellency, as a loyal subject of his Majesty, in view of all that I have stated, I pray and request that you be pleased to grant me said land in the name of his Majesty (whom may God preserve), in order that I may settle upon it so soon as the alcalde himself of Santa Cruz places me in possession, all of which I expect from the charity and justice of your excellency, and I swear by God, our Father, and the sign of the most holy cross, that my petition is not made in malice, but of absolute necessity, and whatever may be necessary, etc. PEDRO SANCHEZ'' [rubric]

829 ANTONIO DE SALAZAR.
Grant. 1714. Reported Claim No. 132, *q. v.*
Was rejected by the court of private land claims.

830 CRISTOBAL DE LA SERNA.
Grant. 1715. Reported Claim No. 109.

831 JUAN GARCIA DE NORIEGA to Salvador de Santiestevan. *Santa Fe*, 1715.
House and land. Juan Garcia de la Rivas, Alcalde. Antonio Duran de Armijo; Juan Manuel Chirinos.

832 MIGUEL DURAN to Domingo Martin Serrano. *Santa Fe*, 1715.
House and land.

833 BARTOLOME SANCHEZ. *Santa Fe*, 1716.
Testimonio of his grant in *La Cañada de Santa Cruz*. No. 824, 827, *q. v.* Juan Garcia de la Rivas, Alcalde.

834 BARTOLOME SANCHEZ. *Santa Fe*, 1716.
Complaint against Salvador de Santistevan. Bartolomé Lobato; Nicolas Griego; Xptobal Crespin; Juan de Mestas. In the matter of their occupancy of his grant. Nos. 824, 827, and 833, *q. v.* No final action. Phelix Martinez, Governor. Nos. 167, 170, 433, 435, 436, and 437, *q. v.*

835 FRANCISCO XAVIER ROMERO to Maria de Selorga. 1718.
House and land in *La Cañada de Santa Cruz*. Francisco Bueno de Bohorquez y Corcuera, Alcalde. Juan de Paz Bustillos; Gregorio Garduño; Diego Arias de Quiros.

836 ANDRES MONTOYA to Bernardino de Sena. *Santa Fe*, 1723.
Land on the other side of *Rio de Santa Fe*. Bohorques, Alcalde. Pedro Lopez Gallardo; Miguel de Sandoval Martinez; Juan Manuel Chirinos.

837 JOSEPH DE SANTIESTEVAN and Josepha Montoya, his wife, to Bernardo de Sena. *Santa Fe*, 1725.
Lands. Miguel Joseph de la Vega y Coca, Alcalde. Juan Joseph Lobato; Juan Manuel Chirinos.

The Cuyamungue Grant, Reported No. 64, was known as the Bernardo de Sena Grant.

When this grant was first surveyed, in 1877, there was a conflict between the survey and those of the grants to the pueblos of Nambé and Pojoaque. The grant was never confirmed by Congress, but the title was confirmed by the court of private land claims October 24, 1895. The case was appealed to the supreme court of the United States, where the decision was reversed, a new survey ordered and a new decree was entered. By this the conflicts were removed. The Cuyamungue is bounded on the north by the Pojoaque and the Nambé grants and on the south by the grant to the pueblo of Tesuque. This grant is sometimes called the Bernardo Sena Grant and should not be confused with the Alfonso Rael de Aguilar or Pueblo of Cuyamungue Grant, Reported No. 81, which was rejected by the court of private land claims.

838 AGUSTIN SAIS. Intestate. *Santa Fe*, 1725.
    Inventory of his property. Miguel Joseph de la Vega y Coca, Alcalde.

839 FRANCISCO RENDON to Antonio Felix Sanches. 1728. *Santa Fe.*
    House and lot on the other side of *Rio de Santa Fe*. Diego Arias de Quiros, Alcalde. Juan Manuel Chirinos.

840 ANDRES MONTOYA, *el viejo*, to Bernardino de Sena. *Santa Fe.*
    Land on the other side of the river *Santa Fe*. 1728. Diego Arias de Quiros, Alcalde.

841 FRANCISCO DE SILVA, *Alburquerque*, vs. NICOLAS DE CHABES. 1733.
    In the matter of the dower of his wife. Gervasio Cruzat y Gongora, Governor. Juan Gonzales Bas, Alcalde. Bernabe Baca; Nicolas Duran; Francisco Antonio Gonzales; Juan Phelipe de Ribera; Pedro Barela; Isidro Sanchez; Antonio de Chabes; Geronimo Jaramillo.

842 MARIA SANCHEZ vs. SALVADOR VIGIL. *Cañada de Santa Cruz*, 1734.
    In the matter of land sold by her deceased husband, Juan Ignacio Mestas, to defendant against the will of herself and her minor children. Fernando Chacón, Governor. Josef Andrés Galles; Antonio José Ortiz, Alcalde; Miguel Garcia, Alcalde.

843 JOSE SANCHES.
    In the matter of the settlement of the estate of his deceased father, Jacinto Sanches. *Alburquerque*, 1735. Juan Gonzales Bas, Alcalde; Geronimo Xaramillo; Pedro Barela; Joseph Gonzales Bas; Alexandro Gonzales; Francisco Antonio Gonzales; Juan Julian Gonzales; Juan Julian Gonzales Bas.

844 LAZARO GARCIA DE NORIEGA, as executor of the estate of his deceased father, to Antonio de Santiestevan. *Santa Fe*, 1739.
    Land on the other side of the *Rio Santa Fe*. Antonio Montoya, Alcalde; Baltazar Montoya; Gregorio Garduño.

845 JOSEPH SALAS vs. MARIA DE SILBA. *Fuenclara,* 1745.
 Trespass. Joachin Codallos y Rabal, Governor. Joseph Baca, Alcalde.

846 MARIA GOMEZ ROBLEDO, widow, and Bernardo de Sena, executors of Diego Arias de Quiros to Manuel Sanz de Garvisu. *Santa Fe,* 1738.
 House and lands. Joachin Codallos y Rabal, Governor. Phelipe Jacobo de Vnuane; Francisco Ortiz; Joseph Romo de Vera.
 On the first page a house is described as being *"contiguous to the tower of the Palace."* The boundaries described on the following page show that this tower was on the *east* end of the building.

847 MIGUEL MARTIN SERRANO vs. LOS VALDESES. *Abiquiú,* 1746.
 Joachin Codallos y Rabal, Governor. Vincente Ginzo Ron y Thobar; Juan de Beytia, Alcalde; Francisco Gomez del Castillo.

848 PUEBLO DE NUESTRA SENORA DE LOS DOLORES DE SANDIA. 1748.
 Proceedings in the establishment of the Mission, etc. Joachin Codallos y Rabal, Governor. Bernardo Antonio de Bustamante, Alcalde (Tagle); Isidro Sanchez Tagle; Fr. Juan Miguel Menchero.
 Petition by Friar Juan Miguel Menchero to Governor Joaquin Codallos y Rabal, asking that lands be distributed to the Moqui Indians who had been gathered together with a view to the reëstablishment of the *pueblo* of Sandia; that the boundaries of the *pueblo* lands be determined; that certain lands which had been granted to Spaniards within the boundaries desired by the Indians be declared to belong to the latter, and that the Spaniards be given lands elsewhere, etc., etc.
 The foregoing petition was presented to the governor on April 5, 1748, together with a communication from the viceroy of New Spain in regard to the reëstablishment of the mission. The governor thereupon commissioned Don Bernardo de Bustamante to go to Sandia and examine the tract needed for the reëstablishment of the new *pueblo*, and to distribute the lands, waters, pastures, etc., neces-

sary for the use of the Indians, setting forth the boundaries, and giving the royal possession to the missionary who might be appointed to manage the *pueblo*. He further directed that for the time being the *pueblo* of Sandia should be attached to Alburquerque, for judicial purposes, and subject to the control of the chief alcalde of that town in such matters. The alcaldes of the various towns were directed to see to it that the Moqui Indians who might be residing in their respective districts should assemble as soon as possible at Sandia, where construction of the new *pueblo* was to be begun by the beginning of the month of May.

On May 14, 1748, Bustamante, who was at Sandia on that date, caused to appear before him three Spaniards, Antonio de Salazar, Joseph Jaramillo, and Salvador Jaramillo, who apparently were the owners of land on the west side of the Rio del Norte (Rio Grande) and opposite the site of Sandia. Bustamante explained to these men that the law allowed the Indians to have a league in each direction from their pueblo, but that he would not measure the league toward the west (which, doubtless, would have included the lands occupied by the Spaniards), but in consideration of this the Spaniards would have to consent to the Indians grazing their stock west of the river on the Spaniards' pasture lands. To this they agreed in the presence of witnesses.

On May 16, 1748, Bustamante called together the owners of lands adjoining those of the Indians on the north and south, and asked them whether they had any objections to make to the giving of possession to the Indians as had been ordered by the governor. They replied that notwithstanding the fact that the measurements included some lands granted to them and others purchased by them, they would give them up without controversy, because of the orders proceeding from superior authority, but they would take legal steps to protect their rights. Bustamante then proceeded to give to the new *pueblo* and mission the name of Nuestra Señora de los Dolores y San Antonio de Sandia, after which he placed the Indians and their pastor, Friar Juan Joseph Hernandez, in possession of the lands.

In making the measurement toward the west (presumably from the site of the new *pueblo*) to the Rio del Norte, there were only 1,440 *varas*, or 3,560 *varas* less than a league.

Bustamante says that in order to make up the distance which was lacking in this measurement, it became necessary to increase in an equal degree the measurements toward the north and south. He further states that he ordered landmarks of mud and stone, as high as a man, with wooden crosses on top of them, to be placed at the following places: On the north opposite the end of what was commonly called the Cañada del Agua, on the south opposite the mouth of the Cañada de Juan Taboso, and on the east the main mountain range called Sandia.

The new *pueblo* was settled by 350 persons, counting adults and children.

849 MARIA TRUXILLO to Antonio Salazar. *Corral de Piedras*, 1750.
 Land. Juan José Lobato, Alcalde. Juan Joseph Jaques.

850 MARIA DE SERNA and Jacinto Martin, her husband to the Heirs of Sebastiana de Serna. *Villa Nueva de Santa Cruz*. 1751.
 Land inherited from Roque Madrid, her grandfather. Juan Joseph Lovato, Alcalde. Antonio Martin.

851 CLEMENTE MONTOYA to Antonio Sandoval. *San Antonio de Padua del Pueblo Quemado*. 1752.
 Land in this Grant. Juan Joseph Sandoval, Alcalde. Alonzo Sandoval.

852 MARIA DE HERRERA to Francisco Saes (Zaes and also Sais). *Santa Cruz del Ojo Caliente*.
 Donation of house and lands. Juan Joseph Lobato, Alcalde. Juan Manuel Dias del Castillo, Vicente Apodaca, José Martin.

853 MARIA DE HERRERA, widow of Captain Antonio Martin, to Gregorio Sandobal. *Santa Cruz del Ojo Caliente*, 1753.
 Donation of house, lot and lands. Juan José Lobato, Alcalde. Francisco Saes.

854 MARIA MAGDALENA DE MEDINA, wife of Juan de Ledesma, absent in *Sonora*, to Maria Francisca de Sena. *Santa Fe*, 1753.

Land in Tesuque. Francisco Guerrero, Alcalde. Manuel Bernardo Garvisu. Santa Fe, 1763. Partition of the above land by Manuel Gallego, Alcalde. Between Francisco de Sena and Maria Tomasa de Sena, minor heirs. Vicente Sena, Antonio Abad Armenta.

855 MIGUEL DE DIOS SANDOVAL.
Francisco Guerrero, Alcalde. Geronimo Esquibel.

856 JUANA SISNEROS.
Francisco Guerrero, Alcalde.

857 SANTIAGO DE ROYBAL, *Vicario y Juez Eclesiastico*, to Phelipe de Sandoval Fernandez de la Pedrera. *Santa Fe*, 1756.
Donation of a flour mill called *Molino de San Francisco* on the *Rio de Santa Fe* above the city. Francisco Guerrero, Alcalde. Bernardo Manuel Garvisu, Lucas Moya.

858 FERNANDO ROMERO to Phelipe de Sandobal Fernandez de la Pedrera.
Land in *Santa Fe*, 1756. Francisco Guerrero, Alcalde. Lucas Moya.

859 MARCELA TRUGILLO to Phelipe de Sandoval Fernandez de la Pedrera, 1758.
Land on the *Rio de Santa Fe* above the city. Francisco Guerrero, Alcalde. Manuel Bernardo Garvisu.

860 BERNARDINO DE SENA.
Will, *Santa Fe*, 1765. Francisco Guerrero, Alcalde. Tomas Antonio Sena.
The testator requests that his remains be buried in the "*Capilla de Señor San Miguel.*"

861 HEIRS of Lucia Gomez Robledo:
Antonio Sandobal, Maria Francesca Rael, Nicolas Rael de Aguilar, Melchora Sandoval, Juan Sandobal, and Phelipe de Sandobal Fernandez to Andres de Sandobal. *Santa Fe*, 1758. Land on right side of the *Rio Santa Fe*. Francisco Guerrero, Alcalde. José Miguel de la Peña.

862 ROSALIA DE GILTOMEY to Antonio de Sena. *Santa Fe*, 1760.
Land. Francisco Guerrero, Alcalde. Juan Esteban Baca.

THE SPANISH ARCHIVES OF NEW MEXICO 239

863 MARIA FRANCISCA DE SENA, widow of Joche Moreno. Intestate. *Santa Fe*, 1763.
    Proceedings in the settlement of her estate. *Santa Barbara de la junta de los Rios.* Manuel Gallego, Alcalde. Joseph Miguel Garduño, Nicolas Rael de Aguilar, Vicente Sena, Antonio de Beytia, Juan Rafael Pineda, Tomas de Armijo, Carlos Joseph Mirabal.

    SANTA BARBARA GRANT. No. 114.
    This grant was surveyed in 1879 for over 18,000 acres. It joins the Pueblo of Picuriés Grant on the east. The title was confirmed by the court of private land claims and under the decree and survey it was found that the area is 31,000 acres. The grant was patented May 5, 1905.

864 FRANCISCO and MARIA PAULA SANCHES vs. JOSEPH SANCHES, Executor of Jacinto Sanches. *Cañada de Santa Cruz*, 1763.
    Claim to property under will of said Jacinto, their grandfather. Tomas Veles Cachupin, Governor. Antonio Baca, Alcalde. No final action.

865 TOMAS SENA. Bartolomé Fernandez. Manuel Duran y Chaves. *Santa Fe*, 1763.
    Registration of a mine. Tomas Veles Cachupin, Governor. Manuel Antonio Lorenz.

866 SIMON SEGURA.
    Francisco Guerrero, Alcalde. Juan Cayetano Vnaue.

867 ISABEL LUJAN, widow of Juan Lucero de Godoy, to Juana de la Cruz Sanz de Garvisu. *Santa Fe*, 1766.
    Donation of land in Santa Fe. Francisco Guerrero, Alcalde. Juan Antonio Alari, Francisco Xavier Fragoso, Geronimo Esquibel.

868 SANTIAGO DE ROYBAL, *Vicario y Juez Eclesiastico* to Antonio de Sandobal. *Santa Fe*, 1766.
    Donation of a rancho between Los Palacios and *Cieneguilla*, said rancho having been acquired by purchase from Bartholo Gutierrez. Francisco Guerrero, Alcalde. Lucas Manuel de Alcala, Juan Francisco Niño Ladron de Guebara.

869 INHABITANTS OF SABINAL vs. INHABITANTS OF BELEN.
    Question of pastures and waters, 1767. Don Tomas Veles Cachupin, Governor and Captain-General.

870 PEDRO MARTIN SERRANO.
    Will. *Corral de Piedra.* 1768. This man was the grantee of the Piedra Lumbre Grant. Antonio Joseph Garcia de la Mora, Alcalde.

871 JULIANA DE SANDOBAL, wife of Miguel Tafoya, vs. Lugarda Tafoya. *Santa Fe,* 1768.
    Question of lands. Don Pedro Fermin de Mendinueta, Governor. Nicolas Ortiz, Teniente General.

872 ANTONIO DE SALAZAR. *Alburquerque,* 1768.
    In the matter of the settlement of his estate. Francisco, Pablo and Cristobal de Salazar, executors and heirs. Joaquin de Luna, husband of Juana Angela de Salazar, heir. Lands in *Corral de Piedra.* Don Pedro Fermin de Mendinueta, Governor and Captain-General.

873 CRISTOBAL MADRID to Joseph Salazar. 1769.
    House and land in *Chama.* Antonio Joseph Ortiz, Alcalde.

874 CAYETANO DE ATENCIO to Joseph Salazar. *Santa Cruz,* 1769.
    House and land on the *Rio Chama.* Antonio Joseph Ortiz, Alcalde.

875 JOSEPH and JUAN DURAN Y CHABES. *Atrisco,* 1769.
    Confirmation of a sale of land made to Jacinto Sanches in 1757. Confirmed to Feliciana Sanches, daughter of said Jacinto and wife of Joseph Hurtado de Mendoza. Francisco Trebol Navarro, Alcalde.

876 JUAN JOSEPH DURAN to Pedro Ignacio Sanches. *Santa Cruz,* 1770.
    Land on the *Rio Chama.* Salvador Garcia de Noriega, Alcalde.

877 INHABITANTS OF BELEN. 1776.
    Complaint against settlers coming in from *Tomé* and

Sabinal. Don Pedro Fermin de Mendinueta, Governor. Diego de Borica, Ten'te G'ral.

878 JUAN CRISTOBAL SANCHES. *Tomé,* 1772.
Question as to whether he has a right to pasturage in the *Nicolas Duran y Chabes Tract.* Don Pedro Fermin de Mendinueta, Governor. Reported No. 155, Nicolas Duran y Chaves Grant, *q. v.*

879 JUAN CASIMIRO PEREA to Bernardo Sena Maese. 1772. *Puesto del Pino.*
Land in *Santa Fe.* Manuel Garcia Pareja, Alcalde.

880 JOSEPH ANTONIO SAIS. *Alburquerque.*
Will, 1770. Joseph Apodaca, Alcalde.

881 MANUEL BACA to Juan José Silva. *Santa Fe,* 1785.
Land in the *Cienega.* Antonio José Ortiz, Alcalde.

882 VILLA NUEVA DE SANTA CRUZ.
Settlement, 1695. Don Diego de Vargas Zapata Lujan Ponce de Leon, Governor and Captain-General.

"Proceedings had in the new town and settlement founded and called 'The Exaltation of the Cross of the Mexicans of the King our Lord Don Carlos II,' established and obtained by the efforts of the governor and captain-general of this kingdom of New Mexico, its new restorer and conqueror, Don Diego de Vargas Zapata Lujan Ponce de Leon, a certified copy of the said proceedings having been sent on May 11, of the said year of 1695, to his excellency the viceroy, the Conde de Galve.

"Don Diego de Vargas Zapata Lujan Ponce de Leon, governor and captain-general of this kingdom and province of New Mexico, its new restorer and conqueror at his own expense, and reconqueror and settler in the same, and castellan of its forces and garrisons, by His Majesty, etc.

"It being now the time when a fixed place of residence must be given to the families which, on the part of His Majesty our Lord, whom may God preserve, in his royal name, by his excellency the viceroy, the Conde de Galve, over all the kingdom of New Spain governor and captain-general and president of the royal audience and court of the City of Mexico and of all this new world, and with the approval of the royal commission and the ministers of the same, have been sent, as well as the others brought by the said governor and captain-general to this kingdom, and all of which are now in this said city, and also as another lot and party are expected, and in order to give them a fixed place of settlement, land for cultivation of their crops, pastures, woods and waters, watering places, commons, and stock ranges, in order that they may have all that they need for raising their large and small stock of all kinds and classes; and I, having been informed of the same, and it being the royal will that I should be placed in charge of the whole in the matter of the location and settlement of the said parties, and that I should procure for such as I considered proper for the service, stability, permanency, security, comfort, and utility, seeking to find the same on lands separate and apart, if possible, from the natives of the tribes and pueblos of this said kingdom and the district of this said city, in order to avoid the troubles and vexations which would arise if they live together with the Spaniards; but, on the contrary, being separated, both would be at peace, and the said natives and Spaniards would live together in concord and harmony, in such manner that by kind and friendly treatment our holy faith might be implanted among them on a firm basis and with the hope that with their example the adjoining barbarous tribes might be converted; and, with this view, I, the said governor and captain-general, having to duly carry out the royal will, which the said most excellent viceroy has so frequently and repeatedly communicated to me in the name of His Majesty, I have done what was necessary, and have not only gone over, passed through, and tried the entrances, exits, routes, courses, and distances, particularly and generally, of all this said kingdom, but with an army of the royal forces of His Majesty under my command as far as the last pueblo and tribe of the Taos of this said kingdom and come out at the mouth of the river Chama at the pueblo of San Juan de los Caballeros, distant ten leagues from the said city, and the said examinations having been made as aforesaid by me, the said governor and captain-general, I found that the said place and settlement of the said party and of the other said party that is expected to arrive should be made of lands which belonged to the Spaniards, who abandoned and left them at the time of the general revolution, in the month of August, in the year 'eighty, in this kingdom, at the places and farms extending from this said city of Santa Fe to the pueblo of Tesuque, and those which extend beyond the pueblos of San Ildefonso and Santa Clara, on the other side of the Rio del Norte, and, on this side, those which lie in front of the mesa de San Ildefonso and extend to the road which leads to the said pueblo of San Juan de los Caballeros, and those which extend to the pueblos established on the said farms, which are San Lazaro and San Cristoval, and those which extend from the latter in the direction of the highway which leads to Picuriés, to the Cañada called the Hacienda de Moraga, and the farms of Captains Luis Martin and Juan Ruis, in front of and at the place and tract of land called Chimayo; and in order that they be examined by my lieutenant-governor and captain-general, who is Colonel Luis Granillo, I order him to proceed with Sergeant Ruiz de Cazeres, because he knows the language of the said tribe of the Teguas, to the two pueblos of the Thanos, San Lazaro, and San Cristobal, with Matias Lujan, their alcalde mayor, because he is also an interpreter, to examine in the first place, the said farms and places separately, making a map showing the names of the places and the names of their former owners, the quality of the lands, and the distances, and he will examine personally and will confer with the above mentioned as to the number of persons who can be settled on the same, giving them lands which they can cultivate and plant advantageously and without inconveniencing one another, with notification that the pastures of the tract and limits of each of the said farms shall be in common and not for individuals, and that the stock which each may have in greater or less number may feed on the same, and only in case of there being an equal number will it be permitted them to appear in order to petition that no one shall have more stock than another; and in this manner he will make the said demarcation, map, computation, and regulation and in respect to the said two pueblos of San Lazaro and San Cristoval, they having been established on the farms and lands which absolutely belonged and did belong to the said Spanish residents, who, because of the said general rebellion of the whole of this kingdom in the month of August, of the year 'eighty, abandoned and left them in order to save their lives, and who left on their farms their household goods, clothing, wares, grain, growing crops, and stock, all of which were taken possession of by the said rebels; and in view of the fact that the aforesaid, of the said tribe of Thanos, left their pueblos, because of the improvements and the fertility of the lands and the greater security of their lives, and came together with those of the Teguas tribe, who were settled at so short a distance, and took advantage of the occasion to obtain the improvements on the said lands, everything being already completed, those of San Cristoval and those of San Lazaro settled upon them, the lands which the Teguas of the said pueblo of San Juan de los Caballeros hold being many, and the number of people of both being small, and it being on the frontier, as it is, and at the entrance of the Apache enemy as well as that of the Ute tribe, they saw fit to admit them and give them the permission, with the general consent of all, to settle, as in effect they did settle and were settled in the said pueblo of San Juan, the land and dwelling houses of which are vacant and standing unoccupied today, because of their having been abandoned only a few years ago on account of their having gone to settle on the lands of the Spaniards, and where they are today living and settled; and whereas I have conferred with the said governors of the said pueblos in regard to the above reasons and the royal will, and I, the said governor and captain-general, not being informed of the settlement which the said natives of San Lazaro, in the said pueblo of San Juan, had granted and designated to their governor, Don Cristoval Yope, the place of Yunque, in order that they might go there in the coming winter, giving them permission and consent to plant the said lands this year, he having a place to go to thereafter with his said people, which number sixteen families, their whole number being one hundred and fifty-five persons, according to what I am informed and as appears by the list of the same made by the reverend father preacher, Brother Antonio Obregon, their father minister, doctrinal teacher, and guardian; I hereby direct my said lieutenant-general and their said alcalde mayor and interpreter, Matias Lujan, to say and intimate to the said natives and their said governor, Don Cristoval Yope, that they must go to their said land which they have in the said pueblo of San Juan, which they had in the same, as well as the lands which were given and partitioned among them by the natives of the same; and I direct my said lieutenant-general, if it should be necessary, to go to the said pueblo of San Juan with the said governor, Don Cristoval Yope, and the war captains of the two pueblos being together in the plaza to inform them of my said order by virtue of the said royal will, which is but just and proper with regard to the said Spaniards, and it being neither unjust nor tyrannical to order them to leave the said lands and town founded by them on their said tract when they have and are provided with a safe dwelling on the portion of land which belongs to them as their own in the pueblo of San Juan, and as they also have their lands sufficient, irrigable, and dependent upon the seasons which are well known, and it is not right that injustice and injury should be done to the Spaniards by keeping them out of their said lands known to be theirs, which through the Divine will promise, on account of their fertility, abundant harvests, wherewith to maintain themselves and secure their support, without running the risk of a failure and the loss of their supplies by working new lands; and these (the Spaniards) even at great cost are not yet secure among the said natives, but are discouraged and intimidated, and have not the measure and the amount of their legitimate value (of the lands), and besides, the risk of a new loss to the royal Crown, and also the labor of working for a year lands wild and unknown, for all of which I, the said governor and captain-general, ought to consider and regard such proper reasons as the near arrival of the above-mentioned lot and branch of the said people and settlers in the said planting season, so as not to have them to break lands, much less not to be troubled with regard to their dwelling houses, they having them secured on the said lands and tracts, as well as their acequias open and prepared, wherefore it is not in my power to give permission to the said natives of San Lazaro to plant and cultivate the same for this year, but they, as well as those of the said pueblo, must vacate them, and go to their said piece of land and dwelling houses in the said pueblo of San Juan and on their said lands and there plant their crops, and he will give them time to move without injuring or tearing down the said houses of the said town until the moon of the coming month, and he will call upon them to consider their having enjoyed for so many years the planting of the said lands as a reason for there being nothing due them on account of their leaving the said town. And with regard to the pueblo of San Cristoval, my said lieutenant-general, together with the said alcalde mayor and interpreter, Matias Lujan, will proceed to the same, and will tell the said governor and captains to go to the said place of Chimayo, where they asked my permission to settle, and I will keep my word to them in all things, and if it be ascertained that the said land which they designated and asked for can be planted at once, and he will remind them that I gave the said permission and promise in regard to the said possession with the understanding that the lands should not be such as to require much time to prepare them for planting, and it having been learned that this could readily be done I made them the said grant under the condition that they should at once take possession and establish their settlement and plant their crops at the said place; and he will give them also, as a term for leaving and moving from their said town until the moon of the coming month, since they have had time sufficient for the same, and the said Spanish settlers, who have made representation and to whom I have made a grant because of their having alleged that the said tract and lands were theirs in the said place of Chimayo, shall go with my said lieutenant-general, in order that in the presence of the said governor and the natives of the said pueblo of San Cristoval they shall identify the tract which they have asked for and the lands which I have granted to them, which are from the said pueblo forward and none towards that which they leave and the road which leads to the said pueblo of San Cristoval, since with this specification I made them the said grant; and I inform, direct, and order the said Spaniards, through my lieutenant-general, not to have any conflict with the said natives, as my word and the importance of the said compact are superior to the grant which I have made to them, since it is uncertain because of having been made on lands designated for the said natives and governor of the said pueblo of San Cristoval, and therefore I will make it up to them in another part and place of equal value; and to the said natives he will make known the said order and will direct that they obey, carry out, and execute the same within the said term in accordance with the reasons justifying the same set forth, and those of them who may have any complaint may appear before me, the said governor and captain-general, in this city to make the same, and to say to them that I will hear them verbally or in writing, they presenting them through their alcalde mayor and interpreter, Matias Lujan, and in order that this said order to my said lieutenant may appear, and for the execution of the same I so provided and signed the same with my civil and military secretary, and it is dated in this city of Santa Fe on the eighteenth day of the month of March, of this present year of one thousand six hundred and ninety-five, to whom, on my order, it was delivered in the original in order that it be returned with the report of its execution.

"DON DIEGO DE VARGAS ZAPATA LUJAN PONZE DE LEON
[rubric]
"ALPHONSO RAEL DE AGUILAR [rubric]
"Civil and Military Secretary."

DEPARTURE FROM THIS CITY OF SANTA FE

"In this city of Santa Fe, on the twentieth day of the month of March, in the year one thousand six hundred and ninety-five, I, Colonel Luis Granillo, lieutenant and captain-general of this kingdom of New Mexico, in fulfilment of and in obedience to the above order and direction of the governor and captain-general of this kingdom, who is Don Diego de Vargas Zapata Lujan Ponze de Leon, left this city in company with the sergeant, Juan Ruiz de Cazeres, and at the distance of two long leagues from the same before arriving at the pueblo of Tesuque, of the Teguas, I came to the farm, which is in ruins, which belonged to Colonel Francisco Gomez, in which there is sufficient agricultural land for one settler only, and pasturage and woodland for the stock of one owner only; and I proceeded from the said pueblo of Tesuque directly to San Lazaro, which is the pueblo named in the said order, and in order to duly execute the same I caused to be assembled its governor, and cacique, Don Cristoval Yope, and the elders and principal men, and the majority of the natives of the said town of the Thano tribe, and in the presence of their alcalde mayor, who is an interpreter, and Sergeant Juan Ruiz, who is also an interpreter and who acted as such, I read to them the said order that they might understand it in their Thano tongue word for word, as was done, and they all answered that they would obey in accordance with what they had asked for and the grant which had been made to them in order that they might settle anew on the place at the end of the Cañada, called Chimayo, adjoining the mountain range, and in order to identify the same and to carry out the said direction contained in the said order I instructed them to proceed to the inspection of the same in my company tomorrow and also to advise as parties interested and adjoining, the governor of San Cristoval, the principal men and the natives of the same and in order that it may so appear, I made it a part of the proceedings, and I signed the same, dated ut supra.   Luis Granillo [rubric]

"The said lieutenant-general proceeds with the said governors of the pueblos to the examination of the tract designated at Chimayo, which was granted to them by the governor and captain-general of this kingdom for their settlement.

"On the twenty-first day of the present month of March, of the date and year, I, the said lieutenant-governor and captain-general, left the said pueblo of San Lazaro with the said alcalde mayor and sergeant, and also its governor and leading Indians, and the majority of the natives, and also those of the pueblo of San Cristoval with their governor, their doctrinal minister, who is Fray Antonio Obregon, also going with them and me, the said lieutenant-general, and at the distance of two long leagues having gone through the Cañada and passed an arroyo or small rivulet (arroyo Riochuelo Pequeño) which comes down from the said mountain range and which lines with the farm of Captain Juan Ruis, up the river, and having gone along a little further, about half a league, where there is a ruin on the left, the said Indians, governors, and caciques showed me the plain which is adjacent to the said ruin which is in a Cañada wide and large enough for their pueblo with sufficient land for irrigation from the arroyos and rivulets which come down from the said mountain range, and I examined the mouth of the ditch and the dam, which the said Indians showed me, and the said rivulet has water sufficient and permanent; and returning to the plain the said Indians again proceeded to mark off and describe the said place for which they had asked the said governor and captain-general, and which

grant he had made and conceded to them, and they marked off the plan for the said town, saying that it was to be of sixty-eight houses, in order that the people of the said two pueblos might occupy the same, and adding to them the Thanos Indians and captive women who had escaped from the city of Santa Fe in case they should desire to come with them, that they would admit and receive them; thus the said lands were given and set off to them they being satisfied with having examined and seen the tract and place for the establishment and site of their pueblo, and in order that it might so appear I made it a part of the proceedings and I signed it, dated ut supra.
"LUIS GRANILLO [rubric]

"The said lieutenant-general departs from the Cañada for the pueblo of San Juan and proceeds to the other side of the Rio del Norte to sleep at Santa Clara.

"And immediately thereafter, on the said day, month and year, I, the said lieutenant-general, took the route and way in order to carry out the tenor of the order and direction aforesaid, proceeding to the examination of the farms and ranches belonging to the Spanish setlers in the Cañada before the general revolution of this kingdom, which were said to be occupied and at the distance of half a league, and on the boundary of said farm of Captain Juan Ruiz, which he has at the said place of the said grant to the said Indians, I found and examined the farm which belonged to the Martinez, the ruins of which consist of the standing walls, and in them were living encamped five persons, with their families, because there were lands and pastures sufficient on the north; and having proceeded in the said direction about three-quarters of a league I found, on the left of the route, the said pueblo of San Lazaro, and crossing the Rio del Norte to the right side I found and saw the farm which belonged to Miguel Lujan, on which the house is still standing, he occupied with his own family only, as there is irrigable land sufficient for one family only and pastures sufficient for such stock as it might possess; and with this farm there lines another house and cultivable lands which were planted by Marcos de Herrera, who had his family on another farm lower down which said place has about as much land as the last named and mentioned; and following this there is another lot of cultivable land which belonged to Nicolas de la Cruz, the house on which is standing and occupied by his widow, the land being sufficient for the support of her family only, and the pastures are in the same proportion; and following this is the land which belonged to Melchor de Archuleta, the ruin of the house only remaining, and there are about sufficient lands for one family, with pastures to correspond; and following along the said plain and meadow there is another farm, which belonged to Juan Griego, and this is a better piece of land than any of the others, because of its extent, it being sufficient for two families, dividing the agricultural land between them and giving them the pastures in common; and next there follows another farm, which belonged to Sebastian Gonzales, and now held by Captain Alonso del Rio, and in this two others had shares, so that there is room for three families to settle on the said tract, and the lands are of superior quality; and next is the farm which belonged to Francisco Xavier, the house in ruins and a little tower standing, and although he lived on it alone, the tract has abundant land for two families; and this is followed by that of Pedro de la Cruz, of whose house there is but one room standing, and it has land sufficient for one family only; and having finished making the inspection of the said farms I, the said lieutenant-general, proceeded to the other part of the arroyo, which lies between them and descends the said Cañada, the Rio del Norte being on the right, and I examined the following farms: first, there is adjoining the said arroyo the farm of which belonged to Bartolomé Montoya, on which there is only the ruin of the house in which he lived, and there are lands sufficient for one family only; and there adjoins this another farm, which belonged to Diego Lopez, and there is a tower left standing which adjoined his house, there being land enough for one family; following this is another farm, which belonged to Marcos de Herrera, and the said farm has land sufficient for one family, the house, because of its being close to the said arroyo or rivulet, was carried away by a heavy freshet; next follows another tract of land, which was held and owned by the community of the pueblo of Santa Clara; following is the farm which belonged to Colonel Francisco Gomez, the lines of the foundation of his house only are visible, and there is room for one family only; next follows the farm which belonged to Ambrosio Saez, in the houses of which there are now living, as they were during the past year of one thousand six hundred and ninety-four, part of the Tegua Indians, rebels from the pueblo of Tesuque making use of the said lands, for which reason the houses are in good condition, and on this farm two other families can be settled; and there is also in the middle of the said meadow the farm on which Agustin Romero was settled during the planting season because he had his cultivable land on the said tract, and here one family can live very well; and so descending along the Rio del Norte and the Mesa de San Ildefonso, the ruins of the said house are seen, and the land is sufficient only for one family; and the said farms are those which are found as aforesaid, from the said mouth of the Cañada as named, with the owners who lived in them and were settled on them; and I, the said lieutenant-general, then returned with Sergeant Juan Ruiz, who accompanied me on the said inspection, and he knows the said places because of always having lived near them and of having been raised there; and the said report is true and certain, and in order that it may so appear, I made it a part of the proceedings, and I signed it, and I proceeded to the pueblo of Santa Clara, in order to sleep there; dated ut supra.

"LUIS GRANILLO [rubric]

"Arrival of the said lieutenant-general at the city of Santa Fe, at which place he returns the order of the said governor and captain-general with the proceedings had in obedience thereto.

"On the twenty-third day of the present month of the date and year, I, the said lieutenant-general, having arrived at the city of Santa Fe, made report of the foregoing proceedings to the governor and captain-general of this kingdom, Señor Don Diego de Vargas Zapata Lujan Ponze de Leon, and by direction and order of his excellency I left and delivered the original into his hands, and in order that it may so appear I signed the same with the said governor and captain-general in the presence of his civil and military secretary.

"DON DIEGO DE VARGAS ZAPATA LUJAN PONZE DE LEON [rubric]

"LUIS GRANILLO [rubric]

"Before me:
 "ALPHONSSO RAEL DE AGUILAR [rubric]
  "Civil and Military Secretary"

PETITION OF THE THANOS TRIBE OF THE PUEBLOS OF SAN
CRISTOVAL

"To THE GOVERNOR AND CAPTAIN-GENERAL:

"The governors of the pueblos of San Lazaro and San Cristoval of the Thanos tribe for themselves and in the name of the people of the said pueblos: We appear before your excellency asking that all the privileges allowed by law be given us, and we say: That your excellency was pleased to order us to move from the said pueblos in order to settle them with Spaniards, and we pray that your excellency will give us time to plant the said lands, which are now open, during the present year, using the acequias of the same, and as soon as we take off the crops we will vacate the said pueblos in order that your excellency may settle them as your excellency pleases. Which said petition your excellency was pleased to grant, and with the same we were gratified. And now we have learned that it is the intention of your excellency to send us to settle and plant in another place, in view of which we submit to the consideration of your excellency the hardships which we are now undergoing, as we have (as is well known) no maize, which is our only food, and now we are not only unable to procure any, but in order to support ourselves up to the present we have sacrificed our clothing, having had to sell it at low prices, and also in order to have seed for this year, and no matter where we may go to settle and plant it will be necessary for the people of both pueblos to occupy all their time in breaking the land and constructing acequias, a thing impossible to do in this year, because we have nothing to live on and we will have to seek it elsewhere, with which the present evil is not remedied, nor that of the future, which is imminent. In view of all that which we have set forth, placing ourselves at the feet of your excellency, with all due respect, we ask and pray that your excellency will consider our need and the remedy for the same, which rests wholly on your excellency's word, and that your excellency will be pleased to permit that for this year we may plant in these pueblos, and on our part we are ready to vacate them as soon as we gather the crops, in which we hope to receive from the powerful hand of your excellency all favor and grace as we have already experienced in things of greater import, and which is just, and for the same, etc.,

"THE THANOS GOVERNORS OF SAN LAZARO
AND SAN CRISTOVAL.

"Presentation of the foregoing petition by the war captains for themselves and in the name of the Thanos tribe of the pueblos of San Lazaro and San Cristoval.

"In this city of Santa Fe, on the twentieth day of the month of March, of the year one thousand six hundred and ninety-five, before me, Don Diego de Vargas Zapata Lujan Ponze de Leon, governor and captain-general of this kingdom and provinces of New Mexico, its new restorer and conqueror at his own expense, and re-conqueror and settler and castellan of its forces and garrisons by His Majesty, etc.

DECREE

"It was presented by the war captains of the natives of the Thanos tribe of the said pueblos of San Lazaro and San Cristoval; and, whereas I have given the order to my lieutenant-general, I direct that it be carried out and executed, since I can only permit that the Indians of the first pueblo, that of San Lazaro, if they do not desire to join and incorporate themselves with those of the pueblo of San Juan de los Caballeros, where they came from and where they left their portion of land, or to return to their old pueblo which they left and which they had and did have before the general revolution of this kingdom in the year 'eighty, and in which they lived for many years afterwards, they shall join and agree to live together in the said second pueblo of San Cristoval, and shall plant their crops on their lands, going as far as the said Cañada of Chimayo and farm of Moraga, where, during the past year because of the second uprising, they made and had their cornfields; and they having lands of their own, there is no reason why the royal will of His Majesty the King, our master, should not be carried out in regard to Spaniards who are expected and who are now on their way here to augment the population and secure the restoration and reconquest of this said kingdom, nor that the provision made for the same out of his royal treasury should be lost by their not being given lands suitable and proper for their making their crops and thereby their support — reasons for not being able to leave exposed to said contingency an enterprise of such magnitude; and besides, in view of the objection of the said natives that the said lands are not in condition to be cultivated, they ought to consider the favor done in giving them the half of the lands belonging to the other said pueblo of San Cristoval, and acknowledge the care and attention given to their relief; and in order that this said decree may appear of record let it be placed, with the petition of the said natives with the decrees and proceedings, which by virtue of the said order my said lieutenant-governor and captain-general shall carry out and make report of the same in order that proper action may be taken, and I signed it in this said city with my civil and military secretary on the said day ut supra.

"Don Diego de Vargas Zapata Lujan Ponze de Leon
[rubric]
"Before me:
"Alphonsso Rael de Aguilar [rubric]
"Civil and Military Secretary."

"Proclamation including therein the grant made to the Mexican-Spanish families and given with the title of Villa Nueva de Santa Cruz de Españoles Mexicanos del Rey Nuestro Señor Don Carlos Segundo, as set forth and the conditions and causes expressed for the carrying out of the same.

"Don Diego de Vargas Zapata Lujan Ponze de Leon, governor and captain-general of this kingdom and provinces of New Mexico, its new restorer, conqueror at his own expense, reconqueror and settler of the same, castellan of its forces and garrisons, by His Majesty, etc.,

"The Thanos Indians, of the pueblo of San Lazaro, having by virtue of my order and direction, as expressed in the same and forwarded for its due execution on the twentieth of March last of this present year to my lieutenant-governor and captain-general, Colonel Luis Granillo, as it appears in the proceedings which by virtue of the said order were had, and the said Indians having consulted with their governors and asked me for the grant of the tract of the Cañada de Chimayo and left to me the said pueblos of San Lazaro and San Cristoval, and I having succeeded in having that of San Lazaro vacated in order to employ and occupy it with the families which his excellency the viceroy, the Conde de Galve, has sent for the settlement of this said kingdom of New Mexico, and they having arrived on the twenty-third of June of the past year one thousand six hundred and ninety-four, their number being in accordance with their list and muster roll, in order that they might be supported and lodged until the said kingdom was safe, and they came into this said city to the number of sixty-six and one-half families, and in order that they may be together without the intrusion of any others, in view of their union, and in order that they may be contented, they having come from one place and country to this said city, I placed them in the first grade, and I designate the said pueblo, its dwelling houses, its cleared agricultural lands, drains, irrigation ditches, and dam or dams which the said native Indians had and did have for irrigation and the security of raising their crops, and I also designate and grant, in the name of His Majesty, the dams which they may leave open and those which they may open, and the woods, pastures, and valleys which the said natives had and enjoyed, without prejudice to the farms and ranches which lie within its limits and district, and all that which it covers and may contain as far as the pueblos of Nambé, Pojoaque, Jacona, San Ildefonso, Santa Clara, and San Juan de los Caballeros, giving these as the boundaries of the tract which the said settlement shall enjoy, hold, and have, and which I make a seat and town, and also possession of the houses which may be given or assigned to them in person; and furthermore, the honorary title of 'Villa Nueva de Santa Cruz de Españoles Mexicanos del Rey Nuestro Señor Carlos Segundo,' which, in the name of His Majesty, I give to the said settlement, and I constitute and grade it as the first new settlement, and as such it shall enjoy priority of settlement, with the understanding that that of this city of Santa Fe is the first, and in it only shall be held the election of the members of the illustrious council, but each shall have its civil authority, which shall be composed of an alcalde mayor and war captain and lieutenant, with the title of captain of militia, alférez, and sergeant, the said settlement being limited to four squad corporals and alguazil de guerra, who shall go out on scouting expeditions with the said captain of militia and other officers, alternating every month, and they shall have this style and form of government because of being on the frontier, and in order that the said Spanish Mexicans may be informed of the grant of the said Villa Nueva made to them, I direct that the same shall be published in the said form, in order that they may acknowledge in due form that I, the said governor and captain-general, have them in this said kingdom and that I have favored them in proportion to my respectful appreciation of the promise contained in the proclamation ordered to be published by his excellency the said viceroy, the Conde de Galve, as in it he promised them and directed that I should be ordered to give them lands on which to settle, and I give them all with appreciable improvements, since I have given them cleared and broken lands and of known fertility, with their drains and irrigating ditches and dams in good condition and with the irrigation secured, and also new houses, because the said pueblo is new, and they have nothing to do but to go and live in them and to make use of the lands which I will designate for them, granting ranches and farms to those who may prefer the same, in order to allow them more room and allow for other settlers who may come in, and which the King our master may be pleased to send, and also those which I, the said governor and captain-general, may deem it proper to send to settle there, and this will also be done with people who may voluntarily ask for a grant, and who may be designated as settlers of the said town, in order that they may enjoy the privileges and rights of the same; and in order that it may so appear and that they may be ready to leave this city of Santa Fe I appoint Thursday, at ten o'clock in the morning, and I will then have in the plaza of this city the packmules which I now have, and I will also furnish some horses to mount, in part, those who may need them, and I will aid them in all things, assuring them that a ration of beef and corn shall not be wanting, as well as half a fanega of corn to each family for planting which I promise to give them, and also implements, such as picks, shovels, hoes, and axes, until those ordered by his excellency the viceroy from the contractors shall arrive, and there shall also be forwarded to their alcalde mayor and war captain, who may be appointed, a supply of firearms, powder, and ball, in order that they may be provided with all that is necessary; and in order that this said proclamation and that which is set forth in it may serve them as a foundation and sufficient title, I order that it be published in military style, with music by the band, and in the presence of the leaders and officers and my lieutenant-governor and captain-general, and also

Don Juan de Acuña, Marqués de Casa Fuerte
Viceroy of Mexico, 1722-34

that part of the illustrious council which is in this city, and its notary, and of my civil and military secretary, and that it be published in the inner and the outer plazas; and I signed it in this said city of Santa Fe on the nineteenth day of the month of April, one thousand six hundred and ninety-five.
"DIEGO DE VARGAS ZAPATA LUJAN PONZE DE LEON
[rubric]
"By order of the governor and captain-general:
"ALPHONSSO RAEL DE AGUILAR [rubric]
"Civil and Military Secretary
"In this city of Santa Fe, on the nineteenth day of the month of April of the year one thousand six hundred and ninety-five, I, Captain Alphonsso Rael de Aguilar, civil and military secretary, certify that on this day this said proclamation was published in the two public plazas of this city in the presence of a large concourse of people in the same and in a loud and intelligible voice by Sebastian Rodriguez, negro drummer, and in order that it may so appear I signed it.
"ALPHONSSO RAEL DE AGUILAR [rubric]
"Civil and Military Secretary."

THE MEXICAN SETTLERS DESTINED FOR THE VILLA NUEVA DE SANTA CRUZ DEPART FROM SANTA FE

"On the twenty-first day of the present month of April of the said year of one thousand six hundred and ninety-five, at the hour designated in the proclamation granting the title of Villa Nueva de Santa Cruz de los Españoles Mexicanos del Rey Nuestro Señor Don Carlos Segundo, the sixty families now in this city of Santa Fe departed at nine o'clock in the morning to settle, as provided in the said proclamation, and, in order that it may so appear, I signed it with my civil and military secretary.
"DIEGO DE VARGAS ZAPATA LUJAN PONZE DE LEON
[rubric]
"Before me:
"ALPHONSSO RAEL DE AGUILAR [Rubric]
"Civil and Military Secretary."

ARRIVAL AT THE VILLA NUEVA DE SANTA CRUZ

"On the twenty-second day of the month of April of the said date and year, I, the said governor and captain-general, Don Diego de Vargas Zapata Lujan Ponze de Leon, of this Kingdom and Provinces of New Mexico, by His Majesty, arrived at this Villa de Santa Cruz de los Mexicanos Españoles del Rey Nuestro Señor Don Carlos Segundo, so named and placed by me the said governor and captain-general, its site and settlement having been vacated by my order by the Thanos tribe, formerly of the pueblo of San Lazaro, and having given it the title and placed it under the protection of the Holy Cross, and they having already arrived with their alcalde mayor and war captain appointed, and the other officers named in the said proclamation, and with the title of Villa published in the same, and ordered to be published on the nineteenth day of the present month and year, and they being drawn up in line with their said captain and other officers designated and appointed, and they were at the entrance of the plaza of the said Villa, and dismounting there near the chapel which served as a church for the natives of the said pueblo, and having ordered the settlers to form in a half circle at my side, the royal alférez being front with the royal standard with my lieutenant-governor and my civil and military secretary, I directed the said alcalde mayor and war captain, Major Antonio Jorge, his lieutenant and captain of militia, Sergeant Nicolas Ortiz, and his ensign, Joseph Valdez, and Sergeant Manuel Ballejo and Antonio Godinez, Alguacil de Guerra and the four squad corporals, Joseph del Balle, Sebastian de Salas, Miguel Fajardo, and Bustos, to step forward from the said line, all of whom were appointed as the government political and military the said Villa being on the frontier, by me, the said governor and captain-general.

POSSESSION GIVEN OF THE SAID VILLA AND OATH MADE

"And I required and directed that they should make the usual oath accepting the said place and settlement, the Nueva Villa of their own nation of the Mexicanos Españoles del Rey Nuestro Señor Don Carlos Segundo, and as loyal vassals to maintain and preserve it, even at the expense of their lives, to which they responded under said oath that they accepted the same and that they would obey and keep the same; and I again made them the grant under the said acceptance and oath, revalidating to them their lands which belong to them and the boundaries set forth, and which limit the pueblos mentioned in the said proclamations of jurisdiction without prejudice to the boundaries of the lands which belong to each one; and also, in order to encourage them, I made them a grant of all the minerals which might be found in the Chimayo mountain range according as they might discover them and that I would carry out and observe the royal ordinances of His Majesty, and that they be of good heart and keep up their courage and that on my part I would assist them; and there being present the reverend father, Fray Francisco de Vargas, ecclesiastical judge in capite of this kingdom and its custodio in this custodia and concourse, and having in his company the reverend father preacher missionary, Fray Antonio Moreno, whom he had chosen as guardian and minister, I, the said governor and captain-general, said to the said settlers that he being the chaplain of His Majesty appointed and named him as their guardian and as such I gave him possession of the said chapel in order that until they rebuilt their church it might serve them as such, and thus I gave possession of the same to the said reverend father, leading him into the same by the hand, and he arranged the altar, going in and out; and for the greater formality and force of the said possession and oath made in regard to the said Villa, I left my said place with my said royal alférez and my lieutenant, directing my royal alférez to place himself in the centre of the plaza, together with my civil and military secretary, in order that he might proclaim that he defended and sustained the possession given by favor of His Majesty at the said granted place and tract with the limits and boundaries given and granted by me, the said governor and captain-general, in the said royal name, to the said settlers with the honorary title of Villa Nueva de los Españoles Mexicanos del Rey Nuestro Señor Don Carlos Segundo; that he came out to defend it as he would defend it with his life, and thus with his drawn sword in his hand he would sustain and did sustain it against all who might oppose it; and I, the said governor and captain-general, with all present, cried out all together, as loyal vassals of His Majesty, saying, 'Long live the King our Lord, whom may God preserve, the Señor Don Carlos II, King of the Spaniards, and all of this New World and this new town of the Mexicans and Spaniards, and which in his royal name was founded with the title of Villa Nueva de los Mexicanos y Españoles, and increased, founded, and settled in the interest of his Royal Crown, may he live for many years and reign over greater domains and monarchies;' and having repeated the said acclamation three times, throwing up our hats, three volleys were fired at the same time, in congratulation upon the installation of the said settlers with such honor and demonstrations of appreciation and jubilee; and they asked me as a favor that I would give them a certified copy and that I would order that they be given the same of the said possession as well as of the proclamation and the quality of the title specified in the same in order that they might hold the same as such for the said Villa; and in order that it may so appear they signed it with me the aforesaid, together with my lieutenant-governor and captain-general and my civil and military secretary.

"DON DIEGO DE VARGAS ZAPATA LUJAN PONZE DE LEON [rubric]

"LUIS GRANILLO [rubric]
"SERGEANT MANL. BALLEJO [rubric]
"ANTONIO BALVERDE DE COSSIO [rubric]
"The Alférez Real: ANTONIO JORGE [rubric]
"Before me:
"ALPHONSO RAEL DE AGUILAR [rubric]
"Civil and Military Secretary."

THE GOVERNOR AND CAPTAIN-GENERAL LEAVES ORDERS WITH THE SAID LIEUTENANT-GENERAL TO PARTITION THE SEPARATE TRACTS BELONGING TO THE SAID SETTLEMENT.

"In this city of Santa Fe, on the twenty-third day of the month of April of the year one thousand six hundred and ninety-five, I, the said governor and captain-general, my personal presence being necessary in the city of Santa Fe, and I having to go to the pueblos of San Cristoval and Nambé, I order and I leave orders with my lieutenant-governor and captain-general that the separate lands of the district and limits of the said Villa Nueva de Santa Cruz, the settlers having been assembled and it having been ascertained which of them have received and have been favored with grants of the tracts and ranches already surveyed, to those to whom such grants have not been made the said separate lands shall be given, marking off for each settler and his family that which may be found to be sufficient for the planting of one-half a fanega of maize, and in it he may plant such other seed as he may have, and the said partition shall be made in such manner as to satisfy the said settlers, and of the lands that may be left over an account shall be made to me, and in order that the said order may appear in this said decree I made it a part of the proceedings, and I signed it, with my civil and military secretary.

"Don Diego de Vargas Zapata Lujan Ponze de Leon
[rubric]
"Before me:
"Alphonso Rael de Aguilar [rubric]
"Civil and Military Secretary"

Arrival of the said governor and captain-general at the pueblo of San Cristoval, and he again requires the native Thanos of the same to plant their crops and to carry their harvest to the new pueblo which they shall build on the said tract of Chimayo, in order that he may settle the said pueblo with Spaniards in the month of October.

"And immediately thereafter, on the said day, month, and year of the date, I, the said governor and captain-general, having repeated to the said Spanish Mexicans of the said Villa Nueva de Santa Cruz the said order, I bade them good-bye and proceeded to the said pueblo of San Cristoval, in the plaza of which place all its people were assembled, together with those who had been settled at the said Villa Nueva, and I confirmed the grant which I had made to them in giving permission to pass this summer on the same and to plant their crops on its lands, and required of them that the crops which God our Lord might be pleased to permit them to gather they should at once carry to the new pueblo, which during this summer they would have to rebuild, since in the month of October they would have to occupy it, leaving that of San Cristoval vacant in order that I might settle it with Spaniards, as I had already informed them, and they replied that they would so do; and I having again confirmed the grant made in their favor of the said tract of Chimayo, I bade them good-bye, leaving them happy; and in order that it may appear of record I made it a part of the proceedings, and I signed it, with my civil and military secretary.

"Don Diego de Vargas Zapata Lujan Ponze de Leon
[rubric]
"Before me:
"Alphonsso Rael de Aguilar [rubric]
"Civil and Military Secretary"

THE SAID GOVERNOR AND CAPTAIN-GENERAL PROCEEDS TO THE PUEBLO OF NAMBÉ, AND IN IT GIVES POSSESSION TO THE MINISTER MISSIONARY, WHO REMAINS THERE AS DOCTRINARIAN.

"On the said day, the twenty-third of April, of the said year, I, the said governor and captain-general, the very reverend father custodian, Fray Francisco de Vargas, having appointed as minister doctrinarian to the mission of the Teguas of the pueblo of Nambé, proceeded with him to give him the possession, and, having entered the said pueblo, its people were assembled to receive me with all politeness, and they being in front of the principal site where they had the chapel and the house adjoining the same for the said minister, I dismounted, and, through the interpreter, I told them that I had come to install the father who was to aid them and administer the holy sacraments, he being the reverend father preacher, Antonio de Acevedo, and in the said form I gave him possession of the said chapel and house, and in testimony of the same I directed that the doxology, etc., be prayed and sung three times, and I ordered the said Indians to aid him in all things and to fulfil their obligations as Christians and to fail in nothing; and in order that the said possession and the reply of the said natives that they would comply with and obey all that I had ordered might appear of record, I signed it with my civil and military secretary.

"DON DIEGO DE VARGAS ZAPATA LUJAN PONZE DE LEON
[rubric]

"Before me:
 "ALPHONSSO RAEL DE AGUILAR [rubric]
  "Civil and Military Secretary"

ARRIVAL OF THE FAMILIES WHICH BY ORDER OF HIS EXCELLENCY THE CONDE DE GALVE WERE PROCURED AND OBTAINED BY CAPTAIN JUAN PAEZ HURTADO, CHIEF COMMISSIONER, APPOINTED BY ME, THE SAID GOVERNOR AND CAPTAIN-GENERAL.

"In this city of Santa Fe, the capital of this kingdom and provinces of New Mexico, on the ninth day of the month of May of the present year of one thousand six hundred and ninety-five, there arrived at this city of Santa Fe, capital which it is of this kingdom and provinces of New Mexico, the families which by order of his excellency the viceroy, the Conde de Galve, with the approval of the general committee of the ministers of the royal treasury and war, in March of the past year of one thousand six hundred and ninety-four, ordered me, the said governor and captain-general of this kingdom, to send a chief commissioner possessing my confidence, to be appointed by me, and Captain Juan Paez Hurtado possessing the same, I gave him the commission and appointment in order that he might carry out the said orders of his excellency the said viceroy, and he proceeded to the kingdom of Galicia and the Real de Zacatecas and other places, and the families which he procured were forty-four, according to the list made of the same and which I, the said governor and captain-general, received in person, and in the presence of the said captain chief commissioner I gave them lodgings in the said city in the houses which the settlers now at the Villa Nueva de Santa Cruz had occupied, and in order that the said arrival may appear of record I signed it, with the said captain chief commissioner and my civil and military secretary.

"Don Diego de Vargas Zapata Lujan Ponze de Leon
[rubric]

"Before me:
"Alphonsso Rael de Aguilar [rubric]
"Civil and Military Secretary"

ACT OF TRANSMITTAL

"In this said city of Santa Fe, on the said day of the date May nine and year one thousand six hundred and ninety-five, I, the said governor and captain-general, Don Diego de Vargas Zapata Lujan Ponze de Leon, having examined these proceedings, in order that his excellency the viceroy, Conde de Galve, which he is of all this kingdom of New Spain, may be informed of what has been done in this said kingdom in the royal service, in which I, the said governor and captain-general have devoted the care and attention necessary for his satisfaction, and in order to make transmittal of the same I directed my civil and military secretary to make a literal copy of the said proceedings, as well as of the letter of transmittal with this said decree, in order that being copied and compared in due form the same transmitted and forwarded to his excellency the said viceroy, and more particularly because the courier despatched on the fourteenth of January of the present year has not returned and the cause of his delay is not known. And I signed it in this said city of Santa Fe on the said day, month, and year, with my civil and military secretary.

"Don Diego de Vargas Zapata Lujan Ponze de Leon
[rubric]

"Before me:
"Alphonsso Rael de Aguilar [rubric]
"Civil and Military Secretary"

"Most Excellent Sir:
"Sir: Captain Juan Paez Hurtado, chief commissioner appointed by me to bring the families which by order of your excellency he procured and obtained in the city of Zacatecas, having arrived at this city of Santa Fe and having entered the plaza of the same to the number of forty-four families, which I received and inspected personally, I going to the said plaza for the purpose, and also to lodge them in the houses which were vacated by the sixty Mexican families which your excellency also sent for the settlement of this kingdom, and having succeeded in all that which I might and could desire for the royal service of His Majesty in the Villa Nueva de Santa Cruz de los Vecinos Mexicanos del Rey Nuestro Señor Don Carlos Segundo in a pueblo which the rebels of the Thanos tribe had newly founded on lands which had belonged to Spaniards, and by the means which I devised for the accomplishment of this difficult enterprise I succeeded, as will be shown by the orders and proceedings had of which I forward a certified copy to your excellency and this, upon examination and consideration, will prove to your excellency that I have been successful, and that I have secured at a short distance another larger town of the said tribe which is vacant and free and I have secured it for the month of October, when, God willing, I will found and settle another town with these said families which we have received and lodged today in this city of Santa Fe, and I will see that both shall plant crops in order that they may be relieved from receiving rations as at present and living on the generosity and magnificence of your excellency, and it is very true that the transportation of maize to this city has caused me much trouble because of the distance of the kingdom of New Biscay and of there being no resources any nearer.

"I am anxious and troubled because the courier whom I despatched on the fourteenth of January of the present year to your excellency has not returned, and this also induces me to send this despatch, in order that I may ascertain the reason of his delay or know whether he has been robbed or murdered; and I beg that your excellency will send me duplicates of the orders and despatches which your excellency may have been pleased to forward to me by the said courier in order that I may on my part duly execute the same; and I also hope that your excellency has received the order that with the same your excellency may decide upon the reply to my letters of consultation forwarded by your excellency to the supreme and royal council of the Indies, as in this expectation I have delayed the said settlers in order that through its means they may be assured of their establishment; and two missions have also been established, Nambé and the said Villa Nueva, the doctrinal father serving the united pueblo of the said Thanos.

"While I was absent from this city there arrived a band of Apaches from the east, who are called Chiyenes, and they told in the town at which they arrived which is of the Picuriés tribe, how some men, white and light-haired, had destroyed a very large tribe of the Apaches Conejeros, living much further inland than their own. The Chiyenes then returned whence they came. This was told to me by the alcalde mayor and the father minister, who came to see me, and I having asked the alcalde mayor why he had not detained them, he replied that the leader of the band had said that he would return with all his people in September, and if God will permit me to live until his return I will hear what he has to say and judge of it accordingly, and I did not wish to omit to give your excellency this information, together with the above, as I desire to serve your excellency in all things; and may God preserve your excellency for many happy years. Done in Santa Fe, on the ninth day of the month of May, one thousand six hundred and ninety-five.

"Most excellent sir, etc.,
"Don Diego de Vargas Zapata Lujan Ponze de Leon"
[rubric]

883 DON FERNANDEZ De TAOS. 1796.
Possession. Reported Claim No. 125.

884 JUAN JOSE SILVIA. *La Cienega.* No date.
Complaint that he is forbidden to graze his stock on the common lands. No action taken.

885 **MATIAS SENA.** *Santa Fe*, 1799.
Will. Fernando Chacón, Governor.

886 **LUIS MAESE** to Augustin Sais. *Santa Fe*, 1799.
Land. Antonio de Aguilera Isasi, Alcalde.

887 **SAN JOSE** DEL **BADO** DEL **RIO** DE **PECOS.** 1803.
Partition of lands to settlers. Names given in this archive. Fernando Chacón, Governor. Pedro Bautista Pino, Alcalde.

888 **MARIANO CASTELO** to Juan Segura. *Santa Fe*, 1812.
Land in the *Cañada del Tio Leonardo*. José Miguel Tafoya, Alcalde.

889 **MARIA POLONIA SILVIA.** *La Cienega*, 1815.
Complaint that her husband sold her land without her consent. Juan Estevan Pino, Alcalde. Alberto Maynez, Governor.

890 **TOWN OF SOCORRO**
Grant. 1817. Reported Claim No. 107, *q. v.*

891 **JUAN RAFAEL ORTIZ.**
Report of Committee of the *Ayuntamiento* against donating certain lands. *Santa Fe*, 1831. Ribera, Talomo, sindico. Armijo.

892 **MATIAS SANDOVAL.** *Santa Fe*, 1822.
Grant of lands in *Galisteo* by the *Ayuntamiento* of *Santa Fe*. Pedro Armendaris, José Maria Baca, Secretary.

893 **RAFAEL SENA.** 1822.
Grant. Same as No. 892.

894 **FELIPE SANDOVAL.** 1822.
Grant; same as 892-893.
The petition in the Town of Galisteo Grant was made in February, 1814, by Felipe Sandoval; José Luis Lobato; Julian Lucero; Matias Sandoval; Pedro Sandoval; José Antonio Alarid, Diego Piñeda, and was addressed to Governor Maynes, who granted them a piece of land at the old abandoned Indian pueblo of Galisteo, reserving to the people of Santa Fe and vicinity, the privilege of

pasturing live stock. Maynes was not governor at the time this petition states. Don José Manrique was governor from 1808 to 1815, and Alberto Maynes in 1815, 1816, and 1817. From the papers on file in this case, in the surveyor-general's office, Donaciano Vigil says that he never held any office under the Spanish government, but under the Mexican government he was continually in office from the year 1824 until the American government took possession in 1846, at which time he was a captain of the line and secretary of the militia commandancy, which latter position he had held ever since the year 1824. That he acted as civil governor of New Mexico from January, 1847, until the first of March, 1851.

895 JOSE MANUEL SANCHES, *Bosque*, 1823, vs. Antonio Martin.
: Question of lands.

896 CABO JOSÉ SALAICE, CABO FRANCISCO GARCIA, CARABINERO JOSÉ BACA, SOLDADO JOSÉ SALAICE, SOLDADO FELIZ GARCIA, SOLDADO ANTONIO JOSÉ RIVERA.
: Petition; 1823, asking the *Jefe Politico* for the *sobrante* of the league between the pueblos of *Santo Domingo* and *San Felipe*. Bartolomé Baca, *Jefe Politico*. Referred to the Provincial Deputation.

897 MIGUEL and FELIPE SENA. *Santa Fe*, 1824.
: Petition for lands on the *Pecos*. No action taken.

898 JOSE RAFAEL SAMORA and 25 others for lands on the *Pecos*. 1824.
: Reported Claim No. 108, *q. v.*

899 MANUEL ANTONIO RIBERA. For himself and Others. 1822.
: Petition for lands adjoining *San Miguel del Bado*. Reported Claim No. 29. *Anton Chico Grant*. Facundo Melgares, Governor. San Miguel del Bado, 1824.

  On the 24th day of January, 1822, Don Salvador Tapia, for himself and sixteen others, filed a petition with the "Tribunal of Independence"— presumably the ayuntamiento of San Miguel del Bado — for the tract of land on the Pecos river, known as Anton Chico. The president of the ayuntamiento referred the petition to the then governor, Facundo Melgares, who on the 13th of February of the same year, sent the petition back to the ayuntamiento with instructions to make application to the Provincial Deputation. On November 9th of that year this was done. Nothing seems to have been done after that until May 2, 1822, when Melgares is supposed to have granted the land to Manuel Rivera and thirty-six men, and directed Manuel Baca, the constitutional justice of El Bado, to place the parties in possession, which was done on May 2d of the same year.

There is another document in this grant, of date March 3, 1834, which purports to be a distribution of lands at Anton Chico by Don Juan Martin, under verbal authority from the constitutional justice of El Bado, Don Juan José Cabeza de Baca. The Manuel Baca, above referred to, was a second cousin of Don Luis Maria Cabeza de Baca. This document states that the original settlers were driven off by Indians.

The original petitioners and settlers were: Salvador Tapia, Francisco Baca, Rafael Duran, Juan Sebastian Duran, Diego Antonio Tapia, Bernardo Ullibarri, Felipe Valencia, Luis Gonzales, Juan Cristobal Garcia, Tomas Martin, Juan José Martin, Miguel Martin, José Medina, Simon Estrada, Lorenzo Tapia, Mariano Aragon, and José Duran.

The name Anton Chico was a slang term, the place being properly known as "Sangre de Cristo."

When possession was given it was done in the presence of "thirty-six" settlers and that of two "aldermen;" Don Ventura Trujillo, second alderman, and Don Miguel Sisneros, third alderman. The conditions were, among others, that the place selected should be common, not only for themselves, but for others who in the future should remove there; and also that the settlers should be equipped "with fire-arms and arrows, and they shall pass muster upon entering upon the land and whenever the justice sent to them shall deem proper." They cried "long life to the independence" and took possession of lands bounded as follows: On the north, the boundary of Don Antonio Ortiz; on the south the ridge of the Piedra Pintada and the little table-land of Guadalupe; on the east, the Sabino Spring, with the Alto de Los Esteros, where the river forms a cañon below, where the men were killed, and on the west, the Cuesta and the Little Bernal Hill; which is the boundary of El Bado.

In 1834 the place was known as "The Avocation of Our Lord and Sangre de Cristo."

It was near this place that the Texas-Santa Fe expedition under McLeod came in 1841; at that time Anton Chico had a population of 600.

Don Juan Bautista Vigil y Alarid, testifying in 1859, says that Colonel Viscarra proclaimed the independence of Mexico in New Mexico; that the Spanish governor, Melgares, was relieved by Colonel Vizcarra, who was appointed upon the petition of the citizens of New Mexico who requested the removal of Melgares and that after the declaration of independence, under the Plan of Iguala, all of the old authorities were relieved by the new officers.

Governor Melgares was superseded by Colonel Vizcarra on the 21st day of December, 1822.

Don Donaciano Vigil, appointed secretary by General Kearny in 1846, afterward governor of New Mexico, declares in his testimony before the surveyor-general, in 1859, that up to the 22d of December, 1822, the independence of Mexico was not known in New Mexico and the same order of things existed and all the authorities exercised their functions under the Spanish government; after the declaration had been promulgated by the general government the latter approved all of the public acts performed by the officers of the country from the date of the declaration to the time it was published in New Mexico; in other words, these acts were "canonized"; they were not approved by statute but they were not disapproved. However, the people of new Mexico considered themselves as separated from the Spanish crown from the date of the declaration, September 27, 1821.

JUAN ÉSTEVAN PINO: Report of Diego Casilla, *Alcalde Constitucional de la Jurisdicion del Bado* in the matter of the giving possession of lands to said Pino in said place and the damage that would result therefrom, etc. Bartolomé Baca, Governor.

This item is of interest in connection with the *Anton Chico* and the *Las Vegas* grants, *q. v.*

900 URSULA CHAVES of *Los Padillas*, in the name of her husband, Antonio Sandoval. 1824.

In the matter of a petition for lands, made by her said husband, situate at Agua Negra. Referred by the Territorial Deputation to the *Jefe Superior Politico* in 1824. No final action. Juan Bautista Vigil, Secretary.

In 1845, the Mexican government granted to Antonio Sandoval, what is known as the Sandoval or Nolan Grant in Valencia county. Sandoval conveyed his title to Gervacio Nolan. The latter died in 1858 and his heirs sold the entire grant to Joel P. Whitney, who afterwards conveyed a half interest to F. H. Story. The surveyor-general of New Mexico found this to be a perfect grant and afterwards, the supreme court of New Mexico, in a suit brought on a homesteader's claim, decided that the action of the surveyor-general as to the validity or invalidity of grants was beyond the power of the supreme court to change and the legal effect of the action of the surveyor-general in declaring the title valid was to "segregate from the public domain all the lands covered by the grant as reported on by him and to except and reserve them from the operation of the homestead and other general laws of the United States providing for the disposal of the public domain."

901 PEDRO ALCANTAR VIGIL, of *Santa Cruz*, and 19 Others. 1845.

Petition for lands on the *Sapello* and *Manuelitas*. Acted upon by the Territorial Assembly and favorably recommended, but there is no record of possession having been given. Reported Claim No. 9—John Scolly, *q. v.* The names of the petitioners are found in this item.

902 DOLORES JALONA to Juan Damasio Salazar. *Santa Fe*, 1834.

903 ANTONIO SENA to George Pratt and William Hague. *Santa Fe*, 1831.

Lease of land. Pablo Montoya, Alcalde.

904 ALEJANDRO SANTIESTEVAN vs. PABLO MONTOYA. *Peña Blanca*, 1832.

Trespass; damage to crops. Juan Garcia, Alcalde; José Miguel Baca, Alcalde; Fernando Aragon, Alcalde.

905 MANUEL SENA vs. MIGUEL and FELIPE SENA, his sons.

THE SPANISH ARCHIVES OF NEW MEXICO 271

In the matter of the sale of a house to the defendants by their mother, Maria de Jesus Campos, without the consent of the plaintiff, her husband. *Santa Fe,* 1832. Juan Garcia, Alcalde. Francisco Rascon, Alcalde.

On the next to the last page there is a reference to a house on *"La calle publica q va para el barrio del Torreon."* This is the only reference to such a place found in the archives. Possibly it may refer to the locality in the neighborhood of the chapel of Rosario, as mention is made in several archives of a *"Torreon"* which stood upon lands in this locality belonging to Lucero de Godoy.

906 MARIA DE JESUS CAMPOS to Miguel and Felipe Sena. *Santa Fe,* 1832.

House and lot in said city. Juan Garcia, Alcalde. No. 905, *q. v.*

907 MANUEL SENA. *Santa Fe.*

In the matter of the sale of a house without his consent; sale by his wife. Abreu, *Jefe Politico.* Juan Garcia, Alcalde. Nos. 905 and 906, *q. v.*

908 MARIA GUADALUPE SANCHEZ.

Will. *Santa Fe.* 1832 or 1833. José Maria Baca y Terrus, Alcalde.

909 MIGUEL SENA vs. JUAN ESTEVAN PINO. *Santa Fe.* 1835.

Complaint in regard to a reservoir or pond. Albino Perez, Governor. Francisco Trujillo, Alcalde.

910 RAFAEL SENA of *Alburquerque* vs. FRANCISCO BACA, a *Navajo.* 1835.

Complains that defendant, of whom he and the other settlers of the *Cebolleta* bought a piece of land at *Cubero,* claims a part of the crops raised on the same. Referred to the Alcalde of Laguna. Albino Perez, Governor.

Petition of August 27, 1835, by Rafael Sanchez to the jefe politico. The petitioner states that in connection with all the other settlers of Cebolleta he had bought a tract of land of Francisco Baca, a Navajo Indian, at the place called Cubero, near the pueblo of Laguna; that possession of said tract had been given to the purchasers by the ex-alcalde, Don Juan Chaves, and the document evidencing that fact was in the hands of the then alcalde;

that this officer wanted to take from the petitioner one-third of the crop which he had raised that year, on the particular portion of the tract which had been assigned to him, in order to give it to the Indians (of Laguna?) who claimed a right to the lands.

In view of the foregoing, the petitioner asks the protection of the jefe politico against the arbitrary action of the alcalde, and in a postscript he adds that the parties interested in the tract had ceded a piece of land to the said Indians, which the latter ignored and left uncultivated.

On September 9, 1835, the jefe politico, Don Albino Perez, ordered the alcalde of Laguna to report in detail on the matters contained in the petition. There are no further proceedings.

911 RAFAELA SANCHEZ vs. Juan Bautista Vigil. *Santa Fe.* 1839.

Question of a corral in said city. Manuel Armijo, Governor.

912 MANUEL SANCHEZ. Intestate. *Santa Fe.* 1839.

Inventory of his estate. Gaspar Ortiz, Alcalde. Gaspar Ortiz Grant, Reported No. 31.

This grant is entirely within the limits of the grant to the *pueblo* of Nambé and its eastern boundary is the western boundary of the grant to the *pueblo* of Pojoaque. It was confirmed by Congress June 21, 1860, but has not been patented.

913 PABLO ORTIZ Y MIERA to José Anastacio Sandobal. *Santa Fe.* 1838.

House and lot in said city. Felipe Sena, Alcalde. Anastacio Sandoval to *Ayuntamiento* of *Santa Fe.* 1842. Donation of the above house and lot. Antonio Sena, Regidor.

914 JUAN JOSE SARRACINO. *Santa Fe.*

Petition for land on the *Pecos.* No date. No action.

915 FRANCISCO SANDOBAL. *Santa Getrudis de lo de Mora.* 1844.

Re-validation of sale of land made to Francisco Sandobal by Juan Antonio Garcia. Tomas Ortiz, *Juez de Primera Instancia.*

916 DIEGO SANDOBAL. *Santa Getrudis de lo de Mora.* 1844.
>Grant. Land on the Mora river. Tomas Ortiz, *Juez de Primera Instancia.*

917 AGAPITO SANDOVAL. *Valle de Santa Getrudis de lo de Mora.* 1844.
>Land on the Mora river. Tomas Ortiz, *Juez de Primera Instancia.* The name of Francisco Sandoval is mentioned in the first part of this grant, but it appears that it must be a mistake as Francisco had land there by purchase from Juan Antonio Garcia. No. 915, *q. v.*

918 FOREIGNERS as SETTLERS on public lands on the *Sapello.* 1845.
>Decision of the Departmental Assembly adverse on the ground that they are frontier lands.
>Bernardo V. Franco, *Secretario de Gobierno.* In this archive are a number of signatures of members of the Assembly.
>The national colonization law of January 4, 1823, by its first article, recites that the Mexican government "will protect the liberty, property, and civil rights of all foreigners who profess the Roman Catholic apostolic religion, the established religion of the empire."
>Pursuant to Article 27, "all foreigners who come to establish themselves in the empire shall be considered as naturalized, should they exercise any useful profession or industry, by which, at the end of three years, they have a capital to support themselves with decency, and are married. Those who, with the foregoing qualifications, marry Mexicans will acquire particular merit for obtaining letters of citizenship."
>By Article 31 it was provided that "all foreigners who may have established themselves in any of the provinces of the empire, under a permission of the former government, will remain on the lands which they may have occupied, being governed by the tenor of the law in the distribution of said lands."
>By virtue of a decree of the Sovereign General Constituent Congress, August 18, 1824, "those territories comprised within twenty leagues of the boundaries of any foreign nation, or within ten leagues of the seacoast, can

not be colonized without the previous approval of the supreme general executive power."

In 1828, it was decreed that "The governors — *Jefes Politicos* — of the territories are authorized in compliance with the law of the General Congress of the 18th of August, 1822, and under the conditions hereafter specified to grant vacant lands in their respective territories to such contractors (*empresarios*), families, or private persons, whether Mexicans or foreigners, who may ask for them, for the purpose of cultivating and inhabiting them."

In 1824, March 16th, the following edict was issued:

"Antonio Lopez de Santa Anna, general of division, *benemerito* of the country, and provisional president of the Mexican Republic, to all the inhabitants thereof:

"KNOW YE: — that after a mature and most cautious examination into the benefits which will result to the Republic from permitting foreigners to acquire property; having heard the opinion of the council of representatives, which with the greatest exactitude examined this subject; the reports of several *Juntas* of the departments, many well informed persons, and the *pro* and *contra* supported in print; having seen the various projects for a law which to this effect have been offered; being also convinced that a frank policy and a well-understood interest demand that there should be no longer delayed a concession which may tend to the advancement of the public, by the increase of population, the extension and division of property, which consequently makes the national wealth the greater; having also in consideration that by these means the safety of the nation may be more and more secured, since foreign proprietors will be so many more defenders of the national rights, at the same time that they are interested in the common property; considering also the impulse which will be given to agriculture, industry, and commerce, which are the sources of public wealth; and finally, that the opinion generally expressed is in favor of the said concessions, I have thought proper exercising the powers conceded in me by the seventh of the bases accorded in Tacubaya, and attested by the representatives of the departments, to decree as follows:

"Art. 1. Foreigners not citizens residing in the republic may acquire and hold town and country property, by purchase, adjudication, denouncement, or any other title established by the laws.

"Art. 2. They may also acquire ownership in mines of gold, silver, copper, quicksilver, iron, and coal, of which they may be the discoverers, in conformity with the ordinance of the branch.

"'Art. 3. Each individual foreigner cannot acquire more than two country estates in the same department, without a license from the supreme government, and only under the boundaries which they now have, each independent of the other.

. . . . .

"Art. 9. These arrangements do not include the departments on the frontier and bordering upon other nations, in regard to which special laws of colonization will be enacted, without the power to foreigners to ever acquire property in them, without the express license of the Supreme Government of the Republic.

"Art. 10. In the departments which are not on the frontier, and which may have coasts, only at five leagues distance from the coasts can foreigners acquire country property.

"Art. 11. In order that foreigners who may have acquired property in the republic may be citizens thereof, it is sufficient that they prove before the political authority of the place of their residence that they are proprietors, that they have resided two years in the republic, and that they have conducted themselves well. The *expediente* drawn up in this manner will be sent to the proper department, by which the certificate of citizenship will be issued.

"Art. 12. Foreigners cannot acquire royal or public lands in all the departments of the republic, without contracting for them with the government which possesses this right as representing the domain of the Mexican nation.

"Wherefore I order that it be printed, published, circulated, and carried into full effect.

"Palace of the National Government, Mexico, 11th March, 1842.   ANTONIO LOPEZ DE SANTA ANNA
"JOSE MARIA DE BOCANEGRA,
  "Minister of Foreign Affairs and Government"

919 AYUNTAMIENTO DE SANTA FE. 1845.
Petition to the Governor for a piece of land in front of the *Palace Garden*. Refused. José Francisco Baca y Terrus, Alcalde. Francisco Ortiz y Delgado, Alcalde.

920 FOREIGNERS as Settlers on public lands on the frontier. 1845.
>Decision of the Departmental Assembly in regard thereto. No. 918, *q. v.* J. Manuel Gallegos; Tomas Ortiz.

921 JOHN SCOLLY. *Santa Fe.* 1845.
>Petition. Asking reconsideration of his petition for lands by the Departmental Assembly. No. 918-920, *q. v.* Chaves, Governor.
>
>On the 27th of March, 1843, John Scolly, Gregorio Trujillo, Santiago Giddings, Agustin Duran, Guillermo Smith, Gabriel Allen, George H. Estes, Mateo Sandoval, Ygnacio Ortiz, Vincente Lopez, and Francisco Romero petitioned Governor Manuel Armijo for ten square leagues of land, situate at the junction of the Sapello and Mora rivers, in what is now Mora county, New Mexico; at the time, this land was in the *partido* or county of Taos; two days later Armijo granted the petition and the justice of the peace of Mora and Las Vegas was directed to put them in possession. On December 4, 1844, Scolly, Trujillo, Giddings, Duran, Smith, and Romero petitioned Governor Martinez, who had succeeded Armijo, for a confirmation of the grant which had been made by the latter, or that a new grant be made to them, as the time specified for cultivation of the lands in the former grant had expired. This had occurred on account of the invasion by the Texans, as well as on account of an order made by Martinez suspending all of the grants of a similar kind made by Armijo to other individuals. Martinez referred the petition to the prefect of the Santa Fe district, and on the 18th of December, the prefect, Don Antonio Sena, recommended that the grant be validated.
>
>Nothing was done until the spring of 1846, when Armijo was again governor, when the same persons, with the exception of Ygnacio Ortiz, again petitioned for the land. By direction of Armijo the persons were directed to be put in possession of as much land as they could cultivate, with other provisos. On May 13, 1846, the justice of the peace of Las Vegas, by order of Governor Armijo, put the persons named in possession of five square leagues, made a certificate of his doings and filed the same, together with a map, with the governor.
>
>Ten square leagues were asked for and five square leagues were given. The words *"cinco leguas cuadradas"* and *"cinco leguas encuadro,"* according to the

THE SPANISH ARCHIVES OF NEW MEXICO 277

testimony of witnesses, were held to be synonymous terms.

In the month of November, 1843, Scolly had already begun the cultivation of the land, according to Judge Joab Houghton. James Bone had a house and cultivated land near what was known as Barclay's Fort, which was situate near the junction of the Mora and Sapello rivers, which was known as Junta de los Rios. Barclay, whose name was Alexander, built his fort in 1849. This fort was still standing in the seventies.

The site of Fort Union was taken possession of in 1851 and was leased by the government from the grantees named in the petition.

Scolly, Giddings, and Smith were foreign born but naturalized Mexican citizens.

Don Donaciano Vigil stated, in 1857, before the surveyor-general, Pelham, that the custom under the Spanish and Mexican laws of measuring lands was to select a common center, from which the measurement was made in each direction, equally to the north, south, east, and west; that *cinco leguas cuadradas* would be two and one-half leagues measured in each direction from a common center.

Domingo Fernandez, in this case, testified that he was seventy-four years of age, by the grace of God; had been a justice of the peace under the Spanish and Mexican governments, a member of the cabildo of Santa Fe under the Mexican government, circuit attorney and keeper of the archives under the government of the United States.

Donaciano Vigil held the office of recorder of land titles under General Kearny's appointment, as well as secretary of New Mexico. General Kearny gave instructions for the recording of these land titles in a book provided for that purpose.

In measuring the lands of the Pueblo Indians, Domingo Fernandez declared that "in the center of the cemetery of every pueblo there is a cross from which the measurements were made in each direction, as the document called for."

John Scolly brought the first modern plows to New Mexico. In his petition, filed with Governor Armijo, he says: "We ordered from the United States plows of a new invention, and other necessary farming implements, which are now on the road and costing a considerable amount for their purchase and transportation; and during the next year we expect merinos and cows to improve the breed.''

922 FELIX MAES to Felipe Sandoval. *Santa Fe.* 1845.
House and lot. Juan Armijo, witness. Tomas Rivera, witness.

923 JUAN SAENZ and others.
Grant. Town of *Chaperito.* File No. 7, *q. v.*

924 AGUSTIN ZAES to Mateo Trujillo. *Santa Fe.* 1700.
Land in the city. *Testimonio.* Certified by Antonio de Aguilera Isasi, Alcalde.

925 ORIGINAL of 924.
Antonio de Aguilera Isasi, Alcalde.

926 DIEGO TRUXILLO. Grant. 1701.
Land on the *Chama.* Don Pedro Rodriguez Cubero, Governor and Captain-General.
Catalina Griego, widow of Diego Truxillo, and Antonio Truxillo, their son. Petition for re-validation of this grant to Salvador Santiestevan and Nicolas de Valverde, their near relations. 1714.
Salvador Santiestevan and Nicolas Valverde. Re-validation. Juan Ignacio Flores Mogollon, Governor.
Possession given by Sebastian Martin, Alcalde.
Bartolomé Lovato. 1714. Possession given in the same place to said Lovato by the same alcalde by order of the same governor. The grants do not conflict. The land is situate near the mouth of the *Chama* river.

927 SEBASTIAN DE SALAS to Juan Trujillo. 1701. *Santa Fe.*
Land. *Pojoaque.* Joseph Rodriguez, Alcalde.

928 SEBASTIAN CANSECO to Juan Trugillo. 1702.
Land in *Pojoaque* called *San Isidro.* Joseph Rodriguez, Alcalde.

929 DIEGO TRUXILLO, for his wife, Catalina Griego, and her sisters, Juana and Maria Griego, vs. Diego Arias de Quiros.
Relative to a tract of land in *Santa Fe.* 1703. *Testimonio* of the proceedings, certified to by Alphonso Rael de Aguilar, Secretary of Government and War.
He also signed himself ''Alonzo.''

930 MATEO TRUXILLO. *Santa Fe.* 1703.
> Protest against grant of a piece of land in *Santa Fe* to Joseph Lopez. El Marqués de la Nava Brazinas, Governor and Captain-General.

931 JOSEPH DE QUIROS to Miguel Thenorio de Alva. *Santa Fe.* 1703.
> Part of a grant made to him by Governor Pedro Rodriguez Cubero in *Pojoaque*. Antonio Montoya, Alcalde.

932 ANTONIO GODINES to Pascual Trujillo. *Santa Fe.* 1705.
> A rancho in the *Cañada*. Juan de Ulibarri, Alcalde.

933 LAZARO DE CORDOBA to José Truxillo. *Villa de Santa Cruz.* 1712.
> *Una carta dote y todo el poder y señoria que tiene en el pedaso de tierra que en dicha carta dote le adjudicaron.*

934 JUAN DE DIOS SANDOBAL MARTINEZ to Mateo Truxillo. *Villa Nueva de Santa Cruz.* 1713.
> House and lands. Juan Garcia de la Rivas, Alcalde.

935 BALTAZAR ROMERO, of *Alburquerque,* to Nicolas de Torres. 1715.
> House, lot, and lands. Diego Arias de Quiros, Alcalde.

936 FELIPE DE TAMARIS. Grant. *Santa Fe.* 1716.
> Land in *Santa Fe*. Re-validation of a grant made by the Marqués de la Nava Brazinas. Phelix Martinez, Governor. Possession given by Francisco Lorenzo Cassados.

937 DIEGO ZAINO to Miguel Thenorio de Alva. *Santa Cruz de la Cañada.* 1712.
> Small tract of land. Francisco Montes Vigil; Juan de Dios Lucero de Godoy; Alphonsso Rael de Aguilar, Alcalde.

938 XPTOBAL TAFOLLA. *Villa Nueva de Santa Cruz.* 1718.
> Will. Bohorques y Corcuera, Alcalde.

939 JOSEPH RODRIGUEZ and Maria Lopez Conejo, his wife, to Antonio de Tafolla. *Santa Fe.*
> House and lot. 1718. Bohorques y Corcuera, Alcalde.

940 RAMON DE MEDINA to Juan Truxillo. *Santa Fe.*
1719.
House and land. Bohorques y Corcuera, Alcalde.

941 XPTOBAL DE TAFOLLA ALTAMIRANO.
Grant. *Valle de Taos.* 1722. Juan Domingo de Bustamante, Governor. No possession given.

942 JUAN and ANTONIO TAFOLLA.
Grant. *Cañada de Santa Clara.* 1724. Juan Domingo de Bustamante, Governor. Xptobal Torres, Alcalde. *Santa Clara* Grant, q. v.

Petition by Juan and Antonio Tafoya for lands in the Cañada of Santa Clara, west of the lands belonging to the Indians of the *pueblo* of that name.

The boundaries asked for in the petition were on the east of whatever belonged to the Indians of the *pueblo*, on the west as far as the high mountain range, on the north a high, wooded, black hill which pointed toward the mountain, on the south a straight line from the little table-land of San Ildefonso.

The grant asked for was made by Governor Juan Domingo de Bustamante on June 8, 1724, and the chief alcalde of Santa Cruz was ordered to place the parties in possession.

On June 10, 1724, Cristobal Torres, chief alcalde and war-captain of Santa Cruz, proceeded to give possession of the tract granted, in the presence of the caciques, governor, and war-captains of the *pueblo* of Santa Clara.

The Indians stated that if the Tafoyas were going to cultivate lands on the tract in question it would result in grave injury to the *pueblo*, as there was scarcely enough water in the stream which flowed through the *cañada* to enable them to cultivate their fields, and consequently they would not consent to the giving of the possession to the Tafoyas until they had presented their objections to the Spanish governor. Thereupon, Cristobal Tafoya, who was present as the representative of the two grantees, his sons, stated that they did not want the tract for agricultural purposes, but only to build corrals and keep their cattle and horses there. To this the Indians agreed, and the possession was given with that understanding.

943 XPTOBAL DE TORRES.
Grant on the *Chama.* 1724. Made by Juan Domingo de

Bustamante, Governor. Re-validated in 1726 by the same official. It appears that the grantee gave lands to the following:

Juana Lujan, Joseph Truxillo, Nicolas Jorge, Josepha de Madrid, widow of Cristoval Tafoya, *el Moso,* Antonio de Sandoval, Juan de Serna, Mateo Truxillo, and Francisco Trujillo, upon condition that they would settle there within a certain time. The original grantee died, and, later on, the settlements not having been made, proceedings were begun to have the grant revoked, and this was done by the governor and captain-general, Gervasio Cruzat y Gongora, in 1733, and the lands were published as *"realengas."* In this archive are:

Xptobal Torres.
Will. 1726.

Angela de Leyba, widow of Xptobal Torres.
Will. 1727. It appears that the revocation was made with notice to all of the parties interested.
No. 950, *q. v.*

There is a grant called Jose Trujillo, Reported No. 12, which was rejected by the court of private land claims. It conflicted with the *pueblos* of Santa Clara, Pojoaque, and San Ildefonso.

944 XPTOBAL TORRES vs. Heirs of Juan de Mestas.
Question of boundaries. *Villa Nueva de Santa Cruz.* 1725.

945 ANTONIO DE GIJOSA to Baltazar Trujillo. *Villa de Santa Cruz.*
Reported Claim No. 109, Antonia Gijosa, *q. v.*

946 ANTONIO DE ULIBARRI to Maria de Tafolla. 1727. *Santa Fe.*
House and lands. Diego Arias de Quiros, Alcalde.

947 PHELIPE DE TAMARIS to Lugarda Tafolla. *Santa Fe.* 1728.
Lands. Diego Arias de Quiros, Alcalde.
The parents of Felipe Tamaris were Francisco de Tamaris and Ysabel Gutierrez.

948 SALVADOR GONZALES to Manuel Thenorio de Alva. *Santa Fe.* 1729.
Two pieces of land. Diego Arias de Quiros, Alcalde.

949 JUAN DE TAFOYA ALTAMIRANO and Antonio de Tafoya.

In the matter of the use of the water of the *Santa Clara* river. 1734. Refused to them by Gervasio Cruzat y Gongora, Governor.

Reported Claim of the *pueblo* of Santa Clara and No. 942, *q. v.*

Petition of Juan de Tafoya and Antonio de Tafoya, asking for the privilege of cultivating land in the Cañada of Santa Clara. They state that they had been settled in the *cañada* for ten years, but had not been permitted to cultivate lands there because of the objections made by the Indians of Santa Clara on account of the scarcity of water in the stream which comes down from the *cañada*; that there was a spring in the *cañada* which they could use without interfering with the water of the river, and numerous pieces of land which produced crops without irrigation. They requested the governor to send some reliable person to investigate the truth of their statements, and, in case the conditions should be as they alleged, they asked that they be allowed to cultivate the lands referred to.

This petition was presented to Governor Cruzat y Gongora on March 4, 1734, and he immediately ordered the lieutenant-general Don Juan Paez Hurtado, to inspect the lands in question, and make report to him.

This was done by Paez Hurtado on March 8, 1834, in the presence of the governor of the *pueblo* of Santa Clara, the interpreter, and five other principal men of the *pueblo*, and also the two Tafoyas, Juan and Antonio.

Paez Hurtado stated that he went up the *cañada* on one side of the river and came down on the other; that he found the spring of water on the south side, about 60 paces from the river, that it discharged its waters into a marsh, and the latter into the river; that he examined the pieces of land which the Tafoyas said could be cultivated without irrigation, and which they had been cultivating for ten years, and that they were under irrigation; that the governor of the pueblo said that it was all irrigated because there were some lateral ditches in the midst of the fields; that the Tafoyas said these ditches were to irrigate some of the more elevated parts of the lands, and this statement was corroborated by an Indian named Antonio, a native of Santa Clara.

The report of Paez Hurtado was transmitted to Governor Cruzat y Gongora on March 10, 1734, and on the 13th of that month he decided that the prayer of the petitioners could not be granted.

950 DIEGO DE TORRES. *Villa Nueva de Santa Cruz.* 1731.

Petition in the matter of the settlement of the grant made to Xptobal de Torres on the Chama. Gervasio Cruzat y Gongora, Governor. No. 943, *q. v.*

951 BALTAZAR ROMERO to Baltazar Truxillo. 1732.

Reported Claim No. 109, *q. v.*

952 JUAN and ANTONIO TAFOYA.

Petition. 1733. For lands in the *Cañada de Santa Clara.* Refused. Gervasio Cruzat y Gongora, Governor. Nos. 972 and 949, *q. v.* Also the *Santa Clara* Grant.

Petition by Juan and Antonio Tafoya to Governor Cruzat, alleging that they had been in possession of a tract of lands in the *cañada de Santa Clara* for eight years, which tract had been granted to them by Don Juan Domingo de Bustamante; that they had cultivated the land all the time; that while they were in quiet and peaceable possession of it, they received a written order from Miguel de Archibeque, chief alcalde of Santa Cruz, to present to him the titles they held to said tract; that having complied with said order, a few days later the alcalde died; that although they had endeavored to recover their title papers they were unable to find them, even in the hands of the executors. In view of all this they ask the governor to make them a new grant of the premises, stating the boundaries to be on the east by the boundaries of the *pueblo* of Santa Clara, on the west by the main mountain range, on the south by a table-land called that of San Ildefonso, and on the north by the lands of Juan de Mestas.

This petition was presented to the governor on November 12, 1733, and he thereupon ordered the petitioners to present witnesses before Antonio de Ulibarri, chief alcalde of Santa Fe, to prove the making of the grant by Governor Bustamante.

Subsequently this was done, the petitioners at different times presenting five witnesses, whose sworn statements were reduced to writing, and made a part of the record. These depositions showed that the grant undoubtedly

had been made by Governor Bustamante; that possession had been given by the chief alcalde, Captain Cristobal de Torres; that the Indians had objected to the grantees being permitted to cultivate any lands on the tract granted, because such cultivation would interfere with the supply of water in the Santa Clara river, on which stream they depended for the cultivation of their own fields; that the Tafoyas then stated they did not want the grant for agricultural purposes but only as a ranch; that the Indians had no objections to it being used for that purpose, and that possession was given with that understanding.

Also it was shown that the Tafoyas had settled the land, built houses, opened up the lands, and even built a chapel.

In view of the foregoing, Governor Cruzat y Gongora, on November 20, 1733, stated that the possession which had been given of the tract should be understood as applying only to a ranch, and not to planting lands.

On November 26, 1733, this decision was made known to the Tafoyas by the chief alcalde of Santa Cruz, Captain Juan Esteban Garcia de Noriega, and the Tafoyas, after hearing and understanding it, stated that they still had some statements to make in regard to the possession.

The document abruptly ends in that way.

953 PHELIPE TAMARIS, for his wife, Magdalena Baca. 1734.

Claim for house and lands against Francisco Guerrero. *Santa Fe.* Compromised. Gervasio Cruzat y Gongora Governor.

Felipe Tamaris was a *vecino* in 1733 and 1734; married Magdalena Vaca, daughter of Ignacio Vaca and Juana de Almazan; there are four of Tamaris's signatures, the last being certified to by Antonio de Ulibarri.

954 SALVADOR DE TORRES, Xptobal Tafoya, Josefa de Torres, Juan Joseph de la Cerda, Miguel Montoya, Juan Truxillo, Miguel Martin Serrano, Francisco Truxillo, Vincente Xiron, and Bartolomé Truxillo.

Petition. 1734. Lands on the *Chama* at *Abiquiú*. Grant made by Gervasio Cruzat y Gongora, Governor. Possession given by Juan Paez Hurtado, Teniente General.

955 JOSEPH ANTONIO DE TORRES. Petition. 1735.

Land at *Abiquiú*. Grant made by Juan Paez Hurtado,

Acting Captain-General. Revoked by Cruzat y Gongora, Governor.

956 TOWN of TOME. Grant. 1739.

Reported Claim No. 2, *q. v.*

The grant to the Town of Tomé was made in the year 1739; the new settlement was called *"Nuestra Señora de la Concepcion de Tomé Dominguez"* and was named for the celebrated Captain Thomé Dominguez de Mendoza, who owned a rancho near by prior to the pueblo rebellion of 1680. The grant is as follows:

"Sir Senior Justice: — All the undersigned appear before you, and all and jointly, and each one for himself, state, that in order that his excellency the governor may be pleased to donate to them the land called Thomé Dominguez, granted to those who first solicited the same, and who declined settling thereon, we therefore ask that the land be granted to us; we therefore pray you to be pleased [eaten by mice] at that time [eaten by mice] said settlers, we being disposed to settle upon the same within the time prescribed by law; we pray you to be pleased to give us the grant which you have caused to be returned, as you are aware that our petition is founded upon necessity and justice, our present condition being very limited, with scarcity of wood, pasture for our stock, and unable to extend our cultivation and raising of stock in this Town of Alburquerque on account of the many foot-paths encroaching upon us, and not permitted to reap the benefits of what we raise, and, in a measure, not even our crops on account of a scarcity of water, and with most of us our lands are of little extent and much confined, etc."

. . . .

The original settlers were: Juan Barela, José Salas, Juan Ballejos, Manuel Carillo, Juan Montaño, Domingo Sedillo, Matias Romero, Bernardo Ballejo, Gregorio Jaramillo, Francisco Sanches, Pedro Romero, Felipe Barela, Lugardo Ballejos, Agustin Gallegos, Alonzo Perea, Tomas Samorra, Nicolas Garcia, Ignacio Baca, Salvador Manuel, Francisco Silva, Francisco Rivera, Juan Antonio Zamora, Miguel Lucero, Joachim Sedillo, Simon Samorra, Xptobal Gallehos, Juan Ballejos, *grande,* Jacinto Barela, and Diego Gonzales.

This petition was presented to Juan Gonzales Bas, chief alcalde of Alburquerque and by him referred to the governor and captain-general, Don Gaspar Domingo de Mendoza, who made the grant, and possession was given on July 30, 1739, by Don Juan Gonzales Bas, the boundaries being: on the west the Rio del Norte; on the south the place commonly called *"Los Tres Alamos"*; on the east the main ridge of the Sandia Mountains, and on the north the point of the Cienega at the hill called *Thomé Dominguez*.

957 FRANCISCO RENDON to Cayetano Tenorio. *Santa Fe.* 1739.
: House and land. Antonio Montoya, Alcalde.

958 MANUEL VELASQUEZ to Bernardino Truxillo. *Santa Fe.* 1739.
: Land on the other side of the *Rio de Santa Fe*. Antonio Montoya, Alcalde.

959 ANTONIO DOMINGUEZ to Antonio Tafoya. *Santa Fe.* 1739.
: Land in *Santa Fe*. Antonio Montoya, Alcalde.

960 DIEGO GAYTAN to Bernardino Truxillo. *Santa Fe.* 1739.
: House and land in *Santa Fe*. Antonio Montoya, Alcalde.

961 PHELIPE TAFOYA.
: Grant. *Santa Fe.* 1742. Land near *Santa Fe* known as the *Rancho de Velasquez*. Gaspar Domingo de Mendoza, Governor. Possession given by Antonio de Ulibarri, Alcalde.

962 TOMAS DE TAPIA. Grant. *Santa Fe.* 1742.
: The land designated in the grant made to Phelipe Tafoya. No. 961, *q. v.* Gaspar Domingo de Mendoza, Governor.

963 JOSEPH DE RIAÑO TAGLE.
: Will. *Santa Fe.* 1743. Also inventory of his estate. *Testimonio* certified by Antonio de Hulibarri, Alcalde.

964 JOSEPH DE RIAÑO TAGLE.
: Will and inventory and partition of his estate. *Santa Fe.* 1743. No. 963.
: Joseph Antonio de la Fuente. *Santa Fe.* 1743. Petition for the settlement of the estate of Ana Maria Baca,

widow of Joseph Griego, she having died intestate. Gaspar Domingo de Mendoza, Governor.

Don José de Riaño y Tagle was a native of the kingdom of Castile, archbishopric of Burgos, mountains of Santander, in the Villa de Santillana. He was the son of Don Jacinto Riaño and Doña Teresa de Tagle Bustamante. His wife was Doña Maria Roybal, daughter of Don Ignacio Roybal and Doña Francisca Gomez Robledo. Of this marriage there was one son, José Riaño. His place of residence was at "El Alamo," in Santa Fe county. He also had a fine residence in the City of Santa Fe, on lower San Francisco street, which had a garden, orchard, and extended from the street to the river. Both of these places he purchased from Doña Maria Fernandez de la Pedrera. Riaño was an intimate friend of Captain Juan José Lobato. The *Juez Eclesiastico* and *vicario* Don Santiago Roybal was his brother-in-law, as was also Don Juan José Moreno.

This will, owing to the sudden illness of the testator and the impossibility of obtaining other, is written upon a small piece of paper. He was a very wealthy man for the period; he was a slave owner (negroes) and owned a land grant at the Piedra Lumbre. Lugarda Lujan was his god-daughter. The will provides that six thousand *pesos* be set aside as patrimony for his son, José, who was *dedicated* to the priesthood. Don José Miguel de la Peña's signature appears in the inventory.

At this period oxen were worth $25.00, bulls $16.00, steers $20.00, calves $6.00, cows $16, mares $15.00; a gun was worth $40.00 and a pair of silk stockings, gold embroidered were worth $8.00; a saddle, silver mounted, was valued at $120.00, and a sword with silver hook and handle, $50.00; a pair of spurs with straps were valued at $30.00. Sheep sold for $2.00, wethers or ewes. The place called *San José del Alamo*, his country residence, was two stories in height, with corridors, and contained thirteen rooms.

965 JOSEPH MARIANO DE LOS DOLORES ITURRIETA and OTHERS.

Petition. Lands at *Xemes*. 1744. Of no effect. Joachin Codallos y Rabal, Governor.

966 JOSE TERRUS.

Will. 1745. *Santa Fe.* Antonio de Hulibarri, Alcalde

288 THE SPANISH ARCHIVES OF NEW MEXICO

967 CRISTOBAL TAFOYA and OTHERS.
> Partition of lands. 1745. Reported Claim No. 109, *q. v. Francisca Antonia Gijosa* Grant.
>
> Gijosa Grant; Reported No. 109, has an area of about 1557 acres, a part of which conflicts with the grant to the *pueblo* of Taos. The grant was confirmed by the court of private land claims and under the decree and survey it was found that the grant had more than 16,000 acres. The conflict under the new survey with the Taos *Pueblo* Grant was entirely eliminated. It was patented October 26, 1908.

968 LUGARDA QUINTANA.
> Will. *Villa Nueva de Santa Cruz.* 1749. Ilario Archuleta, Alcalde.

969 JUAN TOMAS LOBATO to Pedro Antonio Truxillo. 1750. *Santa Fe.*
> Land at *Buena Vista.* Joseph de Bustamante (y Tagle), Alcalde.

970 HEIRS OF MANUEL TRUXILLO and Maria de la Candelaria Gonzales, his wife. *Santa Fe.* 1751.
> Partition of estate. Names of the heirs: Maria Francisca Trujillo, Antonio Marcela Truxillo. Manuel Gallegos, Alcalde.

971 PEDRO TRUXILLO and Bartolomé Martin to Cristobal Truxillo. 1751.
> Lands on the *Rio Pojoaque.* Juan Joseph Lobato, Alcalde.

972 BLAS TRUXILLO to Maria Rosa de Mestas. 1751.
> Lands on the *Rio de Jojoaque.* Juan Joseph Lobato, Alcalde.

973 JUAN TRUXILLLO in the name of Pedro, Francisca, Josepha Truxillo, minor heirs, and for himself to Antonio Truxillo. *Pojoaque.* 1751.
> Lands on the *Rio de Pojoaque.* Juan Joseph Lobato, Alcalde.

974 FRANCISCO ANAYA ALMAZAN to Teresa Tenorio.
> House and land in *Santa Fe,* 1751. Manuel Gallegos, Alcalde.

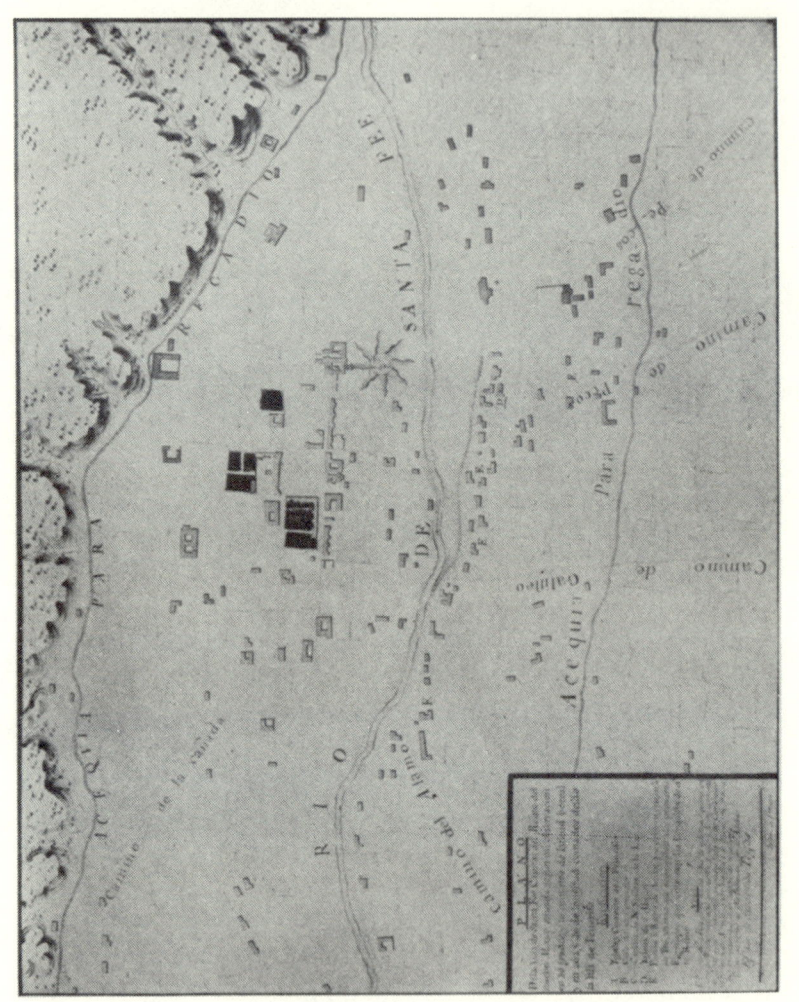

URRUTIA'S MAP OF SANTA FE, 1768

975 *LAS TRAMPAS* GRANT.

Settlement of 1751; Reported Claim No. 27.

Grant and Royal Possession, and Donation of Sebastian Martin, in favor of the resident settlers, included here in at the new settlement of the place called "Santo Tomas del Rio de Las Trampas."

At the Town of Nuestra Señora de la Soledad del Rio Arriba, on the first of July, in the year one thousand seven hundred and fifty-one, before me, Captain Juan José Lovato, chief justice and war-captain of all this jurisdiction, appeared Captain Sebastian Martin, resident of said town, and declared: That, whereas, he has reliable information that Don Thomas Velez Cachupin, governor and captain-general of this kingdom, intends, as good governments should do, to settle the place called Santo Tomas Apostol del Rio de Las Trampas, with twelve families, consisting of the following named citizens; Juan de Arguello, Melchor Rodriguez, Antonio Dominguez, Pedro Felipe Rodriguez, Eusebio de Leyba, Luis de Leyba, Juan José de Arguello, Juan Garcia, Salvador Baca, Ygnacio Vargas, Vicente Lucero, and José de Aragon, and considering that said settlement will redound to the service of His Majesty (whom may God preserve) and to the public weal, he grants, donates, and conveys, according to law, to the above mentioned citizens, a piece of land from his possession, which adjoins said settlement, in order that it may have sufficient land for cultivation on both sides of the Trampas river; that from the Peñasco del Cañoncito to the main road; said piece of land, on being measured, contains one thousand six hundred and forty varas, and in proportion the proper amount of land in a direct line from south to north, to have, use and cultivate it for themselves, their children, heirs and successors, and barter, sell and dispose of the same, for which purpose he assigns and transfers to the aforesaid citizens all the royal and personal title he had to said lands, granting the same to them free of all tax, tribute, mortgage, or other encumbrance, for which neither himself, his children, heirs, or successors will enter suit, dispute, or complaint against them, and if he should do so he requests not to be heard in court or out of court, as said land is donated freely and voluntarily, for the just ends above expressed, and for which he resigns his own rights, residence and vicinity, under the law *cit combenerit*, and the general law in reference to the matter, acknowledging this deed to be good, and (valid) any want of form to the contrary notwithstanding, and for its greater force and validity, he requested me, the aforesaid senior justice, to interpose my judicial decree, which I certify to have interposed, acting as appointed judge, with two attending witnesses, in the absence of public or royal notaries, within the limits provided by law; said conveyor did not sign this document, as he has an impediment in his sight, and it is executed at the aforesaid town on the day and date above mentioned, to all of which I certify.

Este—duplicate—valid. JUAN JOSÉ LOBATO
Acting Judge—attending:
JUAN DOMINGO LOVATO

In the City of Santa Fe, on the fifteenth day of the month of July, one thousand seven hundred and fifty-one, I, Don Thomas Velez Cachupin, governor of this kingdom of New Mexico and castellan of its royal garrison, stated: That whereas, in the general visit made by me, in conformity with royal orders throughout the entire extent of this kingdom, as will appear by reference to several decrees, it appears that the inhabitants of this said city have increased to a great extent, many of whom are yet of a youthful age, consequently there is not land or water sufficient for their support, neither have they any other occupation, trades, or means of traffic, excepting agriculture and the raising of stock; and whereas, in the King's domains which are unoccupied, there are lands which up to this time are uncultivated, and which will yield comforts to those who cultivate them, and where such persons as shall be named in this town, who have no occupation or employment, can settle upon and cultivate such lands as shall be assigned to them, from which the further benefit will result that the hostile Indians will not travel over them, and will serve as a barrier against their entrance to despoil the interior settlements. In view of all which, and whereas one of the said sites is called Santo Thomas Apostol del Rio de las Trampas, situate in the vicinity of the settlement of Santa Barbara, therefore, I hereby assign and distribute said site in the manner and to the persons following:

To Juan de Arguello, one hundred and eighty varas of wheat-growing land, with corresponding water, pastures, and watering places, entrances and exits, without injury to third parties.

To Melchor Rodriguez, the same hundred and eighty varas as the foregoing.

To Antonio Dominguez, the same amount and number of varas as the preceding one.

To Pedro Felipe Rodriguez, the same, one hundred and eighty varas, without variation.

To Eusebio de Leyva is assigned the same amount of land, under the same conditions.

Luis de Leyva is placed on an equality with the others in lands and measurements.

To Juan José de Arguello is assigned the same quantity with the conditions above prescribed.

To Juan Garcia is assigned the same amount of one hundred and eighty varas.

To Salvador Vaca a like grant of land is made, with the measurements and conditions above-mentioned.

To Ygnacio Vargas, in the same manner, are assigned one hundred and eighty varas of land.

To Vicente Lucero will be given the same amount, in comformity with the above.

To Joseph de Arragon, who is the last of the twelve heads of families, the same amount of land, in conformity with the conditions imposed on the balance, above described.

To whom, for the reasons above stated, I grant, in the name of his Majesty, (whom may God preserve) two thousand one hundred and sixty varas of arable land, all of which are wheat-growing and under irrigation, in the cañon and streams of the Trampas river, which runs from east to west, for themselves, their children, successors, and other legal —(torn); to have, cultivate, and reap the benefit of its fruits, crops, and other profits, without injury to third parties; and considering that this quantity of wheat-growing land will not be sufficient, on account of the increase of their families, and as in the cañon or place where they are to settle, from east to west, there are no other lands under irrigation that they can use, and whereas there are two cañons, called De los Alamos and Ojo Sarco, south of the Trampas river, which, although not susceptible of irrigation, are most fertile and of good quality, I also grant them to the above-mentioned persons, to be equally divided between them, in the same manner as the two thousand one hundred and sixty varas, assigning them as boundaries a narrow made by the river, where it joins the mountain, on the east; on the west the narrows (Angostura) of the river, to where the grant made to Sebastian Martin terminates, and drawing a straight line from the Angostura towards the south to the summit of the Cañada del Ojo Sarco; on the north, the boundary of the *pueblo* of Picuriés; and on condition that they shall not sell, transfer or convey, or in other manner dispose of all or a portion of said lands, until the expiration of the four years provided by law, and not even then to ecclesiastics, convents, colleges, or other communities. And Juan Joseph Lovato, the chief justice of the town of Cañada, will give the royal and personal possession to all in common, and to each one in particular, of their respective tracts; and for that purpose and the other purposes herein mentioned, and concerning the authentic documents thereunto appertaining, he is hereby commissioned as the law requires, and after having executed all the necessary acts and decrees in the premises, he will return them complete to this government.

Further, in regard to Sebastian Martin having [torn] made a donation of a piece of land, with what has been before stated, I approve said (donation), and interpose my authority and judicial (decree) including them in the two thousand one hundred and sixty varas, with which they will have sufficient. All of which I, the said governor, have determined, after mature deliberation, desiring the service of the king and the public good. And I so ordered and signed, acting with two attending witnesses, in the absence of a public or royal notary, there being none in this kingdom. To all of which I certify.

THOMAS VELEZ CACHUPIN

THOMAS DE ALVEAR Y COLLADO
THORIBIO ORTIZ

At this place of Santo Thomas Apostol del rio de las Trampas, I, Juan Joseph Lovato, chief justice and war-captain of the new city of Santa Cruz and its districts, by virtue of the commission conferred upon me by Don Thomas Velez Cachupin, governor and captain-general of this kingdom of New Mexico, and in conformity with the directions therein contained, I placed the aforementioned citizens in royal and personal possession, according to the decree of his excellency, after having performed all the ceremonies directed by the royal ordinances. Joseph Zamora, Manuel Martin, and Juan Fresque, being present and acting as instrumental witnesses, having been summoned by me for that purpose, the distribution, centre, and boundaries being as follows [torn]: The residences and dwellings of the twelve families, fifty-seven and one-half varas, were set aside towards (the four points of the compass) leaving for drippings, enclosures, stables, and other objects of that nature [the following fifteen lines in the original are so much torn as to be unintelligible] sixty-one varas in equal parts on the southern side, one hundred and eighty varas belong to Juan de Arguello; one hundred and eighty varas to Eusebio de Leyba; to Vicente Lucero another hundred and eighty varas of land; to Juan Garcia a like one hundred and eighty varas of land; to José Aragon another hundred and eighty varas of land; Juan Joseph Arguello also received one hundred and eighty varas of land; to Melchior Rodriguez the same, one hundred and eighty varas of land; to Pedro Phelipe Rodriguez another one hundred and eighty varas of land; to Salvador Baca, in consequence of the arable land having become narrower as it entered the cañon, were assigned two hundred varas of land; and considering that a gulch in the centre of the fields prevents [torn] the same amount of one hundred and eighty varas which is [torn] received in possession, establishing the boundaries in direct lines, [the remaining portion of the original document, with the exception of the last four lines, is torn in half and illegible], in the absence of a royal or public notary, and it is done at the aforesaid place of Santa Thomas Apostol, on the twentieth day of the month of July, in the year one thousand seven hundred and fifty-one, to all of which I certify.

JUAN JOSEPH LOVATO, Acting Judge.
FRANCISCO ZISNEROS
ANTONIO JOSEPH LOVATO

976 BARTOLOMÉ TRUJILLO.

Grant, 1752. *Rancho de San Joseph de Garcia.* At Santa Rosa de Abiquiú. This is the second time that this land was granted to this grantee, the first having been made in 1734 by Juan Paez Hurtado. Tomas Veles Cachupin, Governor.

977 FRANCISCA CADENA to José Torres. *Santa Fe.* 1753.

House and land. Nicolas Ortiz, Alcalde.

978 MARIA LUISA CADENA to José Torres. *Santa Fe.* 1753.
    Land. Nicolas Ortiz, Alcalde.

979 ANTONIO DE ARMIJO to Josepha Thenorio. *Santa Fe.* 1755.
    House and land. Francisco Guerrero, Alcalde.

980 ISIDRO MARTIN to Getrudis Trugillo. *Santa Fe.* 1757.
    House and land. Francisco Guerrero, Alcalde. Phelipe Sandoval Fernandez.

981 SANTIAGO DE ROIBAL, vicario, etc., to Phelipe Tafoya. *Santa Fe.* 1758.
    Land in *Pueblo Quemado*, about one league distant from Santa Fe. Francisco Guerrero, Alcalde.

982 MANUEL DE SENA to Miguel Tafoya. *Santa Fe.* 1758.
    House and land. Francisco Guerrero, Alcalde.

983 ANTONIO DURAN DE ARMIJO, *el Chico*, to Francisco Trugillo. *Santa Fe.* 1759.
    House and land on *San Francisco* street.

984 LUIS FRANCISCO DE LEYBA to Juan de Tafoya. *Santa Fe.* 1759.
    House and land in *Santa Fe.* Francisco Guerrero, Alcalde.

985 JACINTO PEREA to Juan Tafoya. *Santa Fe.* 1761.
    Land at the place called *El Pino.* Manuel Gallegos, Alcalde.

986 TOMAS ROIBAL to Juan Tafoya. *Santa Fe.* 1762.
    House and land. Manuel Gallego, Alcalde.

987 MARCIAL TORRES of *Taos* Valley. 1762.
    Inventory and partition of his estate. Francisco Marin del Valle, Governor.

988 FRANCISCO RAEL DE AGUILAR to Martin Torres. *Santa Fe.* 1763.
    House and land. Manuel Gallego, Alcalde.

989 PASCUALA VASQUEZ to Cristobal Tapia. *Santa Fe.* 1764.
> Land. Francisco Guerrero, Alcalde.

990 ANTONIO GONZALES of *Alameda.*
> In the matter of the settlement of his estate. Nicolasa Gonzales by her attorney, Antonio Casimiro Trujillo vs. Josepha Barela, her mother-in-law. Tomas Velez Cachupin, Governor.

991 MARIA BACA and Domingo de Luna, her husband, by their attorney, Miguel Thenorio de Alva, to Miguel Tafoya. *Santa Fe.* 1767.
> A tract of land in the *Cañada* called *Guicu,* acquired by said Maria Baca by inheritance from her father, Nicolas Baca. Pedro Fermin de Mendinueta, Governor. Francisco Guerrero, Alcalde.

992 NICOLAS MORAN to Miguel Thenorio de Alva. *Santa Fe,* 1767.
> Land in *Buena Vista.* Francisco Guerrero, Alcalde.

993 JUAN MARTIN to Manuel Teyes (Telles). *Pojoaque.* 1769.
> Tract of land on the *Rio del Norte.* Antonio Joseph Ortiz, Alcalde.

994 MARIA FRANCISCA TRUXILLO. *San Geronimo de Taos.* 1770.
> Will. Antonio Harmijo (Armijo), Alcalde.

995 PHELIPE TAFOYA.
> Will. *Santa Fe,* 1771. Pedro Fermin de Mendinueta, Governor.

996 ANTONIO ELIAS MARTIN to Manuel Trujillo. *Santa Fe.* 1772.
> Land. Manuel Garcia Pareja, Alcalde.

997 CAYETANO TORRES. Intestate. *Sabinal.* 1780.
> Inventory and partition of his estate. Juan Francisco Baca, Alcalde.

998 ANTONIO TAFOYA.
> José Maldonado, Teniente.

999 CARLOS FERNANDEZ to Vincente Troncoso. *Santa Fe.* 1786.
    House in said city. Antonio José Ortiz, Alcalde.

1000 JOSEPH MANUEL TRUJILLO. Will *San Joseph de Chama.* 1770-1785.
    Proceedings in the administration of his estate, etc. Juan Bautista de Anza, Governor.
    The town of Chamita had a grant. Reported No. 36. File No. 64, which lies west of the Rio del Norte and almost entirely within the boundaries of the grant to the *pueblo* of San Juan. It was confirmed June 21, 1860, but has not been patented.

1001 BARBARA TRUXILLO, of the *Vallecito de Xemes,* vs. Bautista Gonzales. 1794.
    In the matter of lands sold to defendant by her father-in-law, Paulin Montoya, etc. Papers incomplete. Miguel Canelas, *Comandante Accidental y Capitan Graduado de este Real Presidio.*

1002 JOSEPH and MARIANO TRUXILLO of *Sabinal* and *Abiquiú,* vs. Adauto Isidro Fresquis. 1801.
    In the matter of title to a certain rancho. Manuel Garcia de la Mora, Alcalde.

1003 MANUEL THENORIO DE *ALVA* vs. Heirs of Juan Domingo Romero. *Santa Fe.* 1810.
    In the matter of a piece of land in the *Cienega.* Manrique, Governor. Bartolomé Fernandez.

1004 HEIRS OF CHRISTOBAL TORRES vs. Ignacio, Juan Lorenzo and Rosalia Valdez. No date.
    Protest against grant of land at *Chama.* No action.

1005 FRANCISCO TRUXILLO, Bartolomé Marquéz, and Diego Padilla.
    Petition for lands on the *Pecos.* No action. 1813.
    This is the *Los Trigos* Land Grant. The original petition was addressed to the governor of New Mexico, May 26, 1814, Don José Manrique. The petitioners asked for a tract of uncultivated land situate in the place called Los Trigos, as far as El Gusano, independent of the league of the Indians of the *pueblo* of Pecos. The matter was

referred to the corporation of Santa Fe, at that time composed of the following:

Matias Ortiz, Antonio Ortiz, Manuel Gallegos, Juan de Dios Sena, Ignacio Ortiz, Manuel Delgado, Juan Esteban Pino, Francisco Ortiz, Felipe Sandoval, Francisco Ortiz, Jr., and Francisco Montoya, Cristobal Ma. was secretary.

The "Ojito de las Ruedas" and " El Gusano" are prominent places mentioned in the papers on file; these were both the sites of old *pueblos,* the ruins of which may still be seen, consisting today of covered mounds of earth; they were undoubtedly occupied in the time of the first Spanish explorers, as these names have come down from the seventeenth century. There is also an "Arroyo de Las Ruedas" which empties into the Rio Pecos.

Don Domingo Fernandez is authority for the statement that in 1822 the place was abandoned because of the hostilities of the Apaches who killed a prominent Mexican, named Vincente Villanueva, near Las Ruedas.

The first man to cultivate lands at Los Trigos was Don Mariano Casados.

1006 FRANCISCO TRUJILLO.

Manrique, Governor. Manuel Garcia de la Mora, Alcalde. Marcos Delgado, Secretary of the Ayuntamiento of Abiquiú. This paper is not complete.

1007 FRANCISCO TRUJILLO. Part of 1006.

No final action.

1008 IGNACIO TAFOYA and others. 1819.

Grant. Reported Claim No. 96. *Cañon de Carnuel.*

1009 TOWN OF TECOLOTE.

Grant, 1824. Reported Claim No. 7.

The citizen, Salvador Montoya, made petition for this grant saying that he had no lands wherein to "scatter a few grains of corn and other seed for my support and that of the large family which I have." This petition was filed with the constitutional justice at San Miguel del Bado, Don Diego Padilla, October 8, 1824. The alcalde thought the petition "rigorously just" and sent the same to the Territorial Deputation, that body at the time being composed of the following: Bartolomé Baca, president; and the Señores Antonio Ortiz, Pedro José Perea, Pedro Bautista Pino, Matias Ortiz and Juan Bautista

Vigil, secretary. The Deputation approved the petition and the same was also approved by the political chief, Don Bartolomé Baca. it was approved by the surveyor-general of New Mexico, December 31, 1856. Don Tomas Sena, the constitutional justice of El Bado (San Miguel) placed the petitioners in possession of the property on the 23d day of April, 1825. This was a noted stopping place on the Old Trail from the Missouri river to Santa Fe.

1010 MANUEL TRUXILLO. *San Miguel del Socorro.* 1827.
>Complaint against Santiago Torres, Alcalde, for ejectment from lands granted to him in said place. Antonio Narbona, Governor. No final action taken.

1011 JOSE TAFOYA vs. José Perea. *Alameda.* 1827.
>Letter of Mariano Sanchez Vergara, Alcalde of Alameda, in relation to a suit between the said parties. No final action.

1012 GETRUDIS TAFOYA vs. Heirs of Santiago Garcia. *Alameda.* 1827.
>In the matter of title to lands inherited from her maternal grandmother, Prudencia Gonzales. Manuel Armijo, Governor. Cleto Miera y Pacheco, Alcalde.

1013 JOSE MANUEL TRUXILLO and 77 others.
>Report of Committee of the Territorial Assembly on their Petition for lands at the *Manzano.* 1829.

1014 DOLORES JALOMO, Ignacio Niño Ladron de Guebara, Marcelino Abreu.
>Registration of a mine. 1833. Antonio Narbona, Governor.

1015 FRANCISCO BACA Y TERRUS.
>Grant. 1839. Reported Claim No. 57.

1016 FRANCISCO BACA Y TERRUS.
>Grant. 1840. Reported Claim No. 57.

1017 JUAN DE URIBARRI. Grant. 1709.
>Land in the jurisdiction of *Alburquerque.* Possession not given. El Marqués de la Peñuela.

1018 JUAN DE URIBARRI. 1709.
Registration of a mine. El Marqués de la Peñuela.

1019 JUAN DE URIBARRI. 1710.
Registration of a mine. El Marqués de la Peñuela.

1020 JUAN DE URIBARRI, Matias Madrid, Sebastian Duran, Bartolomé Lobato, Joseph Madrid, Simon de Cordoba.
Petition for a tract of land near *Chama*. 1710. Granted but no possession given. El Marqués de la Peñuela.

Roque Madrid and others. Petition. 1712. Asking that they be permitted to leave the *Villa Nueva de Santa Cruz* and take possession of the old Villa de *Yunque-Yunque* on the Rio del Norte near *Chama*. Refused on the ground that it would leave Santa Cruz without sufficient defense.

El Marqués de la Peñuela. Juan Paez Hurtado, Teniente General.

Bartolomé Lovato and others. Villa Nueva de Santa Cruz. Petition asking that they be declared the founders of the Villa Nueva de Santa Cruz. 1712. Reply by Juan Paez Hurtado, Teniente General.

BARTOLOME LOVATO and Others.
Villa Nueva de Santa Cruz. No date. Protest to the Captain-General against his giving the land they had asked for to Bartolomé Sanchez. No action taken.

Andres Gonzales, Sebastian Duran, Diego Marquez, Blas Lobato, Simon de Cordoba, Captain Bartolomé Lobato, José Madrid, Tomas de Bejarana, Cristobal de Castran, Matias Madrid, and Ysabel de la Serna, who were residents of the Villa Nueva de Santa Cruz, asked the governor and captain-general, the Marqués de la Peñuela, for a tract of land *"called in ancient times the Town of Yunque"*; the petition was referred to Don Juan Paez Hurtado. So that those interested may know, this archive recites as follows:

"To the ancient place established by the first founders who came with Dn Juan de Oñate, known as San Gabriel and by other name the Town of Yunque."

These petitioners had been residents of the Villa Nueva de Santa Cruz "since the year 1694." General Hurtado declared that if these left Santa Cruz would practically be abandoned and on March 30, 1712, reported adversely;

the report was approved by the governor and captain-general.

This archive also recites that the *pueblo* of Chama was on the west bank of the Rio Grande and on the north side of the Rio Chama. The petition is dated February 22, 1710.

Reference is also made to the reëstablishment of the new *pueblo* of Isleta. Captain Bartolomé Lobato came from Zacatecas. General Hurtado says that Cristobal Rodarte and Cristobal Castro, Matias Madrid and Juan Madrid were soldiers at El Paso in 1695 and that Diego Marquez and Simon Cordoba were at that place also, serving their fathers.

On page 5 the settlement of San Gabriel, made by Don Juan de Oñate in 1598, is referred to also as *La Villa de Yunque.*

1021 ANTONIO DE URIBARRI vs. Xptobal Martin and Antonia de Moraga.

Title to a piece of land in *Chimayo*. Phelix Martinez, Governor. Xtobal Torres, Alcalde.

1022 ANTONIO DE URIBARRI. Grant. 1735.

Land at *Pueblo Colorado*. Made by Juan Paez Hurtado and revoked by Governor Cruzat y Gongora. Miguel Martin Serrano, Juan Estevan Garcia de Noriega.

This is a grant to Antonio de Ulibarri for a small piece of land at a place called *Pueblo Colorado,* somewhere in the district under the control of the chief alcalde of Santa Cruz.

The only thing in the document that relates to *Pueblo* Indians is the statement made by Ulibarri in his petition, where he says that in the year 1733 he presented a petition to Governor Cruzat y Gongora, asking for a tract of land adjoining the lands of the *pueblo* of San Felipe, and the governor answered his petition by saying that he could not make the grant because it would be to the prejudice of the Indians, who had documents showing that they had paid their money for it.

1023 PHELIPE DE APODACA to Juan Cayetano Vnuave. *Santa Fe.* 1766.

House and land. Francisco Guerrero, Alcalde.

1024 ANTONIO URBAN MONTAÑO. *Los Palacios.*
Will. 1772. Manuel Garcia Pareja, Alcalde.

On June 15, 1754, Antonio Urban Montaño, a resident of Santa Fe, registered a tract of land which at one time was occupied by the *pueblo* of San Marcos. In the petition he describes an arroyo in that vicinity known as "Lo de Basquez." One boundary call is the "road leading to the *pueblo* of Galisteo." He was given the property by Governor Cachupin "with the understanding that he shall not damage with his herds the commons and the pasture of the horses of this royal garrison, nor the pasturage for the herds kept for the supply and support of the soldiers of the garrison, which are kept and pastured at those places."

The turquoise mountain of Chalchuihuitl is mentioned in the act of possession. Another boundary call is the *Sabinos Altos de Chuacaco.*

1025 TOMAS URIOSTE. *Santa Fe.* 1820.
Will. José Antonio Alarid, Sargento.

1026 JOSE FRANCISCO URIBARRI. *San Miguel del Bado.* 1844. For himself and others.
Petition for re-validation of a tract of land within the boundaries of Las Vegas called *"La Sanguijuela."* No action taken.

1027. DIEGO DE VARGAS ZAPATA LUJAN PONCE DE LEON, Marqués de la Nava de Brazinas. *Santa Fe.* 1704. Will.

IN THE NAME OF GOD ALMIGHTY — Know all who may see this my last will and testament that I, General Don Diego de Vargas Zapata Lujan Ponce de Leon, Marqués de la Nava Brazinas, Governor and Captain-General of this Kingdom and Provinces of New Mexico, by His Majesty appointed, native of the imperial court of Madrid in the Kingdom of Castile, being sick in bed with the infirmity which God, Our Lord, has been pleased to place upon me, believing as I firmly and truly do in the mystery of the Holy Trinity, Father, Son and Holy Ghost, three distinct persons and only one true God, receiving as I do receive, as my intercessor, the Holy Virgin Mary, mother of the divine and eternal Word, I confide my soul to a most clear career of salvation, interceding with his worthy Son for forgiveness of all my sins, I do make order and dispose and declare this to be my testament in the manner and form following:—

Firstly: I commend my soul to God who created it with the price of His precious blood, and my body to the earth from which it was made.

And if His Divine Majesty shall be pleased to take me away from the present life, I desire and it is my will that a mass be said while the corpse is present in the church of this town of Bernalillo, and afterwards the same shall be taken to the Villa of Santa Fe and placed and suspended in my bed selected as a bier and in the same to be taken to the church of the said town of Santa Fe and buried in said church at the principal altar under the platform where the priest stands; this I ask as a favor, said bier to be covered with honest woolen cloth and buried according to military rites and the title ceremonies and privileges of Castile, leading two horses covered with the same cloth as the bier.

I order that on the said day of my funeral there be distributed among the poor of said Town fifty measures of corn and twelve head of cattle.

I declare, also, that since the eighth day of June of last year, One thousand seven hundred and three, when I left the City of Mexico, I have been indebted to the Royal Treasury of His Majesty for the salary for two years which was advanced to me, which at the rate of two thousand dollars per annum will amount to four thousand dollars, which the Most Excellent Duke of Alburquerque ordered his officers and judges of the Court of Mexico to deliver to me upon my giving a life security, and having given the same with the Captains Don Joseph de Villa Urritia, Knight of the Order of Alcantara, and the Major Don Pedro de Tagle, Knight of the Order of Alcantara, and also with Don Joseph Carrillo, Chief Officer of Factorage of the Royal Exchequer (*Minister of Finance*).

I leave and assign for the payment and satisfaction of the most of the account of which I may be indebted to His Majesty from the day that God Our Lord may be pleased to take me away said salary, and that the aforementioned may not suffer or be compelled to pay any amount, I assign as a special pledge two young negro coachmen, of known age, for whom I paid six hundred and sixty dollars, the excise tax having been paid by me and which is mentioned in the receipts in my possession,

THE SPANISH ARCHIVES OF NEW MEXICO 303

to which I refer; and my attorney will also deliver a white mulatto woman named Josefa de la Cruz, twenty-two years of age, the wife of Ygnacio, one of the two coachmen, who was the slave of Don Juan Cristobal de Palma y Mesa, councilman of the Royal Audience of Guadalajara, the contract showing her value.

In the same manner my attorney and executor, the same being my Lieutenant-General, Don Juan Paez Hurtado, will remit or sell at the best obtainable prices the following silverware:

1st: Thirty small silver dishes, the fifth part taken, and twenty-four sealed with my coat-of-arms and weighing more than two marks.

Two large dishes which weigh twelve marks and ounces.

Six candle-sticks, with my coat-of-arms, and two pairs of candle snuffers, which weigh forty-two marks, more or less.

Twelve silver porringers which weigh twelve ounces, sealed with my coat-of-arms, the one-fifth part taken.

One salver bowl, gilded with a siren, weighing sixteen and seventeen marks, more or less.

One small silver keg, with stopper and chain, the one-fifth part taken, weighing six marks.

One large plain tankard, weighing two marks and six ounces.

Six silver forks and their silver tea-spoons, the fifth part taken and weighing twelve ounces.

Three silver table spoons, weighing about two ounces.

One large silver fountain, engraved, one-fifth part taken and weighing twenty-three marks.

Another small silver fountain, engraved with vine-leaves, the one fifth taken, weighing thirteen marks.

One silver deep bowl, for shaving purposes, the one-fifth taken and weighing twelve marks.

One large silver waiter, weighing fourteen ounces.

One silver basin, with my coat-of-arms, the one-fifth taken and weighing nine marks.

One pair of pearl ear-rings, with eight fine emeralds, each one and its pendants worth five hundred dollars.

One finger ring, with a rose diamond, checkered and enameled in black, worth four hundred dollars.

Another finger ring with two diamonds, enameled in black and gold, worth one hundred dollars.

Said silverware I leave to my testamentary executor to be sold to the person or persons of his approval, the returns to be remitted to the three said gentlemen, my said sureties, in said court and City of Mexico, and in the same manner he shall pay the balance of the freight upon three boxes of gun-powder, whatever it may amount to, together with the cost of hides, ropes and covers, for which said amount I ask him to secure a receipt in full payment.

I also declare as my sons, although not by legitimate wife, Don Juan Manuel de Vargas, of the age of twenty-four years, and Don Alonzo de Vargas, of the age of twenty-three years, and their sister Doña Maria Theresa, who is with her mother in the City of Mexico, of the age of nineteen years, who have been supported on my account and to whom I assign two thousand dollars in cash, which are in a small cedar box, and more to make up said amount there will be found in the silk warehouse, forty-five dollars, it being understood that said amount of two thousand dollars shall be divided among the three, the two brothers and sister, in equal parts.

In the same manner I leave to the said Don Juan and Don Alonzo de Vargas the two saddles which I have used; also two pairs of pistols, with the holsters; the banners of Anselm and Saint Michael, the Great, with the covers and cushions; two cloth suits which I have worn, one whitish and the other blue, with the gold buttons, covered with flesh color, and the whitish with its waist-coat and trousers of brown cloth, adorned with flounces of gold and silver; this I leave to my son, Don Juan Manuel, and the other to my said son, Don Alonzo, together with a jacket of blue brocade, and a pair of trousers of blue plush and enough cloth of silk grogram for another pair; and furthermore of the piece of camlet cloth which I have assigned, each one of my sons will make a new suit of cloth, a coat and two pairs of trousers, lined with the color of their selection of the listed cloth in the warehouse, with silk buttons, and the jackets lined with the same listed cloth; in the same manner I leave them six shirts, embroidered with the best of lace, three to each one; two jerkins with eaten-moth laces, one to each; and of the neckties which I have commonly used, I leave two to each one of my said sons; further, four pairs of stockings of genoba, two pairs to each, and I leave to my said son, Don Alonzo, one pair of blue silk stockings, embroidered with gold, and the pair which are silver curled to my son, Don Juan; I leave them four pairs of bed-sheets, two to each, with the embroidered pillow-cases; I leave them four yards of fine linen, to each of my two said sons; to my said son, Don Alonzo, I leave my two cloaks, one of fine native cloth, and the other of gold color, lined with serge; to my said son, Don Juan, I leave the choice of the color of the cloak lined with serge; I also leave them three pairs of drawers, to each one, and one full piece of fine linen to be used by them for handkerchiefs; and I leave to them the selection, to be taken to their mother and sister, a dress pattern of fine camlet cloth, with the lining of the listed cloth which they may like the best, and a pattern of petticoats of scarlet cloth from England, with the silk and trimmings; one silk mantle with fringe, for each one; furthermore, I leave them the two trunks which I have; and to my said son, Don Alonzo, I leave my fine sword hilt, and to my said son, Don Juan, I leave my small sword; and each one to have a leathern jacket, the one I have used and another from the warehouse; in the same manner to take to the General at Parral one leathern jacket of blue color and the stockings and gloves which I ordered to be made; I also leave to them my leather case, large elbow chair and eight ready mules, selected to the satisfaction of my slave, the negro Andrés, who, for having rendered me good service with his great love and good will ever since the year ninety-one, by this clause, I give him liberty, with the understanding that he shall take my said sons to the City of Mexico and remain with them such time as he may see fit, and to whom will be given and provided a saddle and two mules to his satisfaction, with a gun, cover, cushions, bridle, reins and saddle-bag, hat, jacket and a pair of trousers of cloth, and, in the same manner will be given to my said sons one hundred pounds of chocolate and sugar and twelve measures of wheat-made dried bread, stockings, shoes, soap and hats for the said journey, which they will make two months after my death, or with the messenger who may take this notice of my death and in their company will go Don Antonio Maldonado Zapata, to whom I give four mules for pack animals and two saddle mules, fifty pounds of chocolate and fifty of sugar, four measures of wheat, six pairs of shoes, six bundles of tobacco, six dollars' worth of soap and two hats in order that he may accompany my two sons.

To my secretary of government and war, also, for the

love I bear him, I make him the gift of what he may owe me, and more, I leave him cloth of England enough for a suit of four yards, with its listed linings and buttons, so that with due care and legality he may assist my said lieutenant-general, by these presents appointed my testamentary executor.

To the accounts which I have with the soldiers, corporals and officers of war of this garrison, paid in full their year in advance, and to the others, owing small sums, to pay them in full to their satisfaction upon the settlement of their accounts.

There shall also be made an inventory of all of my property, assigning first to my said Lieutenant-general and compadre, Don Juan Paez Hurtado, the testamentary executor and administrator, my black hat embellished with blue and white feathers and my silver-laced cloak, lined with blue plush, and a new jerkin with grogram and silk lace and my gold cane.

To my said sons I leave my mourning suit and to the said Don Antonio Maldonado Zapata, in consideration of relationship and friendship, I leave to him all that he may owe me on account of salary and furthermore, I give him a pair of stockings of yellow color, embroidered with silver, and one pair of socks.

Out of the inventory of my property when made, there will be paid the parochial fee for the nine masses over the corpse, to the Rev. Fr. Guardian, giving him one hundred candles for the bier and fifty for the altars and those Religious present; I believe there is chocolate of my liking in two baskets amounting to about two hundred and twenty-five pounds, and the balance in what he may ask to be paid in goods which may be left.

Relative to the great quantities of supplies with which I have been supplied by the government and which appear to have come in to the Villa of Santa Fe during the last year, one thousand seven hundred and three, I submit the bill of exchange which I have drawn in favor of said persons. To Don Francisco Dias Tagle, resident of the City of Mexico, I may be indebted as to that which may not have been paid on the salary of one hundred soldiers of the garrison of the Villa of Santa Fe, and their year paid in advance began on the 16th day of December of last year, one thousand seven hundred and three, and will end in the present year, one thousand seven hundred and four, and for the payment of said balance I assign to said chief officer the goods of said inventory and also five hundred and fifty head of cattle, furnishing the said soldiers as usual from said stock and grain which are in my warehouse and in the house of Captain Diego Arias, the portion which appears in the book of accounts, and at La Cañada in possession of Sylvestre Pacheco, and from the one as well as from the others said soldiers shall be supplied, all of which will be administered by my lieutenant promptly, the soldiers making to him their obligations to pay out of their salaries, and the new Governor who shall come to make the payment for said soldiers out of their salaries in the first payment to be made in the present year one thousand seven hundred and four, in order that the said soldiers may not be in need of the necessary support in their aid to the Royal service, for which and in compliance with which the said soldiers shall give to my said lieutenant the notes required by him for what may be given to them and also giving to them thirty head of cattle each month at the pleasure of my said lieutenant.

In the same manner I declare that I am indebted in the City of Mexico to the Captain Don Juan de Bazoco in the sum of two thousand one hundred and ninety dollars, payable at the end of the month of May of the present year. Furthermore, I am indebted to the Count of Fresno de la Fuente as evidenced by a note of seven hundred and some odd dollars, for the amount of my account which his predecessor, Don Mathias de Munaris did not collect, and for the payment of which I ask the Captain Don Antonio de Valverde to pay the same on account of what he owes me and to remit a bill of exchange to my said testamentary executor to be by him enclosed with notice of my death to the said Count de Fresno de la Fuente.

In the same manner will Don Antonio Valverde pay to the Captain Don Francisco Sanchez de Tagle the balance due on account of three boxes of gun-powder which was gotten on my account in Mexico from the general contractor and the lead which I gave as ammunition for the journey, which he will pay at the rate of one dollar and a half for gun-powder and lead.

In the same manner said Captain Antonio Valverde will pay in form convenient to himself and when agreeable, the different accounts furnished to the soldiers of his garrison and also for one box of soap which, at his request, I furnished him at said garrison at El Paso del Norte.

I leave in full force and effect the testament made by me

on the first day of June of last year, one thousand seven hundred and three, in the City of Mexico, before Don Juan de Valdez, Notary Public for His Majesty, in which I declared and as to this I repeat and declare as the successor of my first-born son as Marqués de la Naba Brazinas, my oldest grand-son as therein stated.

I do appoint in my place my Lieutenant general, that as soon as I may die he may govern this kingdom, the political as well as the military, who shall give immediate notice to the Viceroy, the Duke of Alburquerque, and in the same manner, for the discharge of this my testament and its contents, I appoint my said lieutenant, Juan Paez Hurtado, my testamentary executor and the keeper of my goods, and after the discharging of the provisions of my will, having paid and satisfied all as in the same stated, it is my will that the remainder be remitted to my said administrators, Don Miguel de Ubilla and Don Diego Suazo y Cojales, and this I sign, while on the campaign, in the Town of Bernalillo, with the Captain Alonzo Rael de Aguilar, my secretary of government and war, and I, the said secretary say that in my presence it was made by the Marqués de la Naba Brazinas, present governor and captain general of this Kingdom, and I do certify and know that His Excellency is in his entire judgment and natural understanding which God Our Lord has been pleased to give him, and while His Excellency is in the field, and there not being any royal or public notary in this Kingdom and much less there being in this place an alcalde who could ex-officio acknowledge this testament, for said reason, it was ackuowledged by me, the said secretary of government, to give it full faith according to law; His Excellency signing it before me said secretary of government and war and signing as witnesses Lieutenant Juan de Urribarri, Don Antonio Maldonado, Adjutant, and the Captain Felix Martinez, who were present and duly signed as stated. Made in the Town of Bernalillo on the seventh day of the month of April, in the year one thousand seven hundred and four, and written upon ordinary plain paper as there is none which is sealed at this place. Holding of no value persons and seventy head of cattle.

And in the same manner I desire and it is my will that, whereas, I have furnished the Captain Don Felix Martinez what my account books show, that my said administrator do not collect anything from him for I give it to him for the great service and love which he has rendered me, and this clause shall be complied with as all the others, and I sign it before said secretary and witnesses on said day, month and year.

Moreover, I declare that I have another mulatto slave by the name of José de la Cruz, whom also, on account of the time he has served me, lovingly and willingly, I do give to him his liberty, with the understanding that he will serve my said sons Don Juan and Don Alonzo de Vargas five years, and at the end of which time he will be at liberty, as appears by this clause and the declaration made before a notary by my said sons that said José de la Cruz has served the five years. I sign it with said secretary of government and war and the witnesses.

THE MARQUÉS DE LA BRAZINAS [Rubric]

Witnesses:
JUAN DE ULIBARRI [Rubric]
ANTONIO MACARIO MALDONADO ZAPATA [Rubric]
FELIX MARTINEZ [Rubric]
Before me:
ALFONZO RAEL DE AGUILAR [Rubric]
Secy. of Govmt. and War.

On said day, month and year, I, the said Governor and Captain-general, Marqués de la Naba Brazinas, do say; that notwithstanding the long time since I came from New Spain, I have ordered a great number of masses to be said for the repose of my soul, and notwithstanding this testament is closed, I desire and it is my will to have five hundred masses, two hundred applied to the Holy Virgin of Remedies, my protector, for the benefit of my soul, and three hundred for the souls of the poor who died in the conquest of this Kingdom and may have died up to the present day, for which I order my testamentary executor to pay the necessary fees out of my property, requiring a receipt for the payment of the same, and being oppressed with the sickness which his Divine Majesty has been pleased to afflict me, although in my entire judgment and understanding, and not being able to sign this clause it is done for me by the Lieutenant Juan de Uribarri, there being present my secretary of government and war, whom I ask to certify, and I the said secretary, being present, do say that the said Marqués is in his complete judgment and understanding and declares this clause and order for masses, and I sign it with said

Lieutenant Don Juan de Uribarri, the witnesses being the Captain Don Fernando Duran y Chaves, Thomas Olguin and Don Bernardo Duran y Chaves, all present.
By request of The Marques de la Naba Brazinas.
                              JUAN DE URIBARRI [Rubric]
FERNANDO DURAN Y CHAVES [Rubric]
THOMAS OLGUIN [Rubric]
BERNARDO DURAN Y CHAVES [Rubric]
  Before me:
    ALFONZO RAEL DE AGUILAR [Rubric]
        Secy. of Govmt. and War

1028 SEBASTIAN RODRIGUEZ to Micaela de Velasco. *Santa Fe.* 1707.
  Land on the other side of the *Rio de Santa Fe.*

1029 FRANCISCO MONTES VIGIL.
  Grant. 1710. Reported Claim No. 91, *q. v.* Town of *Alameda.*

1030 JUANA DE ZOSA CANELA to Juan Ballejo. *Santa Fe.* 1716.
  Land in *Alburquerque.* Juan Garcia de las Rivas, Alcalde.

1031 JUAN DOMINGO DE BUSTAMANTE, General, to Antonio de Valverde de Cossio, General. *Santa Fe.* 1722.
  Land below the City of *El Paso del Rio del Norte* "*cuyos sitios lindan por la parte del con los sitios de dho Sr. Gen. Dn. Antonio de Valverde y por la otra con el Pueblo de Guadalupe q. fue de los Indios Zumas que es por la parte Poniente y por la del Oriente por una y otra vanda hasta la sierra q. llaman de las Minas, y por la parte del medio dia hasta la sierra por la del Norte Las Salinas, y Sierra Florida en presio y cuantia de Zinco mil pesos de oro,*" etc.
  Francisco Bueno de Bohorques y Corcuera, Alcalde.
  This deed shows that General Don Antonio de Valverde Cossio was the uncle and father-in-law of General Don Juan Domingo de Bustamante, both governors of the Province at different periods.

1032 JUAN RUIS CORDERO to Francisco Velasquez. *Santa Fe,* 1722.
  House and land. Francisco Bueno de Bohorques y Corcuera, Alcalde.

1033 MATEO TRUXILLO to Sebastian de Vargas and Miguel de Dios. 1722.
>House and lands in *Santa Fe*. Francisco Bueno de Bohorques y Corcuera, Alcalde.

1034 LORENZO TRUXILLO to Pedro Vigil. *Santa Fe,* 1724.
>Rancho in *La Cañada de Santa Cruz*. Bohorquez y Corcuera, Alcalde.

1035 CAYETANO and AGUSTIN LOBATO to Domingo Vigil. *Santa Fe,* 1727.
>Land in *Cañada de Santa Cruz*. Diego Arias de Quiros, Alcalde.
>Shows that Santa Cruz de la Cañada was on *south* side of the river; see No. 742 and No. 427.

1036 JUAN LUJAN to Antonio Velasquez. *Santa Fe,* 1730.
>House and lands. Diego Arias de Quiros, Alcalde.

1037 DIEGO GALLEGOS to the *Pueblo* of *Santo Domingo* to Miguel Joseph de la Vega y Coca. *Santa Fe,* 1730.
>One-half interest in a tract of land lying between *Santo Domingo* and *Xemes,* called *San Miguel de la Cruz*. Diego Arias de Quiros, Alcalde.

1038 LUIS ROMERO, *Picuriés* Indian. 1732.
>Permission given him to sell a piece of land near *Embudo* to Pedro Montes Vigil. Gervasio Cruzat y Gongora, Governor.
>Petition by Luis Romero, an Indian of the pueblo of Picuriés, to the governor of New Mexico, asking permission to sell a piece of land which he had at a place called Embudo. Whether he meant the settlement of that name or the stream now called the Embudo river is not clear.
>The petition was presented to Governor Cruzat y Gongora at Santa Fe on February 17, 1732, and by him referred to the Indians of the *pueblo* of Picuriés, in order that they might state whether their interests would be prejudicially affected by the proposed sale.
>On February 25, 1732, the Indians stated that they desired the sale to be made; and the heirs of Luis Romero consented to it, etc.

On February 28, 1732, Governor Cruzat y Gongora, in view of the statement made by the Indians, granted to Romero the permission to make the sale, which, according to the governor's statement, Romero wanted to make to Pedro Montes Vigil.

This document is interesting as throwing some light on the view entertained at its date as to the right of a Pueblo Indian to sell land, although there is nothing in it that makes certain the location of the land, which may have been at or near the settlement of Embudo, miles distant from the Picuriés *pueblo* grant, or at some point on the Embudo river, and possibly within the grant.

1039 JOSEPH DE RIAÑO. *Santa Fe,* 1736.

Presents petition asking that the grants to Mateo Truxillo, made by Governor Cubero, situate between the leagues of the *pueblos* of San Ildefonso and Santa Clara be measured and land-marks set up. Proceedings in the matter, etc. Gervasio Cruzat y Gongora, Governor.

Petition by Joseph de Riaño, asking that the Indians of Santa Clara and San Ildefonso be required to produce any documents that they might have, showing the extent of their holdings, in order that he might know what were the boundaries of a grant, lying between the two *pueblos,* which he had bought from one Trujillo, and which had not been defined by monuments.

On March 15, 1736, Governor Cruzat y Gongora directed General Don Juan Paez Hurtado to measure one league from each of the two *pueblos* in the direction of the ranch which Riaño had bought, and to put up monuments at the proper places.

On March 17, 1736, General Paez Hurtado, in company with Captain Juan Esteban Garcia de Noriega, chief alcalde of the district, Captain Domingo Vigil, Francisco Gomez, and the natives of the two *pueblos*, began at the corner of the plaza of San Ildefonso and measured 4,600 *varas* to the slope of the table-land, and from that point 400 *varas* more "of the lands of Baltazar Trujillo (the party from whom Riaño had purchased) to complete the five thousand *varas* which make the league belonging to said *pueblo* of San Ildefonso." He then proceeded to measure the league belonging to the *pueblo* of Santa Clara, and discovered that it was 169 *varas* less than the full length of 5,000 *varas,* "there remaining to Baltazar Trujillo, between the measurements of said *pueblos,* eighty-four *varas.*"

General Paez Hurtado further states that notwithstanding he had orders to place monuments to mark the lands of the two *pueblos* he would defer doing so until he had reported to the governor what he had already done.

On March 18, 1736, Governor Cruzat y Gongora, in view of the report of Paez Hurtado, decided that nothing new should be done in the matter, and that the monuments should be left at the points where they were established.

1040 JOSEPH XARAMILLO to Leogardo Gallego. *Alburquerque,* 1734.

Lands. Geronimo Xaramillo, Alcalde.

1041 DIEGO DE VELASCO. Grant. 1725.

Land in the *Cañada* called *Cundiyo.* Juan Domingo de Bustamante, Governor. Revoked in 1738 by Enrique de Olavide y Michelena, Governor.

Petition by Diego de Velasco for a tract of land in the *cañada* of Cundiyo, the boundaries of which were on the west a tract called the Potrero, on the east some hills up in the *cañada,* on the north the Rio de en Media, on the south the river of said place of Cundiyo.

This petition was presented to Governor Juan Domingo de Bustamante on July 14, 1725, and he made the grant on condition that it should not be to the prejudice of the Indians or that any third party who might have a better right, and directed the chief alcalde of Santa Cruz, with that understanding, to place the party in possession.

There is no evidence that the possession was ever given.

On the 15th day of September, 1738, Governor Henrique de Olavide y Michelena, being at that date at the *pueblo* of Nambé, on a general inspection tour, attached to the foregoing petition and grant his decree abrogating the same because of representations made to him by the Indians showing that Velasco was causing them great damage; that in all the intervening years he had not received juridical possession of the property.

1042 JUANA DE LOS RIOS to Manuel, Diego, Antonio, and Juana Velasquez. *Santa Fe,* 1739.

Donation of a tract of land. Antonio Montoya, Alcalde.

314   THE SPANISH ARCHIVES OF NEW MEXICO

1043   DOMINGO VALDEZ. *Santa Fe*, 1742.
    Grant. Entrances and exits. Juan Domingo de Mendoza, Governor. Antonio de Hulibarri, Alcalde.

1044   JOSEPH FRESQUI to Manuel Gregorio Vigil. *Santa Fe,* 1750.
    Land. Juan Joseph Lovato, Alcalde.

1045   MANUEL VALERIO to Juan Manzanares. 1751.
    Land on the *Chama*. Juan Joseph Lovato, Alcalde.

1046   JUAN DE DIOS ROMERO to Francisco Montes Vigil. *Santa Cruz,* 1751.
    Land at *San Francisco del Pueblo Quemado*. Juan Joseph Sandoval, Alcalde.

1047   JOSE DE MEDINA to Juan Bautista Vigil. *Chimayo.* 1751.
    Lands. Juan Joseph Sandoval, Alcalde.

1048   SANTIAGO MARTIN to Felix Valerio. *Chimayo,* 1751.
    Land. Juan Joseph Sandoval, Alcalde.

1049   CLARA DE VILLAREAL, wife of Melchor Rodriguez. San Joseph de Garcia. Jurisdiction of Pueblo of *Picuriés.* 1753.
    Inventory and partition of her estate. Made at request of Juan Joseph de Arguello, husband of Joachina Rodriguez, daughter of said Clara de Villareal. Nicolas de Ortiz, Alcalde.

1050   MANUEL VALERIO vs. Lazaro de Atienza. *Santa Cruz de la Cañada.* 1753.
    Question of boundaries. Tomas Velez Cachupin, Governor.

1051   ANTONIO VARELA.
    Grant in *Fuenclara.* 1754. Tomas Velez Cachupin.

1052   JOSEPH RAMO DE VERA. *Santa Fe,* 1753.
    Will. Nicolas Ortiz, Alcalde.

1053   FRANCISCO MONTES VIGIL. Grant. 1754.
    Reported Claim No. 128, *q. v.*

1054 CRISTOBAL VIGIL and Manuel and Joseph Montoya. 1754.
 Petition for land on the *Truchas.* No final action taken. Tomas Velez Cachupin, Governor.

1055 JUAN MONTES VIGIL. *Santa Fe,* 1762.
 Will, inventory, and partition of his estate. Manuel Gallego, Alcalde. Tomas Velez Cachupin, Governor.

1056 MARTIN TORRES to Manuel Vigil. *Santa Fe,* 1762.
 Lands. Manuel Gallego, Alcalde.

1057 NICOLASA VIGIL. *Chama.* 1765.
 Will, proceedings, and partition of her estate. Tomas Velez Cachupin, Governor.

1058 JOACHIN GARCIA DE NORIEGA to Salvador and Ignacio Vigil.
 Land in *Cañada de Santa Cruz.* 1766. Manuel Garcia Pareja, Alcalde.

1059 DIEGO MANUEL BACA and Joaquin Valencia. *Santa Fe,* 1772.
 Exchange of real property in said city. Manuel Garcia Pareja, Alcalde.

1060 MANUEL MONTES VIGIL, alcalde of *Taos,* 1780.
 Proceedings in the settlement of his estate. Juan Bautista de Anza, Governor.

1061 MARINA DE JESUS BACA.
 Will. *Santa Fe.* 1784. José Sandoval; Salvador Ribera; Juan de Abrego.

1062 JOSEPH MANUEL VELARDE and 18 Families.
 Petition to settle at *Ojo Caliente.* No final action. Fernando Chacón, Governor.

1063 PEDRO VIAL (*el Frances*).
 Will and inventory of his estate. *Santa Fe,* 1814. José Antonio Alarid, Sargento. Francisco Ortiz, Alcalde.
 Pedro Vial was a Frenchman and took an important part in some of the affairs of the Province. He died at Santa Fe, and his remains were buried in the Castrense church; he was a bachelor, without any relatives in this

country; he left as his heir, Maria Manuela Martin. From his will, it appears that at times he practiced medicine. He died in 1814. He served as an interpreter to the Comanche Indians for many years.

1064 JOSE ANTONIO VALVERDE and others.
Petition for lands known as the *Rancho de la Xemes* near *Vallecito*, 1815. The parties were put in possession by Ignacio Sanchez Vergara, Alcalde, but the Governor, Maynez, declared his action void because of error in the proceedings.

1065 IGNACIO MARIA SANCHEZ VERGARA.
Petition for land between the *pueblos* of Santo Domingo and San Felipe. 1824. Referred to the Provincial Deputation. Bartolomé Baca, Governor.

1066 SANTIAGO SALAZAR vs. Miguel Velarde.
Question of lands at *Abiquiú*. 1825.

1067 JOSEPH SEDANO vs. Juan Lorenzo Medina. *Santa Fe*, 1731.
Question of title to house and lot. Francisco Bueno Bohorques y Corcuera, Alcalde.

1068 ANTONIO GONZALES DE LA ROSA to José Samorra. *Santa Rosalia del Vallecito. Jurisdiccion de San Geronimo de Taos.* 1763.
Land. Pedro Antonio Martin, Alcalde.

1069 JUAN ANTONIO FRESQUI to José Samorra. *Santa Rosalia del Vallecito.* 1763.
Land. Pedro Antonio Martin, Alcalde.

1070 JOSE SANCHEZ to Joseph Samorra. *Santa Rosalia del Vallecito.* 1763.
Pedro Antonio Martin, Alcalde.

1071 MADALENA DE OGAMA vs. Ramon Garcia Jurado. *Santa Fe*, 1703.
Question of title to land. El Marqués de la Nava Brazinas.

1072 ANTONIO GODINES and MARIA DOMINGUEZ DE MENDOZA, his wife, to Nicolas Ortiz Niño Ladron de Guebarra. *Santa Fe*, 1714.

House and land. Francisco Bueno Bohorques y Corcuera, Alcalde.

Describes a house situate *"en la calle real q ba de la plaza a la Yglesia Nueba q se esta fabricando* — on the main street which goes from the plaza to the new church which is being built" (1714).

1073 NICOLAS ORTIZ NIÑO LADRON DE GUEVARA. *Santa Fe,* 1714.
Possession given of the said property.

1074 PEDRO MONTES DE OCA to Nicolas Ortiz Niño Ladron de Guebara. *Santa Fe,* 1714.
House and land. Diego Arias de Quiros, Alcalde. No. 1072 and 1073, *q. v.*

Describes a house situate *"en la calle real esta Villa que ba a la Yglesia Nueba que seesta haziendo."* December 6, 1714.

1075 JOSEPHA MARTIN to Antonio Olguin. *Santa Fe,* 1719.
House and Land. Francisco Bueno de Bohorques y Corcuera, Alcalde.

1076 JOSEPHA DE ONTIVEROS vs. Pascuala de Concepcion. *Villa Nueva de Santa Cruz.* 1731.
Question of title to a grant of land. Domingo Vigil, Alcalde. Juan Domingo de Bustamante, Governor.

1077 JOSEPHA DE ONTIVEROS. *Villa Nueva de Santa Cruz.*
Grant, 1735. Manuel de la Rosa, Francisco de Baldes, Juan Andrés Gonzales, Juan Feliz Bustillos. Made by Juan Paez Hurtado, Acting Governor. Revoked by Cruzat, Governor.

1078 NICOLAS ORTIZ NIÑO LADRON DE GUEVARA. 1742.
Reported Claim No. 63, *q. v.* Caja del Rio.

Caja del Rio Grant. Reported No. 63. There is a small conflict with the grant to the *pueblo* of Cochiti. When the decree of confirmation was entered by the court of private land claims and a new survey had been made it was found that the conflict had materially increased. The grant was patented February 20, 1897.

1079 NICOLAS ORTIZ NIÑO LADRON DE GUEVARA vs. Juan Estevan Garcia de Noriega.

Trespass. *Santa Fe*, 1754. Don Tomas Velez Cachupin, Governor. Gregorio Garduño, Pedro Sotero, Juan Domingo Lovato, Bernardo de Miera y Pacheco. Antonio de Ulibarri, Alcalde. Juan Joseph Lobato, Procurador. Juan José Jaques, Tomas de Alvear y Collado, Joseph Miguel Garduño.

This tract was granted to Nicolas Ortiz Niño Ladron de Guevara, May 13, 1742, by Gaspar Domingo de Mendosa, as a reward for services performed as a soldier in the reconquest and pacification of the country in 1692-96.

When the son of this reconquistador died on August 2, 1810, whose name was also Nicolas Ortiz Niño Ladron de Guevara, other than his interest in the *Caja del Rio* Grant, he left a house of seven rooms and five hundred varas of land. His wife was Maria Alberta Maes, and they left one son, Francisco Xavier Ortiz, who at his death left the following: Antonio José Ortiz; Juan Antonio Ortiz; the latter deceased and leaving as heirs, Belen Ortiz, wife of José Abeytia; and José Matias Ortiz; the last named left Damacio Ortiz and Ramon Ortiz and Dionicio Ortiz, who married Reyes Tenorio. There were many other heirs, including Miguel Baca y Ortiz, Faustina Baca, Pablo Baca, Severiano Baca, Dolores Baca, and Justo Baca, children of Guadalupe Ortiz.

The original Nicolas Ortiz Niño Ladron de Guevara made his will September 17, 1742, in which he states that he was married to Juana Baca and had three children, Francisco Ortiz, Nicolas Ortiz and Toribio Ortiz. This will is archive 647. In his petition for the grant he states that it is now "forty-nine years since I came with my parents to the reconquest and pacification of this said province as a settler therein, sent by the most excellent Viceroy, the Cónde de Galve, which dignitary promised to supply us with land to cultivate and live upon by the authority of the King himself, which land has not been given me because I was engaged and occupied with all the campaigns and incursions that have taken place from that to the present time, without causing any cost to His Majesty for a load of powder which I furnished at my own expense as well as all kinds of arms and horses, as appears from the documents which I hold in my favor from my superiors."

The boundaries in the grant are described: "On the east the wide Cañada; on the west the Rio del Norte; on the north the point of the mesa situated in the Caja del Rio, and on the south the drainage — (*virtirtiente*) of Santa Cruz. The land lies below the Indian *pueblo* of San Ildefonso. The Indians of San Ildefonso made no objection to the making of the grant. Nicolas Ortiz was known as "Chino" Ortiz. The heirs of Nicolas Ortiz were compelled to abandon this grant in 1818 on account of raids made by the Navajo Indians.

1080 LIST of SETTLERS in the New Town of *San Antonio de MORA*. No date. No signatures. List contains 36 names. List of Settlers *de la Plaza de Santa Getrudis; del Valle de Abajo* contains 34 names. Also list of the *Pobladores que han dehado sus posssesiones y se han salido*. Contains 6 names.

1081 NEMESIO SALCEDO of *Chihuahua* to the Acting Governor of *New Mexico*, 1809 to 1810.

Two letters relating to a piece of land distant seven leagues from *Santa Fe*, of which possession is claimed by Nicolas Ortiz. This action is taken on account of a petition presented by Francisco Ortiz. The land is spoken of as *San Marcos*. The petition is not granted and said Ortiz and Manuel Delgado were forbidden to put their stock on said land, but it was expressly reserved for the poor of *Santa Fe*. Reference is here made to the pasture lands of Galisteo and to those of El Arco.

Reported Claim No. 63, *q. v. Caja del Rio.* No. 1078, 1079, 1271, *q. v.*

1082 ROYAL DECREE giving equal rights to all Americans and Indians in Spanish America. 1811. Published and ordered to be promulgated in Chihuahua in 1821, by Alejo Garcia Cónde, Governor, etc.

Copy, made at Chihuahua on February 20, 1821, of a decree of the Cortes, dated on February 9, 1811, conferring certain rights on the citizens of the Spanish dominions in America, including both Spaniards and *Indians*. These rights were the following:

1st. The right of being represented in the Cortes on the same footing as the inhabitants of Spain.

2d. The right of planting and cultivating all the land

which their ability and circumstances permitted them to do.

3d. The right of eligibility to all public offices and employments in the ecclesiastical, civil, and military branches of the service.

This copy is signed by Alejo Garcia Cónde, governor, commandant general, and superior civil chief of the Internal Provinces of the West, of New Spain.

1083 NUESTRA SEÑORA DE LA LUZ SAN FERNANDO Y SAN BLAS del Rio Puerco. 1770.
Question of boundaries with Antonio Baca. Don Pedro Fermin de Mendinueta, Governor. Carlos Mirabal, Alcalde. *Pajarito* and *Atrisco* Grant, q. v.

1084 INVENTARIO DE DILIGENCIAS *fechas por mi Don Joseph de Bustamante Tagle, alcalde mayor de la Capital Villa de Santa Fe, desde el año de quarenta y nuebe, hasta el presente, de mil septecientos cincuenta y dos y son las siguientes:*
Escritura de venta por el Sindico, Bernardino de Sena, to Don Francisco Ortiz, 1750.
Maria de la Candelaria Gonzales. Will. 1750.
Antonio Dominguez to Phelipe Garduño, 1750.
Julian Rael to Francisco Trujillo. 1750.
Micaela Vasquez, heirs of. Partition of lands. 1750.
Maria de Roibal and Josef de Riaño, her son. Partition of lands. 1750.
Juan Tomas Lobato to Pedro Antonio Truxillo. 1750.
Title deed in favor of Miguel Laso de la Vega.
Manuel Thenorio (de Alva).
Juan Montes Vigil.
There was a grant, Reported No. 38, known as the "Ramon Vigil." This grant is west of the Rio Grande and on the north for a short distance adjoins the San Ildefonso *Pueblo Grant*. The grant was confirmed June 21, 1860, and was patented, April 9, 1908.
Santiago de Roibal.
Ignacio de Roibal.
Miguel Dominguez, Destierro, 1750.
Francisco de Anaya to Theresa Thenorio. 1751.
Manuel de Beitia to Salvador Casillas. 1751.
Domingo de Benavides to Antonio Dominguez. 1751.
Manuel Vaca to Josepha Montoya. 1751.

Don Juan Antonio de Vizarron y Eguiarreta
Viceroy of Mexico, 1734-40

Phelipe Nerio Sisneros to Manuel Gallegos. 1751.
Isidro Montoya, *Carta Segura* in favor of his minors, on account of the death of Manuela Silva. 1751.
Sebastian de Vargas to Antonio Duran de Armijo. 1751.
Antonio Tafoya to Luis Febro. 1751.
Phelipe Rodriguez to Manuel Lopez. 1751.
Manuel Trujillo, heirs of; partition of estate. 1751.
Juana Sisneros to Juan de Chaves. 1751.
Andrés Montoya to Francisco Nieto. 1751.
Juan Antonio Flores to Nicolas Moran. 1751.
José Romo de Vera to Maria Francisca de Sena. 1751.
Catalina Duran. Inventory of her estate. 1751.
Cayetano Pasote. Cause against. 1751.
Joseph Romo. Embargo and other proceedings. 1751.
Maria Diega Garduño. Inventory of her estate. 1751.
Miguel de la Vega de Coca. Will and inventory. 1751.
Deed in favor of Santiago de Roybal. 1752.
Marcial Samora to Melchora de Sandoval. 1752.
Tomas Holguin to Cristobal Madrid. 1752.
Juan Geronimo de Samano. Will and inventory. 1752.
Geronimo de Ortega. Proceedings in the matter of his Minors, 1752.

1085 MANUEL ARMIJO, Political Chief.
Correspondence relating to the palace. 1827.
Two letters from Manuel Armijo, *jefe politico*, to Don Agustin Duran, *comisario substituto*, relative to the occupation of the "Palace" by Colonel Narbona.

1086 PEOPLE of SANTO DOMINGO DE CUNDIYO.
Petition for the establishment of a church. 1754. Not granted. Tomas Velez Cachupin, Governor.

1087 JUAN DE OÑATE. Honorary Title, etc. Copy. 1761.
"Don Felipe, by the grace of God, King of Castile, of Aragon, of the Sicilies, of Jerusalem, of Portugal, of Granada, of Toledo, of Valencia, of Galecia, Mayoria, Sevilla, of Yerdina, Cordova, Coreega, Murrisa, Jaen, Algarbes, of Algesira Gibraltar, Canary Islands, East and West Indies, Islands, and Tierra Firma of the Ocean, Arch-duque of Austria, Duque of Borgora and Milan, Count of Traspur Flanders, and Tirol, of Barcelona, Lord of Viscaya and Molisa, etc., etc.

"Whereas, the viceroy, Don Louis of Velasco, by virtue of a decree of the King, my Lord — may he live in glory — entered in to an agreement and capitulation with

Don Juan de Oñate, relative to the discovery, pacification and settlement of the provinces of New Mexico, which is in New Spain, and among other things he granted to him what is contained in one of the chapters or instructions of new discoveries and settlements of the Indies, which is as follows: 'To those who bind themselves to form said settlements, and shall have done the same, and shall have complied with the agreement, in honor of their own persons and their descendants and of them as first settlers, laudable memory may remain, we make them and their legitimate descendants Hijosdalgos of the lands owned by them, in order that in the settlement established by them, and in any other part of the Indies they may be Hijosdalgos and persons of noble lineage and Lord paramount, and as such they shall be known held and considered, and enjoy all the honors and preeminences, and may do all things that noblemen and gentlemen of the Kingdom of Castile can do, according to the privileges, laws and customs of Spain, should or ought to do and enjoy. And in behalf of the said Juan de Oñate, I have been requested to grant him the grace to command him to approve, notwithstanding the moderation which the Duque of Monterey used relative thereto, and published by him, my Council of the Indies, I have thought proper that the said prerogatives should be understood to continue during the time occupied in said conquest, for five years, and if the said conquerors should terminate the conquest thereof before the expiration of the five years, they, their sons, and descendants shall enjoy the said prerogatives as herein set forth. And I do hereby command that all who may have gone and shall go on the said conquest, pacification and settlement, according to, and in conformity with, the provisions of the said chapter, and shall continue in the conquest for five years; and those who shall prosecute the same who should die before the expiration of five years, there shall be reserved and secured unto their sons and descendants all the preeminences and prerogatives, exemptions, and liberties as aforesaid in conformity to, and as is granted and conferred upon them in the said chapter, entirely and completely, failing in nothing, and charge the Infantes, Prelates, Duques, Marquises, Counts, Nobles, Subjects and Priors of Royal Orders, Prefects, Alcaldes of the Castiles, houses surounded with a moat, and country houses (casas fuertes y lanas), and those of my Councils, Presidents,

THE SPANISH ARCHIVES OF NEW MEXICO 323

Judges, Alcaldes and High Constables of my household and court, and chancery, to my Viceroys and Governors, and to all of my authorities and Judges, as well as those of the Indies and Tierra Firma of the Ocean, and other persons of whatever condition or quality, to observe and comply, and to have obeyed and executed this my franchise and grace, confirmed to the aforesaid, without restricting or increasing nor consent to any infraction of the contents of this my determination, which I desire and it is my will that it shall have the force of law as though it had been decreed and promulgated in court, and it be published in all proper parts and places.

" 'Given at San Lorenzo, on the 8th day of July, 1602.
(Signed) " 'I, THE KING

"Laguna, Armenteros, Doc. Eugenio de Salazar, Benabente de Venavides, Louis de Salcedo. By order of the King, my Lord. Juan de Ibarra. Recorded, Gabriel de Ochoa, Chancellor, Sebastian de la Vega.

"ACT OF AUDIENCE

"In the City of Mexico, June 20, 1604, the President and Judge of the Royal Audience of New Spain being present at the session, also the Mariscal de Campo, Vicente de Saldivar, presented the Royal decree governing to the opposite party and asked that it be compiled with; and being seen by the said Audience, they obeyed the same with all reverence and respects, and replied that it should be observed and complied with, and executed in all its parts as His Majesty commanded; and this it was recorded as their act, and they approved the same by placing their rubric thereto in my presence.
(Signed) "CRISTOBAL OROSIO."

1088 PROCLAMATION requiring Obedience to the new Spanish Constitution of 1820.
Letter from Facundo Melgares, Governor.

1089 DOCUMENT relating to Military Matters.

1090 JOSE RAMON ALARID.
Grant. 1824. At a place called *El Cerrito*. *Cuatro labores que estan inmediatos a la labor de la Cuesta*. Grant made by the Deputacion Provincial. The grantees are: José Ramon Alarid, Roman Garcia, Julian Garcia, Severiano Sanchez, Juan Ignacio Rodriguez, José Tenorio,

Alejandro Sais, Juan Cristobal Garcia, Isidro Flores, Pablo Borrego, Francisco Salas, José Rodriguez, Benito Urtado, Eusebio Garcia.

This document purports to be a copy of the original certified by Francisco Lopez, probate judge of San Miguel county, and dated March 12, 1855.

1091 LIST of GOVERNORS of *New Mexico* from 1770 to 1840.

1092 REPAIRS on Barracks, Santa Fe, 1810.

1093 REPAIRS ON OLD PALACE, 1841.

1094 DOCUMENT (Imperfect) relating to property in the hands of Officials. No date.

1095 LIST of Heads of Families in seventh demarcation, *San Miguel* county, August 3, 1855.

1096 JUAN DE DIOS MAESE and Others.
Grant at *Las Vegas*. 1835. Certified copy by Francisco Lopez, Probate Judge of *San Miguel* County. 1855.

1097 INVENTORY of PAPERS of ARCHIVES in the Office of the Secretary of Government and War, 1715. Fourteen pages. Very interesting.

1098 EL MARQUÉS DE ALTAMIRA, Mexico. 1750.
Relating to re-settlement of the country north and northwest of *Santa Fe*. Don Tomas Velez Cachupin, Governor.

1099 PEDRO DE NAVA, *Chihuahua*, 1798.
Relating to soldiery.

1100 PROCEEDINGS and Order in Relation to the re-settlement of *Abiquiú*. 1750.
Tomas Velez Cachupin, Governor.

1101 MINING REGULATIONS, 1795. Pedro de Nava. Manuel Merino.

1102 PAPERS relating to the PALACE, *Santa Fe*, 1827.
Correspondence relative to the "Palace."

1103 TIERRA AMARILLA GRANT, 1832.
Report of Committee of Territorial Deputation in relation to the same. Martinez, Tenorio, Ortiz.

1104 SETTLEMENT OF LANDS desired by the government.
Circular letter on this subject to the Alcaldes of the Territory. *Santa Fe,* 1815. Alberto Maynez. Socorro is mentioned.

The laws of the Indies relative to towns and communities are quite interesting and give some light on how these municipalities were founded and governed.

The governors and captains-general had the power to appoint in the cities or towns in their districts lieutenants; these bore the title of lieutenant-governor.

Contracts were made with individuals for the founding of towns; if the locality where the proposed town was to be built was found suitable for Spaniards, with a council of alcaldes of ordinary jurisdiction and aldermen, and a person desired to found a town, then he was obliged to make a contract conditioned "that within the term which shall be fixed for him, he have at least thirty persons, and each one of them a house, ten breeding cows, four oxen, or two oxen and two yearlings, one brood mare, one breeding sow, twenty Castilian breeding ewes, and six hens and one cock; he shall also appoint a priest to administer the Holy Sacraments, who shall be chosen by him the first time and thereafter shall be subject to our Royal Patronage; and he shall provide the church with the ornaments and articles for divine worship, and he shall give bond to comply therewith within said time; and if he does not comply therewith he shall lose all that he may have built, cultivated or earned, which we will apply to our Royal Patrimony, and he shall also incur the penalty of one thousand dollars in gold for our Chamber; and if he complies with his obligation, four leagues in boundary and territory, in a square or oblong, according to the quality of the land, may be given him, in such manner that, if it be surveyed, the four leagues be in a square, with the condition that the boundaries of said territory be at least five leagues distant from any city, town or place of Spaniards previously settled, and that it cause no prejudice to any Indian town or private person."

The children and relatives of settlers also were to be considered as settlers under certain conditions; *i. e.* "that they have distinct and separate houses and families and are married.''

The person who undertook to found a city was compelled to make contracts with each individual settler and in doing so the contractor obligated himself to give, in the town designated, lots for building purposes, pasture and farming lands to the extent of as many *peonias* and *caballerias* as each one of the settlers shall obligate himself to build upon; provided, it did not exceed more than five *peonias* or more than three *caballerias* for each settler, according to the distinction, difference, and measurement prescribed in the laws of the title on the distribution of lands, lots, and waters.

A *caballeria* consisted of 105.75 acres of land.

The person contracting to make a new settlement of a town, city, or colony secured the civil and criminal jurisdiction, in the first instance, for the days of his life and for those of a son or heir; he also received authority to appoint alcaldes of ordinary jurisdiction, aldermen, and other officers of the council of the town; and in cases appealed the causes went before a chief alcalde, or the audiencia in the district wherein the settlement or town was made.

Viceroys, audiencias, and governors had no authority to grant city or town titles. See book iv, title viii, law vi, *Laws of the Indies*. ''We order that, for no cause or reason, the Viceroys, Audiencias, Governors, or any other officers of the Indies, however high they may be, give city or town titles to any of the towns or places of Spaniards or Indians, and that they do not exempt them from the jurisdiction of their principal provincial capitals; with the understanding that they will be held responsible at their places of residence, because this favor and power must be asked of our Council of the Indies, and we declare as void the titles which, in contravention of the contents of this law, shall be given to any towns or places; and in regard to new towns or settlements, the provisions of law shall be observed.''

1105 RELATING to a House belonging to the Government in *Santa Fe*. 1733.

Cruzat y Gongora, Governor. Antonio de Ulibarri, Alcalde.

1106 MUNICIPAL ORDINANCES for the Cities and Towns of *New Mexico* prescribed by the Departmental Assembly, 1846.

1107 PRINTED COPY of the Colonization Law of 1823.

1108 TRINIDAD BARCELO.
    Letter to the government in relation to mining matters, 1846.

1109 TRANSLATION of a newspaper article on *New Mexico*.

1110 COMMISSIONS of the Captains-General of *New Mexico*, 1713-1715.

1111 LIST of Heads of Families in the 11th demarcation of *San Miguel* county, 1855.

1112 IGNACIO SANCHEZ VERGARA, 1813.
    Asks whether an Indian may sell land acquired by purchase. No final action by Governor. José Manrique, Governor.
    Letter from Ignacio Sanchez Vergara to Lieutenant-Colonel José Manrique, governor of New Mexico, stating that an Indian woman, who was a native of the *pueblo* of Zia, had negotiated a sale of a piece of land which she owned at San Isidro, and which her husband, then deceased, had bought of a citizen of that place; that the party who proposed to buy the land from her was willing that the woman should name an appraiser, and he desired that the value of the land be fixed so that he could pay for it; that in view of the fact that the owner of the land was an Indian, Sanchez (who was probably an alcalde at that time) thought it necessary to lay the matter before the governor in order that the latter might direct him how to proceed in the premises.
    Immediately following the letter, and on the same sheet (as was the custom at that date—1813), is a rough draft of the governor's reply. He informs Sanchez that no action could be taken in the matter until the future decision of the governor.

1113 S. W. KEARNY, Brigadier General.
    Proclamation, 1846.

328 THE SPANISH ARCHIVES OF NEW MEXICO

1114 SAN CARLOS, New settlement of, on the *Nepeste* River (Arkansas).
 Official letter in relation thereto from Jacobo Ugarte y Loyola, dated *Arispe*, January 22, 1788, to Fernando de la Concha, Governor.
 This is a report to Governor Fernando de la Concha relative to a settlement on the Nepeste (Arkansas) by the Cumanche Lieutenant-General Paruanarimuco. January 22, 1788.
 Refers to the establishment of a town on the Arkansas river composed of Cumanches, who had been aided by the Spaniards in making a permanent settlement there.

1115 RELATING to the disposition of the fees received by the alcaldes for giving possession of lands.

1116 SETTLEMENT of TECOLOTE. 1838.
 Proceedings, etc. Also list of names and quantity of land given to each settler.

1117 PEDRO DE CHAVES, Alcalde *de San Agustin de Isleta*. 1714.
 Acknowledgement of receipt of an order from the Governor.
 It is stated that there were no *"estufas"* or subterranean rooms in the pueblo of *Isleta*.

1118 RELATING to the Removal of the Capitol to a place between *Santo Domingo* and *Cochiti*, etc.
 Galindo Navarro, Arispe, 1781. Antonio Bonilla.

1119 ALAMEDA.
 Question of boundaries between the Garcias and the Tafoyas. Settled by a suit of conciliation, 1827.
 José Alejandro Santistievan, Alcalde. Manuel Armijo Governor.

1120 ROYAL ORDERS. Copies received in *New Mexico*, 1813. Fernando VII and Cortes.

1121 RELATING to the Old Palace in *Santa Fe*.
 Manuel Armijo, Governor.

1122 VENTURA DE MESTAS and ANTONIO DE MESTAS. 1767.

Compromise in the matter of the partition of their lands in *Chama*. Francisco Guerrero, Alcalde. Tomas Velez Cachupin, Governor. Manuel Garcia Pareja, Alcalde.

1123 SAN MIGUEL DEL BADO. *Ayuntamiento*.
Communication in relation to the establishment of a town in a proper place to afford a defense against hostile Indians. 1832.
The members of the ayuntamiento of San Miguel del Bado (Vado) February 8, 1832, were: José Ulibarri, presidente; Vicente Ribera, first alderman; Vicente Romero, second alderman; Juan Estevan Sena, third alderman; Matias, fourth alderman; José Miguel Sanchez, secretary.

1124 NEW MEXICO: Boundaries of.
Order of the Viceroy to establish the same. *Mexico*, 1682.

1125 DEPARTMENTAL ASSEMBLY from January, 1846, to February 12, 1846.
Grant of land made to petitioners at place called *Chaperito*.

1126 PRINTED COPY of Colonization law of August 18th, 1824.

1127 PRINTED COPY of law relating to the examination of surveyors. *Mexico*, 1834.

1128 FRANCISCO G. CONDE. 1845.
Letter to the Governor of the Department in relation to the settlements made by foreigners on the frontier.

1129 ABIQUIU, CHAMA, and SOLEDAD.
Re-settlement of said places. 1751. El Cónde de Revillagigedo, Viceroy. Joseph de Gorraez, *Asesor*.

1130 JUAN ARMIJO, Alcalde. 1821.
Religious question.

1131 JOSE FRANCISCO SENA. *Galisteo*. 1844.
Pasturage of sheep in the common lands of *Galisteo*. Not permitted.

1132 MANUEL ALVAREZ.
Petition for naturalization. 1825.

1133 PRINTED COPY of the Royal Order of 1813 in the matter of reducing the public lands to private ownership.
Letter of Alejo Garcia Cónde, transmitting the same to the Governor of *New Mexico*. 1821.

1134 FRAGMENT of Proceedings of the Departmental Assembly. No date.

1135 PRINTED COPY of law defining the term "finca rustica," Mexico, 1836.
"Bajo la denominacion de *fincas rústicas* á que se contrae la ley de 5 de Julio último, se comprende toda propiedad rural con el nombre de hacienda, rancho, huerta ú otro nombre semajante, cualquiera que sea su ubicacion dentro ó fuera de las poblaciones, con casa ó sin ella cuyas frutas pertenescan á la agricultura, ecepto aquellas sitios en poblado que se cultiven por mero recreo, sin especial utilidad del propietario."

1136 INVENTORY of ARCHIVES of the Cabildo of *Santa Fe*. 1715. As follows:
Lorenzo Rodriguez. Donation of half a *fanega* of corn planting land in the lands of Maria de Tapia. May 2, 1704.
Juan de Mestas. Grant of the *San Buenaventura* rancho at *Pojoaque*, by Don Pedro Rodriguez Cubero. December 9, 1699.
Diego Marquez de Ayala. Grant at or near *Santa Fe* by Juan Ignacio Flores Mogollon. March 11, 1713.
Francisco Martin. Grant on the south side of the *Rio de Santa Fe* by Don Pedro Rodriguez Cubero. March 6, 1703.
Maria Zapata. Grant by Diego de Vargas to Captain José Telles Jiron and confirmed to her husband, Captain Diego de Medina, by Don Pedro Rodriguez Cubero, December 28, 1698. The grant comprises three tracts, one at *Santa Fe*, one called *San Martin*, on the *Rio del Norte*, and one called *San Pablo*.
Ana Maria Romero. *Testimonio* of grant by the Marqués de la Nava Brazinas. November 27, 1703. On October 1, 1699, Maria Cabello made donation of this tract to Pedro de Abila.
Sebastian Martin, captain. Grant by the Marqués de la Penuela, May 23, 1712, confirming that made by the Mar-

qués de la Nava de Brazinas. Situate between *San Juan* and *Embudo.*

Petronila Cubero. Grant by Don Pedro Rodriguez Cubero, May 10, 1700.

Diego Duran. Grant of house and lot by Juan Ignacio Flores Mogollon; also a tract of agricultural land, both situate in *Santa Fe.* August 29, 1713.

José Trujillo, captain. Grant by Don Pedro Rodriguez Cubero, December 29, 1700. Lands formerly belonging to Francisco Jimenez and Ambrosio Saenz. Situate at the *Mesa of San Ildefonso.* Grant by the same on April 23, 1700, of pasture lands in the jurisdiction of the *Villa Nueva de la Santa Cruz.* Grant by Don Francisco Cuerbo y Valdez, May 23, 1707. Small spring on the road between Nambé and the *Villa Nueva de Santa Cruz de la Cañada.*

Juan Trujillo. Grant. [Torn to pieces.] Tract of land near the *Pojoaque* river, sold to him by Sebastian de Salas. *Testimonio* of sale made on October 19, 1701.

Juan Trujillo. Grant to Francisco de Anaya of a tract of land called *San Isidro,* between *Cuyamungue* and *Jacona,* November 27, 1699, by Don Pedro Rodriguez Cubero. Sold by him to Sebastian de Cansua, son-in-law of Anaya, it having belonged to Maria de Anaya, his wife.

Ignacio de Roibal, captain. Grant of house and lands in *Santa Fe* by Don Pedro Rodriguez Cubero, February 15, 1698.

Grant, the place of *Jacona,* the surplus of the grant to Captain Jacinto Pelaez, by Don Pedro Rodriguez Cubero, October 2, 1702.

Grant of a piece of land, which, before the revolution, belonged to the maestro de campo, Francisco Gomez Robledo. The land consisted of five *fanegas* of wheat land, about a quarter of a league below the city of *Santa Fe.* Grant made by Don Pedro Rodriguez Cubero, May 4, 1698.

Mateo Trujillo. Grant of half a fanega of corn land by the Marqués de la Nava de Brazinas, April 7, 1695, to Getrudis de Barrera y Sandoval. Situate in the jurisdiction of the *Cañada.* Sold to Trujillo by the grantee. Also a grant of agricultural and pasture land on the other side of the *Rio del Norte* between *Santa Clara* and *San Ildefonzo,* November 29, 1700. He also presented a grant made by Don Pedro Rodriguez Cubero, on October 6, 1698, to Juan de la Mora Pineda, at a place called *Las Cuevas,* on the *Cañada de San Cristoval* in the jurisdiction of *Villa Nueva.*

Isabel Gonzales, widow of Juan de Archuleta. Grant of a rancho in the jurisdiction of *La Cañada,* formerly belonging to Pedro de la Cruz, made by the Marquéz de la Nava de Brazinas to Manuel Vallejo, on April 6, 1695. This was sold by the said Vallejo to Isabel Gonzales.

Also a grant made to Tomas . . . de Tegeda of a tract of land formerly belonging to Alonzo del Rio, granted on April 6, 1695. Sold to Isabella Gonzales.

Also grant made to Juan de Archuleta, husband of Isabel Gonzales, by Don Pedro Rodriguez Cubero on June 12, 1698, being a *rancho* of eight *fanegas* of wheat land adjoining the lands of the *pueblo* of San Juan.

Cristobal de Torres, ensign. Grant of lands on the *Rio del Norte* adjoining the Pajarito Tract, made by the Marqués de la Nava de Brazinas on May 15, 1695, and a ratification of the same by the Marqués de la Penuela on August 11, 1711.

Also a grant made by Don Pedro Rodriguez Cubero on January 22, 1699, of a tract of land on the *Rio del Norte,* formerly belonging to Sargento Mayor Ambrosio Saenz.

Baltazar Trujillo. Grant of four *fanegas* of land that formerly belonging to the widow of Archuleta, in the valley of *Taos.* Made by Don Pedro Rodriguez Cubero, September 19, 1702.

Cristobal Jaramillo, ensign. Resident of *Alburquerque.* Petition that possession be given him of a house and lands that formerly belonged to Doña Luisa Trujillo. Possession given February 20, 1706.

Antonio Barela. Petition on August 10, 1707, to Captain Martin Hurtado, chief alcalde of *Alburquerque,* asking that possession be given him of the lands that were given him at the time that said town was settled. Possession was given by the alcalde.

Juan de Archuleta. Grant made by Don Pedro Rodriguez Cubero on February 27, 1699, of half a *fanega* of agricultural land at Santa Fe, the boundaries being the lands of "Old" Lucero, Miguel Moran, Pedro Lujan, and Maria de la Encarnacion.

Juan Paez Hurtado. Grant by Don Diego de Vargas Zapata Lujan Ponce de Leon, on March 3, 1704, of the surplus lands between the *pueblos* of Pojoaque and Nambé, bounded by the lands of Juan and Carlos Lopez.

Baltazar Romero. Grant by the Marquéz de la Penuela on September 15, 1707, of house and lands formerly belonging to Doña Isabel Holguin. Salvador Martinez had an interest in the irrigable lands.

THE SPANISH ARCHIVES OF NEW MEXICO 333

Juan Gonzales, captain. Resident of *Bernalillo*. Grant made to Maria Barbara Lujan by the Marqués de la Nava de Brazinas on March 21, 1696, of a tract of land on the *Rio del Norte*, said land having belonged to Estevan Barba, he having purchased the same before the revolution.

Also a grant of the *pueblo* of Puara, made December 31, 1711. Also a confirmation of the grant of the deserted *pueblo* of Alameda, made by Don Juan Ignacio Flores Mogollon, said confirmation being made in view of the land having been given or sold to him by Francisco Montes Vigil, to whom it had been granted by the Marqués de la Penuela.

Cristobal Barela. Resident of *Bernalillo*. Grant at the town of *Alburquerque* of a tract of land granted to him by Captain Martin Hurtado, chief alcalde, bounded on the west by the *Rio del Norte*, south by lands of Lorenzo Carbajal, and north by lands of Antonio Gutierrez.

Pedro Lopez. Grant of a tract of land on the *Rio del Norte* called *San Nicolas* opposite the agricultural lands of *Atrisco* and on the edge of the *Esteros de Mexia*. Granted by Don Diego de Vargas on March 4, 1695. Also a confirmation of the same by Don Pedro Rodriguez Cubero on August 26, 1698.

Sebastian Gonzales. Grant of two *fanegas* of wheat land up the river from *Santa Fe*, by the Marqués de la Nava de Brazinas on January 18, 1704. Also a grant of a piece of land of half a *fanega* by the Marqués de la Nava de Brazinas on March 12, 1695. Confirmation of the same by the Marqués de la Penuela, August 27, 1707.

Melchora de los Reyes. Grant of lands in the *Cañada* . . . to her husband, Luis Martin, by Don Pedro Rodriguez Cubero, on June 25, 1700. Also a grant in the *Cañada* . . . by the Marqués de la Penuela on December 23, 1711. Confirmation of the same by the Marqués de la Penuela, May 4, 1712.

Luis Garcia. Grant of a tract of land called *San Antonio*, on the *Rio del Norte*, formerly the property of his grandfather, to the *maestro de campo*, Alonzo Garcia, by the Marqués de la Penuela, August 30, 1704.

Pedro Montes Vigil. Grant of lands on the *Tesuque* river above the rancho of the Gomez, by Don Juan Ignacio Flores Mogollon. November 10, 1713.

Jacinto Sanchez, captain. Grant in the jurisdiction of the new town of *Santa Cruz*, made to Silvestre Pacheco on March 3, 1704, by the Marqués de la Nava de Brazinas.

Juan Garcia de las Rivas, captain. Grant of three

fanegas of corn land on the other side of the *Rio de Santa Fe*, made to Captain Miguel Garcia, his father, by Don Pedro Rodriguez Cubero. Also grant of the abandoned *pueblo* of San Marcos, by the Marqués de la Penueia on February 12, 1712.

Simon Nieto. Grant of a tract of land one league from the *pueblo* of Galisteo, made to his father, Cristobal Nieto, by Don Pedro Rodriguez Cubero, on January 20, 1700.

Luis Lopez. Grant of lands in the *Cañada de Chimayo* adjoining the lands of Francisco Martin, made on December 10, 1706, by Don Francisco Cuerbo y Valdez.

Maria de Tapia, a widow. Grant of lands on the other side of the *Rio de Santa Fe*, formerly belonging to Fernando Martin, by Don Pedro Rodriguez Cubero, on January 30, 1702.

José Manuel Giltomey. Grant of uncultivated lands on the other side of the *Rio de Santa Fe*, by Don Francisco Cuerbo, August 27, 1706.

Alejo Martin. Resident of *Santa Cruz*. Donation of a *rancho* made to himself and his brothers, Antonio and Maria Martin, by Captain Luis Martin, on July 19, 1700.

Also partition of lands made by Juan Arguello on October 5, 1704, before Captain Nicolas Ortiz, chief alcalde of the *Villa Nueva*.

Petition of himself and Felipe de Aratia to the Marqués de la Penuela on account of a suit and claim of Antonio and Fernando Martin.

Donation of a piece of land at the rancho which he owns on the *Rio del Norte* above the *pueblo* of San Juan, dated June 12, 1712.

Petition to the Marqués de la Penuela praying that Juan Roque Gutierrez, chief alcalde of *La Cañada*, be directed to give possession to the persons to whom Captain Sebastian Martin has made donation of the land.

Order in which said alcalde is directed to give possession to Alejo Martin, Antonio Martin, Francisco Martin, Miguel Martin, Felipe Martin, José Lujan, Felipe de Aratia, and Pedro de Abila, etc., etc.

Diego Lucero. Grant of lands in *Santa Fe*, about half a *fanega* of corn and two of wheat land made by Don Pedro Rodriguez Cubero on July 30, 1697. This grant is also said to have been made to Antonio Lucero de Godoy, father of Diego Lucero.

The petition was filed by Joseph Manuel Gilthomey, who was at that time secretary of the *cabildo* (town council). Under this order all citizens were directed to

THE SPANISH ARCHIVES OF NEW MEXICO 335

present to the *cabildo* within a period of two months, their titles and grants for their lands, houses, and ranches, in order that the *cabildo* might inspect and make note thereof, with a view to preventing litigation in the future.

The order also directed that chief *alcaldes*, before whom instruments might be executed, should not deliver the originals to the parties, but should give certified copies, sending the originals to the *cabildo*, where they were to be permanently filed. The order was promulgated at Santa Fe, Santa Cruz de la Cañada, and Alburquerque, July 24, 30, and August 10, 1713, respectively.

Subsequently memoranda of the documents presented to the *cabildo* in compliance with this order, were made in a book kept for that purpose, known as the *"Libro de cabildo,"* which is archive 1136, which entries are as herein given.

These memoranda contain references to the lands of the Indians in some cases, and these are as follows:

Leaf 1, page 1. Second Entry.

On the first of August, one thousand seven hundred and thirteen, Juan de Mestas presented the grant of the ranch on which he lives at *Pojoaque*, named *San Buenaventura*, made by Don Pedro Rodriguez Cubero, for three *fanegas* of corn-planting land, on the ninth of December, one thousand six hundred and ninety-nine; and the possession given by the maestre de campo, Roque Madrid, lieutenant-governor of this kingdom. And its boundaries are from the slope of a hill as far as the river below the *pueblo* of Pojoaque, and toward the *pueblo* of Jacona from east to west as far as a bluff, and north (to) south as far as the hills which descend from Cuyamungué.

Leaf 2, page 1. Third entry.

Captain Sebastián Martín presented a grant of a tract and farm of cultivable lands, made by the Marquis of La Peñuela, on the twenty-third day of the month of May, of the year one thousand seven hundred and twelve, in which he validates the one that he had, made by the Marquis of Naba de Bracinas, in which he cut off the persons who formerly had said grant, because of the period which His Majesty grants for the settling of new lands having passed; and said grant is countersigned by Cristobal de Gongora, military secretary, who by virtue of a commission from said Marquis de La Peñuela, gave him possession of said tract and farm on the tenth day of the month of June of said year. And its boundaries are on the north side the *Cañada del Embudo de Picuriés*, on the south a cross that is placed at the boundaries of the lands which belong to the *pueblo* of San Juan, and on the west a table-land which is on the other side of the Rio del Norte, and on the east the highway which goes out from *Chimayó* toward the *pueblo* of Picuriés; with entrances and exits, as appears from said grant, which was returned to him.

On the 30th of August, of the year 1713, by virtue of what is commanded by the governor and captain-general of this kingdom, Captain Joseph Trujillo presented a grant made to him by the castellan, Don Pedro Cubero, on the 29th of December, 1700, for the lands which anciently belonged to Francisco Jiménez, close to the *San Ildefonso* table-land and lands of the sargento mayor, Ambrosio Saens, attested by Domingo de Barreda, civil and military secretary; and the possession of said lands, which on the 21st of March, of the year 1701, was given to him by the maestre de campo, Roque Madrid.

And at the same time he presented another grant, made by the same castellan, on the 23d day of April of the same year, for another piece of land for the pasturing of stock, contiguous to that of Francisco Jiménez, in the district of the New Town of Santa Cruz (*Villa Nueva de Santa Cruz*) attested also by said Domingo de la Barreda, and the possession of said piece of land given by said chief alcalde.

As also he presented another grant for a piece of land for pasturing large and small stock, where there is a small spring of water on the *Nambé* road that goes to the New Town (*Villa Nueva*), of which, on the 23d day of May, 1701, General Don Francisco Cuervo made him a grant, countersigned by Don Alonzo Rael de Aguilar, military secretary, with the possession which said maestre de campo, Roque Madrid, gave on the 16th of June, of said year, the boundaries of which appear in said grants, which originals I returned for the protection of his right.

Leaf 3, page 1. Second entry.

On the 30th of August, of the year 1713, before me, General Juan Paez Hurtado, ordinary alcalde, Juan Trujillo, a citizen of the district of *La Cañada* (*Santa Cruz*), appeared and presented a land grant, torn into shreds, for a piece of agricultural lands of about two *fanegas* of corn, which Sebastian de Salas sold to him, on the other side of the *Pojoaque* river, the boundaries of which appear in the certified copy of the deed, which was made before Joseph Rodriguez, ordinary alcalde, at the town of Santa Fe, on the 19th of the month of October, of the year 1701.

Leaf 3, page 1. Third entry.

On the 30th of August, of the year 1713, Juan Trujillo appeared before me, General Juan Paez Hurtado, and presented a grant made to the sargento mayor, Francisco de Anaya, for a tract of agricultural lands between *Cuyamungue* and *Jacona,* called *San Isidro,* made by the castellan, Don Pedro Cubero, on the 27th day of the month of November, of the year 1699, attested by Domingo de la Barreda, civil and military secretary, which Sebastian Cansua, son-in-law of said sargento mayor, sold to him, because of their belonging to his wife, Maria de Anaya; and the possession given by the maestre de campo, Roque Madrid, on the 10th day of December of said year; the boundaries of which appear in said grant, the original of which I returned to him for the protection of his right.

On the 1st of September, of the year 1713, Mateo Trujillo presented before me, General Juan Paez Hurtado, ordinary alcalde of this town of Santa Fe, in virtue of what is commanded by the governor and captain-general of this kingdom . . . a grant of a tract of land for cultivation and the rearing of large and small stock on the other side of the Rio del Norte between the *pueblos* of Santa Clara and Ildefonso, which on the 21st of November, 1700, the castellan, Don Pedro Rodriguez Cubero, gave to him by grant, attested by Domingo de la Barreda, military secretary; and the possession which the maestre de campo, Roque de Madrid, gave on the 9th of September, 1701; the boundaries of which appear in said grant, the original of which I returned to him.

Leaf 4, page 1. Second entry.

On the seventh day of the month of September, of the year one thousand seven hundred and thirteen, Captain Ignacio de Roibal presented three grants of land . . . the second for the place of *Jacona,* district of the Town of Santa Cruz, for the surplus of what Captain Jacinto Pelaez had by grant, also made by the same castellan (Don Pedro Rodriguez Cubero), on the second of October, seventeen hundred and two; attested by Pedro de Morales, civil and military secretary; the boundaries of which appear in said grant, and of which I returned to him the original.

The third for a piece of land which before the revolution of the year eighty (1680) belonged to the maestre de campo, Francisco Gomez Robledo, which may contain five.

fanegas of wheat-planting land, below the Town of Santa Cruz about one-fourth of a league, between the lands of Domingo Martin and Ambrosio Saes, of which lands the said castellan (Don Pedro Rodriguez Cubero) made him a grant on the fourth of May, sixteen hundred and ninety-eight; attested by Domingo de la Barreda, military secretary, which I returned to him with the two preceding ones, to serve him as a formal title.

Leaf 4, page 2. Second entry.

Isabel Gonzales, widow of Juan de Archuleta, on the eleventh day of September, of the year 1713, presented . . . another grant for another ranch of eight *fanegas* of corn-planting land, which adjoins the lands of the *pueblo* of San Juan, made by the castellan, Don Pedro Rodriguez Cubero, to Juan de Archuleta, the husband of said Isabel Gonzales, on the 12th of June, of 1698, attested by Domingo de la Barreda.

Leaf 5, page 2. Fourth entry.

On said day General Juan Paez Hurtado presented a grant, which on March 3, 1704, General Don Diego de Vargas made to him, for the surplus lands which there might be at the *pueblo* of Pojoaque — I mean between the *pueblo* of Pojoaque and that of Nambé; and they adjoin the lands of Juan and Carlos Lopez; and the possession which on the 7th of said month of March and year of the date, Captain Ignacio de Roibal gave to him; the boundaries of which appear in said grant, the original of which I returned to him to serve as a formal title.

MANUEL BACA. Grant of lands at the *Angostura de Bernalillo*, made by Don Diego de Vargas Zapata Lujan Ponce de Leon on January 14, 1695. These lands formerly belonged to his father, Cristobal Baca.

BERNARDINO DE SENA. Grant of lands on the other side of the river at *Santa Fe*, made by the Marqués de la Nava de Brazinas on May 3, 1694.

VICENTE . . . DE ARMIJO. Grant of half a *fanega* of corn land, house and garden, made by the Marqués de la Nava de Brazinas on November 29, 1703.

DIEGO MARQUES DE AYALA. Ensign. Grant of lands made by Don Ignacio Flores Mogollon on July 28, 1713.

On July 21, 1713, a decree was made by the governor and captain-general, Don Ignacio Flores Mogollon, requiring all documents relative to grants of land theretofore made to be presented to the *cabildo* of *Santa Fe*.

THE SPANISH ARCHIVES OF NEW MEXICO 339

1137 COPIES OF LAWS relating to the colonization and settlement of lands of March 12, 1828, November 21, 1828, March 11, 1842.

1138 PETITION of Half-Breed Indians of *Santa Fe.*
   Certified copy dated Arispe, 1780. Certified by Antonio Bonilla. No action taken.
   Bentura Bustamante, lieutenant of the *Genízaros* (half-breed Indians) of the Villa de Santa Fe, by order of his captain, Juan Armijo, and in the name of thirty-three associates of the same class of Indians, filed a protest with the governor and captain-general against being taken away from Santa Fe, where they had built houses, had cultivated fields, etc., to the Cumanche frontier to fight, threatening to leave Santa Fe and the Spaniards and join the hostiles (*gentiles*).

1139 MANUEL DE ALVAREZ. Citizenship.
   Don Manuel Alvarez was one of the most prominent citizens in New Mexico at the time of the American Occupation. In 1839, he held the position of United States consul at Santa Fe. In 1825, in company with a party of French trappers or fur traders, he came to Santa Fe from St. Louis, Missouri. The following year he made application to the Mexican government for citizenship papers. For some reason or other not explained by the archive he was never able to secure Mexican citizenship. At the time of his appointment as American consul at Santa Fe in 1839, he was still a Spanish subject.
   Containing, as they do, a number of points of historical interest, copies of his papers as filed with the Mexican government at the time of his arrival in Santa Fe, are given herewith:

   "Most Excellent Sir:
   "Manuel Alvarez, a native of the village of Abelgas, in the ancient Kingdom of Leon, with due respect appears before Your Excellency and says that having presented two applications, dated June 14, 1825, and May 11th of the present year, asking for papers of naturalization of this Republic, through the Political Chief of this Territory and not having been successful in such purpose, possibly on account of the petition being lost, mislaid, delayed or from other causes unknown to me, to obviate all of which for reasons set forth in my former petition, I am setting forth in this and will say that I address this

to Your Excellency, knowing your solicitude and kindness in such matters, that Your Excellency may be pleased to decide what your petitioner requests.

"Always, Most Excellent Sir, I have been anxious to reside here under a liberal government for which reason for eight years I have remained on this Continent visiting the United States of America and this Republic, whose origin gives guaranty of protection and happiness, and wishing to participate therein, I reiterate to Your Excellency my request, hoping that you will give it early determination and not delay me longer in the sweet satisfaction which will result.

"Your petitioner in order to remove any suspicion or obstacles, causing further delays, would say something in regard to his conduct and manner of living, but even though such statement may be unnecessary, he states to Your Excellency that he speaks the English and French languages; that he has been a trader up to the present time, and proposes in the future to devote himself to the pursuit of agriculture at some convenient locality, all of which was referred to in my petition to the Political Chief which he may have given to Your Excellency.

"To the highest consideration of Your Excellency your petitioner leaves a knowledge of how greatly he will consider the prompt possession of the naturalization papers which he has solicited, and is satisfied that Your Excellency's well known reputation for justice and kindness will prompt you to act satisfactorily and to the end that your petitioner will be content over what has happened.
"MANUEL DE ALVAREZ
"Santa Fe, Nov. 27, 1826."

"TO THE HONORABLE POLITICAL CHIEF.

"The citizen, Manuel de Alvarez, native of the village of Abelgas, of the ancient Kingdom of Leon, at present a resident of this Territory of the Mexican Federation, in the most proper manner, appears before Your Excellency and says: That having left his native land in the year 1818, he had determined to take up his residence either in the United States of North America or in Mexican territory and having gone from Habana to the first mentioned country, he landed at New York as credited by the enclosed passport; I visited the said country and know it not to be a place of convenient residence, but preferring the Mexican Republic I have come here for that purpose.

I request Your Excellency to present my application for citizenship to the Sovereign Constitutional Congress as I desire to become a useful citizen of this country and to its inhabitants, protesting that I am of the Roman Catholic faith, and what may be necessary in order to attain that for which I desire.

"All of which I ask and request Your Excellency to present my application and the attached report to the Supreme Government of the Federation and the Sovereign Constitutional Congress for the attainment of the same.

"The entire lack of sealed paper in this Territory has prevented my application being made upon sealed paper, but I offer to pay its value.   MANUEL DE ALVAREZ.
"Santa Fe, June 14, 1825."

Governor Baca endorsed the application favorably, stating that Alvarez manifested a great zeal for the Catholic faith.

His passport, dated Habana, April 29, 1823, is signed by Don Sebastian Kindelan y Oregan, Knight of the Military Orders of Santiago and Ferdinand, 3d class, of the Cross and City of Hermenejildo, Brigadier of the National Armies, Subaltern Corporal of the Captain-Generalcy of the Island of Cuba, Provisional Captain-General of the same and Superior Political Chief of the City and Province of Habana, etc., etc.

Countersigned by Antonio Maria de la Torre y Cardenas. All of the papers of Alvarez used in connection herewith were certified to by

FRANCISCO PEREZ SERRANO Y AGUIRRE [Rubric]
Provisional Secretary

Accompanying his papers is a passport from Governor Alexander McNair, of Missouri, as follows:

"United States of North America.
"Alexander McNair, Governor of the State of Missouri.
"To all who shall see these Presents, *Greeting*, Be it known that Francis Robidoux, Isidor Roubidou, Antonio LaMarche, Manuel Alvarez, José Martin, Joseph Gervais, Astasio Lasalle, Charles Hotte, Francois Laroque, Francois Quenelle, Joseph Decary, and Antoine Baucheum, traders to Mexico, all citizens of the United States, to me well known as such and that they enjoy and are entitled to all the privileges of citizens of our free and independent Republic.

342 THE SPANISH ARCHIVES OF NEW MEXICO

"In testimony whereof, I have hereunto set my hand and caused the great Seal of the State of Missouri to be Affixed.

"Done at Saint Charles, this 3d day of September A. D. one thousand eight hundred and twenty-four, and of the Independence of the United States the forty-ninth.
(SEAL) "By the Governor. A. McNAIR
"WILLIAM G. PETTUS
"Secretary of State."

"Height, 5 feet 2 inches; color, pale; nose, regular; brows, black; hair, black; no beard."

1140 DECREE of Departmental Assembly in relation to the abandonment of granted lands. 1837.

1141 XEMES, ZIA, and SANTA ANA, 1713.
Receipt of order by Alcalde. Tibursio Ortega, Alcalde. *San Geronimo de Taos.* Receipt of the same. Miguel de Sandoval Martinez, Alcalde.
In the year 1766 "In compliance with the directions of his excellency, Don Tomas Velez Cachupin, governor and captain-general" Bartolomé Fernandez, chief alcalde and war-captain of the pueblos of the Queres, delivered possession to the pueblos of Xemes, Zia, and Santa Ana of a tract of land bounded "from north to south from the place Ventana to the stone ford of the Puerco river, the boundaries also of the citizens of the place San Fernando of Nuestra Señora de la Luz; and from east to west from the pueblo of Zia to the said Puerco river, the eastern edge, the whole valley of the Holy Ghost spring being embraced within the center and within the boundaries of this grant." At the time possession was given there were present the following Indian governors (caciques): Cristoval Naspona, Cristoval Chiguigui, Pedro Chite, Sebastian, Lazaro, and Juan Antonio, and the war-captains Agustin, Tomas, Juan Domingo, and other Indian magistrates.

1142 JUAN OTERO.
Decree of Departmental Assembly revoking grant made Francisco Sarracino. His suspension recommended, 1845.

1143 MINING COURTS in *New Mexico.* 1846.
Decree establishing them. Manuel Armijo, Governor. Tomas Ortiz, President. Miguel de Pino, Secretary.

THE SPANISH ARCHIVES OF NEW MEXICO 343

1144 QUICKSILVER.
Sale of, etc. El Caballero de Croix. Juan Joseph Fernandez de Soria.

1145 PAJARITO.
Complaint of Francisco Lopes that settlers at said place will not take possession of their lands. 1844. Gregorio Vigil, Alcalde.

1146 PRINTED COPY of Land Law of March 11, 1842.

1147 INTERPRETATION of the law of 1813 in relation to reducing the public lands to private ownership.
Printed copy. Letter of transmittal of the same to Governor of *New Mexico*. Bernardo Bonavia.

1148 MADARIAGA. *Tomé.* 1837.
Communication to the Departmental Assembly in relation to settlements abandoned on account of Indian raids.

This archive refers to the settlers at Manzano who abandoned their lands on account of attacks of hostile Indians; also to the settlements at Las Huertas and Carnuel and mentions the building of a large fort at Manzano by all of the settlers.

The Town of Tomé was a regularly organized Villa, had its ayuntamiento and other officers prior to the change from Spanish to Mexican sovereignty and later; it had a "Sala Capitular." This is shown in the granting papers in the Casa Colorada Land Grant. Miguel de Olona was the secretary of the cabildo. The grant known as the Casa Colorada was made upon the petition of José Maria Perea by the Corporation of Tomé and was approved by the Provincial Deputation, September 15, 1823. The original settlers on this grant came from the vicinity of Manzano and were: José Maria Perea, Rafael Perea, Antonio Torres, Dionisio Maldonado, Eugenio Barela, Domingo Lucero, Vincente Torres, Juan Cruz Turietta, Julian Sanchez, Aban Sanchez, Miguel Archuleta, Gregorio Sedillo, José de Jesus Maldonado, José Sedillo, Miguel Lucero, Rafael Cedillo, Guadalupe Perea (widow), Matilda Montoya (widow), Cristobal Jaramillo, Rafael Torres, Buenaventura Sanchez, Manuel Baca, José Baca, Juan Antonio Serna, José Antonio Benavides, Carlos Baca, Juan Agustin Barela, Vincente Moya, Antonio Torres, Sr., Julian Benavides, Tomas Benavides, José Gallegos, José Maria Sedillo, Antonio Torres, 2d, Joaquin

Sanchez, Mariano Pino, Esteban Baca, Andrés Zamora, José Anto Sedillo, Juan Castillo, and Tomas Sanchez.

By virtue of a decree of June 23, 1823, all of the inhabitants in the outlying valleys and mountains and other places liable to attack from hostile Indians were ordered to gather in settlements. These people all came from the vicinity of the Manzano mountains.

1149 SANTA FE PALACE, 1827.

The "Palace" is turned over to the *Jefe Politico*.

1150 BLOTTER in reference to the discovery and working of lead mines.

This lead mine was at Las Huertas; date of letter, August 13, 1818; good for bullets and the defense of the country against the gentile tribes; sent five or six loads (cargas) for use against "los enemigos del estado."

1151 CIENEGA.

Grant to the City of *Santa Fe*. Copy not certified. 1715.

1152 DISCOVERY OF MINERAL among the *Comanches*. 1829.

Bocanegra.

1153 SAN MIGUEL DEL BADO. 1825.

Petition of the people to their Ayuntamiento asking that attention be called to their petition to the Provincial Assembly protesting against the extent of the Tract granted to Juan Estevan Pino.

On December 6, 1823, Juan Estevan Pino, a man of great prominence in New Mexico at that period, filed his petition with the governor of New Mexico asking for lands described as follows: "On the north by the landmarks of the farm or land of Don Antonio Ortiz and the tableland of the *Aguage de la Yegua*; on the south by the Pecos river; on the east by the tableland of *Pajarito*, and on the west by the point of the tableland of the *Chupaines*." The grant was made December 23, 1823, and the land was called the *Hacienda of San Juan Baptista del Ojito del Rio de las Gallinas*. Pino received possession of the property; his heirs disposed of it to Preston Beck, to whose son, Preston Beck, Jr., it was confirmed by Congress, June 21, 1860.

THE SPANISH ARCHIVES OF NEW MEXICO 345

1154 MANUEL TRUGILLO. 1828. *Alburquerque.*
Petition to the Governor in regard to the return of certain papers by the Alcalde of Socorro.

1155 ALAMILLO, 1800.
Account of its re-settlement. Not signed.

1156 JOSEPH XARAMILLO to Barbara, Matilde and Catarina Viviana Ballejos. *Alburquerque*, 1732.
Land. Juan Gonzales Bas, Alcalde.

1157 APPROVAL BY THE KING of the action of the *Superior Junta* of Mexico in the modification of Article 81 of the *Ordenanza de Intendentes*, 1798.
Certified copy by Manuel Merino.

1158 SAN PEDRO TRACT. 1840.
Letter of Antonio Montoya, Alcalde of *Sandia*, to Guadalupe Miranda in reference to the same.

In February, 1844, the governor of New Mexico made a grant to José Serafin Ramirez of lands in the county of Santa Fé described as "bounded on the north by the Placer road that goes down by the yellow timber; on the south, the northern boundary of the San Pedro grant; on the east, the spring of the Cañon del Agua; on the west, the summit of the mountain of the mine known as the property of your Petitioner."

This tract of land as described was confirmed by act of Congress.

In the suit of the *United States vs. The San Pedro and Cañon del Agua Company*, finally determined by the supreme court of the United States, it was held that the mineral underlying the surface of the lands within the limits of this grant were still the property of the United States. That the company when it purchased was fully cognizant of the definite character of the grant which had been made to Ramirez; that when the lands mentioned, at the time of the Treaty of Guadalupe, passed under the dominion of the government of the United States, the title to the mineral lands became vested in the United States government; that Ramirez had a claim to no greater interest than he had obtained from the Mexican government, which had not parted with the title to the mineral underlying the surface; that the Spanish and Mexican governments reserved the rights to minerals unless other-

346 THE SPANISH ARCHIVES OF NEW MEXICO

wise stipulated, and no such express grant had been made to Ramirez.

This decision, affirming the decision of the supreme court of New Mexico, was a great injustice to the persons who had innocently purchased this property.

1159 INVENTORY of DOCUMENTS in the public archives during the time that Gervasio Cruzat y Gongora was Governor, 1736. No. 1136, *q. v.*

1160 PETITION, 1852.

People of *Taos* county in regard to lands occupied by them as pasture lands. Addressed to James S. Calhoun, Governor.

1161 EXPEDITION, 1803, for the discovery of the *Cerro del Oro.*

The Cerro del Oro (Mountain of Gold) was never discovered. Salcedo was deceived by the Indians, to whom he gave money in advance for the information as to the location of the "Mountain."

Second expedition in search of the *Cerro del Oro.*

1162 JUNTA DE FOMENTO DE MINERIA. Mexico, 1844.

Asking information in regard to placer mines of New Mexico. José Del Monte, President.

1163 STATISTICS of *Santo Domingo,* 1845.

1164 EL NACIMIENTO, 1815.

Settlement and partition of lands. Ignacio Sanchez Vergara, Alcalde.

1165 PRINTED POSTER, offering reward for the arrest of the traitor, Mina, 1817.

1166 TREATISE on Political Economy.

1167 BARTOLOMÉ BACA.

Report on Indian Troubles, 1825.

A translation of this important document is as follows:

"I give notice to your excellency that this day arrived the citizen, Manuel Mestas, interpreter, who by order of the militia commander, Don José Viscarra, had visited the Cumanche nation April 5th for the purpose of notifying them of the hostile actions and robberies committed by them at Eleceario and to the north. The Cumanches answered that it was a fact that they had participated in the robberies and had fired upon the Spaniards but the Kiowas were those who had made war on the Spaniards; that the Kiowas now separated from them and had gone to the pueblo of the Jumanes for a council of war for the purpose of attacking those in the north; this is what the Cumanches said and they believed that such separation and going to the Town of the Jumanes is for the purpose of joining the said Town of Jumanes.

"The Kiowas will also march toward the north in October of the present year. The Cumanches also say they will immediately confer with the Kiowas relative to what would happen but by this method possibly the Kiowas would desist and that they would advise us as to the result; that the Cumanches were not concerned in these new hostilities on the part of the Kiowas and that they will prove it; that the hostility of the Kiowas has arisen because 12 of their number including a chief had been killed.

"God and Liberty; El Bado, June 14, 1825.

"Tomas Sena [rubric]

"To the Jefe Politico:
"Don Bartolomé Baca."

The Spanish is *"Pueblo de Jumanes."*

"Several residents of this jurisdiction in my charge have just arrived informing me that, having gone to trade with a band of *Cumanche Pelones* and *Kiowas,* who are at the Rio Nutrias, they met two captives from Paso del Norte, one of them the servant of Don Agapito Alba, who informed them that they were well taken care of and not badly treated by the gentiles, for the reason that they had agreed to accompany them in an attack upon the Town of El Paso, showing them where the cattle of said town were herded, and, adding further, that the Indians had agreed to set them free when this had been done; that they informed them of this on account of their love of country, and requesting that if on this account they were deprived of their freedom, still the information ought to be given to the alcaldes so that the great wrong might be prevented, all of which I communicate to you.

"God and Liberty, June 10, 1825.

"Severino Martinez [rubric]

"To the Hon. Political Chief,
   Santa Fe, N. M."

348 THE SPANISH ARCHIVES OF NEW MEXICO

These letters were sent to Soto la Marina, the commandant at Chihuahua.

1168 TAOS, 1824.
In relation to their wanting the title of *Villa*.

1169 MARIANO MARTINEZ, Governor.
Memorandum of official action taken by him during the years 1844 and 1845.

1170 MINING DECREES, 1843.

1171 RE-SETTLEMENT of the Town of SOCORRO, 1800.
Pedro de Nava.
Juan de Oñate does not mention the existence of the pueblo which stood at *Alamillo*, a few miles north of the present town of Socorro. At the time of the uprising in 1680 there was a church here dedicated to St. Anne, and, according to Vetancurt, the population was about four hundred. In 1681, when Governor Otermín returned to New Mexico, in a vain attempt to reconquer, this pueblo was destroyed by him. See *Autos y Dilijencias hechas,* etc. Testimony of the *maestro de campo*, Francisco Gomez.

1172 NEW MEXICO, 1826.
Report on boundaries, etc. Not signed.

1173 HILARIO MESTAS vs. Pablo Montoya, 1811.
Stock. Ignacio Sanchez Vergara, Alcalde.

1174 DEPARTMENTAL ASSEMBLY, 1845.
Twenty pages of the record of proceedings.

1175 JUAN NAVARRO, Governor of *Durango*. 1824.
Two letters to Bartolomé Baca, in relation to payment of duties on sheep.

1176 JUAN BAUTISTA VIGIL. 1824.
Two letters to Bartolomé Baca on political matters.

1177 JOSEPH DE URQUIDI. 1824.
Letter to Bartolomé Baca. Political.

1178 JUAN ESTEVAN PINO. 1824. To Bartolomé Baca.
Mercantile.

THE SPANISH ARCHIVES OF NEW MEXICO 349

1179 JUAN ESTEVAN PINO, 1823.
   Receipt.

1180 ROYAL CÉDULA. February 14, 1805.
   Relating to the extent of land grants. Copy. Certified by Bernardo Villamil.

1181 JOSE ALVAREZ TOSTADO. 1825.
   Religion. Letter to Bartolomé Baca.

1182 RELIGION. 1825.

1183 RELIGION. 1824.

1184 STAMPED PAPER, Law of. 1823.

1185 MANUEL JOSÉ DE ZULOAGA.
   Political, 1827.

1186 No Consequence.

1187 MISSIONS. 1746.
   Testimonio of order of Viceroy certified by Joachin Codallos y Rabal, Governor.

1188 MANUEL ARMIJO. 1827.
   Letter to Territorial Deputation in relation to monopoly of lands, etc.

1189 FRANCISCO TRUXILLO. 1824.
   Letter to Bartolomé Baca in relation to partition of lands of the *Ojo Caliente* and report of said partition.

1190 FRANCISCO GUERRERO, alcalde, 1766.
   List of deeds made by him belonging to the government archives.

1191 RELIGION. 1808.
   Census.

1192 VALLECITO GRANT. 1809-1813.
   Protest of Manuel Martin and Juan Pedro Duran against settlers of the same for not complying with conditions, etc. Manuel Garcia, Alcalde.

1193 SETTLEMENT of PUBLIC LANDS. 1807.
   Proclamation of the Viceroy. José Ignacio Negreros y Soria. Nemesio Salcedo. No. 1180, *q. v.*

1194 ALAMILLO and SEVILLETA, 1800.
>Re-settlement. Pedro de Nava.

1195 IGNACIO SANCHES DE VERGARA, 1821.
>Letter to Governor Melgares, asking whether he may petition for a tract of land near the *pueblo of Sandia*. Governor replies favorably.

1196 PEDRO DE NAVA. 1798.
>Transmitting *Royal Decree* of March 23, 1798. No. 1157, *q. v.*

1197 JOSE VINCENTE ORTIZ. No date.
>Petition for land. No action.

1198 SANTA FE. 1705.
>Order that houses shall be built. Francisco Cuerbo y Valdez, Governor.

1199 RE-SETTLEMENT of the Town of SOCORRO and those of SENECU, Sevilleta, and Alamillo, 1800. See No. 1171.
>Pedro de Nava.
>In this letter Don Pedro de Nava gives instructions for active war upon the Apaches in the vicinity of Magdalena, N. M. Also at San Mateo.
>Good signature of De Nava.

1200 ROMAN SANCHEZ. *Santa Fe.* 1825.
>*Testimonio* certified by Antonio Narbona, Governor.

1201 PEDRO ANTONIO MESTAS.
>Will. *Santa Fe,* 1826. José Ortega, Cabo.

1202 MATIAS SENA.
>Will. *Santa Fe,* 1826. José Tapia, Cabo.

1203 No Value.

1204 FRANCISCO ANTONIO TORRES.
>Will. 1826. *Santa Fe.* José Tapia, Cabo.

1205 FERNANDO DURAN Y CHAVES and Baltazar Romero.
>Petition. 1708. Asking that soldiers be stationed at *Alburquerque.*

THE SPANISH ARCHIVES OF NEW MEXICO 351

"To the Very Illustrious City Council, Justice and Government:

"The Captains Fernando Duran y Chabes and Baltazar Romero, residents of the Villa of Alburquerque, in the name and with the authority of all of the citizens of the same, appear before your excellency and asking that all the privileges allowed by law be given them, they say that whereas the Señor General Don Francisco Cuerbo y Valdez, who was governor of this kingdom, and who in his time, because it appeared to him to be more advantageous, ordered that the said Villa of Alburquerque be settled in the year of one thousand seven hundred and six, for which object and its due fulfillment he directed us to make public his desire that this kingdom should be greater and that we should increase our estates and not experience in the future the epidemics of the preceding years; he assisted us because we had no lands to plant nor on which to raise our stock (and) although he gave them abundantly at the place where we now are we did not decide to enter upon them because of our poverty and the danger from the enemies which surround us on all sides, reasons which obliged the said general to give us for our guard and defense a squadron of soldiers, in order that they being present we might make some progress, reasons which induced us to leave Bernalillo, where we resided; influenced by the desire to promote our welfare and comfort, we were impelled to make oath and settle the said Villa, and this having been accomplished the said General Don Francisco Cuerbo y Valdez made a report of the same to his excellency the Duke of Alburquerque, to whom he reported and explained the condition of the new Villa [torn — small space] he had settled and that for it he had given us said [torn, same as above] reasons which caused the said viceroy to give [torn as above] an election as appears by his order [torn as above] in our favor, in order that it might so appear, and at the same time he sent sacred vestments and altar furniture and a bell for the said Villa, for which reason we believed that he was well pleased with the said settlement, urging upon the said general with much earnestness the necessity for the preservation and increase of the said Villa of Alburquerque; and now the Señor Marqués de la Penuela, governor and captain-general, at this time has been pleased to take away the said escort, for which reason the enemy, seeing our weakness, have dared barbarously to commit various robberies, every day carrying off our stock, taking it from our corrals, as is shown; and seeing that they are not punished, they may surprise us and destroy us and our wives and children, which may God forbid, and this they did not do before, although it is true that they threatened us from afar, but they did not dare to attack, for they knew that the soldiers were almost upon them, and these are the reasons which have caused us to present a petition for the said citizens to the governor and captain-general, in which it was prayed that he would be pleased to grant them the said squadron because of the circumstances set forth; and he replied in plain words that the petition was not admissible, and he did not grant it, and because of this we are left very disconsolate, and in order that we may not be so in the future we take refuge under the shadow and protection of your Excellency, in order that as you are interested in the welfare and preservation of this community, since it is under your charge, you may present our cause, explaining to the said Marqués, governor and captain-general, the reasons which compel us to make this representation and [torn — small space] admissible to remove [torn as above] said place and to go where we may deem best and that we may never be accused of contumacy, as it is our desire to serve His Majesty; this we do without any mental reservation and we protest the truth of the same; wherefore,

"We ask and Pray that Your Excellency will be pleased, in view of this our statement, to favor us by doing what we ask, since it is just, and we swear by God [torn a small piece from the margin] and the Holy Cross that this is not in bad faith, and the royal aid in [torn as above] we pray, and in that which is necessary, etc.

"FERNANDO DURAN Y CHABES [rubric]
"BALTAZAR ROMERO [rubric]

"In the City of Santa Fe, on the fourteenth day of the month of April of the year one thousand seven hundred and eight, before the Council (Cavildo de Justicia y Regimiento) of the same, this petition was presented by the persons named in it, and it having been examined by us, the members, we admitted it and in compliance with it we proceeded to present it to the governor and captain-general, who said that he would apply the best remedy, and in order that it may so appear we sign this with our secretary of the council, who will place this instru-

THE SPANISH ARCHIVES OF NEW MEXICO 353

ment in the files and papers of our archives for future reference.

    "Ignacio de Roibal   [rubric]
    "Fran. Lorenzo de Cassados [rubric]
    "Phelix Martinez   [rubric]
    "Juan Garcia de la Ri [torn] [rubric]
    "Ju. De Vrribari   [rubric]
    "Juan Paez Hurtado   [rubric]
    "Ante mi [torn]"

1206 JUAN RUIZ CORDERO.
Will. *Santa Fe*, 1723.

1207 JOSE PABLO RAEL. *Santa Fe*.
Will. 1780. Also proceedings in the settlement of his estate. Juan Bautista de Anza, Governor.

1208 PETITION of Half-breeds to settle at deserted Pueblo of *Sandia*. 1733.
Denied. Gervasio Cruzat y Gongora, Governor.

Petition by certain Indians of different tribes, including Jumanes, Apaches, Utes, Kiowas, and Pawnees, who had abandoned their tribal relations and embraced the Catholic religion, and who were living at various towns and pueblos in New Mexico, asking that they be permitted to make a settlement on the site of the then abandoned pueblo of Sandia.

This petition was examined by Governor Cruzat y Gongora on April 21, 1733, and he ordered the petitioners to present to him a list of their names and the tribes to which they belonged. This they did at once, and the governor, after having examined the same and considered their petition, decided that their request could not be granted, but he said that they might settle at the pueblos already established, and if any one of them desired to accept that offer he should appear before the governor in order that a pueblo might be designated as his place of residence.

1209 MEMORANDA, 1844.

1210 HEIRS OF EUSEBIO RAEL, by their attorney, Juan Gonzales, 1826.
Petition to build on land formerly in dispute with the Indians of *Sandia*. Antonio Narbona, Governor.

354 THE SPANISH ARCHIVES OF NEW MEXICO

Letter from Juan Gonzales to Governor Narbona, stating that the heirs of Eusebio Rael had represented to him that they were left without either lands or houses, on account of having paid the debts owed by their father then deceased, etc., and in view of the fact that a controversy between them and the Indians of Sandia had been decided in favor of said heirs, they asked permission to build their house there and go to work to settle other debts, etc.

This letter is dated June 10, 1826, and in the margin thereof is a rough draft of the governor's reply, portions of which are practically illegible. The purport of it, however, appears to be that the heirs of Rael could not build on the land about which they had been disputing with the Indians unless the latter voluntarily agreed to such an arrangement.

1211 LUIS MARIA CABEZA DE BACA. 1821.
His petition for lands referred to in an unsigned letter.

1212 ANDRES ORTEGA.
Will. *Santa Fe*, 1821. Manuel Baca, Sargento.

1213 JOSE JOAQUIN MONTOYA. 1821.
Letter to Governor Melgares in relation to the abandonment of granted lands in the District of *Xemes*.

1214 OJO CALIENTE. 1840.
Discovery of mineral.

1215 ORDENANZA DE INTENDENTES, 1793.
Pedro de Nava. His *letter* to Governor Fernando de la Concha in relation to the provisional approval of action in regard thereto.

1216 SANTIAGO ABREU, 1837. *Cienega. Santa Fe.*

1217 PEDRO ARMENDARIS, 1846.
Protests against the government granting to other persons lands already granted to him.

Don Pedro Armendaris was a prominent citizen of New Mexico, having been alcalde during a long period. In 1820 he made application to the Spanish government for a grant of land lying on the west bank of the Rio Grande, opposite his ranch known as *"Valverde."* The application was granted and the lands were allotted to him; several years later he was driven from the property by the Navajos. Don Pedro left New Mexico and became a citizen of Chihuahua. After the Treaty of Guadalupe Hidalgo, Armendaris made a contract with two American citizens, Hugh N. Smith and Thomas Biggs, whereby, for services rendered in perfecting the title to his grants, Smith and Biggs became the owners of four thousand acres of the land grant, lying opposite the old Armendaris ranch of Valverde — the present town-site of San Marcial, in Socorro county. This grant was confirmed by Congress in 1860, surveyed in 1877, and patented in 1878.

The grants contained 490,000 acres, a large portion of which are situate on the west side of the Rio Grande.

Upon this property the government of the United States is now constructing one of the largest dams and reservoirs for irrigation purposes in the world, the Elephant Butte project. The lands granted to Armendaris are now the property of the Victorio Land and Cattle Company.

1218 JUAN MARTIN BUSTOS. *Santa Cruz de la Cañada*, 1813.
Question of lands with the Madrids.

1219 FRANCISCO DE JESUS DE ESPEXO. *Alburquerque*.
Will. 1733. Also proceedings in the settlement of his estate. Joseph Perez Mangos, Alcalde.

1220 MANUEL VIGIL.
Will. *Santa Fe*, 1733. Antonio de Uribarri, Alcalde.

1221 SALVADOR MARTINEZ.
Petition. *Alburquerque*, 1736. Asks that property inherited by his wife be delivered to her. Gervasio Cruzat y Gongora, Governor.

1222 ANTONIO PACHECO. *Santa Fe*.
Will. No date. Antonio de Ulibarri, Alcalde.

1223 DIMAS XIRON DE TEGEDA. *Santa Fe*.
Will. No date. Antonio de Ulibarri, Alcalde.

1224 PHELIPA DE ROJAS. *Santa Fe*. 1736.
Inventory of her estate. Antonio de Ulibarri, Alcalde.

1225 JUAN GARCIA DE NORIEGA. *Santa Fe*.
Will. No date. Antonio de Ulibarri, Alcalde.

1226 JUANA DE ANAYA ALMAZAN. *Santa Fe.* 1736.
Will. Juan Manuel Chirinos. Manuel Thenorio de Alva.

1227 MIGUEL DE SANDOVAL MARTINEZ to Antonio Truxillo.
Land at *Pojoaque.* 1733. Antonio de Ulibarri, Alcalde.

Deed, dated April 8, 1733, by Miguel de Sandoval Martinez to Antonio Trujillo, for a ranch at Pojoaque.

The grantor states that he acquired the land from Carlos Lopez and the latter's mother, Ana de Tapia, who had it by grant made by Governor Don Pedro Rodriguez Cubero in the year 1701; that he does not attempt to sell all the land described in the grant, because before they sold to him they had sold a portion of the land to the Indians of Pojoaque.

The part sold to the Indians is not described, but the part conveyed by Sandoval to Trujillo had the following boundaries: "On the east side a main ditch which separates the lands of the natives of said pueblo (Pojoaque), on the west side the main road which goes to San Juan, on the north side by the main ditch which crosses the main road, on the south side by a small ditch, before coming to the river, by which the Indians irrigate their little gardens."

1228 ALPHONSO RAEL DE AGUILAR to Juan Joseph Moreno. 1733.
House and lands. *Santa Fe.* Antonio de Ulibarri, Alcalde.

1229 FRANCISCO TRUXILLO to Juan Angel Gonzales. *Santa Fe,* 1733.
House and lands. Antonio de Ulibarri, Alcalde.

1230 JUAN ROMERO. Banished. 1734.

1231 JOSEPH BACA. *Alburquerque.*
Will. 1766. Juan Xptobal Sanchez, Alcalde. Also proceedings before Pedro Fermin de Mendinueta in relation to some sheep.

1232 SANTO DOMINGO.
Claim of Indians to lands adjoining *Cochiti.*

Letter of August 14, 1808, from Friar Antonio Caballero, at the mission of Cochiti, to Don Alberto Maynez, acting governor of New Mexico.

The friar says that the Indians of Santo Domingo, whose mission is under his charge, came to him and asked him to write to the governor for them, because they could not explain themselves clearly; that they were acquainted with the boundaries of their league; that they wanted the governor to know about a piece of land, on the west side of the river (Rio Grande), which extended as far as the old pueblo of Cochiti, and for which they had paid 400 pesos; that the old pueblo of Cochiti was at a place where there was a medium sized hill called Los Chicos, as the governor could see from the recitals in the deed; that this was the land they asked for, and asked for with reason, for they had bought it; that the governor would see from the instrument which they would show to him who it was that had sold it to them; that the writer made this lengthy explanation in order that the governor might not have the trouble of trying to understand the statements made by the Indians.

In a claim filed with the court of private land claims, no record or evidence of which is to be found in the archives, a grant of land was claimed to have been made by the Spanish government on August 2, 1728, to a resident of Alburquerque, named Antonio Lucero; this grant or claim is known as the Cañada de Cochiti. It was located on the mesa of Cochiti, east of the center of the county of Sandoval, and Lucero's petition showed boundaries as follows: On the north by the old pueblo of Cochiti; on the east by the Del Norte river; on the south by the lands of the natives of the pueblo; on the west by the Jemez mountains. The amount of land claimed under this grant was 104,554 acres. The petition gave as the northerly limit the old pueblo to which the Indians retreated during the uprising of 1680. The investigation made by the officials of the department of justice in the court of private land claims showed that the Indians almost unanimously agreed that their traditions were that the retreat mentioned was made to a pueblo located much farther south than that designated in the petition for confirmation of the grant. The court of private land claims, on February 16, 1898, confirmed the grant and ordered the survey to be made, the north boundary to be located through the center of the old pueblo of Cochiti, and the western boundary to follow the crest of the first sierra of the Jemez mountains; the eastern boundary was established at the Rio Grande, and the southern at the northern line of the lands belonging to the Cochiti Indians. The area confirmed was 19,112.78.

1233 TOMAS RIBEROS (Viveros?). *Santa Fe.*
Will. 1843. Santiago Armijo, Alcalde.

1234 SAN FELIPE and SANTA ANA Pueblos. 1819.
Question of lands. Joseph Mariano de la Peña, Alcalde.

Proceedings had in carrying into effect a decision of the Royal Audiencia with regard to the sale of certain lands by the pueblo of San Felipe to Spanish citizens, said lands in fact not being the property of the vendors but really belonging to the Indians of the pueblo of Santa Ana.

On August 5, 1819, Don José Mariano de la Peña, chief alcalde of Alburquerque, who had been appointed by Acting Governor Facundo Melgares to carry out the decision of the Royal Audiencia, called together the people of San Felipe and the citizens to whom they had sold the lands, and explained to the Indians that they must make good to the citizens the sales which they had improperly made to them of lands which had been decided to belong to Santa Ana.

The Indians decided that to Juan Domingo Archiveque, Juan Pablo Archiveque, Francisco Gutierrez, José Garcia, Alonso Garcia, and Blas Chavez, they would give lands which they owned by purchase at Algodones, the purchasers being satisfied with this arrangement.

The value of the lands purchased from the Indians by Don Juan Bautista Gonzales amounted to 2,434 pesos, according to the values recognized at that time. The Indians were willing to make this good, but they objected to giving that amount of land, although they had unimproved lands which they had purchased on the west side of the river. Both the alcalde and the protector of Indians, Don Ignacio Maria Sanchez y Vergara, tried to persuade them that it would be better to give the lands than to pay money, and left them to think over the matter, thus concluding the proceedings for that day.

On August 7, 1819, Peña again took up the matter and proceeded to the lands which the Indians were to give to the citizens in place of those which they had formerly sold to them. He then measured to each purchaser what belonged to him according to the recitals of his deed. In connection with this feature of the case Peña makes the following statement: "and as all purchased uncultivated land and now they delivered it cultivated, for the improvements of them there was assigned respectively to each one the fourth part for his purchase, and both interested parties remained satisfied," etc. If my translation of this statement is not very clear, it is at least as clear as the original, the meaning of which in many places is very obscure.

The next proceeding is dated August 12, 1819. Peña states that the governor of San Felipe and one of the principal men being present, they agreed to give to Juan Bautista Gonzales some of the land which the pueblo owned by purchase on the west side of the river, at a place called Las Lemitas; that he then went to said place and measured from the boundary of the community of Santa Ana toward the north 1,000 varas; that at this point Gonzales and the governor of the pueblo got into a dispute over several points on which they could not agree, so the matter was left in that condition and the parties went home.

On August 13, 1819, Peña ordered the San Felipe people to present to him the deed of purchase of the land which had been in dispute. He states that the document was from the year 1753, and acknowledged before Don Tomas Velez Cachupin, and that the boundary which it cites is the old Angostura on the south, and the boundary of the pueblo of San Felipe on the north, the edge of the river on the west, and the hills on the east.

Peña comes to the conclusion that these boundaries, taken in connection with other matters within his knowledge, show that he was correct in the decision he had made in the month of May when he reported to the Royal Audiencia of the district that the land in question did not belong to San Felipe, but to Santa Ana. He adds that perhaps the mistake made by the San Felipe people in selling the land was made through ignorance. Finally he transmits the proceedings to Governor Melgares for the decision of that officer.

The style of composition of this man Peña is such as to make it very difficult in many instances to understand what he meant, and practically impossible to make an intelligible translation of much that he said.

1235 JOSE ORTEGA. *Santa Fe.*
Will. 1825. Francisco Garcia, Cabo.

360 THE SPANISH ARCHIVES OF NEW MEXICO

1236 GALISTEO.
Petition in regard to the construction of a reservoir. 1840.

1237 MARIA ROSALIA DURAN DE ARMIJO. *Santa Fe.*
Will. 1768. Phelipe Tafoya, Alcalde.

1238 No value.
Relative to the money known as *Pesos de la Tierra*, which the writer says is an *imaginary money?*

1239 No value.

1240 No value.

1241 MATEO GARCIA. 1833.
Report of committee on his petition for land at *Abiquiú.* Suspended because land was in litigation.

1242 No value.

1243 TRANSMITTAL of Cases of Indians of *Cochiti.* The *Ortizes* and *Indians* of Santo Domingo vs. Luis Baca. To the Royal Audience at Guadalajara. 1817.
Rough draft of a letter, dated December 17, 1817, probably by Pedro Maria de Allande, to the attorney, Don Blas Abidiano y Tassol, in the City of Mexico, stating that all the documents in a formal *expediente*, then existing in the government archives, and relating to the Cile (Sile?) ranch, which was in litigation between the Indians of Cochiti and the Ortizes, and the Indians of Santo Domingo with Don Luis Baca, had been sent to the Royal Audiencia of Guadalajara on May 31, 1817, because of their having been requested in a letter, January 31.

1244 ANTONIO ARMIJO and 70 Families.
Draft of title to lands at junction of the rivers *Sapello, Mora,* and *Coyote,* in *Mora* county, 1837. Not signed. Grantees not designated.

1245 INDIANS OF XEMES vs. RAFAEL GARCIA, 1833.
Question of boundaries. Salvador Montoya, Alcalde.
Letter of April 18, 1833, from the alcalde, Salvador Montoya, to the jefe politico, asking for instructions in regard to measuring the league of the pueblo of Jemez.
It appears that the alcalde had already made a measure-

ment at the request of Rafael Garcia, beginning at the church in the pueblo, and measuring the league with a hair rope 50 varas in length. This resulted in the measurement of the league extending over into lands of Garcia about one hundred varas. Thereupon the rope with which the line had been measured was again tested, and it was discovered that it had stretched almost a vara, so the parties agreed that 50 varas of the overlap of 100 should be allowed to Garcia.

Subsequently some question arose between the alcalde and the parties in regard to the payment of the former's fees, and also between Garcia and the Indians as to the proper manner of making the measurement. Garcia was not satisfied, and wanted the distance of 5,000 varas measured anew with poles instead of a rope. The Indians insisted that as they were settled there prior to Garcia, the land should be measured with a rope, as it had been when it was first given to them, and that the measurement should begin from their first church instead of the one in existence at the time of the controversy.

Apparently the contending parties made a good deal of trouble for the alcalde, and he sought the advice of the governor, not only in regard to the proper manner of making the measurement of the league, but also as to his fees in the matter. But he did not get much consolation from that officer. On the back of the letter to the governor is a rough draft of his reply, dated April 23, 1833. He tells the alcalde that it is not the governor's business to resolve doubts that may arise in the minds of the alcaldes with respect to the administration of justice, and that the alcalde had better consult an attorney; that with respect to his fees he should be governed by the schedule of fees in force in his district, or in lack of the latter, to the well established custom in such matters, provided it was not in conflict with the laws.

1246 DOMINGO SANCHES. *Santa Fe.* 1825.
Will. Francisco Garcia, Sargento.

1247 DOMINGO SAENZ. *Santa Fe.* 1827.
Will. Francisco Garcia, Sargento.

1248 TAOS VALLEY, 1753.
Order to fence lands to avoid trouble with Indians. Tomas Velez Cachupin, Governor.

1249 MARIA DE LA LUZ XARAMILLO.
Will. *Santa Fe*, 1825. José de Larañaga, Cabo.

1250 PRIVILEGES of DESCENDANTS of CONQUERORS, 1694.
El Cónde de Galve.

1251 CIENEGA of Santa Fe. 1705. 1717.
Francisco Cuerbo y Valdes, Governor. Juan Paez Hurtado, Governor.

Proclamation prohibiting the pasture of animals in the cienega at Santa Fe, March 27, 1717, by Captain General Juan Paez Hurtado; signed also by Miguel Thenorio de Alba.

Another proclamation by Don Francisco Cuervo y Valdez, governor and captain-general; same prohibition; April 25, 1705; a violation of the order was penalized by *"un mez de carcel"* and the second by two months guarding the horseherd of the royal garrison. This order has a fine signature of Governor Cuervo y Valdez and also of Captain Alonso Rael de Aguilar.

1252 TITLES to Granted Lands. Notice to all persons to present. *Santa Fe*, 1707.
El Marqués de la Penuela.

1253 FRANCISCA ANTONIA DE GUIJOSA. 1715-1716.
Piece of paper belonging to her land grant papers. Reported Claim No. 109, *q. v.*

1254 BALTAZAR ROMERO to Alejo Gutierrez. *Santa Fe*, 1715.
House and land. Order to give grantee *testimonio*. Pedro de Villasur, Lieutenant-Governor.

1255 CIENEGA of *Santa Fe*. **1720.**
Pedro de Villasur, Lieutenant-Governor. Fine signature. April 12, 1720.

1256 FRANCISCO DE MASCAREÑAS and Brothers vs. Juan Rodriguez.
Question of a small tract of land in *Santa Fe*. 1737. Enrique de Olavide y Michelena, Governor. Manuel Sainz de Garvisu. Pedro Joseph de Leon.

THE SPANISH ARCHIVES OF NEW MEXICO 363

1257 NEW MEXICO and NEW BISCAY. 1745. Boundaries.
Joachin Codallos y Rabal, Governor.

1258 INVENTORY of Documents in the government archives delivered by Joachin Codallos y Rabal to Tomas Velez Cachupin, his successor, 1749.

1259 MINING REGULATIONS. 1777. *Comandante General de las Provincias Internas del N. E. Caballero de la Croix.* This officer was the first to hold this office.

1260 EL CABALLERO DE CROIX. 1780.
Letter to Juan Bautista de Anza, Governor.

1261 RECORD of Brands and Land Grants, made apparently by order of Juan Bautista de Anza, Governor. Signed by him. *Santa Fe*, 1787.
The land grants are as follows:
Domingo Romero, Manuel Ortiz, Miguel Ortiz, 1782. The *Mesita de Juana Lopez*. Juan Bautista de Anza, Governor.
This grant was surveyed in 1876 and confirmed by congress January 28, 1879. There was a conflict with the grant to the pueblo of Santo Domingo and a conflict with the Ortiz Mine Grant. The conflict with the Santo Domingo was a strip six miles long and nearly a mile in width of the eastern end of the Pueblo Grant. The confirmation confirms the title to all included within the survey of 1876. In 1907 a new survey of the Pueblo Grant was made and resulted in greatly increasing the conflict with the Mesita de Juana Lopez, the conflict under the last survey being about 20,000 acres. The fact that the Pueblo Grant had been patented seems to have made no difference in the making of the order for the new survey. The Juana Lopez has not been patented, but that, under the wording of the act of confirmation, is considered unnecessary.
Sabinal. Order that the new settlers be put in possession. 1782. Juan Bautista de Anza, Governor.
José Apodaca, Diego Gonzales, Pablo Anaya. Lands at *Alburquerque*. 1782. Juan Bautista de Anza, Governor.
Mateo Roibal. 1782. Grant of lands at *Jacona*, for-

merly granted to Ignacio Roibal in 1702, by Pedro Rodriguez Cubero, Governor. Juan Bautista de Anza, Governor.

This land was at the pueblo of Jacona (*Tewa*) abandoned in 1696. Ignacio Roibal was one of the soldiers under General De Vargas, with the rank of ensign; his wife was Francisca Gomez; a portion of the site of the old pueblo and its lands had already been granted to Captain Jacinto Pelaes, when Ignacio Roibal petitioned for the remainder. Roibal was a man of some means, as he stated to the governor that he had sufficient live stock to use the entire property for grazing purposes; the property was bounded on the east by the lands of Juan de Mestas and lands of *Oyu* (formerly of Francisco Anaya de Almazan) ; on the north by the road which leads to the new village of Jacona and some bluffs above said road; on the west by a cañada, which comes down by a house built by Matias Madrid and some red bluffs near the small mesa of San Yldefonzo; and on the south by the forest between this village and Jacona. The property was given to him October 2, 1702, by the castellan, Pedro Rodriguez Cubero, at the time governor and captain-general. At this time Captain Pelaez was dead and his son had inherited the tract given to the captain. The place has been occupied by the descendants of the original grantee ever since and is now known as "Los Roibales."

Roque Lovato. Grant. Lands at Santa Fe. 1785. Juan Bautista de Anza, Governor.

This grant had for its boundaries, on the north the top of the dividing line or ridge between Santa Fe and Tesuque; on the south the road running along the foot of the hills eastward from the *"Muralla"* in Santa Fe; on the east some black hills, and on the west the road from Santa Fe to Rio Arriba.

Roque Lobato was an armorer in the royal garrison of Santa Fe; the grant was made September 23, 1785, by Juan Bautista de Anza, governor and captain-general, and possession was given by José Maldonado. At this time José Miguel de la Peña was chief alcalde and war-captain of the Villa of Santa Fe and its jurisdiction. Roque Lobato died the same year and his widow, Josefa Armijo, on account of a debt of $450.00, created by her late husband "at the house of José Ortiz," for the payment of which her husband had sold the property to a soldier named José Ribera, deeded the property to Ribera.

The "Muralla" was an old rampart or fort on the outskirts of the City of Santa Fe, in the direction of Tesuque. This property belonged to Don Gaspar Ortiz in 1851.

Lorenzo Marques. Grant. 1785. Lands at the *Cañada de los Alamos*. Juan Bautista de Anza, Governor.

Bartolomé Marquez and Francisco Padilla received a grant of land near the city of Santa Fe from Don Gaspar Domingo de Mendoza in 1742. It contains about 1,300 acres and is described: "On the east the Arroyo of Tierra Blanca; on the west the road leading to Pecos; where the lands of Cayetano, squadron corporal, adjoin; on the south the Arroyo Chamizos; and on the north the high hills, the boundary of the lands of Captain Antonio Montoya, deceased."

A grant was made to Lorenzo Marquez in 1785, by Don Juan Bautista de Anza; the land covered a "surplus to the lands of Captain Sebastian De Vargas; on the south and west it adjoined the little valley called La Cañada de La Tierra; on the east the Pecos road going to the ranchos of *La Cienega*." Possession was given by Don Antonio José Ortiz, senior alcalde of Santa Fe, in the presence of Diego Montoya, Gabriel Ortiz, and Antonio Lujan and the "only adjoining settler," José Maria Montoya. This property was sold by the heirs of Marquez to Simon Delgado, Pablo Delgado, Fernando Delgado, and Felipe Delgado, on June 20, 1856.

Antonio de Armenta. Grant. 1786. Salvador Antonio Sandoval. Lands between the pueblos of *Zia* and *Xemes*. Town of San Isidro Grant. Juan Bautista de Anza, governor.

The Town of San Isidro Grant lies between the Jemez and Zia Grants. The records of the surveyor-general do not show that any patent has ever been issued for this property.

Whenever a grant was applied for, the tract being adjacent to any of the lands belonging to the pueblos, in nearly every instance the "league" of the pueblos is referred to and the consent of the pueblos seems to have been secured before the making of a grant or the putting in possession of the applicant. This clearly appears in the grant to the original settlers of San Isidro de Los Dolores, in the act of possession and in the petition itself. The act of possession is as follows:

"At this point of San Isidro de Los Dolores, on the 16th day of the month of May, in the year one thousand seven hundred and eighty-six, I, Don Antonio Nerio Montoya, senior justice and war-captain of the jurisdiction of San Carlos de la Alameda, by virtue of the commission conferred upon me by Don Juan Bautista de Anza, colonel of cavalry of the royal armies of His Majesty, political and military governor of this Province of New Mexico, being at the aforementioned place, having summoned the natives of the Pueblos of San Diego de Jemez and Cia, who are adjacent residents, and having measured the league belonging to them, with two hundred and sixty-two varas more, with which they expressed themselves satisfied; some of the Indians having planted some small patches and not to offend them, I allowed them to retain possession of them, with your Excellency's permission. I also proceeded to the Pueblo of Cia and measured the league belonging to that pueblo, with the further amount of one thousand six hundred and thirty-two varas which the Indians purchased from Juan Galvan, as shown by the title deeds of said purchase, and the aforementioned lands I assigned and added thereto one thousand varas more, the Indians having asked me for it, and the said Indians having shown to me a sale made by the late Miguel Montoya, which boundaries are in a cañon commonly called El Rito Salado; that this cañon is the pasture ground and summer range of their cattle; the boundaries for which land are the same called for in the title-deed; on the north a red hill; on the south a white table-land, and on the east the Jemez river itself; and having informed myself of the contents of the two deeds, and having found in them only what has been above stated, I gave the two pueblos to understand what belonged to each of them — that of Cia what they had acquired by purchase, and that of Jemez what had been granted to them by His Majesty; and believing that neither of the two Pueblos was entitled to the piece of ground which is unoccupied, and it being the intention of our sovereign that his lands shall be settled upon by his subjects wherever there may be any surplus, and finding no impediment, and by virtue of the commission which I hold from His Excellency, I proceeded to the land lying between the two Pueblos, which, upon being measured, was found to contain two thousand nine hundred varas, and no person appearing who claimed a better right, both Pueblos being present, as well as the Senior Justice, Antonio de Armenta, and the militia sergeant, Salvador Antonio Sandoval, and being informed of all the circumstances, I took them by the hand, walked with them over the land, they pulled grass, threw stones toward the four winds of heaven, and we all exclaimed three times, "Long life to the King, Our Sovereign," (whom may God preserve), in proof of legal possession which I gave them, and they received quietly and peacefully, without any opposition; the boundaries whereof are as follows: on the north the lands of Jemez; on the south the lands of the Pueblo of Zia; on the west the mountain of the Espiritu Santo Spring, at the place commonly called Los Bancos; on the east the lands of the aforementioned senior justice, Antonio Nerio Montoya, which is the road leading from Cochiti to Jemez. And having assigned their boundaries, and no injury resulting thereby, and being satisfied with them, I directed them to erect permanent boundaries; and in order that it may so appear, I, Antonio Nerio Montoya, as commissioner and senior justice, at the same time, signed with two attending witnesses, with whom I act in the absence of a royal or public notary, there being none in this Kingdom; to which I certify.

"NERIO ANTONIO MONTOYA

"Witnesses: TORIBIO GONZALES, SALVADOR LOPEZ."

1262 SOLDIERS' QUARTERS at Santa Fe, 1788, 1790, 1791.

1263 PEDRO DE NAVA. October 22, 1791.

Decision that notwithstanding the provisions of Article 81 of the Ordinances of Intendentes, Captains of Presidios may grant lots and other lands within the four leagues belonging to each presidio.

On October 22, 1791, Don Pedro de Nava, then commandant-general of the *Provincias Internas*, with the approval of the viceroy, promulgated at Chihuahua what is known as the "Order of Pedro de Nava." This order made provision for the allotment of lands by the captains and commandants of presidios within the presidial jurisdiction.

This order of de Nava was revoked on January 19, 1793, because in violation of Article 81 of the "Ordinance of Intendants," which gave those officers exclusive jurisdiction over the sale, allotment, and composition of crown lands in the provinces under their jurisdiction. This order of revocation is as follows:

"In the Superior Board of the Royal Treasury His Excellency, the Viceroy, approved provisionally the course you took on the 22nd of October, 1791, and which I communicated to you on the same date, that, notwithstanding the provisions of Article 81 of the Royal Ordinance of Intendants, the captains and commandants of presidios should continue selling lots and lands to the soldiers and residents who applied for them in order to establish themselves under their protection, limiting this power to the area of four common leagues, measured from the center of the plaza of each one, two to each wind; but to the end that the permanent ruling that is to be observed in the matter may be made in said Superior Board, I was instructed to confer with said Captains and Commandants on the consultation that furnished the occasion for making that declaration. It was restricted substantially, under the provisions of Articles 7, 81, and 306, of said Ordinance of Intendants, to the order to the Captains and Commandants to suspend the apportionment of lands which they were making under Article I, title II, of the regulations of Presidios; since those articles give to said intendants in the whole territory of their several provinces, exclusive cognizance of the transactions that occur in the matter, such as are the sales, compositions and apportionments of crown and vacant lands; and on the contrary, the treasury would be deprived of the fees that belong to it.

"Afterwards, there was brought before His Excellency, the Viceroy, the point that said articles of the Ordinance of Intendants conferred on those who filled those offices absolute political jurisdiction even in the settlements bordering upon the enemy; the opinion being that it was prejudicial for the Captains and Commandants of Presidios to exercise it with prohibition and without the cognizance of the governors-intendants, and that it was less so, for the power to sell and apportion lands to belong exclusively to them.

"The first was based on the belief that the residents would be better governed by the judges whom the Intendant would appoint, they would have less distant, the appeal to the latter than the commandancy general in their complaints and grievances, it would cause them no expense to bring their suits, nor would they suffer the vexation and annoyances the military and civil head officials cause them, by proceeding despotically and arbitrarily in their decisions; so that they saw themselves obliged not a few times to abandon their establishments, or they made them leave them by inflicting banishment upon them without hearing them, besides, also, it would better facilitate the storing of grain, which the troops need, inasmuch, as the Intendant would attend to encour-

THE SPANISH ARCHIVES OF NEW MEXICO 369

aging it among the frontier residents with greater energy than could the captains and commandants; and the second, in that the royal treasury is prejudiced, his Majesty failing to receive the composition fees for the lands that are apportioned in the four jurisdictional leagues of the Presidios.

"In order to comply with the resolution of the Superior Board, you will immediately circulate this order to the Captains and Commandants of Presidios in that Province, to the end that they may report without delay through you (and you will do the same with regard to that of Loreto which is under your charge), whatever occurs and appears to them, together with an individual notice of the settlements contained in the four leagues assigned to each one as its area; and another of the residents and settlers therein, with a statement of the number of persons of both sexes that compose them, besides the troops.

"God preserve you many years.

"PEDRO DE NAVA [rubric]

"Chihuahua, January 19, 1793."

Under and by virtue of the Ordinance of Intendants of December 4, 1786, New Spain, with the exception of the Californias, was divided into twelve Intendancies, as follows: Mexico, Puebla, Guadalajara, Oaxaca, Guanajuato, Merida de Yucatan, Valladolid, San Luis Potosi, Durango, Vera Cruz, Zacatecas, and Sonora and Sinaloa (Arispe).

Each of the foregoing political divisions was entrusted to an officer under the name of intendant, who had jurisdiction in the four departments of justice, police, treasury, and war, but the intendants of Sonora and Sinaloa (Arispe) and Durango, in matters of justice and police, were subordinate to the commandants general of their provinces, and the other ten to the viceroy, and all of them to the Territorial Audiencias.

There was also to be an intendancy general of the army in the City of Mexico, and the intendant general was the delegate in Mexico of the superintendency general of the royal treasury of the Indies.

A superior board of the treasury, to reside in the City of Mexico, was also created and the intendant general was its president.

Under Article 81 of the Ordinance of Intendants, these officers were empowered to make sales and compositions of the crown lands of their several provinces. The original proceedings had by them were to be forwarded to the superior board of the treasury for approval. The intendants issued the titles upon such approval and these were again forwarded to the board of confirmation.

1264 MARIA ANTONIA LUCERO. 1791.
Letter of Francisco Xavier Bernal to Fernando de la Concha in relation to her unwarranted claim to certain lands.

1265 NEW SETTLEMENTS.
Copy of instructions for the formation and management of the same. 1800. Certified by Manuel Merino. 21 pages. Perfect copy. Very legible.

1266 CEVILLETA. 1800.
Draft of letter of the Governor of New Mexico to Don Pedro de Nava.

1267 COLONISTS from *Louisiana*. 1806.
Letter of Nemesio Salcedo in regard to.

1268 XEMES. Juan de Abrego, 1806.
Settlements at *Xemes*. Letter to the Governor.

1269 VALLECITO — Grantees of: 1808.
Two letters of Ignacio Sanchez de Vergara, in one of which the *Vallecito* is mentioned.

1270 LANDS held by purchase, grant, inheritance, etc. 1809.
Draft of a letter of the Governor of New Mexico to Nemesio Salcedo, acknowledging the receipt of a letter informing him that the time designated for the re-settlement of such had expired and no one should be permitted to use them without notice to the authorities.

1271 FRANCISCO ORTIZ. 1809.
Draft of a letter of the Governor of *New Mexico* to Nemesio Salcedo in regard to tract of land asked for by said Ortiz. Also giving account of the custom that had formerly obtained in New Mexico in the manner of making grants. No. 1081, *q. v.*

1272 RESIDENCE of the Governor, *Santa Fe*. 1810.
Describes the bad condition of the palace in 1810, which *had been the residence of the governors.*

1273 SAME subject.
   Salcedo writes to the Governor of New Mexico about the condition of the palace.

1274 CINNABAR MINES in *New Mexico,* 1810. Not known.

1275 RANCHOS DE ALBURQUERQUE. 1811. José Antonio Chaves.
   Objections to the opening of a road through his land.
   Los Ranchos or Helena Gallegos Grant, R. No. 156.
   This property is known as the Ranchos de Alburquerque Grant. Two suits were filed in the court of private land claims which were consolidated for the purposes of the hearing; the grant was confirmed and later surveyed for 35,000 acres. The northern line of this grant touches the southeast corner of the Sandia Grant. It was patented February 25, 1909.

1276 JOAQUIN CASTILLO. 1812.
   Question of certain lands in the *Belen* Grant which he had purchased. José Antonio Chaves, ex-Alcalde.

1277 LA MAJADA Tract. 1813.
   Complaint against Miguel Ortiz.

1278 DOMINGO CHAVES. 1813-1820. *Rancho de Peralta.*
   Question of partition. Manuel Ruvi de Celis, Alcalde. Bartolomé Baca; Facundo Melgares, Governor; Francisco Sarracino; Francisco Xavier Chaves; Manuel Aragon.

1279 INDIANS OF SANTA CLARA vs. Indians *Canjuebes*, 1815.
   Question of lands. Miguel Lopez, Alcalde.
   Letter of November 11, 1815, from Miguel Lopez, alcalde of Santa Cruz, to the acting governor of New Mexico (probably, at that time, Alberto Maynez), stating the opinion of the alcalde as to the merits of a controversy between the Indians of the pueblo of Santa Clara and certain individuals of the tribe, named *Canjuebes*, who had abandoned their tribal relations and become Spanish citizens, but who still claimed lands within the pueblo grant. Apparently this controversy had been passed on by the acting governor and had at last reached the commandant general at Durango.

Evidently the alcalde strongly favored the contention of the *Canjuebes,* and he pretty strongly intimates that the governor had overlooked the justice of their side of the case.

The rough draft of the governor's reply immediately follows the alcalde's letter. It is a scathing rebuke of the latter's interference in a matter which did not concern him. The governor remarks, however, that he is not surprised at it, as the alcalde's ignorance is notorious.

1280 BERNARDO BONAVIA. 1815.

Letter in regard to the question raised in No. 1279.

Letter of December 27, 1815, by Bernardo Bonavia, commandant general at Durango, to the acting governor of New Mexico, approving his decision in the matter of the controversy between the pueblo of Santa Clara and certain individuals of that town who had abandoned their tribal relations, but still desired to hold land within the pueblo grant. This is the same controversy referred to in archive 1279.

Bonavia directs the acting governor to give the Canjuebes to understand that if they want to hold the lands in dispute, they must go back and become part of the pueblo community, but if they want to retain their Spanish citizenship they must buy the lands they need elsewhere, as do other citizens of the Province.

1281 LOS QUELITES. 1817. Juan José Chaves and others.

Petition for the said tract. Refused and recommended to go to *Socorro.* Allande, Governor. Josef Mariano de la Peña, Alcalde. José Gabriel Sanchez.

1282 MILITARY MATTER, 1819.

1283 LUIS MARIA CABEZA DE BACA. 1819.

Costs in Royal Audiencia at *Guadalajara* in the matter of the sale of certain ranchos to the Indians of *San Buenaventura de Cochiti.* Rafael Cuentas.

Detailed statement of costs incurred in the Royal Audiencia at Guadalajara by Don Luis Cabeza de Baca in a suit had with the Indians of Cochiti in relation to the sale of some ranches.

1284 LETTERS (2) of June 19, 1820, by Governor Facundo Melgares, one to Aléjo Garcia Cónde, Commandant General, the other to the Royal Audiencia of Guadalajara.

In relation to certain costs due the employes of that tribunal by Don Luis Maria Cabeza de Baca.

These costs were incurred in the suit with the Cochiti Indians referred to in archive 1283.

The governor says that cash was so scarce that Baca had been unable to raise the amount of the costs in money (192 pesos 7 reales) and consequently had turned over to the soldiers of the company at Santa Fe eight mules, which the governor asks the commandant general to charge to the company, paying to the Royal Audiencia the costs in question.

1285 CEBOLLETA. 1821.

Disposition of land in said settlement which had belonged to Salvador Chaves. It was given to Juan Bautista Chaves by José Manuel Aragon, Alcalde. Mariano Sanchez Vergara, Alcalde.

1286 JOSÉ MARIA ALARID. 1821.

Petition for land at *Las Nutrias, Valencia* county. Not granted. Juan Cruz Baca, Alcalde. Facundo Melgares, Governor.

1287 LUIS MARIA CABEZA DE BACA. 1821.

In the matter of a grant of land asked for by him. Decision of the *Deputation of Durango* giving him the tract called *Las Vegas Grandes*. Diego Garcia Cónde. Miguel de Zubiria.

The early history of the Las Vegas Grant is given in a report of Surveyor-General William Pelham, before whom the grant came for consideration in 1858, and who found, at the time, that there were two claimants to the land, one the heirs of Luis Maria Cabeza de Baca and the other the Town of Las Vegas.

On January 16, 1821, Luis Maria Cabeza de Baca, in his own name and that of seventeen male children, petitioned the Provincial Deputation of the State of Durango, under whose jurisdiction, he avers, the Province of New Mexico then was, for a tract of public land suitable for cultivation and pasture, called the *Vegas Grandes*, on the Gallinas river, in the jurisdiction of El Bado. In this petition he states that a like petition had been made to the authorities of the Province of New Mexico, and that, by a decree of the 18th of February, 1820, the land was granted to him and to eight other persons, but as these persons already possessed land elsewhere they took no interest in its cultivation, and prays that the grant be made to himself and his aforementioned children, with the following boundaries, to-wit:

On the north, the Sapello river; on the south the boundary of El Bado; on the west the summit of the Pecos mountain; on the east the Aguage de la Yegua and the boundary of Don Antonio Ortiz.

Governor Bartolomé Baca, on October 17, 1823, holding the title of political chief, directed the alcalde of El Bado to place Luis Maria Cabeza de Baca in possession of the land called for in his petition, as the eight individuals who accompanied him in his first petition had placed no improvements on the land, and the alcalde was required to certify at the foot of the order the proceedings had by him in the premises.

The claim of the Town of Las Vegas was based upon the following proceedings:

On March 20, 1836, Juan de Dios Maese, Miguel Archuleta, Manuel Duran and José Antonio Casados, for themselves and in the name of twenty-five others, petitioned the ayuntamiento of El Bado for a tract of land for cultivation and pasture, situated in the county of El Bado and bounded as follows: on the north by the Sapello river; on the south by the boundary of the grant to Don Antonio Ortiz; on the east by the Aguage de la Yegua; and on the west by the boundary of the town of El Bado.

On the same day the ayuntamiento of El Bado sent the petition to the Territorial Deputation with the recommendation that the petition be granted.

On March 23, 1835, the grant was made by the Territorial Deputation with the boundaries asked for, with the further provision that persons who owned no lands were to be allowed the same privileges of settling upon the grant as those who petitioned for it.

On March 24, 1835, Francisco Sarracino, acting governor and political chief, directed the constitutional alcalde of El Bado to place the parties in possession, and adding: "It is also convenient to suggest to you that you should select for the settlers a townsite and provide them with lots for residence, together with such other steps as you may deem proper for the security of the inhabitants, who on account of settling on the land indicated will be included in your jurisdiction."

The constitutional alcalde of El Bado made report to Governor Sarracino as follows:

"At Nuestra Señora de los Dolores de Las Vegas, on the sixth day of the month of April, in the year one thousand eight hundred and thirty-five, jurisdiction of San Miguel del Bado, I, citizen José de Jesus Ulibarri y Duran, Constitutional Alcalde, the only one in this jurisdiction, proceeded to this town for the purpose of apportioning the lands to the twenty-five individuals mentioned in the petition dated March 20, 1835, and in general to those who are without lands, not only those within this jurisdiction, but also anyone who may present himself to me, who has no occupation, and, having examined the land, I took the measure from north to south, after which I made the apportionment according to that portion of the colonization law which refers to grant of public lands, each individual received a gratuitous piece of land, according to his means, with the understanding that the lands given to the persons contained in the accompanying list, one should remain uncultivated."

The surveyor-general, Pelham, considered both of these titles good and recommended both for confirmation, leaving to the several claimants the right of adjusting their titles in the courts. But Congress (a Senate committee) did not agree with the surveyor-general as to the best manner in which these conflicting titles should be disposed of. The committee said:

"The claimants under the title to Baca have expressed a willingness to waive their older title in favor of the settlers, if allowed to enter an equivalent quantity of land elsewhere within the Territory; and your Committee cannot doubt that Congress will cheerfully accept the proposal, which, indeed, would undoubtedly have been acceded to by Mexico if the Territory had remained hers, to whose rights and duties the United States have succeeded."

Congress confirmed the grant to the Town of Las Vegas and settled the claim of the Baca heirs in the following language:

"And be it further enacted, that it shall be lawful for the heirs of Luis Maria Baca, who make claim to the said tract of land as is claimed by the Town of Las Vegas, to select, instead of the land claimed by them, an equal quantity of vacant land not mineral, in the Territory of New Mexico, to be located by them in square bodies, not exceeding five in number. And it shall be the duty of the surveyor general of New Mexico to make survey and location of the lands so selected by said heirs of Baca when thereunto required by them: Provided, however, that the right hereby granted to said heirs of Baca shall continue in force during three years from the passage of this act, and no longer." Approved June 21, 1860.

The authority thus given to make locations was afterward exercised by the Baca heirs, and the lands thus acquired are known as "Baca Location" with the number up to five.

In 1887, the title of the town of Las Vegas to this property was attacked by Moses Milheiser and others. The case was finally determined by the supreme court of New Mexico in 1889, Chief Justice Long delivering the opinion of the court. The judicial determination favored the title of the town to the property and that title is now unquestioned. The grant has since been administered by a board of trustees, appointed by the presiding judge of the district court, pursuant to the provisions of legislative enactment.

Don Luis Maria Cabeza de Baca claimed to be a descendant of Alvar Nuñez Cabeza de Vaca, one of the first Europeans to cross the continent from the Gulf of Mexico to the Gulf of California. He came to the Province of New Mexico in the early part of the eighteenth century, with his father, Juan Antonio Cabeza de Vaca. His is the first of the name of Cabeza de Baca to appear in the archives of New Mexico. He was one of the most notable men of his time. In his petition for lands at the *Vegas Grandes*, the present location of the city of Las Vegas, he recites that he makes the request for himself and his *seventeen male children*. He died at Peña Blanca, New Mexico, in 1833. A friend and neighbor, José Francisco Salas, who was present at his death and burial, states that he was killed by a soldier in the Mexican army on account of his having some contraband property in his possession, belonging to an American and which he refused to deliver to the soldier. Mr. Salas, in 1858, testified that he knew Luis Baca, Prudencio Baca, Jesus Baca, Sr., Felipe Baca, Jesus Baca, Jr., Domingo Baca, and Manuel Baca, who were then living and that he had known Juan Antonio Baca, José Baca, José Miguel Baca, Ramon Baca, and Mateo Baca, all of whom were dead.

Don Luis lived at the Vegas Grandes for a period of ten years, in a hut at the place known as the *Loma Montosa*. He was finally driven off by incessant raids of the

Pawnee, Kiowa, and Cumanche Indians. Don Tomas C. de Baca, son of Juan Antonio C. de Baca, was a very prominent man in New Mexico during his career. He left several children, among the rest Don Marcos C. de Baca, several times a member of the New Mexican Legislative Assembly, and a candidate for Congress in 1912. Don Domingo C. de Baca, son of Don Luis Maria, was believed to be connected with the conspiracy against the American officers at Santa Fe, in 1846-7.

A complete list of the children of this notable New Mexican appears elsewhere in this work.

1288 SANTA FE. 1822.
Tract of land next to the house of the *Cura*.

1289 JUAN RAFAEL ORTIZ, *Santa Fe*.
Question of debt. Facundo Melgares, Governor.

1290 AYUNTAMIENTO of *El Paso del Rio del Norte* in regard to the extent of its jurisdiction.
Don Juan Maria Ponze de Leon was secretary of the Ayuntamiento of Paso del Norte.

1291 PROVINCIAL DEPUTATION, 1822-1825.
Inventory of documents in the archives. No. 1258.

In the *Journal* of the Provincial Deputation are many items of interest relative to the lands of the Pueblo Indians, the efforts of people to secure title to some of them, and the disposition of the Mexican authorities is reflected by these entries.

These orders and decisions are as follows:
February 16, 1824. Leaf 86, page 2.

Three petitions, by eighteen different persons, asking for unoccupied agricultural lands belonging to the Indians of Santo Domingo and San Felipe, were taken up for discussion.

It was resolved to appoint Don José Francisco Ortiz to examine the lands, ascertain their extent and also to give the natives to understand that the Deputation could dispose of those lands. The right to decrease the number of applicants was reserved for further discussion.
March 12, 1824. Leaf 88, page 2.

Don José Francisco Ortiz reported that he had examined the surplus land at the pueblos of Santo Domingo and San Felipe, which was three-fourths of a league in extent, and the natives stated that it had been given to them for the pasturing of their animals.

It was decided that the *jefe politico* (governor) should go to the pueblos in question, in company with Ortiz and such other persons as he saw fit to take and should partition to the two pueblos the land which they had held in common up to that time, in order that each might dispose of what belonged to it, with the same liberty as other citizens. The surplus lands were then to be disposed of.

February 16, 1825. Leaf 41, page 2.

There was taken up for consideration a petition by Miguel Rivera and others, in regard to lands on the Pecos river which had been partitioned to them by the alcalde of El Bado (Vado) by order of the *jefe politico* and from which they had been subsequently ejected.

It was decided that the parties must be governed by the decision of the Deputation of February 16, 1824.

In discussing this matter the question was raised whether the Pecos Indians could sell their lands or prevent the Deputation from making donations of those lands which they claimed to own but were not cultivating.

Reference is made to such donations having been rejected in accordance with section 5 of the law of November 9, 1812.

July 19, 1825. Leaf 55, page 2.

A petition from various persons who asked for the surplus lands of the Nambé Indians, was referred to the town council of La Cañada (*Santa Cruz de la Cañada*) for report.

September 15, 1825. Leaf 63, page 1.

On the petition of Juan Diego Sena, asking for the granting of the surplus lands of the San Juan Indians, it was decided not to consider this and similar petitions, until the decision of the Federal government, as to a general rule to be observed in such cases, should be obtained.

The San Juan Indians are referred to in this entry as "Citizens."

November 17, 1825. Leaf 70, page 2.

After considering a petition of the Pecos Indians, asking that they be declared to be the owners of one league of land on each course, which amount of land had been considered to belong to each pueblo of the Territory, it was decided to refer the matter to the Federal government for interpretation of section 5, of the law of November 9, 1812.

July 18, 1827. Leaf 152, page 1.

Two petitions of the Laguna Indians were presented to the Deputation; one relative to the interference of the Acoma Indians with the water rights of the petitioners; the other in regard to the attempt of the people of Cebolleta to deprive the Lagunas of the Paguate ranch, which they claimed by purchase.

The Lagunas also asked for a new grant to the Paguate ranch.

June 25, 1827. Leaf 159, page 1.

Two complaints of the Laguna Indians, presented to the Deputation on June 18, 1827, relative to the water rights dispute with the Indians of Acoma and the dispute with the people of Cebolleta as to the Paguate ranch, were transmitted to the *jefe politico* for his action thereon.

June 27, 1827. Leaf 159, page 2.

A memorial and deeds of Don Francisco Ortiz, relative to lands which he had bought of the Indians of San Ildefonzo, were referred for report to a committee composed of Antonio Ortiz, Francisco Baca y Ortiz, and Pedro Ygnacio Gallego.

February 9, 1829. Leaf 22, page 2.

A petition by Rafael Sanchez and others, asking for lands at San José, near the pueblo of Acoma, was taken up for discussion; it was decided that the constitutional alcalde of Laguna should investigate whether any person had acquired property rights there and whether the water with which the land was to be irrigated was independent of that used for similar purposes by the Indians of Laguna and Acoma.

If such was found to be the case, and there was no obstacle, the parties were to be put in possession.

January 8, 1831. Leaf 56, page 1.

An application of Juan Garcia of Alburquerque for a tract of land at Cubero was referred to the constitutional council of Laguna, with instructions as to points to be covered in their report.

April 14, 1831. Leaf 63, page 1.

A petition of Agustin Duran and others for a tract of land about 3,000 varas in extent between the pueblos of Santo Domingo and San Felipe, was referred to the councils of Cochiti and Sandia for report.

November 12, 1831. Leaf 69, page 1.

A petition of Juan Cristobal Muñiz, a citizen of Jémez,

for some farming land at Vallecito and near the Jémes pueblo, was referred to the council of Jémez.
November 12, 1831. Leaf 69, page 1.
The report of the council of Cochiti on the petition of Agustin Duran and others for lands between Santo Domingo and San Felipe was considered; after which the matter was ordered transmitted for report to the council of Sandia, that being the jurisdiction of San Felipe.
July 16, 1832. Leaf 74, page 2.
Complaint of the Jemez Indians relative to the damages they were suffering as to their common lands, was referred to the council of Jemez for further information.
July 18, 1832. Leaf 76, page 2.
Petition of Antonio Sandobal, asking for pasture land from the Ojo Hediondo as far as the Cañoncito del Cojo. Referred to the council of Laguna.

1292 INDIANS of the Pueblo of *Taos* and the People of *Arroyo Seco.* 1823. Water rights.

Report of the *Ayuntamiento*.

Report of the *ayuntamiento* (town council) of Taos, dated December 30, 1823, to the *jefe politico,* in regard to a suit pending between the residents of Arroyo Seco and the Indians of the pueblo of Taos, as to water rights in the Lucero river.

The *ayuntamiento* states that the Arroyo Seco people acquired their rights to their lands under a grant made by Joaquin Codallos y Rabal, dated October 7, 1745, but the land had not been used until 1815, when they began to build houses, and cultivate their lands, which they irrigated from the Arroyo Seco and also from the Lucero river; that the Indians, in addition to using the waters of the river which ran through their pueblo also used and had always used the water of the Lucero river for irrigating their lands; that moreover they had acquired a new right in the latter stream by having purchased from the descendants of Antonio Martin, the legal owner of the land granted from the league of their pueblo, to the Arroyo Seco, etc.

The general tone of the report is favorable to the priority of the right of the Indians.

There is a crude sketch map with this report, showing the lands purchased by the Indians, the pueblo, the town of Don Fernando, and the streams in that neighborhood.

This archive, I understand, has been translated and used in a suit in which the Indians of Taos are now (1913)

THE SPANISH ARCHIVES OF NEW MEXICO 381

involved with persons claiming under the Antonio Martinez grant.

1293 PETITION of Francisco Xavier Ortiz and three others for lands near *San Ildefonso*. No action.

Petition by Francisco Xavier Ortiz and his three sons, to the jefe politico, for a piece of land for each adjoining the lands of the pueblo of San Ildefonso. The date is February 19, 1824.

The parties ask the jefe politico to forward the petition with a report, if necessary, to the Provincial Deputation.

There is no further action.

1294 LA CIENEGA DE LOS GARCIAS. 1825.

Piece of a letter in regard to the partition of the same.

1295 ALAMEDA TRACT. 1825.

Report of measurement of the same by Perea. Report made to Bartolomé Baca, political chief.

Letter of June 13, 1825, from a certain Perea, at Bernailillo, to the jefe politico, Bartolomé Baca, reporting that he had complied with the latter's order to measure the Alameda Tract from the boundary of the natives of the pueblo of Sandia to the Alburquerque line.

One statement in this letter indicates that the land immediately adjoining the Indians' land (on the south) belonged to Don Eusebio Rael.

1296 JOSE IGNACIO MADRID and Mariano Baldes and Others.

Letter to José Manuel Salazar in the matter of the partition of their lands on the *Rio Chama*. 1826.

1297 CORPORATION OF SANTA FE. 1826.

Record of the proceedings in a suit about lands at Arroyo Seco, near the pueblo of Taos. The petition is addressed to Don Antonio Narbona, governor and political chief. The signatures are those of Juan de Dios Peña, war-captain and chief alcalde; Mariano Peña, Salvador Padilla, José Ma. Ortiz; Juan Domingo Fernandez; Francisco Lobato; Francisco Sanchez; Rafael Antonio de Luna; Pedro Martin; Matias Martin; Juan Antonio Martin; José Miguel Aragon; Mariano Sanchez; José Gonzales.

Bartolomé Baca also appears in the proceeding in June, 1825.

This is a controversy begun in the year 1825, between Felipe Gonzalez and Carpio Cordoba, as complainants, and José Antonio Sanchez and Diego Antonio Sanchez, defendants, in regard to some lands at Arroyo Seco, near Taos.

The manuscript is nearly 40 pages in extent, but it is not necessary to make a full brief of its contents, as the most of it is not of importance to the Indians of Taos.

It appears from these papers that in the year 1816 Manuel and Matias Martin, citizens of Abiquiú, petitioned Don Pedro Martin, chief alcalde of Taos, to restore to them certain lands of which they had been illegally deprived.

They state that it had come to their knowledge that their grandfather, Don Antonio Martin, had had a grant made to him by the king at the Rinconada del Rio de Lucero, and that having been advised to seek for the granting documents at the pueblo of Taos, they discovered that the grant had been sold to the natives of that pueblo by Joaquin Sanches, who had hid said grant from their father, who was the lawful heir to it. They allege that the said Joaquin Sanches was not an heir of their grandfather, and they denounce the sale made by him as being illegal and depriving them and their children of their lawful rights.

The petition of Manuel and Matias was presented to the alcalde, as above stated, and he directed, by his official order of April 26, 1816, that one of the interested parties should take it to the governor of the Province, in order that he should take such action as he saw fit.

That officer, on May 7, 1816, ordered the alcalde to investigate whether the petitioners were lawful heirs, and whether Joaquin Sanchez had usurped their lands.

This the alcalde did, and on May 30, 1816, he made his report to the governor. That part of his report which is most important to the Taos Indians relates to the genealogy of these Martins. The alcalde's investigation revealed the fact that the grandfather of the petitioners, Antonio Martin, had by his own niece, Isabel Pacheco, an illegitimate child, who was named Diego Rafael, and who became the father of Manuel and Matias Martin, the petitioners in the matter now under consideration; that subsequent to the birth of her illegitimate son, Isabel Pacheco married Francisco Sanchez, by whom she had four children, Joaquin, Joseph, Francisco, and Mariano; that Antonio Martin gave a tract of land, which he had by grant from the king, to Isabel and her sister Francisca, by whom also he had had a child, which apparently did not survive the mother; that neither Antonio Martin nor Isabel Pacheco made any will; that Joaquin and José Sanchez, two of the legitimate children of Isabel, sold the land in opposition to the wishes of their brothers, Francisco and Mariano, and their half-brother, Diego Rafael; that some years prior to the date of the alcalde's report, Francisco and Mariano had taken some legal steps, apparently to assert their own rights, but entirely ignoring the rights of their half brother, Diego Rafael; that ultimately Francisco and Mariano decided to compromise the whole matter in order to avoid being involved in law suits; that with that object in view they acknowledged the petitioners, Manuel and Matias Martin (the children of Diego Rafael), as their nephews; that they requested the alcalde to divide the ranch in halves, through the center.

The alcalde then proceeds to describe the measurement which he made of the ranch, and the manner in which it was divided in accordance with the voluntary compromise.

On June 3, 1816, Governor Allande approved the partition of the land.

Another paper in the case indicates that when the Indians of Taos became satisfied that the sale made to them by Joaquin Sanchez was not legal, they gave up the land in consideration of one hundred pesos and an ox, which was given to them by Don Felipe Gonzalez.

This paper is dated at Taos on May 13, 1816.

The original controversy of Felipe Gonzalez and Carpio Cordoba with José Antonio and Diego Antonio Sanchez, of which the papers above described form a part, was apparently decided in favor of Diego Antonio Sanchez, by Governor Antonio Narbona, on May 23, 1826.

1298 JULIAN RAEL vs. Indians of *Sandia*. 1827.

Opinion of Ignacio Maria Sanchez Vergara, Alcalde.

Letter of July 7, 1827, from Ignacio Maria Sanchez Vergara to Manuel Armijo, jefe politico of New Mexico, transmitting an *expediente* of a suit in regard to lands between Don Julian Rael and the Indians of the pueblo of Sandia.

He sets forth at length his opinion in regard to the matter, which was strongly in favor of Rael's contention and which strongly intimated that the Indians were not acting in good faith.

It is possible that Sanchez was personally interested in

the matter, as he requests the return to him of certain documents; and following his signature to the letter is an acknowledgment, also signed by him, of the return of all his documents, at Sandia, August 17, 1827.

One of the statements made by Sanchez seems to indicate that the title under which Rael was claiming had its inception as far back as the time of the Marquis of Penuela, who was governor of the province about 1707 to 1712. This would be many years prior to the grant made to the pueblo of Sandia, the date of which was 1748.

Letter of November 10, 1829, from the office of the minister of justice to the jefe politico of New Mexico, acknowledging the receipt of the copy of the legal proceedings in regard to the restitution of lands to the citizens (*vecinos*) of the pueblo of Sandia. The expediente was forwarded with the jefe politico's letter of October 30, 1829 (?).

A marginal note shows that the alcalde of Sandia was notified of the receipt of this letter of November 10, on December 25, 1829.

1299 PUEBLO OF SANDIA. 1829.
Receipt from the office of the Minister of Justice of the proceedings in the matter of the restitution of lands.

1300 DRAFT OF A REPORT of a Committee of the Territorial Deputation in the matter of granting the *Gotera Tract* to José Guadalupe Romero and Manuel Bustamante.

1301 JUAN CRUZ BACA. *Sabinal,* 1831.
Complains to José Antonio Chaves, political chief, that Ramon Torres, alcalde of *Sabinal,* has taken the lands from the heirs of Geronimo Chaves and given them to his brother.

1302 GERONIMO CHAVES, Heirs of, vs. Roman Torres. *Sabinal,* 1831. No. 1301, *q. v.*

1303 JUAN JOSE LUJAN. 1832.
Lease to Harvey Ellison and Wyatt; land for a tannery. Juan Garcia, Alcalde.

1304 PEDRO MOLINA. 1832.
Letter to the *jefe politico* in regard to sale of lands by Francisco Baca in Encinal and Cubero.

Don Pedro de Castro Figueroa
Duke of the Conquista, Viceroy of Mexico 1740-41

He states that the lands had been purchased and the price paid therefor, which he enumerates in sheep, horses, a cow, etc., with which Baca was satisfied; that the citizens who had purchased them were ready to go to work and were only waiting for the lands to be partitioned among them, etc.

It is likely that the Francisco Baca referred to in this letter was the Navajo Indian whose rights at Cubero were purchased by Mexican citizens prior to the establishment of their town.

1305 MARIANO SANCHEZ. 1833.
Petition that the tract — *Agua Sarca* — formerly granted to Sebastian Martin, his great-grandfather, be partitioned among twenty-five persons.

1306 DECREE of Mexican Congress forbidding the sale of property held in mortmain until further legislation on the subject. 1833.

1307 DECREE of Mexican Congress correcting typographical error. 1834.

1308 VICENTE OTERO. 1834.
Letter to the political chief, Francisco Sarracino, in Valencia, March 9, 1834:

"Most Excellent Sir: Manuel Sanchez, for himself and in the name of nineteen individuals, all residents of Valencia, represents to your excellency that having discovered a tract of land suitable for cultivation at the point of Tajique, which is vacant, and consequently will not be to the injury of any third party, on the contrary, the condition of the petitioners will be bettered on account of the limited amount of land which they can now cultivate, and that your excellency, in compliance with the law which recommends the encouragement of agriculture, be pleased to direct that the above-mentioned land, containing one-half of a league in circumference, be donated to them, protesting to pay all costs in good faith, etc.
"Manuel Sanchez"
"Santa Fe, March 17, 1834.
"The constitutional justice of Valencia, to which jurisdiction Tajique belongs, as I am informed, will make the division asked for, within the boundaries they set forth, provided no injury will result to any third party, the

grant temporarily made by the government, to avoid delay in planting their crops, being subject to the confirmation of the most excellent deputation when it shall meet.

"SARRACINO."

"At this point of Tajique, on the ninth day of April, one thousand eight hundred and thirty-four, in compliance with the provisional order of the political chief to place the parties in possession, in order that the individuals who asked for a grant to said land, containing one-half league in circumference, should not lose their crops, I, Citizen Vicente Otero, constitutional justice of the township of Valencia, proceeded to the place for that purpose, with two attending witnesses, which said office is entitled to, commencing by measuring the one-half league in circumference, having in the first place set aside one hundred and seventy-two varas in the most convenient place for a town site, and from the center thereof the one-half league in the direction of the four cardinal points of the compass was measured in the following manner: the first towards the south, which reached to a thick cedar a little above the cañon called '*De los Pinos*;' the second towards the north, to the cañon *De Las Migas,* where a pine tree was marked with a cross; the third towards the west, to the little table lands of the Cueva, where another pine tree was marked with a cross; the fourth towards the east to the lone pine, said measurements having been made in the presence of twelve of the grantees. The subdivision of the arable land to which each one was entitled to was omitted, on account of the absence of seven of those contained in the granting act, directing the persons present to commence planting their crops, with the understanding that when the proper time arrived I would return to subdivide the land, informing them that no one acquired any right to the land he cultivated excepting those to whom it should fall by lot, with the condition that whosoever received the land which was broken up should break up a like quantity for the first occupant; and for the purpose of placing this on record and other proper objects, I, the aforesaid justice, signed this document, with my attending witnesses, to which I certify. VICENTE OTERO.

"Attending:
  "JACINTO SANCHEZ.
  "JOSE MANUEL MALDONADO.

"At this place of Tajique, on the twenty-fourth day of December, one thousand eight hundred and thirty-four, I, Citizen Vicente Otero, constitutional justice of the jurisdiction of Valencia, in fulfillment of the foregoing document, and in the presence of my attending witnesses, I caused to appear before me the persons to whom this place was granted, who, being present, I informed them of the operation to be performed, as set forth in the foregoing document, and they willingly consented to receive whatever tillable land each one was justly entitled to; whereupon, the calculation being made, I commenced measuring from west to east one hundred and twelve varas to each one; leaving out, in the first place, twelve varas as outlets to the town, having placed them in possession in the following order: 1st. Measured to Maria Gertrudis Chaves, who is bounded by the lands of Antonio Otero. 2d. Antonio Otero, who is bounded by the lands of Maria Gertrudis Chaves and those of Manuel Garcia. 3d. Manuel Garcia, who is bounded by Antonio Otero and José Lorenzo Otero. 4th. José Lorenzo Otero, bounded by Manuel Garcia and Matias Sanches. 5th. Matias Sanchez, bounded by José Lorenzo Otero and José Antonio Zamora. 6th. José Antonio Zamora, bounded by Matias Sanchez and Rafael Sanchez. 7th. Rafael Sanchez, bounded by José Antonio Zamora and Francisco Moya. 8th. Francisco Moya, bounded by Rafael Sanchez and José Maria Maldonado. 9th. José Maria Maldonado, bounded by Francisco Moya and Cristobal Zamora. 10th. Cristobal Zamora, bounded by Jose Maria Maldonado and Lazaro Ramirez. 11th. Lazaro Ramirez, bounded by Cristobal Zamora and Mateo Anaya. 12th. Mateo Anaya, bounded by Lazaro Ramirez and Ignacio Cedillo. 13th. Ignacio Cedillo, bounded by Mateo Anaya and Roman Zamora. 14th. Roman Zamora, bounded by Ignacio Cedillo and Domingo Zamora. 15th. Domingo Zamora, bounded by Roman Zamora and José Chavez. 16th. José Chavez, bounded by Domingo Zamora and Antonio Sanchez. 17th. Antonio Sanchez, bounded by José Chavez; José Sanchez to the west of the temple; Dionisio Vigil to the west of the temple; giving to all the privilege of breaking up such land as they may want, on a line with their own, without going beyond the half league granted to them; it being understood that those having received land which has been broken up by others, within their lot, shall break up an equal quantity for the person entitled to it on unbroken land, by the month of April, 1835; and if said condition is not complied with, they will continue using the land they have broken up originally until other land is broken for them. All having expressed their satisfac-

tion at this and all other matters connected with the division of the land, and in order that they, their heirs and successors, may enjoy the same peaceably and quietly, and in order that they may barter their land or dispose of it to whomsoever they may see proper at the expiration of the period prescribed by law for such grants, I, the aforesaid justice, said I would authorize this document, as I did authorize it, in due form of law, and by virtue of the powers in me vested, signing with those in my attendance, to which I certify. VICENTE OTERO.
"Attending:
"JOSE ANTONIO MALDONADO."

Don Vicente Otero, mentioned in the foregoing archive, was the grandfather of Miguel A. Otero, governor of New Mexico during the McKinley and Roosevelt administrations. His father, Don Miguel A. Otero, 10, was delegate in Congress in the 'fifties. Tajique is the site of an old pueblo, destroyed by the Apaches in the middle of the seventeenth century.

1309 DRAFT of a Letter to the Alcalde of *El Bado* in relation to action taken by the Territorial Deputation in the matter of the petition of Juan de Dios Maese, et al., for a grant of lands at *Las Vegas*. 1835.

1310 JOSE FRANCISCO CHAVES Y BACA. 1835.
Letter to political chief in regard to lands sold by a Navajó Indian, which lands belonged to the Indians of *Laguna*.

Letter of May 26, 1835, written at Laguna, by José Francisco Chaves y Baca, constitutional alcalde of that district, to the *jefe politico*, in regard to a controversy between the natives of Laguna and the parties who had purchased land from the Navajó Indian, Francisco Baca.

He states that Baca had deeded the land to the purchasers, the deed being acknowledged before Don Manuel Gallego, the retiring alcalde; that he had summoned the latter before him and had asked him what reasons he had had for including in the deed lands which belonged to the Indians; that Gallego had answered that at the time in question there was no one to inform him that the property of the complainants was included in the deed; that he was governed by the boundaries which Baca pointed out to him in company with Don Juan Dionicio Chaves, the attorney in fact for the purchasers; that he had no means of knowing whether the statements made in the deed by the Indian were true.

This letter was evidently a letter of transmittal of documents which the Laguna Indians had laid before the alcalde in connection with their attempt to recover lands which they claimed and which had been sold by the Navajó to the people of Cubero, and although it does not reveal the contents of those documents, it shows that the alcalde took the side of the Indians as against the Cubero people and their grantor, Francisco Baca.

1311 SANTA FE. 1835.
> In the matter of a reservoir. Francisco Trujillo, Juan José Lujan, Simon Apodaca, members of the *Ayuntamiento*.

1312 ALBINO PEREZ, Governor. 1835.
> Receipt of official letter.

1313 SANTA FE. 1835-6.
> Destruction of a reservoir maintained by Miguel Sena.

1314 SANTA FE. 1836.
> Names of property owners in the city. Juan Bautista Vigil y Alarid.

1315 JUAN DE DIOS MAESE. *San Miguel del Bado*. 1836.
> Petition to political chief that he take some steps toward compelling the grantees in the *Las Vegas* Grant to take possession of their lands.

1316 PROTOCOL of Manuel Doroteo Pino, First Constitutional Alcalde of *Santa Fe*. 1838.
> Lorenzo Balizan to Lorenzo Provencio. Land at *El Paso*, 1838.
> Ignacio Duran to Gaspar Rivera. Land in *Santa Fe*, 1838.
> Tomas Valencia to Antonio Matias Ortiz. Mortgage. Lands in *Santa Fe*, 1838.
> José Serafin Martin for his father, Antonio Martin, to Juan Rafael Ortiz. House and land in *San José de La Cienega*, 1838.
> Mariano Mares to Blas Ortega. Land in *Santa Fe*. 1838.
> Eusebio Garcia, for his wife, Luciana Martin, to Miguel Tafoya. House and land on the *Rio de Santa Fe*. 1838.

Felipe Coris to Esmeregildo Ortiz. Land in *Santa Fe*, 1838.

Getrudis Sandoval. Partition of her estate. 1838.

1317 MANUEL ARMIJO, Governor.
Book 2d of rough draft of decrees, 1840-1842.

1318 CORNELIO VIGIL. 1842. Juez de Paz.
Transmitting to Guadalupe Miranda, secretary of the government, *expediente* of land suit between the people of *Don Fernando de Taos* and those of *San Francisco del Rancho*.

The Don Fernando de Taos Grant, R. No. 125, was confirmed by the court of private land claims and under a survey pursuant to the decree, the area is found to be more than 1,817 acres. The north boundary of this property is the southern boundary of the Taos Pueblo Grant. Patented, February 25, 1909.

1319 PABLO MONTOYA, deceased. 1842.
Draft of a letter to the governor in regard to the disposition of his property.

1320 VICENTE RIBERA, Juez de Paz, to Guadalupe Miranda, Secretary, 1842.
Announcing that he has placed certain parties in possession of lands at the junction of the *Gallinas* and *Pecos* rivers, and asking whether there shall be given lands to others who may need them. Draft of an affirmative reply on the same paper.

1321 LA CIENEGA of *Santa Fe*. 1844.

1322 MARIANO MARTINEZ, Governor, 1844.
To the president of the Departmental Assembly. Transmitting petition of certain citizens for lands at *Sapello* and *Mora*.

1323 SANTA FE. 1845.
Petition of the first and second alcaldes on behalf of the city, to the governor, for a tract of land. No action.

1324 AGAPITO, NAZARIO, and RICARDO ORTIZ. 1845.
Claim to a house in *Santa Fe*, as heirs of their mother, Maria Rosa Mestas, which had been sold without their consent, by their father, Casimiro Ortiz. Teodoro Gonzales, Juez de Paz. *San Ildefonzo*.

THE SPANISH ARCHIVES OF NEW MEXICO 391

1325 SANDIA Grant. 1846.

Letter of Manuel Armijo, directing Juan Bautista Vigil to send the papers to him. Vigil's letter of transmittal.

A marginal note, signed by the rubric of Vigil, shows that the grant was delivered to Don Tomas Ortiz, on March 20, 1846, which is corroborated by Vigil's letter of that date to Governor Armijo, forming a part of the same archive.

1326 MANUEL DELGADO and JUAN PINO. No date.

Fragment of a document in relation to a controversy as to water rights at the *ranchos* of *Juana Lopez* and *Los Cerrillos*.

1327 COMMUNICATION (3), rough draft, in relation to stationing soldiers at some point in the valley of the Rio Grande.

These are addressed to the viceroy, the Duke of Alburquerque. The apostasy of the Moquis is mentioned.

1328 TESTIMONIO of letter and report relative to an attack made upon the Pueblo of Pecos by the Cumanches, the presence of a hundred lodges of these Indians on the Rio Jicarilla, and the selling of firearms to them by the French, and the proposed construction of a Presidio at the place called "Jicarilla."

The date is 1748; the archive contains 14 pages and bears the signature of Governor and Captain-General Joachin Codallos y Rabal. The fact that a Frenchman named Luis Maria and eight others had been at Taos in 1742 is mentioned; that Luis Maria had been "*apeloleado*" in the plaza at Santa Fe under an order from the superior government of New Spain; that in 1744 a Frenchman, named Santiago Velo, had come to the pueblo of Pecos. The Villasur expedition of 1720 is also mentioned. The names of Fr. Joseph Urquijo, Fr. Juan Miguel Menchero, Fr. Lorenzo and Antonio Duran de Armijo also occur. In addition to the signature of Governor Joachin Codallos y Rabal, those of Phelipe Jacobo de Unanue, J. Miguel de Alire, with rubrics, also appear.

1329 LETTER from the Department of the Interior to the Political Chief of New Mexico, enjoining great caution in the matter of permitting colonists from

392 THE SPANISH ARCHIVES OF NEW MEXICO

the United States of North America to enter. *Mexico*, November 21, 1828. It was received at *Santa Fe*, N. M., January 14, 1829, and answered.

1330 LETTER, *Mexico*, February 12, 1825, from Rafael Mangino to the Commissary-General of Santa Fe, relative to arms for light infantry.

1331 LETTER from General Antonio Lopez de Santa Anna; *Merida*, April 23, 1825, to the Governor of New Mexico, announcing his resignation of the office of Commandant-General of the Free State of Yucatan. Rough draft of letter in reply.

1332 CIRCULAR from the office of the Minister of the Interior, requesting the Governor of New Mexico to furnish information relative to lands suitable for colonization purposes. *Mexico*, September 10, 1838, 1 folio.

1333 LETTER from Don Jacobo Ugarte y Loyola to Governor Don Juan Bautista de Anza in relation to the proper manner of obtaining and retaining the friendship of the Indian tribes. Chihuahua, October 9, 1786.

> There is also a certified copy of an opinion of the asesor, Galindo Navarro, on the same subject, dated September 4, 1786. The letter is only a fragment, and the handwriting is the same in each. The *"Dictamen"* refers to the *bandos* of former governors, mentioning them by name, upon the same subject.
> Fr. Sebastian Antonio of Santa Cruz de la Cañada is also mentioned.
> Relative to obtaining and retaining the friendship of the Indian tribes.

1334 ROYAL DECREE. Cadiz, March 24, 1811, granting to Spanish Americans and Indians perfect equality in political rights with European Spaniards.

> A copy. Chihuahua, October 21, 1811; ordered published in all cities, towns, etc., of the provinces under his charge,

and signed by the commandant-general, Don Nemecio Salcedo. In the lower corner of the last page is found the signature of Don José Maria Ponze de Leon, at that time an officer of the ayuntamiento of Paso del Norte.

1335 PROCLAMATIONS (3) from the Regency to Spaniards, two of them specially directed to Spanish-Americans, in relation to aiding in the prosecution of the war then in progress against the Emperor Napoleon.

The first is dated Cadiz, January 31, 1812, and is signed by Ignacio de la Pezuela, who refers to the war as being for the preservation of the religion, honor, property, and liberty of the Spanish nation. In describing Napoleon he says: *"Estaba reservado al moderno Atila sobrepujar mucho al antiguo en enganos, en ferocidad, en una crueldad calculada, y en el arte infernal de amaestrar en sus perfidias y en sus furores a sus Marescales, a sus Geberales y a todos los demas satelites de su refinada tirania. El ha encendido la guerra en todo el contenente de Europa, el lo ha devastado, lo had empobrecido, y lo quiere hacer volver a la barbarie de los siglos obscuros para dexar asi establicido su cetro de hierro."*

The second, also from Cadiz, dated January 23, 1812, and signed by Don Joachin de Mosquera y Figueroa, is addressed to *"Americanos,"* and concludes with an appeal as follows:

"Lejos de vosotros, O Americanos! tan funesto presagio. Renazcan las dulces ideas de fraternidad y de union que han labrado nuestra comun felicidad durante trescinetos años. Unamos nuestros esfuerzos para sacudir el y go ignominioso que pretenden imponernos nuestros invasores y arrastremos impávidos los obstáculos que puedan presentársenos en la escabrosa senda en que nos vemos empeñados! escabrosa por cierto, pero que debe conducirnos a la inmortalidad."

The third is signed by Ignacio de la Pezuela and is dated Cadiz, January 31, 1812.

1336 LETTER; rough draft; no date; relative to education of the Indians. No signature.

1337 DECREE of the Mexican Congress abolishing titles of nobility, such as *Cónde, Marqués, Caballero,* and "*todos los de igual naturaleza, cualquiera que sea su origen.*" Mexico, May 2, 1826.

(Signed) GUADALUPE VICTORIA
SEBASTIAN CAMANCHO

Published at *Santa Fe*, June 16, 1826, by the governor, Don Antonio Narbona.

1338 ROYAL DECREE.
Appointment of Don Domingo de Cruzate as governor and captain-general of New Mexico. Instructions for the reëstablishment of towns, location of Indians, etc. Grants to the Pueblo tribes authorized. Dated 1684.

1339 PETITION relative to lands of the Pueblo of San Ildefonso. September 18, 1704.
Petition by Captain Alfonso Rael de Aguilar, protector of Indians, on behalf of those of the pueblo of San Ildefonso, complaining that Captain Ignacio de Roybal had acquired by grant all the lands on the other side (the western side) of the Del Norte river opposite the pueblo of San Ildefonso, in violation of the royal ordinances and to the detriment of the Indians, to whom said lands had belonged from ancient times and on which they had squashes and melons planted at the time of making the complaint. Captain Rael requests the governor to make Roybal present his instrument of title for examination, and to give to the Indians the four leagues of land to which they were entitled, and compel Roybal to confine himself to the lands which he had at the pueblo of Jacona and at Santa Fe and other places.

This petition was presented to Acting Governor Juan Paez Hurtado on September 18, 1704, and he immediately ordered Roybal to produce his grant for examination.

This order was served on Roybal on the same day, and the following day he appeared at Santa Fe with his grant, a copy of which is attached to the proceedings.

This grant was made by the Marquis de la Nava de Brazinas (Diego de Vargas) on March 4, 1704.

In the petition for the grant, Roybal had stated that he wanted the lands "for a large and small stock and a horse herd," which practically made it nothing more than a request for a pasturage permit. He described the lands as lying between the lands of the pueblo of Santa Clara and the Caja del Rio (the Caja del Rio is the box cañon below San Ildefonso, sometimes called the Whiterock Canyon), and the Rio Grande on the east, and the mountain on the west.

The governor, in making the grant, called attention to the fact that Mateo Trujillo had a grant extending from the boundary of Santa Clara down to a place where he (the governor) had halted with his camp; that from that point Roybal's grant should extend toward the Caja del Rio.

There was no act of possession following the grant.

On the same day on which he presented his grant for examination, Roybal filed an answer to the petition of Rael, in which answer he denies that his grant interferes with the Indians. He says that he has never prevented their pasturing their stock and horses on the land, but he denies that they have ever cultivated any portion of it.

The acting governor, on September 19, 1704, ordered Antonio de Aguilera Ysasi, in company with Captain Cristobal de Arellano and two attending witnesses, to examine the land and see whether the Indians had ever had on the other side of the river cultivated lands and an irrigating ditch.

On September 22, 1704, Aguilera and others went to the land in question and about three-fourths of a league from the pueblo he found what was apparently a ditch which came out of the river, and some land which appeared to have been cultivated. The Indians stopped at that point and told him that at that place, where some evidences of a monument were discovered, the first Spaniards had designated to them their boundary, before the revolution of 1680.

Aguilera reported his examination to the acting governor, and the latter, on September 25, 1704, ordered Captain Cristobal de Arellano, chief alcalde of the district, to measure one league in each direction (from the pueblo?) and designate monuments for the Indians; that the grant of Roybal should be understood to extend onward from said monuments; that if the measurements to be made by the alcalde should include any of the cultivated lands held by Matias Madrid, said measurements should be understood as effective only from the pueblo as far as Madrid's boundaries; and if the parties were not satisfied with this decision they might appeal to the new governor, who was soon to take charge, or they might appeal to the viceroy.

On September 28, 1704, the governor of the pueblo of

San Ildefonso, Matias Cuntzi, and other officers of the pueblo, presented a statement by their protector, Rael, setting forth that they had occupied the lands in dispute before the Spaniards abandoned the kingdom (in 1680), as could be shown by the evidence of an old Spaniard named Domingo Martin, who knew that Father Antonio de Sotomayor, formerly minister of the pueblo, had planted them; and that Father Felipe Rodriguez, another minister of the pueblo, and Father Francisco de Sandoval also had planted them, and during a time of great famine had compelled the Indians to plant there in order to have food for their subsistence; that they had determined to plant the same lands in the coming year, when they discovered that Roybal had received a grant covering the lands.

They further stated that their old monument could be found a little beyond a place where they had built a house and a tower, and that evidences of their former ditch and cultivated lands could still be seen, although they were dim, as the lands had not been cultivated for ten years. They ask that they be given the customary measurements and that monuments be erected to mark their boundaries.

The acting governor made an indorsement on this statement, to the effect that he had already taken the steps necessary in the matter, and ordered it to be attached to the other proceedings in the case.

On October 9, 1704, the alcalde, Cristobal de Arellano, in compliance with the orders of September 25, went to San Ildefonso to make the measurement of the league. He notified Roybal of the governor's order in the premises in order that Roybal might be present, but the latter declined to come. Arellano then measured one league to the north, half a league to the south, half a league to the west, and another half league on the east. His reasons for not completing the full league in three of his measurements are so badly expressed as to make his meaning very doubtful. I am inclined to think that he meant to say that the measurements in question included only the cultivable land, and that the rest of it was of no value, except for fuel. However, I am not perfectly certain what he meant. The one thing that is perfectly clear is the distance measured toward each of the cardinal points.

The document ends in this way, without any approval of the measurements by the acting governor.

1340 ORDER, August 25, 1705, by Governor Francisco Cuervo y Valdez.
> Prohibiting all Spanish citizens from residing in Indian pueblos, or even entering them without express permission from the governor, and commanding any citizens who were then living in the pueblos to leave them, and to remove therefrom all their property.
> This order was made public at the pueblo of Taos on August 28, 1705, by Felix Martinez, chief alcalde of that district.

1341 TESTIMONIO of an Order of Don Ignacio Flores Mogollon, Governor and Captain-General, giving directions to General Antonio Valverde, El Paso, to locate the Sumas Indians, dated November 10, 1712.
> This archive has a magnificent signature of Captain Roque de Pintto, the secretary of government and war.
> The *Sumas* Indians to be located in pueblos.

1342 ORDER, by the Viceroy of New Spain, October 22, 1704, directing his compliance with a decree of the King relative to the giving of lands to Indians, preventing their being compelled to work without compensation, etc., said decree bearing date, October 15, 1713.
> With this order is a copy of an opinion of the attorney-general at Arispe, to the commandant-general, relating to certain modifications of the laws of the Indies in regard to Spaniards and mixed bloods living in Indian pueblos; said copy being directed to Don Juan Bautista de Anza, then governor of New Mexico.
> The opinion was dated at Arispe, January 23, 1783, and the copy made on the next day.
> Accompanying the copy of the opinion is a letter of transmittal from the commandant-general, De Croix, to Governor Anza, dated January 24, 1783, advising him that in the future he will be governed by the opinion of the attorney-general.
> The last paper in this archive is a copy of the foregoing opinion, made by Governor Anza, to be circulated and promulgated throughout the province, followed by a certificate of the alcalde of each district to the effect that he had publicly proclaimed the same.

1343 STATEMENT by Alfonso Rael de Aguilar, at the Pueblo of Santo Domingo, on June 8, 1722.

> That he had been ordered by Governor Juan Domingo de Bustamante to call together the Indians of Santo Domingo and Cochiti for the purpose of investigating the facts connected with a suit brought by the Santo Domingo people against those of Cochiti in regard to certain lands sold by Doña Juana Baca to the latter; that with this end in view, he summoned Miguel de San Juan, her son, who stated that the lands which his mother had sold were on the other side of the river (the Rio Grande), and were not included in the lands in dispute, as would appear by the deed of sale made by his mother in virtue of her grant titles, which documents were in the possession of the Cochiti Indians; that he thereupon ordered the Indians to produce the documents, which they did; that their inspection showed that on February 20, 1703, Pedro Rodriguez Cubero, the governor of New Mexico, made a grant to Doña Juana Baca of a tract of land on the *other* side of the Del Norte river between the two pueblos, and that she had received the royal possession thereof quietly and peaceably; that he then called upon the Indians to state which were the lands about which they were disputing; that they replied that they were on *this* side of the river midway between to the two pueblos; that thereupon he proceeded to measure one league from the cemetery of the Santo Domingo church straight toward the pueblo of Cochiti, making a temporary mark at the termination of the league; that he then measured one league south from Cochiti, and between the termination of that measurement and the one made northward from Santo Domingo there was a distance of 1,600 varas; that this space between the extremities of the two leagues he divided equally between Santo Domingo and Cochiti, the Indians being perfectly satisfied with the arrangement, and certified copies of the proceeding being given to both parties.

1344 CERTIFIED STATEMENT by Juan Paez Hurtado, dated at Santa Cruz, on June 10, 1724.

> That he had received a message from the governor of New Mexico directing him to ascertain whether Mateo Trujillo had ever settled on the tract of lands granted to him in the year 1700 by General Cubero, on the other side of the Del Norte river, between the pueblos of Santa Clara and San Ildefonso; that he had called together the

principal Indians of "said Pueblo" (which pueblo?) and had administered the oath to them; that they had stated that on two Sundays Trujillo had erected a cross, and on Wednesday of that week he had put up two forked poles, which Paez had seen when he made the measurements in order to give the Indians their league, as they had only 2,200 varas of land on which they were planting, the land being theirs and they always having planted it, as was shown by an irrigating ditch which was on the tract, and they not having in any other direction any place they could plant, there remaining for Trujillo, from the Indians' boundaries to the table-land, about three hundred varas; that the chief alcalde swore to the same thing that the Indians did — that Trujillo had never settled on the land; that the Indians who swore to it were Juan, the governor, Felipe Cherpe, and Juan the general, and that the whole pueblo swore to the same, etc., etc.

1345 BALTAZAR ROMERO. Deed to Pueblo of Santa Ana. The sale was annulled by Governor Cruzat y Gongora, March 1, 1734.

The date of the sale by Romero does not appear, nor is the land accurately described; it is stated that it is a tract of lands and a grove situate on the other side of the river and that it belonged to Bernalillo, *a very ancient settlement of Spaniards*; that the sale was to the prejudice of the settlement and contrary to the royal laws; that if Romero wanted to sell the land he must sell it to Spaniards and not to the Indians, or any community of Indians, etc.

The notice of this annulment was served on the parties to the sale by the chief alcalde of Bernalillo, on March 11, 1734.

1346 DIEGO GALLEGOS. Deed; Grant: uncertified copy.

The grant was made by Governor Don Juan Domingo de Bustamante on January 13, 1730, to Diego Gallegos, a citizen of Bernalillo, for a piece of land opposite Santo Domingo, on the other side of the river, the boundaries of which were described in the petition as follows: "On the north side by the old Pueblo of Cochiti, which is in the mountain; on the south a spring of water, which is in the small cañada which comes down to the little house called Cubero's; on the east by the road which comes down from Jemez to San Felipe; on the west by the lands of Santo Domingo.''

Possession was given by the chief alcalde, Andrés Montoya, after having summoned the Santo Domingo and Cochiti Indians to be present and offer any objections they might have and after they had stated that the grant was not to their injury.

The deed was made by Maria Josefa Gutierres, widow of Diego Gallegos, and by her children, to the Indians of the pueblo of Santo Domingo, November 28, 1748, and conveyed the same property that was granted to Diego Gallegos by the Governor Bustamante on January 13, 1730.

1347 PUEBLO OF SANDIA. January 23, 1748.

This archive consists of five separate papers. The largest of these is a certified copy of proceedings in connection with the decision of the question whether future missionary efforts among the Moquis should be carried on by the Franciscans or the Jesuits. On the first page of leaf 8, there begins a petition of Fr. Juan Miguel Menchero, who asks for the tract of land on which is situate the abandoned mission of Sandia, in order that he might re-settle it with the Moquis, who had come over from their country in 1742 with his missionaries, and who were then living at Jemez and other pueblos. This petition is followed by a grant of land asked for made by the governor, Don Joaquin Codallos y Rabal, on January 23, 1748.

Opinion of the auditor-general of war to the viceroy of New Spain as to whether the missionary work among the Moquis should be given to the Jesuits or to the Franciscans. This archive is interesting as it refers to the Moquis having participated in the revolution of 1680 and advising the resettlement of many abandoned pueblos in the valley of the Rio Grande; also contains a petition by Fr. Juan Miguel Menchero, asking for the abandoned tract of the Sandia mission for the purpose of establishing the *Moquis* who came over in 1742 with his missionaries Delgado and Pino, and who were *then living at Jemez and other pueblos*. The archive contains five documents; the one marked 1347-I is a call for a council of war to decide as to making war on the Utes for having stolen the horse-herd of the Taos Indians. Date October 14, 1716.

1348 JUAN MONTES VIGIL: March 21, 1753.

This archive begins with a statement by Juan Montes y

Vigil, chief alcalde of Santo Domingo, Cochiti, and San Felipe, advising the governor of the province that the Indians of San Felipe had arranged with the heirs of Cristobal Baca to purchase a tract of land at Angostura for 900 pesos, and suggesting that the matter be carried through regularly and the Indians be protected against imposition and fraud; that the governor should appoint one or two honest and competent persons to appraise the land in question.

This petition was presented to Governor Don Tomás Velez Cachupin at Santa Fe, March 21, 1753, and he at once issued his order covering the matter, appointing Miguel Montoya of Atrisco and Geronimo Jaramillo of Los Corrales as appraisers and directed the chief alcalde, Miguel Lucero, to take the sworn statements of the appraisers, separately, after they had examined the land.

The depositions of the appraisers show that they considered the lands were not worth more than 600 pesos, and when this information was laid before the governor, he immediately issued an order giving detailed directions how the sale should be made and the money (600 pesos) paid over by the Indians. The order also shows that the governor was familiar with the customary methods of defrauding the Indians at that date, and did not intend that they should be imposed upon. The document is full of interesting details.

The result of the governor's action was that the owners of the land sold it at the price fixed by the appraisers and the Indians paid for it in cattle, sheep, bucksins, and other articles of barter, there being little or no money in the kingdom at that time.

The vendors executed a deed to the Indians, April 24, 1753, the deed being found on the last two leaves of the manuscript. The lands are described: "And said lands are at the place called the Angostura immediately contiguous to the Pueblo and Mission of San Felipe and on the other side they adjoin the ranch and lands of Cristobal Martin, deceased."

1349 PUEBLO OF SANTA ANA; purchase of lands from Quiteria Contreras, wife of José de Jesus Montaño widow of Cristobal Martinez Gallego, and from her son, Mariano Martinez, et al.

The statement of the boundaries locates the tract east

of the Rio Grande and other recitals place the town of Bernalillo west of the river at that date.

It appears from these proceedings that the Santa Ana Indians appeared before the chief alcalde, Don Bernardo de Miera y Pacheco, and informed him that they desired to buy from Quiteria Contreras a tract of land "which is on the other side (of the river) from Bernalillo," and the prospective vendors also appeared and agreed to sell.

The alcalde ordered each party to select a person to act as an appraiser of the lands. The Indians selected the militia ensign, Pablo Salazar, and the vendors selected Juan Bautista Montaño, who were sworn by the alcalde.

The lands were measured and valued at 3,000 pesos, according to prevailing prices. The sum was paid by the Indians in bulls, cows, oxen, sheep, goats, horses, the animals contributed by each Indian being set forth in a list which forms a part of the proceedings.

The deed was made on July 7, 1763, and the property sold is described as being "on the west side by the Rio del Norte, on the east to the foot of the Sandia mountain, on the north the half of the Angostura, where a cross is placed adjoining the properties of the Pueblo of San Felipe; on the south by the three cottonwood trees which are below the house where said deceased used to live, and from the said cottonwood trees the straight line follows from northeast to southwest to join and re-unite said lands with those which said natives have purchased which formerly belonged to Miranda, and from said cottonwood trees in the direction of the south they reserve, without selling, a piece of land which was sold to said deceased by Josefa Baca, deceased," etc. The "said deceased" was Cristobal Martinez Gallego, first husband of Quiteria Contreras.

The sale was approved by the governor. The Indians were ordered to put up permanent monuments, which they did.

This archive shows that in 1763 *Bernalillo* was on the *west side of the Rio Grande.* Pp. 1, 2, 3, 8, and 9; *q. v.*

1350 DECREE. October 31, 1769. Location of the Sumas Indians.

Don Pedro de la Fuente [rubric]; Don Tomas Velez Cachupin, Governor and Captain-General; Don Carlos Fernandez; Don Joseph Maldonado.

The founding of a pueblo of *Sumas* Indians at *San Lorenzo el Real*.

1351 PUEBLO INDIANS. San Ildefonso; Santa Clara. Lands.

Felipe Tafoya, as attorney for the Indians of San Ildefonso, filed a protest with the governor of New Mexico against the occupancy of certain lands belonging to the Pueblo league by Spaniards who claimed to own them.

The Indians alleged that during the administration of Governor Pedro Rodriguez Cubero their old people had loaned a house lot to Mathias Madrid, in order that he might erect thereon a house; that not only did he build a house, but also began to cultivate lands notwithstanding their protests; that finally he offered to sell the lands to them, but they refused to buy because the lands were already theirs; that he then sold them to Juana Lujan, whose heirs were still in possession, her son, Juan Gomez, having built a house so close to the pueblo that his cultivated land adjoined the garden of the Indians next to the pueblo; that on the other side of the river and within the pueblo boundaries Marcos Lucero, a citizen of Ojo Caliente, also had built a house, under the pretext of being an heir of Francisco Lujan, deceased; that although it was true that the latter had bought a piece of land of an Indian of San Ildefonso the people of the pueblo had made complaint because of the damage done to their planting lands by the cattle and horses of said Lujan and others, and Governor Francisco Marin (Francisco Antonio Marin del Valle) had ordered that the Indian should return what he had received for the land, but the Indian not being able to do so, an Indian from Tesuque named Francisco "El Coyote," put up the money by consent of the pueblo, said Francisco being interested in the lands because he had married a daughter of the interpreter of the pueblo; that after said Marcos Lucero received the money it had not been possible to get him to leave the place, and he was still there to the inconvenience and damage of the Indians; that also, west of the pueblo and within the boundaries of the grant, some of the commons of the pueblo had been granted to Pedro Sanchez, who also had built a house, and although the Indians protested against this grant at the time it was made, no attention was paid to them, and they had suffered great injury because of the stock belonging to Sanchez and that of other persons who claim title under said ranch; that in addition one Antonio

Mestas, a citizen of Chama and son-in-law of Sanchez, proposed to establish a ranch on the other side of the river, opposite the Caja del Rio, at the only place where there is a practical descent from the Pajarito mesa, etc.

In view of all this the Indians asked relief from the damage they suffered and that their league in three directions should be protected and given to them.

The governor, Cachupin, acted and commissioned, February 4, 1763, Don Carlos Fernandez to examine the grants or titles under which Matias Madrid had sold to Juana Lujan; to measure the distance from the church in the pueblo to the ranch; to measure also toward the ranch of Marcos Lucero, ejecting the latter from the land for which the price had been returned without permitting him the slightest recourse; to examine the site of the ranch of Pedro Sanchez as to whether it is on lands which belong or ought to belong to the pueblo; to notify Antonio Mestas not to build a house or make a settlement at the only point for a watering place on the Rio del Norte and to report to the governor what he had done.

On February 17, 1763, Fernandez, chief alcalde of Santa Cruz at the time, made report that he had notified the heirs of Juana Lujan and that they had exhibited to him a grant given to Matias Madrid by Don Pedro Rodriguez Cubero, the possession being given by Roque Madrid with a decree by Don Juan Paez Hurtado; also a deed by Matias Madrid to Juana Lujan, made before Captain Sebastian Martin, and re-validated by the inspector, Juan Paez Hurtado; and also a certified copy of a decision made by the same officer. The alcalde ordered the documents attached to the proceedings in the case. They are found on leaves 5 to 9 of the archive in question.

On February 17, 1763, Fernandez measured the distance from the gate of the cemetery in the pueblo, which gate faced the east, to the boundary of the land claimed by the heirs of Juana Lujan, a distance of 2,200 varas and continuing the measurement in the same direction (east) to the boundary which said heirs recognized as separating them from the lands of the heirs of Ygnacio Roybal, there was a further distance of 1,650 varas. This last boundary was an arroyo, the nearest one to the principal house of Juana Lujan. From the measurements it is evident that the lands claimed by the latter's heirs were within a distance of 3,850 varas from the gate on the east side of the San Ildefonso cemetery.

On the 18th, Fernandez began at the north wall of the

THE SPANISH ARCHIVES OF NEW MEXICO 405

church in San Yldefonzo and measured directly toward the house of Marcos Lucero and at a distance of 4,372 varas he came to the boundary of the land claimed by said "Lucero and other heirs of Francisco Gomez del Castillo." Thence continuing the measurement in the same direction a distance of 628 varas he arrived at a point 5,000 varas, or one Spanish league, from the point of beginning. This distance took in the house and all the lands, except 61 varas, claimed by the heirs of Gomez del Castillo. These 61 varas reached the boundary of Juan Esteban Canjuebe, a citizen of Santa Clara.

While this party who had been present at this measurement were all together on the lands which had been purchased by Marcos Lucero (they were purchased by Francisco Lujan) under whom Lucero claimed by right of inheritance (see the protest at the beginning of the proceedings) the verbal statement was made by the Indian from Tesuque, Francisco (El Coyote) that from the time he paid the money back to Marcos Lucero the latter had not planted the lands, which as a matter of fact were being planted by Francisco, although Lucero was living in the house which he had built, not on the lands purchased but on those he had inherited.

Also, on February 18, 1763, Fernandez began at the western wall of the cemetery of San Ildefonso and measured west therefrom a distance of 3,200 varas, at which point he was north of the house of Pedro Sanchez. He then continued the measurement west 1,800 varas further to the end of the league of 5,000 varas belonging to the pueblo.

In closing the proceedings for that day the alcalde uses the following language: "From measurements it results that there remains to the natives of this said Pueblo all that which the two extremities of the north and west measurements comprise as far as the mountain, which might be four leagues in length, for commons between the two directions mentioned."

On February 20, 1763, the alcalde summoned before him Antonio Mestas, whom the Indians had accused of intending to establish a ranch on the other side of the river at the only place where there was a practical descent from the Pajarito mesa. The alcalde informed Mestas of the order of the governor and Mestas said that he would obey it; that neither then nor at any time had he intended to settle the place.

Having complied with the orders of the governor the

alcalde returned the papers to him and the governor sent them all to the Indians in order that they might make any statement they saw fit in support of their contention.

Felipe Tafoya, as attorney for the Indians, made answer for them stating that he had examined the grant made to Matias Madrid by Governor Cubero and also the deed made by Madrid to Juana Lujan and he did not admit the value of these documents; that he called attention to the decision (see leaf 9 of his archive) in favor of Madrid, dated September 27, 1704, which clearly showed the justice of his client's contention, for said decision stated that the grant made by the Marquis of Naba Bracinas to Ignacio Roybal was made to the injury of the Indians; that that being true with how much more reason did the Indians claim that they were injured by the grant made to Madrid, for the measurements made by the alcalde, Madrid, showed that Fernandez' grant was further within their boundaries than that made to Roybal.

The answer made by Tafoya and the other papers were sent to Juan Gomez and Marcos Lucero, heirs of Juana Lujan, on February 28, 1763, for reply thereto.

The reply was signed by Juan Gomez del Castillo. He denies the statement made by Tafoya, in first presenting the case, that the Indians had loaned the land to Matias Madrid in order that he might build a house thereon. He says that the grant which he had already exhibited proved the contrary; that from the date of the grant to the date of his reply it had been duly held and cultivated without interference by those claiming under it, and he remarks: "If ten years of possession in good faith give a right to the possessor, how much more do sixty-odd years give it to us." He makes quite an argument on the facts developed in the case.

On November 3, 1763, the papers were again ordered to be sent to the attorney for the Indians, Felipe Tafoya, and he made another argument for the Indians.

Following this is an order of November 12, 1763, by Governor Velez Cachupin, directing that the proceedings be transmitted to the licentiate, Don Fernando de Torija y Leri at Chihuahua, in order that he give a legal opinion on the points involved.

The opinion requested is dated October 27, 1764, and, after a brief review of conditions existing, amounts only to a suggestion as to the best and most practicable manner of settling the dispute in an equitable way and without encouraging the same class of controversies in other pueblos.

The licentiate says, in substance, that the best way to settle the matter would be to give the Indians from the unoccupied lands on the north and west, an amount sufficient to make up what they are lacking to complete the full amount to which they were entitled. He also approves the action of the governor relative to the house which Antonio Mestas was accused of intending to erect on the land of the Indians and suggested that monuments should be erected and that the Spanish citizens be ordered to keep their stock outside of those boundaries under the gravest penalties.

This opinion is followed by the decision of the governor, dated April 12, 1765, which is in effect a grant of lands west of the pueblo to the Indians thereof. He says: "In view of the fact that on the west, directly toward the mountain, there are lands free and unoccupied, there is granted to the Indians of the Pueblo of San Ildefonso all the extent necessary and of which they may be in need for pasturing their large stock, of which they have an abundance, and big herd of horses necessary to the rendering of royal service, there being included in their property the ranch that was called that of Pedro Sanchez, now unoccupied, situate in the valley of the little arroyo which they call Los Guages; and as to what relates to the north side, along the edges of the river, upward, the house constructed by Marcos Lucero, a citizen trespassing on the boundaries of the cultivated land of said Pueblo of San Ildefonso, may be destroyed, or the said house may be remain for the benefit of the said Pueblo, to serve as a boundary and stable and known landmark;" etc.

At San Ildefonso, on April 24, 1765, the substitute chief alcalde, Antonio José Ortiz, in compliance with the order of the governor called together the people of the pueblo, their attorney, and all the heirs of Juana Lujan and announced to them the decision of the governor. Thereupon the Indians stated they were in conformity with the decision as to the eastern and western sides, but not as to the northern, because the house of Marcos Lucero, which was designated to them as a boundary, was in the midst of the lands which they had always recognized as theirs, for the boundary which they had always recognized had been an arroyo which had been pointed out to them by Governor Juan Paez Hurtado; that if their landmark should be fixed at that arroyo, they would be satisfied. The heirs of Juana Lujan and Francisco Lujan stated that with regard to the boundary with which the Indians were satisfied they still desired to make further representations, and the heirs of Pedro Sanchez made the same statement.

The next paper in the proceedings is a statement by Felipe Tafoya, on behalf of the Indians, that if they should be given the arroyo designated by General Juan Paez Hurtado, for their boundary on the north they would be satisfied with the decision as to the eastern and western boundaries. He further stated that the Indians said that the monument erected by order of Juan Paez Hurtado had been taken away, but at the foot of the monument they had buried in the ground some stones, in the form of a cross, and that those possibly might still be found, but even if they could not be found the Indians knew the place where they had been buried to mark the boundary.

On June 10, 1756 (1765) Governor Velez Cachupin ordered the Indians to exhibit some documentary evidence of the measurements which they claimed had been made by Governor Paez Hurtado, and also he directed the substitute chief alcalde, Don Antonio José Ortiz, to make an examination as to whether the stones placed in the form of a cross could be found.

On July 21, 1765, the substitute chief alcalde proceeded with the examination ordered, having first asked the Indians to exhibit the instrument that was given to them at the time the boundary was established and to state the names of the witnesses who were present on that occasion. To this request the Indians responded by presenting a document which forms leaves 21 and 22 of the manuscript, the purport of which will be referred to later. The substitute chief alcalde, accompanied by the Indians, the heirs of Francisco Gomez del Castillo, and by Domingo Vigil, who had been summoned as a witness at the request of the Indians, and who had taken part in the proceedings described in the document just presented by the Indians, went to the place where the latter said stones had been buried in the ground. Some of the stones were visible, and when the others were uncovered it was seen that they had been buried in the form of a cross, as the Indians had stated. Domingo Vigil then said to the Indians that the boundary which he had pointed out to them was not there, to which the Indians replied that it was the same one which they had established by command of General Paez Hurtado. When the Indians were asked if he had given them a document they said that they did not know for they were mere boys at that time, but they were certain it was the boundary which was designated by him.

This man, Domingo Vigil, whom the Indians had summoned as a witness, and who, when confronted with the stones set in the ground in the form of a cross, denied that such was the place he had designated, was the chief alcalde (formerly) of Santa Cruz, and while filling that office, had acted officially in a matter which was set forth in a document signed by him and dated April 2, 1731, which document had been presented to the alcalde, Antonio José Ortiz, July 21, 1765, by the Indians and which, as before stated, forms a part of archive 1351, being found on leaves 21 and 22 thereof.

It is shown in this document that the Indians of San Ildefonso made some sort of a complaint to Governor Bustamante about a grant made to Mateo Trujillo between their pueblo and the pueblo of Santa Clara; that the governor sent for Domingo Vigil, then alcalde of Santa Cruz, ordering an investigation of the boundaries and to see that the Indians were paid for the work they had done in taking out the irrigation ditch; that when the alcalde went to examine into the matter the Indians of Santa Clara showed him a decree by Governor Paez Hurtado, June 9, 1724, in regard to a complaint they had made about this same grant to Mateo Trujillo, by which it appeared that the governor (Juan Paez Hurtado) had measured a league south from the pueblo of Santa Clara, said Trujillo being present, and had fixed as the northern boundary of his land the lands of the pueblo of Santa Clara, and as his southern boundary the slope of the San Ildefonso mesa.

Vigil states that in conformity with the decree of Governor Paez he designated as a boundary on the north the slope of the mesa which served as a southern boundary of the lands of Mateo Trujillo; that he commanded monuments to be placed on the boundary, and they were placed; that the Indians agreed not to demand anything for the work they had done on the irrigation ditch, provided the lands should remain in the hands of Baltazar Trujillo or Antonio Tafoya, and in case they wanted to sell them they would sell to the Indians; and with the further understanding that in the meantime the Indians should not be compelled to clean the ditch, all of which was agreed to by Trujillo and Tafoya.

Following the foregoing, which is signed by Domingo Vigil and two witnesses, is an approval of the agreement between the Indians and the Spaniards, signed by Governor Don Gervasio Cruzat y Gongora on July 6, 1732.

This is followed by another action of the same governor, April 7, 1736, showing that he had changed his mind about the matter; that he had come to the conclusion that the agreement was prejudicial to the interests of the Spaniards, because the Indians had not exhibited any grant for their lands and consequently the lawful boundaries thereof were not known with certainty; but he told both parties to respect the boundaries which had been established.

This concludes the document presented to the alcalde, Antonio José Ortiz, on July 21, 1765, by the Indians of San Ildefonso.

The examination having been completed by Ortiz, he returned his report with the papers, and the governor, February 6, 1766, referred them to the attorney for the Indians, Don Felipe Tafoya.

Argument was now made by Tafoya in favor of the Indians, whereupon, May 5, 1766, the governor rendered a second decision. This is recorded in the records of the county of Santa Fe, but it appears that a portion of it is missing, but the most important features are recorded.

The governor decided that the land belonged to the Indians of San Ildefonso as far as the boundary established by Governor Paez Hurtado, where the stones in the form of a cross were found buried; that if the owners of the ranch, including the lands of Mateo Trujillo, should wish to sell it at any time, they must give the Indians the preference in the event they wanted to purchase; that any sale which might have been made to any person other than the Indians was null and void.

Furthermore, the governor ordered the alcalde, Antonio José Ortiz, to place the Indians in possession of the boundary and to give them to understand that they could use, hold, and enjoy the lands which had been usurped by the Spaniards up to that point, which was to be marked by a firm and permanent monument.

The next document is a petition by Ursula Guillen to Governor Velez Cachupin, in which she alleges that she had a ranch between the pueblos of San Ildefonso and Santa Clara, which was bought by her deceased husband, Francisco del Castillo, from Don Joseph de Orcasitas; that she had lived on said ranch in quiet and peaceful possession for twenty-six years; that she still holds possession in spite of the fact that the Ute Indians had attacked the ranch, killed two of her sons, and driven off her stock; that on the 20th of that month (apparently May, 1766) the Indians of San Ildefonso had gone to her ranch while she was engaged in planting, and had told her that Felipe Tafoya had sent them an order that the lands of the ranch should be partitioned among them by their governor; that in view of the fact that they exhibited no order from Governor Velez, and the notification was not brought by any Spanish official, she had not permitted them to make a partition of the lands until she could lay the matter before the Spanish governor. She calls attention to the fact that during a very long period the Indians had failed to make any claim to the ranch when it had been sold and had passed from the possession of one owner to another and that at the time that her husband had been placed in possession of it, the Indians had been summoned to appear and that the boundaries had been designated by Domingo Vigil. In conclusion she states that in order that the governor may understand the matter she transmits with her petition four documents. These do not form a part of this archive, and a subsequent statement by Governor Velez shows that he ordered that they be returned to her.

This petition was examined by Governor Velez on May 24, 1766, and he ordered that it and the four instruments accompanying it be transmitted to Felipe Tafoya, that, as attorney for the Indians, he might reply to the same.

This he did immediately, calling the attention of the governor to the fact that the recitals in the instruments referred to were not of a character to make clear the number of varas contained in the ranch, some of them containing no mention even of the boundaries, or referring to the original grant as giving that information, although the said grant was not attached to the proceedings and consequently was not available for the purposes of the case.

In regard to one of the instruments, which he says did mention the boundaries, as being on the north the lands of the pueblo of Santa Clara and on the south the lands of his clients, the people of San Ildefonso, he says that this simply leaves open the question as to the exact location of those boundaries and that nothing has been presented in the case which militates against the proof already adduced by the Indians in regard to their boundary being at the point where the stones were buried in the ground in the form of a cross.

In conclusion he asks that the governor's previous decision be carried into effect, and that after the landmark shall be established at the proper point, the number of varas from there to the house of Ursula Guillen be measured, as well as the distance from the house to the boundary of the pueblo of Santa Clara.

On May 24, 1766, Governor Velez reviewed the case and ordered that his previous decision be carried into effect, commanding the deputy alcalde and the attorney for the Indians to proceed at once to place the Indians in possession of their ancient boundary, and to measure from there to the ranch house and from the latter to the boundary claimed by the Santa Clara Indians, and to set forth the whole matter in a proper document in order that the claimants of the ranch might not thereafter trespass upon the lands of the Indians.

On May 26, 1766, the substitute chief alcalde, Don Antonio José Ortiz, with Felipe Tafoya, attorney for the Indians, in the presence of the parties interested, and the principal Indians of the pueblos of San Ildefonso and Santa Clara, proceeded to comply with the order of the governor.

At the point where the stones had been buried in the ground in the form of a cross, a landmark of stones and mud was erected and from said landmark a distance of 200 varas was measured in a northerly direction to the corner of the house, and from said corner the measurement was continued toward the north a further distance of 126 varas to the boundary of the pueblo of Santa Clara, making the total distance between the boundaries of the two pueblos 326 varas.

On June 23, 1766, Governor Velez ordered that the preceding instrument be attached to the other papers in the case and that a certified copy of his decisions of April 12, 1765, and May 5, 1766, and also of his last decree of May 24, 1766, be given to the Indians, as well as the proceeding immediately following that decree and the one in which the order is given. He further ordered that the original proceeding should be deposited in the government archives.

1352 EL CAPULIN. Proceedings as to occupation of by Miguel Romero and his brother, Domingo Romero. *Santa Fe*, April 11, 1765.

This manuscript contains first a communication from Bartolomé Fernandez, chief alcalde of the Queres Pueblos, to the governor and captain-general of New Mexico, calling his attention to the fact that certain citizens, named Romero, were settling a place called El Capulin, near the pueblo of Cochiti; that the said place was the summer pasture grounds of the Cochiti Indians and other people; that as long as Fernandez had lived in the kingdom the place had never been settled and he had no knowledge of any grant to cover the place in question.

On April 11, 1765, Governor Velez commissioned Fernandez to visit the place in question and eject the persons who were settling there.

Two days later Fernandez made report that he had informed Miguel Romero of the order and had stated that he would obey but he had certain statements which he would make to that officer in regard to the matter. The report is followed by a statement from Miguel Romero wherein he says that he had had the place for five years and six months and had not been interfered with until that year, when it became known that he had bought those interests in the property that did not belong to him, which had been paid for by him and his brother, Domingo Romero. He states that he presents to the governor in support of his claim a grant and a will left by his grandfather, Andrés Montoya, and adds that the persons who are opposing his occupancy of the land had an opportunity to purchase the interests which he had acquired, but they waited until he had bought them and then took advantage of the occasion to give him trouble.

The grant referred to in Romero's statement is found on leaves 5 and 6 of the manuscript, and the will, which is a certified copy, made June 18, 1740, is found on pages 7, 8, and 9.

The grant, which was made August 18, 1739, by Governor Gaspar Domingo de Mendoza, does not describe the boundaries of the land, but the applicant, Andrés Montoya, stated in his petition that the tract was half way beween the gardens of Cochiti and those of San Ildefonso, on the other side (western) of the Rio del Norte. In describing the boundaries he used the following language: "Said tract is bounded on the north side by said gardens of San Ildefonso, and on the south by those of Cochiti, being distant from each of the two mentioned places of the gardens more than a league; and also it is bounded on the east by the Rio del Norte and on the west by the Cochiti mountains.''

The act of possession, October 7, 1739, signed by Captain Antonio Montoya, chief alcalde of Santa Fe, has this to say about the boundaries: ''And I gave it (the possession) to him with the same boundaries which he designates in his petition, as also his boundaries run on the east the Rio del Norte, on the west by the high mountain which runs from Cochiti, on the north one league farther down from the last trees of the Indians of San Ildefonso, and on the south one league farther up from the gardens of the Indians of Cochiti.''

In the margin, on the act of possession, is a note signed by Governor Mendoza, showing that the grant had been entered on the proper book in the archives.

The will, heretofore referred to, was dated June 17, 1740, one day prior to the making of the certified copy, and in it the land in question is referred to on the third page of the instrument. The testator, in describing two tracts of land which he owned, refers to the second one in these words: ''And the other on the other side of the river Del Norte, which I have not put under cultivation because of my illness, which is between the gardens of the Pueblo of San Ildefonso and Cochiti, the boundaries of said tract being distant from each garden half a league.''

Miguel Romero's statement transmitting this grant to the governor and the will, is followed by an order of Governor Velez, April 18, 1765, directing that his previous order be carried into effect and that the parties be again notified that under no circumstances should they have a house or cultivated land on said tract. However, they were permitted to run their stock on it, as did other citizens, but this was to be done without injury to the Cochiti and San Ildefonso Indians. The chief alcalde of Santa Fe, Don Francisco Guerrero, was directed to carry this order into effect; and the governor further directed that the grant and certified copy of the will filed in the case by Miguel Romero be attached to the other papers and be transmitted to the people of Cochiti and San Ildefonso, to the owners of lands adjoining the Capulin Tract, and to the officers of the cavalry company at Santa Fe, in order that they might state anything favorable to their interests.

On the day this order was issued (April 18, 1765,) the alcalde of Santa Fe, Don Francisco Guerrero, notified the Romeros of the contents of the order and they stated that they would obey, but also that they had certain matters in their defense which they desired to lay before the governor.

The next proceeding, in chronological sequence, is an argument by Bartolomé Fernandez, on behalf of the Indians, criticising the grant filed by the Romeros and showing its defects, as well as those of the will filed, and the inconsistencies existing between recitals in the latter and others in the act of possession, with regard to the boundaries. This argument is on leaf 10 of the manuscript, and is followed by a note, signed by Fernandez, transmitting the papers to the alcalde of La Cañada (Villa Nueva de la Cañada de Santa Cruz) for the latter's compliance with the governor's order of April 18, 1765. The entries by Fernandez are not dated.

On July 7, 1765, Don Manuel Garcia, the alcalde of La Cañada, reported that he had called together the San Ildefonso Indians and the citizens and informed them of the order of the governor, to which they assented, saying nothing whatever.

On October 1, 1766, Lieutenant Tomas Madrid and Ensign Francisco de Esquibel, of the royal garrison of Santa Fe, reported that they had examined the grant and the boundaries therein stated, and had found out that said boundaries did not include the commons used for the horse-herd of the garrison.

Subsequently, Miguel Romero presented a petition to the governor, asking that the proceedings in the case and the instruments which he had presented be delivered to him so that he might present his side of the controversy.

On April 22, 1767, Governor Pedro Fermin de Mendinueta ordered his petition to be attached to the proceedings and delivered to Romero as requested.

Romero then made a statement of his case, alleging their occupancy of the land was not prejudicial to the Indians of Cochiti, because it was more than 3½ leagues distant from their pueblo and that in the space between the two places, were situated more than 40 Spanish families. He says that these families do not in any way damage the Indians, and asks why it should be thought that he and his brother would injure them, etc. He says that so far as San Ildefonso is concerned, no damages result to that pueblo, which is distant about 3½ leagues.

He urges that if the documents he had himself presented as evidencing his right to the place be considered as having no value, his having kept his stock there for five and one-half years is favorable to his contention, and he alleges great damages on account of having been prevented making a settlement at the place in question.

On April 25th, Governor Mendinueta finally decided the case, saying in substance that having examined the proceedings and in view of the nullity of the grant appearing on leaves 5 and 6 thereof, and the convincing arguments of the alcalde, Bartolomé Fernandez, on leaf 10, which clearly showed that the possession given to Andrés Montoya was lacking in the necessary requisite of the summoning of the owners of the adjacent lands, and also because of no settlement having been made within the period prescribed by law, the grant having been made in 1739, and the attempted settlement made by Miguel Romero in 1765, and for other reasons proper to consider, declared the grant to be of no value and that neither Andrés Montoya nor his heirs had acquired any right to the Capulin Tract. He further decided that the fact that Romero had pastured his stock on the tract gave him no right of property therein, because it had been done without just title (*justo titulo*); that he might use it in the same way that it had been used by the natives of Cochiti and the adjoining citizens — as royal domain; that neither Miguel Romero nor anyone else should make settlement on or have the ownership of the tract; that it should be held and considered to be royal domain for the common use of anyone who desired to pasture stock, without excluding Romero, who had been permitted so to do by Governor Tomas Velez Cachupin by his decree of April 18, 1765.

In conclusion he ordered that Miguel Romero be notified of the decision and warned that he must not again present petitions in bad faith, and advised that no appeal would be allowed.

1353 PUEBLOS OF SANTO DOMINGO AND SAN FELIPE.

Grant. Papers transferred to packet containing all pueblo claims.

1354 PROCEEDING IN A DISPUTE between the Indians of Santa Clara and San Ildefonso and certain

Facsimile of Signature of Captain Don Carlos Fernandez.

Facsimile of Signature of Colonel Don Pedro de Villasur.

Facsimile of Signature of Captain Don Manuel Delgado.

Facsimile of Signature of Don Domingo de Labadia.

Spanish citizens relative to a ranch claimed by the Spaniards lying between the two Pueblos.

The Indians of Santa Clara and San Ildefonso presented a petition to the governor of New Mexico, complaining that many years before some Spaniards had established a ranch between the two pueblos on the western side of the Rio del Norte; and had trespassed upon their lands; that complaint had been made to the governor's predecessors, but without avail; that the pueblo of Santa Clara had never had its league measured; that Fr. Sebastian Anton, then deceased, a former minister of that mission, having found in the possession of Juan Pubijua, a Santa Clara Indian, an old document which cleared up the whole matter, and the contents of which were entirely favorable to the Indians, delivered the same to them; that they sent it to the governor, who, after having examined it, returned it to them, and they gave it back to Juan Pubijua, who was living away from the pueblo as a Spanish citizen; that, having then learned that when the governor returned the paper to them he said to the persons who brought it back that if the Indians had any right or request to make they should make it in a formal manner, they invited his attention to it in order that he should compel the return of the paper to them, and in case the paper should not be found, they asked that the league be measured south from the pueblo of Santa Clara, and another league be measured north from the pueblo of San Ildefonso for the purpose of ascertaining whether in the intervening space there was room for a Spanish ranch. In conclusion they asked the governor to decide the matter as he believed to be just and also to approve their selection of Carlos Fernandez as their attorney in the case.

This petition was presented to Governor Juan Bautista de Anza, at Santa Fe, May 6, 1786, and the selection of Fernandez was approved and directed the alcalde of La Cañada, Don José Campo Redondo, in company with Fernandez and in the presence of the governors and *principales* of the two pueblos, and the occupants of the ranch in question, to proceed to measure with a waxed cord, one hundred varas in length, one league south from the cross in the old cemetery at Santa Clara; and the same distance north from a like point in the one at San Ildefonso, placing at the termination of the two lines permanent landmarks, which, for the lack of stone and mortar, were to consist of inclosures of cedar stakes driven into the ground, two varas in circumference, and filled in with four or five cart-loads of stone, so that they could not easily be removed.

In case any land remained between the two landmarks it was to be measured, and the number of varas it contained was to be stated in the report of the alcalde.

On May 10, 1786, the alcalde proceeded to comply with the governor's orders, but states that because he could not find any wax with which to wax the cord he had to moisten it. He says that the distance of 5,000 varas (one league) measured south from the cross of the cemetery of the old church in Santa Clara, included the residence of the citizens who claimed the ranch and that the same distance measured north from San Ildefonso overlapped the first measurement 39¾ varas, so that each of the two leagues was 19 varas and 1½ quarters short. [His calculation is erroneous.]

After the alcalde's report had been returned to the governor, the latter, May 13, 1786, sent it to Carlos Fernandez that he might make any statements which he deemed in the interest of his clients. Fernandez made an argument in favor of the Indians, stating that in view of the fact that the two leagues over-lapped, it was incredible that any predecessor of the governor had made a grant to any citizen of the lands belonging to the two pueblos, unless the same had been based upon a deceptive and fraudulent report; that any sales which had been made did not avail anything, because, if the first vendor had no right, neither had his successors, etc., etc. He goes into the question of the character and extent of the lands owned by the Santa Clara people and other matters, all of which, in view of the final decision of the case, do not appear to be of sufficient importance to be set forth. In conclusion he prays the governor to eject the citizens from the lands and to declare the lands the property of the two pueblos.

This argument was transmitted by the governor, May 16, 1786, to the occupants of the ranch, who made answer, among other things alleging that the lines had not been correctly measured; that the cord had not been waxed and that it was old and patched up with a leather strap; that it broke on two occasions because of being drawn too tight; that the measurement made toward the north from San Ildefonso was not made from the cross in the cemetery, but along the lower side of the wall of the garden of that pueblo; that their statements could be proved by witnesses, who did the measuring. They also referred to proceedings had in the time of Governor Velez, when Carlos Fernandez, then chief alcalde, made what they refer to as the first measurement (see archive 1351). They further stated that subsequently Don Felipe Tafoya, who was acting as attorney for the Indians of San Ildefonso, came to hunt up the old boundary and found the one which the Indians said had been established by order of Governor Juan Paez; that at that time the Indians had been asked to produce any documents they had, and they answered that they had none, but were bound by that anciently established landmark; that the said landmark as then established left the ranch in question 326 varas. (This statement is confirmed by the proceedings of May 26, 1766, by the substitute alcalde, Don Antonio José Ortiz.) (See archive 1351.)

There are other matters touched upon by the statement of the occupants of the ranch, but they are of small consequence and not worth setting out here.

On May 19, 1786, Governor Anza, after having considered the allegations and recitals contained in the documents, but which are not attached to this archive, ordered the lines re-measured by the same alcalde, Don José Campo Redondo, who had measured them on the 10th of the same month; in this second measurement he ordered that a waxed cord be used. He also directed that the space occupied by the houses in San Ildefonso which interfered with running a line straight north from the beginning point in that pueblo, should be carefully measured and included in the distance to be measured toward Santa Clara.

On May 22, 1786, the alcalde, Campo Redondo, measured, with a waxed cord, from the beginning point in the pueblo of Santa Clara in a southerly direction toward San Ildefonso, and at the end of 50 cords, equal to 5,000 varas or one league. discovered that the measurement was 118 varas short of the previous measurement, made May 10th. In order to decide whether this difference was the result of a mistake in the last measurement, he measured from the point he had just reached back to the cross in the cemetery at Santa Clara, and found the distance to be 50 cords of 100 varas each.

On the following day he went to San Ildefonso to measure the league north from that pueblo. He stated that being at the point of beginning, it was not possible to measure a line straight north without cutting a hole through the wall of the church; that he laid out an offset line in order to avoid the church and other rooms of the convent, and thus measured 50 cords toward the north, and at the end of that distance was 118 varas short of the measurement previously made; that, therefore, between the ends of the two lines measured respectively from Santa Clara and San Ildefonso, there was a space of 236 varas; that at the ends of the two lines just mentioned, two stakes were driven into the ground as temporary marks.

The report of the second measurement was transmitted to the governor, who, May 26, 1786, transmitted it and the four documents, filed by the ranch claimants, to the attorney for the Indians.

The latter made a very long argument for the Indians, with the conclusion that under the royal laws of Spain they were entitled to the lands in dispute, and praying for a decision by the executive to that effect.

On May 30, 1786, the governor sent all of the proceedings to the claimants of the ranch and they made another statement in regard to the matter, alleging that they had been injured in the second measurement by the cord being three-fourths of a vara too long, it having been made so by the attorney for the Indians, who took it away from the men who were doing the measuring and lengthened it; that when Miguel Quintana protested against this to the alcalde, the latter refused to allow him to make any statement about it; that this could be proven by Quintana and the witnesses from whom the cord was taken in order to be altered in length, etc.

On June 3, 1786, the governor sent the papers to the alcalde, José Campo Redondo, telling him to report in regard to the alleged treatment of Quintana, and to return the papers with the witnesses referred to by the complainants.

The alcalde complied with this order June 6th, saying that the allegation in regard to the measurement of the cord was false, and that he had not failed to treat both Quintana and all the other parties with justice. In conclusion he stated that he was sending it to the governor with the witnesses requested.

On June 8th, the governor ordered Second Lieutenant José Maldonado to take the depositions of the two witnesses, Juan Ignacio Mestas and Cristobal Maese. This was done at once and the depositions taken fail to support the statements made by the occupants of the ranch, but corroborated each other and that of the alcalde.

On June 10, 1786, Governor Anza decided the case, reviewing the important features. His decision was that the two pueblos were the owners of the lands included within the leagues measured to them by the alcalde, José Campo Redondo, on May 23, 1786, which was the date of the second measurement; that they were immediately to proceed to erect landmarks at the proper points, in compliance with his first decree; that Marcos Lucero and the other occupants of the lands in dispute between the two pueblos, were to be limited, until some other decision of the case, to the 236 varas that had been shortly before measured; that if they desired to sell the land they must sell it to the Indians of San Ildefonso if they wished to purchase; but they must not keep on the land more than four milch cows and the oxen necessary for tilling during the season for cultivation; that if they violated this order or moved the Indians' landmarks they would be subject to a fine of 100 pesos; that the chief alcalde, José Campo Redondo, in company with the attorney for the Indians, was to place all the parties in possession of the lands respectively belonging to each; and that the Spaniards were to pay all the costs of the proceedings and the survey.

On June 19, 1786, the alcalde proceeded to carry into effect the governor's order, Carlos Fernandez not being able to be present because of illness and his place being taken by Don Juan Ignacio Mestas.

At the points where the temporary marks had been set up, the alcalde set into the ground heavy cedar posts in the form of a square, two varas in length, and filled these with about three cart-loads of stone in each; also at the request of the Indians they were permitted to build a wall of stone and mud about a vara in height as a boundary line for the Spanish ranch, and the space occupied by the monuments was on the land of the Indians. The manuscript concludes with an entry by the alcalde sending the proceedings to the governor.

1355 LETTER from Felipe Sandoval, dated August 28, 1812, to Lieutenant-Colonel Joseph Manrique, then Acting Governor of New Mexico.

Sandoval states that the governor of the pueblo of Jemez, and his lieutenant-governor, had appeared before him in the name of the pueblo and had complained that while Don Antonio Armenta was the alcalde of that district he had purchased a corn-field from an Indian of the pueblo, named Cumpa; that this had been done without the knowledge of the people of the pueblo, and that they did not approve of it, but were willing to give an equivalent and have it remain for the benefit of the pueblo; that they wanted Armenta to be compelled to compensate them for all the pieces of land he had sold to various persons, because the lands belonged to the league which they held by grant, which league they wanted to have measured and marked by monuments; that they considered that they had been injured to the extent of a very considerable part of their land.

Sandoval requests the governor to give him orders as to steps he should take to undo the wrong which had been inflicted on the Indians, whose claim he considered just.

There is a marginal note, September 1, 1812, signed by the governor, directing that the communication be transmitted to the lawyer, Don Rafael Bracho, in order that he give his opinion, and sending to him also a document (deed?) in favor of the defendant, Don Antonio Armenta.

There are no further proceedings.

1356 PROCEEDINGS in a dispute between the Indians of Santa Ana and those of San Felipe in regard to certain lands claimed by both Pueblos.

The manuscript begins with a petition by Eusebio Mairo, the governor of the pueblo of Santa Ana, to the protector of the Indians, Don Felipe Sandoval, asking him to secure for them the decision of a dispute between them and the Indians of San Felipe, relative to certain lands which they alleged they owned by purchase, but which the San Felipe Indians have taken from them and sold to different persons. They say that they complained about this matter five years before, to the governor, but had received no decision; that, in the meantime the San Felipe people not only had been selling the lands, but had been destroying the timber; that they had protested to the San Felipe people against the cutting of the timber until it should be decided to whom it belonged, but no attention had been paid to their protests; if there should be much more delay in the matter all of the timber would be destroyed before a decision could be had.

This petition, dated May 5, 1813, was transmitted by

Sandoval to the acting governor, Don Joseph Manrique, on May 10, 1813, and on the same day he directed Don José Pino, one of the alcaldes of Alburquerque, to investigate and settle the dispute, summoning for that purpose the alcaldes of Alameda and Jemez, and requiring the Indians of both pueblos to present such documents as they had in support of their claims respectively.

In a proceeding, dated May 13, 1813, Pino, after copying a letter of transmittal which he had received from Governor Manrique, states that he had notified the alcaldes and the representatives of the pueblos to assemble in the neighborhood of the disputed lands on the day mentioned, on the west side of the Rio del Norte; they did so and showed him their documents.

He says that the document of Santa Ana described its boundaries as follows: "That on the north side it is bounded as far as the outlet of the Angostura, where there is a trunk of a tree which the Indians cut down; on the east by the Rio del Norte; on the south by the junction of the two rivers; on the west by lands of the Pueblo itself."

He further says that the San Felipe document describes the boundaries thus: "On the east the Rio del Norte; on the west by the Cuervillo; on the north the boundary of said Pueblo; on the south by lands of the Pueblo of the Indians of Santa Ana."

After the alcalde had read to them these papers, the Santa Ana Indians wanted their boundary at the trunk of the tree mentioned in their documents, but the alcalde says that the trunk was not in existence and no one present could give any information about it, so he was governed by the first boundary —"the outlet of the Angostura," where a landmark of stone was placed, both pueblos and the alcaldes being satisfied with it.

The headmen (*principales*) of the pueblos stated that they had no objections to make, but they did want to have the boundaries on the other side of the river settled. Consequently, May 14, 1813, at the request of the Indians of Santa Ana, who had informed Pino that the principal object of their complaint was to settle the boundary on the east side of the river, he went there and examined what he describes as a "pocket of old land" which had been formed by the river at the time of a freshet, although he could not learn at what date it had occurred.

He goes on to say that as the papers gave no information about the boundary except that it was the edge of the river, without explaining whether it ran to the Angostura from the west or the east, he saw no way out of the matter except to compromise it by a sort of rough estimate; that after he had made this, they all said they were satisfied; that in accordance with this compromise line which he established there were some pieces of broken land that fell to the share of the Santa Anas, which were held by various citizens of Angostura by purchase from individual Indians of the pueblo of San Felipe; that in view of this fact Pino suggested to Don Cleto Miera y Pacheco (at that time possibly chief alcalde of Alameda) that if any of the purchasers should demand the return of the money they paid to the vendors, the latter, if they had the means, ought to pay it back, as Pino considered the purchases made by the citizens had not been made in good faith, because having bought only pieces of tillable land (without any other right) they had availed themselves of the use of the wooded and pasture lands, like owners thereof, to the injury of both pueblos.

Having this view of the subject, Pino submits to the governor's decision. He further states that the dividing line he had selected was the Santa Ana ditch which was to the west, toward the river, the other ditch going along the hills to the east; that the ditch divided the land in dispute into two parts, the western part for the people of Santa Ana and the eastern for those of San Felipe; that the ditch did not run in a straight line from north to south but made some curves; that these fell to the share of one or the other of the two parties according to their respective sides of the ditch; that in some of those which fell to the share of the pueblo of Santa Ana there were some strips of land planted in wheat, and that he informed the Indians of Santa Ana that they must not take possession of those strips until after the wheat was harvested, but they could take the other pieces; that both pueblos were satisfied with this arrangement and settlement of the boundary.

On May 21, 1813, the governor and lieutenant-governor of San Felipe petitioned Felipe Sandoval, the protector of the Indians, to present to the governor of New Mexico, a statement of the injury they had received by the settlement of the boundary question by the judge (José Pino), who had been appointed to act in the matter by the acting governor, the latter having taken cognizance of it on the petition of the Indians of Santa Ana. They state that the damage done to them was in connection with lands which their ancestors had purchased from the heirs of

Cristobal Baca, deceased; that said lands were at Angostura; that the damage done them consisted in taking from them lands which they considered to be theirs, including both lands they had been cultivating and others which they had sold by the consent of their superiors, and without opposition on the part of the Santa Ana people; that the boundary had been established at the Bernalillo dam, some 500 or more varas above the real Santa Ana boundary.

In conclusion they request Sandoval to go to the tract in question and inform himself as to the facts before presenting the matter to the governor.

On May 29, 1813, Sandoval appended to the foregoing petition a statement to the effect that he had gone to the Angostura and carefully informed himself about the matter, and was convinced that the complaint made was a just one; consequently he transmitted the petition to the acting governor, requesting him to order that the Santa Ana documents be produced in order that each party might have given to him that which belonged to him in accordance with the citation of the boundary of the Angostura in a straight line.

Under date of June 3, 1813, Acting Governor Joseph Manrique appended to the petition a marginal note, directing Don José Maria de Arze, first ensign of the company stationed at Santa Fe, to investigate and report upon the matter.

On June 5, 1813, Arze, after having appointed two attending witnesses, and in the presence of the alcaldes of Alameda and Jemez, and the protector of the Indians, etc., read over the proceedings which had been conducted by José Pino, and asked the parties to the dispute if they had any objections to make thereto.

The protector of the Indians, Felipe Sandoval, then stated, on behalf of the San Felipe people, that they objected to everything appearing in said proceedings on the second page of the second leaf; that what they wanted was that the boundary be given to them straight from north to south, because of the irregularities occurring in the ditch and river, and that the matter be settled according to the recitals in the documents.

The Santa Ana people said that as they had not been injured by what had been done, it might be given to them in the way suggested, if it belonged to them, but in case of any damage being done to them, they would demand that the documents be examined and that each party should have what was his.

Arze says that when he asked the San Felipe people for their documents, they failed to produce any one that fully set forth the boundaries; for the reason that they had none; but they did exhibit to him a certified copy of some proceedings had by the chief alcalde of the pueblos of Santo Domingo, Cochiti, and San Felipe (based on a grant by Governor Don Tomás Velez Cachupin) in which the following occurs: "Immediately adjoining the Pueblo of San Felipe; and on the other side they are bounded by the ranch and lands of Cristobal Martin;" that upon examining the lands it turned out that the San Felipes were trespassing on lands which the Santa Anas had bought from the heirs of Cristobal Martin, as appeared by a certified copy (which the Santa Anas exhibited to him) which stated that the original documents were in the government archive; that having established substantial monuments of stone and mud, it was acknowledged by both pueblos that they were satisfied with them. These monuments formed a southern boundary for the San Felipes and a northern boundary for the Santa Anas, while a thick cottonwood tree which was asked for as a boundary mark by the San Felipes, notwithstanding it was on lands belonging to the Santa Anas, was denied them because their request was unjust.

On June 6, 1813, Arze proceeded to examine into the matter of the establishment of the Santa Ana ditch as a boundary line between the two contending parties, which line, it will be remembered, was established by José Pino May 14, 1813. He says that having asked for the documents of both pueblos, and it being clear from the San Felipe document that the selection of the Santa Ana ditch as a boundary line resulted prejudicially to one of the parties at some points, and to the other at other points, he took from among the papers of the Santa Anas a document drawn up by the chief alcalde of the Queres pueblos, Don Nerio Antonio Montoya, relating to a compromise between the headmen of Santa Ana and San Felipe as to the lands which the river had taken away from them. From this document it appeared that one-half of the space formerly occupied by the river had been partitioned to each pueblo, the western side to Santa Ana and the eastern to San Felipe, which arrangement had been satisfactory to both towns.

Arze then made a reconnoissance of the land in question,

searching for the landmarks of stone which the above mentioned document stated had been ordered to be set in the ground from the point where the river had begun to change its course to the point where it had returned to its bed, but he found only one such landmark. He then made an examination of the old river bed close to the hills on the east, estimating about where its center was, and following its windings, and then having read to the Indians the account of the establishment of the boundary along the center of the old river bed by Don Nerio Antonio Montoya, he asked them if they would be satisfied with the reëstablishment of the line described. They replied that they would, and that they wanted it done in the same way in which it had formerly been done.

Thereupon Arze proceeded to lay out a curved line along what he calculated to be the center of the land which had formerly been occupied by the river, marking it with a great number of landmarks of stone and mud, set into the ground and plainly visible. He instructed the Indians to inspect these monuments frequently, to make all their people acquainted with them, and if any of them should be destroyed by the river or carried away by any persons, they must immediately rebuild them, his object being to secure the perpetuation of the line as he had fixed it without regard to future changes in the course of the river.

Arze then had the document above referred to properly certified, signing it with the attending witnesses, the alcaldes, and the protector of the Indians, and he also made a copy of it for the San Felipes to keep in their possession for their own protection.

After having reduced to writing his report of the proceedings, he inquired of all those present whether they were satisfied with what he had done, and said that if any one of them had any objection whatever to the manner in which the case had been settled that he must speak out and state his views. However, they all said that they were satisfied, and had no opposition to offer, nor would they again raise the question; it being understood that if it was again brought up, no attention would be paid to them and they were to be bound by the proceedings just had in the case.

Arze says that as the boundary which he had established between the Santa Anas on the west and the San Felipes on the east ran through some pieces of land which the former had planted as a result of the partition made by

José Pino, and which pieces by the later adjustment of the boundaries fell to the share of the San Felipes, and also as the latter had sold to some citizens other pieces of land, some by permission of the government and others without, which pieces by the said adjustment now belonged to the Santa Anas, he directed them respectively not to take possession of such lands until after the crops should be gathered; and he also told them that they must reimburse the citizens who had bought lands of them and who were now losing them, either by giving them other lands or by paying back to them the sums they had given for them, and that they should make deeds for the lands for the protection of their owners, said deeds to be approved by the government.

On June 7, 1813, Arze reported his action to the acting governor, saying that what had been done by José Pino in regard to the lands on the west side of the river ought to be approved, but what Pino had done on the east side should be annulled and the boundary fixed by Arze on that side should receive his approval.

On June 18, 1813, Manrique approved the proceedings and ordered that they be filed in the archives.

1357 PROCEEDINGS in a dispute between the Indians of Taos and some Spanish citizens who were occupying lands within the boundaries of the grant claimed by the Indians.

This manuscript begins with a petition by José Francisco Lujan, governor of the pueblo of Taos, to the chief alcalde Don José Miguel Tafoya, in which the Indian governor states that whereas the king had given to them "a league of land in the four directions," they wanted the alcalde to deliver it to them, in order that their families might spread out over the planting lands and have ample pasturage for their animals; and that knowing that the citizens who had usurped their lands would make damaging allegations against them and that the Indians would not know how to properly set forth their rights in the premises, they had requested Fr. Benito Pereyro to represent them.

The petition ends with a prayer for justice.

Following the petition is a statement by the alcalde, April 11, 1815, in which he expresses the opinion that the Indians should apply for relief to the governor of the Province, because the owners of the ranches inside the Indian league would make so great opposition to the granting of their petition that the matter could not be settled except by an order of the governor.

On April 18, 1815, Governor Alberto Maynez issued the following decree:

"The league of five thousand varas measured from the cross in the cemetery in all directions, of which His Majesty made grant to each town of Indians from the beginning of its establishment, is in order that it be conserved for the maintenance of its natives; so that they have the use and can not give nor sell without permission of the King; because of its being a patrimony or entailed estate, so that no judge or governor has the power to sell a part or the whole of said league.

"If it should result that for many years past or in any manner whatever citizens may have intruded to plant and build on the Indians' land, they ought to lose the work done, leaving their ground free to them; but as from this grave injuries might result to the citizens, the chief alcalde of Taos will temper equity with justice so far as possible, hearing the parties and adjusting their differences in such manner that the natives shall not be left injured in the compromise which they may make; and Don Felipe Sandoval, the Protector of the Indians, will set forth after this decree whatever may occur to him in regard to the present petition."

On the same day Felipe Sandoval, speaking on behalf of the Indians, suggested that the matter might be settled by a compromise, the citizens being given to understand that the tract belonged to the Indians' league and that those who had made purchases within the tract had no right to lands of the pueblo.

Following the suggestion of Sandoval is a note by Governor Maynez, to the effect that if the planting permitted to the citizens in the Arroyo Hondo marsh should be prejudicial to the Indians, the citizens should not be allowed to plant; and the alcalde was directed to determine that matter as might be most just and proper.

May 3, 1813, Pedro Martin, who apparently was the alcalde of Taos, reported to Governor Maynez what he had done in the matter under consideration. He says that he measured the league with an ordinary vara, and as a result of the measurement the citizens were deprived of a tract of land one thousand seven hundred varas wide, from east to west, and three thousand nine hundred and fifty varas, from north to south; that all this land had been improved by the citizens, and that included in it there were three villages with about 190 families, and also a church, which the citizens had built.

The alcalde also states that the citizens had represented to him that when the Cumanches were on the war-path, the Indians of Taos gathered the citizens together and treated them with great kindness, in order to have their assistance against the warlike Cumanches; that in addition to this, by a decree dated May 1, 1793, Governor Fernando de la Concha ordered that the league be measured, and the citizens representing the grants included within the league agreed that the boundaries should remain at the customary places with the obligation of the pastures being common.

Also the alcalde says that he proposed to the Indians that they should allow the Spaniards to retain their houses and ranches, and in consideration of that the Spaniards should give them cattle and horses to the number of forty-five; that the Indian governor and his interpreter agreed to it, but when they laid the matter before the Indians, the latter not only refused the proposition, but abused them; that if the Spanish governor should decide that the citizens were to lose their ranches which they had bought in good faith, it was the alcalde's opinion that the Indians should lose what they had bought to the prejudice of the heirs of Sebastian Martin; that these Martin lands would provide a place for the Spaniards where they could be given other lands equivalent to what they were losing.

In conclusion he says that the settlement of the Arroyo Hondo would not injure either the Indians or the Spaniards, because it was more than 10,000 varas distant from the league.

On May 6, 1815, Governor Maynez issued the following decree:

"By no means do I wish any wrong to the Indians of Taos or to the citizens. My foregoing decree of the fifteenth of last April can not be changed, because it is just and well founded; it is sufficiently ample for the alcalde and the Rev. Father Missionary to average things so as to leave them by compromise in permanent peace; and the Arroyo Hondo will be settled by farmers, if it can be done without prejudice to third parties."

On May 20, 1815, the alcalde, Pedro Martin, and the missionary priest, Fr. Benito Pereyro, made report to the governor of what they had done in trying to bring about a compromise between the Spaniards and the Indians and also made certain recommendations in the matter. They say that they urged the Spaniards to give the Indians fifty horses and cattle in consideration of the landmarks being left at their customary places; that the Indians rejected this proposal and demanded their league, etc.

They then state that in their opinion the league might be given to the Indians, but the latter ought to pay for the Spanish improvements and give to them the lands which the Indians had purchased in the tract which formerly belonged to Captain Sebastian Martin; that the Indians have the best land in the Province, but do not cultivate it at all, and rent portions of it to the Spaniards; that the latter, being the conquering nation, ought to have those lands which the Indians do not improve or cultivate, and also the Sebastian Martin tract.

In conclusion they say that they would have decided the case, had it not been that the Indians requested that the governor should determine its merits; therefore they transmit the papers with the statement made by the attorney for the Spaniards.

This statement, May 15, 1815, is directed to the alcalde and is signed by José Romero, who states that he has been appointed the defender of the citizens. He says that the damage done to the citizens applies to forty-four tracts of land and two villages containing about 200 families with a church built by the Spaniards; that the surrender of this property would be an annulment of the grants made to their forefathers in the name of the king; that they can exhibit documents and deeds showing that they had purchased the lands, and that furthermore, the Indians not only permitted the making of the grants, but kindly treated the Spaniards in order to get their assistance in defending the pueblo against the savage Cumanches. These are not the only arguments used by Romero, but are probably the most important. He intimates that if the Spaniards should be deprived of their property they will be placed in a position of so hopeless character that they may be driven to some act of desperation. This language evidently accounts for one of the statements in the governor's final decree, which bears date May 22, 1815, and is as follows:

"My foregoing decrees of the 15th of April and 6th of May cannot be better founded in principles of right and justice, nor more expressive to the end of inclining the parties to compromise and tranquility; and if the alcalde, the parish minister and Don José Romero find means of placing them in permanent peace without claims by either party, I give to them all of my authority for the purpose of mediation and compromise, for it is my intention that there be no more writing and that it all be remedied by verbal decisions, if it should be possible.

"When matters are conducted by legal steps, and without violence, there are no results to be feared, and to proclaim them is the same as to speak with little respect for the lawful authorities. It is a matter which if it is not cut short by a verbal decision, I shall take special care to settle it without any order from the General Commandant or from the Royal Audiencia, to whom, because of its gravity, its decision belongs. This occasion I should not wish to arise, considering the distance and the expense to the parties, and I shall appreciate it if the parties make a compromise for the good and tranquility of all, to which I shall contribute in the cases in which the Indians of Taos apply to me. But it being laid down as a principle that their rights to the league which His Majesty granted to them are incontestable, it is to the interest of the citizens to placate them, because if an ordinary trial be had it appears that the right is on the side of the Indians."

This archive has been used in the courts of Taos county in sustaining the rights of the Indians to the league of land given them by the Spanish crown.

1358 LETTER from Juan Antonio Baca to Governor Alberto Maynez relative to a suit in regard to lands claimed by an Indian named Quintana, who belonged to the Pueblo of Cochiti.

The writer of this letter did not in all places express himself with perfect clearness, but apparently the matter he was discussing was in relation to a suit between his family and the Cochiti Indian, Quintana, in which the Indian had secured a favorable decision, or at any rate seemed to have the better of the litigation up to the time when Baca wrote his letter, March 14, 1815.

He says that he had received an order not to use the land included within the landmark or monument which Governor José Manrique had directed the alcalde, Juan José Gutierrez, to build, which he had done; that, although the suit had turned on the question whether the boundary is farther above or farther below (some point understood by the writer but not named) shortly before the governor had ordered that the boundary be removed to where it had stood in the beginning when the land had been purchased, as was evidenced by deeds of sale which were in his possession.

Facsimile of Signature of Captain Francisco Trebol Navarro, Governor of New Mexico, 1778.

Facsimile of Signature of Governor Don Fernando de la Concha, 1789-1794.

Facsimile of Signature of Don Francisco Antonio Marin del Valle, Governor and Captain-General, 1754-60.

Facsimile of Signature of Don Pedro Fermin de Mendinuueta, Governor and Captain-General, 1767, 1778.

Facsimile of Signature of Don Tomas Velez Cachupin, Governor and Captain-General, 1749-1754.

Facsimile of Signature of General Don Juan Bautista de Anza, Governor of New Mexico, 1778-1789.

Apparently the Bacas had lands and houses within the boundary claimed by Quintana and were obliged to give them up, so Baca says in his letter that they could do nothing more than to demand reimbursement for their property, which he estimates at a value of 4,000 pesos in coin, and go elsewhere to find other lands. He refers also to Don Pedro Pino as being a person familiar with the case, and who could give the governor information about the boundaries, as he had measured the pueblo league, and had experience in other matters in the premises.

Concluding, he says that a short time before he had gone to the governor of the pueblo to learn what he could about the unfounded complaint that had been made by Quintana, and the Indian governor had told him that he knew nothing about it and the people of his pueblo did not mix up in it; that only Quintana and his partisans were those who had made the trouble.

The location of the land is not fixed in the letter; as it is dated at Peña Blanca, it is possible the land was in that vicinity.

1359 LETTER from José Gutierrez, dated at Bernalillo, March 3, 1816, to Governor Alberto Maynez, in regard to lands belonging to the Indians of Sandia, which they had loaned to some Spanish citizens.

Gutierrez says that he had received the governor's decree of the 23d of the preceding February, it having been shown to him by the Sandia Indians along with a preceding report by Don Felipe Sandoval, the protector of the Indians, based upon information received from the Indians; that the report is lacking in truth, and if the protector of the Indians had made a personal examination of the premises instead of depending on hearsay, the Indians would not have presented these unfounded charges.

Gutierrez discusses the matter with great detail. According to his statement the Indians, in the year 1814, loaned to more than 20 Spaniards, who were poor and had no lands of their own, certain pieces east of the Rio Grande and about 2,000 varas from the intake of the Sandia irrigating ditch; they were loaned for a period of five years. Six of the Spaniards had built some huts on the land in order to have some place in which to live while farming, and in two years' time they had begun to get some return for their labors. Then the governor of the pueblo began to make trouble and demand that the Spaniards give up the land, notwithstanding the fact that most of the people of the pueblo were willing that they should retain it to the end of the period of five years. He states that he believes it proper that the Spaniards should be allowed the use of the lands at least for the year 1816, in order that they might have the benefits of three years' worth of work of the five years; the latter period is, he says, the customary one in the country.

1360 LETTERS (2). This consists of two separate documents.

One is a letter from Alberto Maynez, who was a colonel in the Spanish army and had been previously acting as governor of New Mexico, dated September 17, 1817, and directed to Felipe Sandoval, protector of the Pueblo Indians of New Mexico, stating that the attorney who was defending the Indians in the City of Mexico, evidently under the impression that Maynez was still exercising executive powers, had directed to him the official communication which he was forwarding to Sandoval.

The other is the official communication referred to, which is by Don Blas Abadiano, under date of February 8, 1817, to Don Alberto Maynez, acting governor of New Mexico, requesting that the latter would have the Indians of Cochiti make a petition for a certified copy of the deed of sale which they made to Mr. Alencaster for the Cile (Sile?) ranch and of the one which the latter made to the Ortizes; also that they make another petition asking that Captain Don Anacleto Miera Pacheco produce the order which he received from Mr. Alencaster for them to sell a ranch to Don Luis Baca, or to give information as to its whereabouts and contents.

1361 PROCEEDINGS in land suit.

Copy made by Rafael Cuentas, special notary of the Royal Audiencia of Guadalajara, of certain proceedings had in that tribunal in connection with a suit about the annulment of a sale of real property made by the Indians of Cochiti, dated January 31, 1817.

It appears that the king's attorney, as protector of the Indians, desired to push a suit in which the Indians of Cochiti were interested, which related to the annulment of the sale of the Peña Blanca ranch, situate within the Pueblo Grant and then occupied by Don Luis Baca and also to the return to them of the ranch known as the Santa Cruz Spring, which they had purchased in 1744, for the sum of 1,500 pesos; that not being able to verify all the matters alleged by the Indians, the king's attorney asked the Audiencia to require the governor of New Mexico to transmit all the papers at Santa Fe in any way relating to the matter. This request of the attorney was made January 16, 1817, and the Audiencia granted it the 25th of that month.

At the end of this document, in the handwriting of the governor, Pedro Maria de Allande, is the following: "Answered, and the *Expediente* transmitted on May 31, 1817.
"ALLANDE" [rubric]

1362 DOCUMENTS referring to litigation then before the Royal Audiencia of Guadalajara, between the Indians of Santo Domingo and Cochiti, one side, and Don Antonio Ortiz and Don Luis Maria Cabeza de Baca, on the other; the dispute with Ortiz being in regard to the Sile tract, and that with Baca being in relation to the Peña Blanca and Santa Cruz tracts. Rough drafts.

The entire document is in the handwriting of the governor, Don Pedro Maria de Allande.

The first draft is that of an order by Governor Allande, directing that the lands of the two pueblos be measured, in order to settle the questions which had arisen between them and their opponents. The order appoints a considerable number of persons as commissioners, attending witnesses, attorneys in fact, etc., and directs that the measurements be made in accordance with the opinion of Don Francisco Antonio de Landa, December 31, 1816, and with a view to reporting the results to the Royal Audiencia. It is dated at Santa Fe, May 10, 1817.

The second rough draft is that of a proceeding announcing the conclusion of the *expediente*, and directing that it be sent to the Royal Audiencia, in order that that tribunal should decide the matter in dispute. This is dated at Santa Fe, May 28, 1817.

It is stated that the proceedings made two books, one of 84 leaves and the other of 51 leaves.

The third draft is of a letter of transmittal, dated May 31, 1817, sending to Don Rafael Cuentas, secretary of the Audiencia, the *expediente* above referred to.

1363 DOCUMENTS relative to Indians.
>This manuscript is a copy of various documents in the archives of the Royal Audiencia at Guadalajara, treating principally of the need of having the Indians instructed in Christian doctrine, and deploring the results which had arisen from the action of the Spanish Córtes in abolishing the teaching of the doctrine in the Spanish language by Indians who had been instructed for that purpose, and who were known in the pueblos as *Fiscales de Doctrina*.
>
>The subject appears to have been called to the attention of the Audiencia by communications received from the local protector of the Indians of New Mexico, and incidentally connected therewith are references to some land matters affecting some of the New Mexican pueblos.
>
>On page 1, of leaf 3, it is stated that the pueblo of Santa Ana was situated on very bad land, and that its inhabitants, in order to support themselves, were compelled to farm lands on the Rio del Norte, at a distance of four leagues from the pueblo; that the Indians of San Felipe had usurped some pieces of these lands without any authority or right and had sold them to three or four Spanish citizens; that the nullity of these sales was particularly fixed by a decision of the Royal Audiencia made public in the city of Guadalajara on April 19, 1817; that the member of the Audiencia who was responsible for the protection of the Indians had requested, among other things, that the governor of New Mexico be directed to restore the lands in question to their rightful owners and to give a hearing to the persons who had bought them, with a view to providing other lands for them on the royal domain and entirely separated from the lands of the Indians.
>
>This request was made March 26, 1818, and on the following day it was approved by the Audiencia.
>
>The governor of New Mexico was informed of this action May 20, 1818. Apparently no answer was received from him, and assuming that the communication sent to him had never been received, the present manuscript, containing all the proceedings in the archive up to that time, was prepared by the secretary of the Audiencia, Don Rafael Cuentas, January 14, 1819.

1364 LETTER from Ignacio Maria Sanchez Vergara, April 14, 1819, to Lieutenant-Colonel Facundo Melgares (either Governor or Acting Governor of New

Mexico at that time) referring to communications received from the Royal Audiencia of Guadalajara, etc.

In regard to the land suit between Santa Ana and San Felipe, etc., and suggesting as a solution of the dispute that the two pueblos should abide by the action of Don José Pino, deceased, and that the pieces of land included within the boundaries established at that time should be given to the Indians of Santa Ana; that the persons in possession of the lands should give them up, and recover the price they had paid for them from the Indians of San Felipe, who had sold them.

In the margin of this letter, under date April 22, 1819, is a rough draft of the reply to it. The governor says that he has determined that the decision of the Royal Audiencia shall be fully complied with without loss of time. He directs Sanchez to go to the land in question, and in company with the chief alcalde of Alburquerque, who was to represent the governor, to make proper distribution of the lands; also he tells him to tell the parties in interest (holders of the land) that he will grant them at Socorro better and more fertile lands than those they are losing.

He adds that as the Indians of San Felipe probably sold lands that did not belong to them, that it would be well for them to make some suggestion as to the manner in which they should make restitution for that which they had taken mistakenly or improperly.

1365 PUEBLOS. Sales of Lands.

This archive contains eleven separate papers, eight of which are numbered in red ink, thus "1365-1." The other three are numbered, also in red ink, "1365-2." The eight papers referred to have nothing whatever to do with the Santa Ana or San Felipe pueblos or any other lands; they relate only to ecclesiastical matters. The three papers, numbered "1365-2" relate to the dispute between the Indians of Santa Ana and those of San Felipe, arising from sales made by the latter of lands belonging to the former.

The first of these three papers shows that Josef Mariano de la Peña, chief alcalde of Alburquerque, had been commissioned by the acting governor of New Mexico, Don Facundo Melgares, to carry into effect the decision of the Royal Audiencia of Guadalajara in regard to the matter in controversy; that with that object in view he went to the land in question and on May 7, 1819, in the presence of the litigants and the local protector of the Indians, Don Ignacio Maria Sanchez Vergara, proceeded to examine the boundary in dispute; having done this and having made inquiries as to the former situation of the river, and having had exhibited to him a document made by Don José Maria de Arze, dated July 6, 1813 (perhaps June 6, 1813; see archive 1356), he finally came to the conclusion that permanent landmarks should be established along the eastern edge of the old bed of the Rio del Norte to designate the boundary between the lands of San Felipe and those of Santa Ana. He explains that his reason for establishing the boundary along the eastern edge of the old river bed was that when the river left that bed and cut a new channel for itself farther west, it damaged to that extent the lands of the Santa Anas, but did not damage those of the San Felipes.

On May 8, 1819, Peña inquired into the matter of the sales made to Spaniards by the Indians of San Felipe. He says that Don Juan Bautista Gonzales exhibited five deeds, dated from 1782 up to 1816; that the sum of the amounts paid for four different purchases, and one for which there was no deed, amounted to more than 2,700 pesos in the current prices of the country, which sum had been paid in sheep, cattle, horses, money, etc.; that Gonzalez obeyed the order to surrender the land, but requested that the vendors should return what he had paid for it, or that he be given land on the royal domain, on the eastern side of the river, between the pueblos of Santo Domingo and San Felipe.

Don José Francisco Silva, who also was willing to give up the land he was occupying, stated that he was not its owner; that it belonged to Juan Estevan Pino, of Santa Fe, in whose possession the deeds would be found.

Miguel Lopez, in obeying the order to vacate, stated that it was not his; that he was working it under a lease from the owner, Don Pablo Montoya, a citizen of Las Golondrinas, in the District of Santa Fe, who was in possession of the deeds.

Peña notified Don José Garcia, Alonso Garcia, Juan Domingo Archibeque, Pablo Archibeque, Diego Chaves, Francisco Gutierrez, and Rev. Fr. Jeronimo Riega, some of whom were absent and others ill, that they must return the lands belonging to the pueblo of Santa Ana and that in compensation they would be granted others at Socorro.

The second paper is a letter from Peña to Melgares,

May 8, 1819, which in a general way reviews the action taken and set forth in his report. He states that the protector of the Indians, Sanchez Vergara, and the Santa Ana people, were satisfied with what he had done but the San Felipe Indians were not; that to have settled it in any other way would have been to the injury of the Santa Anas who had already been damaged by the river changing its course, while the San Felipes had suffered no loss on that account; that the citizens understood that the sales made to them by the San Felipes were declared to be null; that as there was not sufficient time for them to dig new irrigating ditches that season on the lands which might be given them in lieu of those they were giving up, they requested that they might be allowed to plant and gather on the latter the harvests of that year.

In the margin of the letter, under date, May 11, 1819, is the rough draft of the reply, in which it is stated that the planting and harvesting of the crops is a matter which the Santa Ana people may decide as they see fit.

The third paper is a letter, dated May 9, 1819, from the protector of the Indians, Ignacio Sanchez Vergara, to Melgares, covering about the same ground as the letter of Peña to the governor.

In the margin of the letter, May 11, 1819, is a rough draft of Melgares' reply. He directs Sanchez to go back with the alcalde of Alburquerque and make the San Felipe Indians pay back the money they had received from the persons to whom they had illegally sold the lands, or else make restitution by giving them other lands. He says that in case there are any lands belonging to the royal domain between San Felipe and Santo Domingo, they will be given to the citizens who asked for them at that place.

The last paragraph of this rough draft is not perfectly clear; it seems, however, to mean that the Indians of San Felipe were obligated to pay into the royal treasury the amount they had illegally received from any Spaniard, who, having given up to the Santa Anas the land he had purchased from the San Felipes, subsequently had been given other lands in lieu thereof out of the royal domain.

1366 PETITION by Ignacio Sanchez Vergara, Protector of the Indians, on behalf of the Indians of Santa Ana, to the Governor of New Mexico, dated June 4, 1819.

According to the statements of the protector, the Indians of Santa Ana, on account of the poor quality of the land in the neighborhood of their pueblo, requested permission to come down to the edge of the Rio del Norte, where they had their planting lands, and there establish the pueblo. They also offered to give for the lands at Algodones, in the San Felipe lands, the same amount which the Indians of San Felipe had paid for them. They assumed that the San Felipes did not need the Algodones lands because they had made numerous sales of them to citizens.

There is nothing to show that any action was ever taken in this matter.

1367 PETITION by the Indians of the Pueblo of San Juan to the Commandant-General at Chihuahua, requesting his protection in the matter of various abuses of which they complain.

Relative to land matters they say they had learned of a proclamation relating to the cutting down of the lands of the pueblos; that their lands did not extend in a direction as far as a league; that they, however, had been more loyal vassals of the king than had the other pueblos who had their leagues in full.

The entire document is badly composed, disconnected, and is a rambling protest against any reduction of their possessions, the payment of tithes, and being refused burial in the church.

In the margin, under date October 11, 1821, is an order of the commandant-general, Garcia Cónde, directing the acting governor of New Mexico to see to it that the Indians were not molested in any manner, maintaining them in the possession of their lands, and not permitting any changes in the government of the pueblos, the preservation of the church, and the contributions they made for that purpose.

This document contains a statement by the Indians of San Juan giving the reasons why the title of "*Caballeros*" was given to them.

1368 PUEBLO OF ISLETA. Jurisdiction of, in August 16, 1822.

José Antonio Chaves Duran [rubric]; Juan Gutierrez [rubric].

1369 PUEBLO OF PECOS.

Question as to lands; contest with Domingo Fernandez and others. 1830. Letter from José Maria Paredes, secretary of the *"Segunda Sala de la Suprema Corte de Justicia."* Mexico, February 17, 1830, to Don Ramon Abreu, secretary of the Diputacion Provincial.

A claim in regard to the title to lands by the pueblo of Pecos which claim had been before the supreme court of justice in the City of Mexico.

1370 PECOS INDIANS.

Petition relative to their lands, to the Diputacion. *Pecos*, March 12, 1826. Alcalde Rafael Aguilar, Subteniente, Juan Domingo Vigil, General José Manuel Armenta. 1730. Rough draft of letter to the supreme government.

Citizens to whom lands had been given at the pueblo of Pecos must not sell them until the question of title had been decided by the supreme government.

1371 REPORT as to the area of the Pueblo of Pecos, to the Minister of the Interior, *Mexico*, October 10, 1826.

Draft of a report by the governor of New Mexico to the minister of domestic and foreign relations giving information as to the lands and the population of the pueblo of Pecos and relative to the communal system of the Pueblos generally.

1372 PETITION by three Laguna Indians, who acted by authority of and in the name of the people of their pueblo, asking relief in the matter of the interference of the Acomas with their water rights.

The document is dated June 15, 1827, and complains that the Acomas are interfering with the rights of the Lagunas by enlarging the Acoma farming lands at Cubero, thus impeding the flow of the water in the little stream which flows from the Gallo spring, on which stream the pueblo of Laguna is situated; that the Acomas have always bothered the Lagunas about the water, although the governors (of New Mexico) had ordered the Acomas not to shut off the water and to confine themselves to a limited area of cultivated land so as not to interfere with the flow; and that the Lagunas have always enjoyed the right of preference to the water.

They ask that an end be put to further encroachment on the part of the Acomas by declaring that the Lagunas are entitled to the preference in the use of the waters of the stream.

In the margin of the petition, under date of June 25, 1827, there is an entry made in the office of the secretary of the Territorial Deputation of New Mexico, signed by Francisco Perez Serrano, a member and the secretary of that body, directing that in accordance with the action of the deputation the petition be transmitted to the jefe politico (governor) in order that the proper steps to the doing of justice should be taken.

1373 PETITION of June 15, 1827, by three Laguna Indians, acting by authority of and in the name of their pueblo, asking relief from the enroachment of the Cebolleta people on the Paguate ranch, which belonged to the Lagunas.

The petitioners state that the pueblo of Laguna had held the Paguate ranch from time immemorial, having bought it from a native of the pueblo from whom the ranch received its name; that the people of Cebolleta were trying to take the ranch from them and add it to the lands they already had, and that they were being aided in this by the ayuntamiento (town council) of Cebolleta; that in view of this condition the pueblo of Laguna petitioned the Territorial authorities to make to it a grant of the ranch in question with the following boundaries: "on the north by the grant conceded to Cebolleta, which is the Gavilan tableland (Mesa Del Gabilan); on the south by the league belonging to the pueblo; on the east the little butte called the Cojo (el Serrito nombrado del Cojo); and on the west the limits of the pueblo of Acoma."

The petitioners further state that they transmit with their petition three documents, numbered respectively 1, 2, and 3.

In the margin of the first page of the petition is an entry made in the office of the secretary of the Territorial Deputation, dated June 25, 1827, and signed by Francisco Perez Serrano, a member and the secretary of that body, directing that in accordance with the action of the deputation the petition be transmitted to the jefe politico (governor) in order that the proper steps to the doing of justice be taken.

Document one (1), of the three above referred to, is a communication from Lorenzo Romero, governor, Juan Miguel *Cacique*, and Blas, war-captain, to the civil and

THE SPANISH ARCHIVES OF NEW MEXICO 443

military governor of New Mexico, dated at Santa Fe, August 28, 1826, stating that they appeared before him with documents of the properties belonging to the pueblo of Laguna, in order that he should give to them his official approval, in order to avert future claims and injuries.

There is an endorsement on this communication, dated August 28, 1826, signed "Narbona" (Antonio Narbona was at that time the jefe politico, or governor, of New Mexico) and in these words: "Let it be done as is requested; returning all to the parties in interest for the use which may be to their benefit."

Document two (2) is an undated copy, made by Eusebio Aragon, of an original which he states was torn and much handled, which original appears to have been a document made on May 15, 1796, by Antonio Sedillo, chief alcalde, in which he relates that one Pascual Pajarito, who had a grant made by the governor (of New Mexico) for a house and tillable lands, had attempted to drive Juan Paguasti away from the latter's ranch, and that Sedillo had called the parties together, with the *cacique* and other principal men and had read to them the act of possession which Pajarito had, and had settled the dispute between them, Pajarito being entitled to his house and tillable lands, but the pasture and wood lands, which he had claimed as his, were declared to be common to all. Sedillo says that he made the document as an evidence of the settlement of the dispute; that Paguasti was an older settler than Pajarito, and that the former and his brothers were well behaved Indians, etc. Furthermore, Sedillo orders that the document be presented to the governor on his general inspection tour, in order that it might receive his approval.

At the end of the document is the following:

"Santa Fe, August 28, 1826.
"This document approved in so far as belongs to this government, and according to the merit and formality with which it appears. (Signed) NARBONA [rubric]"

Document three (3) is made by Ignacio Maria Sanchez Vergara, the official protector of Indians, on June 1, 1820, at the pueblo of Jémez.

This officer states that the Indians named in the document presented the same to him, which document had been drawn up by the former alcalde, Antonio Sedillo, in regard to a suit between Juan Paguate and Pascual Pajarito, in which the alcalde had ordered the disputants to confine themselves to their individual holdings and not to interfere with each other.

Then he goes on to refer to the fact that the pueblo had acquired the Paguate ranch by "just title," and that after the alcalde, José Manuel Aragon, had given the possession to the people of Cebolleta, of the grant made to them, the Paguate ranch still remained undisturbed with its ancient boundaries, the boundary in the direction of the new settlement (Cebolleta) being the table-land called the Gavilan, with which the new Cebolleta colonists were satisfied.

This is followed by a deal of language about the Paguate ranch being about the only valuable land left to the Lagunas, etc., etc., and finally Sanchez says that he gives this document to the Indians for their protection.

Following the document is an endorsement in these words:

"Santa Fe, August 28, 1826.
"This document approved in so far as belongs to this government, and according to the merit and formality with which they appear. (Signed) NARBONA [rubric]"

1374 PETITION by Mariano Rodriguez to the Jefe Politico of New Mexico, on his own part and in behalf of the Indians of the Pueblo of Picuriés protesting against the giving of possession of lands within the common lands of the Pueblo to Rafael Fernandez and Miguel Gonzales, and requesting that the steps already taken in the matter be revoked.

The petitioner says among other things, that it is the custom of the parties whom he names to ask for the possession of lands, and as soon as the same have been granted to them to dispose of them, thereafter asking for other lands with the intention of repeating the operation.

The petition is dated at Picurié, on May 14, 1829.

In the margin is an order dated June 5, 1829, signed by Ramon Abreu, secretary of the Territorial Deputation, setting forth the action of that body in regard to the matter. It is stated that the right of ownership to the lands for which they had asked is not given to Rafael Gonzalez [this is a mistake as to the name of the petitioner] and his associates; that as soon as they harvest the crops from the lands they were allowed to plant for that year, they shall go away from the place; that the order directing this action be presented by the protestant to the proper alcalde, who shall make it known to the parties affected by it, and shall cause it to be complied with.

This paper is followed by another, dated March 4, 1830, which apparently is a report of a committee of the Territorial Deputation, which, after reviewing and quoting the decision of that body, dated June 6, 1829, reports that the application of the petitioners ought not to be granted.

There is also another report of another committee, dated April 14, 1831, which simply amounts to an approval of the previous action of the Territorial Deputation and the report of the committee of March 4, 1830.

1375 DEPOSITION COPY, which was transmitted to the Supreme Government. Dated July 1, 1829. The copy bears the signature of José Antonio Chaves, who was the *Jefe Politico* (or Governor) of New Mexico somewhere about that date.

The first part of the document is a copy of the deposition of Don Andrés Romero and Don Juan José Gurierrez, taken at Bernalillo, May 18, 1829, on the petition of the natives of Sandia, by the constitutional alcalde, Pedro José Perea.

The deponents were respectively 69 and 66 years of age. They state that for years they had known that the *"lands in litigation"* had no other owner than those of the pueblo; that they also know, from information received from their forefathers, that when there was a great famine among the Moquis a priest who had learned of it reported the matter to the government, with a view to having those Indians brought within the fold of the Church; that an adequate escort was sent to the Moquis, and they were told that if they wanted to become Christians lands would be given to them upon which they could support themselves; that sixty odd families left the Moqui pueblo, and having adopted the Christian religion, were settled at the pueblo of Sandia.

The foregoing is followed by a somewhat complicated and vague statement rather difficult to thoroughly understand. However, I gather from it that the deponents meant to state that the settlement of the Indians at Sandia was made known to the citizens of Bernalillo and those of Alameda, and that they agreed to it, with the understanding that the western boundary of the Indians' lands was to be the Del Norte river; also it seems likely that the lands herein before referred to as the *"lands in litigation"* were situated outside of the boundaries of the pueblo of Sandia, and extended for half a league in the direction of Alameda; and that all this was understood by the citizens, and for years the Indians had had no suit in regard to said lands, and had not sold them.

The second part of the document is a copy of a deposition of Rafael Miera, made at Bernalillo, May 15, 1829, before the constitutional alcalde, Pedro José Perea.

The deponent states that he was 37 years old; that some 12 or 13 years before the date of his deposition he was at the house of his father-in-law, Don Eusebio Rael, in company with some of his brothers-in-law, when Don Ignacio Sanchez came to the house, and, after having conversed for some time with Don Eusebio Rael, took from his pocket the grant of the Sandia Indians; that the deponent saw that Sanchez was reading the grant, and pinching out of it certain words and putting in others with a pen he had in his hand; that also on that same occasion deponent heard Sanchez say that now they could bring suit for the lands claimed by the pueblo of Sandia, and he promised Don Eusebio Rael that if he got the land he would give him the half of it; that while the suit was going on deponent's brother-in-law asked him what he was going to put up to assist in paying for the paper and other expenses which might arise, and he replied that in view of what he had witnessed, he would not contribute even half a real.

1376 PUEBLOS OF SANTO DOMINGO and SAN FELIPE. 1831.

Grant to. Papers transferred to, reported No. 142. File No. 200.

1377 COMPLAINT of Ursula Chaves. Santa Fe, July 5, 1835.

Dispossession of certain lands near Los Padillas. The signature of Governor Perez is very finely executed.

1378 LETTER from Agustin Duran, Second Alcalde of San ta Fe, dated at Santo Domingo, February 26, 1836, to Don Gregorio Sanchez, First Alcalde of Santa Fe.

Duran informs Sanchez that the attorney in fact of the

pueblo of Santo Domingo has laid claim to certain lands on behalf of the pueblo, alleging that they had been usurped by Don Antonio Ortiz; that said lands were at the *Sile* ranch, which occupied a part of the league belonging to the said pueblo; and he requests Sanchez to direct Ortiz to appear at Santo Domingo on the following day, either personally or by attorney, to answer the charge made against him and to restore to the Indians their property.

Following this letter is the rough draft of Sanchez's reply, informing Duran that Ortiz had gone to Pojoaque, and on that account can not make a prompt appearance, but that he would do so as soon as he returned to the city. This rough draft is dated also on February 26, 1836.

In the margin of the first page is a memorandum showing that the letter was sent to Ortiz, at Pojoaque, on the 27th of the same month.

1380 PROCEEDINGS in regard to the measurement of the league to the north of the Pueblo of Santo Domingo.

On August 23, 1844, Miguel Antonio Lobato, attorney in fact for the pueblo of Santo Domingo, petitioned the governor and commandant-general of New Mexico to order a survey of the league belonging to that pueblo. He represented that the old monuments which marked the boundaries had been entirely destroyed; that because of this his clients, the Santo Domingo Indians, had had frequent disagreements with José de Jesus Sanchez, who was occupying the adjoining lands; that, with a view to obviating such disagreements and in order to avoid a ruinous suit, he requested the governor to order that the league which had been adjudicated to them by the Spanish government be measured, after summoning the owners of the adjoining lands; and that this be done in accordance with the measurements made in the year 1815, by Don Juan José Gutierrez, the alcalde of Alameda, who had acted under orders of Don Alberto Maynes, as appeared by a document which the petitioner transmitted with his petition, etc.

On August 26, 1844, Governor Martinez ordered the prefect, Don Francisco Sarracino, to make the measurements, after first summoning the owners of the adjoining lands, in order to avoid future controversies.

On September 3, 1844, Sarracino, having previously

summoned the owners of the adjoining lands, proceeded to measure a distance of 5,000 varas toward the north from the cross which stood in the center of the cemetery at the pueblo of Santo Domingo. At the point where this measurement terminated he ordered that the natives should place a firm monument of stone, and he says that in the meantime they dug two trenches in the form of a cross, and filled them with stones, as a temporary mark for the spot. Also he says that at that point there were found the foundations of three monuments which had previously existed there; that some of the Indians had predicted that he would find these if he made the measurement impartially and without error.

The report of the measurement was transmitted by Sarracino to Governor Martinez on September 8, 1844, and on the 9th of October, of the same year, the latter ordered that a certified copy of the whole proceedings be issued to the parties in interest, which was immediately done.

1381 PROTEST of March 27, 1845, by the Indians of the Pueblo of Isleta, against the granting of the Ojo de la Cabra Tract to Don Juan Otero.

This protest is directed to the governor of New Mexico by two Indians of the pueblo of Isleta, acting in behalf of their whole community. It appears that they had learned that the legislative body of New Mexico, the Departmental Assembly, had granted to Don Juan Otero a tract of land situated at the Cabra spring, which tract and spring they alleged had always been recognized as the property of their pueblo. They strongly protest against this violation of their rights, and request the governor to lay their protest before the Assembly.

This was done, and on the same day of the date of the petition that body ordered the prefect of the Third district of the Department, in concurrence with the ayuntamiento, to report upon the matter, and at the same time to direct the proper justice of the peace to do likewise. This action of the Departmental Assembly is signed by its president and secretary.

This is followed by the report of the prefect, Francisco Sarracino, dated May 15, 1845, in which, among other things, he says that the Cabra spring is outside of the Isleta league; that the land is not the lawful property of any settlement; that the spring is very small, and during

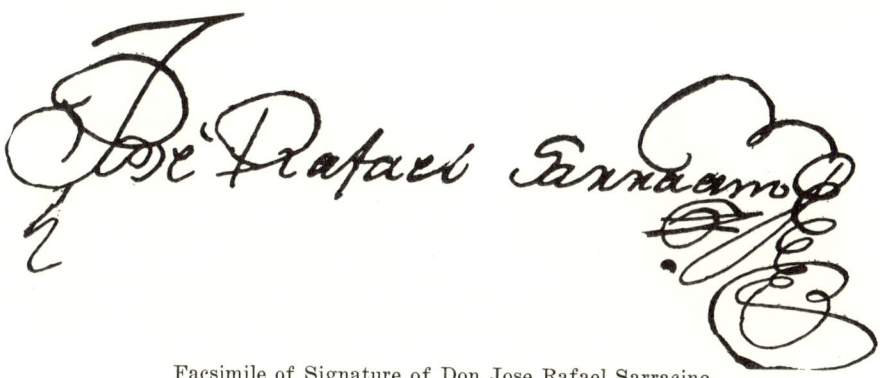

Facsimile of Signature of Don Jose Rafael Sarracino.

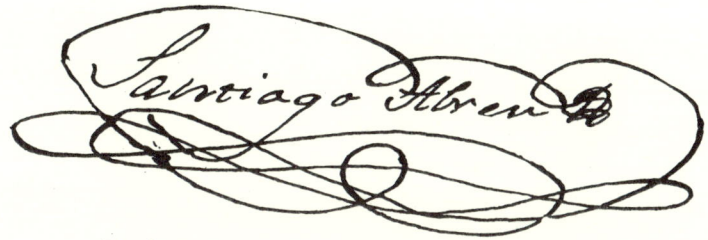

Facsimile of Signature of Don Santiago Abreu.

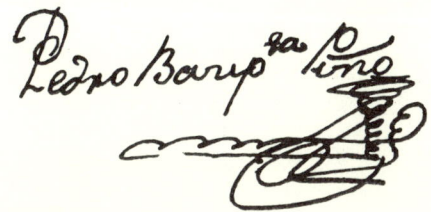

Facsimile of Signature of Don Pedro Bautista Pino, Delegate from New Mexico to the Spanish Cortes.

Facsimile of Signature of Don Carlos Beaubien.

Facsimile of Signature of Don Nicolas Ortiz.

the greater portion of the year does not furnish enough water for one horse; that the land has been considered as commons for the people of Valencia, Isleta, Padillas, and Pajarito, and for all others who have wanted to make use of it; and he concludes his report by saying that he therewith transmits the report made by the justice of the peace.

Sarracino's report is followed by the record of the action taken thereon, on June 29, 1845, by the Departmental Assembly, in which that body states that being convinced by the prefect's second report, dated May 15th, that the place of the Cabra spring had been considered as a part of the commons of the pueblo and other places mentioned in the report, it repealed the decree of the 14th of the previous March, by which the place had been granted to Don Juan Otero, and declared the same to be null and void. It also ordered that its action in the matter be communicated to the governor, in order that he might notify the parties in interest, and cause the same to be complied with.

On July 7, 1845, the governor issued his order that the decree of the Departmental Assembly should be observed in all particulars by the parties whom it concerned.

There are two other separate papers in this archive, each referring to the proceedings above set forth. The first is a communication dated June 2, 1845, from Ramon Luna to the prefect of the district, in which he makes it plain that, although he believes the Indians have always owned the Cabra Spring Tract, he does not feel that he ought to or can report on the matter until he has before him the petition presented by the Indians, and the report of the prefect in concurrence with the ayuntamiento. The second of these papers is a fragment of the proceedings of the Departmental Assembly on June 29, 1845, followed by a rough draft of a letter of transmittal informing the governor of the action which the Assembly had taken in the matter.

1382 OJO DE LA CABRA GRANT.

This archive consists of three papers, all of which have to do with the Ojo de la Cabra Grant to Don Juan Otero, the revocation thereof, and kindred matters.

The first of the three is a report of a committee of the Departmental Assembly, dated September 28, 1845, and signed by A. Duran and Sena.

It was called forth by a petition, drawn up in the interest of Don Juan Otero, by his attorney, Don Manuel Muños, who evidently had argued that the tract of land known as the Cabra Spring Tract having been granted to Don Juan Otero by the governor of New Mexico could not be revoked by the Departmental Assembly of that Department.

The committee is of the opinion that the grant was not made by the governor, but by the Assembly, and assuming the correctness of Muños's contention that the governor alone has the power to grant lands, suggests that the only thing that can be done for the relief of Otero is to present a new petition to that officer praying for a grant of the lands in question.

The second paper is also a report of the same committee on the same subject, but dated one day previous to the first report. It covers substantially the same ground, and is followed by the action of the Departmental Assembly, signed by the president and secretary, approving the report and returning it to the governor with other papers in the case. The approval is dated September 28, 1845.

The third paper is an unsigned fragmentary report of a committee of the Assembly in regard to the same matter. It ends with a recommendation that the assembly adopt a resolution to the effect that the Cabra Spring Tract shall not be granted to anyone, but shall remain, as it had been from time immemorial, as common for the settlements of Isleta, Valencia, Padillas, and Pajarito; that no appeal shall be allowed to Don Juan Otero or the natives of Isleta on the subject of the dispute as to the direct ownership of the tract; and that the resolution be carried into effect as soon as it should reach the hands of the governor.

1383 REPORT of a Committee of the Department Assembly, dated April 29, 1846.

In regard to matters arising from the dispute as to the ownership of the Cabra spring property. It appears that the governor of the Department, on April 16, 1846, directed an official communication to the Assembly, inclosing a decree of the superior tribunal of the Department of Chihuahua, referring to some action had in the supreme court of justice at Mexico City, based on a complaint by Antonio José Otero, a citizen of Valencia, New Mexico, that he had been violently dispossessed of his property at the Ojo de la Cabra.

The report of the committee purports to give a full history of the case, beginning with the petition of Otero to the prefect of the Third district, on January 22, 1845, and ending with the governor's approval of the revocation of the grant, on July 7, 1845.

It is stated also that subsequently the prefect was suspended because of the bad faith he had exhibited in connection with the matter.

The report concluded with an explanation of the causes which have prevented the establishment in New Mexico of the superior tribunal of Second and Third instance, provided for by the supreme decrees of February 28, and March 2, 1843.

The details of the controversy about the Cabra spring property are much more interesting than important, in view of the final disposition of this case by the United States government. The claim based on this grant was rejected by the United States court of private land claims on November 29, 1896. Subsequently, on May 22, 1897, it was appealed to the supreme court of the United States by the plaintiffs, and that court thereafter dismissed the appeal, January 18, 1899, mandate on file in the office of the United States surveyor-general at Santa Fe, New Mexico, in cause No. 167, C. P. L. C. — the *Ojo de la Cabra* Grant.

1384 BARTOLOME LOBATO v. XPTOBAL DE ARELLANO.

Suit for the possession of an Apache slave. The petition is addressed to the Marques de la Naba Brazinas, and the order is signed by the Marques and by his secretary of government and war, Alfonso Rael de Aguilar.

LIST OF GRANTS OR ALLOTMENTS OF LANDS

TO THE

PUEBLO INDIANS

WITH HISTORICAL, DESCRIPTIVE, AND OTHER

NOTES

R. No. A PUEBLO OF JEMEZ.

Grant. 1689, September 20th. Made by Governor and Captain-General Don Domingo Jironza Petriz de Cruzate. Certificate by Don Pedro Ladron de Guitara, Secretary of Government and War.

It will be noted that this instrument was executed at El Paso, where the Spaniards maintained headquarters after the revolution of 1680, Governor Antonio Otermín and all of the Spanish colonists and inhabitants of New Mexico having been driven out by the Pueblos in the month of August of that year. At the time this grant is supposed to have been made the Pueblos were still hostile.

Inasmuch as all the alleged granting instruments made by Governor Cruzate are practically the same in wording, I give this, which is in the words and figures and abbreviations following, to wit:

1689. *En el Pueblo de Nra. Sa. de Guadalupe del Passo del Rio del Norte en veinte dias del mes de Septe. de mil seissientos y ochenta y nueva años el Señor Gouer. y Capn. Genl. Dn. Domingo Jironza Petriz de Cruzate dijo por quanto en el alcanze que se dió en el reino de la Nueva Mexco. de los Yndios Queres, y los Apostatas, y los Teguas y de la Nacion Thanos y despues de hover pele ado con todos los demas Yndios de todos pueblos un Yndio del Puo. de Zia llamado Bartolome de Ojeda que fue el que fue. el que mas se señalo en la vatalla acudiendo á todos partes se rindio biedose huedo de un valazo y un Yechasso, lo cual como dicho es mandé que denajo Juranto. declare como se alla el Puo. de Jemez que fueron unos Yndios Apostatas de aquel reino de la Nueva Mexico. pues fue el que le dió la muerte el Padre Fr. Juan de Jesus Morador. Preguntado que si este Puo. volvera en algun tiempo á Apostatarse como ha sido costumbre entre ellos y dice el confesante que no que ya está muy medio en temor, que aunque estavan abilantados con lo que les havia susedido á los de el Puo. de Zia el año pasado jusgana que era inposible ue dejaran de dar la obedienzia, por lo cual se consedió por el Señor Gouer. y Capn. Genl. Dn. Domingo Jirenza Petriz de Cruzate, los linderos que aqui anocto: para el el norte una legua y para el oriente una legua y para el poniente una legua y para el sur una legua midiendo estas de las cuatro esquinas del templo que queda en medio del Puo. assi lo proveyó, mandó, y firmó su ssa. á mi el presente Cecretario de Gov. y Ga.*

DOMINGO JIRONZA PETRIZ DE CRUZATE.

Ante mi:
DON PEDRO LADRON DE GUITARA,
Sec. de Gn. y Guea.

A literal translation of which document is as follows, to-wit:

1689. In this village of Our Lady of Guadalupe del

Paso del Rio del Norte, on the twentieth day of the month of September, in the year one thousand six hundred and eighty-nine, His Excellency, Don Domingo Jironza Petriz de Cruzate, governor and captain-general, stated that, whereas, in overtaking the Queres Indians and the Apostates, and the Teguas and those of the Thanos nation, in the kingdom of New Mexico, and after having fought with all the Indians of all the other pueblos, an Indian of the pueblo of Zia, named Bartolomé de Ojeda, one of those who was most conspicuous in the battle, rendering assistance everywhere, being wounded by a ball and an arrow, surrendered, who, as formerly stated, I ordered to declare under oath the condition of the Pueblo of Jemez, who were apostate Indians of that kingdom, having killed their priest, Fr. Juan de Jesus Morador. Being interrogated whether this Pueblo would rebel in the future, as it had been customary for them to do in the past, the deponent answered no; that they were very much terrified, and, although they were concerned with the Indians of Zia in what had occurred in the year previous, he was of the opinion that it would be impossible for them to fail in giving their allegiance.

Whereupon, His Excellency, Don Domingo Jironza Petriz de Cruzate, granted them the boundaries herein set forth: on the north one league, on the east one league, on the west one league, and on the south one league, to be measured from the four corners of the temple which stands in the center of the pueblo. His Excellency so provided, ordered, and signed before me, the present secretary of government and war, to which I certify.

DOMINGO JIRONZA PETRIZ DE CRUZATE.

Before me:
DON PEDRO LADRON DE GUITARA,
Secretary of Government and War.

The Indians of Zía belonged to the Queres stock. The battle referred to in this archive was fought by General Reneros de Posada in 1688. The present village of *Cia* is surrounded by ruins of old pueblos. Espejo says (1582) *"hallamos otra provincia que llaman los Punames, que son cinco pueblos, que la cabecera se dice Sia."* Onate calls them *"el gran pueblo de Tria."*

Jemez is north of Zia. Until about 1650, the Indians of Jemez inhabited a number of pueblos along the Jemez river. It is probable that ten pueblos were then occupied by the Jemez. The pueblos of the Jemez were abandoned after 1622 and re-occupied before 1627. Benavides, *Memorial*, p. 27, q. v.

The revolution of 1680 began at Jémez, and the alcalde mayor, Luis Granillo, sent word to General Garcia, who lived near the site of the present city of Alburquerque, to come to his aid. Garcia had only a very few men, but with them he saved Granillo and the surviving priest of Jémez, as well as the priest at the pueblo of Zía or Cia, as this pueblo is generally called today.

The reference to what occurred at the pueblo of Zía the year previous is the assaults on the pueblos of Santa Ana and Zía in the year 1688 by General Reneros de Posada, at the time acting governor at El Paso, who made a dash into New Mexico and appeared before these villages, demanding their surrender; the Indians refused; an assault was made, the villages captured, portions burned, and some of the Indians were incinerated. It is likely that this event occurred in 1687, because Reneros de Posada says himself that it transpired on the 6th of October of that year. It is difficult to reconcile this statement as to the year and date with the several certified statements made by Cruzate in 1689, every one of which says that this battle occurred the "year previous." Reneros de Posada was an officer under Cruzate. There is no doubt that the pueblo of Zía was entirely destroyed by Governor Cruzate, and that its destruction occurred later than the making of this grant to the Jémez. Cruzate's battle at Zía was undoubtedly the bloodiest of all in the re-conquest. Escalante says that this battle took place in September, 1689; it is possibly so, but being in El Paso on September 20, 1689, Cruzate would hardly have had time to lead his forces as far north as Zía, and we know that he was still in El Paso on the 25th of September. Grant to the *pueblo of Pecos*, q. v. Escalante says: "*Por Setiembre del año siguiente entró D. Domingo Gironza á la misma reducion de los rebeldes. Tuvo una sangrienta batalla en el dicho pueblo de Cia, en que los rebeldes se defendiéron con tal valor y desesperado arrojo, que muchos se dejaron quemar vivos sobre las casas por no rendirse; el numero de Queres, asi del dicho pueblo como del de Santa Ana, y de otros que vinieron de socorro á los sitiados, que quedaron muertos en esta batalla, llegó á 600 de ambos sexos y de diferentes edades. Solo cuatro ancianos se cogieron vivos; en la misma plaza del pueblo fueron arcabuzeados.*"

I have said that the Jémez abandoned their pueblos in

THE SPANISH ARCHIVES OF NEW MEXICO 455

1622; this was done because of the wars and raids of the Navajos. They came back in 1627, because of the protection guaranteed by Fr. Martin de Arvide. The celebrated Fr. Zarate-Salmeron lived at Jémez in 1618.

There is an old church at Jémez; it was probably built subsequent to 1627.

Barrionuevo, an officer under Coronado, was the first Spaniard to visit Jémez; he was there in 1541.

There were two villages of the Jémez in 1680, because there were two priests there, one of whom, Juan de Jesus Morador, was killed.

Don Fernando de Arguello, governor, hung twenty-nine of the Jémez on account of their having killed a Spaniard. Governor Ugarte put down an incipient rebellion among them. This was in 1650.

Fr. Juan de Jesus, killed in 1680, was murdered at the pueblo of the Jémez known, among the Indians, as *Ginseua, or San Diego de Jémez,* close to the Jémez Hot Springs. The one who escaped with Granillo was Fr. Francisco Muñoz. The remains of Fr. Juan de Jesus were found by De Vargas in 1694, exhumed and carried to Santa Fe and buried with great ceremony in the parish church. He fought a battle there in 1694; the Indians offered desperate resistance, but eighty-four were killed in the engagement, several of them perishing in the flames of their burning dwellings; he took 361 prisoners. See *Autos de Guerra* De Vargas, July 23, 1694, fol. 60. In 1696, they killed another frayle, named Francisco de Casaus. The Spaniards again attacked the Jémez, and in this battle, in which the Spaniards were led by Captain Miguel de Lara, the Indian, mentioned in the grant to the Jémez, Bartolomé de Ojeda, aided the Spaniards and led a part of the attacking force; his war-like conduct on this occasion was very distinguished. Forty Indians were killed.

With this archive is found a deposition by Don Donaciano Vigil, as follows:

"Donaciano Vigil, late Secretary of the Territory of New Mexico, being duly sworn, declares that since the year 1840, the period when he received the charge of the public archives of the Territory of New Mexico *there were no title-deeds of grants made to the Indian pueblos of New Mexico in the archives* under his charge from that date up to the present time. That, occupying the position he did, as secretary as well as recorder of public documents, and having had occasion to examine them very often, he had every opportunity of knowing if they were in the archives or not. The said deponent further says that the lands held by the Indian pueblos of *Tesuque, Nambé, Santa Clara,* and *San Ildefonso,* were always recognized as belonging to said Indians, by virtue of grants made to them by the authorities of the Spanish government towards the close of the seventeenth century. That from time immemorial they have continued in the pacific and quiet enjoyment of the lands they occupy without any question being raised as to their legal right thereto.

"DONACIANO VIGIL

"Subscribed and sworn to before me, this 21st day of June, 1856.   WM. PELHAM,

"Surveyor General of New Mexico."

This affidavit is of importance (historically) for several reasons; Vigil was a very sagacious man; he was well read; took a pronounced interest in these state papers; if anyone knew anything about them at that time he did; when the office of surveyor-general was created in 1854, Vigil assisted in going over all of the old archives which had been in his sole possession, for the purpose of delivering to the surveyor-general those which were deemed of importance in the administration of the affairs of his office, which was done; it was many years later when the archives not so turned over to the surveyor-general were supposed to have been burned and sold by Governor Pyle. I do not believe that any were so burned or lost that were of consequence; many were stolen and carried off *after* Pyle's time — that is certain.

The grant to the pueblo of Jémez was confirmed by the Congress of the United States, December 22, 1858.

The Don Pedro Ladron de Guevara who signs with Cruzate was one of the Spanish officers who were driven from New Mexico in the revolution of 1680. His full name was Pedro Ortiz Niño Ladron de Guevara. [Note that the archive shows "Guitara." There was no such officer.]

R. No. B PUEBLO DE ACOMA.

Grant. 1689. Made by Governor and Captain-General Don Domingo Jironza Petriz de Cruzate, September 20th.

This archive is somewhat lengthier and contains some historical information not found in the archive, R. No. A (**grant** to the *Pueblo of Jémez*), so I will give it in full, translated. As will be seen it is signed by Bartolomé de Ojeda, as well as by the governor and his secretary.

1689. In the village of our Lady of Guadalupe del Paso del Rio del Norte, on the twentieth day of the month of September, in the year one thousand six hundred and eighty-nine, his excellency, Don Domingo Jironza Petriz de Cruzate, governor and captain-general, stated that whereas in the overtaking which was had in the pueblo of Acoma, and the power which he has over the Queres Indians and over the apostates in New Mexico, he provided that an Indian named Bartolomé, who was the most conspicuous in the battles, lending his aid everywhere, and surrendered, having been wounded by a ball and an arrow, and being already crippled, I ordered him to state the truth, and declare in his confession the condition of the pueblo of Acoma and that of the other apostates in that kingdom, and as the Indian is well versed in the Spanish language, intelligent, and can read and write, he was examined before General Don Pedro Reneros de Posada, who had returned from New Mexico, having been at the pueblo of Acoma, and the maestro de campo, Dominguez Mendoza, having also been called, in order that the Indian, Bartolomé de Ojeda, might give his name.

Having been asked if he is disposed to confess the truth as to what he knew and about which he might be asked, and having been asked his name, of what place he is a native, his age and what office he has, and whether he knows the condition of Acoma and Laguna, who are neighbors, he said that his name was Bartolomé de Ojeda; that he is a native of the pueblo of Zia, in the province of New Mexico; that he is twenty-one or two years of age, more or less; that he has had no other office than that of soldier (warrior) and that he knows the condition of Acoma and Laguna because he was an apostate in the Province of New Mexico; and this he answered.

Having been asked how it happened that Laguna and Acoma, being neighbors, disagreed so much, and how was it that they had moved to the Peñol, being such arrogant Indians, and why had they left their pueblo, he responded saying that the Acomas had moved to the Peñol because they were very proud and had moved to the Peñol because of the many wars these Pueblos had, one with the other; and this was his answer.

Having been asked why it was that these Pueblos lived near to each other, what agreement there was between them and why they disagreed, he answered that Laguna moved close to Acoma because of the abundance of water there was at that pueblo, but always for the purpose of collecting the surplus remaining from the pueblo of Acoma; and this he answered.

Having been asked what are the existing boundaries of Acoma, and to how much is each pueblo restricted, he said that the Prieto mountain is on the north, that the Gallo spring is on the west, and that the Cubero mountain is opposite the old pueblo of Acoma and that the Peñol is on the south side and that when the Indian Poc-Pec (Po-pé) visited the pueblos he confirmed the above because he is an Indian of the Tegua nation and a native of the pueblo of San Juan, to whom all the land gave obedience at the time of the insurrection, and was in company with Alonzo Catiti; and Don Luis Tu-pa-tu, and many other chiefs of those pueblos had declared that the water belonged to the pueblo of Acoma, and that Laguna was to collect the surplus remaining from the pueblo; and this is his answer.

Having been asked if he knows any more than he has stated, and if Laguna has any other defense to make concerning the water, he answered that he had not; that although the pueblo had removed to the Peñol it had not lost its right to the water, and that the Laguna Indians were not ignorant of the fact as it is notorious; and that what he has stated is the truth, under the oath which he has taken, which he affirms and ratifies. This grant being read and explained to him he signed it with his excellency, the governor and captain-general, aforesaid, before me, the present secretary of government and war, to which I certify.   DOMINGO JIRONZA PETRIZ DE CRUZATE
         BARTOLOME DE OJEDA

Before me:
    DON PEDRO LADRON DE GUITARA,
        Secretary of Government and War.

From this it will be seen that Reneros de Posada *"had returned from Acoma;"* that Bartolomé de Ojeda had been wounded with a ball and an arrow and was crippled, had surrendered, having been conspicuous for his conduct in battle, etc., why can we not harmonize the conflicting dates as to the time when Zía was assaulted and destroyed by the conclusion that this affidavit and deposition was made AFTER the return from New Mexico to El Paso? Mr. Tipton's conclusion that it is spurious is the best solution.

THE SPANISH ARCHIVES OF NEW MEXICO 459

It does not necessarily follow when Ojeda says of the Jêmez *"and although they were concerned with those of Zia in what had occurred in the previous year"* that he had reference entirely to the battle fought by Posada; he may have had in mind the conduct of the several Pueblo tribes *"the year previous"* in which those of his own pueblo of Ziá had a part.

It will be noticed that there are no "granting" words in this instrument, although it is declared to be a grant *"read and explained"* to Ojeda.

The grant was confirmed to the pueblo of Acoma by the Congress of the United States on December 22, 1858.

The three Indians mentioned by Ojeda — Poc-Pec, Catit, and Tupatu — were the leaders of the revolution of 1680. Poc-Pec is also and more familiarly known as Po-pé. He was a native of San Juan and killed his son-in-law just before the uprising, for fear that he would make known what was going on to the Spaniards.

Don Juan Dominguez de Mendoza was lieutenant-general under Otermín when the latter made his effort to regain the Province. He had been an officer in the army in New Mexico for many years prior to the revolt. He came north in 1681 as far as Cochiti and had an interview with Catiti, who professed regret for the events of the year before.

On January 1, 1682, Otermin and the invading army having retired as far south as Isleta, believing that they could not hold the province with the force with them, retired to El Paso.

Poc-Pec or Po-pé was an Indian of the pueblo of San Juan. Catiti belonged to Santo Domingo, and Tu-pa-tu was of the pueblo of Picuriés.

Acoma is the *"Hacus"* of the Fr. Marcos. The present pueblo, we may safely assert, was standing in its present location in the fifteenth century. Acoma was only abandoned when the Indians went to the Peñol. In all probability it is the most ancient of the pueblos of New Mexico.

It is said that the last settlement of this pueblo prior to the one now occupied by them, was upon the celebrated *"Mesa Encantada,"* standing nearly in the center of the valley in the southwest corner of which is the *Rock of Acoma*. The *Enchanted Mesa*, it is claimed, was accessible many centuries since; at some period — entirely in Acoma tradition — dangerous crevices made their appearance in the road to the top, and a large number of the people left; those remaining were suddenly deprived of the power to reach the plain, owing to a fall of the rock and those died of hunger. This ancient pueblo was reached by Mr. F. W. Hodge, in 1897, who made the ascent, where he found enough remains to justify the tradition that a pueblo had once stood on top of the rock.

The use of the water referred to by Ojeda was not only for domestic, but for purposes of irrigation. These Indians understood the use of water for irrigation in pre-Spanish times. It is true that corn and beans did not necessarily require irrigation, as these crops grow and mature on the high mesas today without water artificially supplied. Around ruins, known to be pre-Spanish, evidences of irrigating ditches are found. Espejo in his narrative, says: *"Y de todo esto hay sementeres de riego y de temporal con muy buenas sacas de agua y que lo labran como los Mexicanos."* The Acomas did not raise cotton; they bought it either from the Moquis or from the pueblos of the Rio Grande.

The Spanish authorities, prior to the *"grants"* made by Cruzate, never allotted any specific tracts of land to the many *pueblos* in the Province.

Strange as it may seem, the Pueblo Indian, while known as of sedentary habits, thought nothing of abandoning a pueblo and building another in a different locality, and it was doubtless the policy of Cruzate, in making these allotments, to curb this tendency to move and ramble about. I do not consider the word "sedentary" as entirely satisfactory. It is true that they were agriculturists and built permanent homes, *i. e.*, permanent until something might happen which induced them to move and change their habitations; the great number of ruins are no index of a great population; one hundred Pueblo Indians were capable of building twenty-five pueblos (villages) in a century; if by chance anything happened to his water supply, forthwith he moved; if his pueblo was sacked by enemies, he built another, but rarely in the same place. All of this finds abundant documentary proof.

The Pueblos have always contended that they hold their lands by titles even superior to that of the United States government, and that they are absolute citizens of the United States, and have managed themselves and their affairs for hundreds of years, having built up customs and a local form of municipal government consisting of a vast number of officials, each of whom has a special duty to perform with regard to the management and control of the internal affairs of the pueblos.

These views are referred to in some of the decisions of the supreme court of New Mexico deciding Pueblo matters, as witness the following quotation from a decision rendered by Kirby Benedict, chief justice, in the case of *De la O vs. The Pueblo de Acoma,* decided in 1857, viz:

"Having closed our view of the merits of this case, we may be indulged in reflecting that of the highly interesting causes we have had to consider and determine during the present session, this is the second in which this Pueblo has been the party complainant. The first keenly touched the religious affections of these children of the Rock of Acoma. They had been deprived by neighboring Pueblos of the ancient likenesses in full painting of their patron or guardian saint, San José. However much the philosopher or more enlightened Christian may smile at the simple faith of these people in their supposed immediate and entire guardian of the Pueblo, to them it was a Pillar of Fire by night and a Pillar of Cloud by day, the withdrawal of whose light and shade crushed the hopes of these sons of Montezuma and left them victims to doubt, to gloom and fear. The cherished object of the veneration of their long line of ancestors, this court permanently restores, and by this decree confirms to them, and throws around them the shield of the law's protection of their religious love, piety and confidence. In this case the title that Spain had given this people, confirming to them the possession and ownership of their lands, and the rock upon which they have so long lived, was found in the hands of one professing to be of a better instructed and more civilized race, and turned by him into the means of extortion and money gathering from the inoffensive inhabitants.

"It is gratifying to us to be the judicial agents through which an object of their faith and devotion, as well as the ancient manuscript, that is the written evidence that established their ancient rights to their soil and their rock, are more safely restored and confirmed to their possession and keeping."

In early times the Acomas, among other ceremonial dances, performed the *Snake Dance,* similar to the one now given by the Moquis. Don Antonio Espejo saw one of these dances at Acoma—"*Hicieronnos un mitote y baile muy solemne, saliendo la gente muy galana y hacien-*

do muchos juegos de manos, algunos dellos artificios con vivoras vivas, que era cosa de ver lo uno y le otro."

The Indians of Acoma, under the leadership of a chief named Zutucapan, conspired to kill Don Juan de Oñate at the time of his visit to the pueblo by enticing him into an estufa. Oñate declined to be trapped.

Later on these Indians had an encounter with Zalvidar, a lieutenant under Oñate, in which Zalvidar was slain by Zutucapan; this fight occurred on top of the rock of Acoma; when Zalvidar was slain, five surviving Spaniards fled to the brink of the mesa and leaped down, four of them reaching the plain alive. Don Vicente Zalvidar, a brother of Juan who had been slain, resolved to avenge the death of his brother. In a battle which lasted three days, the Indians were decisively defeated, the buildings of the pueblo were partially burned, and hundreds killed each other rather than yield to the Spanish arms. Oñate says that Acoma had about three thousand population at this time, of whom only six hundred survived. This battle occurred on the 22d, 23d, and 24th of January, 1599.

R. No. C PUEBLO OF SAN JUAN.

Grant. September 25, 1689, made by Governor and Captain-General Don Domingo Jironza Petriz de Cruzate. The paper is signed by

DOMINGO JIRONZA PETRIZ DE CRUZATE.
BARTOLOME DE OJEDA.

DON PEDRO LADRON DE GUITARA,
Secretary of Government and War.

Ojeda says that this pueblo was the first to rebel in 1680. That all of the San Juan Indians were well versed in the Spanish language and could read and write and that at the time of the first conquest they had saved the life of their missionary.

Additional evidence that Ojeda's affidavit is spurious. In 1708, it is shown by a number of trials for witchcraft that numbers of these Indians could not read or write.

This grant was confirmed to the pueblo by the Congress of the United States on the 22d day of December, 1858. The boundaries are: on the north, the Rio Bravo del Norte, completing one league on both sides of the river, measuring from the northern corner of the temple of the pueblo on the east, and on the west one league and on the south one league.

The text of this archive is practically the same as that of Archive R. No. A.

Almost directly opposite this pueblo is the place where Don Juan de Oñate established his capital in 1598, at the place called *San Gabriel del Yunque*. Torquemada says (*Monarquia*, vol. i, p. 672) : "*Despachados Don Juan de Oñate, y los suios, para la jornada del Nuevo Mexico, siguieron su camino, en demanda de aquellas tierras, en llegando á aquellas partes, tomaron posesion por el Rei, en ellas, y el Pueblo donde Don Juan de Oñate, Governador, y Capitan General de esta entrada, hizo asiento y puso su Real, se llama San Gabriel el qual sitio está en treinta y siete grados de altura del norte, y está situado entre dos rios, y con las aguas del menor de los dos, so riegan los trigos, cevada y maiz . . . El otro rio es grande, que llaman del Norte, ques es de mucho, y muy buen pescado.*"

The first irrigation ditch constructed by the Spaniards in New Mexico was built by the colonists under Oñate and the water was taken out of the Chama river at this point. The first capital of New Mexico was here, and because the inhabitants of *Yunque* gave up their pueblo to the colonists and settled in the pueblo of San Juan, across the Rio Grande, they were known as the pueblo of *San Juan de los Caballeros*.

The *pueblo* of *Yunque* was visited by nearly all the earlier Spanish explorers or some of their soldiers and captains.

The town of Chamita of today stands close to the old pueblo of *Yunque*. I believe the place called "*Pueblito*" across the river from San Juan is very close to the old pueblo of *Yunque*; *Pueblito* is owned by Indians of San Juan.

Oñate moved the capital from this place to Santa Fé about the year 1605.

The settlers of Santa Cruz at one time tried to obtain a grant of the old pueblo of Yunque.

R. No. D PUEBLO OF PICURIES.

Grant. September 25, 1689. Made by Governor and Captain-General, Don Domingo Jironza Petriz de Cruzate, at El Paso. The archive is signed by

DON DOMINGO JIRONZA PETRIZ DE CRUZATE.
BARTOLOME DE OJEDA.

DON PEDRO LADRON DE GUITARA,
Secretary of Government and War.

The text is almost identical with that of Archive R. No. C. The Indians are declared by Ojeda to be of a very rebellious spirit.

The boundaries of the grant are—one league, north, east, south, and west, measured from the four corners of the temple situated on the western side of the village.

The grant was confirmed by the Congress of the United States on the 22d day of December, 1858.

The Rio del Pueblo and the Rio Peñasco unite about a mile below the pueblo of Picuriés. This pueblo, so far as inhabitants are concerned, is now a very small affair. It is situate in a beautiful spot.

Tu-pa-tu, one of the leaders of the revolution of 1680 was a native of this pueblo.

The mission at this pueblo was called *San Lorenzo de Picuriés.* The priest who was murdered by the Indians here in 1680 was the Rev. P. Fr. Mathias Rendon.

When the Indians made their attack on Santa Fe, during the first day's fighting Otermín was successful, but on the day following the Tehuas of the north and from Picuriés, led by Tu-pa-tu, arrived and Otermín retired into the old palace, where he was under siege for five days. The besiegers numbered over three thousand; they burned the church and the convent; also the chapel of San Miguel. On the 20th Otermín determined, with his small force, to make a desperate assault upon the besiegers; he did so, killing three hundred and capturing about fifty, who, when their depositions had been taken, were shot.

During the siege the Spanish loss was five killed, but many were wounded, including Otermín. On the 21st it was determined to abandon the city, which was done; their departure was not disturbed by the Indians who watched them from the surrounding hills. They marched south by way of the pueblo of Santo Domingo, on the Galisteo, where they found the bodies of three friars and five other Spaniards who had been murdered.

The frayles whose bodies were found at Santo Domingo were those of Fr. Francisco Antonio Lorenzana, a native of Galicia; Fr. Juan de Talabán, custodio habitual, a native of Seville, who had been a missionary almost twenty years and Fr. Joseph de Montesdoca, a native of Querétaro.

Facsimile of Signature of Don Facundo Melgares, Governor of New Mexico, 1818-1822.

Facsimile of Signature of Colonel Antonio Narbona, Governor of New Mexico.

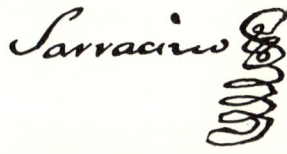

Facsimile of Signature of Don Francisco Sarracino, Governor of New Mexico

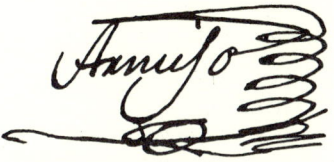

Facsimile of Signature of General Don Manuel Armijo, Governor of New Mexico.

Facsimile of Signature of Governor Francisco Xavier Chavez, 1822-23.

Facsimile of Signature of Colonel Albino Perez, Governor of New Mexico

Facsimile of Signature of Don Mariano Martinez, Governor of New Mexico.

R. No. E PUEBLO OF SAN FELIPE.

Grant. September 20, 1689. Made by Governor and Captain-General Don Domingo Jironza Petriz de Cruzate, at El Paso. The archive is signed by

DOMINGO JIRONZA PETRIZ DE CRUZATE.
BARTOLOME DE OJEDA.

DON PEDRO LADRON DE GUITARA,
Secretary of Government and War.

The text is almost identical with that of Archive R. No. A. The boundaries as given are: on the north, the *Bosque Grande* which is toward the east, and on the east one league, and on the west one league, and on the south a little grove which is in front of a hill called *Culcura*, opposite the fields of the Indians of Santa Ana.

The grant was confirmed to the *pueblo of San Felipe* by the Congress of the United States December 22, 1858.

The San Felipe Pueblos were Queres. The present village is not built upon the site of the ancient village. The old pueblo was built at the foot of the mesa of *Tamita*. In 1607, Fr. Cristobal Quiñones was at this pueblo. He built the first mission; he died there in 1609, and was buried in the church which had been erected under his supervision. In 1636, Fr. Cristobal de Quiros was located here; he was father custodian of the Franciscans. The Indians occupied the original site until three years after the revolt in 1680.

When De Vargas came in 1692, he found them on top of the *Black Mesa*, just above their present village. The old ruin which one sees on top of this mesa, just after crossing the big arroyo which comes down from *Tunque*, is all that is left of the church which was built in 1694.

When Otermín and the refugees came down the Rio Grande valley by way of Santo Domingo they passed by this place. No frayles or Spaniards were murdered at San Felipe in 1680; all of the Indians of San Felipe had gone to Santo Domingo, where the missionaries referred to in notes to Archive R. No. D lived; they served Cochiti, Santo Domingo, and San Felipe; these Indians, however, murdered many Spaniards between San Felipe and the site of the present town of Algodones. As Otermín passed down the valley great numbers of the Indians watched them from the top of the *Black Mesa*.

There is nothing left of the old pueblo which stood at the foot of *Tamita*. The *Tunque* arroyo has washed everything into the Rio Grande. The confluence of the arroyo with the Rio Grande is only a short distance above the present pueblo.

The ruins on top of the mesa are quite extensive, although the pueblo was not a very large one. The name of this ruined pueblo is *Katishtya*.

In 1696, at the time of the second rebellion of the Pueblos, a frayle from the neighboring pueblo of Cochiti fled to this pueblo of *Katishtya* and was saved by the San Felipe Indians from death; his name was Fr. Alonzo. There is a complete list of the frayles serving here from 1696 to date. The register is quite valuable; it is the book showing the interments by this mission.

R. No. F PUEBLO OF PECOS.

Grant. El Paso. September 25, 1689. Made by Governor and Captain-General Don Domingo Jironza Petriz de Cruzate. The archive is signed by

DON DOMINGO JIRONZA PETRIZ DE CRUZATE.
BARTOLOME DE OJEDA.
DON PEDRO LADRON DE GUEVARA,
Secretary of Government and War.

The exact wording of this archive is as follows:

1689. *En el Pueblo de Nrs. Sa. de Guadalupe del Passo del Rio del Norte, en veinte y cinco dias del mes de Septe. de mil sessientos y ochenta y nueve años, el Señor Gouer. y Capn. Genl. Dn. Domingo Jironza Petriz de Cruzate, dijo que por quanto en el alcanze que se dió en los de la Nueva Mexco. de los Yndios Queres, y los Apostatas, y los Teguas y de la nacion Thanos, y despues de haver peleado con todos los demas Yndios de todos pueblos, un Yndio del Pou. de Zia, llamado Bartolomé de Ojeda que fue mas se señalo en la vatalla á cudiendo á todas partes, se rindió biendose herido de un valaso y un flechasso lo cual como dicho es, mandé que denajo de juramto. declare como se halla el Puo. de Pecos, aun queda muy metido á honde el sol sale y fueron unos Yndios Apostatas de aquel reino de la Nueva Mexico.*

Preguntando: que si este Puo. volvera en algun tiempo, como ha sido costumbre en ellos, y dise el confesante que no; que ya esta muy metido en temor que aunque estaban abilantados con lo que habia susedo a los de el Puo. de Zia en año pasado jusgana que era un inposible que dejaran de dar la obediencia; por lo cual se consedieron por el Señor Gouer. y Capn. Genl. Dn. Domingo Jironza Petriz

de Cruzate, los linderos que aqui anoto; para el norte una legua, y para el oriente una legua, y para el poniente una legua, y para el sur una legua; y medidas estas cuatro lineas de las cuatro esquinas del Puo. dejando á salus el templo que queda al medio dia del Puo., y asi lo proveyó, mandó y firmó su ssa. á mi el presente Secretario de gouer. y guerra, que de ello doi fee.
    Don Domingo Jironza Petriz de Cruzate.
    Bartolome de Ojeda.
Don Pedro Ladron de Guitara,
 Sec. de Gn. y Gua.

 There is nothing left of this old pueblo today other than the debris of the fallen walls; these are leveled to the ground; the old wall which surrounded the pueblo may be traced by the stones; the old church is also a ruin; a portion of the walls remains. The last of the Indians of the pueblo is still alive living at Jemez, where the few remnants of the pueblo migrated in 1835. Disease and attacks from the *Ute, Apache,* and *Comanche* destroyed the people. Its name was *Tshiquite* and was first visited by the Spanish officer, Hernando de Alvarado, in 1540. Espejo visited it in 1583, and descended the Pecos river from this locality. Castaño de Sosa was here in 1590-91; he called the Pecos river the "*Saladó.*" Castaño assaulted the pueblo because the Indians had fought with some of his soldiers who were on a scouting expedition. It is not believed that Castaño assaulted the large pueblo of Pecos but one of the smaller ones, possibly that known as *Ruedas,* which lies near Rowe station on the Atchison, Topeka and Santa Fe Railway; this pueblo is just about three-quarters of a mile from the Pecos river.

 The church at Pecos was one of the finest in New Mexico; it is said to have had six towers at one time.

 Francisco Vasquez Coronado visited the pueblo several times; when he left the country for Mexico, one of the Franciscan frayles remained behind at this place; it is not known what was his fate; he was doubtless murdered by the Indians.

 In 1680, these Indians revolted and killed their missionary, Fr. Domingo de Vera, who was a native of the City of Mexico.

 Fr. Ayeta, who escaped, being in Mexico at the time, gives a list of the frayles who perished in the revolution; also some biographical information; the full list is given in a funeral sermon delivered in the City of Mexico one year after the revolt.

Four days after the revolt commenced the Spaniards ascertained that five hundred of the Pecos and other eastern Pueblos were on their way to Santa Fe; on the 15th of August, 1680, these Indians were seen in the *"milpas"* of *San Miguel*, in the neighborhood of the chapel of that name, in the present City of Santa Fe.

One of the Indians, Juan, entered the city and told the Spaniards they could no longer remain in the country; they must leave or fight; Governor Otermín determined to fight and began the engagement which lasted all day and resulted in favor of the Spaniards.

The Pecos Indians say that they came from the southeast, but their origin was in the north; they spoke the same language as the Jemez and were their kinsmen. Harrington says they were not.

The Pecos Indians were buffalo hunters and traded their buffalo hides with the Pueblos living farther south and west. The Pecos also bartered with the plains Indians for hides, which they in turn traded with the Indians to the west.

This grant to the Pecos Indians was confirmed by Congress long after every Indian had left the pueblo. It is now the property of D. C. Collier, who has given the Archaeological School at Santa Fe a deed to the site of the old pueblo and church.

With this archive is filed another which is a report from a committee of the Territorial Deputation, appointed to investigate and report upon a petition filed with the Deputation by the Indians of Pecos asking that the Mexican settlers on the Pecos river be required to vacate and restore to the Indians the lands which they have taken.

Date, 1825.   PINO [rubric]
              ARZE [rubric]
              BACA [rubric]

The name of this pueblo was *Cicuye*, which was probably the *Tigua* name for it. It was during the administration of Oñate that a mission was first established at Pecos. Pecos was the *Keresan* name of the pueblo. In the Sixteenth century they occupied several pueblos in and adjacent to the Pecos river beginning at a point near the present Pecos town and extending as far down the river possibly as *La Cuesta*. It is claimed also that they had a pueblo near the old Spanish town of Golden, in Santa Fe county. The old ruins near *Ojo de Vaca* have not been certainly identified as having been occupied by these Indians, although living in such close proximity.

No. R. G PUEBLO DE COCHITI.

Grant. 1689. Made by Governor and Captain-General Don Domingo Jironza Petriz de Cruzate, September 25th, at El Paso. Signed

DOMINGO JIRONZA PETRIZ DE CRUZATE.
BARTOLOME DE OJEDA.

Before
DON PEDRO LADRON DE GUITARA,
Secretary of Government and War.

The text of this archive is practically the same as that of R. No. A.:

The Cochiti were Queres. There are many ruins in the Cañada de Cochiti.

Close by is the celebrated *Potrero Viejo*. There is a settlement of Mexican people in the cañada. The title to the lands held by the Mexicans dates 1728, when a grant was made to them by Governor and Captain-General Juan Domingo de Bustamante. See this grant — *Merced de la Cañada de Cochiti* — in office of surveyor-general. The Mexicans were always troubled by the Navajo until about the time of the American Occupation. It was temporarily abandoned in 1835, owing to the Navajo attacks.

About a mile below the settlement are found the ruins of the pueblo called *Qua-pa*. There is not much left to this ruin, and from all indications it is much older than those on the *potrero*. The Indians claim that their ancestors moved from *Qua-pa* to their present village in the valley of the Rio Grande. It is believed that the ancestors of the *Cochiti* at one time lived and occupied the dwellings and pueblos in the valley of the *Rito de los Frijoles*. They were driven out of the *Rito* by the *Tehuas*.

It is my opinion that the *Queres* of *Cochiti* inhabited the cañada, as did also the Indians of San Felipe and that it was from the cañada that they finally moved to their present village. The oldest men of the pueblo have told me this. De Vargas found the *Queres* of *Cochiti* and of San Felipe and the *Tanos* of the pueblo of San Marcos on the *potrero* in 1692. They also told him they had come there because of their enemies, the *Tehuas, Tanos,* and the *Picuriés*.

It will be remembered that from the time the Spaniards were driven out in 1680, there was a great period of hostility between these various tribes of the Pueblos.

This particular locality is very important in the deeds of the *reconquistadores* under General De Vargas. The present village of *Cochiti* was occupied as early as 1598. *Doc. de Indias,* vol. xvi, p. 102. q. v. Vetancurt in his *Cronica* says that it was located *"al lado izquierdo del Rio del Norte tres leguas de Santo Domingo."* They retired to the cañada when they received word that Otermín was on his way back to re-conquer the country. The *maestro de campo* states, 1681, that an Indian told him at San Felipe *"Al qual le preguntó en su lengua por la gente del pueblo, y respondió haberse ido huyendo á la Cieneguilla, ó Pueblo de Cochiti."*

Mendoza was taken to task by Otermín because of his retreat from *Cochiti* in 1681. Mendoza knew his force was too small to risk a battle with these Indians and retreated to the pueblo of *Puara,* near Bernalillo.

When Otermín went back to El Paso in 1681, the pueblos were all re-occupied by the Indians in this vicinity.

When De Vargas visited them in 1692, they all promised to give in their allegiance, with which statements De Vargas was satisfied.

When De Vargas returned to New Mexico, in 1693, the people of *Cochiti* had not kept their agreement and were still on the potrero along with those *Tanos* of San Marcos. De Vargas fought several very severe engagements before he succeeded in reducing these people. It was in one of these that the Indian of Zia, Bartolomé de Ojeda, distinguished himself. The battle was fought on the 17th of April. It was Ojeda that showed a new trail by which the *potrero* could be ascended. Escalante, in his *Relacion,* p. 160, gives a detailed report of this fight; he says: *"Cayeron en gran numero y cercaron el pueblo, pusieron a los nuestros en gran aprieto y como los nuestros eran tan pocosa atendian y solamente a defender las bocas calles del pueblo, y asi tuvieron lugar de huir ciento cincuenta de los prisioneros; lo cual visto por los reveldes, se retiraron juzgando que ya habian librado a todos sus hijos y mugeres."*

Escalante refers to a fight, in the nature of a surprise to the Spanish troops, which occurred after the *potrero* had been gained and the Indians defeated. In this surprise De Vargas lost 150 of his prisoners or *"Chusma."* This was only about one-half of the Indians captured in the fight of the preceding 17th; this surprise occurred on the 20th. De Vargas burned the pueblo on the *potrero* before he left for Santa Fe and it was never again occupied.

R. No. H PUEBLO OF SANTO DOMINGO.

Grant. September 20, 1689.

Made by Don Domingo Jironza Petriz de Cruzate, Governor and Captain-General, at El Paso.

The wording in this grant is practically the same as in the others; the translation on file is very poorly done. The archive is signed by

DON DOMINGO JIRONZA PETRIZ DE CRUZATE.
BARTOLOME DE OJEDA.

Certified before

PEDRO LADRON DE GUITARA,
Secretary of Government and War.

The boundaries as given are: On the north the *Lomas Pelados* — barren hills, near a rivulet running from where the sun rises, and empties into the Rio Bravo del Norte, and to the east some water which is said to be the property of Alonzo Catiti, near a white hill of alabaster, and to the west a little hill which is on the bank of the dry bed of a stream and where there is a cave on the south, to the side of a hill having the name of *Blanca Pelado* towards the east.

The Indians of Santo Domingo are of very pugnacious disposition; they resent any interference, in any way, with any of their customs or manners.

There never has been a time in the history of New Mexico when the inhabitants of this pueblo may have been considered tractable.

When the Atchison, Topeka and Santa Fe Railway was built, the located line was surveyed and built through the lands of these people in the valley of the Rio Grande; being a community grant, there was no way in which the title could be obtained by the railway company except by a proceeding to condemn; this was done, the attorney for the United States appearing for the pueblo; a decree was made and the company paid into court the sum of fifteen hundred dollars for the right of way; this money the Indians refused to accept and it remained in the custody of the court for nearly twenty years, when Mr. C. J. Crandall, Indian agent, persuaded the Indians to accept the money.

At one time, some of the Indians of this pueblo were constantly stealing ties, bridge timbers, and other material from the railway company; they were caught, tried, and convicted and sent to jail at Alburquerque; this did no good; one day the governor of the pueblo, who was a very honest man, said to the writer, who was attorney for the company, "the next time you catch any of the Indians stealing the property of the company, try them before the justice of the peace, and if convicted, send them to me, not to the jail at Alburquerque;" "they like to be sent there," said he, "but I will show you how to break off this thievery." In a short time two Indians were detected, duly tried and convicted, and turned over to the governor, who, having summoned his *capitan de la guerra*, or chief of police, tied the Indians to a stake in front of the *kiva* of the pueblo and proceeded to administer to them one hundred lashes which were laid on with great force; there has never been any stealing of company property since that time by these Indians.

The Indians of Santo Domingo formerly lived at a place called *Guy-pu-y*, the ruins of which lie about five miles south of the settlement of *Peña Blanca*, in Sandoval county. These ruins are nearly two miles east of the railway station called "*Domingo*;" they are upon the bank of the Galisteo river. The waters of the Galisteo (floods) destroyed the pueblo of *Guypuy*.

Castaño de Sosa visited this pueblo and made it his headquarters; he says that it stood on the banks of the Rio Grande. The pueblo of Santo Domingo which was visited by Juan de Oñate, in 1598, stood very nearly where the present village is situate. Otermín when he left the country, in 1680, also says that the village at that time stood on the river bank, east side.

The first church built in Santo Domingo was built by the Fr. Juan de Escalona, who was commissary of the Order of Franciscans; he died at Santo Domingo and was buried in the church which he had built. The location of this church building can not now be ascertained; it was built in 1607 and has been washed away by the floods from the Galisteo.

This village was visited by Major Pike in 1807 and by General Kearny in 1846.

THE SPANISH ARCHIVES OF NEW MEXICO 473

The Indians of Santo Domingo have always been averse to the education of the children, particularly the education provided for since the American Occupation. They endeavor in every way to prevent any of the young people going to the Indian school at Santa Fe or the one at Alburquerque. It was always a difficult matter to get any to go to Carlisle.

There is a government school at this pueblo which was established in 1896. The attendance of children at this school when it was first opened was very disappointing; the *"principales"* would not permit any of the girls of the pueblo to attend the school. The Indian agent, at that time an army officer, visited the pueblo for the purpose of an inspection and noticing that there were no girls at the school, asked the governor why this state of affairs existed; the governor replied, "Education might be all very well for boys, but it wouldn't do for girls, who as soon as they got educated wanted to run off."

These Indians are great dancers; they have a great feast on the 4th of August of each year. When some of the more religious dances are carried on they will not allow anyone, not a member of the pueblo, to remain in the village. They are also very much averse to having pictures taken of any of their ceremonial dances, and by force have driven persons off the pueblo lands who have sought to take pictures, breaking their cameras if unable to get rid of them in any other manner. They are very jealous of the secret mysteries of their dances.

On the evening of the 3d of August church services are held in the mission church; this service is always well attended by the Indians. The Indian women spread handkerchiefs or towels on the adobe floor, upon which they kneel, so that their neat clothing is in nowise soiled; the men take off the head-bands which they usually wear instead of hats. The walls of the church are decorated with rude paintings of corn plants, some with birds perched on the ears of corn; in several places one sees rude pictures of the moon and stars and other symbols understandable only to the Indian. The altar is very crude and simple; its decorations tawdry, but they are the best the Indians can afford.

On the 4th, it is the custom to perform wedding ceremonies; at this service also women come in with great baskets of bread which they take to the altar as an offering; when the mass is over a procession is formed and the

Indians march to an open-air altar in the street; acolytes head this procession and just behind an image of Santo Domingo is carried under a muslin canopy. Behind these come officers of the church and then the Indians — Pueblos, Apaches, Navajos, Mexicans, Americans who may be visiting here at the time and who are helping to celebrate the feast. Out in the street on the rude altar the image of the saint is placed and it is guarded by four Indians armed with muskets.

About noon eight dancers appear on the roof of one of the *kivas* of the pueblo and execute some very peculiar evolutions, whereupon they descend and march around the streets of the village. These are called *Koshare*; they are what Mr. Bandelier calls the *Delight-makers*. Everywhere they go they make fun for the multitude, crack jokes and cut up all sorts of antics. The dancers are almost naked; the arms are painted white and black in stripes; so is almost all of the body; a band of everegreen encircles the waist; there are fur wristlets on the forearm and bands of fur are crossed upon the breast; the face is painted like a mask — hideous to behold, and there are black marks around the eyes and mouth; the hair is drawn up and parted in two masses above his ears, and carries decorations of corn shucks; in one hand is carried a gourd rattle and clusters of deer and sheep hoofs are around the waist; pretty soon he goes back into the *kiva*. Presently, from another *kiva*, come more *Koshare*, and these announce the coming of the dancers; these look like the *Delight-makers*, only they have evergreens instead of fur on their breasts and the faces are striped longitudinally in black and brown, and the hair is in one mass above the head and carries feather and corn decorations. When these have marched around a bit, there comes a band of about sixty singers and one *tombe* beater from behind an *estufa* or *kiva*; following them comes a man with a long pole, on which is tied a scarf — a sort of standard, from which also float many feathers and some skins of foxes are hung on the pole; following him come ninety dancers all in ceremonial garb; the women are in black with red waistbands, and green tablets stand upright on the head of each; they carry bunches of cedar or piñon; the hair is loose and their wrists are daubed with luminous paint; the bodies of the men are painted a sort of reddish brown from the waist up and from the knees down, but the forearm and thigh are painted white with lines on them; about the hips they wear ceremonial skirts and sashes with knotted fringes, and in the hand of each is a gourd rattle, in the other bunches of cedar or piñon; the hair is loose and is ornamented with feathers; on their feet are moccasins trimmed with white and black fur. In front and behind from the waist hang beautiful fox and coyote skins and around their necks all sorts of beads are strung.

The dancers march to the open space left for them and begin to dance, while the chorus gives the music. The standard bearer is the leader, or seems to be, for every once in a while he lowers the pole, and every time this is done the figure changes; the women advance, retreat, and wheel around with short steps; their forearms are outspread, their bodies erect, their feet keeping perfect time to the chorus; the men do not keep time; they hop and skip around, shout and shake their gourds; all is very graceful, however, and they make no mistakes in the figures, and these are very complicated.

Altogether this dance is a very quaint and weird performance.

The authority for making these grants, in the manner in which they *seem to have been made,* and the grant to the *pueblo* of Sandia, as well, is to be found in the *Royal Cédulua* of June 4, 1687, two years prior to Cruzate's alleged acts at El Paso.

An extract from the decree mentioned is as follows:

"WHEREAS, as in my Royal Council of the Indies, they are advised that the Marqués de Falces (Don Gaston de Peralta) Cónde de San Estevan, Viceroy of the Province of New Spain, issued an ordinance on May 28, 1567, by which he ordered that each of the Indian Pueblos as might need lands upon which to live and sow, should have given to them five hundred varas, and more should it be necessary; and that from that time forward there should not be granted to anyone lands or grounds unless they should be located a thousand varas, cloth or silk measure, away from and separate from the pueblos and houses of the Indians, and the lands five hundred varas removed from said settlement, as is obvious from the evidence of said ordinance which has reached the council — have been contrary to custom, order and practice — have been encroached upon by owners of estates and lands, thereby depriving the Indians of them, and seizing upon them sometimes violently, sometimes fraudulently, for which cause the miserable Indians have lost their houses and towns, which is what the Spaniards seek for and desire; and obtaining these thousand or five hundred varas, which have to be apart from the towns they measure from the church or public house (ermita) which the people generally have in the center of the place, and which happens to comprehend in them the whole plat of the town, whereby they lose what had been given to them, it being necessary to understand the last five hundred varas by the four winds, which is arranged and commanded in the Laws XII and XVIII, title xii, lib. iv *de la Nueva Recopilacion de Indies*; and on account of the many difficulties, losses, and injuries which thus befell these poor natives, it has been thought proper to command that such Indian Pueblos as might need lands to live upon and cultivate, should have given them not only five hundred varas, as the said ordinance provides, but whatever might be necessary, measuring them from the farthest limits and houses of the place, outwards by the four winds — thus five hundred varas east, as many west, north and south, leaving always the plat of the pueblos included as vacant place, giving these five hundred varas of land not only to the chief or capital pueblo, but all the rest that may ask for and need them, as well in the pueblos already inhabited as those which might hereafter be founded and peopled; so that thus all might have land to cultivate, and upon which their flocks may graze and feed, it being just and of my royal charity to have a regard for the Indians, who, I am informed, suffer so much injustice and trouble in view of their being those who render more services, and enriching my royal crown and all my vassals; with which design, and seeing what in view of them and the said testimony and Laws XII and XVIII of the *Nueva Recopilacion de Indies*, the acting-general of my said council of the Indies has said and alleged, I have thought it best to order and command, as by these presents I do, that in conformity with the ordinances which the Viceroy, cónde de San Esteban formed and decreed on the 24th of May. 1567, and the compiled laws referred to, that there shall be given and assigned generally to all the Indian Pueblos of New Spain for their farming lands, not only the five hundred varas around the place of settlement, and these measured from the church, but from the farthest house of the place, as well eastward as westward as north and south; and not only the said five hundred varas, but a

THE SPANISH ARCHIVES OF NEW MEXICO

hundred varas more, up to full six hundred varas; and should the place or settlement be more than ordinarily contracted, and should not seem sufficient for all, my Viceroy for New Spain, and my Royal Court of Mexico, shall take care, as I now charge and command them to do, to set them apart a much larger quantity, and they shall mark off and assign to the said place and settlements, as many more varas of land as shall be necessary, without limitation.

"And as regards the pasture land, it is my will and order that there shall not only be separated from the settlement and Indian places, the thousand varas mentioned in the said Ordinance of May 24, 1567, but even a hundred varas more, and that these one thousand one hundred varas shall be measured from the last house of the settlement or place, and not from the church."

This was a decree of Felipe II, originally, and was renewed by Carlos II.

There seems to be small doubt today that the alleged grants made to the Pueblo Indians by Governor and Captain-General Don Domingo Jironza Cruzate, at El Paso, in 1689, are spurious. There can also be no doubt that had this fact been known to Congress when these "grants" were confirmed and later patented, such action would not have been based upon the so-called "grants," copies of which I have given on previous pages. It is not believed, however, that Congress would have refused to confirm to the several pueblos their "league" of land. The fact that each pueblo was entitled to a league of land seems to be beyond question, as many of the archives, petitions for other lands made to the several governors and captain-generals, always recognize the "league" of the Indians whenever it appeared that there was apt to be a conflict as to boundaries.

After the organization of the court of private land claims and the attorney for that court had become more or less familiar with the archives, signatures of officers, historical data, etc., aided by his able assistants, he came to the conclusion that every one of the El Paso papers bearing the signature of Cruzate, Ojeda, and others were forgeries. This discovery was made by Mr. Will M. Tipton, a recognized authority on such matters.

Mr. Tipton has prepared a resume in regard to all of the "Pueblo Grants," the first to be prepared in such concise form and for that reason given here as follows:

Pueblo of Jémez.

There are two Spanish documents in this case, dated in 1689, and both are spurious; as, in fact, are all the grants in New Mexico which purport to have been made to Indian Pueblos in that year.

It was surveyed in 1859 for a fraction over 17,510 acres and was patented in 1864.

Pueblo of Acoma.

There is one Spanish document in this case, dated 1689. It refers to the Laguna Indians having moved near to the Acomas on account of the water which the latter had for irrigating. This statement purports to have been made in the year 1689, whereas, it is a *well-established historical fact* that the pueblo of Laguna was not in existence at that date and was not founded until ten years later.

It was surveyed in 1877 for a fraction over 95,791 acres and was patented November 19, 1877.

Pueblo of San Juan.

There are two Spanish documents, both of 1689, neither of which is genuine. Document "B" refers to the pueblo of Laguna ten years before it was founded. The grant was surveyed in 1859 for a fraction over 17,544 acres and was patented in 1864.

Pueblo of Picuriés.

The Spanish muniment in this case is also dated in 1689 and is not genuine. The grant was surveyed in 1859 for a fraction over 17,460 acres and was patented in 1864.

Pueblo of San Felipe.

The Spanish document marked "A," dated 1689, is not genuine. The Spanish document marked "B," dated 1770, formerly with this case, is a genuine document and has been transferred to Private Land Claim Reported No. 142, the Santo Domingo and San Felipe Grant. The grant was confirmed December 22, 1858, surveyed in 1859 for a fraction over 34,766 acres, and patented in 1864; it was re-surveyed in 1907 for a fraction over 33,692 acres.

Pueblo of Pecos.

The Spanish document "A," dated 1689, is not genuine. The Spanish document marked "B," which is a report of a committee of the Territorial Deputation of New Mexico, see page ——, is a genuine document. The document was probably executed between 1828 and 1830. The grant was surveyed in 1859 for a little over 18,763 acres and was patented in 1864.

Pueblo of Cochiti.
The Spanish document, dated in 1689, is not genuine. The property was surveyed in 1859 for a fraction over 24,256 acres and was patented in 1864.

Pueblo of Santo Domingo.
The Spanish documents in this case are lettered from "A" to "H" inclusive. All of these are genuine, except document "G," 1689, which is spurious. This document contains several phrases that are taken bodily from the *Ojeda sobre Nuevo Mejico*, by Antonio Barreyro, Puebla, Mexico, 1832.

This fact seems to show that the date at which this document, alleged to have been written in 1689, was actually written was not earlier than 1832.

The grant was surveyed in 1859 for a small fraction over 74,743 acres and was re-surveyed in 1907 for an area of a little more than 92,398 acres. It was patented in 1864.

Pueblo of Taos.
There is no granting document in this case and the testimony of the Taos Indians, taken before the surveyor-general, August 2, 1856, shows that they did not have any grant for their pueblo lands.

The only Spanish paper in the case is a letter from Governor Alberto Maynez to Rev. Fr. José Benito Pereyro, the priest at Taos, dated April 15, 1815, informing the latter that the governor had received his letter of the 11th of that month, in regard to the measurement of the "Taos League" and that he had issued a decree on April 15, 1815, to the chief alcalde of that district in regard to the matter. See Archive 1357. The grant was confirmed December 22, 1858, was surveyed the followig year for a fraction more than 17,360 acres and was patented in 1864.

Pueblo of Santa Clara.
There is no Spanish document in this case and the testimony of the Indians themselves, taken before the surveyor-general, June 16, 1856, shows that the witnesses had never seen any grant, although the old men of the pueblo said that there had been such a grant, which had been lost.

It was surveyed in 1859 for a little over 17,368 acres and was patented in 1864.

Pueblo of Tesuque.
There is no Spanish document in this case. The testimony of witnesses taken June 14, 1856, before the sur-

veyor-general, shows that what they refer to as the "title deeds to the pueblo" were taken from the Indians by the Mexican government to have copies made of them, with a view to their validation, the originals being much torn and that the papers were never returned to them. The grant was surveyed in 1859 for 17,471 acres and was patented in 1864.

Pueblo of San Ildefonso.

There is no Spanish document in this case. The testimony of the Indian witnesses, taken before the surveyor-general in 1856, shows that the grant which the Indians claim to have had, was taken to Santa Fe by the priest of the pueblo, whose name was Tagle, for the purpose of having a certified copy made of it, the original being torn and scarcely legible and that it was never again seen by the Indians; they do not fix the date of this occurrence, but say "This took place many years ago."

The grant was confirmed in 1858, surveyed in 1859 for a fraction over 17,292 acres, and patented in 1864.

Pueblo of Pojoaque.

There is no Spanish document in this case. The Indians testified, June 28, 1856, before the surveyor-general that about forty years prior to that date the "title deed" of the pueblo was presented in evidence in a suit between the pueblo and a Mexican, which suit was tried before Bautista Vigil, the *alcalde* of Chimayó, and that the document had not again been heard of. The grant was confirmed in 1858, was surveyed in 1859 for a fraction over 13,520 acres, and was patented in 1864.

Pueblo of Zía.

The Spanish document marked "A" dated 1689, is not genuine. The document marked "2" is apparently an English translation of the Spanish document "A," in private land claim "TT," in the name of the pueblos of Zía, Santa Ana, and Jemez. The grant was confirmed in 1858, along with the other pueblo grants, was surveyed in 1859 for a fraction over 17,514 acres, and was patented in 1864.

Pueblo of Sandia.

The two Spanish documents in this case are geniune. The grant was confirmed in 1858, surveyed in 1859 for a fraction over 24,187 acres, and was patented in 1864.

Pueblo of Isleta.

There is no Spanish document in this case. The testi-

Facsimile of Signature of Don Alberto Maynez, Governor of New Mexico.

Facsimile of Signature of Don Joaquin Real Alencaster, Governor of New Mexico, 1805-1808.

Facsimile of Signature of Don Joseph Manrique, Governor of New Mexico, 1810-1814.

Facsimile of Signature of General Bartolome Baca, Governor of New Mexico, 1823, 1825

mony of the Indians, taken before the surveyor-general in 1856, shows that the grant had been deposited in the archives of the Territory, and that a man named Miguel Antonio Lobato had told the Indians that not long before he had the grant in his hands; that it was in the possession of a man at Polaverda or Socorro, etc. The grant was surveyed in 1859 for a fraction over 110,080 acres, and was patented in 1864.

Pueblo of Nambé.

There is no Spanish document in this case. The Indians testified before the surveyor-general, September 29, 1856, that the grant was delivered to the acting governor of the Territory in connection with a case in which some Mexican citizens were alleged to have trespassed upon the lands of the Indians and was never thereafter seen or heard of. It was confirmed in 1858, surveyed in 1859 for a fraction over 13,586 acres and resurveyed in 1903 for a little over 13,590 acres, and was patented in 1864.

Pueblo of Laguna.

The two Spanish documents in this case (A and B) are both dated 1689 and are spurious.

One reason for the belief that document "B" is not genuine is that on its fourth page is a disconnected, rambling statement in regard to matters more or less intimately connected with the early history of New Mexico, written in the same hand as the three preceding pages and containing a number of statements couched in precisely the same words as those found in the book entitled *Ojeada sobre Nuevo Mejico*, Antonio Barreyro, *op. cit*. In fact, the first four words on page 4 of document "B" are those which form the name of the book — "*Ojeada sobre Nuevo Mejico*," which means "Glance over New Mexico."

"The contents of this fourth page of document 'B,'" says Mr. Tipton, "has nothing to do with a grant to the pueblo of Laguna; the handwriting establishes the fact that it was written by the same person who wrote the so-called grant of 1689; its contents shows that it contains statements taken bodily from a book published in 1832; the signatures of the governor, his secretary and the Indian witness, Bartolome Ojeda, are in the same handwriting; the signature of the governor, when compared with his signatures on Archive 1 and Archive 1124, in the U. S. Surveyor-General's Office, at Santa Fe, and with others on numerous documents formerly in the Territorial Library at Santa Fe and now in the Library of Congress, in Washington City, are clearly shown to be spurious; the surname of the secretary who purports to sign the alleged grant with the governor appears as 'GUITARA,' while it is a well known fact that no person of that name filled that position at that or any other period in New Mexican history.'

"In view of the present status of this case these statements in regard to this paper may not be important, but they are true; as it is also true that all the Indian grants in New Mexico, purporting to have been made in 1689, were written by the same hand which wrote this so-called grant to Laguna, and are equally spurious."

The claim of a grant based on this document "B" was recommended to Congress by the surveyor-general for confirmation on November 22, 1872, but Congress took no action.

A preliminary survey was made in 1877 for an area of more than 125,000 acres.

Many years later the claim was filed in the court of private land claims and confirmation was sought upon the same basis.

Inasmuch as the United States attorney for the court of private land claims was convinced from the investigation he had made that the pueblo of Laguna was not founded until 1699 — ten years after the date of the muniment in question, he informed the attorney for the Indians that he was prepared to prove that that document was not genuine.

After making an investigation the attorney for the Indians, becoming convinced that he could not establish the geunineness of the paper, abandoned the attempt to do so and proceeded upon an entirely different theory in the trial of the case. The court confirmed the grant in October, 1897. Under the decree of the court, it was surveyed for an area of a fraction more than 17,328 acres and patent issued in 1909.

Pueblo of Santa Ana.

There is no Spanish document in this case. The Indians, so they testified, had a "tradition" that they once had a document or grant, but it had become mislaid. The grant was confirmed in 1869 and was surveyed in 1876 for a fraction over 17,360 acres. It was patented April 25, 1883.

Pueblos of Zía, Santa Ana, and Jémez.

This grant was made jointly to the three pueblos by the Spanish governor of New Mexico in 1766.

THE SPANISH ARCHIVES OF NEW MEXICO 483

The granting decree shows that the object of the grant was to provide the Indians with lands for "pasturing the stock and horses of the aforesaid three pueblos."

The surveyor-general approved the claim February 2, 1874, and recommended it to Congress for confirmation. No action was taken on the recommendation. In 1877, a preliminary survey was made for an area covering 382,849 acres.

The claim was filed with the court of private land claims and in August, 1883, the case was tried and the claim rejected.

Pueblo of San Cristobal.

The Spanish document in this case is not genuine. There are no other papers except a translation into English of the spurious document. The pueblo was abandoned many years ago. It was situated near Galisteo and was abandoned some time after the revolution of 1680. They moved to a place above the site of the present town of Santa Cruz, near the present pueblo of San Juan.

Pueblo of Zuñi.

There are two Spanish papers in this case. The one dated 1689 is spurious. The claim was approved by the surveyor-general in 1879, but Congress never acted upon the claim. The surveyor-general believed that the signature of Governor Cruzate was genuine. The claim was never filed with the court of private land claims. The grant was surveyed in 1880 for an area of 17,581 acres.

484 THE SPANISH ARCHIVES OF NEW MEXICO

	PRIVATE LAND CLAIMS — NEW MEXICO	OFFICE OF SURVEYOR-GENERAL	REPORTED NUMBERS, ETC.
1	Ojito del R. Gallinas	Juan E. Pino	Preston Beck, Jr.
2	Tome, Town of	J. Varela et al	
3	Tierra Amarilla	M. Martinez & sons	
4	Sangre de Cristo	Lee & Beaubien	
5	Casa Col. town	R. Gutierrez et al	
6	Bracito	J. A. Garcia et al	
7	Tecolote, town	S. Montoya et al	
8	Los Trigos	F. Trujillo et al	
9	La Junta	John Scolly et al	
10	Nra Sra de la Luz	C. Herrera	Bishop Lamy
11	Chilili, town	S. Padilla et al	
12	Agua Negra	Ant. Sandoval	
13	Belem, town	D. T. Salazar et al	
14	S. Pedro	J. Miera et al	J. S. Ramirez
15	Cimarron or Rincon	Beaubien et al	
16	Los Esteros	P. J. Perea	
17	Las Animas	Vigil & St. Vrain	
18	Cañon de Pecos	J. D. Pena et al	{ Alex Valle { J. Estevan et al
19	S. Cristobal	Dom. Fernandez	E. W. Eaton
	Vaca Location 1	L. M. Vaca	Heirs of Vaca
	Vaca Location 2	L. M. C. Vaca	Heirs of Vaca
	Vegas Grandes	L. M. C. Vaca	Heirs of Vaca
20	Las Vegas, town	J. D. Maese et al	
21	Tajique, town	M. Sanchez et al	

THE SPANISH ARCHIVES OF NEW MEXICO 485

22	Torreon, town	N. A. Montoya et al	
23	Manzano, town	J. M. Trujillo et al	
24	S. Isidro, town	Armenta et al	
25	Cañon de S. Diego	Garcia de Noriega et al	
26	Jornada del Muerto	A. J. Rivera et al	
27	Las Trampas, town	J. Arguello et al	
28	S. Joaq. Nacimiento	S. Martin	
29	Anton Chico, town	S. Tapia et al	
30	Laguna tracts		Rep. V. Duran et al G. Ortiz
31	Mora, town	V. Duran de Armijo	
32		J. Tapia et al	
33	Valverde & Fr. Cristobal	P. Armendariz	Heirs of Armendariz
34		P. Armendariz	Heirs of Armendariz
35	Bosque del Apache	A. Sandoval	
36	Chamita, town	A. Trujillo	
37	Tejon, town	S. Barreras et al	
38		P. Sanchez	Ramon Vigil
39	Cañoncito or Sta Clara	Gerv. Nolan	
40	Cañon del Agua	J. S. Ramirez	
41		P. Montoya	
42	Gallinas	Ant. Ortiz	
43	Ortiz Mine	Ortiz & Cano	E. Whittlesey et al
44	Espirito Santa Springs	L. M. C. Vaca	
45	Añil Springs	J. Sutton	
46	Cebolleta, town	F. Aragon et al	
47	Los Luceros	P. Vigil de S. et al	
48	Rio Don Carlos	G. Nolan	Ant. Leroux
49	S. Fern & S. Blas	B. M. Montaño et al	
50	Cañada de Apaches, or Alamos	A. Sedillo	

PRIVATE LAND CLAIMS — NEW MEXICO — OFFICE OF SURVEYOR-GENERAL — REPORTED NUMBERS, ETC.

51	Middle Spring	N. A. Montoya
52		Roque Lobato
53	Cañada de Alamos, or Apaches	L. Marquez
54	Cuyamungue	B. Sena et al
55	J. B. Valdes	
56	La Gotera	J. D. Peña et al
57	Cañada S. Francisco	J. F. Vaca et al
58	R. Rio Grande	J. Mirabal et al
59	Los Cerrillos	J. M. Peña et al
60	Galisteo, town	F. Sandoval et al
61	Cebolla	J. C. Santistivan et al
62	Cieneguilla	J. Sanchez et al
63	Caja del Rio	N. Ortiz
64	Mesita de J. Lopez	D. Romero et al
65	Cajon de R. Tesuque	J. Gabaldon
66	S. Joaq. Nacimiento	J. Luna et al
67	S. Clemente	Ana Sandoval
68	Chamisos Hill	L. Armenta
69	Alamitos	J. Salas et al
70	Estancia	A. Sandoval
71	Cañon de Chama	F. A. Salazar et al
72	Apache Springs	V. Trujillo
73	Piedra Lumbre	P. Martin
74	Chamizos Arroya	Marquez & Padilla
75	Sierra Mosca	I. L. Ortiz
76	S. Ant. Rio. Col., town	R. Archuleta et al
77	Ojo Caliente, town	L. Duran et al

78	S. Miguel Springs	B. Fernandez	
79	S. Lorenzo Arroyo	A. Chavez	
80		J. Mestas	
81	Cuyamungue, pueblo	A. R. Aguilar	
82	Cerros Negros	S. Gonzalez	
83	Bernalillo, town	F. Gutierrez	
84	Angostura	J. J. Gonzalez	
85	Ancon de D. Ana	Colonists	
86	Mesilla	Colonists	
87	Sierra Mosca	V. Duran de Armijo	G. Ortiz
88	Santa Fé, city	City	
89	Talaya	M. Trujillo	
90	Refugio	Colonists	
91	Alameda, town	F. M. Vigil	
92	Jacona, town	Roibal et al	
93	Canon del R. Col.	A. E. Armenta et al	
94	Una de Gato	Bernal & Lopez	
95	Sevilleta	C. Gabaldon et al	
96	Chaco Mesa	I. Chavez et al	
97	Sta Teresa de Jesus	I. Mestas	
98	Cañada de Alamos	Miera Y Pacheco et al	
99	Nra Sra del Pilar	F. Tafoya et al	
100	Bosque Grande	M. & S. Montoya	
101	Lagunitas	Ant. Vaca	
102	S. Mateo (Marcos) Springs	A. U. Montaño	
103	Agua Salado	L. Jaramillo	
104	Encinal	B. Vaca & sons	
105	Petaca	J. J. Martinez et al	
106	Goat Spring	J. Otero	

PRIVATE LAND CLAIMS — NEW MEXICO — OFFICE OF SURVEYOR-GENERAL — REPORTED NUMBERS, ETC.

107	Socorro, town	J. Garcia et al
108	Vallecito de Lobato	J. R. Zamora
109	Rancho Taos	F. A. Gijosa
110	S. Cristobal	S. & A. Martinez
111	Santa Teresa	F. Garcia
112	Mesilla	J. Trujillo
113	Arroyo Seco	J. Trujillo
114	Can. Pedernales	J. B. Valdez
115	Santa Barbara	V. Martin et al
116	Cieneguilla	F. A. Almazan
117	Lucero de Godoy	A. Martinez
118	Orejas del Llano	J. J. Lucero
119	Ojo de Borrego	N. A. Montoya
120	S. Mig. del Vado	L. Marquez et al
121	Maragua	J. Dominguez
122	Cañon de S. Diego	Vaca et al
123	S. Isidro	F. & J. A. Garcia
124	Peña Blanca	I. S. Vergara
125	S. Fern. De Taos	J. M. Vigil
126	Torreon	Inhabitants
127		B. Vaca
128	Las Truchas	B. E. Edwards
129		F. M. Vigil
130	Alburquerque	J. M. Sanchez
131	Polvadero	Inhabitants
132	Hermosa Estrella	J. P. Martin
		C. Ant. Salazar

133			Ant. R. Lujan
134	S. Mateo Springs	S. Duran y Chavez	
135	Can. de Cochiti	Ant. Lucero	
136	La Madera	S. Ramirez	
137	Arroyo Hondo	Seb. Bargas	
138	Can. Santa Clara	Indians of pueblo	
139	Sto Tomás Iturbide	Colonists	
140	Abiquiú, town	Inhabitants	
141		Dom. Valdez	
142	Sto Dom. & S. Felipe	Inhabitants	
143	Ocate	Man. Alvarez	
144	Las Huertas	A. Aragon et al	
145	Atrisco	Inhabitants	
146	El Tajo	D. Padilla	
147		J. A. Lucero	
148	Plaza Blanca	Man. Bustos	
149	Plaza Colorado	R. J., & J. Valdes	
150	Can de Carnué	J. A. Lafoya et al	
151	El Rito	Town	
152	Guadalupita	P. A. Gallegos et al	
153		P. Gallegos & M. Maes	
		ADDITIONAL GRANTS	
4	Cienega	City of Santa Fe	
5		J. Ortiz	
7	Chaperito, town	S. Martin et al	
23	Angostura de Pecos	J. M. Sanchez et al	
26	Cubero, town	Settlers	
35	Mora tract	E. Sandoval et al	
37	Sta. Rosalia	I. Cano	

490 THE SPANISH ARCHIVES OF NEW MEXICO

PRIVATE LAND CLAIMS — NEW MEXICO — OFFICE OF SURVEYOR-GENERAL — REPORTED NUMBERS, ETC.

59	Vallecito, town	Settlers
71	Rio Picuries	R. Fernandez et al
72	Macho Bend	F. Gonzalez et al
75	Arquito	R. Archiveque
76	Angostura	Jer. Gonzalez
77	S. Antonito	C. Jaramillo
79	Rito de So. Jose	P. Gonzalez et al
80	Conejos	J. M. Martinez
81	Arroyo Hondo	N. Sisneros et al
82	Cañ. De Mesteñas	V. Trujillo et al
86	Talaya	J. M. Tafoya et al
90	Cardillal	J. Chavez et al
91	S. Ant. Embudo	J. Marquez et al
92		G. Davalos et al
94	Guadalupita	G. Gold et al
98	Rio Tesuque	Settlers
99	Ranchose and towns	Settlers
100	Arkansas Colony	Royuela et al
101	Lo de Vasquez	J. Ortiz
103	Sta. Cruz	L. M. Vaca
104		A. R. de Aguilar
105	Guadalupe, town	Settlers
106	Frijoles	A. Montoya
107	Sta. Rita del Cobre	F. M. Elguea
108	Sta. Teresa	
109		C. D. Serna
110	S. Geron. De Taos	F. A. Luejosa

112	Rio del Oso	J. A. Valdez
113	Peña Blanca, town	J. Pelaez
114	Mesilla Valley	M. Guerra et al
183	Vallecito	J. G. Mora et al
185	S. Jose Springs	
186	La Naza	M. Lucero
190	S. Mateo Springs	
191		A. Salazar
192		A. Jacques et al
194	Elguea	
195	Sitio de Navajo	Joaq. Garcia
197	El Rito	J. J. Lobato
198	Pueblo Colorado	

492 THE SPANISH ARCHIVES OF NEW MEXICO

No.	Claimants	Name	Location	Claimed Area	Confirmed Area	Rejected Area
1	Juan Chaves et al	Town of Cubero	Valencia county	47,743.00	16,490.94	31,252.06
2	J. M. Chaves et al	Plaza Colorado	Rio Arriba county	19,200.00	7,577.92	11,622.08
3	(Transferred to Arizona District)					
4	Francisco A. Montoya	San Antonio del Rio Colorado	Taos county	18,955.00		18,955.00
5	Julian Martinez et al	Arroyo Hondo	Taos county	23,000.00	20,000.38	2,370.62
6	Louise J. Purdy et al	Sebastian de Vargas	Santa Fe county	42,000.00	13,434.38	28,565.62
7	Charles W. Lewis	Bernabe M. Montaño	Bernalillo county	151,000.00	44,070.66	106,929.34
8	City of Alburquerque	Villa de Alburquerque	Bernalillo county	13,381.00		13,381.00
9	Francisco Martinez et al	Lucero de Godoy	Taos county	61,605.48	61,605.48	
10	Tomas Torres et al	Rancho del Rio Grande	Taos county	109,043.00	91,813.15	17,229.85
11	Alejandro Sandoval et al	Alameda	Bernalillo county	106,274.00	89,346.00	16,928.00
12	Katie McIrvine	José Duran	Santa Fe county	425.85		425.85
13	City of Socorro et al	Town of Socorro	Socorro county	17,371.18	17,371.18	
14	Salvador Romero et al	Francisco Montes Vigil	Rio Arriba county	35,000.00	8,253.74	26,746.26
15	Louis Huning	Antonio Sedillo or Cañada de los Apaches	Bernalillo and Valencia counties	152,879.00	86,249.09	66,629.91
16	Feliz Romero	Gijosa	Taos county	20,000.00	16,240.64	3,759.36
17	Pueblo of Santa Clara	Cañada de Santa Clara	Rio Arriba county	9,000.00	490.62	89,509.38
18	Matias Dominguez	Pacheco	Santa Fe county	581.29	581.29	
19	See case No. 80					
20	J. Franco Chaves	Nerio Antonio Montoya	Valencia county	3,546.00		3,546.00
21	Juan de Dios Romero	Cristobal de la Serna	Taos county	30,000.00	22,232.57	7,767.43
22	Lehman Spiegelberg et al	San Marcos Pueblo	Santa Fe county	1,895.44	1,895.44	
23	Clinton N. Cotton	Santa Teresa de Jesus	Bernalillo county	3,623.00		3,623.00
24	Numa Reymond	Doña Ana Bend Colony	Doña Ana county	35,399.017	35,399.017	
25	Julian Sandoval et al	San Miguel del Vado	San Miguel county	315,300.00	5,024.30	310,275.70
26	Leandro Sandoval et al	Rancho de Galban	Bernalillo county	30,000		30,000.00
27	Manuel Crespin et al	San Antonito	Bernalillo county	32,000.00		32,000.00
28	Pedro José Gallegos	Nuestra Señora del Rosario San Fernando	Rio Arriba county	20,000.00	14,786.58	5,213.42
29	(Transferred to Arizona District)					

THE SPANISH ARCHIVES OF NEW MEXICO 493

30	Aniceto Martinez et al	Casas de Riano or Piedra Lumbre	Rio Arriba county	49,747.89	49,747.89
31	Jesus Armijo y Jaramillo et al	Luis Jaramillo or Agua Salada	Bernalillo county	18,000.00	10,693.98	7,306.02
32	J. M. C. Chaves et al	Plaza Blanca	Rio Arriba county	16,000.00	8,955.11	7,044.89
33	City of Isleta	Pueblo of San Antonio de Isleta	Doña Ana county	65,628.00		65,628.00
34	Walter P. Miller	Ignacio Chaves	Bernalillo county	243,056.00	47,258.71	195,797.29
35	Desiderio Gomez et al	Jacona	Santa Fe county	46,241.00	6,952.844	39,288.156
36	Cassandra E. Baird et al	Baird's Ranch	Bernalillo county	33,696.00		333,696.00
37	Martin B. Hayes	Antonio Chaves	Socorro county	130,138.00		130,138.00
38	Carlos Lewis	Cañada de los Alamos	Santa Fe and Bernalillo counties	148,862.00	4,106.66	144,755.34
39	Felipe Delgado et al	Caja del Rio	Santa Fe and Bernalillo counties	66,848.783	66,848.783	
40	(Transferred to Arizona District)					
41	George N. Fletcher et al	Rito de los Frijoles	Bernalillo county	23,000.00		23,000.00
42	(Transferred to Arizona District)					
43	Frank Perew et al	Polvadera	Rio Arriba county	35,761.14	35,761.14	
44	James Corrigan	Las Animas	State of Colorado	4,096,346.00		4,096,346.00
45	Town of Atrisco	Town of Atrisco	Bernalillo county	82,728.72	82,728.72	
46	Heirs of Wm. Pinkerton	Gervacio Nolan	Mora county	575,968.00		575,968.00
47	(Transferred to Arizona District)					
48	Benjamin Hodges et al	Corpus Christi	State of Colorado	698,960.00		698,960.00
49	Marcos Valdez et al	Domingo Valdez	Santa Fe county	500.00		500.00
50	Pueblo of Zia et al	Ojo del Espiritu Santa	Bernalillo county	276,000.00		276,000.00
51	Donaciano Gurule et al	Elena Gallegos or Ranchos de Alburquerque	Bernalillo county	70,000.00	35,084.78	34,915.22
52	Reyes Gonzales et al	Abiquiu	Rio Arriba county	16,708.16	16,708.16	
53	Francisco A. Manzanares	Cañada de los Alamos	Santa Fe county	13,706.00	12,068.39	1,637.61
54	Luciano Chaves et al	Galisteo	Santa Fe county	22,000	260.79	21,739.21
55	Felipe Peralta et al	Cevilleta	Socorro county	261,187.90	261,187.90	
56	Roman Martinez et al	Medina or Black Mesa	Rio Arriba county	25,000	19,171.35	5,828.65

494 THE SPANISH ARCHIVES OF NEW MEXICO

No.	Claimants	Name	Location	Claimed Area	Confirmed Area	Rejected Area
57	J. Chaves y Gallegos et al	Nicolas Duran de Chaves	Valencia county	50,000	46,244.94	3,755.06
58	Eloisa L. Bergere et al	Bartolomé Baca	Valencia county	500,000		500,000
59	J. B. Cessna et al	Juan Jid or John Heath	Doña Ana county	108,000		108,000
60	Levi P. Morton (see No. 25)					
61	Roman A. Baca et al	Bartolomé Fernandez	Bernalillo and Valencia counties	25,424.28	25,424.28	
62	Maria Cleofes Boné et al	Boné	Mora county	6,000		6,000
63	Frank Huning	Diego de Padilla or El Tajo	Bernalillo and Valencia counties	24,800		24,800
64	J. Franco Chaves	San Clemente	Valencia county	95,000	37,099.29	57,900.71
65	Juan Fernandez et al	Rio del Pueblo	Taos county	20,000		20,000
66	Clinton N. Cotton	M. & S. Montoya or Bosque Grande	Bernalillo county	3,253		3,253
67	Roman A. Baca	Felipe Tafoya	Bernalillo county	22,000	4,340.23	17,659.77
68	Maria L. Lucero et al	Antonio de Abeita or Baltazar Cisneros	Rio Arriba county	8,000	721.42	7,278.58
69	Maria M. Baca et al	Lucero Spring	Valencia county	70,000		70,000
70	Mariano S. Otero	Nuestra Señora de la Luz de las Lagunitas	Bernalillo county	43,653	39,184.446	4,468.554
71	(Transferred to Arizona District)					
72	Rosario Corkins et al	Arroya de los Chamisos	Santa Fe county	1,500		1,500
73	Tomas C. Gutierrez et al	Pajarito Tract	Bernalillo county	45,000	28,724.22	16,275.78
74	Pablo Crespin et al	Cañon de Carnue	Bernalillo county	90,000	2,000.59	87,999.41
75	Roman A. Baca	San Mateo Spring	Bernalillo county	4,340.276	4,340.276	
76	J. W. Akers et all (see No. 38)					
77	Justo R. Armijo	Montano	Bernalillo county	151,056		151,056
78	Beatriz P. de Armijo	Los Cerrillos	Santa Fe county	2,284	1,478.81	805.19
79	Beatriz P. de Armijo	Sitio de los Cerrillos	Santa Fe county	572.04	572.04	
80	City of Santa Fe	The City of Santa Fe	Santa Fe county	17,361		17,361
81	Juan Nieto et al	El Pino	Santa Fe county	2,000		2,000
82	Beatriz P. de Armijo	Sitio de Juana Lopez	Santa Fe county	1,366	1,085.53	280.47
83	Nasario Gonzales et al	Gotera	Santa Fe county	1,800		1,800

THE SPANISH ARCHIVES OF NEW MEXICO 495

84	Lehman Spiegelberg et al	Cieneguilla	Taos county	43,961		43,961
85	Abraham Gold, et al	Salvador Gonzales	Santa Fe county	25,000	200.82	24,799.18
86	Thomas B. Catron	Juan de Gabaldon	Santa Fe county	11,619	10,690.05	928.95
87	Luis M. Ortiz et al	Sierra Mosca	Santa Fe county	33,250		33,250
88	Jesus Maria Olguin	Ojo Caliente	Rio Arriba county	40,000	2,244.98	37,755.02
89	Benigno Ortiz et al	La Majada	Santa Fe and Bernalillo counties	54,404.10	54,404.10	
90	Jose H. Gurule	San Antonio de las Huertas	Santa Fe and Bernalillo counties	130,000	4,763.85	125,236.15
91	Thomas B. Catron	Juan Salas or Alamitos	Santa Fe and Bernalillo counties	2,500	297.55	2,202.45
92	Mariano S. Otero	José Garcia	Bernalillo county	76,000		76,000
93	Lorenzo Lobato	Salvador Lobato	Taos county	2,500		2,500
94	Antonio Joseph (see No. 88)					
95	Jose Albino Baca et al	Ojo del Borrego	Bernalillo county	75,000	16,079.80	58,920.20
96	Nepomuceno Martinez et al	Santa Barbara	Taos county	30,638.28	30,638.28	
97	Anastacio C. de Baca et al	Barranca	Rio Arriba county	25,000		25,000
98	Nasario Gonzales	Cañada de San Francisco	Santa Fe county	1,590		1,590
99	Antonio Serafin Pena et al	La Petaca	Rio Arriba county	186,977	1,392.10	185,584.90
100	Amado Chaves et al	Canyon de San Diego	Bernalillo county	9,752		9,752
101	May Hays	Ojo del Apache	San Miguel county	47,743		47,743
102	J. A. Romero et al	Antonio Armijo	Santa Fe county	900		900
103	Jose M. Lobato	Juan Cayetano Lobato	Santa Fe county	1,000		1,000
104	Juan de Archuleta	Archuleta and Gonzales	Santa Fe county	1,000		1,000
105	Albino Dominguez et al	Antonio Dominguez	Santa Fe county	800		800
106	T. G. Gutierrez (see case No. 51)					
107	The Rio Arriba Land and Cattle Company	Canyon de Chama	Rio Arriba county	472,737	1,422.62	471,314.38
108	Clarence P. Elder et al	Juan Carlos Santistevan	Taos county	17,159		17,159
109	Cresencio Valdez	Conejos	State of Colorado	2,500,000		2,500,000
110	James A. Peraltareavis	Peralta	Arizona and New Mexico	12,467,456		12,467,456
111	Guadalupe Montoya	Town of Real de Dolores	Santa Fe county	17,361		17,361

496 THE SPANISH ARCHIVES OF NEW MEXICO

No.	Claimants	Name	Location	Claimed Area	Confirmed Area	Rejected Area
112	M. de la P. V. de Conway	Cuyamungue	Santa Fe county	5,000	604.27	4,395.73
113	Ponciano Lucero et al	Chupaderos de la Lagunita	San Miguel county	4,340		4,340
114	Margarita Baca et al	San José del Encinal	Valencia county	30,000		30,000
115	Manuel Archuleta et al	Arroyo Seco	Santa Fe county	6,000		6,000
116	Jacob Gold et al	Talaya Hill	Santa Fe county	1,003	319.20	683.80
117	Juan B. Lucero et al	Lucero	Santa Fe county	700		700
118	Jacob Gold et al	Bernal Spring	San Miguel county	20,000		20,000
119	Vicente Velarde et al	Catarino Maese	Santa Fe county	300		300
120	José Anto. Rodriguez et al	Juan Rodriguez	Santa Fe county	2,000		2,000
121	J. A. Romero et al	De Vera	Santa Fe county	300		300
122	Higinio Lujan et al	Peñasco Largo or Santiago Ramirez	Santa Fe county	6,165	272.168	5,892.832
123	Manuel Romero y Dominguez	Rio Tesuque or Juan Benabides	Santa Fe county	7,300		7,300
124	Juan A. Romero et al	Juan José Archuleta	Santa Fe county	500		500
125	Esquipula Flores et al	Juan Antonio Flores	Santa Fe county	1,500		1,500
126	David Trulillo et al (see Case No. 61)					
127	Eutimio Montoya	Town of Socorro	Socorro county	843,259		843,259
128	Thomas J. Allen et al (see case No. 44)					
129	(Transferred to Arizona District)					
130	Florencio Sandoval et al	Ojo de San José	Bernalillo county	30,000	4,336.91	25,663.09
131	Maria A. Gallegos et al	Guadalupita	Colfax and Mora counties	47,743		47,743
132	(Transferred to Arizona District)					
133	Pueblo of Laguna	Pueblo of Laguna	Valencia county	101,510	17,328.91	84,181.09
134	Pueblo of Santo Domingo et al	Santo Domingo and San Felipe	Bernalillo county	40,000	1,070.688	38,929.312
135	Geo. W. Thompson et al	(See No. 44)				

THE SPANISH ARCHIVES OF NEW MEXICO 497

136	Anastasio P. De Castillo		Bernalillo and Valencia counties	511,000	511,000
137	Rafaela C. Barela et al	Santo Tomas Y Yturbide	Doña Ana county	10,000	9,622.34	377.66
138	Corporation of José Manuel Sanchez Baca	Manuel Sanchez Baca	Doña Ana county	3,601	3,530.60	70.40
139	Josiah F. Crosby	Miranda	Doña Ana county	4,751		4,751
140	J. I. Martinez et al	Juan José Lobato	Rio Arriba county	205,615.72	205,615.72	
141	J. I. Martinez et al	Vallecito de San Antonio	Rio Arriba county	38,000		38,000
142	Merejildo Martinez et al	Vallecito de Lobato	Rio Arriba county	114,000		114,000
143	Lewis Lutz et al	José Sutton	San Miguel county	69,445		69,445
144	Ramon Garcia et al	San Pablo y Nacimiento	Bernalillo county	131,000		131,000
145	Pedro Perea	Arquito	Bernalillo county	2,000		2,000
146	Pedro Perea	Luis Garcia	Bernalillo county	11,674		11,674
147	Mariano S. Otero	Nuestra Señora de Los Dolores Mine	Santa Fe county	42		42
148	Benito Borrego et al (No. 122)					
149	Juan Santistevan et al	Fernando de Taos	Taos county	1,889	1,817.24	71.76
150	Grant of the Colony of Refugio et al	Grant of the Colony of the Refugio	Doña Ana county	26,000	11,524.30	14,475.70
151	Corporation of Mesilla	Mesilla Colony	Doña Ana county	21,628.52	21,628.52	
152	Joel P. Whitney et al	Estancia	Valencia county	415,036		415,036
153	L. Z. and M. Z. Farwell (No. 99)					
154	Los Animas Land Grant Co. (No. 44)					
155	Pinito Pino et al	Hacienda del Alamo	Santa Fe county	50,000		50,000
156	Florencio Sandoval et al	Las Lamitas	Bernalillo county	120,000		120,000
157	Pueblo of Santa Anna et al	Pueblo of Santa Anna or El Ranchito	Bernalillo county	87,360	4,945.24	82,414.76
158	Felicita Crespin	San Acasio	Socorro county	18,000		18,000
159	Antonio Baca et al	Mesita Blanca	Santa Fe county	18,000		18,000
160	Roman A. Baca et al	Ancon Colorado	Bernalillo county	800		800
161	Juan N. Armijo et al	La Peralta	Bernalillo county	400,000		400,000
162	(Transferred to Arizona District)					

498 THE SPANISH ARCHIVES OF NEW MEXICO

No.	Claimants	Name	Location	Claimed Area	Confirmed Area	Rejected Area
163	Julian Martinez et al	Cañada de Las Mestenas	Taos county	16,000		16,000
164	Nicolas Pino	Ojito de Galisteo	Santa Fe county	25,000		25,000
165	Eduardo Otero et al	Guadalupe Mine	Valencia county	16,000		16,000
166	C. P. Elder	Cañon del Rio Col.	Taos county	43,939		43,939
167	Mariano S. Otero	Ojo de La Cabra	Bernalillo county	4,340		4,340
168	M. R. Pendell et al	Santa Teresa	Doña Ana county	9,861	8,478.51	1,382.49
169	Smith H. Simpson et al	Oreja del Llano de Los Aguajes	Taos county	150,000		150,000
170	Alex Grezlachowski et al	Sanguijuela	San Miguel county	20,000		20,000
171	Abran de Herrera et al	Pueblo Quemado	Santa Fe county	900		900
172	Pueblo de Cochiti	Juana Baca	Bernalillo county	20,000		20,000
173	Antonio Griego et al	El Embudo	Rio Arriba county	25,000		25,000
174	Jose N. Martinez	Jose Ygancio Martinez	Taos county	500		500
175	Juan Antonio Valdez	Felipe Medina	Taos county	300		300
176	Manuel Espinosa	Manuel Fernandez	Taos county	300		300
177	José Luis Valdez	Rio del Oso	Rio Arriba county	5,000		5,000
178	Felipe Delgado et al	Lo de Basquez	Santa Fe county	76,000		76,000
179	José L. Valdez et al	Juan Bautista Valdez	Rio Arriba county	60,000	1,468.57	58,531.43
180	Magdalena L. de Ortiz et al	Roque Lobato	Santa Fe county	1,620		1,620
181	Tomas C. de Baca et al	Santa Cruz	Bernalillo county	60,000		60,000
182	José Albino Baca (No. 130)					
183	Kate Sullivan (No. 91)					
184	Pueblo de Santo Domingo (No. 134)					
185	Pueblo de San Felipe (No. 134)					
186	William Frazer	Miguel Chavez	Taos county	15,000		15,000
187	Refugio Aguilar	Felipe Tafoya	Santa Fe county	500		500
188	Francisco Lujan et al	Manuel Tenorio	Santa Fe county	600		600
189	Juan de Dios Tapia et al	Tomas Tapia	Santa Fe county	500		500
190	Jose A. Ribera	Diego Arias de Quiros	Santa Fe county	2,000		2,000
191	Refugio Aguilar et al	Alfonzo Rael de Aguilar	Santa Fe county	500		500
192	Luis Ribera et al	Felipe Pacheco	Santa Fe county	500		500

THE SPANISH ARCHIVES OF NEW MEXICO   499

193	Jesus Ochoa et al	(No. 150)			
194	Frank Becker et al	Santa Cruz	Santa Fe county	48,000	4,567.60	43,432.40
195	Amado C. de Baca et al	(No. 95)			
196	Ambrosio Pino et al	(No. 136)			
197	Antonio J. Ortiz et al	El Badito	Santa Fe county	1,350		1,350
198	Juan Marquez et al	(No. 25)			
199	José M. Nieto et al	Santa Fe Canon	Santa Fe county	6,000		6,000
200	Luis Chavez et al	The Alamo	Santa Fe county	2,000		2,000
201	(Transferred to Arizona District)				
202	William T. Russell (No. 86)				
203	R. H. Longwill et al (No. 144)				
204	S. Endicott Peabody (No. 142)				
205	Joel P. Whitney et al	Cañada de Cochiti	Bernalillo county	104,554	19,112.78	85,441.22
206	Eloisa Bergere et al (No. 165)				
207	Mariano S. Otero et al (No. 38)				
208	Manuel Gurule et al	Town of Bernalillo	Bernalillo county	47,743		47,743
209	John Gwinn, Jr. (No. 69)				
210	Ambrosio Pino (No. 136)				
211	José A. Vigil et al	Santo Domingo de Cundiyo	Santa Fe county	2,137.08	2,137.08	
212	Jose de G. Trujillo et al	Pueblo Quemado	Rio Arriba county	288,000		288,000
213	S. H. Simpson (No. 144)				
214	Feliciano Montoya et al	Cieneguilla	Santa Fe county	45,245	3,202.79	42,042.21
215	John B. Salpointe	Bishop's Ranch	Santa Fe county	600		600
216	Louise J. Purdy et al (No. 44)				
217	José M. Chavez et al	Town of Bernalillo	Bernalillo county	11,674.37	3,404.67	8,269.70
218	Maria M. De Berry et al (No. 107)				
219	Marcos A. Chavez et al	Rancho de Los Comanches		95,380		95,380
220	Clotilda de Spencer et al	Rancho Rio Puerco	Bernalillo county	95,480		95,480

500 THE SPANISH ARCHIVES OF NEW MEXICO

No.	Claimants	Name	Location	Claimed Area	Confirmed Area	Rejected Area
221	Luciano Chavez et al	Rancho de Los Comales or Corrales		95,380		95,380
222	Clotilda Spencer et al	Rancho de la Gallina		95,480		95,480
223	N. M. de Aragon	Rancho		95,480		95,480
224	Tomasa T. de Quintana	Rancho El Rito		95,480		95,480
225	Isabel J. de Romero et al	Rancho		95,480		95,480
226	Agapito Ortega et al	Rancho	Rio Arriba county	1,000		1,000
227	Juan A. Quintana	José Ignacio Alarid	Rio Arriba county	10,000		10,000
228	José P. Jaramillo et al	Roque Jacinto Jaramillo	Bernalillo county	2,300	1,579.48	720.52
229	Jesus M. Castillo et al	Angostura	Socorro county	4,000		4,000
230	Matias Contreras	Francisco Garcia	Mora and Colfax counties	69,440		69,440
231	Eugenio Alverez et al	Manuel Alvarez				
232	Jesus Crespin et al	Cristobal Crespin	Rio Arriba county	3,000		3,000
233	José A. Garcia (No. 99)					
234	Vicente Romero et al	Alfonzo Rael de Aguilar	Santa Fe county	17,361		17,361
235	Bernardo Salazar	Antonio de Salazar	Rio Arriba county	23,351		23,351
236	José S. Y Ortiz et al (No. 142)					
237	Atanacio Romero et al	Juan de Mestas	Santa Fe county	3,000		3,000
238	Albino Lopez	La Nasa	Rio Arriba county	2,000		2,000
239	Agapito Sena	Tacubaya (No. 205)	Santa Fe county	3,000		3,000
240	Manuel Hurtado et al					
241	Antonio G. Gomez et al	Hurraza or Paraje del Rancho	Taos county	90,000		90,000
242	Apolonio Vigil	Las Manuelitas (No. 214)	San Miguel county	200,000		200,000
243	Zenon Sandoval et al					
244	N. M. de Aragon et al	La Gallina		434,000		434,000
245	N. M. de Aragon et al	Rancho del Rio Arriba		434,000		434,000
246	N. M. de Aragon et al	Rancho Los Rincones		434,000		434,000
247	N. M. De Aragon et al	Rancho Abiquiu		434,000		434,000
248	N. M. De Aragon et al	El Coyote		434,000		434,000
249	Juan Garcia	Manuel Garcia de Las Ribas	Rio Arriba county	7,577		7,577

THE SPANISH ARCHIVES OF NEW MEXICO 501

250	Juan Torres et al	Cristobal de Torres	Rio Arriba county		205,615
251	Antonio Vigil	Diego de Belasco.	Rio Arriba county		5,000
252	Feliciano Montoya (No. 144)				
253	Juan Ramon Duran	Juan de Ulibarri	Rio Arriba county		500
254	Andres Garcia et al	Juan Y Garcia de Noriega	Santa Fe county		5,000
255	José Torres et al	José A. Torres	Rio Arriba county		5,000
256	Refugio Valverde et al	Santo Toribio de Jems	Bernalillo county		100,000
257	Bartolome Trujillo et al	San Jose de Garcia	Rio Arriba county		2,000
258	Pedro Perea (No. 217)				
259	Pedro Perea	San José Spring	Bernalillo county		182,130
260	Crecencio Moreno et al	Juan José Moreno	Bernalillo county		35,000
261	Antonio de Urribari	Pueblo Colorado	Taos county		1,000
262	Francisco A. Romero	F. X. Romero (No. 257)	Rio Arriba county		300
263	Francisco Serna et al				
264	Bartolome Sanchez et al	Bartolome Sanchez (No. 97)	Rio Arriba county	4,469.828	10,000
265	Juan A. Martin et al				
266	Francisco Tafoya	Juan Tafoya	Rio Arriba county		86,000
267	Valentin C de Baca et al	Santa Rosa de Cubero	Bernalillo county	1,945.496	5,000
268	Manuel Archuleta et al	Mesilla Tract (No. 90)	Santa Fe county		6,000
269	Antonio Jose Gallegos et al				
270	Mariano S. Otero et al	Virtientes de Navajo	Bernalillo county		11,480
271	(Transferred to Arizona District)				
272	Guadalupe Montoya et al	Bosque Grande or M. and S. Montoya	Bernalillo county	2,967.574	4,340
273	Pueblo de Isleta	Lo de Padilla	Valencia county		51,940.82
274	J. Franco Chavez	Antonio Gutierrez	Valencia county		22,636.92
275	J. Franco Chavez	Joaquin Sedillo	Valencia county		
276	Peregrina Campbell et al	Maragua	Santa Fe county		1,042
277	(Transferred to Arizona District)				
278	Mariano F. Sena	José De Leyba	Santa Fe county		18,000
279	J. Maria Mestas	Joaquin de Mestas	Bernalillo county		3,632
280	Blaza Alvarez de Sanchez	Sanchez	Doña Ana county		4,428

No.	Claimants	Name	Location	Claimed Area	Confirmed Area	Rejected Area
281	Romulo E. Varela et al	Barela	Doña Ana county	4,428		4,428
282	Manuel M. Martin et al	Galban or Ygnacio Sanchez Vergara	Bernalillo county	30,000		30,000
			Total,	34,653,340.616	1,934,986.39	32,718,354.226

This tabulated statement of the business pending before the Court of Private Land Claims and disposed of by that tribunal is taken from the report of Matt G. Reynolds, United States Attorney.

INDEX

INDEX

Abadiano, Blas, 434
Abalos, Pedro de, 1
Abalos, Antonio de, 2
Abenbua, Lucas de, 7
Abeytia, Antonio de, 205
Abiquiú, inhabitants of, 25, 26, 27, re-settlement, 28, 31, 32, 43, 76, 77, pueblo, 141, re-settlement, 324, 329
Abrego, Juan de, 93, 113, 370
Abreu, Marcelino, 215, 298
Abreu, Ramon, 32, 122
Abreu, Santiago, 46, 62, 354
Acoma, pueblo, 180, 181, 456-462, 478
Aganza, José Balentin de, 100
Aguilar, Eusebio de, 133
Aguilar, Juan Bautista, 193
Aguilar, Juan de, 30, 193
Aguilar, Luis, 66
Aguilar, Nasario, de, 33
Aguilar y Lopez, 49
Aguilera, Antonio de, 5
Aguilera y Issasi, Antonio, 97, 104, 145, 187
Alameda, people of, 27, 29, 166
Alameda tract, heirs of, 29, 99, 166, 310, 328, 381
Alamillo, re-settlement, 345, 350
Alamo de Culebra, 70
Alamo, rancho, 50, 71, 126
Alaraguia, José, 181
Alari, Juan Antonio, 112, 190, 239
Alari, Manuel, 113
Alarid, Ignacio, 29
Alarid, Jesus Maria, 50
Alarid, José Antonio, 30
Alarid, José Ignacio, 28
Alarid, José Nepomuceno, 33
Alarid, José Ramon, 32, 49, 323, 373
Alba, Agapito de, 30
Alburquerque, 29, 30, 66, 68, ranchos, 371
Alburquerque, Duke of, petition as to soldiers, 391
Alcala, Lucas Manuel de, 239
Alderete, Juan de, 5
Alderete, Joaquin de, 28
Alencaster, Joaquin Rael de, governor, 166, 180, 181, 434

Alire, Juan Lorenzo, 33, 164
Alire, Miguel de, 105, 178
Alire, Tomás, 29
Allande, Pedro Maria de, governor, 30, 77, 180, 435
Altamira, Marques de, 324
Altamirano, Antonio Tafoya, 25
Alto del Pino del Virgen, 120
Alvarez del Castillo, Juan Miguel, 141
Alvarez, Manuel, 329, citizenship, etc., 339-342
Alvear, Tomás de, 176
Alvear y Collado, Tomàs de, 41, 292
Analco, 36, 37
Analla, Antonio, 143
Anaya Almazan, Francisco, 5, 147, 288
Anaya Almazan, Juana de, 356
Anaya, Francisco de, 27
Anaya, Juan de, 153
Ancon del Tejedor, 81
Angel, Francisco, 20
Angel, Francisco Xavier, 20
Angel, José Manuel, 33
Angel, Manuel, 33
Angel, Marcial, 28
Angostura, 34
Ansures, Salvador, 32
Ansures, Teresa, 19
Anton Chico, grant, 267, 268, 269
Anza, Juan Bautista de, governor, 45, 76, 110, 113, record of grants, 363
Apaches, Faraon, 12
Apaches, Jicarillas, 20
Apaches, Navajos, 140, 159
Apaches, raids of, 189
Apodaca, Felipe de, 300
Apodaca, Inez de, 28
Apodaca, José, 196
Apodaca, Juan de, 205
Apodaca, Juan Estavan de, 12, 19
Apodaca, Nicolas de, 27, 86
Apodaca, Sebastian, 103, 178
Apodaca, Vicente, 27
Aragon, Eusebio, 184
Aragon, Fernando, 270
Aragon, José, Manuel, 30, war captain, 181
Aragon, José Miguel, 118

Aragon, Manuel, 182, 371
Aramburu, Antonio, 103, 105, 207
Aratia, Felipe de, 66, 68, 89
Archibec, Juan de, 6, 9 inventory of estate, 12, story of, 113, 114, 115
Archibeque, Agustin de, 20
Archibeque, Maria de Guadalupe de, 29, 85
Archiveque, Maria de, 206
Archiveque, Miguel de, 19
Archives, inventory, 1715, 324, Cabildo, 330-338
Archuleta, Ana de, 4, 5
Archuleta, Gregorio, 4
Archuleta, Hilario, 74
Archuleta, J. Andrés, 80, 169
Archuleta, Juan Antonio, 21, 90, 189, 211
Archuleta, Juan de, 98
Archuleta, Juan José de, 20
Archuleta, Marcial, 119
Archuleta, Miguel, 80
Archuleta, Pascual, 119
Archuleta, Salvador, 212
Arco del arrogo de Galisteo, 33
Arellano, Cristobal, 451
Arellano, Cristobal de, 145, 155
Arguello, Juana de, 152
Arias de Quiros, Diego, 5, reservoir, 10, 11, 12, 17, 19, 33, 66, 68, 69, 98, 135, 136, 152, 197, 278
Aricara, Indians, 21
Arkansas, river, settlement on, 328
Armendaris, Pedro de, 30, 46, 115, 354
Armenta, Antonio de, 29, 140, 164
Armenta, Joseph, 140
Armenta, Luis de, 38, 108
Armenta, Simon de, 179
Armijo, Antonio de, 28, 32, 118, 123, 294, 360
Armijo, Concepcion, 33
Armijo, Getrudis de, 29
Armijo, Isabel de, 28
Armijo, José Nestor, 47
Armijo, Josepha, 33, 92
Armijo, Joseph de 19
Armijo, Juan, 46, 329
Armijo, Juan Antonio, 31, 50, 96, 122
Armijo, Juan Cristobal, 197
Armijo, Julian de, 107
Armijo, Manuel, political chief, 28, 321, governor, 62, 321, 349, 390
Armijo, Manuel de, 165
Armijo, Manuel, Segundo, 85
Armijo, Salvador, 30
Armijo, Vicente, 112
Armijo, Vincente Ferrer de, 123

Arroniz, Juan Francisco de, 209
Arroyo de en Media, 42
Arroyo de San Lorenzo, 79
Arroyo Seco, water rights, 380, 381
Arteaga, Gregorio de, 32
Arteaga, Manuel, 45, 76, 113, 141
Arvisu, José de, 202
Arze, Antonio, 113
Ascencion, Josepha de la, 28
Aspitia, Inez de, 5
Atencio, Antonio, 207
Atencio, Juan de, 164
Atencio, Lazaro, 29
Atienza Alcala y Escobar, Joseph de, 145
Atienza, Antonio de, 84
Atienza, Joseph de, 15, 100, 123, 150
Atienza, Juan de, 6, 7, 100, 123, 146
Atienza, Juan de Alcala, 231
Atienza, Lazaro de, 19, 324
Atrisco Tract, 43, 69, 75, 76, 90, 91, 101, 189, 320
Attencio, Antonio de, 83
Attencio, Cayetano de, 240
Autentica pre fide Jurobus, 137
Ayeta, Fr. Francisco de, 1
Ayuntamientos, 30, 32, 49, 50, 86, 87, 123, 143, 170, 329
Azuela, Manuel de, 180

BACA, Antonio, 41, 75
Baca, Baltazar, 44, 71, 104
Baca, Barbara, 45
Baca, Bartolomé, governor, 45, 46, 168, 169, 213, 346, 348
Baca, Bernabe, 40, 74
Baca, Cristobal, 40
Baca, Diego Manuel, 35, 315
Baca, Estevan, 46
Baca, Francisco, Navajo, 271
Baca, Ignacio, 213
Baca, Isabel, 45
Baca, Jōsé, 46, 267
Baca, José Francisco, 47, 49, 50
Baca, Josef Maria, 45, 46
Baca, Joseph, 28, 43, 44, 160, 356
Baca, Josepha, 40
Baca Juan, 82
Baca, Juan Antonio, 142
Baca, Juan Cruz, 384
Baca, Juan Esteban, 49, 112
Baca, Juan Francisco, 111
Baca, Juan José, 49
Baca, Juan Manuel, 50
Baca, Juana, 73
Baca, Juana Maria, 45
Baca, Lorenzo, 111

INDEX

Baca, Magdalena, 284
Baca, Manuel, 41, 46, 157, 241
Baca, Maria, 295
Baca, Maria Miquela, 50
Baca, Marina, 44
Baca, Marina de Jesus, 44, 315
Baca, Miguel, 44, 45, 142
Baca, Pablo, 42
Baca, Simon, 35
Baca, Tomás, 49, 50
Baca, Vicente, 89
Baca y Ortiz, Francisco, 62, 87
Baca y Pino, Francisco, 87
Baca y Terrus, Francisco, 275, 298
Badito del Arroyo, 32
Baldez, Ana, 66
Baldez, Domingo de, 200
Baldez, Mariano, 381
Ballejo, Antonio, 35
Ballejo, Bernardo, 101
Ballejo, Juan, 310
Ballejo, Manuel, 198
Ballejos, Barbara, 345
Ballejos, Catarina, 345
Ballejos, Matilda, 345
Bandelier, A. F., 13
Bancroft, H. H., 2, 4, 5, 12
Barba, pueblo of, 26
Barcelo, Marin Getrudes, 62
Barcelo, Trinidad, 50, 327
Barclay's Fort, 277
Barela, Felipe, 105
Barela, José Francisco, 80
Barela, Manuel Ramos, 208
Barela, Pedro, 29
Barela, Salvador, 40, 41
Barela, Tiburcio, 41
Barela, de Posada, Antonia, 133
Barela, de Posada, Pedro, 201
Bargas, Maurilo, 143
Barracks, Santa Fe, 324
Barreda, Domingo de la, 4, 33, 97
Barrera, Manuel de la, 50, 73
Barrio de Analco, 67
Barrio del Torreon, Santa Fe, 271
Barrios, Juan Antonio, 4
Bas Juan Gonzales, 30, 40, 82
Basquez, Joseph, 35
Basquez, Michaela, heirs of, 106
Beaubien, Carlos, 62, genealogy, 65
Bejar, Simona de, 35
Bejarana, Tomás de, 299
Bejil, Miguel, 113
Belarde, Francisco, 145
Belen Tract, 43, first settlers, 43, 73, 240
Bellijo, Fr. Manuel, 46

Benavides, Domingo, 84, 164
Benavides, Francisco Xavier, 99
Benavides, Fray, 78
Benavides, Jesus, 46, 47
Benavides, José Maria, 123
Benavides, Juan, 32, 40, 163
Benavides, Juana, 29, 40
Benavides, Juana de Ojeda, 140, 163
Benavides, La, 35
Benavides, Luis, 49, 39
Benavides, Miguel, 175
Benavides, Nicolas, 35
Benavides, Rafael, 47
Benavides, Tomás, 40, 41
Benjamin, J P., 62
Bercera, Tomás Antonio, 118
Bernal, Antonio, 188
Bernal, Barbara, 114
Bernal, Julian, 46
Bernal, Tomás, 46
Bernalillo, 29, 399
Beytia, Antonio de, 43, 154
Beytia, Diego de, 98, 145
Beytia, Juan de, 25
Beytia, Manuel, 156
Beytia, Rosalia de, 106
Bigil, Antonio, 33
Bitton, Gaspar, 27, 109
Blasquez, José, 126
Bocanegra, José Maria de, 275
Bohorquez y Corcuera, Francisco Joseph Tomás de, 67, 68
Bohorquez y Corcuera, Joseph, 12, 19, 35, 37, 41, 62, 135, 151, 152, 187, 188
Bonanza, 12
Bonavia, Bernardo, 77, 343, 372
Bone, Santiago, 62
Borica, Diego de, 241
Borrego Diego, 45, 70
Borrego, Diego Basquez, 41
Bosque Grande, 169
Bosque Redondo, 80
Brito, Juan de Leon, 36, 37
Brito, Manuel, 44
Brito, Manuela, 29, 44, 84, 139
Brojas, Juan Rico de, 100
Burgos, Fr. José de, 93
Bustamante, Don Juan Domingo de, governor, 15, trial, 17, 35, 36, 37, 38, 52, 64, 65, 68, 131, 132, 134, 135, 310
Bustamante, Joseph, 124
Bustamante, Josepha, 45
Bustamante, Manuel, 50, 215
Bustamante, Phelipe, 155
Bustamante, Ventura, 339
Bustamante, de, Bernardo, 112, 113

Bustamante de Tagle, Bernardo, 25, 105, 178
Bustamante Tagle, Joseph, inventory, etc., 74, 105, 106, 220, 321
Bustamante y Tagle, Pedro Antonio, 28
Bustillos, Juan de la Paz, 187
Bustos, Cristobal, 49
Bustos, José Antonio, 45, 169
Bustos, Juan Martin, 355

CABALLERO, Fr. Antonio, 357
Caballero de Croix, 363
Cabeza de Baca, Luis Maria R. C. No. 20, children, 47, 354, court costs, 372, Las Vegas, 373, 435
Cabeza de Baca, Tomás, 81, 122
Cabrera, Gabriel de 133
Cabrera, Maria de, 66
Caceras, Clara Ruiz de, oldest archive, 201
Cachupin, Don Tomás Velez, governor, 27, 28, 41, 43, 74, 75, 77
Cadena, Francisco, 293
Cadena, Maria Luisa, 294
Cadena, Pedro Velasquez de, 3
Cadiz, city, 393
Caja del Rio, grant, 19, 319
Calles, Josef Andrés, 165
Campo Redondo, José, 45, 113, 180
Campos, Maria de Jesus, 291
Cañada de Cochiti, 357
Cañada de Cundiyo, 313
Cañada de Los Apaches, 70
Cañada de Santa Clara, 283
Cañada del Tio Leonardo, 201
Candelaria, Bentura de, 100
Candelaria, Blas de la, 141
Candelaria, Felix de la, 142
Candelaria, Francisco de la, 199
Candelaria, Juan, 116
Candelaria, Maria de la Luz, 79
Candelaria, Ventura de, 68
Canela, Juan de Sosa, 147
Canela, Juana de Sosa, 310
Caño, Ignacio, 185
Cañon de Jemez, 77, 167
Cañon de San Diego, 167, first settlers, 167
Canoñes de Riano, 119
Canjuebe, Antonio, 77
Canjuebe, Francisco, 7, 8
Canjuebes, Indians, 371
Canseco, Sebastian, 278
Capilla de San Miguel, 238
Capitol, removal to Santo Domingo, 328

Captains-General, 1713-1715, commissions, 327
Capulin, El, 413
Carabajal, Lorenzo de, 66
Carbono, Luis, 80
Cardenas, Petrona de, 75
Carillo, Juan, 71
Carillo, Miguel, 67
Carmona, Francisco de, 133
Carnuel tract, 29, claim, 76, 150, Cañon, 297
Carrizal, 76
Carros, Juan de, 126
Carson, Christopher, testimony, Maxwell Grant, 60
Casa Colorado, 106
Casados, Antonio, 73
Casados, Francisco Joseph, 4, 5, 11, 66, 67, 206
Casados, Francisco Lorenzo de, 35, 66
Casados, José Antonio, 49, 50
Casillas, Bernardo, 12
Casillas, Diego, 269
Casillas, Manuel, 206
Casillas, Salvador, 74
Casillas, Tomás, 74
Castela, Getrudis, 142
Castela, Mariano, 266
Castellanos, José, 132, 145
Castillo, Ana Maria del, 80
Castillo, Joaquin, 371
Castrense, Capilla, 177
Castrillon, Antonio Alvarez, 4, '100
Castrillon, Manuel Alvarez, 147
Cebolleta, grant, 49, 76, 373
Cédula, Real, 6
Cerda, Juan Josef de la, 284
Cerrillos, 12, grant at, 15, 28
Cerrito, grant, 323, 324
Cerro Colorado, 70
Cerro del Oro, 346
Cevilleta, town, claim, 95, 78, 367
Chaco Mesa, 111, 159
Chacon, Fernando, governor, 45
Chacon, Francisco, 75
Chacon, Medina Villaseñor, Joseph, governor, 146, 198
Chama, 329
Chama, Partido de, 74
Chama, river, 67
Chambers, Samuel, 80
Chaperito, 81, 329
Chavez, Antonio, of Belen, 79
Chavez, Antonia de, 102, 234
Chavez, Antonio de, 69, 75
Chavez, Buenaventura, 77
Chavez, Clara de, 66

INDEX

Chavez, Diego Antonio, 76
Chavez, Domingo, 77, 371
Chavez, Fernando, 43, 83
Chavez, Francisco, 80
Chavez, Francisco Antonio, 76
Chavez, Francisco Xavier, 71, 371
Chavez, Geronimo, 384
Chavez, Ignacio, 75, 80
Chavez, Joaquin, 80
Chavez, José, 71, 80
Chavez, José Antonio, 32, 77, 80, 142, 324
Chavez, José de la Cruz, 80
Chavez, General José Maria, 114
Chavez, Leogarda, 32
Chavez, Maria, widow of Sebastian Martin, 75
Chavez, Maria Antonia, 69
Chavez, Maria de, 82
Chavez, Miguel, 75
Chavez, Nicolas de, 40, 43, 69, 74, 75, 155, 234
Chavez, Pedro, 69, 75, 328
Chavez, Quiteria, 75
Chavez, Tomás, 75
Chavez, Ursula, 77, 79, 269, 270, 446
Chavez, Ventura, 142
Chavez, Vicente, Cura, 80
Chavez y Baca, José Francisco, 388
Chavez y Duran, José Antonio, 32
Chelli, 185
Cheyennes, 265
Chico, Payemo, 206
Chimayo, 88, 208
Chiriños, Juan Manuel, 73, 76, 84, 92, 104, 133, 136, 151, 152, 153
Church, parish, 73, 147, 148, 187, 207, 317
Cienega, pueblo, 4, 12, 43, puesto, 123, 178, 203
Cienega, Santa Fe, 10, 68, 81, 143, grant, 345, 354, 362, 390
Cienega, de Los Garcias, 381
Cieneguilla, 12, 170
Cinnabar, 371
Cit Combenerit, 289
Coca, Don Miguel de, 37, 67, 178
Cochití, pueblo, 46, 49, 74, 156, notes, 469-471, 360, 432, 434, 435, 478
Codallos y Rabal, governor, 21, 25, 26, 73, 74, 77, French and Comanches, 148, 149, 150, 151, 363
Colonists, 391
Colonization, lands, 392
Colonization laws, 273, 274, 275, 1823, 327, 329, 339

Comanches, 20, 148, 149, 150, attack on Taos, 200, 328, 347
Concepcion, Pascuala de, 317
Concha, Don Fernando de la, governor, 15, 29, 44, 45, 113
Cónde, Francisco Garcia, 329
Conejo, Maria Lopez, 279
Congress, Mexican, 385, decrees, titles, 393
Conquerors, rights of descendants, 362
Constitution, 1820, 323
Contreras, Casilda, 206
Contreras, Joseph de, 145
Copas, José Manuel, 122
Coquindo, Juan, 80
Cordero, Juan Ruiz, 310, 353
Cordoba, Ana Maria, 74
Cordoba, José Manuel, 172
Cordoba, Joseph, 74
Cordoba, Juan de Jesus, 80
Cordoba, Juan Ruiz, 66, 68
Cordoba, Lazaro de, 66, 74, 279
Cordoba, Pedro, 74
Cordoba, Simon de, 129
Corral de Piedra, 108, 157
Cortes, Teresa, 76
Corvera, José Ibanez, 112
Cossio, Antonio Valverde de, 100, 144, 310
Crespin, Cristobal, 67, 68, 134, 135
Crespin, Diego, Antonio, 33
Crespin, Francisco, 33
Crespin, Gregorio, 71, 75, 209
Crespin, Rafael, 33
Cristobal, Fray, 1
Cruciaga, Antonio de, 36, 37, 38
Cruciaga, Manuel de, 152
Cruz, Juana de la, 67
Cruzat y Gongora, Don Gervacio, governor, 19, 35, 82, 346
Cruzate, Domingo Jironza de, 1, 2, 3, 394
Cubero, Don Pedro Rodriguez de, governor, 6, 18
Cubero, Rancho de, 79, 385
Cuervo y Valdez, Don Francisco, governor, 12, 18, 81, 397
Cuesta del Oregano, 136
Cuma, Camino Real de, 201
Cuyamungue, pueblo, 9, 45, 233

De Dias, Miguel, 311
De la Cruz, Leonardo, 157
De la Fuente, Joseph Antonio, 286
Delgado, Fray Carlos, *informe*, 17, 156
Delgado, Manuel, 45, will, 86, 113, 165, 180, 391

Del Norte, river, 5
Del Rio, Alonzo, 97
Departmental Assembly, members, 60, 175, foreigners, 276, 329, 330, 348
Deputation, Durango, 373
Deputation, Provincial, 86, 185, 213, 215, 377, Indians, 378-380
Deputation, Territorial, 31, 47, 87, 88, 185, 195, 196, 213, 214, 215, 384, 388
De Vargas, Alonzo, 304
De Vargas, Don Diego Zapata Lujan Ponce de Leon, 2, 4, 5, 12, 15, 16, 18, Relacion Sumaria, 26, 34, 36, coat of arms, 144, will, 301, 310
De Vargas, Juan Manuel, 304
De Vargas, Sebastian, 27, 36, 67, 71, 75, 132, 176, 241-264, 311
Dias del Castillo, Juan Manuel, 237
Dias del Castillo, Manuel, 158
Dimas, Joseph de, 92
Dolores, Nuestra Señora de Los, 28
Dominga, Maria, 86
Dominguez, Ana Maria, 81
Dominguez, Antonio, grant, 82, 106, 286
Dominguez, Benito, 81
Dominguez, Captain Thomé, 1
Dominguez, José, 81
Dominguez, Joseph, 81
Dominguez, Juana, 82, 132
Dominguez, Leonor, 82
Dominguez, Pablo, 213
Doña Ana, colony, grant, 88
Don Fernando de Taos, grant, 390
Doniphan, A. W., 4
Dubus Res de Vendi, 137
Duran, Agustin, 61, 87, 197, 446
Duran, Antonia, 82
Duran, Antonio, 40
Duran, Cristobal, 42
Duran, Diego, 205
Duran, Joseph, grant, 82
Duran, Josepha, 126
Duran, Juan, 84
Duran, Juan Joseph, 42, 85, 86, 240
Duran, Luis, 41
Duran, Matias, 31
Duran, Miguel, 68
Duran, Nicolas, 82
Duran, Salvador, 86
Duran, Sebastian, 299
Duran, Vicente Ferrer, 118
Durana, Chatalina, 84
Duran de Armijo, Antonio, 6, 7, 8, 22, 77, 83, 84, 132, 145, 207, 294
Duran de Armijo, Fray Antonio, letter to governor, 148, 149

Duran de Armijo, Manuel, 85
Duran de Armijo, Maria Gertrudes, 83
Duran de Armijo, Maria Rosalia, 360
Duran de Armijo, Rosa, 82
Duran de Armijo, Vicente, grant, 21
Durango, Bishop of, 19
Duran y Chavez, Antonio de, 112
Duran y Chavez, Fernando, 81, 350
Duran y Chavez, José, 86, 240
Duran y Chavez, Juan, 240
Duran y Chavez, Manuel, 239
Duran y Chavez, Nicolás, tract, 241
Duran y Chavez, Pedro, 1

EATON, E. W., grant, San Cristobal, 94
Education, Indians, 393
Eguijosa, Francisco Antonio de, 11, 88
El Bado, 32, meaning, 154
El Canyon, 96
El Chopo, 144
Ellison, Harvey, 384
El Paso, 1, 2, 25, 76, meaning, 154, 189, ayuntamiento, 377
El Rito, rancho, 79
El Sitio del Pueblo de la Cienega, 203
El Tajo, 187
Embudo, 311
Encinal, 169, 185
Engle, 2
Enriquez, Miguel, 83
Escalante, Fr., 2
Escobedo, Juan Leon Oneto, 105
Esperanza, Pedro Buen-Amigo, 89
Espexo, Francisco de Jesus, 355
Espinosa, Miguel de, 208
Espinosa, Salvador de, 88, 208
Espinosa, Tadeo, 208
Esquibel, Antonio A., 89
Esquibel, Buenaventura, 93
Esquibel, Clemente, 89
Esquibel, Francisco, 90
Esquibel, José, 88, 111
Esquibel, Ventura, 88
Estiercoles, Taos, 171
Estrada, Bartolomé, de, 3
Estrada, José, 89
Estufas, Isleta, 328

FAMILIES, heads of, San Miguel County, 1855, 324, 327
Fe-Jiu, pueblo, 26
Fernandez, Bartolomé, 76, 94, 140, 159, 239
Fernandez, Carlos, 90, 92, 111, 112, 295
Fernandez, Domingo, 93, 94; Eaton Grant, 94, 96, 97; 122, 143, 201, 214

INDEX 511

Fernandez, Felipe Sandoval de, 159
Fernandez, José D., 122
Fernandez, Juan Antonio, 93, 111
Fernandez, Juliana, 92
Fernandez, Martin, 89, 157
Fernandez, Rafael, 96, 215
Fernandez, Rosa Martina, 157
Fernandez, Santiago, 79, 93
Fernandez de la Pedrera, Bartolomé, 110
Fernandez de la Pedrera, Maria, 89, 111
Fernandez de la Pedrera, Phelipe de Sandoval, 238
Fernandez de Salazar, Juan Joseph, 90
Fernandez de Taos, 265
Figueroa, Ignacio Cornelio, 111
Finca Rustica, 330
Flores, Candelaria, 49
Flores, Juana Gertrudes, 163
Flores, Juana Teresa, 163
Flores, Juliana, 163
Flores, Lucas, 89
Flores Mogollon, Don Ignacio, governor, Sumas Indians, 397
Flores, Santiago, 144
Foreigners, 273, departmental assembly's decision, 276
Fragoso, Francisco Xavier, 90, 138, 159, 210, 239
Fragoso, Gabriel, 90
Frayles, revolution of 1680, 231
Frenchmen, 20, 21, 148, 149, 150, firearms, 391
Fresques, Adauto Isidro, 296
Fresques, Antonio, 66
Fresques, José, 35, 176
Fresquis, Joseph, 314
Fresquis, Juan Antonio, 316
Fuenclara, 20, 128
Fuenclara, Condé, de, 73
Fuera, Luiz, 106

GALISTEO, 15, 30, ayuntamiento, 46, 266, 267, pueblo, 301, 360
Gallegos, Antonio, 100
Gallegos, Cristobal, 112
Gallego, Diego, 101, 311, 399, grant, 400
Gallegos, Domingo, 119
Gallegos, Domingo, Segundo, 119
Gallegos, Francisco, 119
Gallegos, Helena, grant, 371
Gallegos, José Marcelo, 111
Gallegos, José Maria, 120
Gallegos, Juan, 107, 110
Gallegos, Juan Roque, 112

Gallegos, Juan Tomasa, 108
Gallegos, Julian, 119
Gallegos, Manuel, 27, 28, 42, 106, 119
Gallegos, Maria de la Luiz, 122
Gallegos, Miguel, 113
Gallegos, Pedro, 118
Gallegos, Ramon, 119
Gallegos, Tomás Antonio, 118
Gallardo, Pedro, Lopez, 135, 233
Galvan, Mariano, 8
Galvana, Juana, 75
Gamboa, Cristobal, 108
Garcia, Alonzo, 1
Garcia, Antonia, 102, 113
Garcia, Antonio, grant, 113, 114
Garcia, Antonio, José, 119
Garcia, Cristobal, 68
Garcia, Felix, 267
Garcia, Francisco, 30, 70, 97, 98, 101, 109, 112, 113, 119, 267
Garcia, Fray Andrés, 112
Garcia, José Domingo, 122
Garcia, José Victor, 122
Garcia, Joseph, 102, 103
Garcia, Juan, 50, 71, 118
Garcia, Juan Cristobal, 113
Garcia, Juan Estevan, 101
Garcia Jurado, Barbara, 106
Garcia Jurado, José, 5
Garcia Jurado, Ramon, 105, 127, 128, 132, 145, 316
Garcia Jurado, Toribio, 111
Garcia, Lazaro, 102
Garcia, Luciano, 114
Garcia, Luis, 81, 105
Garcia, Marcial, 207
Garcia, Martin, 66, 97
Garcia, Mateo, 360
Garcia, Miguel, 122
Garcia, Nicolás, 107
Garcia, Pablo, rancho, 79
Garcia Pareja, Manuel, 42, 44, 75
Garcia, Rafael, 360
Garcia, Ramon, 112
Garcia, Salvador, 112
Garcia, Santiago, heirs of, 298
Garcia Villegas, Juan Ignacio, 42
Garcia, Xavier, Socorro tract, 115
Garcia de la Mora, Antonio Josef, 111
Garcia de la Mora, José, 114
Garcia de la Mora, Juan, 25, 102
Garcia de la Mora, Juan Eusebio, 120
Garcia de las Rivas, 102
Garcia de Las Rivas, Juan, 4, 11, 12, 35, 66, 67, 98, 99, 100, 123, 124
Garcia de Las Rivas, Juan José, 97

Garcia de Las Rivas, Miguel, 127
Garcia de Los Reyes, Juan, 107
Garcia de Noriega, Joaquin, 111, 135, 315
Garcia de Noriega, Juan, 1, 19, 99, 133, 176, 231, 355
Garcia de Noriega, Juan Estevan, 19, grant, 101, 102, 106, 188, 300
Garcia de Noriega, Lazaro, 102, 234
Garcia de Noriega, Luis, 105
Garcia de Noriega, Maria, 66, 97
Garcia de Noriega, Rosalia, 106
Garcia de Noriega, Salvador, 200, 240
Garduño, Bartolomé, 4, 84
Garduño, Eduarda Rita, 113
Garduño, Felipe, 106
Garduño, Francisco, 25, 112
Garduño, Gregorio, 25, 36, 37, 38, 135
Garduño, Joseph, 107
Garduño, Joseph Miguel, 105, 107, 112
Garduño, Julian, 123
Garduño, Maria Diega, 107
Garvisu, Manuel, 43
Garvisu, Manuel Bernardo, 41, 238
Garvisu, Manuel Sanz de, 103, 112, 178
Gavaldon, Maria Antonia, 112
Gavaldon, Juan, 103, grant, 107
Gavaldon, Juan Manuel, 105
Gayegos, Julian, 33
Gaytan, Diego, 286
Genizaros, 26, 27
Gilthomey, José Maria, 123
Gilthomey, Joseph Antonio, 98
Gilthomey, Joseph Manuel, 4, 67, 98, 99, 176
Gilthomey, Rosalia, 28, 238
Giron, Dimas, 110
Giron, Juan Antonio, 41
Giron de Tejeda, Dimas, 206
Godines, Antonio, 100, 147, 279, 316
Gomes del Castillo, Juan, 158
Gomez, Diego, 107
Gomez, Petrona, 100
Gomez de Chavez, Pedro, 40
Gomez del Castillo, Francisco, 127, 158
Gomez Robledo, Francisco, 1
Gongora, Cristobal de, 66, 67, 74, 79, 145, 146, 161, 162, 193, 197, 198
Gongora, Gregorio de, 103
Gonzales, Alejandro, 102
Gonzales, Antonio, 124, 295
Gonzales, Antonio Bas, 98
Gonzales, Bautista, 296
Gonzales, Cristobal, 118
Gonzales, Diego, 97, 98, 102
Gonzales, Felipe, 120
Gonzales, Francisco, 44, 111

Gonzales, Isabel, 97
Gonzales, Joseph, 102
Gonzales, Juan, 99, 132, 353
Gonzales, Juan Angel, 102, 356
Gonzales, Juan Bas, 101, 102
Gonzales, Juan Francisco, 112
Gonzales, Leonardo, 21
Gonzales, Marcial, 27
Gonzales, Maria, 71
Gonzales, Maria Candelaria, 106
Gonzales, Miguel, 215
Gonzales, Nicolasa, 295
Gonzales, Pedro Antonio, 112
Gonzales, Prudencia, 298
Gonzales, Rafael, 122
Gonzales, Rosalia, 111
Gonzales, Salvador, 103, 281
Gonzales, Sebastian, heirs of, 103
Gonzales, Theodora, 102
Gonzales de la Cruz, Francisco, 106
Gonzales de la Rosa, 316
Gonzales de Parral, Juan Antonio, 208
Gorraez, Joseph de, 329
Gotera tract, 384
Governors, list of, 1770-1840, 324
Granillo, Luis, 202
Granillo, Maria, 67
Grants, abandoned, 342
Griego, Alonzo, 102
Griego, Catalina, 278
Griego, Faustin, 126
Griego, José Antonio, 113
Griego, Josefa, 99, 113
Griego, Juan, 197
Griego, Juana, 98, 278
Griego, Lorenzo, 19
Griego, Luis, 123
Griego, Maria, 98, 99, 104, 278
Griego, Nicolás, 19, 99, 134
Griego, Pedro, 99
Groslee, Santiago, 13
Guadalajara, Royal Audiencia, 42
Gruciaga, Antonio, 35, 82
Guejosa, Francisco Antonia, 100, 205, 206, 287, 362
Guerrero, Antonio, 177
Guerrero, Francisco, 27, 28, 41, 43, 107, 169, 170, 174, 208, 238, 349
Guerrero, Fr. Joseph Antonio, 104
Guijosa, Antonio de, 281
Gurule, Antonio, 105
Gurule, Juan Antonio, 212
Gurule, Toribio, 118
Gusano, El, 296
Gutierrez, Alejo, 100, 133, 206
Gutierrez, Antonio, 101
Gutierrez, Bartolomé, 138

INDEX

Gutierrez, Clemente, 77, 113
Gutierrez, Felipe, 81
Gutierrez, Francisco, 103
Gutierrez, Gregorio, 105
Gutierrez, heirs of, 193
Gutierrez, José, 115, 433
Gutierrez, Juan Isidro, 115
Gutierrez, Lorenzo, 77
Gutierrez, Maria, 100, 133, 206
Gutierrez, Maria de los Reyes, 123
Gutierrez, Maria Victoria, 115
Gutierrez, Mateo, 163
Gutierrez, Pedro Miguel, 115
Gutierrez de Figueroa, Antonio, 5
Gutierrez de los Rios, Gaspar, 66, 99

HACIENDA de San Juan Bautista del Ojito del Rio de Las Gallinas, 344
Hague, William, 270
Half breeds, Santa Fe, 339, settle at Sandia, 353
Hall's *Mexican Law*, 8
Hemenway expedition, 13
Hernandez, Joseph Anastacio, 168
Hernandez, Fray Juan Joseph, 156
Herrera, Antonio de, 181
Herrera, Domingo de, 158
Herrera, Francisco, 88
Herrera, Joseph de, 102, 124
Herrera, Juan Bautista de, 124
Herrera, Juan Manuel de, 88, 124, 127
Herrera, Maria de, 27, 35, 107, 158, 176, 237
Herrera, Mariano de, 168
Herrera, Miguel de, 161
Herrera, Sebastian, 2, 201, 202, 203
Herrera, Teresa de, 185
Herrera, Tomás de, 187
Herrera y Sandoval, Teresa, 123
Herrera y Sandoval, Tomás, 123
Holiba, Pedro de, 208
Holguin, Juan de la Cruz, 111
Homayo, pueblo, 26
Hosio, Fray Francisco de, 94, 113
Houghton, Joab, 276
Houiri, pueblo, 26
House, government, Santa Fe, 326
Hoyo de Mendoza, Joseph Gonzales, 147
Hulibarri, Antonio de, 36, 71
Hulibarri, Juan Antonio de, 104
Hurtado, Bartolo, 124
Hurtado, Joseph, 158
Hurtado, Juan, 158
Hurtado, Juan Paez, governor, 12, colonists, 18; 67, 69, 81, 83, 88, 123, 124, 398

Hurtado, Maria, 124
Hurtado, Martin, 66, 200
Hurtado, Miguel, 168
Hurtado, Miguel Geronimo, 168
Hurtado de Mendoza, Joseph, 128

ICUZA Y ELIZONDO, Juan Joseph de, 124
Idalgo, Nicanor, 80
Inventario de Diligencias, 320
Ipalenzia, Manuel Ramon, 146
Irigoyen, Fr. Joseph, 105
Irigoyen, Martin, 113
Isleta, pueblo, 45, 70, 71, 143, 187, 188, 189, reëstablished, 305, 440, 448, 480
Iturrieta, Joseph Mariano de Los Dolores, 287
Iturrieta, Pedro, 32, 43, 111

JACONA, pueblo, 8, 204
Jalona, Dolores, 270
Jaquez, Juan Joseph, 237
Jaramillo, Cristobal, 34
Jaramillo, Geronimo, 40, 70
Jaramillo, Ignacio, 90
Jaramillo, Joseph, 128
Jaramillo, Juan Barela, 34
Jaramillo, Juan de, 128
Jaramillo, Luis, 128
Jaramillo, Ramon Jacinto, 127
Jaramillo, Xavier, 128
Jemez, Cañon de, 77
Jemez, pueblo, 2, 92, 311, 421, 422, 451, 452, 453, 477, 478, 481
Jicarilla, post, 391
Jiron, Dimas, 92, 206
Jiron, Maria, 97
Jiron de Xeda, Tomás, 97
Jollanga, Bonifacio, 141
Jorge de Bera, Isabel, 126
Jo-so, 26
Jo-so-ge, pueblo, 26, 27
Juanatilla, 74
Juanjuebe, Juan Esteban, 128
Juan Toboso, Cañada de, 237
Jumanes, pueblo de, 347
Junta de Fomento de Mineria, 346
Junta de Guerra, 1
Jurado, Catalina, 128
Jurado, Francisco, 119

KA-PO, pueblo, 13
Kearny, Stephen W., brigadier-general U. S. A., proclamation, 327
Kiowas, Indians, 347

LABADIA, Domingo, 164
La Cuesta, 31

514 THE SPANISH ARCHIVES OF NEW MEXICO

La Cueva de Los Pescadores, 80
Ladron de Guevara, Ignacio, 215, 298
Ladron de Guevara, Miguel, 97, 98
La Garza, Florencio, 123
Lain, Joaquin, 112
Lago, Juan Gabriel, 165
Laguna, Marqués de La, 3
Laguna, pueblo, 30, 76, 180, 388, 389, 441, 442, 443, 481
Laguna purchases, 184
Lagunita del Rio Puerco, 159
La Lande, Juan Bautista, 21
La Lusera, 112
La Majada, tract, 49, 168, 230, 371
Lamelas, Fernando, 165
Lamy, grant, 214
Land grants, 363
Land laws, 1842, 343
Land of Sunshine, 148
Lands, purchase, etc., 1, 370
Lands, settlement, 325, 326
Langham, John S., 143
Larragoite, Benito Antonio, 175
Larrañaga, Cristobal, 113, 180
La Salle, Robert, Cavalier, expedition, 13
Las Trampas, grant, 289
Las Trampas, rancho, 83, 142, 143
Laureano, Juan, 86
Leal, Nicolás, 107
Ledesma, Juan de, 28, 165, 210
Leon, Alonzo de, governor, 13
Leon, Juan, 27
Leon, Pedro Joseph, 188, 362
Lerud (Leroux), Antonio, 143, 144
Leyba, Angela de, 281
Leyba, Antonio de, 132
Leyba, Carmen, 144
Leyba, Joseph de, 136
Leyba, Juan Angel, 136
Leyba, Luis Francisco, 294
Leyba, Simon de, 136, 139
Leyba y Mendoza, Maria de, 123
Limpia Concepcion, 20
Lisarras y Gamboa, José Joaquin, 86
Lobato, Agustin, 138, 311
Lobato, Antonio Joseph, 293
Lobato, Bartolomé, 67, 132, 133, 230, 299, 451
Lobato, Blas, 209
Lobato, Cayetano, 135, 311
Lobato, Domingo, 106
Lobato, Gregorio, 158
Lobato, José Manuel, 140
Lobato, Juan Cayetano, 138
Lobato, Juan Domingo, 290

Lobato, Juan Joseph, 27, 40, 41, 290, 293
Lobato, Juan Tomás, 288
Lobato, Maria Francisca, 143
Lobato, Miguel Antonio, 172
Lobato, Pedro, 47
Lobato, Roque, 92, 179
Lobera, Francisco, 179
Lo de Basquez, 35, 301
Lo de Padia, 71, 143
Lopez, Antonio, 133
Lopez, Antonio José, 140
Lopez, Blas, 77
Lopez, Carlos, 82
Lopez, Geronimo, 138, 139, 140
Lopez, José, 132
Lopez, José Antonio, 111
Lopez, Juan, 132
Lopez, Manuel, 138
Lopez, Maria Josepha, 112, 136, 138
Lopez, Pedro, 36, 37
Lorenz, Manuel Antonio, 239
Losano, Ignacio, 19, 140
Losano, Joseph, 138
Losano, Juan, 138
Losano, Maria Manuela, 138
Los Corrales, 33
Los Lunas, 77, 141
Los Quelites, 70, 200, Comanche attack, 20, 372
Los Valles de Santa Getrudis de Lo de Mora, 33, 143, 144
Los Trigos, 296
Louisiana, colonists, 367
Lucero, Bernardo, 142, 143
Lucero, Diego, 144
Lucero, Juan, 143, 207
Lucero, Julian, 144
Lucero, Manuel, 28, 102
Lucero, Manuela, 102
Lucero, Maria Antonia, 367
Lucero, Miguel, 27, 111, 138
Lucero, Nicolás, 82
Lucero, Pedro, 68, 82
Lucero de Godoy, Antonio, 97, 130, 131
Lucero de Godoy, Antonio, or Antonio Martinez, 130, 131, 145, 203, 231
Lucero de Godoy, Francisco Mateo, 5
Lucero de Godoy, Juan, 202, 129, 239
Lucero de Godoy, Juan de Dios, 17, 203
Lucero de Godoy, Nicolás, 201
Luis Marie, 391
Lujan, Ana, 33, 144, 145
Lujan, Antonio, 31
Lujan, Francisco, 140
Lujan, Isabel, 140, 239

INDEX

Lujan, Josepha, 68, 99, 133, 145
Lujan, Juan, 101, 138, 311
Lujan, Juan Antonio, 106, 156
Lujan, Juan José, 138, 143, 384
Lujan, Juana, 133
Lujan, Miguel, 135
Luna, Antonio, de, 141, 142, 164, 165, 200
Luna, Domingo de, 76, 105, 141, 295
Luna, Joaquin de, 115, 240
Lucero, Antonio de Jesus, 179
Lucero, Antonio Salado, 110

MADARIAGA, Francisco Ignacio de, 94, 343
Madrid, Antonio, 161
Madrid, Antonio Xavier, 168
Madrid, Cristobal, 160, 163, 240
Madrid, José Ignacio, 45, 169, 381
Madrid, Joseph, 299
Madrid, Lorenzo, 4, 5, 97, 126, 145, 230
Madrid, Matias, 299
Madrid, Roque, 4, lead mine, 18, 98, 144, 146, 152, 169
Madrid, Tomás, 25, 112, 128, 163, 165
Maese, Antonia, 19
Maese, Bernardo de Sena, 164, 241
Maese, Catarina, 155
Maese, Felix, 278
Maese, Francisca, 19
Maese, Francisco, 207
Maese, Joseph, 164
Maese, Juan de Dios, 324, 388, 389, 175
Maese, Luis, 144
Maese, Maria Micaela, 166
Maldonado, José, 92, 111, 159, 163, will, 165, 180
Maldonado, José Manuel, 386
Maldonado, José Miguel, 180
Mallet Brothers, 20
Mangino, Rafael, 392
Manrique, José, governor, 45, 77, 114, 421
Manuelita, grant, 175
Manzanares, Andrés, 164
Manzanares, Juan, 315
Manzanares, Manuel, 164
Manzano, 119, 298
Mares, José, 138, 165
Mares, Manuel, 166
Mares, Nicolás, 161
Marie, Louis, 20, 266
Marin, Joaquin, 105
Marin de Valle, Francisco, Antonio, 42, 43

Margue, Diego Antonio, 128
Marques, Antonia, 6
Marques, Bartolomé, 158, 163, 296
Marques, Pedro, 1
Marques de Ayala, Joseph Miguel, 153
Marquez, Ana Maria, 200
Marquez, Diego Antonio, 138
Marquez, de Ayala, Maria, 166
Martin, Alejo, 145
Martin, Antonio, 19, 27, 152, 155, 157, 161, 188, 237
Martin, Antonio Elias, 295
Martin, Cristobal, 11, 119, 146, 147, 152, 153, 154, 158
Martin, Diego, 123, 204
Martin, Diego Antonio, 168
Martin, Domingo, 144
Martin, Francisco, 146, 147, 152, 153, 154, 157, 161, 206
Martin, Geronimo, 154, 160
Martin, Getrudis, 160
Martin, Hernando, 28
Martin, Ignacio, 154
Martin, Isidro, 138, 159, 200, 294
Martin, Jacinto, 154, 155, 237
Martin, José, 42, 138, 160
Martin, José Antonio, El Renegado, 169
Martin, Josepha, 152, 317
Martin, Juan, 200, 295
Martin, Juan Francisco, 155, 162, 165
Martin, Juan Manuel, 166
Martin, Juan Pablo
Martin, Juana, 19, 68
Martin, Lorenzo, 157
Martin, Magdalena, 40
Martin, Manuel, 27, 112, 142, 147, 157
Martin, Marcial, 75, 164
Martin, Marcos, 158
Martin, Margarita, 155
Martin, Maria, 164, 206
Martin, Maria Rosa, 88
Martin, Maria Viviana, 167
Martin, Matias, 81
Martin, Miguel, 153
Martin, Monica Tomasa, 164
Martin, Pedro, 122, 157, 166, 168
Martin, Rosa, 41
Martin, Santiago, 160, 315
Martin, Sebastian, 41, 67, 68, 75, 121, 145, 160, 188, 189, 190, 278
Martin, Vicente, 165
Martin y Sandoval, Juan de Dios, 204
Martinet, Chaffie, 175
Martinez, Antonio, grant, Taos, county, 131, 152
Martinez, Fr. Antonio José, 60

Martinez, Bernardo, 169
Martinez, Felix, governor, 9, 68, 81, 145, 154
Martinez, Joaquin, 107
Martinez, José Maria, 31, 143
Martinez, Juan de Jesus, 170
Martinez, Margarita, 175
Martinez, Mariano, governor, 11, 33, 348, 390
Martinez, Miguel, de Sandoval, 99, 133
Martinez, Nazario, 33
Martinez, Salvador, 127, Sandia Vega, 156, 355
Martinez, Santiago, 170
Martinez, Severino, 347
Mascareñas, Francisco, 362
Mascareñas, Miguel, 172, Mora, 173, 174
Maxwell Grant, 51-60, 62, 63, 64
Maxwell, Lucien B., 60
Maynez, Alberto, governor, 76, 86, 147, 193, 194, 195, 432
McNair, Alexander governor of Missouri, 342
Medina, Antonia de, 85
Medina, Joseph de, 128, grant, 128, 158, 315
Medina, Juan Lorenzo de, 316
Medina, Maria Magdalena de, 155
Medina, Ramon de, 280
Medrano, Fray Joseph, 142
Melgares, Don Facundo, governor, 30, 46, 79, 115, 372, 373
Menchero, Juan Miguel, Fray, 155, 235, 236
Mendoza, Antonio Dominguez, 155
Mendoza, Don Gaspar Domingo de, governor, 20, 21, 23, 37, 38, 71, 72, 81, 82
Mendoza, Maria Dominguez, 316
Mendinueta, Don Pedro Fermin de, governor, 28, 29, 43, 44, birthplace, 177
Merino, Manuel, 345
Mesilla Colony, settlers, ceremonies, 172
Mesita de Juana Lopez, 185, 186
Mesita del Alamillo, 79
Mesnier, Pedro, 13
Mestas, Antonio de, 328
Mestas, Casilda de, 158
Mestas, Cristobal, 157
Mestas, Francisco Xavier, 154
Mestas, Hilario, 348
Mestas, Joaquin de, 42, 159, 160, 162
Mestas, Josepha, 165

Mestas, Juan de, 134, 204, grant, 204, 205, heirs, 281
Mestas, Maria, 211
Mestas, Maria de Rosa, 288
Mestas, Mateo, 157, 161
Mestas, Pedro Antonio, 350
Mestas, Tomás, 119
Mestas, Ventura de, 154, 156, 157, 158, 328
Mier, José Maria, 215
Miera, Anacleto, 112
Miera, Francisco, 79
Miera y Pacheco, Bernardo, 104, 163, 180
Miera y Pacheco, Cleto, 15, 86, 113, estate, 114, 164, 165, 166
Mina del Toro, 15
Mina traitor, 346
Mines and mining, 1, 15, 66, regulations, 324, courts, 342, lead, 344, 346, decrees, 348, regulations, 363, 371
Miñon, Juan, 159
Mirabel, Carlos José Perez de, 71, 178
Mirabel, Fr. Juan, 20
Mirabal, Maria Nieves, 168
Mirabal, Miguel, 166
Miranda, Francisco Xavier, 101, 165
Miranda, Guadalupe, 62, 63, 64, 65, 171, 390
Misquia, Francisco de, 147
Misquia, Lazaro de, 5
Missions, 349
Mississippi, river, 20
Missouri, river, 20
Mogollon, Don Juan Ignacio Flores, governor, 6, 7, Cienega, 10, 11, 67, 81
Molina, Pedro de, 384
Molina, Simon de, 302
Mondragon, Juan Alonzo de, 11, 14, 205
Mondragon, Sebastian de, 97, 187, 231
Montaño, Antonio Urban, 301
Montaño, Bernabel Manuel, 91
Montaño y Cuelar, Bernabel, 90
Montaño, Joseph, 27, 153
Montaño, Juan Bautista, 71, 162
Montaño, Juana Barbara, 167
Montaño, Leonor, 69
Montaño, Vicente, 167
Montes de Oca, Valentina de, 35, 40
Montesdoca, Pedro de, 132, 147, 317
Montes y Vigil, Domingo, 135
Montes y Vigil, Francisco, Alameda, 99, 146, 148, 165, 166, 310, grant, 314
Montes y Vigil, Getrudis, 153

INDEX

Montes y Vigil, José Victorino, 170
Montes y Vigil, Juan, 400
Montes y Vigil, Pedro, Rio Lucero, 170
Montezuma, origin of story, 26
Montoya, Andrés, 153, 155, 177, 231, 234
Montoya, Antonio, 20, 40, 66, 89, 145, 151, 154, 155, 159
Montoya, Barbara, 83, 84
Montoya, Clemente, 147, 237
Montoya, Diego, 5, 34, 50, 81
Montoya, Eutimio, 115
Montoya, Felipe, 175
Montoya, Isabel, 102
Montoya, José, 167
Montoya, José Francisco, 153
Montoya, José Joaquin, 354
Montoya, José Pablo, 33
Montoya, Josepha, 152, 157, 161
Montoya, Juan José, 175
Montoya, Manuel, 40, 208
Montoya, Marcial, 168
Montoya, Maria, 136
Montoya, Maria Getrudis, 170
Montoya, Mariano, 169
Montoya, Miguel, 161, claim, 163
Montoya, Nerio Antonio, 142, 162, 163
Montoya, Nicolasa, 138
Montoya, Pablo, 50, 168, 169, 170, 270, 390
Montoya, Paulin, 163, 166
Montoya, Santiago, 161, claim, 100, 163, 177
Montoya, Salvador, 146, 153
Montoya, Tomás Manuel, 142
Moqui, 26, 27
Mora, Francisco de la, 4, 97
Mora, Francisco Alberto de la, 35
Mora, town of, 172, settlement, 173, 174, 175, grant, 174, 175, 390
Moraga, Antonio de, 147, 300
Moraga, Felipe, 152
Morales, Pedro de, 152
Moran, Nicolás, 295
Moreno, Joche, 239
Moreno, Joseph, 42
Moreno, Juan Joseph, 159, 209, 356
Moreto, Antonio, 140
Moya, Juan Francisco, 159
Moya, Lucas, 108, 159, 163
Moya, Lucas Manuel de, 15, 106, 138
Moya, Manuel, 163
Moya, Maria de, 153
Moya, Santiago, 115

Naba, Maria de, 176
Nacimiento, 346
Nambé, pueblo, 8, 21, 23, 481
Napoleon, emperor, 393
Naranjo, José Antonio, 176
Narbona, Antonio, governor, 31, 45, 49, 182
Nava, Pedro de, 324, 325, 350, 367
Nava de Brazinas, Marqués de la, 34
Navajó Apaches, 71
Navarro, Francisco Trebol, governor, 29, 43, 112, 177
Navarro, Galindo, 328
Navarro, Juan, governor of Durango, 348
Negreres y Soria, José Ignacio, 349
New Biscay, 363
New Mexico, boundaries, 1, 2, 3, 13, 329, 348, 363
Newspaper (clipping), 327
Nieto, Cristobal, 176
Nieto, Francisco, 177
Nieto, Simon, 176
Niño Ladron de Guevara, Juan Francisco, 112, 161, 239
Nombre de Dios, river, 3
Non Numerata Pecunia, 136
Nuanez, Phelipe Jacobo, 77
Nuestra Señora de La Concepcion de Tomé Dominguez, 285
Nuestra Señora de La Luz, Lamy Grant, 214
Nuestra Señora de La Luz, San Fernando y San Blas, 43, 90, 128, 189, 320
Nuestra Señora de La Luz y San Blas, 43, 90, 128, 189, 320
Nuestra Señora de La Soledad, 112
Nuestra Señora de La Soledad del Rio Arriba, 289
Nuestra Señora de Los Dolores de Sandia, 235
Nuestra Señora del Pilar de Zaragoza, 103
Nuestra Señora del Rosario, San Fernando y Santiago, 209
Nuñes de Aro, Tomás, 102

Ogama, Magdalena de, 146, 316
Ojeda, Bartolomé de, 2, 4
Ojeda, Juana de, 163
Ojito de Las Ruedas, 297
Ojo Caliente, sitio de, 19, inhabitants of, 25, re-settlement, 178, 179, settlers, 179, 180, grant, 180, 315, 349, 354
Ojo de La Cabra, 186, 187, 448, 449, 450
Ojo de La Jara, 79

Ojo del Coyote, 136
Ojo del Oso, 32
Olavide y Michelena, Don Enrique, governor, 188
Olaya de Oton, 5
Olguin, Bartolomé, 178
Olguin, Maria Manuela, 211
Olguin, Miguel, 179
Oñate, Juan de, 78, honorary titles, 321, 322, 323
Ontiveros, Josefa de, 317
Ordenal, Juan Antonio, 84
Ordenanza de Intendentes, 345, 354
Ordenanzas de Terras y Aguas, 8
Ordinances, municipal,1846, 327
Ortega, Antonio, 138, 178, 179, 180
Ortega, Andrés, 185, 354
Ortega, Francisco, 179, 180
Ortega, Geronimo, 101, 103
Ortega, José Vivian de, 180
Ortega, Lucia, 179
Ortega, Mateo de, 147
Ortega, Tomás de, 178, 179
Ortiz, Agapito, 390
Ortiz, Antonio, grant, 201
Ortiz, Casimiro, 390
Ortiz, Cristobal, 180
Ortiz, Francisco, 25, 88, 207, 370
Ortiz, Francisco Xavier, 381
Ortiz, Gaspar, 25, grant, 272
Ortiz, Gertrudis, Teodora, 45
Ortiz, Ignacio, 185
Ortiz, José Antonio, 15, 28, 29, 45, 180
Ortiz, José Francisco, 185
Ortiz, José Ignacio, 185
Ortiz, José Rafael, 122, 185
Ortiz, José Vicente, 30, 180, 350
Ortiz, José Vitervo, 143
Ortiz, Juan de Medina, 123
Ortiz, Juan Rafael, 185, governor ad interim, 197, 266, 377
Ortiz, Marcelino, 123, 213
Ortiz, Matias, 180, 196
Ortiz, Miguel, 180
Ortiz, mine grant, 185
Ortiz, Nazario, 390
Ortiz, Nicolás, 74, 111
Ortiz, Pablo, 50
Ortiz, Ricardo, 390
Ortiz, Teodora, 45
Ortiz, Tomás, 33, 172
Ortiz, Torribio, 106, 178, 210, 211
Ortiz y Delgado, Francisco, 197, 295
Ortiz y Miera, Pablo, 272
Ortiz Niño Ladron de Guevara, 2
Ortiz Niño Ladron de Guevara, Francisco, 178
Ortiz Niño Ladron de Guevara, Nicolás, 19, 67, genealogy, 177, will, 177, 178, 316, 317, 318
Otermín, Don Antonio de, 1, 2, 4, 201
Otero, Antonio José, grant, 186, 450, 451
Otero, Juan, 186, 342, 448
Otero, Miguel Antonio, 388
Otero, Vicente, letter, 385

PACHECO, Felipe, lands, Taos, 121
Pacheco, Francisco, 122
Pacheco, Geronimo, 28
Pacheco, Isabel, 122
Pacheco, Joseph, 190
Pacheco, Juan, 188, 189
Pacheco, Juan José, 188
Pacheco, Marcos, 189
Pacheco, Sylvestre, 146, 187
Pacheco, Valentina, 104
Padilla, Bernardo, 77
Padilla, Diego, 31, 187, grant, 187, 188, will, 188, 189, 197, 296, 213
Padilla, Estevan, 77
Padilla, Francisco, 77, 189
Padilla, José Antonio, 193
Padilla, José Martin, 196
Padilla, Juan, 190
Padilla, Juan Manuel, 111
Padilla, Luis, 77
Padilla, Maria Antonia, 197
Padilla, Maria Feliciana, 180
Padilla, Pascual, 20
Padilla, Rafael, 197
Padilla, Victoriano, 143
Paguati, Antonio, 181
Paguati Purchase, 76, 181, 184, 442, 443, 444
Pajarito, Pascual, 181
Pajarito tract, 40, 45, 113, 153, 343
Pajarito, Vicente, 181
Palace of the Governors, towers, 235, repairs, 324, papers, 324, 328, 344, in 1810, 370, 371, earliest reference, 98, irrigation ditch, 146
Palacios, 301
Palacios y Bolivar, Maria de, 124
Palomino, Tomás, 97, 187, 230
Pankey, B. F., 96
Pareja, Manuel Garcia, 29
Parkman, Francis, 13
Parral, City of, 3
Parrida, Arroya de la, 115
Partido del Bado, 166
Paruanarimuco, Comanche chief, 328
Pawnee, villages, 21
Paz, Andrés de la, 205

INDEX

Paz, Marina de la, 140
Pecos, pueblo of, 2, 30, 31, 46, 47, 94, 97, 195, 267, 296, Comanche attack, 391, 441, 466, 467, 468, 478
Pecos, river, 46, 47, 49, 94, 95, 96, 97, 212, 213
Pelaez, Jacinto, 204
Peña, Diego de la, 113, 163
Peña, José Agustin, de la, 77
Peña, José de la, 193
Peña, Josef Mariano de la, 113, 115, 168
Peña, Josef Miguel de la, 15, 45, 90, 107, 113, 210
Peña, Juan de Dios, 113, 143, 193
Peña Redonda, Mattheo, de, 112, 140, 164
Peñasco Blanco, de las Golondrinas, 136
Peñuela, Marqués de la, 8, 66, 83, 146, 193, coat of arms, 193, 199
Peralta, Felipe, 79
Perea, Eugenio, 179, 190
Perea, Jacinto, 177, 294
Perea, José, 298
Perea, Juan Casimiro, 241
Perea, Juana de la, 20
Perea, Maria de, 187
Perea, Maria Manuela, 196
Perea, Mariano, 113
Perea, Nicolasa, 197
Perea, Pedro José, 115, 196
Pereyro, Fr. Josef Benito, 26
Perez, Albino, governor, 50, 143, 271, 272, 389
Perez, José Miguel, 196
Pesos de la Tierra, 360
Phillip 2d, 6
Picuriés, pueblo, 103, 144, 170, 444, 463, 478
Piedra Lumbre, 141
Pike, Zebulon M., 21
Pilabo, pueblo, 115
Piñeda, Juan de la Mora, 68, 83, 133, 188, 199
Pino, Felix, 118
Pino, heirs of, 193
Pino, Joaquin, 49, 79, 180
Pino, Juan Estevan, 196, 197, 269, 271, 348, 349
Pino, Manuel Doroteo, 389
Pino, Maria Catarina de, 164, 165
Pino, Mateo, 70
Pino, Miguel, 342
Pino, Pedro Bautista, 30, 45, 119, 266
Pino, Fr. Pedro, 156
Pintto, Roque de, 11, 67, 146

Piro, pueblos, 78, 79
Plows, 277
Pojoaque, pueblo, 6, 23, 50, 480
Poñil, settlers, 62, 80
Political economy, treatise on, 346
Portillo Urrisola, Manuel de, 42
Potrero Viejo, 4
Pratt, George R., 196, 270
Private land claims, 484, 491, court of, 492, 502
Proclamation, constitution, 1820, 323, Kearny, 1846, 327
Protector of Indians, 6
Provencio, Francisco, 123
Provincial deputation, 46
Pueblo Colorado, 101
Pueblo Quemado, 25, 28, 43, 44, 74, 144, 146, 177, 200, 209, 237
Pueblo de Jumanos, 347
Pueblo de San Antonio del Biquiú, 43
Pueblo de San Antonio del Guyquiu, 43
Pueblos, 2, 6, 12, 13, 21, 23, 25, 26, 28, 30, 31, 40, 43, 46, 47, 48, 78, 91, 92, 94, 141, 378, 379, 380, education, 393, grants, 394, Sumas, 403, sales of land, 437, 451, 483
Puente, Pedro de la, 189
Puesto de la Cienega, 123
Puesto del Pino, 241
Puesto de Nuestra Señora de la Soledad del Rio Arriba, 74

QUARTERS, soldiers', 367
Quaron, Lorenzo Antonio, 189
Quicksilver, 343
Quintana, Cochití Indian, 432
Quintana, Francisco, 102
Quintana, Gabriel, 28
Quintana, José Alejandro, 79
Quintana, Joseph de, 152, 153, 200
Quintana, Leonisio, 200
Quintana, Luis, 73
Quintana, Lugarda, 288
Quintana, Manuel, 200
Quintana, Maria de Los Angeles, 201
Quintana, Miguel de, 102, 153, 201
Quintana, Teodosio, 49, 201
Quiros, Joseph de, 6, 7, 8, 279

RAEL, Eusebio, 169, heirs, Sandia, 353
Rael, Julian, 383, 384
Rael, José Pablo, 45
Rael, Juan Pablo, 353
Rael, Maria Francisca, 238
Rael, Nicolás, 45
Rael de Aguilar, Alonzo or Alphonso,

1, 7, 8, 9, 10, heirs, 15, grant, 16, 17, 34, lieutenant-general, 68, 103, 132, 133, 145, 153, 203, grant, 203, 205, 207, 356, 398
Rael de Aguilar Antonio, 126
Rael de Aguilar, Francisco de, 158, 294
Rael de Aguilar, Juan, 153
Rael de Aguilar, Julian, 27
Rael de Aguilar, Manuela, 209
Rael de Aguilar, Nicolás, 210
Ramirez, Jorge, 215
Ramirez, Santiago, 143, 197
Ramirez y Casanova, José Serafin, 143
Ramos, Manuel, 208
Ramos, Ursula, 127, 204
Rancho de Cuberos, 93
Rancho de Peralta, 371
Rancho de Velasquez, 286
Rascon, Francisco, 271
Rascon, José Ignacio, 30
Raynolds, A. W., 96
Real de Los Dolores, 32, 66, 88
Real de San Francisco del Tuerto, 175
Religion, 349
Rendon, Francisco, 205, 206, 234, 286
Rendon, Maria Estela Palomino, 211
Reneros de Posada, Pedro, 2
Revilla Gigedo, Cónde de, 329
Reyes, Melchora de los, 97
Riaño, Cañones de, 119
Riaño, Joseph de, 154, 206, 207, 208, 312
Riaño, Tagle, Joseph de, 286
Ribera, Antonio, 209
Ribera, Antonio José, 267
Ribera, Francisco de, 147
Ribera, Joseph Manuel, 211
Ribera, Juan de, 66
Ribera, Juan Felipe de, 133, 206
Ribera, Manuel, 213
Ribera, Manuel Antonio, 267
Ribera, Maria Luisa, 213
Ribera, Miguel, 213
Ribera, Salvador Matheo de, 67, 145
Ribera, Vicente, 390
Ribera, Tomás, 358
Rico, Francisco, 145
Rincon, Joseph, 158
Rio Arriba, 11, 27, 88
Rio Chiquito, 27, 67, 126, 132, 138, 188
Rio Colorado, 92
Rio Colorado del Rincon de la Cinta a La Trinchera, 169
Rio Lucero, 170, 171
Rio Puerco, settlers, 41, 42, 128, 162, 189

Rio de Chama, 133
Rio de Las Trampas, 83, 207
Rio del Oso, 127
Rios, Gaspar Gutierrez de los, 146
Rios, Juan de los, 204, 313
Rivas Palacio, 13
Roa y Carillo, Francisco, de, 77, 103, 155, 207
Robledo, Lucia Gomez, 238
Robledo, Maria Gomez, 235
Roche, Maria de la, 145
Rodelo, Juan, 27, 203
Rodriguez Cubero, Don Pedro, governor, 130, 131
Rodriguez, Felipe, 138, 204
Rodriguez, Francisco Xavier, 210
Rodriguez, Getrudes, 86
Rodriguez, Isidor, 211
Rodriguez, Joseph, 6, 33, 74, 279
Rodriguez, Juan, 206
Rodriguez, Juan Antonio, 211
Rodriguez, Juan Felipe, 71
Rodriguez, Lorenzo, 205
Rodriguez, Manuel, 210, 211
Rodriguez, Marcos, 90, 138, 212
Rodriguez, Melchor, 207, 314
Rodriguez, Santiago, 93
Rodriguez, Sebastian, 310
Rodriguez, Vicente, 210, 211, 212
Romero, Andrés, 83, 207
Romero, Baltazar, 100, 206, 279, 283, 350, 362, 399
Romero, Diego, 83, 84, 207, 210
Romero, Domingo, 413, 416
Romero, Felipe, 27, 43
Romero, Fernando, 238
Romero, Francisco, 83, 210
Romero, Francisco Xavier, 205, 207, 210
Romero, Juan José, 206
Romero, José Dolores, 215
Romero, Jose Guadalupe, 213, 215
Romero, Juan, 74, 356
Romero, Juan Bautista, 211
Romero, Juan Domingo, 296
Romero, Juan de Dios, 208, 315
Romero, Juana, 209
Romero, Juana Maria, 206
Romero, Luis, Picuriés Indians, 311
Romero, Maria, 84, 210
Romero, Maria Rosalia, 210
Romero, Matias, 206
Romero, Miguel, 211, 212, 413-416
Romero, Pablo, 168, 213
Romero, Pablo Antonio, 168
Romero de Pedraza, Francisco, 5, 33, 144

INDEX 521

Romero, Santiago, 205
Romo de Vera, Joseph, 103, 207, 314
Ron y Thobar, Vicente Ginzo, 127
Rosa, Manuel de la, 157
Roubidoux, Antonio, 215
Royal decrees, 319, orders, 328, 330, 342, 349, 392, 394, Sumas Indians, 402
Roybal, Ignacio, 146, 147, 159, 204, 205, 206
Roybal, José Maria, 31
Roybal, Juana, 211
Roybal, Manuela, 212
Roybal, Rafael, 31
Roybal, Santiago, 77, 209, 238, 294
Roybal, Tomás, 209, 294
Roybal, Vicente, 123, 213
Roxas, Pedro de, 4, 100, 133, 355
Rubin de Zelis, Alonzo Victores, 25
Ruiz, Antonio Villegas, 113

SABINAL, inhabitants, 240
Sabinos Altos, 301
Sacramento, river, 3
Saenz, Domingo, 361
Saenz de Garvisu, Juan, 278
Saenz de Garvisu, Juana de la Cruz, 239
Saenz de Garvisu, Manuel, 178
Saes, Agustin, 6, 234, 266, 278
Sais, Francisco, 237, 197, 205, 237
Sais, Joseph Antonio, 241
Sais, Juliana, 197
Salaises, Joseph, 30, 267
Salas, Joseph, 235
Salas, Sebastian de, 187, 278
Salazar, Antonio de, 67, 73, 134, 142, 232, 237, 240
Salazar, Joseph, 240
Salazar, Juan Angela, 240
Salazar, Juan Domingo, 270
Salazar, Pablo, 210
Salazar, Santiago, 316
Salcedo, Nemesio, 30, 349, 370, 319
Sales of land, pueblos, 437
Samorra, José, 316
Samorra, José Rafael, Pecos, 267
San Andrés de Los Padillas, 77
San Antonio de Carnue, 118
San Antonio de Mora, 319
San Antonio de Padua del Pueblo Quemado, 237
San Antonio del Embudo, 161
San Buenaventura de Chimayo, 107
San Buenaventura de Cochití, 74, 392
San Carlos, 328
San Carlos de Alameda, 86

San Clemente, 141, 142
San Cristobal, grant, 94, 98
San Cristobal, pueblo, 483
San Diego de Tesuque, pueblo, 40
San Felipe, pueblo, 34, 46, 79, 87, 93, 116, 117, 118, 151, 185, 267, 300, 316, 358, 416, 422, 439, 446, 465, 478
San Fernando del Rio Puerco, 162, 189
San Francisco de Sandia, 127
San Francisco, street, 10, 99
San Francisco Xavier del Bosque Grande, 98
San Francisco Xavier del Pueblo Quemado, 27, 74, 208
San Gabriel, pueblo, 26
San Gabriel de Las Nutrias, 177, 210, 211
San Geronimo de Taos, 83, 84, 148, 149, 150, 151, 342, 413
San Ildefonzo, 204, 381, 394, 395, 396, 403-5, 406, 413, 416-21, 480
San José de la Laguna, 180, 181
San José de Las Huertas, 79, 114
San José del Bado del Rio Pecos, 266
San José del Encinal, 44
San Josef de Garcia, rancho, 293
San Joseph, Maria de, 206
San Joseph de Chama, 85
San Joseph de Los Corrales, 127
San Juan, pueblo, 2, 462, 463
San Juan de Los Caballeros, 145, 176, 177, 440, 478
San Lazaro, Sierra de, 32
San Lorenzo, 189
San Lorenzo de Picuriés, 170
San Lorenzo de la Toma del Rio del Norte, 201
San Lorenzo del Real de Dolores, 86
San Marcos, 171, 172, 301, 319
San Miguel del Bado, 45, 196, 329, 389, ayuntamiento, 49, 50, 301, 344
San Miguel del Socorro, 298
San Pedro de Chamita, 80
San Pedro, tract, 345
San Pedro de Chama, 42, 160
San Pedro de Chamita, 80
Santa Ana, 92, 116, 117, 118, 342, 358, 359, 399, 422-428, 439, 482
Santa Ana del Sabinal, 122
Santa Anna, General Antonio Lopez de, 275, 392
Santa Barbara, 106, 239, grant, 239
Santa Barbara de la Junta de Los Rios, 239
Santa Clara, Cañada, 283, 312, 371, 403-5, 416-421

Santa Clara, pueblo, 13, 77, 78, 280, 282, 479
Santa Cruz de La Cañada, 4, 7, 11, 15, 45, 66, 68, 74, 75, 80, south of river, 182, 205, 241, 242, 264
Santa Cruz del Ojo Caliente, 27, 237
Santa Fe, ayuntamiento, 30, 143, 185, proceedings, 187, names, 187, 197, 266, 275, 381, cabildo, 5, 10, 87, 123, 143
Santa Fe, city, 1, 4, Cienega, 10, 11, 21, grant, 215, 228, cabildo archives, 330, 338, houses, 350, 377, reservoir, 389, property owners, 389, petition for lands, 390
Santa Fe, river, 82
Santa Getrudis, 319
Santa Rosa de Abiquiú, 162
Santa Rosa de Cubero, 92
Santa Rosa de Lima, 103
Santa Rosalia del Vallecito, 316
Santa Teresa de Jesus, 159
Santa Toribio de Jemez, 114
Sandoval, Agapito, 273
Sandoval, Andres, 238
Sandoval, Antonia, 239
Sandoval, Diego, 273
Sandoval, Francisco, 272
Sandoval, Gregorio, 27, 237
Sandoval, José, 143
Sandoval, Juan, 238
Sandoval, Juan Josef, 27, 41
Sandoval, Juan Joseph, 74
Sandoval, Juliana, 240
Sandoval, Maria de Los Dolores, 50
Sandoval, Matias, 266
Sandoval, Melchora, 238
Sandoval, Miguel de Dios, 238
Sandoval, Nicolás, 33
Sandoval, Pedro de, 230
Sandoval, Phelipe, 43, 162, 193, 238, 266, 278, 421, 423
Sandoval, Salvador de, 90
Sandoval, Santiago, 49
Sandoval Martinez, Juan de Dios, 279
Sandoval Martinez, Miguel de, 356
Sandoval y Manzanares, Ana de, 141
Sandoval y Manzanares, Mateo de, 141
Sangil, Marcial Martin, 164
Sanguijuela, 301
Santistievan, Alejandro, 270
Santistievan, Antonio de, 234
Santistievan, Joseph de, 233
Santistievan, Salvador de, 67, 133, 231, 278
Sapello, 89, 380

Sarracino, Francisco, governor, 50, 385
Sarracino, José Rafael, 113
Sarracinol, Juan José, 272
Sausal, 193
Scolly, John, grant, 270, 276
Sebastian, Fr. Antonio, 392
Sebolleta, 30, 32
Sedano, Antonio, 126
Sedano, Joseph, 152, 316
Sedano, Josepha, 135, 152, 188
Sedillo, Antonio, 44, 70, 181
Sedillo, Joaquin de, 70, grant, 71
Sedillo, Juana de, 70
Segura, Juan, 201, 266
Segura, Simon, 239
Selorga, Maria de, 233
Sena, Antonio de, 28, 270
Sena, Bernardino de, 9, 21, 231, 233, 234, 235, 238
Sena, Felipe, 267, 270
Sena, Francisco de, 238
Sena, José Francisco, 329
Sena, Josepha, 89
Sena, Juan Diego, 143
Sena, Manuel, 270, 271
Sena, Maria Francisca de, 237, 239
Sena, Maria Tomasa, 237
Sena, Matias, 266, 350
Sena, Miguel, 80, 271
Sena, Rafael, 266, 271
Sena, Tomás, 180, 239
Sena, Vicente de, 112, 163, 237
Senecú, 360
Serna, Antonia de la, 88
Serna, Cristobal de la, 83, 207, 210, 231
Serna, Joseph de la, 211
Serna, Juana de la, 84
Serna, Sebastiana de la, 84
Serrano, Blas Martin, 178
Serrano, Domingo Martin, 203, 231
Serrano, Francisco Perez, 93, 180
Serrano, Miguel Martin, 158, 235, 284
Serrano, Pedro Martin, 141, 240
Serrito de Lara, 21
Servantes, Manuel de, 231
Settlements, 325, 349, 367, instructions to Cruzate, 394
Sevilleta, grant, 79, 350
Shapellote (Sapello), 89
Silva, Antonio de, 30, 100, 230
Silva, Francisco de, 234
Silva, José, 123
Silva, Juan, 123
Silva, Juan José, 241, 265
Silva, Maria, 105, 235
Silva, Maria Polonia, 266
Silva, Santiago, 113

INDEX 523

Sisneros, Antonio, 68, 73, 166
Sisneros, Heremenigildo, 68
Sisneros, Juan Pedro, 158
Sisneros, Juana, 68, 238
Sisneros, Maria Manuela, 166
Sisneros, Phelipe Nerio, 68, 106
Sisneros, Roman, 123
Socorro, 79, 115, 266, 348, 350
Solano, Antonio, 164
Soldiers' quarters, 367
Soledad, 329
Sopena, Fr. Manuel de, 153
Sossa Canela, Juana de, 67
Springer, Frank, argument, Maxwell, land grant case, 53-60
Stamped paper, law, 349
Sumas, Indians, 397, 402
Supreme Tribunal of Justice, 49, 50

TAFOYA, Altamirano Cristobal, 280
Tafoya, Altamirano Juan, 282
Tafoya, Antonio, 68, 106, 139, 279, 280, 282, 283, 286, 295
Tafoya, Cristobal, 68, 100, 279, 284
Tafoya, Felipe, 29, 43, 73, 105, 106, 139, 286, 294, 295
Tafoya, Getrudes, 298
Tafoya, Ignacio, 297
Tafoya, José, 298
Tafoya, Juan, 42, 68, 280, 283, 294
Tafoya, Lugarda, 44, 240, 281
Tafoya, Maria, 102, 281
Tafoya, Miguel, 240, 294
Tafoya, Pedro, 112, 138, 209
Tafoya, Pedro Antonio, 138
Tajique, settlers, 387
Talache Coyote, 210
Tamaris, Felipe, 15, 110, 279, 281, 284
Tamaris, Francisco, 281
Tamaris, Joseph, 102
Taos, pueblo, 26, 29, 83, 121, ayuntamiento, 143, 170, Comanche attack, 200, 265, 348, fences, 361, water rights, 380, 428, 432, 479
Tapia, Cristobal, 295
Tapia, Josef, 114
Tapia, Maria de, 66
Tapia, Tomás de, 84, 286
Tecolote, 297, 328
Tehua, 27
Tejeda, Dimas Xiron de, 81
Telles, Manuel, 295
Tenorio, Cayetano, 286
Tenorio, Josepha, 294
Tenorio, Teresa, 288
Tenorio de Alva, Manuel, 38, 296
Tenorio de Alva, Matthias, 140

Tenorio de Alva, Miguel, 6, 7, 8, 68, 83, 104, 131, 136, 140, 131, 136, 140, 279, 295
Territorial Assembly, 51, 298
Territorial Deputation, 50, 79, 80
Terrus, José Francisco, 32
Terrus, Joseph de, 36, 38, 72, 83, 103, 287
Tesuque, pueblo, 479, river, 29
Tesuque, San Diego de, 40, 45
Thanos, 253, 263, 264
Thorre, Joseph Antonio de la, 155
Tierra Amarilla, 168, report, 325
Tipton, Will M., 4, 118
Titles, grants, 362
Tlascalan, Indians, 36
Toledo, Fray Juan José, 26, 105, 110
Tomé Dominguez, 142
Tomé tract, 43, 45, inhabitants, 241, grant, 285, 286, 343
Torres, Carlos, 33
Torres, Cayetano, 295
Torres, Cristobal, grant, 127, 135, heirs, 296, 280
Torres, Diego, 73, 142, 176, 206, 283
Torres, Francisco, 89
Torres, Francisco Antonio, 350
Torres, José, 89, 293, 294
Torres, Josef Antonio, 284
Torres, Josefa, 284
Torres, Juan Geronimo, 122
Torres, Manuel, 71
Torres, Marcos, 294
Torres, Martin, 294, 315
Torres, Ramon, 80, heirs, 384
Torres, Salvador, 156, 284
Tostado, José Alvarez, 349
Tournier, Juan, 66
Troncoso, Vicente, 86, 110, 296
Trujillo, Antonio, 133, grant, 134, 288
Trujillo, Baltazar, 6, 7, 281, 282
Trujillo, Barbara, 296
Trujillo, Bartolomé, 85, 138, 142, 158, 284, 293
Trujillo, Bernardino, 286
Trujillo, Blas, 288
Trujillo, Cristobal, 97
Trujillo, Diego, 278
Trujillo, Francisca, 29, 288
Trujillo, Francisco, 284, 294, 296, 297, 349, 356
Trujillo, Getrudis, 294
Trujillo, José, 279
Trujillo, José Manuel, 80, 296, 298
Trujillo, Joseph, 7, 72, 296
Trujillo, Josepha, 288
Trujillo, Juan, 8, 84, 278, 288

Trujillo, Lorenzo, 311
Trujillo, Manuel, 295, 298
Trujillo, Marcela, 28, 238
Trujillo, Maria, 237
Trujillo, Maria Francisca, 295
Trujillo, Mariano, 296
Trujillo, Mateo, 279, 311
Trujillo, Pascual, 82, 231, 279
Trujillo, Pedro, 288
Trujillo, Pedro Antonio, 104, 288
Trujillo, Santiago, 111
Trujillo, Sebastiana, 11, 205
Turquoise Mines, 12

UGARTE, Diego de, 101, 154
Ugarte y Loyola, Jacobo, 392
Ulibarri, Antonio de, 281, 300
Ulibarri, Juan de, 66, 94, 101, 127, 195, 196, 204, 298, 299
Ulibarri, Santiago, 49
Unanuez, Juan Antonio de, 82, 101, 109, 153, 154
Unanuez, Juan Cayetano, 300
Unanuez, Phelipe Jacobo de, 105
United States, colonists from, 391
United States v. San Pedro Co., 345
Uribarri, Antonio de, 10, 20, 21, 38, 40, 82, 300
Uribarri, José Francisco, 301
Urioste, Tomás, 301
Urquidi, Joseph de, 348
Utes, Indians, 26

VACA, José, 42
Vaca, Manuel, 71, 81
Valdez, Antonio Feliz, La Vandera, 85
Valdez, Domingo, 314
Valdez, Ignacio, 296
Valdez, Joseph Luis de, 66
Valdez, Juan Lorenzo, 296
Valdez, Los, 235
Valdez, Rosalia, 296
Valdez y Bustos, Francisco, 188
Valencia county, 30
Valle, Francisco del, 193
Valle de Santa Getrudes de Lo de Mora, 80, 89, 172, 273
Vallecito, grant, 114, 316, 349, 370
Vallecito de Xemes, 114, 316
Valerio, Felix, 315
Valerio, Manuel, 142, 314
Valverde, José Antonio, 316
Valverde, Josepha, 127
Valverde Nicolas de, 67, 134, 278
Valverde de Cossio, Antonio de, 310
Varela, Antonio, 314
Varela, Benito, 123

Varela, Eusebio, 45
Varela, José, 45
Varela, José Manuel, 28
Varela, Mariano, 66
Vasquez, Pascuala, 295
Veccia Diego de, 33, 97
Vega y Coca, Maria de la, 43
Vega y Coca, Miguel Josef de la, 124, 136, 178, 188
Velarde, Joseph Manuel, 315
Velarde, Miguel 316
Velasco, Diego de, 66, 313
Velasco, Micaela de, 126, 310
Velasquez, Antonio, 311, 313
Velasquez, Diego de, 99, 113
Velasquez, Francisco, 310
Velasquez (Blasquez), Joseph, 99
Velasquez, Manuel, 286 313
Velo, Santiago, 149
Venavides, Domingo de, 44
Vergara, Ignacio Sanchez de, 114, 316, 327, 350, 436, 439
Veytia, Manuela de, 74
Vial, Pedro, will, 315
Viceroy, New Spain, Indians, 397
Victoria, Guadalupe, 394
Vigil, Donaciano, governor, 61
Vigil, Francisco, 127, 142
Vigil, Juan Nepomuceno, 47
Vigil, Manuel, 29
Villasur, Pedro de, 15, 100
Villa Nueva de Santa Cruz, 84, 228, 229, 241, 264
Villanueva, Don Vicente, 30
Villapando, Pablo Francisco, 178
Villapando, Maria Antonio, 210
Villareal, Clara de, 314
Virgen, Joseph de la, 67
Viscaya, Province, 3
Vitton, José Gabriel, 27

WEAVERS' BEND, 81

XARAMILLO, Cristobal, 82, 206
Xaramillo, Geronimo, 19, 213
Xaramillo, Getrudes, 158
Xaramillo, Joseph, 313, 345
Xaramillo, Luiz, 128
Xaramillo, Maria de La Luz, 362
Xaramillo, Salvador, 119
Xemez, pueblo, 311, rancho, 316, 342, 360, 370
Xiron, Antonia, 127
Xiron, Antonio, 179
Xiron, Vicente, 284
Xiron de Texeda, Dimas, 153, 355

YUNQUE, pueblo, 135, 299

INDEX

Zaes, Francisco, 107
Zaino, Diego, 279
Zanez, Manuel, 43
Zanez, Manuel Garvisu, 43
Zapata, Antonio Maldonado, 306
Zaragosa, Nuestra Señora del Pilar de, 1

Zembrano, Fray Manuel, 103
Zena, Bernardo de, 112
Zia, pueblo, 2, 75, 92, 342, 480, 481
Zisneros, Francisco, 293
Zuloaga, Manuel José, 349
Zuñi, pueblo, 483

THE CHICANO HERITAGE

An Arno Press Collection

Adams, Emma H. **To and Fro in Southern California.** 1887

Anderson, Henry P. **The Bracero Program in California.** 1961

Aviña, Rose Hollenbaugh. **Spanish and Mexican Land Grants in California.** 1976

Barker, Ruth Laughlin. **Caballeros.** 1932

Bell, Horace. **On the Old West Coast.** 1930

Biberman, Herbert. **Salt of the Earth.** 1965

Casteñeda, Carlos E., trans. **The Mexican Side of the Texas Revolution (1836).** 1928

Casteñeda, Carlos E. **Our Catholic Heritage in Texas, 1519-1936.** Seven volumes. 1936-1958

Colton, Walter. **Three Years in California.** 1850

Cooke, Philip St. George. **The Conquest of New Mexico and California.** 1878

Cue Canovas, Agustin. **Los Estados Unidos Y El Mexico Olvidado.** 1970

Curtin, L. S. M. **Healing Herbs of the Upper Rio Grande.** 1947

Fergusson, Harvey. **The Blood of the Conquerors.** 1921

Fernandez, Jose. **Cuarenta Años de Legislador:** Biografia del Senador Casimiro Barela. 1911

Francis, Jessie Davies. **An Economic and Social History of Mexican California** (1822-1846). Volume I: Chiefly Economic. Two vols. in one. 1976

Getty, Harry T. **Interethnic Relationships in the Community of Tucson.** 1976

Guzman, Ralph C. **The Political Socialization of the Mexican American People.** 1976

Harding, George L. **Don Agustin V. Zamorano.** 1934

Hayes, Benjamin. **Pioneer Notes from the Diaries of Judge Benjamin Hayes, 1849-1875.** 1929

Herrick, Robert. **Waste.** 1924

Jamieson, Stuart. **Labor Unionism in American Agriculture.** 1945

Landolt, Robert Garland. **The Mexican-American Workers of San Antonio, Texas.** 1976

Lane, Jr., John Hart. **Voluntary Associations Among Mexican Americans in San Antonio, Texas.** 1976

Livermore, Abiel Abbot. **The War with Mexico Reviewed.** 1850

Loyola, Mary. **The American Occupation of New Mexico, 1821-1852.** 1939

Macklin, Barbara June. **Structural Stability and Culture Change in a Mexican-American Community.** 1976

McWilliams, Carey. **Ill Fares the Land:** Migrants and Migratory Labor in the United States. 1942

Murray, Winifred. **A Socio-Cultural Study of 118 Mexican Families Living in a Low-Rent Public Housing Project in San Antonio, Texas.** 1954

Niggli, Josephina. **Mexican Folk Plays.** 1938

Parigi, Sam Frank. **A Case Study of Latin American Unionization in Austin, Texas.** 1976

Poldervaart, Arie W. **Black-Robed Justice.** 1948

Rayburn, John C. and Virginia Kemp Rayburn, eds. **Century of Conflict, 1821-1913.** Incidents in the Lives of William Neale and William A. Neale, Early Settlers in South Texas. 1966

Read, Benjamin. **Illustrated History of New Mexico.** 1912

Rodriguez, Jr., Eugene. **Henry B. Gonzalez.** 1976

Sanchez, Nellie Van de Grift. **Spanish and Indian Place Names of California.** 1930

Sanchez, Nellie Van de Grift. **Spanish Arcadia.** 1929

Shulman, Irving. **The Square Trap.** 1953

Tireman, L. S. **Teaching Spanish-Speaking Children.** 1948

Tireman, L. S. and Mary Watson. **A Community School in a Spanish-Speaking Village.** 1948

Twitchell, Ralph Emerson. **The History of the Military Occupation of the Territory of New Mexico.** 1909

Twitchell, Ralph Emerson. **The Spanish Archives of New Mexico.** Two vols. 1914

U. S. House of Representatives. **California and New Mexico:** Message from the President of the United States, January 21, 1850. 1850

Valdes y Tapia, Daniel. **Hispanos and American Politics.** 1976

West, Stanley A. **The Mexican Aztec Society.** 1976

Woods, Frances Jerome. **Mexican Ethnic Leadership in San Antonio, Texas.** 1949

Aspects of the Mexican American Experience. 1976
Mexicans in California After the U. S. Conquest. 1976
Hispanic Folklore Studies of Arthur L. Campa. 1976
Hispano Culture of New Mexico. 1976
Mexican California. 1976
The Mexican Experience in Arizona. 1976
The Mexican Experience in Texas. 1976
Mexican Migration to the United States. 1976
The United States Conquest of California. 1976
Northern Mexico On the Eve of the United States Invasion:
    Rare Imprints Concerning California, Arizona, New Mexico, and Texas, 1821-1846. Edited by David J. Weber. 1976